BEING IN THE WORLD

AN ENVIRONMENTAL READER FOR WRITERS

Most people are on the world, not in it—have no conscious sympathy or relationship to anything about them—undiffused, separate, and rigidly alone like marbles of polished stone, touching but separate.

John Muir, Journal Entry,
July 16, 1890

SCOTT H. SLOVIC
Southwest Texas State University

TERRELL F. DIXON
University of Houston

Macmillan Publishing Company
New York

This book is printed on recycled, acid-free paper.

To our students and colleagues,
fellow readers and writers of nature

Editor: Barbara A. Heinssen
Production Supervisor: Ann-Marie E. WongSam
Production Managers: Muriel Underwood and Su Levine
Text Designer: Blake Logan
Cover Designer: Tom Mack
Cover illustration: Bridal Veil Fall, Yosemite National Park, California, c. 1927. Photograph by Ansel Adams. Copyright ©1992 by the Trustees of the Ansel Adams Publishing Rights Trust. All Rights Reserved.
Photo Researchers: Chris Migdol and Suzanne Skloot

This book was set in Futura Light and Palatino by Publication Services, Inc., and was printed and bound by Halliday Lithograph.
The cover was printed by New England Book Components, Inc.

Copyright acknowledgments appear on pages 718–722, which constitute a continuation of the copyright page.

Macmillan Publishing Company
866 Third Avenue, New York, New York 10022

Macmillan Publishing Company is part of
the Maxwell Communication Group of Companies.

Maxwell Macmillan Canada, Inc.
1200 Eglinton Avenue East
Suite 200
Don Mills, Ontario M3C 3N1

Library of Congress Cataloging-in-Publication Data

Being in the world: an environmental reader for writers/[edited by]
    Scott Slovic, Terrell Dixon
        p.   cm.
    Includes index.
    ISBN 0-02-411761-7 (paper)
    1. Readers—Nature.   2. Environmental protection—Problems,
exercises, etc.   3. Readers—Environmental protection.   4. Nature—
Problems, exercises, etc.   5. English language—Rhetoric.
6. College readers.   I. Slovic, Scott, 1960–.   II. Dixon, Terrell
PE1127.S3B45 1993
808'.0427—dc20   92-14929
                                                              CIP

Printing: 1 2 3 4 5 6 7   Year: 3 4 5 6 7 8 9

FOREWORD

Let me put it bluntly. Environmental problems should be our nation's, indeed the world's, very top priority. Preserving the integrity of our life-sustaining resource base is society's most important challenge. And, over the long haul, it will be in the field of education and in the political arena where we will succeed or fail to meet this challenge.

The purpose I had in mind when I organized Earth Day in 1970 was to create a nationwide demonstration of concern for the environment so large that it would shake the political establishment out of its lethargy and finally force this issue permanently into the political arena. It was a gamble but it worked. An estimated twenty million people participated in peaceful demonstrations all across the country on the first Earth Day. Ten thousand grade schools and high schools, two thousand colleges, and one thousand communities were involved.

My other purpose was to establish an annual educational event which would be observed in schools and communities around the country, and that has taken place for more than twenty years now. It's important to take an inventory every year of where we are, what we've done, and where we're going.

The President, the Congress, the media, and community leaders around the nation devote almost all of their time and energy to discussing events and issues of immediate concern—the economy, jobs, wars, the budget deficit, crime in the streets, the worldwide unraveling of the communist system. Strangely, an issue that is immeasurably more important receives comparatively scant attention. The most important political reality today is that all industrial nations are rapidly degrading and dissipating their life-sustaining resource base. The economist Herman Daly cogently summarized this evolving tragedy when he said, "There's something fundamentally wrong in treating the earth as if it were a business in liquidation."

As a society and as individuals, we must begin addressing long-term issues. We must somehow reorganize our political institutions in order to keep in mind the needs of future generations, not only the issues of the next election. Today's college students will soon be playing important leadership roles in our society as politicians, scientists, writers, business people, media representatives, teachers, and many other kinds of professionals. Already, as voters, many students are actively helping to shape society. A writing textbook like *Being in the World: An Environmental Reader for Writers* offers students many ways of developing skills as writers and thinkers. But just as importantly, I think, it helps to focus attention on how human beings live on—or "in"—the world, an issue that will determine what kind of world future generations will inherit.

Gaylord Nelson
Former U.S. Senator (D.-Wisconsin),
Current Counselor of The Wilderness Society

ABOUT THE EDITORS

Scott Slovic was born in Chicago, Illinois, but grew up in Oregon. On the occasion of the first Earth Day in 1970, he presented a speech about zero population growth to his fellow fourth graders at Edgewood Elementary School in Eugene. Slovic earned a B.A. in English at Stanford University in 1983, and then attended graduate school at Brown University, where he completed his Ph.D. in English in 1990. In 1986–1987, he was a Fulbright Scholar at the University of Bonn in West Germany, studying German nature writing and in particular the exploration narratives of Alexander von Humboldt. The author of numerous articles, reviews, and conference papers, he has also published *Seeking Awareness in American Nature Writing: Henry Thoreau, Annie Dillard, Edward Abbey, Wendell Berry, Barry Lopez,* which appeared in 1992. He coedited the special issue of *The CEA Critic* devoted to "The Literature of Nature" in 1991, and a year later became the editor of *The American Nature Writing Newsletter.* In 1992 he helped to create the Association for the Study of Literature and Environment, serving as the organization's first president. Since 1990 Slovic has been an assistant professor of English at Southwest Texas State University in San Marcos, where he teaches freshman composition, American literature, and nature writing workshops for M.F.A. students.

Terrell Dixon was born in Texas and grew up in Oklahoma. He graduated from the University of Oklahoma with a B.A. in Letters (English, history, philosophy, and classics) in 1962 and won a Woodrow Wilson Fellowship for graduate study at Indiana University, where he earned his Ph.D. in English in 1971. He has taught at Indiana University, at Southern Methodist University, and at the University of Houston where he teaches composition, literary nonfiction, and literature and the environment. He has been director of graduate studies in the department there, and since 1980 he has served as chair. Currently, Dixon is a member of the Executive Committee of the Association of Departments of English. He is editing a book on chairing the department for the Modern Language Association, and he is also editing an interdisciplinary, multi-genre collection on the changing views of the grizzly bear in American culture. Dixon has presented many conference papers on exploration and nature writing and contributed essays and reviews on nature literature for such publications as *The CEA Critic* special issue on nature writing, the 1992 volume *A Wilderness Tapestry* (Eds. Mikel Vause, William McGrath, and Samuel Zeveloff), and *The American Nature Writing Newsletter.* He is on the board for the Association for the Study of Literature and Environment.

PREFACE

Being in the World is a thematic anthology derived from the assumption that, as John Muir put it, "most people are *on* the world, not in it." This collection is designed to make available to writing teachers and students many examples of the best American nature writing since Thoreau; we have selected almost exclusively nonfiction essays, letters, and journals, and nearly always complete, non-excerpted pieces, but four short works of fiction have been included as well. The goal of this project has been to move beyond the many existing anthologies of American nature writing—most of which are historically organized, offer minimal gender and ethnic diversity among contributors, and provide no teaching apparatus other than scant headnotes—in preparing a reader specifically to guide student writers. *Being in the World* is intended to meet the needs of students in both beginning composition courses and advanced workshops in literary nonfiction, offering opportunities to experiment with a wide range of rhetorical modes, from narrative to argumentation. This book will enable teachers to develop courses even in disciplines other than English—for instance, Environmental Studies courses with substantial student writing—that encourage students to become more conscious of their relationship to the natural world, to consider the possibility of living *in* the world, not merely *on* it.

The four parts of *Being in the World* ("Nature: 'Out There,' " "Human Visitors," "Belonging to the World," and "Abstractions: Thinking About the Environment") are divided into three or four chapters, each presenting an average of six readings. The structure is meant to suggest an evolving human relationship to the natural world, from detachment to intermittent contact, to genuine familiarity, to internalization. The specific thematic groupings emphasize interaction of one kind or another with nature, but they encompass experiences and issues that should, in most cases, be familiar even to the most emphatically indoor reader. For instance, although many students and instructors may never have climbed a mountain, they will still take an interest in such topics as companionship, joyful solitude, danger and catastrophe, and self-exploration which emerge in the chapter "Climbing: Mountain Narratives." Other chapters, such as "Public Statements: Polemics, Conjectures, Records of Conflict," include a wide range of subtle and provocative issue-oriented readings, not just predictable positions on environmental topics—and our apparatus is designed to offer students opportunities to question the readings and actively debate both environmental issues and issues of literary technique.

The readings do display predominantly positive attitudes toward nature, but they nonetheless represent an extraordinary range of moods and prose styles. Many of the anthologized writers (for example, Annie Dillard, Loren Eiseley, and Alice Walker) will be familiar to writing instructors and to advanced students, while others (such as Gloria Anzaldúa, Mary Austin, Rick Bass, Gretel Ehrlich, Sue Hubbell, Richard Nelson, David Quammen, Edwin Way Teale, and Eudora Welty) are among the most distinctive nonfiction stylists of this century and will be welcome additions to the models currently available to writing students. Many of the authors whose work appears in this anthology took the time to explain, through correspondence or over the phone, their own experiences and their ideas about writing as we worked on our headnotes—their comments have added an engaging dimension to the book. These writers include Gloria Anzaldúa, Arlene Blum, John Daniel, Paula DiPerna, Baruch Fischhoff, John Elder, Stephen Harrigan, Betsy Hilbert, David Brendan Hopes, John Janovy, Jr., Randall Kenan, Larry Littlebird, Wangari Maathai, Susan Mitchell, Michael Pollan, Stephen J. Pyne, Chet Raymo, Scott Russell Sanders, John Tallmadge, and Joy Williams.

Because our goal has been to provide useful models and stimuli for writers and not to present a systematic historical survey of American nature writing, we have included primarily twentieth-century texts, with occasional selections from the second half of the nineteenth century; several of the chapter introductions offer historical explanations for interested readers. This book also presents a far more diverse group of writers in terms of gender, ethnicity, and writing style than any comparable collection. In addition, we have managed to provide an "indepth" component; multiple selections by ten writers, including Henry David Thoreau, John Muir, Annie Dillard, David Quammen, Scott Russell Sanders, and Barry Lopez, will enable students to compare and contrast the writers' approaches to different topics.

Being in the World is a medium-sized reader with 83 selections and substantial apparatus. The book's apparatus includes the following features:

- A general introduction to environmental writing
- Substantial chapter introductions and biographical/critical headnotes, designed to illustrate the salient themes and stylistic issues in the anthologized texts
- Topics for discussion and suggested writing assignments, ranging from brief exercises to full-length essays, following each reading selection

- Rhetorical and geographical alternative contents
- A glossary of critical terms commonly used in discussing nature writing
- Black-and-white photographs before each chapter and a full-color insert with related writing and discussion topics, adding a rich visual dimension to the book

Our recommended writing assignments come from a belief in eclecticism rather than from a single guiding rhetorical philosophy; in connection with each anthologized text, we have proposed writing tasks for students that encourage not only the imitation of rhetorical and/or thematic emphases in the model texts but, in many cases, the launching of analytical, argumentative, and research-based projects that move beyond the goals of the texts themselves. We ourselves tend to be skeptical of textbook apparatus, particularly of suggested topics for discussion and writing. Our responses to the anthologized texts should serve merely as starting points, indicating issues that we, as nature-writing scholars and teachers of nonfiction writing, find interesting and potentially useful in the classroom. Individual instructors will want to emphasize different things about the texts they ask their students to study, and students will come up with their own questions and interpretive angles.

Acknowledgments

We owe a tremendous debt to the many people who helped us during the preparation of this book, either by providing direct encouragement, advice, information, and services or simply by tolerating our frenzied obsessiveness for the past year.

Barbara Heinssen, our editor at Macmillan, has been enthusiastically involved with this project since the initial proposal stage. Her clear-sighted monitoring of our work has kept us close to schedule and has frequently helped us to anticipate the needs of the book's potential users. Rachel Wolf, also at Macmillan, has ably and cheerfully assisted with the comings and goings of drafts and ideas. Joe Samodulski performed the crucial service of negotiating permissions for the texts reprinted in this book. Chris Migdol, Macmillan's director of photo research, helped us select many of the book's distinctive illustrations. Our first contact with Macmillan came through Neil Barry and Doug Day, and we have appreciated their advice and support at every stage of the project.

This project was boosted in its early stages by discussions with scholars and teachers who have gathered in recent years to discuss environmental literature at the Society for Literature and Science Conference, the annual North American Interdisciplinary Wilderness Conference in Ogden (Utah), the College English Association Conference, and the Western Literature Association Conference.

A number of reviewers have contributed valuable responses to our selections and the preliminary apparatus: Chris Anderson, Oregon State University; Cheryll Burgess-Glotfelty, University of Nevada–Reno; Barbara Lounsberry, University of Northern Iowa; James Pickering, University of Houston; John Ruszkiewicz, University of Texas–Austin; Sandra Stephan, Youngstown State University; and Joseph F. Trimmer, Ball State University. Other friends, writers, educators, and nature writing scholars who have supported this project with suggestions and words of encouragement include Steve Barry, University of New Mexico; Linda Bergmann, Illinois Institute of Technology; Ralph Black, New York University; Karen Brennan, Southwest Texas State University; Allan Chavkin, Southwest Texas State University; Michael Hennessy, Southwest Texas State University; David Laurence, Association of Departments of English; Erika Lindemann, University of North Carolina at Chapel Hill; Glen Love, University of Oregon; Thomas J. Lyon, Utah State University; Michael McDowell, Portland Community College; Nicholas O'Connell, University of Washington; Sean O'Grady, University of California–Davis; Steve Olsen, Association of Departments of English; Elizabeth Porter, University of Michigan; Ann Ronald, University of Nevada–Reno; William Rossi, University of Oregon; Barton St. Armand, Brown University; Don Scheese, Gustavus Adolphus College; Nancy Sommers, Harvard University; Bill Stephenson, Northland College; Stephen Trimble, freelance writer and photographer; Mikel Vause, Weber State University; Anita Walsh; Miles Wilson, Southwest Texas State University; Nancy Wilson, Southwest Texas State University; and Steve Wilson, Southwest Texas State University.

Many members of the English Department at the University of Houston have contributed to this book through informal discussions of environmental and writing issues; we would like, in particular, to thank Marianne Cooley, Peter Gingiss, Anne Christensen, John McNamara, Maria Gonzalez, Robert Phillips, Sherry Zivley, Carl Lindahl, Patricia Yongue, and other dedicated teachers of freshman and sophomore courses for their advice. At Southwest Texas State University, the members of interdisciplinary faculty reading group known as the Live Oak Society offered enthusiastic advice as we searched for suitable texts for this anthology; we appreciate the help of Tom Arsuffi, Mark Busby, Susan Hanson, Dick Heaberlin, Dick Holland, Jim Sherow, and Rich Warms. The Faculty Advancement Center at Southwest Texas has provided extremely useful computer and copying facilities, and an ever-helpful staff. Administrative colleagues whose support and understanding have helped us find the time to do this anthology include Harmon Boertien, Nancy Ford, James Pipkin, Roberta Weldon, and Nancy Tynan from the University of Houston and G. Jack Gravitt and Nancy J. Grayson from Southwest Texas.

Several friends, relatives, and colleagues have contributed wonderful photographs (or advice about photographs) for the black-and-white chapter openers. We would like to thank Cheryll Burgess-Glotfelty, Susan Hanson, Sean O'Grady, David Robertson, Mikel Vause, and Linda Walsh for their help with this part of the book.

Elizabeth Kessler took time away from her work as a graduate student at the University of Houston to help with the headnote research for *Being in the World*. Margaret Chelette, also at Houston, worked very hard to keep us in contact with each other—by phone and FAX—despite our busy schedules. Bobby Horeka pitched in with vital clerical assistance at Southwest Texas. We thank all of our writing students at the University of Houston, Brown University, and Southwest Texas, who allowed us to "field test" many of the readings and writing assignments.

As so often happens during time-consuming partnerships like ours, our families have had to tolerate frequent trips and incessant late-night phone calls. Linda Walsh has participated in the making of this book by offering her views on our approach to the project and by proofreading the manuscript. Analinda and Jacinto Camacho-Slovic have watched the entire book-making process with amusement and patience, and have helped to put all of the work into perspective.

Scott H. Slovic
Terrell F. Dixon

CONTENTS

Part Four   Abstractions: Thinking About the Environment   561

RHETORICAL CONTENTS

Cause and Effect

Comparison and Contrast

Definition

Description

Division and Classification

Humor

Narration

Process Analysis

GEOGRAPHICAL
CONTENTS

Midwest

Northeast

Pacific Northwest

South

Southwest and California

Transcontinental (North America)

INTRODUCTION

Where were you, your brothers and sisters, or your parents on April 22, 1970? Many of you who are now college undergraduates had probably not even been born when twenty million Americans participated in the first Earth Day. The mood on that day was hopeful but sober. By 1970 Americans and people throughout the world had already become conscious of the many ways in which modern civilization was contributing to the rapid destruction of the natural environment, the final result of which would include the loss of natural resources needed to sustain human life. Rachel Carson had published *Silent Spring,* her important exposé of the dangers of spraying crops and yards with the pesticide DDT, in 1962. A year later, at the urging of Senator Gaylord Nelson of Wisconsin, President John F. Kennedy toured the United States, speaking about the importance of conserving natural resources. But the public was not interested. In 1968, Paul Ehrlich, the biologist from Stanford, published *The Population Bomb,* identifying the excessive growth of human population throughout the world as the principal cause of the environmental crisis. Even this information failed to change the behavior of the average American. Then in 1969, en route to deliver a speech at the University of California at Berkeley, Senator Nelson read a *Ramparts* magazine article on teach-ins against the Vietnam War, and he quickly developed this idea into what has become an annual "environmental teach-in," an event to honor the earth and raise public awareness of environmental issues.

In conjunction with Earth Day 1970, Garrett De Bell edited *The Environmental Handbook: Prepared for the First National Environmental Teach-In* (Ballantine/Friends of the Earth). Many of the articles in this book emphasize the direness of the environmental crisis, seeking to prompt new awareness—and subsequent changes in behavior—among readers and Earth Day participants with strident warnings and critiques of modern society. But there is also an implicit hopefulness in even the bleakest of these essays, a belief that increased consciousness will somehow help the world avert, or at least delay, what Ehrlich calls "eco-catastrophe." The main way of achieving this consciousness is through education. In his article "Education and Ecology," De Bell asserts that

> Education, particularly higher education, is critically important to solving our ecological crisis. At present, universities do much of the spe-

cialized research which develops the technology that is raping the earth and threatening our survival. They do this job devastatingly well. Yet the knowledge and wisdom to apply technology wisely is neglected .... In many, if not in most of our universities, there is little criticism of the basic assumptions and value judgments that underline our current priorities. (p. 129)

Essential to our ability to think critically about nature itself, about modern technology, and about our own attitudes and values—and to exchange our ideas lucidly and effectively—are the processes of reading and writing. For several years during the early 1970s, college composition teachers around the country used such books as *Ecological Crisis: Readings for Survival* (1970), *There Is No "Away": Readings and Language Activities in Ecology* (1971), and *Beyond Survival* (1971) in hopes of encouraging students to develop their writing skills by considering environmental issues and even by taking direct environmental action, such as writing letters to members of Congress. For the past decade or so, however, universities in general and writing programs in particular have emphasized issues of multiculturalism and gender, neglecting environmental concerns. Meanwhile, pollution, urban sprawl, global warming, overpopulation, and other problems have worsened.

It is time for us to recognize that social and environmental issues are fundamentally linked and that we need to work consistently with everyone in our society if we are to make headway in solving vast problems of any kind. In the past few years Earth Day participants have begun to include numerous members of African-American, Latino, Native American, and Asian-American communities. In an article called "The Many Colors of Green" (*San Francisco Bay Guardian*, August 14, 1991), David Spero noted that the largest 1991 Earth Day event in the San Francisco area occurred in the Bayview District of the city, and the participants were mainly African-Americans. "People realize ecology cannot be separated from issues of economics, power, and racism," said Carl Anthony, the director of the Urban Habitat Project, based in San Francisco. At present, the transcultural importance of environmental issues has barely begun to influence the kinds of people who put their pens and word processors to use in writing about experiences and issues related to the natural world. But our society does need multicultural nature writing, and we hope this anthology will begin to attract student writers from all backgrounds to writing in general, especially to the contemplation of nature.

When representatives from 178 nations gathered in Rio de Janeiro in June of 1992 for the first Earth Summit, the mere occurrence of the meeting demonstrated a new willingness on the part of world leaders to acknowledge and respond to the gravity of the planet's environmental crisis. Delegates at the Earth Summit drafted—and sometimes signed— new treaties to curb global warming, help developing countries improve their economies without further degrading the environment, and protect endangered species. But, above all, the Rio conference showed the impossibility of quick, simple solutions to these problems. Today's college students, in the United States and abroad, will soon be called upon to articulate new philosophies and draft new policies that will help to preserve our fragile environment. Now is the time to gain the knowledge and skills necessary for these complex tasks.

The contemporary environmental writer John Nichols has stated that "to save the world, first we must love it." *Being in the World* echoes this idea, aiming to encourage fascination with the natural world, not merely to generate fear about the jeopardy of the planet. Similarly, we believe that to write well, first we must understand and take pleasure in the process of writing—and not *fear* it. The diverse and lively readings in this anthology reflect the renaissance in American nature writing that has occurred since the late 1960s and the growing interest in this genre among scholars, teachers, and students. With this new textbook we seek to foster appreciation among college students for both the natural environment and the process of writing. The reading selections in the anthology are intended to be appealing and interesting—worthy models for student writing. But they're just a beginning. As the hefty lists of suggestions for further reading indicate, much more wonderful nature writing is available than a single anthology can contain. Individual students and teachers will certainly have their own favorite writers among those included (and excluded) here, and we encourage all users of this book to pursue their personal affinities with a passion. Just as the reading of nature writing will only begin with this book, so, too, the process of learning to write with grace and vigor will need to continue once the current writing course ends. We hope this book will generate an excitement about writing that will linger—and inspire students to produce journals, letters, and essays independent of classroom assignments—long after the final grades are in.

Where were you on April 22, 1990, when the nation observed the twentieth anniversary of Earth Day? Did your school or community offer any special programs to increase environmental awareness? In the Earth Day anniversary issue of *Smithsonian* magazine, Wallace Stegner noted that "there was an environmental movement before Earth Day, a long, slow revolution in values of which contemporary environmentalism is a consequence and a continuation." But the process is far from complete, he added: "We are still in transition from the notion of Man as master of the Earth to the notion of Man as a part of it." By considering the issues raised in this anthology, and by developing a deeper and more constant awareness of our own places in the natural world, perhaps we can learn to honor the earth every day, not just once a year or once every twenty years.

PART ONE

Nature: "Out There"

Richard Harrington/Freelance Photographer's Guild

CHAPTER ONE

Encounters with the Otherness of Nature

John Muir used to claim that in going to the mountains, to the wilderness, he was actually going home. But often writers do not feel utterly at home in the nonhuman world. Indeed, many people struggle to make sense of the seemingly alien realm of nature, to get their bearings in landscapes devoid of human markings, to tolerate and even appreciate things in the world that exist independently of human needs and desires. This chapter emphasizes the idea that the natural world is "out there," alien, something *other* than what's familiar and human. This otherness causes distress, confusion, and even revulsion for some of the following essayists, and yet it also poses an intriguing psychological challenge: how to understand what defies easy description and explanation. Henry David Thoreau confesses facetiously on the opening page of *Walden* (1854) that "I should not talk so much about myself if there were any body else whom I knew so well. Unfortunately, I am confined to this theme by the narrowness of my experience." The authors of the following selections attempt to tell us not only about themselves, but about the outside world. Yet, like Thoreau, they frequently find themselves in front of a mirror, explaining, exploring, and critiquing their own responses to otherness. The object of good essay writing is not merely to have all of the answers in mind when the writing begins and simply lay them out on the page in an orderly manner. Good writing often seems erratic and exploratory—it bears traces of the authors' mental adventures, impasses, detours, and discoveries.

It is fitting that the first reading selection in this book displays the explorer Matthew A. Henson's struggle to describe the strange landscape he and his companions encountered en route to the North Pole in 1908 and 1909. In a sense, all writers must grapple with the inadequacy of language, but sometimes even reports of this difficulty can make for engaging essays. The next two writers, Rachel Carson and John Janovy, Jr., are scientists by training, and yet they, too, demonstrate their awareness of the aesthetic dimensions of the natural world in the process of explaining its intricacies and peculiarities. Carson instructs us in "The Marginal World" to pay attention to the subtle, easily overlooked aspects of nature. Janovy, in his essay "Tigers and Toads," uses his discussion of two obscure creatures as an opportunity to illuminate the process of scientific investigation. For Robert Finch, Annie Dillard, and David Quammen, various encounters with natural otherness become opportunities to explore human consciousness and issues of ethics and aesthetics. What is it about mysterious phenomena, Finch asks in "Very Like a Whale," that so captivates the human imagination? Dillard stares down a weasel, only to lament the difference between her self-conscious human mind and the immersion in the present that she ascribes to the animal. Quammen confesses his uneasiness with the physical appearance of spiders but then wrestles with the ethical implications of his own intolerance for otherness.

MATTHEW A. HENSON

From **A Black Explorer at the North Pole**

Orphaned as a child, the black explorer Matthew A. Henson (1866–
1955) spent most of his life traveling and trying to survive in extreme
environmental conditions. At the age of thirteen, he went to sea, where
he became an able seaman and also learned to read and write. While
still a teenager, Henson met Robert E. Peary, a U.S. Navy civil engineer,
who took Henson with him on an engineering survey to Nicaragua. But
the two men were ultimately to become famous for their adventures in
the Arctic rather than in the tropics. The pair undertook six expeditions to
Greenland between 1891 and 1907 before Peary decided they should try
to be the first men to reach the North Pole. On April 6, 1909, after months
of enduring the unpredictable ice and severe cold of the region, six
men and their dogs stood at the northernmost point on the earth. Their
claim to have been the first to reach the North Pole, however, was later
contested by Frederick A. Cook, who said that his own expedition had
reached the Pole on April 21, 1908. Nonetheless, the saga of Henson
and Peary, recorded in Henson's 1912 book, *A Black Explorer at the
North Pole,* remains a classic example of the lure of even the world's
harshest, most inhospitable places.

Certainly the desire for glory motivated the Peary–Henson expedition to a great extent, but in the following description of the Arctic's
"magnificent desolation," we can see how the power of the landscape
provided its own compensations. With unusual vividness, Henson shows
the ambivalent response to the natural world that many people, including such writers as Henry David Thoreau and Annie Dillard, display in
much milder conditions. Perhaps it is fitting to begin an environmental
reader for writers with Matthew Henson's confession that "words proper
to give you an idea of [the Arctic's] unique beauty do not come to mind."
In a larger sense, the failure of language to describe the strangeness,
the otherness, of the natural world — or the contortion of language into
such oxymorons as "gorgeous bleakness" and "beautiful blankness" —
demonstrates with compelling eloquence both the desire to "be in the
world" and the difficulty of doing so.

[Magnificent Desolation]

While we waited here, we had time to appreciate the magnificent desolation about us. Even on the march, with loaded sledges and tugging dogs to engage attention, unconsciously one finds oneself with wits wool-gathering and eyes taking in the scene, and suddenly being brought back to the business of the hour by the fiend-like conduct of his team.

There is an irresistible fascination about the regions of northernmost Grant Land that is impossible for me to describe. Having no poetry in my soul, and being somewhat hardened by years of experience in that inhospitable country, words proper to give you an idea of its unique beauty do not come to mind. Imagine gorgeous bleakness, beautiful blankness. It never seems broad, bright day, even in the middle of June, and the sky has the different effects of the varying hours of morning and evening twilight from the first to the last peep of day. Early in February, at noon, a thin band of light appears far to the southward, heralding the approach of the sun, and daily the twilight lengthens, until early in March, the sun, a flaming disk of fiery crimson, shows his distorted image above the horizon. This distorted shape is due to the mirage caused by the cold, just as heat-waves above the rails on a railroad-track distort the shape of objects beyond.

The south sides of the lofty peaks have for days reflected the glory of the coming sun, and it does not require an artist to enjoy the unexampled splendor of the view. The snows covering the peaks show all of the colors, variations, and tones of the artist's palette, and more. Artists have gone with us into the Arctic and I have heard them rave over the wonderful beauties of the scene, and I have seen them at work trying to reproduce some of it, with good results but with nothing like the effect of the original. As Mr. Stokes said, "it is color run riot."

To the northward, all is dark and the brighter stars of the heavens are still visible, but growing fainter daily with the strengthening of the sunlight.

When the sun finally gets above the horizon and swings his daily circle, the color effects grow less and less, but then the sky and cloud-effects improve and the shadows in the mountains and clefts of the ice show forth their beauty, cold blues and grays; the bare patches of the land, rich browns; and the whiteness of the snow is dazzling. At midday, the optical impression given by one's shadow is of about nine o'clock in the morning, this due to the altitude of the sun, always giving us long shadows. Above us the sky is blue and bright, bluer than the sky of the Mediterranean, and the clouds from the silky cirrus mare's-tails to the fantastic and heavy cumulus are always objects of beauty. This is the description of fine weather.

Almost any spot would have been a fine one to get a round of views from; at Cape Sheridan, our headquarters, we were bounded by a series of land marks that have become historical; to the north, Cape Hecla, the point of departure of the 1906 expedition; to the west, Cape Joseph Henry, and beyond, the twin peaks of Cape Columbia rear their giant summits out to the ocean.

From Cape Columbia the expedition was now to leave the land and sledge over the ice-covered ocean four hundred and thirteen miles north—to the Pole!

Analyzing and Discussing the Text

1. Is the phrase "magnificent desolation" negative or positive? Explain Henson's attitude toward the Arctic landscape.
2. What seems to be the purpose of the author's elaborate apology in the second paragraph? How does this description of the landscape actually succeed and what are its shortcomings?
3. Does Henson emphasize any precise physical details in the Arctic landscape? If so, try to list the physical characteristics you learn about the Arctic from this text. What else does he seem to emphasize?

Experiencing and Writing About the World

1. Can you "define" the landscape where you are currently located? What are its physical elements, what mood does it inspire, what are its positive and negative attributes? Devote two or three pages to a detailed landscape description in which you record, in separate paragraphs, the details of the place itself and your own intellectual and emotional response to it.
2. The natural world, like the human realm, often strains a writer's descriptive skills—its subtlety, complexity, strangeness, and even familiarity make it hard for us to pin it down in words or sometimes even to *perceive* it adequately. In the preceding description, Matthew Henson clearly feels overwhelmed by the combination of pleasure and abhorrence he feels when viewing the Arctic landscape. Look closely at your own immediate surroundings and then attempt to describe, perhaps with Henson-like oxymorons, the "nature" of the place.
3. Choose at least one of the other essays in this chapter to compare or contrast with Henson's. Which of the essays use similar descriptive techniques or display similar difficulty in coming to terms with nonhuman phenomena?

RACHEL CARSON

The Marginal World

"I can remember no time when I wasn't interested in the out-of-doors and the whole world of nature," Rachel Carson (1907–1964) said in 1954, recalling her childhood on a farm near Pittsburgh, Pennsylvania. Born in the town of Springdale, Carson grew up exploring the nearby woods and fields, but it was for her poetic evocations of the sea that she eventually became famous. When Carson entered the Pennsylvania College for Women (now Chatham College), she already had plans to become a writer; she started out as an English major until she became so fascinated with her required sophomore biology class that she began to consider science as an alternative to writing. "It never occurred to me, or apparently to anyone else," she later reported, "that I could combine the two careers." Carson switched her major to zoology as a junior and graduated magna cum laude in 1928. She went on to earn an M.A. in zoology at Johns Hopkins University.

Since her death in 1964, Carson has become equally well-known for her dramatic exposé of environmental abuse (*Silent Spring*, 1962) and her popularizations of oceanography and marine biology (for instance, *Under the Sea Wind*, 1941, and *The Sea Around Us*, 1951). Both strands of her work, one emphasizing warning and the other wonderment, represent important contributions to the study of nature and, in particular, the relationship between humanity and nature. In her book *The Sense of Wonder* (published posthumously in 1965), Carson yearns to give "each child in the world . . . a sense of wonder so indestructible that it would last throughout life." The following essay, called "The Marginal World," is the introductory chapter of *The Edge of the Sea* (1955). Here the forty-eight-year-old Carson expresses her intense fascination with one of her favorite places in the world: neither the sea nor the inland forests, but the edge, the margin, where the two intersect.

The edge of the sea is a strange and beautiful place. All through the long history of Earth it has been an area of unrest where waves have broken heavily against the land, where the tides have pressed forward over the continents, receded, and then returned. For no two successive days is the shore line precisely the same. Not only do the tides advance and retreat in their eternal rhythms, but the level of the sea itself is never at rest. It rises or falls as the glaciers melt or grow, as the floor of the deep ocean basins shifts under its increasing load of sediments, or as the earth's crust along the continental margins warps up or down in adjustment to strain and tension. Today a little more land may belong to the sea, tomorrow a little less. Always the edge of the sea remains an elusive and indefinable boundary.

The shore has a dual nature, changing with the swing of the tides, belonging now to the land, now to the sea. On the ebb tide it knows the harsh extremes of the land world, being exposed to heat and cold, to wind, to rain and drying sun. On the flood tide it is a water world, returning briefly to the relative stability of the open sea.

Only the most hardy and adaptable can survive in a region so mutable, yet the area between the tide lines is crowded with plants and animals. In this difficult world of the shore, life displays its enormous toughness and vitality by occupying almost every conceivable niche. Visibly, it carpets the intertidal rocks; or half hidden, it descends into fissures and crevices, or hides under boulders, or lurks in the wet gloom of sea caves. Invisibly, where the casual observer would say there is no life, it lies deep in the sand, in burrows and tubes and passageways. It tunnels into solid rock and bores into peat and clay. It encrusts weeds or drifting spars or the hard, chitinous shell of a lobster. It exists minutely, as the film of bacteria that spreads over a rock surface or a wharf piling; as spheres of protozoa, small as pinpricks, sparkling at the surface of the sea; and as Lilliputian beings swimming through dark pools that lie between the grains of sand.

The shore is an ancient world, for as long as there has been an earth and sea there has been this place of the meeting of land and water. Yet it is a world that keeps alive the sense of continuing creation and of the relentless drive of life. Each time that I enter it, I gain some new awareness of its beauty and its deeper meanings, sensing that intricate fabric of life by which one creature is linked with another, and each with its surroundings.

In my thoughts of the shore, one place stands apart for its revelation of exquisite beauty. It is a pool hidden within a cave that one can visit only rarely and briefly when the lowest of the year's low tides fall below it, and perhaps from that very fact it acquires some of its special beauty. Choosing such a tide, I hoped for a glimpse of the pool. The ebb was to fall early in the morning. I knew that if the wind held from the northwest and no interfering swell ran in from a distant storm the level of the sea should drop below the entrance to the pool. There had been sudden ominous showers in the night, with rain like handfuls of gravel flung on the roof. When I looked out into the early morning the sky was full of a gray dawn light but the sun had not yet risen. Water and air were pallid. Across the bay the moon was a luminous disc in the western sky, suspended above the dim line of distant shore—the full August moon, drawing the tide to the low, low levels of the threshold of the alien sea world. As I watched, a gull flew by, above the spruces. Its breast was rosy with the light of the unrisen sun. The day was, after all, to be fair.

Later, as I stood above the tide near the entrance to the pool, the promise of that rosy light was sustained. From the base of the steep wall of rock on which I stood, a moss-covered ledge jutted seaward into deep water. In the surge at the rim of the ledge the dark fronds of oarweeds swayed, smooth and gleaming as leather. The projecting ledge was the path to the small hidden cave and its pool. Occasionally a swell, stronger than the rest, rolled smoothly over the rim and broke in foam against the cliff. But the intervals between such swells were long enough to admit me to the ledge and long enough for a glimpse of that fairy pool, so seldom and so briefly exposed.

And so I knelt on the wet carpet of sea moss and looked back into the dark cavern that held the pool in a shallow basin. The floor of the cave was only a few inches below the roof, and a mirror had been created in which all that grew on the ceiling was reflected in the still water below.

Under water that was clear as glass the pool was carpeted with green sponge. Gray patches of sea squirts glistened on the ceiling and colonies of soft coral were a pale apricot color. In the moment when I looked into the cave a little elfin starfish hung down, suspended by the merest thread, perhaps by only a single tube foot. It reached down to touch its own reflection, so perfectly delineated that there might have been, not one starfish, but two. The beauty of the reflected images and of the limpid pool itself was the poignant beauty of things that are ephemeral, existing only until the sea should return to fill the little cave.

Whenever I go down into this magical zone of the low water of the spring tides, I look for the most delicately beautiful of all the shore's inhabitants—flowers that are not plant but animal, blooming on the threshold of the deeper sea. In that fairy cave I was not disappointed. Hanging from its roof were the pendent flowers of the hydroid Tubularia, pale pink, fringed and delicate as the wind flower. Here were creatures so exquisitely fashioned that they seemed unreal, their beauty too fragile to exist in a world of crushing force. Yet every detail was functionally useful, every stalk and hydranth and petal-like tentacle fashioned for dealing with the realities of existence. I knew that they were merely waiting, in that moment of the tide's ebbing, for the return of the sea. Then in the rush of water, in the surge of surf and the pressure of the incoming tide, the delicate flower heads would stir with life. They would sway on their slender stalks, and their long tentacles would sweep the returning water, finding in it all that they needed for life.

And so in that enchanted place on the threshold of the sea the realities that possessed my mind were far from those of the land world I had left an hour before. In a different way the same sense of remoteness and of a world apart came to me in a twilight hour on a great beach on the coast of Georgia. I had come down after sunset and walked far out over sands that lay wet and gleaming, to the very edge of the retreating sea. Looking back across that immense flat, crossed by winding, water-filled gullies and here and there holding shallow pools left by the tide, I was filled with awareness that this intertidal area, although abandoned briefly and rhythmically by the sea, is always reclaimed by the rising tide. There at the edge of low water the beach with its reminders of the land seemed far away. The only sounds were those of the wind and the sea and the birds. There was one sound of wind moving over water, and another of water sliding over the sand and tumbling down the faces of its own wave forms. The flats were astir with birds, and the voice of the willet rang insistently. One of them stood at the edge of the water and gave its loud, urgent cry; an answer came from far up the beach and the two birds flew to join each other.

The flats took on a mysterious quality as dusk approached and the last evening light was reflected from the scattered pools and creeks. Then birds became only dark shadows, with no color discernible. Sanderlings scurried across the beach like little ghosts, and here and there the darker forms of the willets stood out. Often I could come very close to them before they would start up in alarm—the sanderlings running, the willets flying up, crying. Black skimmers flew along the ocean's edge silhouetted against the dull, metallic gleam, or they went flitting above the sand like large, dimly seen moths. Sometimes they "skimmed" the winding creeks of tidal water, where little spreading surface ripples marked the presence of small fish.

The shore at night is a different world, in which the very darkness that hides the distractions of daylight brings into sharper focus the elemental realities. Once, exploring the night beach, I surprised a small ghost crab in the searching beam of my torch. He was lying in a pit he had dug just above the surf, as though watching the sea and waiting. The blackness of the night possessed water, air, and beach. It was the darkness of an older world, before Man. There was no sound but the all-enveloping, primeval sounds of wind blowing over water and sand, and of waves crashing on the beach. There was no other visible life—just one small crab near the sea. I have seen hundreds of ghost crabs in other settings, but suddenly I was filled with the odd sensation that for the first time I knew the creature in its own world—that I understood, as never before, the essence of its being. In that moment time was suspended; the world to which I belonged did not exist and I might have been an onlooker from outer space. The little crab alone with the sea became a symbol that stood for life itself—for the delicate, destructible, yet incredibly vital force that somehow holds its place amid the harsh realities of the inorganic world.

The sense of creation comes with memories of a southern coast, where the sea and the mangroves, working together, are building a wilderness of thousands of small islands off the southwestern coast of Florida, separated from each other by a tortuous pattern of bays, lagoons, and narrow waterways. I remember a winter day when the sky was blue and drenched with sunlight; though there was no wind one was conscious of flowing air like cold clear crystal. I had landed on the surf-washed tip of one of those islands, and then worked my way around to the sheltered bay side. There I found the tide far out, exposing the broad mud flat of a cove bordered by the mangroves with their twisted branches, their glossy leaves, and their long prop roots reaching down, grasping and holding the mud, building the land out a little more, then again a little more.

The mud flats were strewn with the shells of that small, exquisitely colored mollusk, the rose tellin, looking like scattered petals of pink roses. There must have been a colony nearby, living buried just under the surface of the mud. At first the only creature visible was a small heron in gray and rusty plumage—a reddish egret that waded across the flat with the stealthy, hesitant movements of its kind. But other land creatures had been there, for a line of fresh tracks wound in and out among the mangrove roots, marking the path of a raccoon feeding on the oysters that gripped the supporting roots with projections from their shells. Soon I found the tracks of a shore bird, probably a sanderling, and followed them a little; then they turned toward the water and were lost, for the tide had erased them and made them as though they had never been.

Looking out over the cove I felt a strong sense of the interchangeability of land and sea in this marginal world of the shore, and of the links between the life of the two. There was also an awareness of the past and of the continuing flow of time, obliterating much that had gone before, as the sea had that morning washed away the tracks of the bird.

The sequence and meaning of the drift of time were quietly summarized in the existence of hundreds of small snails—the mangrove periwinkles—browsing on the branches and roots of the trees. Once their ancestors had been sea dwellers, bound to the salt waters by every tie of their life processes. Little by little over the thousands and millions of years the ties had been broken, the snails had adjusted themselves to life out of water, and now today they were living many feet above the tide to which they only occasionally returned. And perhaps, who could say how many ages hence, there would be in their descendants not even this gesture of remembrance for the sea.

The spiral shells of other snails—these quite minute—left winding tracks on the mud as they moved about in search of food. They were horn shells, and when I saw them I had a nostalgic moment when I wished I might see what Audubon saw, a century and more ago. For such little horn shells were the food of the flamingo, once so numerous on this coast, and when I half closed my eyes I could almost imagine a flock of these magnificent flame birds feeding in that cove, filling it with their color. It was a mere yesterday in the life of the earth that they were there; in nature, time and space are relative matters, perhaps most truly perceived subjectively in occasional flashes of insight, sparked by such a magical hour and place.

There is a common thread that links these scenes and memories— the spectacle of life in all its varied manifestations as it has appeared, evolved, and sometimes died out. Underlying the beauty of the spectacle there is meaning and significance. It is the elusiveness of that meaning that haunts us, that sends us again and again into the natural world where the key to the riddle is hidden. It sends us back to the edge of the sea, where the drama of life played its first scene on earth and perhaps even its prelude; where the forces of evolution are at work today, as they have been since the appearance of what we know as life; and where the spectacle of living creatures faced by the cosmic realities of their world is crystal clear.

Analyzing and Discussing the Text

1. What is Carson's attitude toward the "intertidal area" at the edge of the sea? Which adjectives does she use to describe this zone?
2. Try to identify the specific topic of each paragraph in this essay. How does the essay as a whole seem to be structured? Is there a discernible progression of ideas or merely a random sprawl? Look for patterns.
3. What do you know about the speaker in this essay? Can you tell if it's a man or a woman? Does gender seem to matter?
4. Is this essay written in the first or the third person? How does the perspective change the overall effect of the piece?
5. Is the narrator concerned with science or aesthetics? Use specific examples from the text in your discussion.
6. Do the observer's thoughts remain confined to the present? Explain what happens at the end of this essay—how are these parting thoughts appropriate for the conclusion?

Experiencing and Writing About the World

1. Prepare a generalized, 250-word description of a special place you have visited. Try to define the specialness of the place. Intentionally avoid using precise details in this description. What seem to be the value and the limitations of such a description?
2. In 500–750 words, break down the physical characteristics of this place into specific categories—devote separate paragraphs to each category (plantlife, animals, sounds, locations, and so forth). Leave

out an overarching, explanatory dimension. How successful is this essay without an integration of the specific observations?

3. Compose a brief narrative about one of your own visits to this place. Try, like Carson, to use the pronoun *I* to represent an attentive viewer, but not an overly emotional participant in the scene. Make the external world, not the human observer, the subject of the narrative.

4. Now try knitting together the impersonal descriptions and the personal narrative. Does it work best to intertwine the two or to proceed neatly from one to the next? Check Carson for a model. Try to turn the three separate essays suggested in the previous assignments into a more complex, multidimensional essay that includes specific descriptions; integrative commentary; and a dramatic, humanizing narrative.

JOHN JANOVY, JR.

Tigers and Toads

Although a scientist by training, John Janovy, Jr. (1937–   ), writes with the kind of wit and ingenuous enthusiasm for his subject that compels interest even among his less scientifically minded readers. Janovy was born in Houma, Louisiana, but grew up in Oklahoma, eventually earning three degrees (a B.S. in mathematics and an M.S. and Ph.D. in zoology) from the University of Oklahoma. He spent a year at Rutgers University on a postdoctoral fellowship before beginning his teaching career at the University of Nebraska in 1966. As a biologist, Janovy studies parasites; he has performed much of his research on "population dynamics" in Keith County, Nebraska, the area three hundred miles west of his home in Lincoln that has also inspired most of his literary work. Although he says he has "always been writing these essays," it was not until the mid-1970s that he decided to try "speaking to different audiences" by publishing them. Janovy, the Varner Distinguished Professor of biology at Nebraska, has shown his versatility as a writer with successful books on a wide range of topics; these books include *Keith County Journal* (1980), *Yellow Legs* (1981), *On Becoming a Biologist* (1986), *Fields of Friendly*

Strife (1988), and most recently *Vermilion Sea: A Naturalist's Journey in Baja California* (1992).

Perhaps it is not so important that the average reader come away from an essay like "Tigers and Toads" (from the 1981 volume *Back in Keith County*) with an intricate knowledge of the Rocky Mountain toad and the tiger beetle, although a good deal of information does emerge in the essay. More important is the attitude toward the natural world that is both demonstrated and analyzed in the piece. The "toad" and the "tiger" represent nature's otherness, its distance from the human observer—one is so "truly ugly," the other so "truly beautiful" as to be radically inhuman. Nonetheless, rather than feeling disdain, indifference, or awe toward these creatures, the biologist/writer is moved by *curiosity* to pay close attention. But the real goal, writes Janovy, "is the generation of a curiosity that always asks a question that in turn spurs one on to a physical act in pursuit of an answer." In this way, Janovy differs from the less aggressively analytical appreciators of otherness, from writers such as Robert Finch and Annie Dillard, who prefer to observe and contemplate the world without interfering. Like Gilbert White, the eighteenth-century British "parson naturalist" who in a famous 1776 narrative tells a story about killing a "large viper" and discovering "the abdomen crowded with young," Janovy's goal is to move from passive curiosity to close, analytical scrutiny of such things as the stomachs of toads. To achieve such close observation, or simply to catch the desired animal, requires what Janovy calls "the correct approach," and this approach leads the human observer, paradoxically, to imitate the nonhuman world. In this essay, patient, toadlike waiting proves the best way to trap the speedy beetle: "acting like an animal to get close to an animal, acting like a plant to get close to an animal, those are things biologists do." Yet Janovy concludes his essay on a more universal note, suggesting that the appreciation of anything, whether human or inhuman, requires "*the* correct approach, *the* correct frame of mind...."

The Rocky Mountain toad may be one of the world's truly ugly creatures, also slow and ungainly, showing no outward sign of intelligence, and reproducing in obscene numbers on the sandy shores of Arthur Bay. The tiger beetle may be one of the world's truly beautiful creatures, also exceedingly fast and graceful, running as well as flying, exhibiting behavior suggestive of style and class, stalking the sandy shores of Arthur Bay. There could be no two creatures more illustrative of the extremes to be found within the animal kingdom. Yet, they spend their days in the tightest of life and death relationships: the toads eat the tigers, and in gluttonous numbers, right there on the sandy shores of Arthur Bay.

Surely there is some lesson I am supposed to learn from this! was my first reaction to the above observations. The occasion was routine enough: a tapeworm had been discovered in toads of Arthur Bay. Tapeworms of land animals often must exist for a time in lower animals, insects, for example. The insect is eaten by the land vertebrate and the worm is freed to continue its development into an adult in the vertebrate's intestine. I don't remember the origin of that move to examine the stomach contents of the Rocky Mountain toad, but that move was obviously motivated by a curiosity about toad diet. In retrospect, I do strongly wish I could remember that moment I decided to look into a toad's stomach. That is a moment I would like to repeat again and again at other times, in other arenas, in other laboratories, with problems other than toads.

Some combination of events, of circumstances, of people there at the moment, some spark of interest struck by a previous event, all worked together to generate the question: Wonder what toads eat to get those worms? How I do wish I could put together at will a set of circumstances that would produce similar thoughts about other things! Oh, I've generated plenty of curiosity about those other things; the generation of curiosity has never been a problem. The problem is the generation of a curiosity that always asks a question that in turn spurs one on to a physical act in pursuit of an answer. And I do wish this physical act of observation would, not just once in a while, but *always*, have the lasting power of the sight of a toad's stomach full of tiger beetles.

It was years ago, very near the end of our annual stay in Keith County, when I made the observation about tigers and toads. But at that very moment, the first paragraph of this essay was written in my mind and has stayed there ever since with virtually no change in wording. You see, tiger beetles have a certain reputation among those who know them only slightly, or have tried to catch them. The reputation is one of speed coupled with almost purposeful behavior, a sort of halting run, that makes a tiger beetle simply very hard to catch by normal means. One does not walk up to a tiger beetle and pick it up. Nor does one easily sweep up a tiger beetle with a net skimmed over the white blistering surface of Arthur Bay dunes. No, the way to catch a tiger beetle is to act like a toad. The way to catch speed, grace, beauty, elegance, is to act dumb, slow, ugly, ungainly? No, patient. The Rocky Mountain toad is a packet of patience. But there is something deeper here: Patience is nothing more than the correct approach, and therein lies the lesson of this beauty and this beast. *The* correct approach, regardless of outward appearance, is the one attribute that will always net the prey.

And into how many other circumstances can this rule be inserted? Into many, is the answer. On many barren dunes will the correct approach capture beauty and grace. All one has to do is develop *the* approach. Now there is a challenge! We are not always born with it, latent, awaiting only time, warmth, and water, as are those black polywogs out near Arthur Bay. But we can plan for the correct approach. We can develop the correct approach on purpose, or teach it to others. There is more beauty and grace than that of the tiger beetle awaiting! You do understand that I am resisting the drive to preach too early a personal sermon: The lamination of early decision, of sealed-off options, of the euryphobia attending false security, elitism, or lack of confidence, are all the things that prevent us from accomplishing what a Rocky Mountain toad can do. No, I'll save that sermon for later, if at all. Instead, I will extend this tale into the absurdity of toadal aspirations. Toads, regardless of their beastly countenances, have access to beauty and grace, but not to the beauty and grace of the swallow. Can you not envision that cowboy toad, baking out on the flats of Arthur Bay, watching barn swallows above, watching *their* beauty and grace that more than equals those of the tiger beetle, and saying to himself (or to another toad) "One day I catch *that*."

Let us shift for a few paragraphs to a discussion of *Rana catesbeiana*, the bullfrog, not a toad, but a relative of the toad. Then we'll come back to Mr. *Bufo woodhousei*, dry land cousin of *R. catesbeiana*, the green, waterlogged, euphagous bullfrog. You've tasted bullfrog legs; they're delicious, sort of like rattlesnake, better than chicken, sort of frog-leggy. Around here, the bullfrog is big, capable, on the lists of game animals with *seasons*. You must know that *seasons* set the bullfrog apart in the mind of a human, apart from the other anurans of cowboy country. To me, however, it is his name that sets him apart in a way no season could. *Catesbeiana*—now there is a name of all names. I have no idea who Woodhouse was. I'm sure he was famous in some circles. But I know the name Catesby well.

Mark Catesby was a naturalist, antedating Audubon, and by all standards of modern cultural ethics, was a bum. He came to the United States of America on the bum, married the daughter of a wealthy landowner to support his bummery, moved onto his father-in-law's land, and spent the rest of his days in the woods of what is now North Carolina, collecting plants and animals, drawing pictures of the specimens he'd collected, sending those pictures to the leading biologist of his day, a fanatic named Carl von Linné, and generally pursuing a life of pleasure. This was all done without malice, according to his biographers, but not without forethought. Nobody, to my knowledge, finances a scientific career in that manner today. But then science has grown large, sophisticated, somehow apart from the run of regular society. So I've never heard an aspiring young biologist admit outright he'd like to find a wealthy young landed lady to support him so that he could pursue his studies. But some have come close.

The point of this discussion about the bullfrog, however, is that upon its list of edibles is birds. Now I find myself wondering if there is not some anuran interlanguage, some set of croaks by which *B. woodhousei* could be told that upon the list of his cousin's edibles is birds.

Modern biologists tell me of the impossibility of such interlanguage. Toad calls, frog calls, are wondrously specific, say these folks, and indeed recorded anuran calls, and their respective answers when those recordings are played out in the weeds, are stock in trade of those who study "isolating mechanisms." Such a shame that the independent and asocial anurans should live with that separation of language, that dearth of intercommunication, and in so doing should not be able to tell a single *B. woodhousei* who would have a swallow of swallow that the lofty ambition was indeed lofty, but at least worth a good try! Such fortune, that in the life of that most social of animals, *H. sapiens*, whose interlanguages infect all layers of society, the binding communication between individuals of different ilks is the very element that opens the *idea* of opportunity, that passively sanctions the lofty individual aspiration beyond which immediate companions would strive.

I tested my limits one day, out on those white sands of Arthur Bay. I took upon myself the task of getting close to a tiger beetle. The idea that morning was to establish a photographic record of the tiger-toad relationship. That relationship would make a good subject for a charming lecture to some civic group. After all, Beauty and the Beast has stood the test of time; and tigers and toads is a sort of beauty and the beast kind of tale. But the tiger proved more elusive than the toad, the beauty more elusive than the beast, until, of course, I acted like a beast. So here is a short biology lesson for those of you who will never crawl around in the Arthur Bay sand: In order to photograph the tiger you must be patient and slow, always giving the beauty time to adjust to your presence. You must not all at once present too much of a difference from your surroundings. And, it helps immeasurably to get down on the same level as the beauty. With those simple techniques, *the* correct approach, you can come as close to beauty as your beastly desires want. I was too close for my lenses. I lay in the sand of Arthur Bay eye-to-eye with a tiger beetle, and successfully resisted the temptation to eat it, sensing, somehow, that my tongue might not be as sticky as a toad's. I stood then, to full posture, brushing away the sand, and beauty flew away many yards. But my eyes had adjusted and suddenly there were hundreds of tiger beetles everywhere, ones I had not seen before getting eye-to-eye with one.

I'm sure the recreational folks of Arthur Bay saw me as different from themselves that day. And I'm just as sure that my behavior required no great measure of courage. No, acting like an animal to get close to an animal, acting like a plant to get close to an animal, those are things biologists do. But still, the decision to act like a toad is a decision not everyone would make, and furthermore, I would not make except on the sands of some Arthur Bay. I don't crawl along city sidewalks. But I am very alert to that tiger beetle beauty wherever it can be found. And I am very aware that there *are* options, behavioral and cultural options, that will lead me to that beauty regardless of the form that beauty takes.

The elegant experiment, is that not beauty? The clean glassware; the perfect culture medium; the student who follows your best lecture with a most penetrating question; your child making a decision that makes you, in turn, so proud; the wren that actually uses the house *you* built; the title remembered from a hazy past but plucked from a browser's library shelf; are those not also things of beauty? And do those things not also require *the* correct approach, *the* correct frame of mind, *the* purposeful circumstance that brings out not only their beauty, but also your own willingness to see that beauty? Yes, to all those questions. And cannot you remember times when pursuit of that beauty, maybe beyond the tiger beetle, maybe the beauty of that swallow seemingly beyond you, required some special approach? Of course you remember the time, for you are human, and those opportunities to aspire come many times a day. And you must know that the continuous opportunity to be a toad, to have a tiger, to wish for a swallow, and to feel for those who don't also wish for swallows, that continuous opportunity is your own Keith County.

Analyzing and Discussing the Text

1. What is it about the relationship between the Rocky Mountain toad and the tiger beetle that so intrigues the author of this essay? Can you think of any other relationships in the natural world that might provoke similar interest in the scientist/writer?
2. Does the narrator sound like a scientist or an artist? What are the signs of each in the language of the text?
3. What is "the correct approach"? Is this approach necessary for a writer, too? What do "toadal aspirations" have to do with the aspirations of a nature writer?
4. Is this a serious essay or a humorous one? Why do you think Janovy selects such a tone?

Experiencing and Writing About the World

1. Using whatever resources are available to you, try to discover a quirky fact about the natural world that you can develop into a lively 500-word essay explaining this "quirk of nature." If possible, include both library research and actual field study as sources of information.
2. The combination of patience, knowledge, and attentiveness is essential to good nature writing. Take your notebook and sit somewhere

outside for as long as possible (at least an hour), observing, taking notes, trying to notice more and more details of your surroundings the longer you stay. You might wish to take a camera with you during this exercise in patient observation. Try to take several photographs to accompany a 500-word essay describing the appearance and behavior of a specific natural phenomenon—perhaps that of an insect or a readily observable animal, such as Janovy's toads.

3. Practice close observation by lying on the ground and inspecting the minute phenomena—insects, seeds, small plants, rocks, soil—you encounter. Write down these observations in the form of detailed notes. If you're unable to identify the things you see, go to the library and look them up in appropriate field guides. Type up your notes, combining vivid descriptions with accurate scientific terminology.

4. Ambitious writers might want to try using a natural phenomenon as a metaphor for a particular type of human experience. Devote approximately 250 words to the natural metaphor, 100 words to the transition from the natural to the human, and then another 250 words to human nature. Does your essay give equal weight to the human and the inhuman?

ROBERT FINCH

Very Like a Whale

Like Rachel Carson, Robert Finch (1943–   ) has made a name for himself through his writings about the sea, and, specifically, the *edge* of the sea. His three collections of essays—*Common Ground: A Naturalist's Cape Cod* (1981), *The Primal Place* (1983), and *Outlands: Journeys to the Outer Edges of Cape Cod* (1986)—display a combined fascination with the details of the natural world and the human observer's intellectual and emotional response to it. Finch has not always lived on Cape Cod or even in Massachusetts. He grew up "along the glass-littered, oil-sheened banks of the Passaic River in industrial New Jersey" and, after graduate school in Indiana, taught briefly at Oregon State University. In 1971 he returned to Massachusetts, where he settled with his family in West Brewster (on the Cape) because of the lure of its natural landscape and its literary tradition. Finch currently lives only a short distance from where the poet Conrad Aiken once lived, and he purchased the land where his house stands from John Hay, another contemporary nature writer. Although he now devotes most of his time to writing, Finch has worked as the publications director for the Cape Cod Museum of Natural History and has taught at Cape Cod Community College and the Bread Loaf Writers' Conference in Vermont. In addition to his own books, he co-edited *The Norton Book of Nature Writing* (1990).

Unlike Carson, Finch's academic background is in the humanities; he was an undergraduate English major at Harvard. "Most of what I would call nature writing is not done by scientists or formally trained naturalists," he says in an essay called "Being at Two with Nature" (1991), "but by writers who slip through the back door of the humanities." Finch's writing demonstrates both an understanding of the natural phenomena he encounters during his wanderings—by foot or by boat—on the beaches and coastal waters of the Cape and a profound respect for the mysterious otherness of these phenomena, an uneasiness with the human inclination to control and appropriate what initially defies our ideas of order and usefulness. In "Very Like a Whale," for instance, he goes so far as to say, "This sense of otherness is, I feel, as necessary a requirement to our personalities as food and warmth are to our bodies."

One day last week at sunset I went back to Corporation Beach in Dennis to see what traces, if any, might be left of the great, dead finback whale that had washed up there several weeks before. The beach was not as hospitable as it had been that sunny Saturday morning after Thanksgiving when thousands of us streamed over the sand to gaze and look. A few cars were parked in the lot, but these kept their inhabitants. Bundled up against a sharp wind, I set off along the twelve-foot swath of trampled beach grass, a raw highway made in a few hours by ten thousand feet that day.

I came to the spot where the whale had beached and marveled that such a magnitude of flesh could have been there one day and gone the next. But the carcass had been hauled off and the tide had smoothed and licked clean whatever vestiges had remained. The cold, salt wind had lifted from the sands the last trace of that pervasive stench of decay that clung to our clothes for days, and now blew clean and sharp into my nostrils.

The only sign that anything unusual had been there was that the beach was a little too clean, not quite so pebbly and littered as the surrounding areas, as the grass above a new grave is always fresher and greener. What had so manifestly occupied this space a short while ago was now utterly gone. And yet the whale still lay heavily on my mind; a question lingered, like a persistent odor in the air. And its dark shape, though now sunken somewhere beneath the waves, still loomed before me, beckoning, asking something.

What was it? What had we seen? Even the several thousand of us that managed to get down to the beach before it was closed off did not see much. Whales, dead or alive, are protected these days under the Federal Marine Mammals Act, and shortly after we arrived, local police kept anyone from actually touching the whale. I could hardly regret this, since in the past beached whales, still alive, have had cigarettes put out in their eyes and bits of flesh hacked off with pocket knives by souvenir seekers. And so, kept at a distance, we looked on while the specialists worked, white-coated, plastic-gloved autopsists from the New England Aquarium, hacking open the thick hide with carving knives and plumbing its depths for samples to be shipped to Canada for analysis and determination of causes of death. What was it they were pulling out? What fetid mystery would they pluck from that huge coffin of dead flesh? We would have to trust them for the answer.

But as the crowds continued to grow around the whale's body like flies around carrion, the question seemed to me, and still seems, not so much why did the whale die, as why had we come to see it? What made this dark bulk such a human magnet, spilling us over onto private lawns and fields? I watched electricians and oil truck drivers pulling their vehicles off the road and clambering down to the beach. Women in high heels and pearls, on their way to Filene's, stumbled through the loose sand to gaze at a corpse. The normal human pattern was broken and a carnival atmosphere was created, appropriate enough in the literal sense of "a farewell to the flesh." But there was also a sense of pilgrimage in those trekking across the beach, an obligation to view such a thing. But for what? Are we really such novices to death? Or so reverent toward it?

I could understand my own semiprofessional interest in the whale, but what had drawn these hordes? There are some obvious answers, of course: a break in the dull routine, "something different." An old human desire to associate ourselves with great and extraordinary events. We placed children and sweethearts in front of the corpse and clicked cameras. "Ruthie and the whale." "Having a whale of a time on Cape Cod."

Curiosity, the simplest answer, doesn't really answer anything. What, after all, did we learn by being there? We were more like children at a zoo, pointing and poking, or Indians on a pristine beach, gazing in innocent wonder at strange European ships come ashore. Yet, as the biologists looted it with vials and plastic bags and the press captured it on film, the spectators also tried to *make* something of the whale. Circling around it as though for some hold on its slippery bulk, we grappled it with metaphors, lashed similes around its immense girth. It lay upside down, overturned "like a trailer truck." Its black skin was cracked and peeling, red underneath, "like a used tire." The distended, corrugated lower jaw, "a giant accordion," was afloat with the gas of putrifaction and, when pushed, oscillated slowly "like an enormous waterbed." Like our primitive ancestors, we still tend to make images to try to comprehend the unknown.

But what were we looking at? Or more to the point, from what perspective were we looking at it? What did we see in it that might tell us why we had come? A male finback whale—*Balaenoptera physalus*—a baleen cetacean. The second largest creature ever to live on earth. An intelligent and complex mammal. A cause for conservationists. A remarkably adapted swimming and eating machine. Perfume, pet food, engineering oil. A magnificent scientific specimen. A tourist attraction. A media event, a "day to remember." A health menace, a "possible carrier of a communicable disease." A municipal headache and a navigational hazard. Material for an essay.

On the whale's own hide seemed to be written its life history, which we could remark but not read. The right fluke was almost entirely gone, lost in some distant accident or battle and now healed over with a white scar. The red eye, unexpectedly small and mammalian, gazed out at us with fiery blankness. Like the glacial scratches sometimes found on our boulders, there were strange marks or grooves in the skin around the anal area, perhaps caused by scraping the ocean bottom.

Yet we could not seem to scratch its surface. The whale—dead, immobile, in full view—nonetheless shifted kaleidoscopically before our eyes. The following morning it was gone, efficiently and sanitarily removed, like the week's garbage. What was it we saw? I have a theory, though probably (as they say in New England) it hardly does.

There is a tendency these days to defend whales and other endangered animals by pointing out their similarities to human beings. Cetaceans, we are told, are very intelligent. They possess a highly complex language and have developed sophisticated communications systems that transmit over long distances. They form family groups, develop social structures and personal relationships, and express loyalty and affection toward one another. Much of their behavior seems to be recreational: they sing, they play. And so on.

These are not sentimental claims. Whales apparently do these things, at least as far as our sketchy information about their habits warrants such interpretations. And for my money, any argument that helps to preserve these magnificent creatures can't be all bad.

I take exception to this approach not because it is wrong, but because it is wrongheaded and misleading. It is exclusive, anthropocentric, and does not recognize nature in its own right. It implies that whales and other creatures have value only insofar as they reflect man himself and conform to his ideas of beauty and achievement. This attitude is not really far removed from that of the whalers themselves. To consume whales solely for their nourishment of human values is only a step from consuming them for meat and corset staves. It is not only presumptuous and patronizing, but it is misleading and does both whales and men a grave disservice. Whales have an inalienable right to exist, not because they resemble man *or* because they are useful to him, but simply because they do exist, because they have a proven fitness to the exactitudes of being on a global scale matched by few other species. If they deserve our admiration and respect, it is because, as Henry Beston put it, "They are other nations, caught with ourselves in the net of life and time, fellow prisoners of the splendour and travail of life."

But that still doesn't explain the throngs who came pell-mell to stare and conjecture at the dead whale that washed up at Corporation Beach and dominated it for a day like some extravagant *memento mori*. Surely we were not flattering ourselves, consciously or unconsciously, with any human comparisons to that rotting hulk. Nor was there much, in its degenerate state, that it had to teach us. And yet we came—why?

The answer may be so obvious that we have ceased to recognize it. Man, I believe, has a crying need to confront otherness in the universe. Call it nature, wilderness, the "great outdoors," or what you will—we crave to look out and behold something other than our own human faces staring back at us, expectantly and increasingly frustrated. What the human spirit wants, as Robert Frost said, "Is not its own love back in copy-speech, / But counter-love, original response."

This sense of otherness is, I feel, as necessary a requirement to our personalities as food and warmth are to our bodies. Just as an individual, cut off from human contact and stimulation, may atrophy and die of loneliness and neglect, so mankind is today in a similar, though more subtle, danger of cutting himself off from the natural world he shares with all creatures. If our physical survival depends upon our devising a proper use of earth's materials and produce, our growth as a species depends equally upon establishing a vital and generative relationship with what surrounds us.

We need plants, animals, weather, unfettered shores and unbroken woodland, not merely for a stable and healthy environment, but as an antidote to introversion, a preventive against human inbreeding. Here in particular, in the splendor of natural life, we have an extraordinary reservoir of the Cape's untapped possibilities and modes of being, ways of experiencing life, of knowing wind and wave. After all, how many neighborhoods have whales wash up in their backyards? To confine this world in zoos or in exclusively human terms does injustice not only to nature, but to ourselves as well.

Ever since his beginnings, when primitive man adopted totems and animal spirits to himself and assumed their shapes in ritual dance, *Homo sapiens* has been a superbly imitative animal. He has looked out across the fields and seen and learned. Somewhere along the line, though, he decided that nature was his enemy, not his ally, and needed to be confined and controlled. He abstracted nature and lost sight of it. Only now are we slowly realizing that nature can be confined only by narrowing our own concepts of it, which in turn narrows us. That is why we came to see the whale.

We substitute human myth for natural reality and wonder why we starve for nourishment. "Your Cape" becomes "your Mall," as the local radio jingle has it. Thoreau's "huge and real Cape Cod . . . a wild, rank place with no flattery in it," becomes the Chamber of Commerce's "Rural Seaside Charm"—until forty tons of dead flesh wash ashore and give the lie to such thin, flattering conceptions, flesh whose stench is still the stench of life that stirs us to reaction and response. That is why we came to see the whale. Its mute, immobile bulk represented that ultimate, unknowable otherness that we both seek and recoil from, and shouted at us louder than the policeman's bullhorn that the universe is fraught, not merely with response or indifference, but incarnate assertion.

Later that day the Dennis Board of Health declared the whale carcass to be a "health menace" and warned us off the beach. A health menace? More likely an intoxicating, if strong, medicine that might literally bring us to our senses.

But if those of us in the crowd failed to grasp the whale that day, others did not have much better luck. Even in death the whale escaped us: the tissue samples taken in the autopsy proved insufficient for analysis and the biologists concluded, "We will never know why the whale died." The carcass, being towed tail-first by a Coast Guard cutter for a final dumping beyond Provincetown, snapped a six-inch hawser. Eluding further attempts to reattach it, it finally sank from sight. Even our powers of disposal, it seemed, were questioned that day.

And so, while we are left on shore with the memory of a deflated and stinking carcass and of bullhorns that blared and scattered us like flies, somewhere out beyond the rolled waters and the shining winter sun, the whale sings its own death in matchless, sirenian strains.

Analyzing and Discussing the Text

1. The author repeatedly asks the question, "What had we seen?" Why?
2. How does Finch explain the attraction of several thousand people to the dead finback whale? Is this an essay about whale behavior or human behavior?
3. "Man, I believe, has a crying need to confront otherness in the universe," Finch suggests. What does this mean? Why does Finch use the example of the dead whale to demonstrate this need? Do you feel this same need? Explain how the whale functions as a symbol of otherness.

4. Finch (or his narrator) seems "nourished" somehow by his encounter with the whale, his participation in the whole spectacle. How does he benefit?
5. Why conclude by recounting the Coast Guard's failure to dispose of the whale carcass as planned?
6. What does Finch mean when he writes "the whale sings its own death in matchless, sirenian strains"?

Experiencing and Writing About the World

1. In 500–750 words, present an encounter of your own with an awesome, inexplicable, or simply bizarre natural phenomenon. First try to describe this phenomenon—a wild animal (living or dead), a sheer cliff or raging river, or a particularly memorable storm—by using matter-of-fact language. Does this seem to work? If not, try "grappl[ing] it with metaphors." Does figurative language help or obstruct your ability to convey the inhuman otherness of the phenomenon, its vastness, its wildness, or its mysteriousness? Attempt to interpret the phenomenon, to suggest what it means.
2. After trying to describe the otherness of a natural phenomenon, revise your essay to include intermittent analysis of your own descriptive language. Try to explain the purpose of using language to describe something that by definition defies human comprehension.
3. What recent experience (outdoors or not) have you had that at once intrigued and baffled you? Write a brief account/inquiry (500–750 words) concerning this experience, using abundant rhetorical questions to emphasize the questioning, investigatory purpose of your essay.
4. Have you ever been part of a spectacle like the discovery of a dead whale? Have you ever joined a crowd of onlookers after a tornado, an oil spill, a house fire, or a car accident? Write an essay in which you attempt to analyze and explain the motivations of the crowd.

ANNIE DILLARD

Living Like Weasels

Born and raised in Pittsburgh, Pennsylvania, educated at Hollins College in Virginia (B.A. in 1967, M.A. in 1968), and employed as a teacher of poetry and creative writing for several years at Western Washington University in Bellingham, Annie Dillard (1945–   ) has been writer-in-residence at Wesleyan University in Middletown, Connecticut, since 1979. Although she has become famous for her intensely colorful and often outlandish renderings of the natural world in such books as *Pilgrim at Tinker Creek* (1974), *Holy the Firm* (1977), and *Teaching a Stone to Talk* (1982), she claims in *The Writing Life* (1989), "[I]t should surprise no one that the life of a writer—such as it is—is colorless to the point of sensory deprivation. Most writers do little else but sit in small rooms recalling the real world." She explains that her 1974 Pulitzer-winning study of the Virginia countryside was actually written in the Hollins College Library with the shades intentionally closed, because "appealing workplaces are to be avoided. One wants a room with no view, so imagination can meet memory in the dark." Dillard concludes *The Writing Life* with an extended account of a stunt pilot's artistry, subtly using the pilot's aerial acrobatics as a metaphor for the writer's work, the semiconscious process of achieving verbal flamboyance. Indeed, Dillard's own prose style is known for its energy and idiosyncrasies, notable among the work of contemporary American essayists for its routine blending of terms borrowed from religion, science, and popular culture (such as advertising). The metaphors she uses to describe the natural world are often stunning, eye opening; for instance, when she writes in *Pilgrim at Tinker Creek*, "I have seen the mantis's abdomen dribbling out eggs in wet bubbles like tapioca pudding glued to a thorn." Dillard's dreamlike, metaphor-filled descriptions of the natural world, both its extravagant beauties and its grotesqueness and violence, transform the everyday into the extraordinary. Through language, she snaps herself (and her readers) alert to the world and to the peculiar workings of the human mind.

Although her work often focuses on encounters with the natural world, Dillard's underlying concern is always with the mind, especially with the concept of "waking up." The mental movement into and out of awareness, she writes in her 1982 essay "Total Eclipse," "is a transition we make a hundred times a day, as like so many will-less dolphins, we plunge and surface, lapse and emerge." The following selection, "Living Like Weasels," also appeared in the 1982 volume *Teaching a Stone to Talk: Expeditions and Encounters*. This essay demonstrates many of Dillard's stylistic and thematic trademarks, including the use of an encounter with strikingly alien nature as a way of understanding more profoundly her own mental habits. The otherness of nature (in this case, the weasel's mind) thus becomes, for Dillard, not a mirror exactly, but a necessary stimulus—a means of provoking an intriguing psychological response in herself.

A weasel is wild. Who knows what he thinks? He sleeps in his underground den, his tail draped over his nose. Sometimes he lives in his den for two days without leaving. Outside, he stalks rabbits, mice, muskrats, and birds, killing more bodies than he can eat warm, and often dragging the carcasses home. Obedient to instinct, he bites his prey at the neck, either splitting the jugular vein at the throat or crunching the brain at the base of the skull, and he does not let go. One naturalist refused to kill a weasel who was socketed into his hand deeply as a rattlesnake. The man could in no way pry the tiny weasel off, and he had to walk half a mile to water, the weasel dangling from his palm, and soak him off like a stubborn label.

And once, says Ernest Thompson Seton—once, a man shot an eagle out of the sky. He examined the eagle and found the dry skull of a weasel fixed by the jaws to his throat. The supposition is that the eagle had pounced on the weasel and the weasel swiveled and bit as instinct taught him, tooth to neck, and nearly won. I would like to have seen that eagle from the air a few weeks or months before he was shot: was the whole weasel still attached to his feathered throat, a fur pendant? Or did the eagle eat what he could reach, gutting the living weasel with his talons before his breast, bending his beak, cleaning the beautiful airborne bones?

I have been reading about weasels because I saw one last week. I startled a weasel who startled me, and we exchanged a long glance.

Twenty minutes from my house, through the woods by the quarry and across the highway, is Hollins Pond, a remarkable piece of shallowness, where I like to go at sunset and sit on a tree trunk. Hollins Pond is also called Murray's Pond; it covers two acres of bottomland near Tinker Creek with six inches of water and six thousand lily pads. In winter, brown-and-white steers stand in the middle of it, merely dampening their hooves; from the distant shore they look like miracle itself, complete with miracle's nonchalance. Now, in summer, the steers are gone. The water lilies have blossomed and spread to a green horizontal plane that is terra firma to plodding blackbirds, and tremulous ceiling to black leeches, crayfish, and carp.

This is, mind you, suburbia. It is a five-minute walk in three directions to rows of houses, though none is visible here. There's a 55 mph highway at one end of the pond, and a nesting pair of wood ducks at the other. Under every bush is a muskrat hole or a beer can. The far end is an alternating series of fields and woods, fields and woods, threaded everywhere with motorcycle tracks—in whose bare clay wild turtles lay eggs.

So. I had crossed the highway, stepped over two low barbed-wire fences, and traced the motorcycle path in all gratitude through the wild rose and poison ivy of the pond's shoreline up into high grassy fields. Then I cut down through the woods to the mossy fallen tree where I sit. This tree is excellent. It makes a dry, upholstered bench at the upper, marshy end of the pond, a plush jetty raised from the thorny shore between a shallow blue body of water and a deep blue body of sky.

The sun had just set. I was relaxed on the tree trunk, ensconced in the lap of lichen, watching the lily pads at my feet tremble and part dreamily over the thrusting path of a carp. A yellow bird appeared to my right and flew behind me. It caught my eye; I swiveled around— and the next instant, inexplicably, I was looking down at a weasel, who was looking up at me.

Weasel! I'd never seen one wild before. He was ten inches long, thin as a curve, a muscled ribbon, brown as fruitwood, soft-furred, alert. His face was fierce, small and pointed as a lizard's; he would have made a good arrowhead. There was just a dot of chin, maybe two brown hairs' worth, and then the pure white fur began that spread down his underside. He had two black eyes I didn't see, any more than you see a window.

The weasel was stunned into stillness as he was emerging from beneath an enormous shaggy wild rose bush four feet away. I was stunned into stillness twisted backward on the tree trunk. Our eyes locked, and someone threw away the key.

Our look was as if two lovers, or deadly enemies, met unexpectedly on an overgrown path when each had been thinking of something else: a clearing blow to the gut. It was also a bright blow to the brain, or a sudden beating of brains, with all the charge and intimate grate of rubbed balloons. It emptied our lungs. It felled the forest, moved the fields, and drained the pond; the world dismantled and tumbled into that black hole of eyes. If you and I looked at each other that way, our skulls would split and drop to our shoulders. But we don't. We keep our skulls. So.

He disappeared. This was only last week, and already I don't remember what shattered the enchantment. I think I blinked, I think I retrieved my brain from the weasel's brain, and tried to memorize what I was seeing, and the weasel felt the yank of separation, the careening splash-down into real life and the urgent current of instinct. He vanished under the wild rose. I waited motionless, my mind suddenly full of data and my spirit with pleadings, but he didn't return.

Please do not tell me about "approach-avoidance conflicts." I tell you I've been in that weasel's brain for sixty seconds, and he was in mine. Brains are private places, muttering through unique and secret tapes—but the weasel and I both plugged into another tape simultaneously, for a sweet and shocking time. Can I help it if it was a blank?

What goes on in his brain the rest of the time? What does a weasel think about? He won't say. His journal is tracks in clay, a spray of feathers, mouse blood and bone: uncollected, unconnected, loose-leaf, and blown.

I would like to learn, or remember, how to live. I come to Hollins Pond not so much to learn how to live as, frankly, to forget about it. That is, I don't think I can learn from a wild animal how to live in particular—shall I suck warm blood, hold my tail high, walk with my footprints precisely over the prints of my hands?—but I might learn something of mindlessness, something of the purity of living in the physical senses and the dignity of living without bias or motive. The weasel lives in necessity and we live in choice, hating necessity and dying at the last ignobly in its talons. I would like to live as I should, as the weasel lives as he should. And I suspect that for me the way is like the weasel's: open to time and death painlessly, noticing everything, remembering nothing, choosing the given with a fierce and pointed will.

I missed my chance. I should have gone for the throat. I should have lunged for that streak of white under the weasel's chin and held on, held on through mud and into the wild rose, held on for a dearer life. We could live under the wild rose wild as weasels, mute and uncomprehending. I could very calmly go wild. I could live two days in the den, curled, leaning on mouse fur, sniffing bird bones, blinking, licking, breathing musk, my hair tangled in the roots of grasses. Down is a good place to go, where the mind is single. Down is out, out of your ever-loving mind and back to your careless senses. I remember muteness as a prolonged and giddy fast, where every moment is a feast of utterance received. Time and events are merely poured, unremarked, and ingested directly, like blood pulsed into my gut through a jugular vein. Could two live that way? Could two live under the wild rose, and explore by the pond, so that the smooth mind of each is as everywhere present to the other, and as received and as unchallenged, as falling snow?

We could, you know. We can live any way we want. People take vows of poverty, chastity, and obedience—even of silence—by choice. The thing is to stalk your calling in a certain skilled and supple way, to locate the most tender and live spot and plug into that pulse. This is yielding, not fighting. A weasel doesn't "attack" anything; a weasel lives as he's meant to, yielding at every moment to the perfect freedom of single necessity.

I think it would be well, and proper, and obedient, and pure, to grasp your one necessity and not let it go, to dangle from it limp wherever it takes you. Then even death, where you're going no matter how you live, cannot you part. Seize it and let it seize you up aloft even, till your eyes burn out and drop; let your musky flesh fall off in shreds, and let your very bones unhinge and scatter, loosened over fields, over fields and woods, lightly, thoughtless, from any height at all, from as high as eagles.

Analyzing and Discussing the Text

1. Why does the author devote the first two paragraphs of this essay to miscellaneous accounts of weasel behavior? What characteristics of weasels does she emphasize? How does she work the transition to the next section of the essay?
2. Why, in the second section, does Dillard place so much emphasis on the location of her encounter with the weasel—"suburbia"?
3. What can we infer about the narrator when she tells us she likes to visit Hollins Pond at sunset and sit on a particular tree trunk? Why do we need to know this?
4. Analyze Dillard's descriptive language in the first paragraph of the third section. What seems to be the goal of the weasel description?
5. What is Dillard's point when she writes that "His journal is tracks in clay, a spray of feathers, mouse blood and bone: uncollected, unconnected, loose-leaf, and blown"?
6. Why was Dillard's encounter with the weasel so important to her?
7. What does it mean to live like a weasel? Is this how *you* live?

Experiencing and Writing About the World

1. Discuss in 500 words an encounter you had with a wild creature of some kind. Try, like Dillard, to exaggerate the momentousness of the confrontation. Go out of your way to use dramatic metaphors and similes in describing the animal, to experiment with freewheeling language. If you have never had any contact with an animal, make an effort to go out and meet one—if not a weasel or a bear, then

perhaps a squirrel or a pigeon. The kind of animal is less significant than what you make of the encounter in your own mind and prose.

2. Think of an animal who embodies, in myth or reality, certain characteristics that humans admire and would like to demonstrate in their own lives. Write a brief essay entitled "Living Like _____," in which you move from vivid, concrete description of the animal you select to an explanation of what humans have to gain from living in this way.

3. Often, extraordinary discoveries occur in the midst of everyday activities. Can you recall a discovery you've made while walking to class, eating dinner, or sitting on a tree trunk at sunset? Write a brief account of this moment of revelation.

4. What other essays in this anthology emphasize the value of living intensely and in the present moment? Find one or two essays besides "Living Like Weasels" that idealize this way of living/thinking and write an analytical essay in which you compare the techniques of persuasion used by each author.

DAVID QUAMMEN

The Face of a Spider

For all of their eloquence and insight, nature writers sometimes seem short on humor. This is not so in the case of David Quammen (1948–   ), the wry and sometimes scathingly sarcastic author of *Outside* magazine's science column, "Natural Acts" (this is also the title of Quammen's 1985 book of essays). Born in Cincinnati, Ohio, and educated at Yale University (B.A., 1970), Oxford University (B. Litt., 1973), and the University of Montana (he studied aquatic entomology at the latter), Quammen frequently grapples with ethical issues regarding the effects of human behavior on the nonhuman natural world. However, Quammen's approach to these tricky philosophical matters is impressive because he resists extremist ideologies and simple solutions, and also because he manages to discuss complex ideas with clear, straightforward, and witty language. In addition to his essays, Quammen has authored three novels and a collection of short fiction. He published his first novel, *To Walk the Line* (1970), a study of the friendship between "an ivy leaguer and black militant," at the age of twenty-two. *The Zolta Configuration* (1983), his second novel, is a historical thriller about the development of the first hydrogen bomb. Critics have raved about *Blood Line: Stories of Fathers and Sons* (1987), comparing Quammen's prose to that of Ernest Hemingway and William Faulkner. In addition to his Rhodes Scholarship (thus his degree from Oxford), Quammen has received a National Magazine Award for essays and criticism (1987) and a Guggenheim Fellowship (1988). He lives in Bozeman, Montana, where he continues to write his column for *Outside* and is now preparing a study of evolution and extinction on islands.

In the introduction to his second book of essays, *The Flight of the Iguana: A Sidelong View of Science and Nature* (1988), Quammen asserts, "it seems to me that almost nothing bears more crucially upon the future of this planet than the seemingly simple matter of human attitudes toward nature." Yet in the following selection from *The Flight of the Iguana*, he confesses and attempts to explain an example of his own "*xenophobia*: fear or hatred of what is foreign or strange" — his innate queasiness at the appearance of spiders. The goal of Quammen's writing, its humor notwithstanding, goes beyond merely entertaining, appeasing, or informing readers; in revealing his own responses to a variety of natural phenomena, many of them admittedly freakish and unsettling, Quammen seeks to provoke his readers, to get them to question *their* attitudes toward nature's otherness.

One evening a few years ago I walked back into my office after dinner and found roughly a hundred black widow spiders frolicking on my desk. I am not speaking metaphorically and I am not making this up: a hundred black widows. It was a vision of ghastly, breathtaking beauty, and it brought on me a wave of nausea. It also brought on a small moral crisis—one that I dealt with briskly, maybe rashly, in the dizziness of the moment, and that I've been turning back over in my mind ever since. I won't say I'm *haunted* by those hundred black widows, but I do remember them vividly. To me, they stand for something. They stand, in their small synecdochical way, for a large and important question.

The question is, How should a human behave toward the members of other living species?

A hundred black widows probably sounds like a lot. It is—even for Tucson, Arizona, where I was living then, a habitat in which black widows breed like rabbits and prosper like cockroaches, the females of the species growing plump as huckleberries and stringing their ragged webs in every free corner of every old shed and basement window. In Tucson, during the height of the season, a person can always on short notice round up eight or ten big, robust black widows, if that's what a person wants to do. But a hundred in one room? So all right, yes, there was a catch: These in my office were newborn babies.

A hundred scuttering bambinos, each one no bigger than a poppyseed. Too small still for red hourglasses, too small even for red egg timers. They had the aesthetic virtue of being so tiny that even a person of good eyesight and patient disposition could not make out their hideous little faces.

Their mother had sneaked in when the rains began and set up a web in the corner beside my desk. I knew she was there—I got a reminder every time I dropped a pencil and went groping for it, jerking my hand back at the first touch of that distinctive, dry, high-strength web. But I hadn't made the necessary decision about dealing with her. I knew she would have to be either murdered or else captured adroitly in a pickle jar for relocation to the wild, and I didn't especially want to do either. (I had already squashed scores of black widows during those Tucson years but by this time, I guess, I was going soft.) In the meantime, she had gotten pregnant. She had laid her eggs into a silken egg sac the size of a Milk Dud and then protected that sac vigilantly, keeping it warm, fending off any threats, as black widow mothers do. While she was waiting for the eggs to come to term, she would have been particularly edgy, particularly unforgiving, and my hand would have been in particular danger each time I reached for a fallen pencil. Then the great day arrived. The spiderlings hatched from their individual eggs, chewed their way out of the sac, and started crawling, brothers and sisters together, up toward the orange tensor lamp that was giving off heat and light on the desk of the nitwit who was their landlord.

By the time I stumbled in, fifty or sixty of them had reached the lampshade and rappelled back down on dainty silk lines, leaving a net of gossamer rigging between the lamp and the Darwin book (it happened to be an old edition of *Insectivorous Plants*, with marbled endpapers) that sat on the desk. Some dozen others had already managed dispersal flights, letting out strands of buoyant silk and ballooning away on rising air, as spiderlings do—in this case dispersing as far as the bookshelves. It was too late for one man to face one spider with just a pickle jar and an index card and his two shaky hands. By now I was proprietor of a highly successful black widow hatchery.

And the question was, How should a human behave toward the members of other living species?

The Jain religion of India has a strong teaching on that question. The Sanskrit word is *ahimsa*, generally rendered in English as "noninjury" or the imperative "do no harm." *Ahimsa* is the ethical centerpiece of Jainism, an absolute stricture against the killing of living beings—*any* living beings—and it led the traditional Jains to some extreme forms of observance. A rigorously devout Jain would burn no candles or lights, for instance, if there was danger a moth might fly into them. The Jain would light no fire for heating or cooking, again because it might cause the death of insects. He would cover his mouth and nose with a cloth mask, so as not to inhale any gnats. He would refrain from cutting his hair, on grounds that the lice hiding in there might be gruesomely injured by the scissors. He could not plow a field, for fear of mutilating worms. He could not work as a carpenter or a mason, with all that dangerous sawing and crunching, nor could he engage in most types of industrial production. Consequently the traditional Jains formed a distinct socioeconomic class, composed almost entirely of monks and merchants. Their ethical canon was not without what you and I might take to be glaring contradictions (vegetarianism was sanctioned, plants as usual getting dismissive treatment in the matter of rights to life), but at least they took it seriously. They lived by it. They tried their best to do no harm.

And this in a country, remember, where 10,000 humans died every year from snakebite, almost a million more from malaria carried in the bites of mosquitoes. The black widow spider, compared to those fellow creatures, seems a harmless and innocent beast.

But personally I hold no brief for *ahimsa*, because I don't delude myself that it's even theoretically (let alone practically) possible. The basic processes of animal life, human or otherwise, do necessarily entail a fair bit of ruthless squashing and gobbling. Plants can sustain themselves on no more than sunlight and beauty and a hydroponic diet—but not we animals. I've only mentioned this Jainist ideal to suggest the range of possible viewpoints.

Modern philosophers of the "animal liberation" movement, most notably Peter Singer and Tom Regan, have proposed some other interesting answers to the same question. So have writers like Barry Lopez and Eugene Linden, and (by their example, as well as by their work) scientists like Jane Goodall and John Lilly and Dian Fossey. Most of the attention of each of these thinkers, though, has been devoted to what is popularly (but not necessarily by the thinkers themselves) considered the "upper" end of the "ladder" of life. To my mind, the question of appropriate relations is more tricky and intriguing—also more crucial in the long run, since this group accounts for most of the planet's species— as applied to the "lower" end, down there among the mosquitoes and worms and black widow spiders.

These are the extreme test cases. These are the alien species who experience human malice, or indifference, or tolerance, at its most automatic and elemental. To squash or not to squash? Mohandas Gandhi, whose own ethic of nonviolence owed much to *ahimsa*, was once asked about the propriety of an antimalaria campaign that involved killing mosquitoes with DDT, and he was careful to give no simple, presumptuous answer. These are the creatures whose treatment, by each of us, illuminates not just the strength of emotional affinity but the strength, if any, of principle.

But what is the principle? Pure *ahimsa*, as even Gandhi admitted, is unworkable. Vegetarianism is invidious. Anthropocentrism, conscious or otherwise, is smug and ruinously myopic. What else? Well, I have my own little notion of one measure that might usefully be applied in our relations with other species, and I offer it here seriously despite the fact that it will probably sound godawful stupid.

Eye contact.

Make eye contact with the beast, the Other, before you decide upon action. No kidding, now, I mean get down on your hands and knees right there in the vegetable garden, and look that snail in the face. Lock eyes with that bull snake. Trade stares with the carp. Gaze for a moment into the many-faceted eyes—the windows to its soul—of the house fly, as it licks its way innocently across your kitchen counter. Look for signs of embarrassment or rancor or guilt. Repeat the following formula silently, like a mantra: "This is some mother's darling, this is some mother's child." *Then* kill if you will, or if it seems you must.

I've been experimenting with the eye-contact approach for some time myself. I don't claim that it has made me gentle or holy or put me in tune with the cosmic hum, but definitely it has been interesting. The hardest cases—and therefore I think the most telling—are the spiders.

The face of a spider is unlike anything else a human will ever see. The word "ugly" doesn't even begin to serve. "Grotesque" and "menacing" are too mild. The only adequate way of communicating the effect of a spiderly countenance is to warn that it is "very different," and then offer a photograph. This trick should not be pulled on loved ones just before bedtime or when trying to persuade them to accompany you to the Amazon.

The special repugnant power of the spider physiognomy derives, I think, from fangs and eyes. The former are too big and the latter are too many. But the fangs (actually the fangs are only terminal barbs on the *chelicerae*, as the real jaw limbs are called) need to be large, because all spiders are predators yet they have no pincers like a lobster or a scorpion, no talons like an eagle, no social behavior like a pack of wolves. Large clasping fangs armed with poison glands are just their required equipment for earning a living. And what about those eyes— big ones and little ones, arranged in two rows, all bugged-out and pointing everywhichway? (My wife the biologist offers a theory here: "They have an eye for each leg, like us—so they don't *step* in anything.") Well, a predator does need good eyesight, binocular focus, peripheral vision. Sensory perception is crucial to any animal that lives by the hunt and, unlike insects, arachnids possess no antennae. Beyond that, I don't know. I don't *know* why a spider has eight eyes.

I only know that, when I make eye contact with one, I feel a deep physical shudder of revulsion, and of fear, and of fascination; and I am reminded that the human style of face is only one accidental pattern among many, some of the others being quite drastically different. I remember that we aren't alone. I remember that we are the norm of goodness and comeliness only to ourselves. I wonder about how ugly I look to the spider.

The hundred baby black widows on my desk were too tiny for eye contact. They were too numerous, it seemed, to be gathered one by one into a pickle jar and carried to freedom in the backyard. I killed them all with a can of Raid. I confess to that slaughter with more resignation than shame, the jostling struggle for life and space being what it is. I can't swear I would do differently today. But there is this lingering suspicion that I squandered an opportunity for some sort of moral growth.

I still keep their dead and dried mother, and their vacated egg sac, in a plastic vial on an office shelf. It is supposed to remind me of something or other.

And the question continues to puzzle me: How should a human behave toward the members of other living species?

Last week I tried to make eye contact with a tarantula. This was a huge specimen, all hairy and handsomely colored, with a body as big as a hamster and legs the size of Bic pens. I ogled it through a sheet of plate glass. I smiled and winked. But the animal hid its face in distrust.

Analyzing and Discussing the Text

1. Is this a serious essay? If Quammen's basic question— "How should a human behave toward the members of other living species?"—is serious, why does he address it in such a funny way? Locate and examine humorous passages in the essay, assessing whether the humor enhances or undermines the author's argument.
2. "A hundred scuttering bambinos, each one no bigger than a poppyseed," writes Quammen. Why is this effective prose? Does the diction seem appropriate for a natural history writer? Is there a tension between the words and the subject matter? Explain this.
3. What techniques does Quammen use to make the black widows vivid to readers who possibly have never actually seen such spiders?
4. How do you feel about the concept of *ahimsa*? If the Jain religion takes the idea of "doing no harm" to a seemingly impossible extreme, where then should we—should *you*—draw the line between necessary destruction of other life and "ruthless squashing and gobbling"?

5. Quammen says you should "Make eye contact with the beast, the Other, before you decide upon action." How useful is this strategy for solving the ethical question, "To squash or not to squash?" Does ugliness or alienness seem an appropriate rationale for violence? Could something more than this have motivated Quammen's decision to kill the baby spiders in his office? Explain your response.

Experiencing and Writing About the World

1. Describe the face of a spider in a paragraph or two (hunt around your dorm room or another building for an example, or try to locate a closeup photograph in a book about spiders). Use not only precise physical details but also appropriate figurative language (metaphors and similes) to capture your response to the appearance of this creature.
2. Respond in your own way, earnest and/or funny, to Quammen's philosophical question: "How should a human behave toward the members of other living species?"
3. Recall an experience that gave you, as Quammen puts it, "an opportunity for some sort of moral growth." Did you take advantage of the opportunity or squander it? If the latter, tell your story in a mock-confessional style like Quammen's.
4. When did you last make eye contact with something that seemed hideously ugly to you? In imitation of Quammen, describe this confrontation in an exaggeratedly flippant style, emphasizing the pain, the awkwardness, the difficulty of eye contact.

Suggestions for Further Reading

Ackerman, Diane. *A Natural History of the Senses.* New York: Random, 1990.
Bowden, Charles. *Blue Desert.* Tucson: U of Arizona P, 1986.
Bradford, William. "Of Their Voyage, and How They Passed the Sea; and of Their Safe Arrival at Cape Cod." *Of Plymouth Plantation 1620–1647.* 1856. New York: Random, 1981.
Fabre, J. Henri. *The Insect World of J. Henri Fabre.* 1949. Ed. Edwin Way Teale. Boston: Beacon, 1991.
Hoagland, Edward. *Notes from the Century Before: A Journal from British Columbia.* 1969. San Francisco: North Point, 1982.

Krutch, Joseph Wood. "The Moth and the Candle." *The Voice of the Desert: A Naturalist's Interpretation.* New York: William Sloane, 1954.

Nabhan, Gary Paul. *The Desert Smells Like Rain: A Naturalist in Papago Indian Country.* San Francisco: North Point, 1982.

Pyle, Robert Michael. *Wintergreen: Listening to the Land's Heart.* Boston: Houghton, 1986.

Seltzer, Richard. "A Worm from My Notebook." *Taking the World in for Repairs.* New York: Morrow, 1986.

Stap, Don. *A Parrot Without a Name: The Search for the Last Unknown Birds on Earth.* Austin: U of Texas P, 1991.

Swain, Roger B. *Field Notes: Journal of an Itinerant Biologist.* New York: Scribner's, 1983.

———. *Saving Graces: Sojourns of a Backyard Biologist.* Boston: Little, 1991.

Warner, William. *Beautiful Swimmers: Watermen, Crabs, and the Chesapeake Bay.* Boston: Little, 1976.

Zwinger, Ann. *The Mysterious Lands: The Four Deserts of the United States.* New York: Dutton, 1989.

Galen Rowell/Mountain Light Photography

CHAPTER TWO

Fecundity and Mortality

Life and death, fertility and decay—what could be more fundamental to the natural order than these apparently opposing processes? By carefully observing the world, we come to realize fecundity and mortality are not rare and cataclysmic phenomena that occur only to the fanfare of birth and death announcements in newspapers. The very concept of life must encompass *change*, which means both *becoming* and *disappearing*. In the natural world, living things must nourish themselves, reproduce, and eventually die; this process occurs everywhere, constantly. And yet to the average human eye both birth and death often appear strange and disturbing, somehow improper because they involve such pain, violence, and uncertainty. We have developed elaborate religious explanations of what happens after we die, possibly to reinforce the idea that humans are not quite natural. Other creatures may consume each other or decay by roadsides until their remains melt into the earth and enrich the soil for grass and wildflowers, but not humans. People have a hard time thinking about fecundity and mortality, which is all the more reason that essayists have found these concepts so interesting.

In this chapter we begin with Mary Austin's study of scavengers in the southwestern desert, emphasizing the absolute naturalness of what many humans may regard as a disgusting phenomenon. Her descriptions of the living feeding off the dead show the complementarity of life and death, the interconnectedness of the two extremes. Lewis Thomas, like John Daniel later in the chapter, points out the commonness of death and urges us to accept death more easily as part of the cyclical process of life, to accommodate ourselves somehow within the life cycle we know occurs throughout the nonhuman world. Daniel brings the issue to a more personal level than Thomas, contending with the implications of death for the individual thinking person. Annie Dillard, in the excerpted chapter from *Pilgrim at Tinker Creek* (1974), finds the rampant, often startling, fecundity of nature every bit as grotesque and unnerving as the loss of life. Stephen Harrigan, writing from an omniscient viewpoint that enables us to fly with a hawk and burrow with clams, reveals that nature is indeed considerably more fecund than most of us, casually glancing at a deserted beach as we drive along a coastal highway, realize. Although some forms of death may be entirely commonplace and "natural," there are other instances so widespread, sudden, and permanent that they force us to wonder why they occurred and what their implications are. Stephen Jay Gould addresses such a case when he considers several compelling explanations for the extinction of dinosaurs, using his account both to demonstrate scientific methodology and to warn his readers that the "climatic consequences" of an all-out nuclear war could produce for humanity a fate like that of the dinosaurs.

MARY AUSTIN

The Scavengers

Mary Hunter Austin (1868–1934) was born and grew up in Carlinville, Illinois; she graduated from Blackburn College in 1888. After she finished college, she and her family moved to a homestead in the San Joaquin Valley of California. She married Stafford Wallace Austin several years later and moved around the state as he looked for work. In 1899, at the age of thirty-one, she sold a story to Bret Harte's San Francisco literary magazine, *The Overland Monthly,* in which John Muir also first published his work. Inspired by the possibility of supporting herself as a writer and dissatisfied as the wife of an unsuccessful farmer, Austin left her husband and went on her own to San Francisco, Carmel, New York City, and finally Santa Fe, New Mexico, where she spent the final years of her life. She was a prolific writer, publishing thirty-one books during her life in addition to stories, poems, plays, essays, and anthropological treatises. *The Land of Little Rain* (1903) is her best-known work of "nature writing," but even this book is unusual in its frequent emphasis on human inhabitants of the desert rather than the region's inhuman aspects alone. Her other important sketches of the American Southwest include *Lost Borders* (1909) and *The Land of Journey's Ending* (1924). In 1932 she published an autobiography called *Earth Horizon.*

The issue of "fecundity and mortality" is primarily one of economy—the death of one animal contributes to the life of another, and the hunter in turn becomes the prey in yet another encounter. Yet Austin, writing *The Land of Little Rain* long before the surge of ecological consciousness in the years since the 1960s, concludes her chapter "The Scavengers" with a powerful acknowledgement of how mankind disrupts the "economy of nature" by failing to leave behind scavengeable waste: "There is no scavenger that eats tin cans," she writes, "and no wild thing leaves a like disfigurement on the forest floor." In blunt yet understated comments like this and in her precise accounts of the desert Southwest, Austin is at her best as a writer. Edward Abbey has suggested that "if [Austin's language] seems too fussy, even prissy at first, you are soon absorbed by the accuracy of her observational powers and learn to overlook, then ignore, and finally forget the pretty archaisms, the invertebrate verbs...."

The plain, blunt, direct style which most of us prefer today may seem merely another affectation in the eyes of readers soon to come." The prose in the following selection does suffer occasionally from prissiness ("it is a very squalid tragedy"), but frequently it achieves a directness and simplicity ("Cattle once down may be days in dying") that appeal to the modern reader.

Fifty-seven buzzards, one on each of fifty-seven fence posts at the rancho El Tejon, on a mirage-breeding September morning, sat solemnly while the white tilted travelers' vans lumbered down the Canada de los Uvas. After three hours they had only clapped their wings, or exchanged posts. The season's end in the vast dim valley of the San Joaquin is palpitatingly hot, and the air breathes like cotton wool. Through it all the buzzards sit on the fences and low hummocks, with wings spread fanwise for air. There is no end to them, and they smell to heaven. Their heads droop, and all their communication is a rare, horrid croak.

The increase of wild creatures is in proportion to the things they feed upon: the more carrion the more buzzards. The end of the third successive dry year bred them beyond belief. The first year quail mated sparingly; the second year the wild oats matured no seed; the third, cattle died in their tracks with their heads towards the stopped watercourses. And that year the scavengers were as black as the plague all across the mesa and up the treeless, tumbled hills. On clear days they betook themselves to the upper air, where they hung motionless for hours. That year there were vultures among them, distinguished by the white patches under the wings. All their offensiveness notwithstanding, they have a stately flight. They must also have what pass for good qualities among themselves, for they are social, not to say clannish.

It is a very squalid tragedy, — that of the dying brutes and the scavenger birds. Death by starvation is slow. The heavy-headed, rack-boned cattle totter in the fruitless trails; they stand for long, patient intervals; they lie down and do not rise. There is fear in their eyes when they are first stricken, but afterward only intolerable weariness. I suppose the dumb creatures know nearly as much of death as do their betters, who have only the more imagination. Their even-breathing submission after the first agony is their tribute to its inevitableness. It needs a nice discrimination to say which of the basket-ribbed cattle is likest to afford the next meal, but the scavengers make few mistakes. One stoops to the quarry and the flock follows.

Cattle once down may be days in dying. They stretch out their necks along the ground, and roll up their slow eyes at longer intervals. The buzzards have all the time, and no beak is dropped or talon struck until the breath is wholly passed. It is doubtless the economy of nature to have the scavengers by to clean up the carrion, but a wolf at the throat would be a shorter agony than the long stalking and sometime perchings of these loathsome watchers. Suppose now it were a man in this long-drawn, hungrily spied upon distress! When Timmie O'Shea was lost on Armogosa Flats for three days without water, Long Tom Basset found him, not by any trail, but by making straight away for the points where he saw buzzards stooping. He could hear the beat of their wings, Tom said, and trod on their shadows, but O'Shea was past recalling what he thought about things after the second day. My friend Ewan told me, among other things, when he came back from San Juan Hill, that not all the carnage of battle turned his bowels as the sight of slant black wings rising flockwise before the burial squad.

There are three kinds of noises buzzards make,—it is impossible to call them notes,—raucous and elemental. There is a short croak of alarm, and the same syllable in a modified tone to serve all the purposes of ordinary conversation. The old birds make a kind of throaty chuckling to their young, but if they have any love song I have not heard it. The young yawp in the nest a little, with more breath than noise. It is seldom one finds a buzzard's nest, seldom that grown-ups find a nest of any sort; it is only children to whom these things happen by right. But by making a business of it one may come upon them in wide, quiet cañons, or on the lookouts of lonely, table-topped mountains, three or four together, in the tops of stubby trees or on rotten cliffs well open to the sky.

It is probable that the buzzard is gregarious, but it seems unlikely from the small number of young noted at any time that every female incubates each year. The young birds are easily distinguished by their size when feeding, and high up in air by the worn primaries of the older birds. It is when the young go out of the nest on their first foraging that the parents, full of a crass and simple pride, make their indescribable chucklings of gobbling, gluttonous delight. The little ones would be amusing as they tug and tussle, if one could forget what it is they feed upon.

One never comes any nearer to the vulture's nest or nestlings than hearsay. They keep to the southerly Sierras, and are bold enough, it seems, to do killing on their own account when no carrion is at hand. They dog the shepherd from camp to camp, the hunter home from the hill, and will even carry away offal from under his hand.

The vulture merits respect for his bigness and for his bandit airs, but he is a sombre bird, with none of the buzzard's frank satisfaction in his offensiveness.

The least objectionable of the inland scavengers is the raven, frequenter of the desert ranges, the same called locally "carrion crow." He is handsomer and has such an air. He is nice in his habits and is said to have likable traits. A tame one in a Shoshone camp was the butt of much sport and enjoyed it. He could all but talk and was another with the children, but an arrant thief. The raven will eat most things that come his way,—eggs and young of ground-nesting birds, seeds even, lizards and grasshoppers, which he catches cleverly; and whatever he is about, let a coyote trot never so softly by, the raven flaps up and after; for whatever the coyote can pull down or nose out is meat also for the carrion crow.

And never a coyote comes out of his lair for killing, in the country of the carrion crows, but looks up first to see where they may be gathering. It is a sufficient occupation for a windy morning, on the lineless, level mesa, to watch the pair of them eying each other furtively, with a tolerable assumption of unconcern, but no doubt with a certain amount of good understanding about it. Once at Red Rock, in a year of green pasture, which is a bad time for the scavengers, we saw two buzzards, five ravens, and a coyote feeding on the same carrion, and only the coyote seemed ashamed of the company.

Probably we never fully credit the interdependence of wild creatures, and their cognizance of the affairs of their own kind. When the five coyotes that range the Tejon from Pasteria to Tunawai planned a relay race to bring down an antelope strayed from the band, beside myself to watch, an eagle swung down from Mt. Pinos, buzzards materialized out of invisible ether, and hawks came trooping like small boys to a street fight. Rabbits sat up in the chaparral and cocked their ears, feeling themselves quite safe for the once as the hunt swung near them. Nothing happens in the deep wood that the blue jays are not all agog to tell. The hawk follows the badger, the coyote the carrion crow, and from their aerial stations the buzzards watch each other. What would be worth knowing is how much of their neighbor's affairs the new generations learn for themselves, and how much they are taught of their elders.

So wide is the range of the scavengers that it is never safe to say, eyewitness to the contrary, that there are few or many in such a place. Where the carrion is, there will the buzzards be gathered together, and in three days' journey you will not sight another one. The way up from Mojave to Red Butte is all desertness, affording no pasture and scarcely a rill of water. In a year of little rain in the south, flocks and herds were driven to the number of thousands along this road to the perennial pastures of the high ranges. It is a long, slow trail, ankle deep in bitter dust that gets up in the slow wind and moves along the backs of the crawling cattle. In the worst of times one in three will pine and fall out by the way. In the defiles of Red Rock, the sheep piled up a stinking lane; it was the sun smiting by day. To these shambles came buzzards, vultures, and coyotes from all the country round, so that on the Tejon, the Ceriso, and the Little Antelope there were not scavengers enough to keep the country clean. All that summer the dead mummified in the open or dropped slowly back to earth in the quagmires of the bitter springs. Meanwhile from

Red Rock to Coyote Holes, and from Coyote Holes to Haiwai the scavengers gorged and gorged.

The coyote is not a scavenger by choice, preferring his own kill, but being on the whole a lazy dog, is apt to fall into carrion eating because it is easier. The red fox and bobcat, a little pressed by hunger, will eat of any other animal's kill, but will not ordinarily touch what dies of itself, and are exceedingly shy of food that has been man-handled.

Very clean and handsome, quite belying his relationship in appearance, is Clark's crow, that scavenger and plunderer of mountain camps. It is permissible to call him by his common name, "Camp Robber": he has earned it. Not content with refuse, he pecks open meal sacks, filches whole potatoes, is a gormand for bacon, drills holes in packing cases, and is daunted by nothing short of tin. All the while he does not neglect to vituperate the chipmunks and sparrows that whisk off crumbs of comfort from under the camper's feet. The Camp Robber's gray coat, black and white barred wings, and slender bill, with certain tricks of perching, accuse him of attempts to pass himself off among woodpeckers; but his behavior is all crow. He frequents the higher pine belts, and has a noisy strident call like a jay's, and how clean he and the frisk-tailed chipmunks keep the camp! No crumb or paring or bit of eggshell goes amiss.

High as the camp may be, so it is not above timberline, it is not too high for the coyote, the bobcat, or the wolf. It is the complaint of the ordinary camper that the woods are too still, depleted of wild life. But what dead body of wild thing, or neglected game untouched by its kind, do you find? And put out offal away from camp over night, and look next day at the foot tracks where it lay.

Man is a great blunderer going about in the woods, and there is no other except the bear makes so much noise. Being so well warned beforehand, it is a very stupid animal, or a very bold one, that cannot keep safely hid. The cunningest hunter is hunted in turn, and what he leaves of his kill is meat for some other. That is the economy of nature, but with it all there is not sufficient account taken of the works of man. There is no scavenger that eats tin cans, and no wild thing leaves a like disfigurement on the forest floor.

Analyzing and Discussing the Text

1. Look closely at Austin's descriptions of buzzards. Try to explain where these descriptions seem objective or detached and where they seem anthropomorphic. Why does the author mix these perspectives?

2. What seems to be the point of all of the information about scavengers? Does the author ever come right out and tell us why we ought to know all of this? How does she introduce the essay?
3. What is the role of the author herself in this essay? Do we detect her personality anywhere? Does she give us any narratives? Any *personal* narratives? Is this essay concrete or abstract? Explain why these issues might be relevant to the central goals of the writer.
4. "Probably we never fully credit the interdependence of wild creatures," writes Austin, "and their cognizance of the affairs of their own kind." Explain what she means in this sentence and how this idea contributes to the rest of her discussion of scavengers.

Experiencing and Writing About the World

1. Anthropomorphism, or the attribution of human traits to animals, is often frowned upon by contemporary readers of nature writing. Nonetheless, this approach to describing nonhuman inhabitants of the natural world can be a way of beginning to understand other animals, and it is also a good exercise for the imagination. Write an expository essay on one particular aspect of animal behavior (scavenging, parenting, sleeping, hunting, or something else) in which you anthropomorphically describe several different creatures (birds, cats, insects, or other living things you happen to encounter). Alternatively, you could focus on one particular animal and describe its behavior in various situations. Try, like Austin, to de-emphasize your own participation in the events you describe. You may not find this style of natural description comfortable or easy (or even morally acceptable), but this exercise should help to make you more conscious of various descriptive strategies.
2. Write your own essay on the phenomenon of scavenging. What does the process involve? What specific instances of scavenging have you observed? What is the function of scavenging in the maintenance of a natural community? How do humans resist or participate in this process? Write this paper (500–1,000 words) by combining personal observation with information gathered by research, but avoid using first-person narrative. Instead, aim for lively, but depersonalized description, narration, and explanation.
3. Examine the subtle critique of humanity in the final section of Austin's essay and compare her critical style with the implied or overt critiques of human civilization elsewhere in this anthology. Write an essay explaining the particular virtues and disadvantages of the subtle critique.

LEWIS THOMAS

Death in the Open

Lewis Thomas (1913–   ), although trained as a scientist, has achieved fame as a writer who uses his knowledge of biology to enrich the nonexpert's understanding of the world. A native of Flushing, New York, Thomas studied at Princeton as an undergraduate and later earned his M.D. at Harvard; he subsequently received an M.A. at Yale. His early essays appeared in the *New England Journal of Medicine* and *Nature*, then were collected in such books as *Lives of a Cell: Notes of a Biology Watcher* (1974) and *The Medusa and the Snail: More Notes of a Biology Watcher* (1979), the first of which won the National Book Award. In 1983 Thomas published both *The Youngest Science* (a memoir of his life as a doctor) and *Late Night Thoughts on Listening to Mahler's Ninth Symphony*. His most recent book is *Et Cetera, Et Cetera: Notes of a Word-Watcher* (1990). In addition to his career as a writer, Thomas worked as a research pathologist and a medical administrator at several university hospitals before becoming president of the Memorial Sloan–Kettering Cancer Center in New York in 1973. He is currently a scholar-in-residence at the Cornell University Medical College.

The essay "Death in the Open" shows Thomas's habit of combining everyday observations, common sense, and precise scientific knowledge (or estimates) in explaining his thoughts about a universal biological phenomenon—in this case, death. Why is it, Thomas asks, that death so seldom occurs in the open? Because *life* is so abundant on this planet, *death* must also be commonplace, even if it is often invisible or concealed. After first contemplating the inconspicuousness of death in the nearby natural world, death among insects and birds and squirrels, Thomas comes to address the meaning of death for human beings. He suggests that in the future we might actually take some comfort in recognizing the "synchrony" of our life cycles with the rest of the organic world.

Most of the dead animals you see on highways near the cities are dogs, a few cats. Out in the countryside, the forms and coloring of the dead are strange; these are the wild creatures. Seen from a car window they appear as fragments, evoking memories of woodchucks, badgers, skunks, voles, snakes, sometimes the mysterious wreckage of a deer.

It is always a queer shock, part a sudden up-welling of grief, part unaccountable amazement. It is simply astounding to see an animal dead on a highway. The outrage is more than just the location; it is the impropriety of such visible death, anywhere. You do not expect to see dead animals in the open. It is the nature of animals to die alone, off somewhere, hidden. It is wrong to see them lying out on the highway; it is wrong to see them anywhere.

Everything in the world dies, but we only know about it as a kind of abstraction. If you stand in a meadow, at the edge of a hillside, and look around carefully, almost everything you can catch sight of is in the process of dying, and most things will be dead long before you are. If it were not for the constant renewal and replacement going on before your eyes, the whole place would turn to stone and sand under your feet.

There are some creatures that do not seem to die at all; they simply vanish totally into their own progeny. Single cells do this. The cell becomes two, then four, and so on, and after a while the last trace is gone. It cannot be seen as death; barring mutation, the descendants are simply the first cell, living all over again. The cycles of the slime mold have episodes that seem as conclusive as death, but the withered slug, with its stalk and fruiting body, is plainly the transient tissue of a developing animal; the free-swimming amebocytes use this organ collectively in order to produce more of themselves.

There are said to be a billion billion insects on the earth at any moment, most of them with very short life expectancies by our standards. Someone has estimated that there are 25 million assorted insects hanging in the air over every temperate square mile, in a column extending upward for thousands of feet, drifting through the layers of the atmosphere like plankton. They are dying steadily, some by being eaten, some just dropping in their tracks, tons of them around the earth, disintegrating as they die, invisibly.

Who ever sees dead birds, in anything like the huge numbers stipulated by the certainty of the death of all birds? A dead bird is an incongruity, more startling than an unexpected live bird, sure evidence to the human mind that something has gone wrong. Birds do their dying off somewhere, behind things, under things, never on the wing.

Animals seem to have an instinct for performing death alone, hidden. Even the largest, most conspicuous ones find ways to conceal themselves in time. If an elephant missteps and dies in an open place, the herd will not leave him there; the others will pick him up and carry the body from place to place, finally putting it down in some inexplicably suitable location. When elephants encounter the skeleton of an elephant out in the open, they methodically take up each of the bones and distribute them, in a ponderous ceremony, over neighboring acres.

It is a natural marvel. All of the life of the earth dies, all of the time, in the same volume as the new life that dazzles us each morning, each spring. All we see of this is the odd stump, the fly struggling on the porch floor of the summer house in October, the fragment on the highway. I have lived all my life with an embarrassment of squirrels in my backyard, they are all over the place, all year long, and I have never seen, anywhere, a dead squirrel.

I suppose it is just as well. If the earth were otherwise, and all the dying were done in the open, with the dead there to be looked at, we would never have it out of our minds. We can forget about it much of the time, or think of it as an accident to be avoided, somehow. But it does make the process of dying seem more exceptional than it really is, and harder to engage in at the times when we must ourselves engage.

In our way, we conform as best we can to the rest of nature. The obituary pages tell us of the news that we are dying away, while the birth announcements in finer print, off at the side of the page, inform us of our replacements, but we get no grasp from this of the enormity of scale. There are 3 billion of us on the earth, and all 3 billion must be dead, on a schedule, within this lifetime. The vast mortality, involving something over 50 million of us each year, takes place in relative secrecy. We can only really know of the deaths in our households, or among our friends. These, detached in our minds from all the rest, we take to be unnatural events, anomalies, outrages. We speak of our own dead in low voices; struck down, we say, as though visible death can only occur for cause, by disease or violence, avoidably. We send off for flowers, grieve, make ceremonies, scatter bones, unaware of the rest of the 3 billion on the same schedule. All of that immense mass of flesh and bone and consciousness will disappear by absorption into the earth, without recognition by the transient survivors.

Less than a half century from now, our replacements will have more than doubled the numbers. It is hard to see how we can continue to keep the secret, with such multitudes doing the dying. We will have to give up the notion that death is catastrophe, or detestable, or avoidable, or even strange. We will need to learn more about the cycling of life in the rest of the system, and about our connection to the process. Everything that comes alive seems to be in trade for something that dies, cell for cell. There might be some comfort in the recognition of synchrony, in the formation that we all go down together, in the best of company.

Analyzing and Discussing the Text

1. As you read this essay, try to pick out the source of information Thomas is relying on in each section: everyday experience or scientific research. Need one be a trained scientist or an M.D. to write such an essay? Why or why not?

2. Why do we feel such uneasiness when we see "death in the open"? How does Thomas explain this emotion?
3. What does Thomas mean when he calls death "a kind of abstraction"? How can such a physical process also be abstract?
4. Most of this essay concerns nonhuman death. What is the connection Thomas suggests between nonhumans and humans?
5. Does Thomas believe we should "have [death] out of our minds" or make a point of thinking about it? How does the title of this essay, indeed the essay as a whole, suggest Thomas's view of this issue?
6. According to Thomas, what is it that most disturbs us about death? Should it necessarily bother us? How can we come to terms with our own mortality?
7. Do you find this essay argumentative or neutrally meditative? If the former, try to explain how Thomas seeks to persuade you to think in one way or another.

Experiencing and Writing About the World

1. Think about an instance when you've witnessed death in the natural world, either the moment of death or the aftermath. Devote approximately 250 words to describing your own feelings about the experience. Did it make any impression on you at all? If not, why? Did the death seem unusual or wasteful, "natural" or "unnatural"?
2. Choose one of Thomas's assertions—such as the idea that "We will need to learn more about the cycling of life in the rest of the system, and about our connection to the process"—and either elaborate on this idea or refute it in approximately 250 words.
3. Does the awareness of death in the nonhuman world really help us to be more philosophical about the death of *people* we care about? Consider, in 250–500 words, the value of learning about nature in helping us to understand ourselves as biological entities. Does Thomas's essay tend to erase the distinction between the human and the nonhuman? Is this comforting or more disturbing?
4. What is the relationship between life and death, fecundity and mortality? Examine Thomas's discussion of this connection and then write your own study of this issue.

ANNIE DILLARD

From **Fecundity**

For biographical information, see the headnote for "Living Like Weasels" in Part One, Chapter One.

The following selection from *Pilgrim at Tinker Creek* (1974) demonstrates both Dillard's extraordinary imaginative investment in the significance of natural phenomena and her lack of mushy adoration for the world. The world, for her, is as grotesque and "appalling" as it is beautiful. In an essay called "Why I Live Where I Live" (*Esquire*, 1984), Dillard once said, "I distrust the forest, or any wilderness, as a place to live. Living in the wilderness, you may well fall asleep on your feet or go mad. Without the stimulus of other thinkers, you handle your own thoughts on their worn paths in your own skull till you've worn them smooth." The following excerpt from the essay "Fecundity" shows how Dillard combines the stimuli of the natural world and other thinkers' ideas about the world—having safely stepped back from Tinker Creek to her confines in the library at Hollins College (Virginia), she can compose her thoughts on nature's own unnaturalness, its "freakish," mind-boggling fertility. Dillard cautioned early readers of *Pilgrim at Tinker Creek* that she wrote the book "consciously, off of hundreds of index cards, often distorting the literal truth to achieve an artistic one. It's all hard, conscious, terribly frustrating work! But this never occurs to people. They think it happens in a dream, that you just sit on a tree stump and take dictation from some little chipmunk!"

I wakened myself last night with my own shouting. It must have been that terrible yellow plant I saw pushing through the flood-damp soil near the log by Tinker Creek, the plant as fleshy and featureless as a slug, that erupted through the floor of my brain as I slept, and burgeoned into the dream of fecundity that woke me up.

I was watching two huge luna moths mate. Luna moths are those fragile ghost moths, fairy moths, whose five-inch wings are swallow-tailed, a pastel green bordered in silken lavender. From the hairy head of the male sprouted two enormous, furry antennae that trailed down past his ethereal wings. He was on top of the female, hunching repeatedly with a horrible animal vigor.

It was the perfect picture of utter spirituality and utter degradation. I was fascinated and could not turn away my eyes. By watching them I in effect permitted their mating to take place and so committed myself to accepting the consequences—all because I wanted to see what would happen. I wanted in on a secret.

And then the eggs hatched and the bed was full of fish. I was standing across the room in the doorway, staring at the bed. The eggs hatched before my eyes, on my bed, and a thousand chunky fish swarmed there in a viscid slime. The fish were firm and fat, black and white, with triangular bodies and bulging eyes. I watched in horror as they squirmed three feet deep, swimming and oozing about in the glistening, transparent slime. Fish in the bed!—and I awoke. My ears still rang with the foreign cry that had been my own voice.

For nightmare you eat wild carrot, which is Queen Anne's lace, or you chew the black seeds of the male peony. But it was too late for prevention, and there is no cure. What root or seed will erase that scene from my mind? Fool, I thought: child, you child, you ignorant, innocent fool. What did you expect to see—angels? For it was understood in the dream that the bed full of fish was my own fault, that if I had turned away from the mating moths the hatching of their eggs wouldn't have happened, or at least would have happened in secret, elsewhere. I brought it upon myself, this slither, this swarm.

I don't know what it is about fecundity that so appalls. I suppose it is the teeming evidence that birth and growth, which we value, are ubiquitous and blind, that life itself is so astonishingly cheap, that nature is as careless as it is bountiful, and that with extravagance goes a crushing waste that will one day include our own cheap lives, Henle's loops and all. Every glistening egg is a memento mori.

After a natural disaster such as a flood, nature "stages a comeback." People use the optimistic expression without any real idea of the pressures and waste the comeback involves. Now, in late June, things are popping outside. Creatures extrude or vent eggs; larvae fatten, split their shells, and eat them; spores dissolve or explode; root hairs multiply, corn puffs on the stalk, grass yields seed, shoots erupt from the earth turgid and sheathed; wet muskrats, rabbits, and squirrels slide into the sunlight, mewling and blind; and everywhere watery cells divide and swell, swell and divide. I can like it and call it birth and regeneration, or I can play the devil's advocate and call it rank fecundity—and say that it's hell that's a-poppin'.

This is what I plan to do. Partly as a result of my terrible dream, I have been thinking that the landscape of the intricate world that I have painted is inaccurate and lopsided. It is too optimistic. For the notion of the infinite variety of detail and the multiplicity of forms is a pleasing one; in complexity are the fringes of beauty, and in variety are generosity and exuberance. But all this leaves something vital out of the picture. It is not one pine I see, but a thousand. I myself am not one, but legion. And we are all going to die.

In this repetition of individuals is a mindless stutter, an imbecilic fixedness that must be taken into account. The driving force behind all this fecundity is a terrible pressure I also must consider, the pressure of birth and growth, the pressure that splits the bark of trees and shoots out seeds, that squeezes out the egg and bursts the pupa, that hungers and lusts and drives the creature relentlessly toward its own death. Fecundity, then, is what I have been thinking about, fecundity and the pressure of growth. Fecundity is an ugly word for an ugly subject. It is ugly, at least, in the eggy animal world. I don't think it is for plants.

I never met a man who was shaken by a field of identical blades of grass. An acre of poppies and a forest of spruce boggle no one's mind. Even ten square miles of wheat gladdens the hearts of most people, although it is really as unnatural and freakish as the Frankenstein monster; if man were to die, I read, wheat wouldn't survive him more than three years. No, in the plant world, and especially among the flowering plants, fecundity is not an assault on human values. Plants are not our competitors; they are our prey and our nesting materials. We are no more distressed at their proliferation than an owl is at a population explosion among field mice.

After the flood last year I found a big tulip-tree limb that had been wind-thrown into Tinker Creek. The current dragged it up on some rocks on the bank, where receding waters stranded it. A month after the flood I discovered that it was growing new leaves. Both ends of the branch were completely exposed and dried. I was amazed. It was like the old fable about the corpse's growing a beard; it was as if the woodpile in my garage were suddenly to burst greenly into leaf. The way plants persevere in the bitterest of circumstances is utterly heartening. I can barely keep from unconsciously ascribing a will to these plants, a do-or-die courage, and I have to remind myself that coded cells and mute water pressure have no idea how grandly they are flying in the teeth of it all.

In the lower Bronx, for example, enthusiasts found an ailanthus tree that was fifteen feet long growing from the corner of a garage roof. It was rooted in and living on "dust and roofing cinders." Even more spectacular is a desert plant, *Ibervillea sonorae*—a member of the gourd family—that Joseph Wood Krutch describes. If you see this plant in the desert, you see only a dried chunk of loose wood. It has neither roots nor stems; it's like an old gray knot-hole. But it is alive. Each year before the rainy season comes, it sends out a few roots and shoots. If the rain arrives, it grows flowers and fruits; these soon wither away, and it reverts to a state as quiet as driftwood.

Well, the New York Botanical Garden put a dried *Ibervillea sonorae* on display in a glass case. "For seven years," says Joseph Wood Krutch, "without soil or water, simply lying in the case, it put forth a few anticipatory shoots and then, when no rainy season arrived, dried up again, hoping for better luck next year." That's what I call flying in the teeth of it all.

(It's hard to understand why no one at the New York Botanical Garden had the grace to splash a glass of water on the thing. Then they could say on their display case label, "This is a live plant." But by the eighth year what they had was a dead plant, which is precisely what it had looked like all along. The sight of it, reinforced by the label "Dead *Ibervillea sonorae*," would have been most melancholy to visitors to the botanical garden. I suppose they just threw it away.)

The growth pressure of plants can do an impressive variety of tricks. Bamboo can grow three feet in twenty-four hours, an accomplishment that is capitalized upon, *legendarily*, in that exquisite Asian torture in which a victim is strapped to a mesh bunk a mere foot above a bed of healthy bamboo plants whose wood-like tips have been sharpened. For the first eight hours he is fine, if jittery; then he starts turning into a collander, by degrees.

Down at the root end of things, blind growth reaches astonishing proportions. So far as I know, only one real experiment has ever been performed to determine the extent and rate of root growth, and when you read the figures, you see why. I have run into various accounts of this experiment, and the only thing they don't tell you is how many lab assistants were blinded for life.

The experimenters studied a single grass plant, winter rye. They let it grow in a greenhouse for four months; then they gingerly spirited away the soil—under microscopes, I imagine—and counted and measured all the roots and root hairs. In four months the plant had set forth 378 miles of roots—that's about three miles a day—in 14 million distinct roots. This is mighty impressive, but when they get down to the root hairs, I boggle completely. In those same four months the rye plant created 14 *billion* root hairs, and those little strands placed end-to-end just about wouldn't quit. In a single *cubic inch* of soil, the length of the root hairs totaled 6000 miles.

Other plants use the same water power to heave the rock earth around as though they were merely shrugging off a silken cape. Rutherford Platt tells about a larch tree whose root had cleft a one-and-one-half ton boulder and hoisted it a foot into the air. Everyone knows how a sycamore root will buckle a sidewalk, a mushroom will shatter a cement basement floor. But when the first real measurements of this awesome pressure were taken, nobody could believe the figures.

Rutherford Platt tells the story in *The Great American Forest,* one of the most interesting books ever written: "In 1875, a Massachusetts farmer, curious about the growing power of expanding apples, melons and squashes, harnessed a squash to a weight-lifting device which had a dial like a grocer's scale to indicate the pressure exerted by the expanding fruit. As the days passed, he kept piling on counterbalancing weight; he could hardly believe his eyes when he saw his vegetables quietly exerting a lifting force of 5 thousand pounds per square inch. When nobody believed him, he set up exhibits of harnessed squashes and invited the public to come and see. The *Annual Report of the Massachusetts Board of Agriculture,* 1875, reported: 'Many thousands of men, women, and children of all classes of society visited it. *Mr. Penlow* watched it day and night, making hourly observations; *Professor Parker* was moved to write a poem about it; *Professor Seelye* declared that he positively stood in awe of it.'"

All this is very jolly. Unless perhaps I were strapped down above a stand of growing, sharpened bamboo, I am unlikely to feel the faintest queasiness either about the growth pressure of plants, or their fecundity. Even when the plants get in the way of human "culture," I don't mind. When I read how many thousands of dollars a city like New York has to spend to keep underground water pipes free of ailanthus, ginko, and sycamore roots, I cannot help but give a little cheer. After all, water pipes are almost always an excellent source of water. In a town where resourcefulness and beating the system are highly prized, these primitive trees can fight city hall and win.

But in the animal world things are different, and human feelings are different. While we're in New York, consider the cockroaches under the bed and the rats in the early morning clustered on the porch stoop. Apartment houses are hives of swarming roaches. Or again: in one sense you could think of Manhattan's land as high-rent, high-rise real estate; in another sense you could see it as an enormous breeding ground for rats, acres and acres of rats. I suppose that the rats and the cockroaches don't do so much actual damage as the roots do; nevertheless, the prospect does not please. Fecundity is anathema only in the animal. "Acres and acres of rats" has a suitably chilling ring to it that is decidedly lacking if I say, instead, "acres and acres of tulips."

The landscape of earth is dotted and smeared with masses of apparently identical individual animals, from the great Pleistocene herds that blanketed grasslands to the gluey gobs of bacteria that clog the lobes of lungs. The oceanic breeding grounds of pelagic birds are as teeming and cluttered as any human Calcutta. Lemmings blacken the earth and locusts the air. Grunion run thick in the ocean, corals pile on pile, and protozoans explode in a red tide stain. Ants take to the skies in swarms, mayflies hatch by the millions, and molting cicadas coat the trunks of trees. Have you seen the rivers run red and lumpy with salmon?

Consider the ordinary barnacle, the rock barnacle. Inside every one of those millions of hard white cones on the rocks—the kind that bruises your heel as you bruise its head—is of course a creature as alive as you or I. Its business in life is this: when a wave washes over it, it sticks out twelve feathery feeding appendages and filters the plankton for food. As it grows, it sheds its skin like a lobster, enlarges its shell, and reproduces itself without end. The larvae "hatch into the sea in milky clouds." The barnacles encrusting a single half mile of shore can leak into the water a million million larvae. How many is that to a human mouthful? In sea water they grow, molt, change shape wildly, and eventually, after several months, settle on the rocks, turn into adults, and build shells. Inside the shells they have to shed their skins. Rachel Carson was always finding the old skins; she reported: "Almost every container of sea water that I bring up from the shore is flecked with white, semitransparent objects. . . . Seen under the microscope, every detail of structure is perfectly represented. . . . In the little cellophane-like replicas I can count the joints of the appendages; even the bristles, growing at the bases of the joints, seem to have been slipped intact out of their casings." All in all, rock barnacles may live four years.

My point about rock barnacles is those million million larvae "in milky clouds" and those shed flecks of skin. Sea water seems suddenly to be but a broth of barnacle bits. Can I fancy that a million million human infants are more real?

What if God has the same affectionate disregard for us that we have for barnacles? I don't know if each barnacle larva is of itself unique and special, or if we the people are essentially as interchangeable as bricks. My brain is full of numbers; they swell and would split my skull like a shell. I examine the trapezoids of skin covering the back of my hands like blown dust motes moistened to clay. I have hatched, too, with millions of my kind, into a milky way that spreads from an unknown shore.

I have seen the mantis's abdomen dribbling out eggs in wet bubbles like tapioca pudding glued to a thorn. I have seen a film of a termite queen as big as my face, dead white and featureless, glistening with slime, throbbing and pulsing out rivers of globular eggs. Termite workers, who looked like tiny longshoremen unloading the *Queen Mary*, licked each egg as fast as it was extruded to prevent mold. The whole world is an incubator for incalculable numbers of eggs, each one coded minutely and ready to burst.

The egg of a parasite chalcid wasp, a common small wasp, multiplies unassisted, making ever more identical eggs. The female lays a single fertilized egg in the flaccid tissues of its live prey, and that one egg divides and divides. As many as two thousand new parasitic wasps will hatch to feed on the host's body with identical hunger. Similarly—only more so—Edwin Way Teale reports that a lone aphid, without a partner, breeding "unmolested" for one year, would produce so many living aphids that, although they are only a tenth of an inch long, together they would extend into space twenty-five hundred *light-years.*

Even the average goldfish lays five thousand eggs, which she will eat as fast as she lays, if permitted. The sales manager of Ozark Fisheries in Missouri, which raises commercial goldfish for the likes of me, said, "We produce, measure, and sell our product by the ton." The intricacy of Ellery and aphids multiplied mindlessly into tons and light-years is more than extravagance; it is holocaust, parody, glut.

The pressure of growth among animals is a kind of terrible hunger. These billions must eat in order to fuel their surge to sexual maturity so that they may pump out more billions of eggs. And what are the fish on the bed going to eat, or the hatched mantises in the Mason jar going to eat, but each other? There is a terrible innocence in the benumbed world of the lower animals, reducing life there to a universal chomp. Edwin Way Teale, in *The Strange Lives of Familiar Insects*—a book I couldn't live without—describes several occasions of meals mouthed under the pressure of a hunger that knew no bounds.

You remember the dragonfly nymph, for instance, which stalks the bottom of the creek and the pond in search of live prey to snare with its hooked, unfolding lip. Dragonfly nymphs are insatiable and mighty. They clasp and devour whole minnows and fat tadpoles. Well, a dragonfly nymph, says Teale, "has even been seen climbing up out of the water on a plant to attack a helpless dragonfly emerging, soft and rumpled, from its nymphal skin." Is this where I draw the line?

It is between mothers and their offspring that these feedings have truly macabre overtones. Look at lacewings. Lacewings are those fragile green insects with large, rounded transparent wings. The larvae eat enormous numbers of aphids, the adults mate in a fluttering rush of instinct, lay eggs, and die by the millions in the first cold snap of fall. Sometimes, when a female lays her fertile eggs on a green leaf atop a slender stalked thread, she is hungry. She pauses in her laying, turns around, and eats her eggs one by one, then lays some more, and eats them, too.

Anything can happen, and anything does; what's it all about? Valerie Eliot, T. S. Eliot's widow, wrote in a letter to the London *Times:* "My husband, T. S. Eliot, loved to recount how late one evening he stopped a taxi. As he got in the driver said: 'You're T. S. Eliot.' When asked how he knew, he replied: 'Ah, I've got an eye for a celebrity. Only the other evening I picked up Bertrand Russell, and I said to him, "Well, Lord Russell, what's it all about," and, do you know, he couldn't tell me.'" Well, Lord God, asks the delicate, dying lacewing whose mandibles are wet with the juice secreted by her own ovipositor, what's it all about? ("And do you know . . .")

Planarians, which live in the duck pond, behave similarly. They are those dark laboratory flatworms that can regenerate themselves from almost any severed part. Arthur Koestler writes, "during the mating season the worms become cannibals, devouring everything alive that comes their way, including their own previously discarded tails which

were in the process of growing a new head." Even such sophisticated mammals as the great predator cats occasionally eat their cubs.
A mother cat will be observed licking the area around the umbilical
cord of the helpless newborn. She licks, she licks, she licks until something snaps in her brain, and she begins eating, starting there, at the
vulnerable belly.

Although mothers devouring their own offspring is patently the
more senseless, somehow the reverse behavior is the more appalling.
In the death of the parent in the jaws of its offspring I recognize a
universal drama that chance occurrence has merely telescoped, so that
I can see all the players at once. Gall gnats, for instance, are common small flies. Sometimes, according to Teale, a gall gnat larva, which
does not resemble the adult in the least, and which has certainly not
mated, nevertheless produces within its body eggs, live eggs, which
then hatch within its soft tissues. Sometimes the eggs hatch alive even
within the quiescent body of the pupa. The same incredible thing occasionally occurs within the fly genus *Miastor*, again to both larvae and
pupae. "These eggs hatch within their bodies and the ravenous larvae
which emerge immediately begin devouring their parents." In this case,
I know what it's all about, and I wish I didn't. The parents die, the next
generation lives, *ad majorem gloriam*, and so it goes. If the new generation hastens the death of the old, it scarcely matters; the old has served
its one purpose, and the direct processing of proteins is tidily all in the
family. But think of the invisible swelling of ripe eggs inside the pupa
as wrapped and rigid as a mummified Egyptian queen! The eggs burst,
shatter her belly, and emerge alive, awake, and hungry from a mummy
case which they crawl over like worms and feed on till its gone. And
then they turn to the world.

"To prevent a like fate," Teale continues, "some of the ichneumon
flies, those wasplike parasites which deposit their eggs in the body
tissues of caterpillars, have to scatter their eggs while in flight at times
when they are unable to find their prey and the eggs are ready to hatch
within their bodies."

You are an ichneumon. You mated and your eggs are fertile. If
you can't find a caterpillar on which to lay your eggs, your young will
starve. When the eggs hatch, the young will eat any body in which they
find themselves, so if you don't kill them by emitting them broadcast
over the landscape, they'll eat you alive. But if you let them drop over
the fields you will probably be dead yourself, of old age, before they
even hatch to starve, and the whole show will be over and done, and
a wretched one it was. You feel them coming, and coming, and you
struggle to rise. . . .

Not that the ichneumon is making any conscious choice. If she
were, her dilemma would be truly the stuff of tragedy; Aeschylus need

have looked no further than the ichneumon. That is, it would be the stuff of real tragedy if only Aeschylus and I could convince you that the ichneumon is really and truly as alive as we are, and that what happens to it matters. Will you take it on faith?

Here is one last story. It shows that the pressures of growth gang aft a-gley.[1] The clothes moth, whose caterpillar eats wool, sometimes goes into a molting frenzy which Teale blandly describes as "curious": "A curious paradox in molting is the action of a clothes-moth larva with insufficient food. It sometimes goes into a 'molting frenzy,' changing its skin repeatedly and getting smaller and smaller with each change." Smaller and smaller . . . can you imagine the frenzy? Where shall we send our sweaters? The diminution process could, in imagination, extend to infinity, as the creature frantically shrinks and shrinks and shrinks to the size of a molecule, then an electron, but never can shrink to absolute nothing and end its terrible hunger. I feel like Ezra: "And when I heard this thing, I rent my garment and my mantle, and plucked off the hair of my head and of my beard, and sat down astonied."

Analyzing and Discussing the Text

1. Dillard describes her dream of the mating moths as "the perfect picture of utter spirituality and utter degradation." What is "spiritual" about fecundity and what is "degrading"?
2. Why does Dillard find the reproductive process horrible? As she puts it, what is it "about fecundity that so appalls"?
3. What, according to Dillard, is problematic about the abundance and complexity of the natural world (including us)? "In this repetition of individuals is a mindless stutter, an imbecilic fixedness that must be taken into account," she writes. Explain this idea by referring to specific passages in Dillard's text.
4. Why, for Dillard, is the fecundity of the "eggy animal world" more disturbing than that of the plant world?
5. If Lewis Thomas was philosophical and mildly optimistic in his study of death, how would you describe the tone and overall approach of Dillard's piece? What is the role of emotion in this contemplation of the natural world? How, for Dillard, is fecundity bound up with mortality?
6. Does Dillard rely mostly on personal observation or information from reading? How do the two sources of ideas work together in this text?

[1] gang aft a-gley: Scottish for "gone awry." —Eds.

7. Dillard tends to enjoy using hyperbole: sensational, exaggerated descriptions. Identify examples of this and explain how they contribute to the effect of her writing.
8. How does Dillard associate fecundity in the external world with human existence?

Experiencing and Writing About the World

1. "Fecundity is anathema only in the animal." Interpret this sentence and use it as a springboard to consider your own personal response to the rampant abundance of the biological world. Describe one or more occasions when you have encountered scenes of extraordinary fertility or scarcity, exploring your own *emotional* responses to these events. Do you sympathize with Dillard's reaction or feel differently?
2. One of the fun things about Annie Dillard's writing is her playful use of extravagant examples. Find a guidebook to nature—perhaps even Edwin Way Teale's *The Strange Lives of Familiar Insects*—and select three or four examples that seem especially surprising or unusual to you. Then prepare your own brief essay on fecundity or some other fundamental issue raised in Dillard's essay—individuality, parents and children, mystery—in which you use repeated allusions to your guidebook and perhaps even to Dillard as springboards for your own reflections.
3. It is hard to derive a coherent "argument" from Dillard's essay (unlike Thomas's study of mortality), except perhaps the implicit idea of wonderment as the appropriate way of responding to nature. Write a 500-word argumentless meditation on the natural world in which you intentionally leap from idea to idea, displaying vivid emotion—wonder, revulsion, affection— without trying to persuade your reader to agree with anything you say.

STEPHEN JAY GOULD

Sex, Drugs, Disasters, and the Extinction of Dinosaurs

Born in New York City, Stephen Jay Gould (1941–   ) earned his B.A. in 1963 at Antioch College and his Ph.D. four years later at Columbia University. "A lot of paleontologists began life as dinosaur nuts," he told one interviewer; Gould's interest began at the age of five when he saw Tyrannosaurus rex at the American Museum of Natural History in New York. He is currently professor of geology and curator of invertebrate paleontology at the Museum of Comparative Zoology and Alexander Agassiz Professor of Zoology at Harvard University, and writes monthly columns called "This View of Life" for *Natural History* magazine. These columns have been collected in numerous books, including *Ever Since Darwin: Reflections in Natural History* (1977), *The Panda's Thumb: More Reflections in Natural History* (1980), *Hen's Teeth and Horse's Toes: Further Reflections in Natural History* (1985), and *The Flamingo's Smile: Reflections in Natural History* (1985). More recently he has published *Time's Arrow, Time's Cycle* (1987), *Wonderful Life: The Burgess Shale and the Nature of History* (1989), and *Bully for Brontosaurus: Reflections in Natural History* (1991). Gould's many honors include the National Book Critics Circle Award in general nonfiction for *The Mismeasure of Man* and the American Book Award in science for *The Panda's Thumb*, both in 1981. He has received honorary degrees from more than twenty colleges and universities.

Like Loren Eiseley, Gould's fascination with the intricacies of evolutionary theory and the physical manifestations of evolution in the visible world has led him to focus persistently on this concept in his writing. "Evolution," he writes in the prologue to *The Flamingo's Smile*, "is one of the half-dozen shattering ideas that science has developed to overturn past hopes and assumptions, and to enlighten our current thoughts. Evolution is also more personal than the quantum, or the relative motion of earth and sun; it speaks directly to the questions of genealogy that so fascinate us—how and when did we arise, what are our biological relationships with other creatures?" The essay "Sex, Drugs, Disasters, and the Extinction of Dinosaurs," which first appeared in *Discover* magazine in 1984, considers the same process of extinction that enabled our own species to begin its evolutionary process. In examining several popular theories about dinosaur extinction, Gould explains the importance of methodology in both scientific investigation and popular science writing. The popular science columnist David Quammen has praised Gould's "methodology" as a writer, noting that "when he writes about such bio-logical oddities as the inverted jellyfish Cassiopea, the praying mantis's mating habits, the giant panda's extra 'thumb' or the flamingo's inverted jaw, he does so with a double purpose—to entertain us with fascinating details while teaching us a few general concepts. . . . Every oddity he describes stands on its own as a discrete fact of nature, an individual mystery, as well as yielding an example of some broader principle." The following essay makes precisely this use of the various theories about dinosaur extinction.

Science, in its most fundamental definition, is a fruitful mode of inquiry, not a list of enticing conclusions. The conclusions are the consequence, not the essence.

My greatest unhappiness with most popular presentations of science concerns their failure to separate fascinating claims from the methods that scientists use to establish the facts of nature. Journalists, and the public, thrive on controversial and stunning statements. But science is, basically, a way of knowing—in P. B. Medawar's apt words, "the art of the soluble." If the growing corps of popular science writers would focus on *how* scientists develop and defend those fascinating claims, they would make their greatest possible contribution to public understanding.

Consider three ideas, proposed in perfect seriousness to explain that greatest of all titillating puzzles—the extinction of dinosaurs. Since these three notions invoke the primally fascinating themes of our culture—sex, drugs, and violence—they surely reside in the category of fascinating claims. I want to show why two of them rank as silly speculation, while the other represents science at its grandest and most useful.

Science works with testable proposals. If, after much compilation and scrutiny of data, new information continues to affirm a hypothesis, we may accept it provisionally and gain confidence as further evidence mounts. We can never be completely sure that a hypothesis is right, though we may be able to show with confidence that it is wrong. The best scientific hypotheses are also generous and expansive: they suggest extensions and implications that enlighten related, and even far distant, subjects. Simply consider how the idea of evolution has influenced virtually every intellectual field.

Useless speculation, on the other hand, is restrictive. It generates no testable hypothesis, and offers no way to obtain potentially refuting evidence. Please note that I am not speaking of truth or falsity. The speculation may well be true; still, if it provides, in principle, no material for affirmation or rejection, we can make nothing of it. It must simply stand forever as an intriguing idea. Useless speculation turns in on itself and leads nowhere; good science, containing both seeds for its potential refutation and implications for more and different testable knowledge, reaches out. But, enough preaching. Let's move on to dinosaurs, and the three proposals for their extinction.

1. Sex: Testes function only in a narrow range of temperature (those of mammals hang externally in a scrotal sac because internal body temperatures are too high for their proper function). A worldwide rise in temperature at the close of the Cretaceous period caused the testes of dinosaurs to stop functioning and led to their extinction by sterilization of males.

2. Drugs: Angiosperms (flowering plants) first evolved toward the end of the dinosaurs' reign. Many of these plants contain psychoactive agents, avoided by mammals today as a result of their bitter taste. Dinosaurs had neither means to taste the bitterness nor livers effective enough to detoxify the substances. They died of massive overdoses.

3. Disasters: A large comet or asteroid struck the earth some 65 million years ago, lofting a cloud of dust into the sky and blocking sunlight, thereby suppressing photosynthesis and so drastically lowering world temperatures that dinosaurs and hosts of other creatures became extinct.

Before analyzing these three tantalizing statements, we must establish a basic ground rule often violated in proposals for the dinosaurs' demise. *There is no separate problem of the extinction of dinosaurs.* Too often we divorce specific events from their wider contexts and systems of cause and effect. The fundamental fact of dinosaur extinction is its synchrony with the demise of so many other groups across a wide range of habitats, from terrestrial to marine.

The history of life has been punctuated by brief episodes of mass extinction. A recent analysis by University of Chicago paleontologists Jack Sepkoski and Dave Raup, based on the best and most exhaustive tabulation of data ever assembled, shows clearly that five episodes of mass dying stand well above the "background" extinctions of normal times (when we consider all mass extinctions, large and small, they seem to fall in a regular 26-million-year cycle). The Cretaceous debacle, occurring 65 million years ago and separating the Mesozoic and Cenozoic eras of our geological time scale, ranks prominently among the five. Nearly all the marine plankton (single-celled floating creatures) died with geological suddenness; among marine invertebrates, nearly 15 percent of all families perished, including many previously dominant groups, especially the ammonites (relatives of squids in coiled shells). On land, the dinosaurs disappeared after more than 100 million years of unchallenged domination.

In this context, speculations limited to dinosaurs alone ignore the larger phenomenon. We need a coordinated explanation for a system of events that includes the extinction of dinosaurs as one component. Thus it makes little sense, though it may fuel our desire to view mammals as inevitable inheritors of the earth, to guess that dinosaurs died because small mammals ate their eggs (a perennial favorite among untestable speculations). It seems most unlikely that some disaster peculiar to dinosaurs befell these massive beasts—and that the debacle happened to strike just when one of history's five great dyings had enveloped the earth for completely different reasons.

The testicular theory, an old favorite from the 1940s, had its root in an interesting and thoroughly respectable study of temperature tolerances in the American alligator, published in the staid *Bulletin of the American Museum of Natural History* in 1946 by three experts on living and fossil reptiles—E. H. Colbert, my own first teacher in paleontology; R. B. Cowles; and C. M. Bogert.

The first sentence of their summary reveals a purpose beyond alligators: "This report describes an attempt to infer the reactions of extinct reptiles, especially the dinosaurs, to high temperatures as based upon reactions observed in the modern alligator." They studied, by rectal thermometry, the body temperatures of alligators under changing conditions of heating and cooling. (Well, let's face it, you wouldn't want to try sticking a thermometer under a 'gator's tongue.) The predictions under test go way back to an old theory first stated by Galileo in the 1630s—the unequal scaling of surfaces and volumes. As an animal, or any object, grows (provided its shape doesn't change), surface areas must increase more slowly than volumes—since surfaces get larger as length squared, while volumes increase much more rapidly, as length cubed. Therefore, small animals have high ratios of surface to volume, while large animals cover themselves with relatively little surface.

Among cold-blooded animals lacking any physiological mechanism for keeping their temperatures constant, small creatures have a hell of a time keeping warm—because they lose so much heat through their relatively large surfaces. On the other hand, large animals, with their relatively small surfaces, may lose heat so slowly that, once warm, they may maintain effectively constant temperatures against ordinary fluctuations of climate. (In fact, the resolution of the "hot-blooded dinosaur" controversy that burned so brightly a few years back may simply be that, while large dinosaurs possessed no physiological mechanism for constant temperature, and were not therefore warm-blooded in the technical sense, their large size and relatively small surface area kept them warm.)

Colbert, Cowles, and Bogert compared the warming rates of small and large alligators. As predicted, the small fellows heated up (and cooled down) more quickly. When exposed to a warm sun, a tiny 50-gram (1.76-ounce) alligator heated up one degree Celsius every minute and a half, while a large alligator, 260 times bigger at 13,000 grams (28.7 pounds), took seven and a half minutes to gain a degree. Extrapolating up to an adult 10-ton dinosaur, they concluded that a one-degree rise in body temperature would take eighty-six hours. If large animals absorb heat so slowly (through their relatively small surfaces), they will also be unable to shed any excess heat gained when temperatures rise above a favorable level.

The authors then guessed that large dinosaurs lived at or near their optimum temperatures; Cowles suggested that a rise in global temperatures just before the Cretaceous extinction caused the dinosaurs to heat up beyond their optimal tolerance—and, being so large, they couldn't shed the unwanted heat. (In a most unusual statement within a scientific paper, Colbert and Bogert then explicitly disavowed this speculative extension of their empirical work on alligators.) Cowles conceded that this excess heat probably wasn't enough to kill or even to enervate the great beasts, but since testes often function only within a narrow range of temperature, he proposed that this global rise might have sterilized all the males, causing extinction by natural contraception.

The overdose theory has recently been supported by UCLA psychiatrist Ronald K. Siegel. Siegel has gathered, he claims, more than 2,000 records of animals who, when given access, administer various drugs to themselves—from a mere swig of alcohol to massive doses of the big H. Elephants will swill the equivalent of twenty beers at a time, but do not like alcohol in concentrations greater than 7 percent. In a silly bit of anthropocentric speculation, Siegel states that "elephants drink, perhaps, to forget . . . the anxiety produced by shrinking rangeland and the competition for food."

Since fertile imaginations can apply almost any hot idea to the extinction of dinosaurs, Siegel found a way. Flowering plants did not evolve until late in the dinosaurs' reign. These plants also produced an array of aromatic, amino-acid-based alkaloids—the major group of psychoactive agents. Most mammals are "smart" enough to avoid these potential poisons. The alkaloids simply don't taste good (they are bitter); in any case, we mammals have livers happily supplied with the capacity to detoxify them. But, Siegel speculates, perhaps dinosaurs could neither taste the bitterness nor detoxify the substances once ingested. He recently told members of the American Psychological Association: "I'm not suggesting that all dinosaurs OD'd on plant drugs, but it certainly was a factor." He also argued that death by overdose may help explain why so many dinosaur fossils are found in contorted positions. (Do not go gentle into that good night.)

Extraterrestrial catastrophes have long pedigrees in the popular literature of extinction, but the subject exploded again in 1979, after a long lull, when the father-son physicist-geologist team of Luis and Walter Alvarez proposed that an asteroid, some 10 km in diameter, struck the earth 65 million years ago (comets, rather than asteroids, have since gained favor. Good science is self-corrective).

The force of such a collision would be immense, greater by far than the megatonnage of all the world's nuclear weapons. In trying to reconstruct a scenario that would explain the simultaneous dying of dinosaurs on land and so many creatures in the sea, the Alvarezes proposed that a gigantic dust cloud, generated by particles blown aloft in the impact, would so darken the earth that photosynthesis would cease and temperatures drop precipitously. (Rage, rage against the dying of the light.) The single-celled photosynthetic oceanic plankton, with life cycles measured in weeks, would perish outright, but land plants might survive through the dormancy of their seeds (land plants were not much affected by the Cretaceous extinction, and any adequate theory must account for the curious pattern of differential survival). Dinosaurs would die by starvation and freezing; small, warm-blooded mammals, with more modest requirements for food and better regulation of body temperature, would squeak through. "Let the bastards freeze in the dark," as bumper stickers of our chauvinistic neighbors in sunbelt states proclaimed several years ago during the Northeast's winter oil crisis.

All three theories, testicular malfunction, psychoactive overdosing, and asteroidal zapping, grab our attention mightily. As pure phenomenology, they rank about equally high on any hit parade of primal fascination. Yet one represents expansive science, the others restrictive and untestable speculation. The proper criterion lies in evidence and methodology; we must probe behind the superficial fascination of particular claims.

How could we possibly decide whether the hypothesis of testicular frying is right or wrong? We would have to know things that the fossil record cannot provide. What temperatures were optimal for dinosaurs? Could they avoid the absorption of excess heat by staying in the shade, or in caves? At what temperatures did their testicles cease to function? Were late Cretaceous climates ever warm enough to drive the internal temperatures of dinosaurs close to this ceiling? Testicles simply don't fossilize, and how could we infer their temperature tolerances even if they did? In short, Cowles's hypothesis is only an intriguing speculation leading nowhere. The most damning statement against it appeared right in the conclusion of Colbert, Cowles, and Bogert's paper, when they admitted: "It is difficult to advance any definite arguments against this hypothesis." My statement may seem paradoxical— isn't a hypothesis really good if you can't devise any arguments against it? Quite the contrary. It is simply untestable and unusable.

Siegel's overdosing has even less going for it. At least Cowles extrapolated his conclusion from some good data on alligators. And he didn't completely violate the primary guideline of siting dinosaur extinction in the context of a general mass dying—for rise in temperature could be the root cause of a general catastrophe, zapping dinosaurs by testicular malfunction and different groups for other reasons. But Siegel's speculation cannot touch the extinction of ammonites or oceanic plankton (diatoms make their own food with good sweet sunlight; they don't OD on the chemicals of terrestrial plants). It is simply a gratuitous, attention-grabbing guess. It cannot be tested, for how can we know what dinosaurs tasted and what their livers could do? Livers don't fossilize any better than testicles.

The hypothesis doesn't even make any sense in its own context. Angiosperms were in full flower ten million years before dinosaurs went the way of all flesh. Why did it take so long? As for the pains of a chemical death recorded in contortions of fossils, I regret to say (or rather I'm pleased to note for the dinosaurs' sake) that Siegel's knowledge of geology must be a bit deficient: muscles contract after death and geological strata rise and fall with motions of the earth's crust after burial—more than enough reason to distort a fossil's pristine appearance.

The impact story, on the other hand, has a sound basis in evidence. It can be tested, extended, refined and, if wrong, disproved. The Alvarezes did not just construct an arresting guess for public consumption. They proposed their hypothesis after laborious geochemical studies with Frank Asaro and Helen Michael had revealed a massive increase of iridium in rocks deposited right at the time of extinction. Iridium, a rare metal of the platinum group, is virtually absent from indigenous rocks of the earth's crust; most of our iridium arrives on extraterrestrial objects that strike the earth.

The Alvarez hypothesis bore immediate fruit. Based originally on evidence from two European localities, it led geochemists throughout the world to examine other sediments of the same age. They found abnormally high amounts of iridium everywhere—from continental rocks of the western United States to deep sea cores from the South Atlantic.

Cowles proposed his testicular hypothesis in the mid-1940s. Where has it gone since then? Absolutely nowhere, because scientists can do nothing with it. The hypothesis must stand as a curious appendage to a solid study of alligators. Siegel's overdose scenario will also win a few press notices and fade into oblivion. The Alvarezes' asteroid falls into a different category altogether, and much of the popular commentary has missed this essential distinction by focusing on the impact and its attendant results, and forgetting what really matters to a scientist—the iridium. If you talk just about asteroids, dust, and darkness, you tell stories no better and no more entertaining than fried testicles or terminal trips. It is the iridium—the source of testable evidence—that counts and forges the crucial distinction between speculation and science.

The proof, to twist a phrase, lies in the doing. Cowles's hypothesis has generated nothing in thirty-five years. Since its proposal in 1979, the Alvarez hypothesis has spawned hundreds of studies, a major conference, and attendant publications. Geologists are fired up. They are looking for iridium at all other extinction boundaries. Every week exposes a new wrinkle in the scientific press. Further evidence that the Cretaceous iridium represents extraterrestrial impact and not indigenous volcanism continues to accumulate. As I revise this essay in November 1984 (this paragraph will be out of date when the book is published),[1] new data include chemical "signatures" of other isotopes indicating unearthly provenance, glass spherules of a size and sort produced by impact and not by volcanic eruptions, and high-pressure varieties of silica formed (so far as we know) only under the tremendous shock of impact.

My point is simply this: Whatever the eventual outcome (I suspect it will be positive), the Alvarez hypothesis is exciting, fruitful science because it generates tests, provides us with things to do, and expands outward. We are having fun, battling back and forth, moving toward a resolution, and extending the hypothesis beyond its original scope.

As just one example of the unexpected, distant cross-fertilization that good science engenders, the Alvarez hypothesis made a major contribution to a theme that has riveted public attention in the past few months—so-called nuclear winter. In a speech delivered in April 1982, Luis Alvarez calculated the energy that a ten-kilometer asteroid would release on impact. He compared such an explosion with a full nuclear exchange and implied that all-out atomic war might unleash similar consequences.

This theme of impact leading to massive dust clouds and falling temperatures formed an important input to the decision of Carl Sagan and a group of colleagues to model the climatic consequences of nuclear holocaust. Full nuclear exchange would probably generate the same kind of dust cloud and darkening that may have wiped out the dinosaurs. Temperatures would drop precipitously and agriculture might become impossible. Avoidance of nuclear war is fundamentally an ethical and political imperative, but we must know the factual consequences to make firm judgments. I am heartened by a final link across disciplines and deep concerns—another criterion, by the way, of science at its best[2]: A recognition of the very phenomenon that made our evolution possible by exterminating the previously dominant dinosaurs and clearing a way for the evolution of large mammals, including us, might actually help to save us from joining those magnificent beasts in contorted poses among the strata of the earth.

---

[1] *The Flamingo's Smile* (1985)— Eds.
[2] This quirky connection so tickles my fancy that I break my own strict rule about eliminating redundancies from [this essay]. . . . —Author's note.

Analyzing and Discussing the Text

1. How does Gould define "good science"? What is the role of "speculation" in science—for instance, in the Alvarez hypothesis? Why should these matters concern science writers?
2. Does Gould agree with all three speculations about the extinction of dinosaurs (sex, drugs, rock and roll—or rather, disasters)? Why does he bother describing each theory in such detail?
3. Consider Gould's use of parenthetical comments in this essay. How does he use them and why?
4. Explain the structure of this essay. Why do you think Gould opts for a repetitive, braiding pattern rather than a less complicated examination of one theory at a time?
5. Gould suggests that "fertile imaginations can apply almost any hot idea to the extinction of dinosaurs." What are the implications of this statement for the way humans think about the natural world in general? Is there a subtle warning here? If so, what?
6. Does Gould treat the extinction of dinosaurs merely as an interesting scientific example or does he suggest a more profound link between dinosaurs and humans? Explain your response.

Experiencing and Writing About the World

1. Find a scientific question for which there are several conflicting answers, then write an essay of 500–750 words in which you summarize each theory and evaluate it according to how well it satisfies Gould's criteria for good science.
2. Gould's essay concludes with the ominous speculation that the extinction of dinosaurs may directly herald the fate of humanity if we don't act soon to avert the possibility of a "nuclear winter." Although we now seem to be easing our way out of the cold war era, write a letter to your local congressperson, using Gould's description of the probable effect of nuclear war as part of a brief argument for the continued reduction of nuclear arsenals. Keep it short and to the point. You might consider citing Gould's essay to give your argument authority.
3. Do research on one or more other endangered species and then write a "popular presentation" of this information in which you try to remain faithful to the scientific accounts you've read while still using language with clarity, energy, and humor. If, as with the dinosaurs, the predicaments of the endangered species have clear implications for human behavior (how can this *not* be the case?), try to develop these "ethical and political imperative[s]."

STEPHEN HARRIGAN

The Secret Life of the Beach

The novelist and essayist Stephen Harrigan (1948–   ) worked for many years as an editor and staff writer with *Texas Monthly* magazine. Harrigan attended the University of Texas at Austin in the late sixties (graduating in 1970), then "foundered" for several years, mowing lawns and writing poetry before becoming a freelance journalist and publishing articles in such magazines as *Rolling Stone*, the *Texas Observer*, and eventually *Texas Monthly*. In the preface to his 1988 essay collection, *A Natural State*, Harrigan writes: "I suppose I might rather have written about places radiant with uncorrupted natural beauty, where the beaches were not filled with trash and birds did not bathe in roadside oil slicks, where I could have imagined myself as the chronicler of a laboratory-pure wilderness. But I don't come from those places, and it seems to me that a city-bred Texan with an ambivalence about camping and an unsure way with a field guide can be a fair enough witness to a sullied and complicated natural heritage." Harrigan's ambivalence about the Texas landscape began when he moved from his hometown of Oklahoma City, Oklahoma, to Abilene, on the desolate plains of West Texas, at the age of five. The essay "What Texas Means to Me" recalls his early and continued resistance to the landscapes of his adopted state, first to the low hills and dreary lake near his home in Abilene and later to the humidity and stillness of Corpus Christi on the Gulf Coast, where he moved when he was ten. But Harrigan stayed to attend college in Austin, the city where he still lives. For all of his resistance, he has, as he puts it, "built up without meaning to a certain equity of place." Both of Harrigan's novels are Texas novels: *Aransas* (1980), set on the Gulf Coast, is about dolphins, the people who exploit them, and those who appreciate their beauty and mystery; *Jacob's Well* (1984) is about divers who are compelled to explore the treacherous caverns of an aquifer in central Texas. More recently he wrote the screenplay for "The Last of His Tribe" (based on Theodora Kroeber's book *Ishi: The Last of His Tribe*), which aired on HBO in 1992. *Water and Light: A Diver's Journey to a Coral Reef*, an account of two months Harrigan spent diving in the waters off Grand Turk Island near the Bahamas, also appeared in 1992. Having left his position as senior editor at *Texas Monthly* to give himself more time for writing, he is currently at work on articles for *Life* and *Audubon* magazines and on a historical novel about the Alamo.

"The Texas landscape is not always beautiful, and in some places, at some moments, it is hardly bearable," writes Harrigan. "But it is resonant and full of secrets." "The Secret Life of the Beach," also from *A Natural State*, reveals some of these secrets in the form of the abundant, furtive wildlife on a coastal island in the Gulf of Mexico. Life and death, as always, are bound up together in this peek at the inhuman world. Like many of Harrigan's essays, this piece reflects his sense that "the duty of the nature writer is to use imagination to create some way of thinking about the world." Sometimes, as we see here, even anthropomorphism becomes a way "to penetrate things with the human imagination, to bring them to life."

A white-tailed hawk has spent the night at the summit of a solitary live oak behind the dunes. There is dew on the hawk's wings; he is sluggish and cold. He turns around and around on the branch, positioning himself to catch the warmth of the sun rising into a clear sky over the Gulf.

The tree on which the hawk sits bends elaborately leeward. It stands at the center of the island in a kind of valley, a deflation flat, between the stabilized dunes near the beach and a bare active dune field that backs up to the narrow lagoon separating the island from the mainland.

The isolation of the tree suits the hawk. It gives him a sense of prominence, from which he derives a sense of security. Even at rest, uncommitted to anything except basking torpidly in the early morning sunlight, the hawk gives off an impression of awesome capability and utter indifference. He looks out over the grassland, blinking. His stolid body is clearly marked: a warm gray above, with rufous streaks on the wings, and a clean white underside and tail, which is traversed at the tip by a precise black band.

When the sun is a little higher, he begins his diurnal rounds, rising from the tree with a few powerful surges of his wings and almost immediately entering an updraft. The hawk artfully conforms to the movement of the warm air, letting it support him, adjusting the tension in his wings for direction and height. The same economy that guides his flight guides his will: there is neither wasted motion nor wasted thought. The hawk's mind is as clear as the air in which he flies. He scans the ground and notes without concern the high-packed burrows of pocket gophers, the scattered yellow flowers of beach morning glory, his own reflection in the water of a tidal pool. Far below him on the highway that runs the length of the island lies a dead mother possum, surrounded by the three embryonic forms that were knocked from her pouch when she was struck during the night by a car. The possum babies are pink, with black, skin-covered bulges of incipient eyes and well-developed forelimbs, which they had used to climb from their mother's vagina to her pouch, knowing the way by the trail of saliva she had deposited.

None of this concerns the hawk. It is movement that excites him. The sharpness of his vision, the expert trim of his body in the air—sensations that would produce a state of rapture if transferred to a human being—are part of the package of the hawk, instruments for locating snakes and rabbits and frogs. But within the range of his vision the narrow island is encompassed: it revolves around the steady axis of his perception. When the hawk flies north the open Gulf is at his right wing tip and the muddy lagoon at his left.

The island is little more than a mile wide and only a few hundred yards from the mainland. Though it is twenty miles long, its northern and southern boundaries are almost abstract landmarks, the sites of natural passes that barely interrupt the continuity of a long strip of offshore islands that shadows the Texas coast for some two hundred miles, from the Brazos to the Rio Grande. This island, like the others that make up the chain, is a barrier island, a sandbar that serves as a buffer between the turbulence of the open Gulf and the calm estuarine waters. Above its base of Pleistocene mud the island is an accumulation of sediment washed down from rivers, fanned along the coast by currents, and pounded into a semblance of geological form by the surf. The island's shoreface is paralleled by three submerged bars, with deep troughs between them, that are the last easily discernible features of the sea bottom before it planes out for its long, monotonous drop along the continental slope. The smooth, wind-generated waves of the ocean, coasting along the consistent upgrade of the bottom, trip over the outermost bar, regenerate somewhat in the trough, and then break and reform again for the next two series, finally reaching the shore itself with a weary, slouching motion. Because of the bars the surf is predictable but sloppy, the waves rebuilding and expending themselves all in a distance of a few hundred feet.

The beach itself is several hundred feet wide, and beyond it are the high and stable foredunes, secured by spartina grass and sea oats from the constant scouring of the wind. The grass flats behind the dunes are stable too, in their way, having been eroded down to ancient sand deposits whose surprisingly regular stratigraphy has been spoiled by the ceaseless disturbance of burrowing animals and rooting plants. But beyond this savannah the dunes are clean and virginal, expanses so utterly without shade or protection that practically no living thing interferes with their architectural purity. The dunes are lower than the foredunes, and blindingly white. And though constantly moving, they are not arbitrary forms. Their complex structure is implied by the wind ripples and slip faces that mark their surfaces. Beyond the dune field is a tidal flat, overgrown with marsh grass, that shelves with no particular demarcation into the lagoon and the deep mud that underlies it.

All this is within the field of the hawk's exquisite vision. High up in the sky the full moon is still visible, as pale as a cloud. At this time of the day the moon is simply a receding ornament, but its effects upon the creatures of the island are profound. All of the waters of the world fall a little toward the moon, as gravity demands. The oceans bulge outward, lagging in their momentum as the earth spins beneath, generating immense longitudinal waves that, when they reach land, are known as tides.

It is high tide now, on this island a visually unspectacular event, since the water rarely rises or falls more than a foot or two. The swash line—the farthest boundary of the surf—has advanced several yards up the beach, leaving a string of muddy, deflated foam and a new wave of detritus: broken shells, mangrove pods from the Yucatán, worm tubes, parts of crabs, plastic rings that once held six-packs of beer together, seaweed, light bulbs, gooseneck barnacles slowly dying of exposure on a piece of driftwood.

To the creatures that live within the surf zone the tide is a critical occurrence. Most of them live either beneath the sand or somehow secured to it and would be helpless if dislodged. They have no way of controlling themselves in the violence of the waves, no way to go in search of the tiny planktonic forms upon which their existence depends. The tides bring the plankton to them, and the creatures use whatever means they have for extracting it from the environment. Sand dollars, traveling just beneath the sand of the outermost trough, trap the plankton in minute spines that cover their sturdy, chambered bodies and move it along to their mouths. Nearly microscopic creatures called larvaceans construct a kind of house around their bodies, with which they trap and filter protein. Bivalves like the coquina clam open their shells just enough to send up a siphon to draw in the plankton.

In their makeshift burrows just inside the surf a colony of coquinas is monitoring the violence of the waves above them. They can feel the power of the water, and the relative cessation of that power, by the intensity of the tremors it sends through the unstable sand in which they are buried. The clams read the disposition and duration of each wave. They hold themselves down in the sand by extending a powerful muscle, known as a foot, from their shells and then clenching it to give them purchase in the shifting sediment of the bottom.

A wave breaks above them, shaking the tiny clams in their burrows. They are aware of the calm of the receding wave, and they are impelled to reduce the tension in their feet and use the muscle instead to boost themselves up above the sand, where they extend their siphons and suck in the water, with its oxygen and nutrients.

Sometimes they miscalculate and rise out of the sand to find themselves fruitlessly siphoning the open air, having been stranded on the beach by low tide or an especially powerful outgoing wave. At such times the tiny, pastel-colored clams look like a handful of pebbles half-buried in the sand. But the illusion is momentary: the coquinas turn the sharp ends of their wing-shaped shells downward, extend their feet, and hitch themselves down into the security of the wet sand.

They are such dim, shapeless creatures within their shells; they are hardly imaginable, hardly recognizable as living beings. The shells are the calcified secretions of the clam, built layer by layer like the flowstone of a cave. The creatures themselves are as impalpable as the shells are exact: a blob containing viscera, gills, muscles that control digestion and motion, and muscles that hold the wings of the shell shut with remarkable tenacity to protect the helpless protoplasm inside. The clam's brain consists of a few specialized ganglia strung out along a neural cord. The creature has no eyes, no sense of smell, no hearing. Yet in some way it is as ardent about its existence as the bottle-nosed dolphin that has ridden the tide over the highest bar and is chasing a school of mullet now in the trough. Within the intertidal zone, as well as upon the island itself, there are no degrees of existence, only a range of mysteries, secrets of perception that every species withholds from all others.

Coquina clams lives for about a year if they do not fall victim to the wide range of predators that swarm or swim or walk within the surf. Bottom-feeding fish like drums or croakers cruise above the sand, probing with the barbels on their chins for buried mollusks and then popping the creatures into their mouths with impressive speed. Willet feed on the coquinas in the receding waves, grabbing the still-extended feet of the clams in their bills. With a twist of their heads, the birds then snap the adductor muscles that hold the shell together. Coquinas also fall prey to other mollusks, carnivorous snails that have the gift of locomotion.

One such creature is making its way now toward a colony of coquinas. It is a shark's eye, named for the center point in the whorled design of its shell. The shell rides on the back of the mollusk, which is an almost liquid mass of such volume that it is difficult to imagine how it could ever work itself back inside. Far in advance of the shell are the creature's tentacles, and below them, almost invisible, are two "eyes," blotches of sensitive pigment through which it can sense gross changes in the quality of light. The mollusk glides along on its foot, secreting a film of mucus to smooth the way. Its flesh is formless and almost transparent. The shark's eye burrows easily into the sand and comes out again, unimpeded by the underwater terrain. Though its tentacles are waving rhythmically ahead, more than just the sense of touch they provide guides the snail. It is drawn forward by the smell of the clams, a sense that comes to the snail through a minute organ near its gills.

It tracks the clams relentlessly and thoughtlessly, pulled along by its own appetite. The coquina that it will destroy is unaware of its presence and unequipped to escape anyway. Perhaps in the seawater it draws through its siphon the clam can detect the one-part-per-billion presence of the snail, but such an advance warning cannot mitigate its helplessness.

The snail closes in so slowly that its victim's death seems ordained, and the action itself monumental, as if the mollusks were two land-masses drifting together. When the snail finally reaches the clam it unhesitatingly smothers it with the mass of its body and begins the process of boring a hole through the shell, rasping in a circular motion with the minute denticles in its mouth. When the hole is drilled the snail inserts its proboscis and begins the process of absorbing the clam. It takes hours to accomplish this, and all the while the other members of the coquina colony pop up and down in accordance with the rhythm of the waves.

Strewn all along the beach are the empty shells of coquinas and cockles, each with a neat hole drilled through it. The evidence of pre-dation and destruction is everywhere. The sea brings an astonishing variety of creatures, pulverized or whole and dying, onto the beach. A hardhead catfish washes up onto the sand, its sharp dorsal fin rising up and down with the heaving of its gills; a yellow sea whip, a thin rope of polyps uprooted from its anchoring place, ends up entwined on the beach with the tendrils of a Portuguese man-of-war; a small sprig of brown sargassum floats up on the tide, the host to a doomed and in-credibly diverse community of hydroids, nudibranchs, crabs, shrimps, worms, and fish.

Perhaps nowhere else is the fact of death so obvious and unremit-ting. The most imposing feature of the seashore is the spectacle of life worn down and out, pummeled into its component parts. The dynamic of the littoral is a constant process of disintegration, a process evident even in the sand itself, whose grains are the result of the seemingly infinite weathering and grinding of rocks.

Most of the active life of the beach is hidden, secreted away in burrows or calcified tubes, covered with sand, cemented to or tun-neled into driftwood. The only consistently visible creatures on the shore are birds. Standing at the surf line, looking seaward with con-centration, is a mixed population of laughing gulls and rather large, stocky terns—Caspian terns. The gulls are in their summer plumage, their heads hooded with black. The terns' heads are white, but with a black crest flattened back against their heads by the offshore wind. When they are not standing on shore the terns fly low and fast over the water, their wings canted sharply backward. They are diving birds, with the characteristic of dropping into the water as if they had been suddenly shot out of the sky. Whenever a tern manages to catch a fish in this fashion he must then defend it in an exhaustive aerial dispute with the gulls, who are more aggressive and persistent and are capable of running a tern almost to ground.

But standing together on the beach, the terns and gulls are at peace, narcotized by the rhythm of the surf. Sanderlings poke around near their feet, and just above the water a frigate bird soars, a strange dihedral kink in each wing and a quality of reserve in the manner in which it simply bends down and extracts a fish from the waves. There are black skimmers out there too, and spring migrants—swallows and Baltimore orioles and a chuck-will's-widow—that have flown all the way across the Gulf with instinctive reckoning and endurance.

Within the crowd of shorebirds there are occasional desultory episodes of mating. A male tern bobs his head, struts about, and hops onto a female's back, grabbing her by the neck and then flapping his wings and squawking. When it is over the male hops down and looks out to sea again, his fervor of a moment earlier completely forgotten.

It is the mating season for other vertebrate inhabitants of the island as well. Back behind the dunes a keeled earless lizard skims over the loose sand as lightly as a water bug. The lizard skitters forward for a few feet and then stops, bobbing his head in much the same way as the birds on the beach, advertising himself to whatever females may be around. The lizard is preoccupied with the urge to mate. His skin has broken out in black nuptial bars that run along either side of his body. Somewhere in the same dune field there is a female, but she is already gravid from an earlier encounter with this same male. She is, however, still flushed with her own mating display—an understated suffusion of yellows and oranges where the male has his black bands. Her body is swollen with the eggs she will soon deposit without ceremony into the sand.

The male lizard continues to bob his head, casting about in the vast dune field for another mate. Then he moves on, unfulfilled but undeterred, over the crest of a dune and out to a bed of hard sand where his long digits leave no tracks but where the prints of coyotes, foxes, and skunks are deeply impressed. Beneath a mat of vegetation at the edge of a clear expanse of dunes, the lizard stops, filled with the primal knowledge that to cross the barren sand would be suicidal. Overhead, the white-tailed hawk is circling, stable in the thermals, scanning the brush for a signal, for movement such as the lizard will give when he bobs his head in autonomic longing.

As the day wears on, the lizard becomes progressively less active, finding relief from the heat in the shade of the dune grass. During the afternoon most of the terrestrial inhabitants of the island are likewise holed up, waiting for the cycle of predation and opportunity that the coolness of the evening will bring about. The cycle continues, of course, in the ocean, and in the tidal marshes at the back of the island, where hermit crabs stagger about beneath the weight of the abandoned gastropod shells they have taken over, to which they have fitted themselves almost as firmly as the original inhabitants. The crabs are, for the most part, very small, their hind parts carefully contorted into the inner chambers of moon shells and whelks. Only their claws are visible, and with these claws they pull themselves along the mud bottom of the flat or up the sheer faces of rocks.

When, at length, the sun begins to go down, the hermit crabs are not aware of it, but to many other creatures the coolness and the beginning of darkness are signals to come out of their torpor and hiding and into their nocturnal wakefulness.

In the grasslands midway between the dunes and the mud flats there is a large, brackish pond and several acres of outlying marshland. In a red-winged blackbird's abandoned nest, slightly elevated in the vegetation beside the pond, a rice rat is nursing her five offspring. It is dark in the nest. The rat has reinforced it with bits of grasses and sedges and left a solitary side entrance that lets in some of the fading light. The babies are two days old, and already they are active and demanding. In only a few days they will be on their own, making exploratory trips from the nest and then, on the tenth or eleventh day of their lives, being booted out by their mother. The rat will then mate again and lose no time in driving away the male whose presence she has endured only for the sake of procreation. None of this, of course, does the rat plan. It simply happens, and for now she is wholeheartedly a mother, as devoted to the little squirming forms at her belly as it is in her power to be.

But the babies are draining her reserves of strength and she is hungry. Before they are quite finished she stands up on her whispery little feet and drops out of the door of the nest. She scoots around a miniature inlet of the pond and wanders for a while through the thick jungle of the marsh grass before returning to the shoreline. She finds an insect to eat, a small crab and a jackknife clam, and then, because she is so hungry from the nursing, feeds for a while on the partially decomposed carcass of a lizard. She works her way up and down the muddy fringes of the pond, and then her hunger drives her farther back into the vegetation than she would normally go. Suddenly, in some unspecific way, she is alarmed; she quivers for a fraction of a second, her heart seizes up, and then every muscle and nerve of her body come together in one great convulsive leap as a pair of fangs plow into the sand where a moment earlier she was standing.

The rat does not bother to follow the shoreline now. She splashes headlong into the water and submerges, holding her breath and swimming beneath the murky water. She careens off the shell of a turtle and, closer to shore, swims between the legs of a reddish egret. She makes it to the opening of her nest with an easy leap and lies inside on her belly, with her heart pounding and the baby rice rats trying to burrow down to her nipples.

The massasauga rattlesnake that put the rice rat through such trauma is moving away from the marshland and into the drier grass flats. The failure with the rat has cost him no loss of momentum or determination. His passage over the loose sand is swift and rhythmic. He can see and hear and sense heat, and yet another sense originates in his tongue, which he sends out ahead of him to record the particulate density of prey in the air. This information is stored on the tongue and processed through an organ at the back of the mouth. The resulting knowledge comes to the snake as taste. Already now he is receiving an intimation, the subtlest bouquet of kangaroo rat. The sensation gets stronger, until it is accompanied by the thumping of the creature's feet, a noise that the snake hears through the ground. He positions himself in a coil just off the kangaroo rat's path. He is very still and trancelike. The massasauga is a small snake, and for a rattlesnake has a small mouth. But then his venom—a neurotoxin—is much stronger than most other rattlesnakes'.

When the kangaroo rat comes down the path the snake strikes him in mid-stride, injecting the venom and then removing the fangs before the rat has even had time to become aware of the danger. Once he has registered the fact that he has been struck the rat leaps high into the air and hops away at top speed. The massasauga does not follow or seem concerned. He simply stays where he is, gathering his body together in a loose coil, resting until some internal timer tells him that the poison has done its work.

For long minutes the snake does not stir, and then finally he begins crawling in the direction of the rat. He moves his head from side to side, flicking his tongue and catching a strong taste of rat urine and fear. About a dozen yards down the path he finds the rat on the ground, convulsing. When the body is still the snake moves up to it, running his tongue along it and then slowly opening his jaws to take it in. But then the rat makes one last effort, leaping from the snake's mouth, landing a foot away, and then twitching until he is still again. This time the snake waits awhile before finally moving in to begin the process of swallowing the rat head first.

Back at the pond several dozen diamondback terrapins have risen to the surface, their heads stippling the smooth surface of the water. The heads appear disembodied, and in their fixed, identical expressions they have a hallucinatory quality, as if the mood expressed in those reptilian faces were the true disposition of the pond. The turtles secrete saltwater from their eyes, take in air through their nostrils, and bask indolently in the last remaining light of day. Soon they will swim over the bank and bury themselves in mud for the night.

At this late hour the pond and the surrounding marsh are congested with bird life: willet, avocets, Louisiana herons, black-necked stilts, American bitterns. They are all feeding, after their fashions, or stalking about, or simply standing still in the water, breathing in the calmness of twilight. Except for the bird cries and the sudden flights of blackbirds and terns across the pond, the marsh is mute and still, the blood of its creatures at low tide.

Now, as if entering a stage that has been set for them, come two roseate spoonbills. They are soaring low above the marsh, banking and teetering and coasting in the invisible element of the air. Their pink plumage, deepened by the quality of the remaining light, is gorgeous and alien. The spoonbills cruise low over the shallow marsh water, ease down within a foot of each other, and begin feeding with their heads submerged, moving their odd, spatulate, primitive beaks through the mud. There is a strong but tranquil breeze rippling the surface of the water where they stand and ruffling their feathers. The burst of color they bring to the subtle camouflage shading of the marsh is startling; the color of the spoonbills seems a mistake, or a conscious provocation, or some sort of benevolent gift. Even after the sun has gone down the birds are charged, for a long moment, with its light.

In the darkness the massasauga moves across the highway, the kangaroo rat still an undigested bulge in the center of his body. The asphalt has retained heat and the rattlesnake pauses to absorb it. All at once he hears a monumental commotion from the substratum that actually shakes him a little from side to side. The snake's concern is uncomplicated and cold, but very real. He tries to get away but moves forward just exactly enough for a moving car to crush his head. Some moments later a solitary coyote, after checking the highway for headlights, walks out and picks the snake up in his teeth, then carries the carcass to the side of the road and eats it, heartened by the bonus of the kangaroo rat.

Darkness has come over the beach with little transition. A cottontail rabbit moves about the shoreward face of the dunes, which is pocketed with the fresh burrows of ghost crabs. From one of these burrows a crab emerges, extending its reticulated limbs and wiping the sand from its eyes with its antennae. The crab needs to replenish the seawater it stores within its gills; it is short of breath. It moves across the sand and down to the swash line, positioning itself there for a low, spent wave from which it can extract the water it needs to survive its terrestrial life. Hundreds of other ghost crabs are doing the same thing, or foraging about near the surf for smaller crabs and for stranded coquina clams whose shells they can chip away with their claws.

Several of the crabs stop to feed on the long tendrils of a beached Portuguese man-of-war. There are other men-of-war in the surf, helpless to control their fate in the choppy waves. Beyond the outermost bar, however, is a large flotilla of these creatures, their purple sacs driven by the wind across the surface of the water. The men-of-war are not individual animals, they are strange aggregates of other organisms, all of them too highly specialized to exist on their own. Small fish swimming through the man-of-war's trailing tentacles are injected with a powerful toxin and then eaten by the countless solitary forms.

For all its biological divisiveness, the man-of-war's will is single. In some way it recognizes the danger to its existence from the prevailing wind and adjusts the puckered "sail" on the top of its gas-filled float to compensate, allowing itself to tack steadily seaward.

As the man-of-war fleet moves away from the beach the tendrils trail across the form of a pilot whale dying of natural causes at the edge of the bar. Unlike the men-of-war, the whale brims with awareness, though he is old and emaciated and no longer alert to his dying. He has been drifting aimlessly for days, and the overpowering loneliness and fright he had felt earlier have been replaced by waves of delirium interrupted by lucid moments of resignation. The whale is twenty feet long, his deep black color unrelieved by markings of any kind. He can feel the breakers trying to lift his bulk over the bar, he can feel his bulbous forehead scraping on the broken shells in the sand bottom. The vertigo he feels brings with it a not entirely unpleasant suggestion of diffusion, and he sees his own death as a process of absorption by the sea.

A half-mile away the white-tailed hawk, perched in his tree, can make out the slick black form of the whale in the waves. He can see also the bioluminescence in each wave face, the collective glow of millions upon millions of protozoan forms. The hawk understands neither of these phenomena, but all that the hawk does not know is irrelevant. It is what he knows that counts. The same is true for the manta ray cruising outside the surf, for the mole tunneling beneath the dunes, for the beachcomber walking along the swash line. They know what they need from the island, and they sense that although the sea continually progrades and erodes it, its life is a greater constant than their own.

Analyzing and Discussing the Text

1. Why does Harrigan refer to the creatures that live on or near the beach as "secret life"?
2. In what sense does Harrigan's essay seem a study of natural fecundity? Mortality? Does he view these concepts in the same way as Dillard or Thomas?
3. How, for Harrigan, is life connected to death? Do his comments about death seem emotional or dispassionate? Why do you think he chooses this perspective?

4. Who is the narrator of this long, descriptive essay? Is it told from a human perspective? Explain your answer and discuss why Harrigan might have written the piece in this way. Do you think the author actually watched everything he describes? If not, where does he get his information?
5. Does Harrigan's description of nature seem orderly or disorderly? How does this style contribute to our understanding of fecundity and mortality?
6. Late in the essay Harrigan writes that a "whale brims with aware-ness," that "he sees his own death as a process of absorption by the sea." Does this notion seem anthropomorphic or unrealistic? Why does Harrigan attribute such consciousness to the whale?
7. Discuss the role of the white-tailed hawk in this essay.

Experiencing and Writing About the World

1. Choose a relatively small natural place and do research to learn about the animals, insects, plants, climate, and geological formations likely to exist there; this "research" ought to be a combination of direct ob-servation and library work. Then try to write an account of the "life," secret or otherwise, of this place from an impersonal, omniscient per-spective. This description can be either as brief as a single paragraph or as lengthy and elaborate as Harrigan's essay.
2. Read through Harrigan's essay and write down every unusual word you find, then define each of these words. What does "leeward" mean? "Torpidly"? "Stolid"? "Rufous"? "Diurnal"? Does this lan-guage seem extravagant or essential? In your own description of a natural place, try to use new words— Harrigan's or some others—as a way of vivifying your prose.
3. Produce a brief description of several animals/insects in which you speculate, as unobtrusively as possible, about the states of conscious-ness of these living things (notice how Harrigan does this). Then incorporate these descriptions into an analytical essay in which you consider how such writing affects the way you or your reader thinks about the place as a whole or at least about these conscious features of the place. What does such descriptive writing suggest about the way humans value consciousness? Do your discoveries have any im-plications for people who want to write about nature in order to protect it?

JOHN DANIEL

Some Mortal Speculations

John Daniel (1948–   ), who lives in Portland, Oregon, is the poetry editor for *Wilderness* magazine and regularly publishes literary essays in such periodicals as *Wilderness, Sierra,* the *North American Review, Orion Nature Quarterly,* and *High Country News.* His first collection of essays, *The Trail Home,* appeared in 1992. After growing up in the suburbs of Washington, D.C., Daniel migrated west to Oregon in the late 1960s to attend Reed College. He dropped out of Reed after four semesters and began a succession of jobs in Oregon and California, including work as a chokersetter for Weyerhauser and as a "poet in the schools" in remote eastern Oregon. A Wallace Stegner Fellowship in poetry was the "bolt from the blue" that brought Daniel to Stanford University in 1982, and after the one-year fellowship ended Daniel stayed on at Stanford for five years as a Jones Lecturer in poetry and a lecturer in freshman English, in the process of which he earned an M.A. in English/Creative Writing. His poetry, which frequently contemplates the relationship between humans and nature, has appeared in numerous publications and was collected in the volume *Common Ground* in 1988. A new collection of poetry called *All Things Touched by Wind* is now in progress.

The following essay, which first appeared in *Wilderness* (Summer 1989) and was reprinted in *The Trail Home,* focuses on several specific incidents that provoke Daniel's "mortal speculations." The graceful vacillation between anecdote and meditation is Daniel's characteristic essay structure—a pattern in language that at once acknowledges the minute details of the natural world (a spider's belly, the feeding of owls at dusk) and explores the significance of such details to the human imagination. The working title of this essay, "Looking," emphasized the perception of external phenomena, whereas the published title (proposed by an editor at *Wilderness*) emphasizes the subsequent reflections. The two approaches together make for a more complete experience of the world than either, by itself, would allow. Although Daniel's work frequently emphasizes the way individual human beings experience the natural world rather than analyzing more abstract environmental issues, he is acutely conscious of the connections between the concrete and the abstract—indeed, of the dangers of regarding nature purely from an abstract, analytical perspective. "Since *Silent Spring* and the environmental bloom of the late sixties and early seventies, awareness of environmental issues has clearly expanded," he has written. "But," he continues, "are we *living* with greater ecological responsibility?...And as long as global warming is a story we read in the paper or see on TV, and not the presence of salt in our drinking water or the absence of bread on our tables, it's an abstraction. Practically everyone is *aware* of it. But how many have changed their way of life because of that awareness?" It is with this understanding of the troublesome gap between rarefied ideas and actual experience in mind that Daniel composes his essays on such topics as gardening, the relationship between humans and "other lives," the meaning of "home," radical approaches to "ecodefense," and, in this next essay, mortality.

As I stepped into the shed yesterday morning looking for a rake, a silent commotion caught my eye. A blue fly was floundering in a web by the door—wings blurring, its abdomen curling almost to its head as it strained to pull loose, rocking and bouncing and tearing the web. And the spider was just above, dancing with all its legs, dancing down and nimbly retreating. Half the fly's size, a dull red color, it descended and climbed, never still. Once as it came down it might have managed to jab in its venom; in any case the fly weakened, arching feebly as the spider wrapped its legs and started to carry it away. The damaged web tore under the spider's weight, and tore again. The spider left its bundle and laid new strands, but they too gave way, and for a moment it was still. Slowly then, ceremoniously I thought, it placed its legs round the fly's head and clasped it to its belly. For a moment the spider moved slightly, as if adjusting a ritual posture, then spider and fly were still.

When I returned half an hour later, and at intervals throughout the afternoon, the spider hadn't moved but both had changed. The fly seemed shrunken, the spider swollen. The fly's blue gloss had gone dull; the spider's abdomen shone. And I might have imagined it—the light was too poor to be sure—but it seemed to me that the spider's red belly now had a blue tinge. This morning when I looked there was only the fly's dry husk, a dot of white web attached to one eye.

As I watched that encounter, I felt wildly different things: pity at the fly's helplessness, respect for the spider's mastery, the horror of a life sucked out of its shell. But if such an event is horrible, it is the most commonplace horror in this world. It occurs billions of times every second, *this* second, countless lives slipping into the lives of others—field mouse swelling the king snake, krill becoming body of blue whale, deer disappearing into coyote and magpie and the blooming generations of microbes that carry dead life into darkness and return it to the light. Horrible? Cruel? No more so than the compost, that black distillation of death that I spade into the garden. If it is cruel that a red spider should sustain itself, and thus survive to make more red spiders, and so spin its evolutionary line a little deeper into the openness of time, then cruelty must be part of the very genius that brought spiders and flies and other creatures into being, and which continues to elaborate life into unlikely and beautiful forms.

And yet—some weeks ago, on the brick walkway along the end of the house, I almost stepped on a small beetle. I stooped to get a better look at its odd jerky movements and saw that it was trying, without much success, to shake off a mob of black ants that were darting all around and over it. When the beetle managed to free one leg, a new ant would immediately clamp on and hang, a dragging weight. Sometimes two or three at once gripped a leg; others raced over the beetle's body, trying its armor, as the awkward creature flicked and shook and attempted to walk.

I watched for as long as I could, and even those few seconds were almost unbearable—though I don't know why. I have a fairly strong stomach for the depredations of animals. The cat torments a gopher for half an hour before killing it, or sits with a lizard's twitching tail hanging out of its mouth, and I don't mind watching. I understand the cat to be sharpening its nerves through such playful delay, much as it sharpens its claws on the porch post, and I admire its keen intelligence. But weren't the ants that swarmed the beetle displaying their own intelligence? Weren't they acting out their own instinctive genius, not too distant from the genius I admire in the cat? In fact, as they worked together to bring down their enormous prey, didn't they mirror my own ancestors of fifty thousand years ago, those little dodging men who harried and pricked the groaning mastodon until it fell?

I rescued the beetle, or tried to. I took a pine needle and poked off the ants, rubbed them out, and turned the beetle loose some twenty feet away. Almost immediately, other ants clamped on to its legs. I carried it around the corner of the house and set it down again, and within seconds it was attacked by three ants. That beetle was rife with distress, and any ant could smell it. Finally, I dropped it in the dry grass of the field. It walked away, spry-seeming, but as I watched it I didn't have much confidence either in its longevity or in my reflexive gesture that had temporarily kept it alive.

It seems likely that humankind is the only animal capable of the altruism to rescue a member of a different species from death. But I wouldn't have saved that beetle from a towhee. If I had stepped on it accidentally I would have felt a twinge of remorse, but nothing more. Clearly my concern rose less from pure altruism than from a horror of ants, or some still deeper source. And so I find myself squarely in the middle of a contradiction, unable, or unwilling, to be reconciled with a fundamental truth of nature: that a beetle's death by ants is as proper and seemly as a death by towhee or a death by old age. In the natural economy, any death is proper that nourishes other life, which means that any death is proper. A beetle, a fly, a million dinosaurs—where they fell other life rose, if only in waves of microbes and a new exuberance of flora.

We humans, as always, want to exempt ourselves. In life we increasingly encapsulate our bodies from the organic processes of nature, as if we had no connection with them, and in death we attempt the same, armoring our remains in crypts and coffins and steel ash boxes. Like altruism, our respectful treatment of our dead has been cited as a quality that defines us as human, something more than the animals. But what it chiefly defines, it seems to me, is simply our discontent with mortality. We don't like to die; and if we have to die, we don't like to think of our own dead bodies feeding other creatures.

In evolution's long streaming through time, individual lives don't count for much. Nature thinks in populations, in species, in systems and relationships. It thinks in process and continuation. Individuals are bubbles in the current, briefly here and gone, important only as expressions of what has come before and as constituents of what will follow. That plight presents no emotional problems for pine trees or sparrows, but it does for us because we are aware that we are bubbles. What actually best defines us, and accounts for our other defining characteristics, is our acute consciousness.

The beetle obviously was aware of its plague of ants, and wanted them off. No doubt it felt the stings of their jaws, and possibly even the scurry of their feet across its back. Maybe it even felt an indistinct kind of rage or fear, but almost certainly it felt no horror at its impending death. It was I, watching, who felt the horror—and not so much for the beetle's sake, I now realize, as for my own. The swarming ants repulsed me because I saw a sign of my own fate there. Someday my body will feed other life, and it won't be a towhee that it feeds.

Ever since I've been aware of death I've been intensely afraid of it. As a child, lying awake in bed, I used to imagine it as an endless drifting among icy stars—and my terror came not from that cold vision but from knowing that even the vision was a lie, that death meant seeing nothing, feeling nothing, no consciousness ever again, no *me*. There was no consolation, only the eventual distraction of other thoughts, and sleep.

As Darwin saw, there is grandeur in the prospect of evolutionary time. To be part of this unlikely process, this varied ongoing river that rises out of mystery and tends into further mystery, is a kind of consolation. But it's an abstract consolation. I can't see the fullness of evolutionary time, and except in rare ecstatic moments, I don't feel part of it. Its grandeur is an idea, its beauty as coolly remote as the stars. And both its grandeur and its beauty dissolve all too easily in my fearful mind and leave me thinking of a grotesque parade, a slow blind wave that raises bits of life to sentience and then buries them forever—individuals, families, entire species wandering their weather of chances and then going under as the blind wave rolls on, indifferent, meaningless as clouds of dust in the absolute zero of infinite space.

But that too, of course, is abstraction. What I know for sure is nothing as large as that, whether beautiful or terrifying or both, and nothing as remote. My mind, like my hands, is best suited to the grasping of smaller things, things that happen close in front of me, things I can see and turn slowly in memory and see again, in imagination's second light. It is only a tenuous bubble that I inhabit, but how bright and various the world looks from within it. How vividly I see the beetle I could hardly bear to watch before, how it flicks and lurches, how quickly the tiny black ants dart over its shell, how clearly I recall the shiny spider, and dull shrunken fly—they and a thousand other things that my eyes have gathered are lit by my need to see them, to see into the mystery to which each is a clue, the mystery whose answer somehow is death.

I remember my first winter in eastern Oregon, awaking one night to an intensely strange and moving sound, a frenzied chorus of falsetto yips and howls—the cold starlit dark on fire with coyote cries. I lay warm in bed, my entire body tingling. It was a killing song, of course. A deer or sheep lay bleeding on the snow, never to rise, but what ecstatic music the coyotes made of that life they had claimed. In an alchemy that lasted only seconds, it seemed to me that the blood of the dead and the ancient strain of the coyotes' own blood rose together, transformed wholly into song. I can't say what that singing meant to the coyotes. Its intensity, its quality of utter emptying into sound, made me think that it meant more to them than mere food. But whatever they felt in their singing, for me it was not horror but fierce beauty. It was joy that rose in me, like some forgotten song of my own.

Death must have been both clearer and more mysterious—and perhaps easier to face—when I was one of those dodging men who swarmed with spears around the mastodon. When we killed our meat or else starved, and sometimes died in the killing, when things flared with spirit and every movement of the world was magic, there must have been moments when our own throats burned with involuntary cries, when our own blood surged up and sounded itself in the quiet of the land. In those moments we sang triumph, fear, awe—all the feelings we had no words for, or not words enough. And, perhaps more than the coyotes, we sang our loneliness, our sense of isolation in a world from which we had already begun to separate ourselves, our smallness and transience in the depths of night.

Whether or not it was my own distant past that moved me in those coyote cries, I know, in any case, that they were beautiful. I suppose that beauty, like cruelty, is a category of the human mind, a projection that we cast about with our consciousness. Yet beauty seems so abundant in nature, things seem so thoroughly and extravagantly filled with it, that I have to think it *is* in things, their fundamental fact—and that I've learned to appreciate it in coyotes but not completely yet in ants and spiders. They too are beautiful, and the deaths of other lives compose their beauty, as the deaths of other lives compose our own. All of us are in motion, rising out of previous forms and advancing into new ones, and beauty is the best name I know for the ways in which our shape-shifting nature pursues its changes.

And that is abstraction again, an attempt to say more than I know. What I know, finally, and can't shake loose from, is that the bubble breaks for all of us. For me. The beauty of things will go on, but I will not be alive to witness it. When other lives rise on what I was, the familiar light of my awareness will not rise with them. I who hold the world in mind will then be held in the world, without a mind, lost in what I once looked upon. And so at forty I look carefully at things that live, because everything I see is hieroglyphic of what I might become. Scrub jay scratching in the underbrush, gray squirrel leaping the gap of limbs, the exact aimlessness of blowing leaves—I will be there, and deep in the burrowings of roots and worms, in the ants' long marches and the lizard's crouch, in the spider's stillness and its nimble dance.

I look, and nature answers, speaking in a thousand things. It is alive to my longing, it repays my vanishing in advance. This evening, just before sundown, I heard a whistling out in the field. After a few minutes walking and looking I found the source: two great horned owls, an adult and a young, facing away on the outreaching limb of a solitary oak. They were moving, rocking forward and turning toward each other, and I thought perhaps they were preening. Then suddenly— maybe because the mother heard my approach—they turn on the limb and face me, and I see what they are doing.

The mother tilts forward and rips off a piece of some kind of prey that she holds against the limb with her talons. As she straightens with food in her bill, the fledgling, whistling hoarsely, grabs it with his bill and bolts it down. And so they continue their meal, the mother tearing the small animal without pause or hurry, the fledgling whistling and eating, as the last slant sun turns their mottled brown and white to reddish gold. When they have finished, the mother flies from the limb and the young one follows, the two of them drifting on motionless wings, low and silent over the dry grasses and down the hill, disappearing in the darkening trees.

Analyzing and Discussing the Text

1. Does Daniel seem to make a single, coherent point about mortality in this essay? Using specific passages from the text, explain whether this essay is argumentative or more neutral and speculative. Does the title correctly describe the content?
2. What is the relationship between concrete narrative and abstract meditation in this piece? How exactly does Daniel build his ideas on an "experiential core"?
3. The initial scene of this essay depicts a spider and a fly, describing their struggle as ceremonious and ritualistic. Does Daniel casually accept this incident, perhaps pleased in some way by its elegant drama? Is there a conflict between the author's rational understanding of the event and his emotional turmoil? Explain this.
4. "We humans, as always, want to exempt ourselves," Daniel claims. How does Daniel resist this impulse here? Does Lewis Thomas resist the same impulse in "Death in the Open"?
5. Does Daniel simply equate humans and nonhumans? How, for instance, does he compare his own attitude toward death to the assumed attitude of a beetle? Why is this a significant critical issue?
6. "And so at forty I look carefully at things that live," writes Daniel, "because everything I see is hieroglyphic of what I might become." What does this suggest about the relationship between life and death? Does the author take comfort from this idea? Do *you*?

Experiencing and Writing About the World

1. Think of a specific natural event that started you thinking about some important aspect of your own life. Recreate the scene, then attempt a smooth transition to the more abstract consideration of yourself. This could be a fecundity/mortality issue or perhaps something about family relationships, territoriality, living in the present versus dwelling on the past/future, or love.
2. Daniel seems to derive a mixture of consolation and uneasiness from his observations of the natural world, and he attempts in his essay to show this compelling mixture of emotions. Think of an issue that creates a similar ambivalence in you; start out by simply writing an abstract statement of these feelings, but then deepen and clarify this expression by rooting it in specific episodes of your life (encounters with nature or nonnature).
3. Write an essay comparing Daniel's personal contemplation of the phenomenon of death with Lewis Thomas's impersonal approach. Why does each author seem to have chosen his particular style? How do the essays affect you in different ways?

Suggestions for Further Reading

Douglas, Marjorie Stoneman. "Grass." *The Everglades: River of Grass.* New York: Holt, 1947.

Finch, Robert. "Death of a Hornet." *The Bread Loaf Anthology.* Hanover, NH: UP of New England, 1989.

Graves, John. "Hoof and Paw, Tooth and Claw, Little Creatures Everywhere." *Hard Scrabble: Observations on a Patch of Land.* New York: Knopf, 1974.

Hay, John. *The Run.* New York: Norton, 1959.

Knutson, Roger. *Flattened Fauna.* Berkeley, CA: Ten Speed, 1987.

Lopez, Barry. "Apologia." *Witness* 3.4 (1989): 75–79.

———"A Presentation of Whales." *Crossing Open Ground.* New York: Scribner's, 1988.

McPhee, John. "Travels in Georgia." *Pieces of the Frame.* New York: Farrar, 1975.

Nichols, John. *On the Mesa.* Salt Lake City: Gibbs M. Smith, 1986.

Palmer, Thomas. "The Snakebite." *Outside* Mar. 1992: 98–109.

Saner, Reg. "Technically Sweet." *Georgia Review* 42.4 (1988): 719–50.

Stein, Sara B. *My Weeds: A Gardener's Botany.* New York: Harper, 1988.

Steinbeck, John. *The Log from the Sea of Cortez.* New York: Viking, 1951.

Wallace, David Rains. *The Klamath Knot.* San Francisco: Sierra Club, 1984.

CHAPTER THREE

Birds and Beasts

In *The Outermost House* (1928), Henry Beston wrote that "we need another and a wiser and perhaps a more mystical concept of animals. . . . We patronize them for their incompleteness," he continued, "for their tragic fate of having taken form so far below ourselves. And therein we err, and greatly err. . . . They are not brethren, they are not underlings; they are other nations, caught with ourselves in the net of life and time, fellow prisoners of the splendour and travail of the earth." That we now seek to be engaged in such a relearning of our relationships with animals is evident in several ways. Society sanctions, for example, the expenditure of much money and time in the quest to gather more scientific data about members of the animal world. However, our increasing wisdom with regard to animals is most readily apparent in our growing willingness to acknowledge that even such former competitors as the wolf and the grizzly bear have the right to survive in the wild. This implied treaty with large, wild mammals is paralleled in our society's attitudes toward the rights of other, less distant animals. The use of animals for furs, for testing, for zoo exhibitions, and for food is now the subject of much more heated discussion than we could have imagined a few years ago. We should also take note that we are relearning our relationships with animals from the other direction as well: a new, wiser concept of animals acknowledges the ways in which we humans resemble them.

Sally Carrighar's essay in this chapter exemplifies the field-study approach to learning about birds and beasts; by watching carefully and describing in her essay how bird parents actually raise their young, she breaks up old clichés about bird behavior. Edward Hoagland examines the behavior of our pet dogs to ascertain how they still resemble the wolves who are their wilder ancestors, suggesting that dogs are for us "an avenue of animality," a way of reconnecting with our own wildness. Peter Matthiessen's search for the snow leopard is in part an effort to accumulate field data about animals, but it is primarily a spiritual quest, one rooted in the belief that the search itself can, if done properly, illuminate our own place in "the net of life and time." For Scott Russell Sanders, the attempt to engage in conversations with owls on their own terms lures us "out of ourselves" and exposes us to lives that are utterly independent of human purpose. When Sue Hubbell writes humorously about her own impulses toward "becoming feral," she jokes that she is wilder than her dogs; as an "older woman," she is somehow released from "the social scheme of things" to live any way that she pleases, to write a novel and swim naked in the river. Alice Walker's story of her friendship with a horse called Blue is a clear argument for the view that ethical consideration should be extended to animals, that even nonhumans have rights.

SALLY CARRIGHAR

From **Wild Heritage**

Born in Cleveland, Ohio, Dorothy Wagner (1898–1985) survived a hostile relationship with her mother to become well-known as the naturalist, essayist, and novelist "Sally Carrighar." Carrighar's mother urged her to commit suicide and almost strangled her when she was a child, and this childhood trauma led the writer to begin seeking solace in nature at an early age. Her first acquaintance with the outdoors came from examining the animals and plants at the home of her grandparents in Ohio; she later traveled in northern Michigan, the Ozarks, and the Rockies. Carrighar attended Wellesley College but later claimed that "two years was enough—I knew I had to get into the wilds somehow." After leaving Wellesley, she worked as a fishing guide in the Ozarks, spent three years as a production secretary in Hollywood, and then studied biology at the University of California, Berkeley, and the California Academy of Sciences for another three years. She began her career as a wildlife writer in 1937. With the publication of her first book, *One Day on Beetle Rock* (1944), she won instant critical recognition. The *New York Times* called this study of the natural history of Sequoia National Park in California's Sierra Nevada Mountains "a book of rare distinction." It was followed by the equally successful *One Day at Teton Marsh* (1947), a description of marsh animals caught in a storm. A Guggenheim Fellowship, together with the earnings from her writings, then enabled her to begin a study of Arctic animals and people. Her ensuing nine years in the village of Unalakleet led to three more books: *Icebound Summer* (1953), *Moonlight at Midday* (1958), and *Wild Voice of the North* (1959). *Home to the Wilderness*, her moving autobiography, was published in 1973. Carrighar's final book, *The Twilight Seas: A Blue Whales's Journey*, was written in 1975 on the island of Guernsey. She died in Monterey, California, having spent her final years in Carmel.

When she received the Wellesley College Alumnae Achievement Award in 1977, Carrighar wrote: "I have discovered that I have chosen an extremely pleasant way to live: to begin a book with a year's background investigation, then a year in the animal's own world, and finally, when I have notebooks full of factual information about the characters, return to civilization and write the book." In *Wild Heritage* (1965), the book from which the following essay is excerpted, Carrighar seeks to relate animal and human behavior, to look at "the whole question of what ways, and to what extent, human beings behave like the simpler creatures from which we evolved."

[Parent Birds]

Birds are the world's most famous wild parents. Every child is told how the father and mother birds feed their nestlings "with worms" until they are old enough to fly; and how, then, on that very day, the baby birds "are pushed out of the nest." Up to this point the parents have been described as models of noble virtue, and young listeners, I think, often suspect this tale as being partly propaganda to win appreciation for the unselfishness of all parents. If it is, it backfires, because our own parents show little sympathy for the nestlings dismissed so abruptly.

And one wonders where the story arose that all baby birds are pushed out of the nest. Was it our parents' subconscious wish, a normal reaction to our often-exasperating behavior? The facts are otherwise. Actually the only bird I know of that evicts an unwilling offspring is the wandering albatross (the world's largest bird, with a wingspread of almost twelve feet). The young one is fed on an oily substance derived from its parents' partly digested diet of fish, and on this nourishment the nestling— there is only one in a season—grows hugely fat. It may be so heavy that it could not fly if it wanted to; but it doesn't. The parents leave it, just sitting there, for a period of four months, one hears, a period of pitiful loneliness, during which the nestling trims down. This treatment may arrest the young one's psychological development, for when the parents come back, even then it is reluctant to launch from the nest. So they drive it out. After that event the fledgling spends some time with its father and mother, swimming around on the ocean learning how to catch fish.

The truth about the devotion of parent birds is that most of them spend an immense proportion of their life energy in raising their young. In effect, many probably give their lives for them. Many birds that have been reared in captivity, safe from natural hazards, remain alive for ten years or more—some large birds much longer. In the wilds the small species rarely survive for more than a year or two. Banding records have shown that the age of the English robins at death averages 13.3 months: they have lived only long enough to rear one summer's young. The life span of other birds has been studied, and none of them in the natural environment had survived more than a fraction of its possible years—with exceptions of course. People who provide nest boxes know that the same birds may come back on succeeding springs. This human benevolence may be one of the reasons why they do not succumb sooner. But why do so many of the rest die just after they reach maturity?

The chief reasons are weather, disease (not much of that), predators, and starvation. The toll that these take depends largely on the condition, the health, of the birds. It may be significant, then, that a large number of the lives seem to be lost near the end of the first breeding season, after an effort in raising their broods which is so great that the parents often become exhausted, even emaciated.

And no wonder! At the start of a nestling's life, when it is growing fast, it must be given considerably more than its own weight of food every day. When it is heavier the proportion of food to its weight diminishes, but during the two weeks, approximately, that an average bird stays in the nest, it receives a daily ration of half its mean weight. If there are four, five, six, or more young in the brood, the nourishment needed would seem enormous.

The infants of land birds are fed almost entirely on insects. Finding these would not be too difficult in the early weeks of the season, when most insects are slow-moving larvae like slugs and caterpillars. Later, when the larvae become insects that fly, they have less bulk, so that more of them are required to fill nestlings' stomachs.

The adult birds that normally live on insects themselves, like swifts and swallows, are skilled in catching this kind of prey, but many more birds are seed-eaters. Seeds are abundant and found in predictable places. What a change for these seed-eaters, now, to be seeking insects, which do not stay put! The parent bird, setting out in the morning, leaves a nestful of gaping, ravenous mouths, and to satisfy them requires not only continuous effort but searching—the chancy element of finding victims who themselves are foraging actively.

Tree sparrows, nesting in Canada where summer days are long, have as many as six young in one brood, and to keep them fed hunt from three o'clock in the morning till ten at night. Blue titmice, tiny birds related to chickadees, weigh only half an ounce when full-grown; yet a pair of these feathered mites have been known to carry food to their nestlings 475 times in a single day. A careful study showed that a song thrush caught 10,080 larvae and insects in one month's time, an average of 336 per day; and a pair of English robins nesting near Oxford did even better. Between dawn and dark they were seen to visit their young 29 times every hour and to bring two or three caterpillars each trip. It was estimated that in that period the parents had caught at least 1000 caterpillars.

We are talking here about parent birds with only one family of young in a summer. Some of them will have two, even three, with at least two broods being fed while their infancy overlaps. Usually the mother bird builds a new nest and lays the second clutch before the first brood are out of *their* nest. From then on the male takes responsibility for the earlier young and also helps feed the second brood when they hatch. Even then the father won't push out his nestlings. Edwin Way Teale has made an interesting suggestion: that the way baby birds flutter their wings when begging for food may lift the young suppliant almost automatically, especially after he starts to stand on the edge of the nest where the fluttering can be wider. Suddenly he is in the air—he has discovered that he can fly! After that he will rarely go back into the nest. If he would, if the nestlings all would, the father's task might be easier, for he is far from through with the task of feeding them. Parent birds of the species familiar in gardens continue to find their fledglings' food for two and a half to five weeks after they fly and are physically able to get it themselves. The reason, of course, is their need of time to learn how.

Insect-eaters like swallows and swifts feed their young in the air for a while, at first beak to beak as they hover on quivering wings. Later the morsels are dropped to them as the parent passes in flight. Soon the fledgling is catching the point as well as the tidbit and begins to acquire the speed and skill he will have to have in snapping up darting and skimming prey.

Birds that feed on the ground do not need such fine muscular control. The act of picking up is much easier and is an inborn tendency, but even the seed-eaters have to experiment: at the start they don't know what is edible. During the period of their learning the parents continue to bring them food, less every day until about the nineteenth day out of the nest in most species, when the fledgling himself will be getting about half his requirements. After that the parents' attentions fall off very fast. They still accompany their offspring, only now they swallow the food they find. The young will protest; however, parent birds don't let the fledglings make fools of them. The young have been fed so well by then that most of them weigh more than their parents do. They can stand a lean time.

They can be very mad about it. Last year the robins who raised young in our maple tree had one nestling that was much more demanding than the three others. He got more than his share and became large and fat—and spoiled. I sympathized with his parents, for I like to sit under the tree, which is near the brook, and long after that overgrown bird could look after himself, he perched in the maple and shrieked his resentment because no one came and put food in his mouth. By then his parents had left the neighborhood, rather early, and as I picked up my chair day after day and withdrew, I was sure I knew why.

By the time that they disappeared, the elder robins looked very bedraggled, surely not in the best condition to dodge an attacker or to survive a storm. Seeing them one could believe that most birds live to only a tenth of their possible lifetimes.

Analyzing and Discussing the Text

1. Notice that Carrighar starts with a capsule summary of prevalent human "bird lore," a story that has been told and retold to generations of children, and then provides field observations to give a detailed and engaging overview of how birds actually parent their young. This strategy of exploding a widespread cultural myth by comparing the myth with observations from the field is one way that Carrighar builds the reader's interest in her field work. What other techniques does she use to engage our interest?
2. Analyze the way Carrighar structures her essay on "the world's most famous wild parents." If we divide the essay into introduction, body, and conclusion, where does the body of the essay begin? The conclusion?
3. How does the tone change as this essay moves from section to section? Explain whether these shifts contribute to the effectiveness of her essay.
4. Notice the use of division and classification in this essay. What does Carrighar's essay gain from her skillful use of this rhetorical mode?
5. Discuss the role of anthropomorphism in Carrighar's essay. Is it an effective tool for her? Does she overuse this device? Explain your responses.

Experiencing and Writing About the World

1. Carrighar's focus on the feeding efforts of the bird parents points out the richness of the natural world that people often fail to notice. Spend some time carefully observing a specific aspect of bird or animal life near you and recording the details of these activities in your journal. To what extent do these detailed observations give you a new understanding of wildlife?
2. Fashion your journal notes into a thorough prose description of the natural life you have observed. Be aware of the kinds of changes that you make as you move from field notes to a more polished, although still journal-like, presentation of your observations.
3. Choose some aspect of bird or animal life that has become commonplace—for instance, "busy as a beaver" or "a dog's life"—and then, in a brief essay, compare your knowledge (firsthand or from other sources) of that animal to the cliché.
4. Write an analytical paper describing how Carrighar's technique for describing the life of birds compares and contrasts with the approach in Scott Russell Sanders's essay later in this chapter. Would you describe them as two different kinds of essays? Use specific passages from the texts to support your claims.

EDWARD HOAGLAND

Dogs, and the Tug of Life

Edward Hoagland (1932–   ) was born in New York City and grew up in Connecticut. Since graduating from Harvard in 1954, Hoagland has divided his time between New York City, rural Vermont, and wherever else his inquisitiveness about the natural world, especially his curiosity about animals, has taken him. Hoagland has written five collections of essays, five works of fiction, and four travel books; his subject matter ranges from circus animals in his 1956 novel *Cat Man* to turtles in the essay collection called *The Courage of Turtles* (1971). He studies the landscape and people of the Stikine River country in the vast wilds of British Columbia in *Notes from the Century Before: A Journal from British Columbia* (1969), also contemplating his own responses to the wilderness as a displaced New Yorker. Hoagland's early work was collected in *The Edward Hoagland Reader* (1979). *The Tugman's Passage*, an essay collection, appeared in 1982, followed in 1986 by the novel *Seven Rivers West*. However, the essays in *Walking the Dead Diamond River* (1973) and *Red Wolves and Black Bears* (1976) are the work for which he is best known.

Hoagland's essays are marked by his own personality, his sense of humor, and his candor; they reflect both his delight in the natural world and his attraction to curious stories and strange, minute details about his subjects. In his own essay on the nature of the essay, "What I Think, What I Am" (1982), he argues that "the extraordinary flexibility of essays is what has led them to ride out rough weather and hybridize into forms that suit the times." Hoagland suggests that the "personal essay is like the human voice talking, its order the mind's natural flow, instead of a systematized outline of ideas." Indeed, his own style is so marked by detour, by seeming digression, by the apparently random remembrance, that one critic commented that the essays "meander like streams." Throughout his diverse work, Hoagland has sought to rediscover and to communicate to us what he calls "the commonality of animals and man." He believes that when we lose our awareness of animals, we also lose "some of the intricacy and grandeur of life." In the following essay called "Dogs, and the Tug of Life," Hoagland addresses these concerns in a discussion of dogs and humans.

It used to be that you could tell just about how poor a family was by how many dogs they had. If they had one, they were probably doing all right. It was only American to keep a dog to represent the family's interests in the intrigues of the back alley; not to have a dog at all would be like not acknowledging one's poor relations. Two dogs meant that the couple were dog lovers, with growing children, but still might be members of the middle class. But if a citizen kept three, you could begin to suspect he didn't own much else. Four or five irrefutably marked the household as poor folk, whose yard was also full of broken cars cannibalized for parts. The father worked not much, fancied himself a hunter; the mother's teeth were black. And an old bachelor living in a shack might possibly have even more, but you knew that if one of them, chasing a moth, didn't upset his oil lamp some night and burn him up, he'd fetch up in the poorhouse soon, with the dogs shot. Nobody got poor feeding a bunch of dogs, needless to say, because the more dogs a man had, the less he fed them. Foraging as a pack, they led an existence of their own, but served as evidence that life was awfully lonesome for him and getting out of hand. If a dog really becomes a man's best friend his situation is desperate.

That dogs, low-comedy confederates of small children and ragged bachelors, should have turned into an emblem of having made it to the middle class—like the hibachi, like golf clubs and a second car— seems at the very least incongruous. Puppies which in the country you would have to carry in a box to the church fair to give away are bringing seventy-five dollars apiece in some of the pet stores, although in fact dogs are in such oversupply that one hundred and fifty thousand are running wild in New York City alone.

There is another line of tradition about dogs, however. Show dogs, toy dogs, foxhounds for formal hunts, Doberman guard dogs, bulldogs as ugly as a queen's dwarf. An aristocratic Spanish lady once informed me that when she visits her Andalusian estate each fall the mastiffs rush out and fawn about her but would tear to pieces any of the servants who have accompanied her from Madrid. In Mississippi it was illegal for a slave owner to permit his slaves to have a dog, just as it was to teach them how to read. A "Negro dog" was a hound trained by a bounty hunter to ignore the possums, raccoons, hogs, and deer in the woods that other dogs were supposed to chase, and trail and tree a runaway. The planters themselves, for whom hunting was a principal recreation, whooped it up when a man unexpectedly became their quarry. They caught each other's slaves and would often sit back and let the dogs do the punishing. Bennet H. Barrow of West Feliciana Parish in Louisiana, a rather moderate and representative plantation owner, recounted in his diary of the 1840s, among several similar incidents, this for November 11, 1845: In "5 minutes had him up & a going, And never in my life did I ever see as excited beings as R & myself, ran 1/2 miles & caught him dogs soon tore him naked, took him Home Before the other negro[es] at dark & made the dogs give him another over hauling." Only recently in Louisiana I heard what happened to two Negroes who happened to be fishing in a bayou off the Blind River, where four white men with a shotgun felt like fishing alone. One was forced to pretend to be a scampering coon and shinny up a telephone pole and hang there till he fell, while the other impersonated a baying, bounding hound.

Such memories are not easy to shed, particularly since childhood, the time when people can best acquire a comradeship with animals, is also when they are likely to pick up their parents' fears. A friend of mine hunts quail by jeep in Texas with a millionaire who brings along forty bird dogs, which he deploys in eight platoons that spell each other off. Another friend, though, will grow apprehensive at a dinner party if the host lets a dog loose in the room. The toothy, mysterious creature lies dreaming on the carpet, its paws pulsing, its eyelids open, the nictitating membranes twitching; how can he be certain it won't suddenly jump up and attack his legs under the table? Among Eastern European Jews, possession of a dog was associated with hard-drinking *goyishe* peasantry, traditional antagonists, or else with the gentry, and many carried this dislike to the New World. An immigrant fleeing a potato famine or the hunger of Calabria might be no more equipped with the familiar British-German partiality to dogs—a failing which a few rugged decades in a great city's slums would not necessarily mend. The city had urbanized plenty of native farmers' sons as well, and so it came about that what to rural America had been the humblest, most natural amenity— friendship with a dog—has been transmogrified into a piece of the jigsaw of moving to the suburbs: there to cook outdoors, another bit of absurdity to the old countryman, whose toilet was outdoors but who was pleased to be able to cook and eat his meals inside the house.

There are an estimated forty million dogs in the United States (nearly two for every cat). Thirty-seven thousand of them are being destroyed in humane institutions every day, a figure which indicates that many more are in trouble. Dogs are hierarchal beasts, with several million years of submission to the structure of a wolf pack in their breeding. This explains why the Spanish lady's mastiffs can distinguish immediately between the mistress and her retainers, and why it is about as likely that one of the other guests at the dinner party will attack my friend's legs under the table as that the host's dog will, once it has accepted his presence in the room as proper. Dogs need leadership, however; they seek it, and when it's not forthcoming quickly fall into difficulties in a world where they can no longer provide their own.

"Dog" is "God" spelled backwards—one might say, way backwards. There's "a dog's life," "dog days," "dog-sick," "dog-tired," "dog-cheap," "dog-eared," "doghouse," and "dogs" meaning villains or feet. Whereas a wolf's stamina was measured in part by how long he could go without water, a dog's is becoming a matter of how long he can *hold* his water. He retrieves a rubber ball instead of coursing deer, chases a broom instead of hunting marmots. His is the lowest form of citizenship: that tug of life at the end of the leash is like the tug at the end of a fishing pole, and then one doesn't have to kill it. On stubby, amputated-looking feet he leads his life, which if we glance at it attentively is a kind of cutout of our own, all the more so for being riskier and shorter. Bam! A member of the family is dead on the highway, as we expected he would be, and we just cart him to the dump and look for a new pup.

Simply the notion that he lives on four legs instead of two has come to seem astonishing—like a goat or cow wearing horns on its head. And of course to keep a dog is a way of attempting to bring nature back. The primitive hunter's intimacy or telepathy with the animals he sought, surprising them at their meals and in their beds, then stripping them of their warm coats to expose a frame so like our own, is all but lost. Sport hunters, especially the older ones, retain a little of it still; and naturalists who have made up their minds not to kill wild animals nevertheless appear to empathize primarily with the predators at first, as a look at the tigers, bears, wolves, mountain lions on the project list of an organization such as the World Wildlife Fund will show. This is as it should be, these creatures having suffered from our brotherly envy before. But in order to really enjoy a dog, one doesn't merely try to train him to be semihuman. The point of it is to open oneself to the possibility of becoming partly a dog (after all, there are plenty of sub- or semi-human beings around whom we don't wish to adopt). One wants to rediscover the commonality of animal and man—to see an animal eat and sleep that hasn't forgotten how to enjoy doing such things—and the directness of its loyalty.

The trouble with the current emphasis on preserving "endangered species" is that, however beneficial to wildlife the campaign works out to be, it makes all animals seem like museum pieces, worth saving for sentimental considerations and as figures of speech (to "shoot a sitting duck"), but as a practical matter already dead and gone. On the contrary, some animals are flourishing. In 1910 half a million deer lived in the United States, in 1960 seven million, in 1970 sixteen million. What has happened is that now that we don't eat them we have lost that close interest.

Wolf behavior prepared dogs remarkably for life with human beings. So complete and complicated was the potential that it was only a logical next step for them to quit their packs in favor of the heady, hopeless task of trying to keep pace with our own community development. The contortions of fawning and obeisance which render group adjustment possible among such otherwise forceful fighters—sometimes humping the inferior members into the shape of hyenas—are what squeezes them past our tantrums, too. Though battling within the pack is mostly accomplished with body checks that do no damage, a subordinate wolf bitch is likely to remain so in awe of the leader that she will cringe and sit on her tail in response to his amorous advances, until his female coequal has had a chance to notice and dash over and redirect his attention. Altogether, he is kept so busy asserting his dominance that this top-ranked female may not be bred by him, finally, but by the male which occupies the second rung. Being breadwinners, dominant wolves feed first and best, just as we do, so that to eat our scraps and leavings strikes a dog as normal procedure. Nevertheless, a wolf puppy up to eight months old is favored at a kill, and when smaller can extract a meal from any pack member—uncles and aunts as well as parents—by nosing the lips of the adult until it regurgitates a share of what it's had. The care of the litter is so much a communal endeavor that the benign sort of role we expect dogs to play within our own families toward children not biologically theirs comes naturally to them.

For dogs and wolves the tail serves as a semaphore of mood and social code, but dogs carry their tails higher than wolves do, as a rule, which is appropriate, since the excess spirits that used to go into lengthy hunts now have no other outlet than backyard negotiating. In addition to an epistolary anal gland, whose message-carrying function has not yet been defined, the anus itself, or stool when sniffed, conveys how well the animal has been eating—in effect, its income bracket—although most dog foods are sorrily monotonous compared to the hundreds of tastes a wolf encounters, perhaps dozens within a single carcass. We can speculate on a dog's powers of taste because its olfactory area is proportionately fourteen times larger than a man's, its sense of smell at least a hundred times as keen.

The way in which a dog presents his anus and genitals for inspection indicates the hierarchal position that he aspires to, and other dogs who sniff his genitals are apprised of his sexual condition. From his urine they can undoubtedly distinguish age, build, state of sexual activity, and general health, even hours after he's passed by. Male dogs dislike running out of urine, as though an element of potency were involved, and try to save a little; they prefer not to use a scent post again until another dog has urinated there, the first delight and duty of the ritual being to stake out a territory, so that when they are walked hurriedly in the city it is a disappointment to them. The search is also sexual, because bitches in heat post notices about. In the woods a dog will mark his drinking places, and watermark a rabbit's trail after chasing it, as if to notify the next predator that happens by exactly who it was that put such a whiff of fear into the rabbit's scent. Similarly, he squirts the tracks of bobcats and of skunks with an aloof air unlike his brisk and cheery manner of branding another dog's or fox's trail, and if he is in a position to do so, will defecate excitedly on a bear run, leaving behind his best effort, which no doubt he hopes will strike the bear as a bombshell.

The chief complaint people lodge against dogs is their extraordinary stress upon lifting the leg and moving the bowels. Scatology did take up some of the slack for them when they left behind the entertainments of the forest. The forms of territoriality replaced the substance. But apart from that, a special zest for life is characteristic of dogs and wolves — in hunting, eating, relieving themselves, in punctiliously maintaining a home territory, a pecking order and a love life, and educating the resulting pups. They grin and grimace and scrawl graffiti with their piss. A lot of inherent strategy goes into these activities: the way wolves spell each other off, both when hunting and in their governess duties around the den, and often "consult" as a pack with noses together and tails wagging before flying in to make a kill. (Tigers, leopards, house cats base their social relations instead upon what ethologists call "mutual avoidance.") The nose is a dog's main instrument of discovery, corresponding to our eyes, and so it is that he is seldom offended by organic smells, such as putrefaction, and sniffs intently for the details of illness, gum bleeding, and diet in his master and his own fellows, and for the story told by scats, not closing off the avenue for any reason — just as we rarely shut our eyes against new information, even the tragic or unpleasant kind.

Though dogs don't see as sharply as they smell, trainers usually rely on hand signals to instruct them, and most firsthand communication in a wolf pack also seems to be visual — by the expressions of the face, by body English and the cant of the tail. A dominant wolf squares his mouth, stares at and "rides up" on an inferior, standing with his front legs on its back, or will pretend to stalk it, creeping along, taking its muzzle in his mouth, and performing nearly all of the other discriminatory pranks and practices familiar to anybody who has a dog. In fact, what's funny is to watch a homely mutt as tiny as a shoebox spin through the rigmarole which a whole series of observers in the wilderness have gone to great pains to document for wolves.

Dogs proffer their rear ends to each other in an intimidating fashion, but when they examine the region of the head it is a friendlier gesture, a snuffling between pals. One of them may come across a telltale bone fragment caught in the other's fur, together with a bit of mud to give away the location of bigger bones. On the same impulse, wolves and free-running dogs will sniff a wanderer's toes to find out where he has been roaming. They fondle and propitiate with their mouths also, and lovers groom each other's fur with tongues and teeth adept as hands. A bitch wolf's period in heat includes a week of preliminary behavior and maybe two weeks of receptivity — among animals, exceptionally long. Each actual copulative tie lasts twenty minutes or half an hour, which again may help to instill affection. Wolves sometimes begin choosing a mate as early as the age of one, almost a year before they are ready to breed. Dogs mature sexually a good deal earlier, and arrive in heat twice a year instead of once — at any season instead of only in midwinter, like a wolf, whose pups' arrival must be scheduled unfailingly for spring. Dogs have not retained much responsibility for raising their young, and the summertime is just as perilous as winter for them because, apart from the whimsy of their owners, who put so many of them "to sleep," their nemesis is the automobile. Like scatology, sex helps fill the gulf of what is gone.

The scientist David Mech has pointed out how like the posture of a wolf with a nosehold on a moose (as other wolves attack its hams) are the antics of a puppy playing tug-of-war at the end of a towel. Anybody watching a dog's exuberance as he samples bites of long grass beside a brook, or pounds into a meadow bristling with the odors of woodchucks, snowshoe rabbits, grouse, a doe and buck, field mice up on the seedheads of the weeds, kangaroo mice jumping, chipmunks whistling, weasels and shrews on the hunt, a plunging fox and a porcupine couched in a tree, perhaps can begin to imagine the variety of excitements under the sky that his ancestors relinquished in order to move indoors with us. He'll lie down with a lamb to please us, but as he sniffs its haunches, surely he must remember atavistically that this is where he'd start to munch.

There is poignancy in the predicament of a great many animals: as in the simple observation which students of the California condor have made that this huge, most endangered bird prefers the carrion meat of its old standby, the deer, to all the dead cows, sheep, horses, and other substitutes it sees from above, sprawled about. Animals are stylized characters in a kind of old saga— stylized because even the most acute of them have little leeway as they play out their parts. (*Rabbits*, for example, I find terribly affecting, imprisoned in their hop.) And as we drift away from any cognizance of them, we sacrifice some of the intricacy and grandeur of life. Having already lost so much, we are hardly aware of what remains, but to a primitive snatched forward from an earlier existence it might seem as if we had surrendered a richness comparable to all the tapestries of childhood. Since this is a matter of the imagination as well as of animal demographics, no Noah projects, no bionomic discoveries on the few sanctuaries that have been established are going to reverse the swing. The very specialists in the forefront of finding out how animals behave, when one meets them, appear to be no more intrigued than any ordinary Indian was.

But we continue to need—as aborigines did, as children do—a parade of morality tales which are more concise than those that politics, for instance, later provides. So we've had Aesop's and medieval and modern fables about the grasshopper and the ant, the tiger and Little Black Sambo, the wolf and the three pigs, Br'er Rabbit and Br'er Bear, Goldilocks and her three bears, or Little Red Ridinghood, Pooh Bear, Babar and the rhinos, Walt Disney's animals, and assorted humbler scary bats, fat hippos, funny frogs, and eager beavers. Children have a passion for clean, universal definitions, and so it is that animals have gone with children's literature as Latin has with religion. Through them they first encountered death, birth, their own maternal feelings, the gap between beauty and cleverness, or speed and good intentions. The animal kingdom boasted the powerful lion, the mothering goose, the watchful owl, the tardy tortoise, Chicken Little, real-life dogs that treasure bones, and mink that grow posh pelts from eating crawfish and mussels.

In the cartoons of two or three decades ago, Mouse doesn't get along with Cat because Cat must catch Mouse or miss his supper. Dog, on the other hand, detests Cat for no such rational reason, only the capricious fact that dogs don't dote on cats. Animal stories are bounded, yet enhanced, by each creature's familiar lineaments, just as a parable about a prince and peasant, a duchess and a milkmaid, a blacksmith and a fisherman, would be. Typecasting, like the roll of a metered ode, adds resonance and dignity, summoning up all of the walruses and hedgehogs that went before: the shrewd hillbilly image of Br'er Rabbit to assist his suburban relative Bugs Bunny behind the scenes. But now, in order to present a tale about the contest between two thieving crows and a scarecrow, the storyteller would need to start by explaining that once upon a time crows used to eat a farmer's corn if he didn't defend it with a mock man pinned together from old clothes. Crows are having a hard go of it and may eventually receive game-bird protection.

One way childhood is changing, therefore, is that the nonhuman figures—"Wild Things" or puppet monsters—constructed by the best of the new artificers, like Maurice Sendak or the *Sesame Street* writers, are distinctly humanoid, ballooned out of faces and torsos met on the subway. The televised character Big Bird does not resemble a bird the way Bugs Bunny remained a rabbit—though already he was less so than Br'er or Peter Rabbit. Big Bird's personality, even her confusion, haven't the faintest connection to an ostrich's. Lest she be confused with an ostrich, her voice has been slotted unmistakably toward the prosaic. Dr. Seuss did transitional composites of worldwide fauna, but these new shapes—a beanbag like the *Sesame Street* Grouch or Cookie Monster or Herry Monster, and the floral sorts of creations in books— have been conceived practically from scratch by the artist ("in the night kitchen," to use a Sendak phrase), and not transferred from the existing caricatures of nature. In their conversational conflicts they offer him a fresh start, which may be a valuable commodity, whereas if he were dealing with an alligator, it would, while giving him an old-fashioned boost in the traditional manner, at the same time box him in. A chap called Alligator, with that fat snout and tail, cannot squirm free of the solidity of actual alligators. Either it must stay a heavyweight or else play on the sternness of reality by swinging over to impersonate a cream puff and a Ferdinand.

Though animal programs on television are popular, what with the wave of nostalgia and "ecology" in the country, we can generally say about the animal kingdom, "The King is dead, long live the King." Certainly the talent has moved elsewhere. Those bulbous Wild Things and slant-mouthed beanbag puppets derived from the denizens of Broadway—an argumentative night news vendor, a lady on a traffic island—have grasped their own destinies, as characters on the make are likely to. It was inevitable they would. There may be a shakedown to remove the elements that would be too bookish for children's literature in other hands, and another shakedown because these first innovators have been more city-oriented than suburban. New authors will shift the character sources away from Broadway and the subway and the ghetto, but the basic switch has already been accomplished—from the ancient juxtaposition of people, animals, and dreams blending the two, to people and monsters that grow solely out of people by way of dreams.

Which leaves us in the suburbs, with dogs as a last link. Cats are too independent to care, but dogs are in an unenviable position, they hang so much upon our good opinion. We are coming to *have* no opinion; we don't pay enough attention to form an opinion. Though they admire us, are thrilled by us, heroize us, we regard them as a hobby or a status symbol, like a tennis racquet, and substitute leash laws for leadership— expect them not simply to learn English but to grow hands, because their beastly paws seem stranger to us every year. If they try to fondle us with their handyjack mouths, we read it as a bite; and like used cars, they are disposed of in the scurry of divorce or when the family relocates or changes what it's "into." The first reason people kept a dog was to acquire an ally on the hunt, a friend at night. Then it was to maintain an avenue to animality, as our own nearness began to recede. But as we lose our awareness of all animals, dogs are becoming a bridge to nowhere. We can only pity their fate.

Analyzing and Discussing the Text

1. "Essays," Hoagland has written, "belong to the animal kingdom, with a surface that generates sparks, like a coat of fur, compared with the flat, conventional cotton of the magazine article writer, who works in the vegetable kingdom, instead." Does this metaphor adequately describe the language of "Dogs, and the Tug of Life"? If so, try to define more precisely what kind of "sparks" this essay gives off and how they are generated.

2. Although Hoagland's essay is discursive and digressive, it is not disconnected. Reread the essay, noting carefully how and where the author ties the strands of his piece together. Are there underlying organizational patterns that were not apparent in your first reading?

3. The essay begins with a humorous sociological history of dog ownership in the United States. Among the numerous observations in these first five paragraphs, can you find one or two underlying themes? If so, how do they tie in with the material in the rest of the essay?

4. Characterize the vocabulary that Hoagland uses in his discussion of dogs and humans. Use specific examples from the text.

Experiencing and Writing About the World

1. Do you agree with Hoagland's description of "a dog's life" in the sixth paragraph? If not, write a paragraph expressing your own views on that topic.

2. One of Hoagland's arguments in this essay is that we are losing the important role that the animal kingdom once played in our cultural imagination. Make the case for the other side of this argument, persuading your reader that this is not happening, that, in fact, the animal world is becoming an increasingly important part of contemporary culture.

3. Much of Hoagland's essay develops by comparing dogs to their wolf ancestors. Prepare a brief analytical essay explaining how he sets the two in relation to each other.

4. Hoagland asserts that "to keep a dog is a way of attempting to bring nature back." Choose another prominent aspect of contemporary life that seeks "to bring nature back" and write an essay assessing whether this effort succeeds or not. Carefully monitor the tone of your own argument. Does it have the same cynicism that marks Hoagland's essay?

5. Think about this essay in conjunction with Alice Walker's "Am I Blue?" (later in this chapter). Both authors urge readers to respect animals, but their arguments differ in important ways. Write an essay that analyzes the attitudes of Hoagland and Walker toward domestic animals (dogs and horses) and at the same time states your own attitude, which might differ from those of the authors.

PETER MATTHIESSEN

From **The Snow Leopard**

Peter Matthiessen (1927–   ) was born into a well-to-do family in New York City. He first became interested in nature when he and his brother caught and studied snakes (mostly copperheads) and birds on the family property in Connecticut. Matthiessen was educated at the Hotchkiss School and at Yale University, where, as an English major, he also took courses in biology and ornithology. He received his degree in 1950 and, along with William Styron, George Plimpton, James Baldwin, and others, soon became an important part of the group of expatriate American writers who lived in Paris in the early 1950s. In 1951, he cofounded the *Paris Review* and became its first fiction editor. Matthiessen has also worked as a commercial fisherman; as the captain of a charter boat for deep-sea fishing; and as a member of expeditions to Alaska, Peru, New Guinea, and various parts of Africa. He began his writing career as a novelist, and his fiction, including such works as *At Play in the Fields of the Lord* (1965), *Far Tortuga* (1975), and *Killing Mr. Watson* (1990), frequently develops the same themes that characterize his nonfiction: a concern for ways of life, places, and species that are threatened by a less valuable, but nonetheless steadily encroaching, civilization. When he is not traveling, Matthiessen lives on Long Island, New York.

Although he seems to value his fiction more than his nonfiction and even goes so far as to describe his literary nonfiction as "cabinet-work or carpentry," Matthiessen is still best known for his work in such non-fiction classics as *The Tree Where Man Was Born* (1972) and *The Snow Leopard* (1978). *The Snow Leopard*, which won the National Book Award in 1979, is his most acclaimed book and is generally acknowledged as a masterpiece of contemporary American writing about nature. The book is based on the journals of his 1973 trip to the Himalayas with the naturalist George Schaller. The expedition had two goals: to observe the rut of the Himalayan blue sheep (and through these observations to be able to trace the ancestry of that little-known species) and to see the snow leopard, an animal whose rareness has given it an almost legendary aura. However, *The Snow Leopard* also reflects Matthiessen's personal situation and philosophical concerns. He wrote it during a time when he was seeking a way to accept his second wife's death from cancer and when he was first becoming deeply involved in the meditative philosophy of Zen Buddhism. He has said, in fact, that because he had only intermittent contact with any Zen teachers during this trip, he attempted to make the writing of *The Snow Leopard* his Zen practice. The journey to see the elusive snow leopard thus becomes an effort to separate the permanent from the transient, a quest to find in nature some form of spiritual illumination.

November 15

All morning the moon hangs frozen on the sky, and the wind-bell rings unheard on the hard east wind. The robin accentor has perished, or fled south across the mountains, since it no longer turns up in my yard. To the cook hut, in the bitter cold, comes Namu with a blanket wrapped around her head, to take a cup of tea: ordinarily, her wild black hair blows free. The days are shorter now. The sun is gone by midafternoon, when this primordial woman fills the mountain dusk with her wild cries, calling her black *dzo*, scaring off wolves.

I climb early to the northwest ridge of Somdo mountain, from where I can watch all the trails, scan all the valleys of the western slopes, beyond Black River: if the snow leopard is abroad, then I may see it, and if it makes a kill, I shall see birds. GS has crossed the river early to look for more fresh signs: he tries not to let the leopard interfere with his study of blue sheep, but the great cats have a strong hold on him, and the snow leopard is the least known of them all. It is wonderful how the presence of this creature draws the whole landscape to a point, from the glint of light on the old horns of a sheep to the ring of a pebble on the frozen ground.

Since it is too cold to sit in one position, I roam up and down the ridge, scanning the west walls every little while, and keeping an eye on the blue sheep of Somdo, which seem well behind the Tsakang herd in the progress of the rut. On this slope there are many fossils, mostly spiraled ammonites, and in the river lie wild rocks of great beauty. I love wild rocks, I covet them, but they are too big to carry away over the passes. Perhaps I shall take a few shards of broken prayer stones; the river rocks will stay where they belong.

With the wind and cold, a restlessness has come, and I find myself hoarding my last chocolate for the journey back across the mountains—forever getting-ready-for-life instead of living it each day. This restlessness is intensified by the presence of the extra sherpas, who can do little besides use up precious food; they sleep and sit around, waiting to go.

Like heralds of the outside world, Tukten and Gyaltsen arrived with the full moon. Now the moon is waning, and the fine lunar clarity of life at Shey swiftly diminishes. Exciting days have occurred since their arrival, and yet a kind of power is winding down, a spell is broken.

And so I, too, prepare to go, though I try hard to remain. The part of me that is bothered by the unopened letters in my rucksack, that longs to see my children, to drink wine, make love, be clean and comfortable again—that part is already facing south, over the mountains. This makes me sad, and so I stare about me, trying to etch into this journal the sense of Shey that is so precious, aware that all such effort is in vain; the beauty of this place must be cheerfully abandoned, like the wild rocks in the bright water of its streams. Frustration at the paltriness of words drives me to write, but there is more of Shey in a single sheep hair, in one withered sprig of everlasting, than in all these notes; to strive for permanence in what I think I have perceived is to miss the point.

Near my lookout, I find a place to meditate, out of the wind, a hollow on the ridge where snow has melted. My brain soon clears in the cold mountain air, and I feel better. Wind, blowing grasses, sun: the dying grass, the notes of southbound birds in the mountain sky are no more fleeting than the rock itself, no more so and no less—all is the same. The mountain withdraws into its stillness, my body dissolves into the sunlight, tears fall that have nothing to do with "I." What it is that brings them on, I do not know.

In other days, I understood mountains differently, seeing in them something that abides. Even when approached respectfully (to challenge peaks as mountaineers do is another matter) they appalled me with their "permanence," with that awful and irrefutable *rock*-ness that seemed to intensify my sense of my own transience. Perhaps this dread of transience explains our greed for the few gobbets of raw experience in modern life, why violence is libidinous, why lust devours us, why soldiers choose not to forget their days of horror: we cling to such extreme moments, in which we seem to die, yet are reborn. In sexual abandon as in danger we are impelled, however briefly, into that vital present in which we do not stand apart from life, we *are* life, our being fills us; in ecstasy with another being, loneliness falls away into eternity. But in other days, such union was attainable through simple awe.

My foot slips on a narrow ledge: in that split second, as needles of fear pierce heart and temples, eternity intersects with present time. Thought and action are not different, and stone, air, ice, sun, fear, and self are one. What is exhilarating is to extend this acute awareness into ordinary moments, in the moment-by-moment experiencing of the lammergeier and the wolf, which, finding themselves at the center of things, have no need for any secret of true being. In this very breath that we take now lies the secret that all great teachers try to tell us, what one lama refers to as "the precision and openness and intelligence of the present."[1] The purpose of meditation practice is not enlightenment; it is to pay attention even at unextraordinary times, to be of the present, nothing-but-the-present, to bear this mindfulness of *now* into each event

---

[1]Chögyam Trungpa, *Cutting Through Spiritual Materialism* (Boulder: Shambhala, 1973).— Author's note.

of ordinary life. To be anywhere else is "to paint eyeballs on chaos."[2] When I watch blue sheep, I must watch blue sheep, not be thinking about sex, danger, or the present, for this present—even while I think of it—is gone.

November 16

The snow leopard has been hunting in the night, for part of the Tsakang herd has fled off toward the north, taking shelter in the yard of Dölma-jang, and the rest have crossed the ridges to the west; from Somdo, a calligraphic track up Crystal Mountain can be seen that disappears at the white rim, into blue sky. Having dispersed the Tsakang herds, the leopard crossed over the Black River—or perhaps a second leopard has arrived—for here on Somdo, the big herd is also scattered, with males and females reverting to their separate bands. As we climb the broad mountainsides above the village, a lone band of nine male animals is in sight.

Not a thousand feet above our tents at Shey, on the path that I walked yesterday, a leopard has made its scrape right in my boot print, as if in sign that I am not to leave. The leopard may still be present on this slope, for the rams are skittish. Even so, the rut is near, activity is constant, and GS scribbles in his notebook. "Oh, there's a penis-lick!" he cries. "A beauty!" The onanism is mingled here and there with fighting, especially among the older rams, which rear repeatedly on their hind legs; remarkably, another rears at the same instant, and the two run forward like trained partners, coming down together with a crash of heads. For most creatures, such an encounter would be fatal, but bharal are equipped with some two inches of parietal bone between the horns, together with a cushion of air space in the sinuses, thick woolly head hair, and strong necks to absorb the shock, and the horns themselves, on the impact side, are very thick and heavy. Why nature should devote so many centuries—thousands, probably—to the natural selection of these characters that favor head-on collisions over brains is a good question, although speaking for myself in these searching days, less brains and a good head-on collision might be just the answer.

Watching blue sheep in the sun and windlessness is pleasant, and reminds us that this pleasantness must end. We discuss logistics briefly, and also the implications of our journey, and our great good fortune. Last night at supper, GS remarked that this was one of the best trips he had ever made, "tough enough so that we feel we have really accomplished something, but not so tough that it wiped us out entirely." I feel the same.

This morning, expressing his relief that such good bharal data have come in, GS refers again to his dread of failure, of the satisfaction that

[2]Dogen Zenji, *Shobogenzo* (San Francisco: Japan Publications, 1977).—Author's note.

his peers might take in his first mistake, and after two months I feel I know him well enough to point out how often this refrain occurs in his conversation, and how baseless his apprehension seems to be: no matter how badly he might fail on any expedition, his abilities and good reputation are beyond dispute. GS recognizes his mild paranoia, and discusses it quite frankly as he stands there, observing the blue sheep's world through his faithful spotting scope; he is more open and relaxed each day. When I say so, he looks doubtful, and I quote his remark about the snow leopard: "Maybe it's better if there are some things that we *don't* see." He nods grudgingly, as if in disapproval, but later he resists the implications of his repeated observation at Tsakang that mountains move. "Well," he mutters, "from a certain point of view, I mean, geologically, of course, the Himalaya is still rising, and then there is a downward movement due to erosion—" I interrupt him. "That's not what you meant," I say. "Not at Tsakang." Still squinting into the telescope, my partner grins.

GS feels that our journey has had the quality of adventure because we depend entirely on ourselves; that this is an old-fashioned expedition in the sense that we are completely out of touch with our own world, with our own century, for that matter—no vehicles, no doctor, and no radio, far less airdrops or support teams or other such accoutrements of the modern "expedition." "This is the way I like it," GS says. "You haven't got the whole goddamned society backing you up, you're on your own: you have to take responsibility for your mistakes, you can't blame the organization. And inevitably, you make mistakes—you just hope they aren't too serious." I like it, too, for the same reasons, and also because the penalty for error makes me mindful as I walk among these mountains, heeding the echo of my step on the frozen earth.

At midmorning, when the blue sheep have settled for their rest, we walk a long eastward traverse, then west again, hoping to jump the leopard from a gully. On the stony ground, the few prints are indistinct, with nothing fresh enough to indicate where the creature might be lying. If this is the Tsakang cat, then it is hungry, and there is a chance that it will kill tonight. Since it will stay close enough to guard its kill from the lammergeiers and griffons, this is my last hope of seeing it.

With the herds scattered, it appears unlikely that full rut will get under way in the next fortnight; if the leopard is gone, it is not apt to return again in the next week. And so I have put aside my doubts about departing here the day after tomorrow, and have asked Tukten to obtain stores and a few utensils from Phu-Tsering for the outward journey. We can take little, for the camp is running short; in Saldang, perhaps, some *tsampa* and potatoes can be obtained.

GS feels that I make too much of Tukten's spiritual propensities and, like Jang-bu, warns me to beware of him. On both points he is probably right. Still, I am glad that Tukten will be with me, for unlike all but the head sherpa, he anticipates problems and deals with them unasked. Gyaltsen has no wish to travel on in life with Tukten, preferring to remain at Shey with Jang-bu; Dawa will go out with us instead. Dawa's morale has been uncertain since his two bouts of snow blindness, and as a rule he appears happiest when by himself: I hear him singing every time he passes my stone wall, bound down to the White River to fetch water. He rarely joins the other sherpas at the fire, preferring to set back in the shadows by the wall; though they like him, the others tease him and order him about, and he smiles shyly, as if grateful that they don't pretend he isn't there.

November 17

Last night, the snow leopard left tracks just outside the monastery, on the Saldang path that I shall take tomorrow; like the scrape found yesterday over my bootprint, it is hard not to read this as a sign. Then the cat recrossed the Black River—either that, or there are two leopards in the region, as we think. Followed or preceded by a solitary wolf—perhaps the same elusive beast that circled the prayer wall here last week—this leopard or another has prowled the Tsakang trail, and on my last day here, as the sun rises from the ice horizon, we climb the westward slopes in hopes of locating a kill. Part of the main bharal herd has come back across the snows to graze warily just above Tsakang, and another band—many animals are still missing—steps daintily along the ledges of the cliff below the hermitage, the sunrise bright on their white knees. The only other time the bharal have been seen on the steep cliff face was the morning they were chased there by the wolves, but they may have come here of their own accord, since a few are licking alkali salts from the icicles in the small caves, and others are nibbling at stunted barberry in the crannies.

A young ram tries halfheartedly to mount a ewe, but it now appears that it will be the first days of December before the females come fully into estrus and the height of the rut occurs. After all these weeks of itch and foreplay, only a few dominant males will take part in copulation, which will last but a few seconds at each encounter.

GS is satisfied that the bharal is neither sheep nor goat but a creature perhaps very close to the ancestral goatlike animal of about twenty million years ago from which *Ovis* and *Capra* evolved. ("The behavioral evidence," he wrote later, "confirms the morphological evidence that bharal are basically goats. Many of the sheep-like traits of bharal can be ascribed to convergent evolution, the result of the species having settled in a habitat which is usually occupied by sheep. . . . The species has straddled an evolutionary fence, and if it had to make a choice of whether to become an *Ovis* or a *Capra* it could become either with only minor alterations. Like the aoudad, the bharal probably split early from the ancestral goat stock. If I had to design a hypothetical precursor from which the sheep and goat lines diverged, it would in many ways resemble a bharal in appearance and behavior."[3])

GS continues up the valley to the herd near snow line, while I return slowly down the ridges, wishing to spend most of this last day on the home mountain. At each stupa on the canyon points, the prayer stones are lit by fire-colored lichens; in the shine of thorn and old carved stones, the print of leopard and thick scent of juniper, I am filled with longing. I turn to look back at Tsakang, at the precipices and deep shadows of Black Canyon, at the dark mountain that presides over Samling, which I shall never see. Above the snowfields to the west, the Crystal Mountain thrusts bare rock into the blue; to the south is the sinuous black torrent that comes down from Kang La, the Pass of Snows. And there on the low cliff above the rivers, silhouetted on the snow, is the village that its own people call Somdo, white prayer flags flying black on the morning sun.

On the river islands, winter ice has stilled the prayer wheels, but under the bridge the water is deep, gray, and swift, hurrying away west to the great Karnali. On the bluff, I pay my last respects to the white stupas and make a bow to bright-blue Dorje-Chang. I would enter and give the *mani* wheels a spin, and send OM MANI PADME HUM to the ten directions, but Ongdi the Trader has turned up again and locked the doors, in the hope of realizing a small gain by charging us admission. Accompanying Ongdi on this trip is the owner of the yard where my tent is pitched; he has no wish to charge me rent, merely goes about the walls adjusting prayer stones, in dour sign that I must treat his dung heaps with respect. This dung extends from one wall to the other, my tent is pitched in it, for all I know it may be centuries deep. Yet the householder points at a stone-like coprolith frozen in the dung in the yard corner, and I am existentially embarrassed: there is no way to explain that this phenomenon of dung-on-dung occurred but once, in dire straits of night emergency and bitter cold. No, really, I am mortally offended, with no earthly target for my wrath: what has this dismal lump to do with those transparent states high on the mountain?

The stranger and I stand shoulder to shoulder, glaring downward in the wind and silence, as if the *dorje* lay before us, the adamantine diamond, ready to deliver up some Tantric teaching: *Take care, O Pilgrim, lest you discriminate against the so-called lower functions, for these, too, contain the inherent miracle of being. Did not one of the great masters attain enlightenment upon hearing the splash of his own turd into the water? Even transparency, O Pilgrim, may be a hindrance if one clings to it. One must not linger on the Crystal Mountain—*

[3]George B. Schaller (ms. in progress).—Author's note. [Later published as *Mountain Monarchs: Wild Sheep and Goats of the Himalaya* (Chicago: University of Chicago Press, 1977).—Eds.]

Enough! I am not far enough along the path to perceive the Absolute in my own dung—yours, maybe, but not mine. Shit is shit, as Zen would say, or rather, *Shit!* I boot this trace of my swift passage through the world out of the yard. Then I thank the man for his hospitality and show him a rock that contains a pretty fossil, but having no idea what I require of him, he is indifferent to my thanks and stones.

Slowly I pass along the field of prayer stones to the picturesque low door of Crystal Monastery, with its old prayer wheels, one of copper, one of wood, inset in the walls on either side. Over the door is a small Buddha of worn stone, bright-painted in the reds and blues of earth and sky. Unless Tundu comes this afternoon, bringing the key, I shall never pass through this small door into Shey Gompa. The entrance stupas and Lama Tupjuk's chapel at Tsakang have given me a clue to the interior, and tomorrow, with luck, I shall visit the temple at Namgung, five hours hence across the eastern mountains, which is also a Karma-Kagyu gompa. All the same, it seems too bad not to have seen the inside of the Crystal Monastery, having traveled so far to such a destination.

(Not long after my departure, Tundu's wife turned up with the key to the monastery, demanding one hundred rupees to open the door. GS ignored her, and on the eve of his departure, she let him enter for five rupees. According to his notes and floor plan, Shey Gompa contains a number of fine bronze Buddhas, hanging drums, old swords and muzzle loaders from the bandit days, and the heavy printing blocks that made the "wind pictures" given me by Lama Tupjuk. Otherwise, the gompa differs mostly in its large size from others in the region, excepting one bizarre and unaccountable detail: on a hanging cloth, with a wolf, Tibetan wild asses, and an owl, there is a picture of a female yeti.

This drawing at the Crystal Monastery is more curious than first appears. Pictures of yeti have been reported to exist in remote lamaseries, but they are in fact extremely rare; the only other I have ever heard of in Nepal is found at Tengboche Monastery, under Mount Everest. That such a drawing should exist well to the west of where yetis have been heretofore reported deepens the enigma of that sunny morning in the forests of the Suli Gad, and the strange dark shape that sprang behind a boulder.)

I climb to my old lookout, happy and sad in the dim instinct that these mountains are my home. But "only the Awakened Ones remember their many births and deaths,"[4] and I can hear no whisperings of other lives. Doubtless I have "home" confused with childhood, and Shey with its flags and beasts and snowy fastnesses with some Dark

[4]Bhagavad-Gita.—Author's note.

Ages place of forgotten fairy tales, where the atmosphere of myth made life heroic.

In the longing that starts one on the path is a kind of homesickness, and some way, on this journey, I have started home. Homegoing is the purpose of my practice, of my mountain meditation and my daybreak chanting, of my *koan*: All the peaks are covered with snow—why is this one bare? To resolve the illogical question would mean to burst apart, let fall all preconceptions and supports. But I am not ready to let go, and so I shall not resolve my *koan*, or see the snow leopard, that is to say, *perceive* it. I shall not see it because I am not ready.

I meditate for the last time on this mountain that is bare, though others all around are white with snow. Like the bare peak of the *koan*, this one is not different from myself. I know this mountain because I am this mountain, I can feel it breathing at this moment, as its grass tops stray against the snows. If the snow leopard should leap from the rock above and manifest itself before me—S-A-A-O!—then in that moment of pure fright, *out of my wits*, I might truly perceive it, and be free.

Analyzing and Discussing the Text

1. The journal entry immediately preceding the November 15th entry concludes with the exchange: "'Have you seen the snow leopard?' 'No. Isn't that wonderful?'" How do the journal entries included in the selection elaborate on the meaning of these two questions?

2. What does Matthiessen mean when he says "all is the same"? How is this thought connected to his concern with permanence and transience throughout the journal? How does it tie in specifically with his focus on the present in the last four sentences of the November 15th entry and the final two paragraphs of the November 17th entry? Elaborate on what Matthiessen means when he says, in the sixth paragraph of his entry for November 15th, "the beauty of this place must be cheerfully abandoned."

3. Trace out the progression of ideas and descriptions in the November 15th entry from the first paragraph to the final paragraph and phrase. How does the arrangement of ideas help him persuade us to accept what he says? Find and describe other examples of Matthiessen's narrative craft in these selections. What is the effect when Matthiessen juxtaposes the three paragraphs on dung with his section on the Crystal Monastery?

4. Describe the character of GS as he appears in these pages. How does this picture of Matthiessen's companion fit with the themes that are developed here? What other functions does his appearance serve in the narrative?
5. The dramatic final paragraph of these selections suggests the possibility of attaining freedom. Discuss what constitutes freedom for Matthiessen and the process by which he feels such freedom might be attained. How do these ideas relate to the notions of other nature writers you have studied?
6. Explain the importance of animals—birds, snow leopards, wolves, blue sheep—even when they remain unseen. How do animals contribute to the intense focus of the author's attention?

Experiencing and Writing About the World

1. Does Matthiessen's Zen-inspired concern with living in the present, with those moments in which "we are life" rather than detached from it, seem applicable to your own experience of current American life? If you have had experiences similar to the one he seeks, describe one of them. Although few settings can be as dramatic as the backdrop provided by the Himalayas, careful description of any environment will still help to involve your reader. Use Matthiessen's descriptions of the world around him as a model for your essay.
2. Go on a walk in your own neighborhood, keeping a sharp lookout for any signs of animal life, wild or not. Record your observations and thoughts in a notebook, then return home and expand the terse notebook entries into more substantial narrative and meditative passages, just as Matthiessen did when he returned home from Asia and prepared a preliminary version of *The Snow Leopard* as a series of articles for the *New Yorker*. As you develop your journal notes into more complete explanations of what you have observed, you might explicitly compare your own approach to writing about animals with Matthiessen's approach. He and his companion, GS, have very clear reasons for their observations of the *bharal* and their search for the snow leopard. Is your search for animal life similarly focused and purposeful? If not, what is the value of this current exercise in observation, note-taking, and reflection? Spend at least two hours in the field before heading indoors again.
3. Write a personal essay about the relationship between your own spiritual values and the natural world. Is nature an important part of your spiritual life? How does your religion perceive the world of nature? Is there conflict or harmony between your own sense of

nature and the concept of the natural world presented in formal religion?

4. Mountain travel in the Himalayas serves several functions for Matthiessen. Do you see important connections between the way he views mountains and the viewpoints of some of the essayists in the mountaineering chapter of this anthology? If so, analyze one or two of the mountaineering essays in conjunction with Matthiessen's essay.

SCOTT RUSSELL SANDERS

Listening to Owls

Scott Russell Sanders (1945–   ) was born in Memphis, Tennessee. His father came from a family of cotton farmers in Mississippi, his mother from an immigrant doctor's family in Chicago. His early childhood was spent in Tennessee and his school years in Ohio; Sanders later moved to Rhode Island to major in physics and English as an undergraduate at Brown University. After considering graduate school in both theoretical physics and literature, he chose to study English at Cambridge University; he completed his Ph.D. there in 1971. Since then he has taught in the English Department at Indiana University in Bloomington, where he also writes literary criticism, fiction, and personal essays. Sanders has published fourteen books, including *Wilderness Plots* (1983), *Wonders Hidden* (1984), *Terrarium* (1985), *Hear the Wind Blow* (1985), *The Engineer of Beasts* (1988), and *The Invisible Company* (1989). In 1985 he published *In Limestone Country*, his first book of essays. His second collection, *The Paradise of Bombs* (1987), won the Associated Writing Programs Award for Creative Nonfiction. A third essay collection, *Secrets of the Universe*, appeared in 1991. His awards include a Marshall Scholarship (1967–1971), a Woodrow Wilson Fellowship (1976–1978), and a National Endowment for the Arts Fellowship (1983–1984).

Sanders's writing is often concerned with our relationship to nature, with issues of war and peace, and with tracing out the sources of violent behavior. In his introduction to *The Paradise of Bombs*, where "Listening to Owls" appears (it was first published in the *North American Review*), Sanders states that the essays are his "effort at remembering where we truly live—not inside a skull, a house, a town or nation, not inside any human creation at all, but in the creation." Despite all of the literary and rhetorical skill he brings to this subject, Sanders, like many other successful essayists, sees the essay as a means of exploration and discovery. For him, the writing of a personal essay is "like finding my way through a forest without being quite sure what game I am chasing, what landmark I am seeking." This spirit of discovery emerges in the following essay, which is set literally in a forest, in the dark of night. Sometimes discovery comes as a result of *no* contact, of the wild creatures' very elusiveness. "If the owls choose to remain invisible and silent," writes Sanders, "then, like the gods, silent and invisible they will remain. There are no switches you can throw to make them perform." The otherness of the birds, their apparent indifference to the would-be human observers, becomes the principal lesson of a night spent "listening to owls."

On the morning after the winter solstice, two hours before sunrise, moon full, I stood on frozen feet beside a pine grove in southern Indiana and listened for owls. The pine boughs were dark featherings on darkness. Every winter weed and bush in the meadow cast a pale moon-shadow. Burst milkweed pods hung upon last year's stems like giant commas. Breath haloed about my face in the five-degree air. In such stillness an owl could hear the footpads of mice, the rustling of rabbits, but I with my clumsy ears could hear nothing.

The friend who had brought me to this owl country—Don Whitehead, a husky man with sun-creases around his eyes, who indulges his passion for the outdoors by teaching ecology—cupped gloved hands to his mouth and uttered a long cry, rather like the noise a strangled rooster might make. This was the barred owl's call, which bird books will tell you sounds like a guttural rendering of "Who cooks for you, who cooks for you all?" But don't let the cozy sentences fool you. The cry of the barred owl, even the counterfeit cry my friend Don was making, resembles no human speech. It is night-speech. So there we stood, on the longest night of the year, two grown men hooting into the darkness and listening.

Presently a cow answered, lowing mournfully. Next a dog yapped, then two more, then a fourth, all at a great distance from us and seemingly from all four points of the compass. We were surrounded by domestication. When a rooster chimed in, I began to despair of owls. Gingerly, afraid my iced toes might shatter, I rocked from foot to foot.

Don motioned for me to keep still. Dogs, cow, and rooster obligingly hushed. A moonlit smile stole across his face. He pointed, away from the pine woods and across the meadow, toward a cedar-topped ridge. I faced where he pointed, shut my eyes, and listened, listened so hard my shivering body grew calm. What I heard sounded at first like a distant creek splashing over rocks. I disappeared into my listening. The water-sound grew sharper, divided into syllables, spoke to me at last in the sixty-million-year-old voice of an owl.

Sixty million years is only an estimate, of course, and might be off by an eon or two. The bones of owls, like those of all other birds, are hollow and flimsy, and consequently make poor fossils. Reading the rocks, scientists find dinosaurs by the truckload, seashells and gigantic ferns by the long ton, but scant trace of birds. Some dinosaurs had wings, but they must have been clumsy fliers. Maybe they could not truly fly, but had to climb trees or cliffs and then leap in one hungry swoop onto their prey.

Some one hundred and eighty million years ago, one of these winged dinosaurs lay down in the mud and left its fossilized imprint, including a toothed jaw, a long bony tail, and the ghostly trace of feathers. Feathers! Here was a new invention, and a durable one, to judge by the chickadee on my windowsill. Life shoving through the sluggish bodies of dinosaurs—so the scientists theorize—chopped off the heavy tail, feathered the wings, hollowed the bones, and eventually produced birds. Holding dinosaur and bird together in the mind takes some getting used to: a lumbering swamp monster on one side and an ounce of fluff on the other, with a dotted line connecting them. But next time you get close to a pigeon or some other patient bird, next time you clean a chicken, notice the reptilian scales on its legs and see if you don't catch a whiff of ancient mud.

While the barred owl called, I shook, as if I were a plucked string. Of course the five-degree weather probably had something to do with my shaking. But mainly it was that night-voice plucking at the strings of wonder and dread in me. Listening in that moon shadowed meadow, the grasses and weeds curling from the soil like delicate brush strokes, I understood why so many ancient peoples regarded the owl's cry as an omen of death.

In the old days, when the Chinese heard that cry, they called it "digging a grave" and knew an owl was on its way to snatch some dying soul. Australian aborigines believed that owls trafficked only in the souls of women, the souls of men being reserved for bats. Sicilians used to say that an owl cry meant an ailing person would die within three days. If nobody in the neighborhood was sick, then somebody would come down with tonsil trouble. No point in wasting an evil omen. The Old Testament warned the Israelites not to eat owls, lumping them with vultures as pariahs of the wastelands. Sumerians and Hebrews associated owls with Lilith, the goddess of death, who struck in the night. In the Middle Ages this death-dealing hag became a witch, and the owl one of her familiars, a worker of wickedness.

"Death's dreadful messenger"—that's what Edmund Spenser called the bird. And Shakespeare found it difficult to murder anyone on stage without the help of a preliminary announcement from owls. The king's murder in *Macbeth*, for example, is accompanied by the shriek of an owl, "the fatal bellman which gives the stern'st goodnight."

Even the word *owl* is funereal, coming as it does from a Latin root meaning "to howl," the same root that gives us *ululation* (the sound of wailing and lamentation). The birds have not helped their reputation any by showing a fondness for nesting in ruins and graveyards. Their flight is silent, thanks to the downy edge of their primary feathers and oversized wings. Like death, they arrive unannounced and gobble their victims whole.

These are not comforting details to recollect at two hours before sunrise, with your extremities frozen and ice forming in your arteries and the whole universe seized by a winter that might last forever—not comforting at all, especially if you are given, as I am, to brooding about death even in daylight and without the aid of owls.

Don yelped his strangled-rooster cry again. I flinched. He grinned. Not at me, it turned out, but at the voice of a second barred owl that joined the first in a courting duet. The twin songs spiraled about one another, twisting the birds together in a rope of desire. At the far end of that rope, if things worked out, would be a nest, eggs, four weeks of incubation, and two or three owlets looking like handfuls of dandelion fluff. So here were voices crying at the other gate, the gate of birth rather than death. Night and eros also go together. A century ago, in the streets of London, if you had inquired about "owls" you would have been led to a brothel. Night hags bring the big death; nightwalkers bring the small one.

Once they tuned up, our pair of lovers kept hooting yearnfully, like Romeo and Juliet in their balcony scene. What business did I have eavesdropping on this erotic serenade? How would I like finding them perched one midnight on my bedroom windowsill, their radar-dish ears catching every rustle of my sheets? But I had no intention of budging from that icy meadow so long as they kept singing. Now that love had been introduced, I could hear enough gaiety in their call to understand why Audubon, trailing barred owls in the swamps of Louisiana, compared their cry "to the affected bursts of laughter which you may have heard from some of the fashionable members of our own species."

If you listen to recordings of owls you will hear an eerie babel of moans and cackling, snores and screeches. There are about one hundred thirty species worldwide in sizes ranging from sparrow to eagle, and they speak in as many dialects as people do. Some of the voices are liquid trills. Others resemble the harsh buzz of locusts. Some make you think of murder victims, sirens, the sickening squeal cars make before a crash. Defending their nests, many owls snap their bills, clicking like Geiger counters. Burrowing owls, which like to set up house in abandoned prairie dog tunnels, scare away predators by hissing like a rattlesnake. With wings spread and tail ruffled, a hissing owl might remind other predators rather uncomfortably of a wildcat. Saw-whet owls derive their name from the saw-sharpening whine they make. More than one early traveler in the American wilderness reports having been fooled by this bird whistle into thinking a sawmill was just ahead.

Owls do all this muttering for purposes of courtship, as our yearnful pair of barreds were doing, and also for establishing territory. Wolves mark out the boundaries of their turf by urinating and defecating. Humans build fences and guard-posts. Owls, more fastidious than either, embroider the edges of their territory with song. They also fly their boundaries, regular as mailmen. When threatened, they will cry out like sirens to announce alarms. Nestlings clamor for food in the universally raucous manner of the young. Nocturnal owls often sing for a spell at dusk before the evening's hunt, like children at hide-and-seek counting to twenty before going in search of victims.

They probably conduct other business with their hoots and gurgles— commenting on the weather, say, or estimating the population of field mice. Altogether, the vocabulary of owls is about as complex as that of the average telephone conversation. Once you've spoken about hunger and fear, weather and territory, sex and death, what more is there to say?

Listening to screech owls beside Walden Pond, Thoreau was reminded of wailing women and mournful lovers, as if their call "were the dark and tearful side of music." Others have heard melancholy in these voices. The Kootenay Indians used to warn that children crying in the night would be mistaken by owls for their own young and be carried away. (I tried this warning on my three-year-old, but he seemed to like the idea of being snatched out of bed and flown high above the night-country.) A brooding and sometimes melancholy bird himself, Thoreau welcomed the screech owls, saying. "They give me a sense of the variety and capacity of that nature which is our common dwelling."

Screech owls do not actually screech, but gently whinny, or give a voiceless, quavering whistle like the syncopated whooshing sound of a revolving door. Fans of science-fiction movies might be reminded of the sounds flying saucers are supposed to make. My friend Don had perfected that call as well. He had spent his teen years in the Adirondacks imitating birds, the way ordinary teenagers imitate television comedians or rock singers. When the barred owls tired of their love-duet and fell silent, Don gave a tremulous whistle. Within moments a screech owl whistled back, as if to say, "I thought you'd never call." This time the voice rose from the pine woods, so we shifted around to face the shaggy boughs. It would most likely be a solitary male, staking out his territory. The whistling came only once more. Here I am, he was announcing. This is my realm of bugs and frogs and field mice. Don spoke back to him, but the owl apparently had said his say. The pines bristled silently in the moonlight.

Audubon once carried a live screech owl in his coat pocket from Philadelphia to New York, over land and water, feeding it by hand. Audubon did things like that. On one occasion he was presented with a live duck. Lacking any other place to store it, he carried the bird half a day under his top hat. (I specify that both duck and owl were alive, since Audubon's ordinary method of studying birds, like that of all early ornithologists, was to shoot first and ask scientific questions later. "I have not shot but have seen a Hawk of great size entirely *new*" he wrote to his wife from Florida, and then added hopefully, "may perhaps kill him tomorrow." He sometimes shot upwards of three hundred birds to secure one fine specimen for illustration.) He once fell into quicksand while chasing a great horned owl. The slime was up to his armpits before someone heard his cries and pulled him out. Audubon held no grudge against the bird, to judge from his portrait of a male and female pair. They stare at you regally from the page, "ear" tufts erect, yellow-rimmed eyes somewhat crossed, feathers subtle as fine-threaded tapestry.

Studying those eyes, you can see where owls get their reputation for wisdom. We guess at the intelligence of strangers by watching their eyes. Here are two strangers, these Audubon owls, who bore holes through you with their stare. You could use either face for a mantra and lose yourself among the concentric rings of feathers. Their eyes proclaim that they know exactly who they are and what they are about. They have seen to the heart of things, while we grope around on the surface. Since the eyes of owls are fixed in their sockets, the bird must swivel its entire head in order to look to the side or rear. You receive no sly glances from an owl, but always a full stare. Its neck is so flexible that it can even gaze directly behind itself, thus keeping watch on the past. When a cartoon owl gazes at me and poses its cartoon question — "Whooo?" — I wish I had as clear an answer as the owl appears to have. Like all wild creatures, owls are serenely and unambiguously themselves. They do not suffer from existential angst. They do not wake themselves up four hours early and fly into town in hopes of hearing the overtones of truth in human chatter.

But are owls wise? The Greeks thought so, identifying them with Athena, goddess of wisdom. In medieval illustrations, owls accompany Merlin and share in his sorcery. In fairy tales they rival the fox for cunning. Children's picture books show them wearing spectacles, mortarboard, and scholar's gown. Soups and other confections made from owls have been credited with curing whooping cough, drunkenness, epilepsy, famine, and insomnia. The Cherokee Indians used to bathe their children's eyes with a broth of owl feathers to keep the kids awake at night. Recipes using owl eggs are reputed to bestow keen eyesight and wisdom. Yet these birds are no smarter, ornithologists assure us, than most others—and other birds don't set a very high standard.

A museum guide in Boston once displayed a drowsy-looking barn owl on his gloved wrist, explaining to those of us assembled there how small the bird's brain actually was. "You'll notice the head of this live specimen appears to be about the size of a grapefruit," he said, "but it's mostly feathers." Lifting his other hand, which cradled a round ball of bone, he added, "the skull, you see, is the size of a lemon. There's only room enough inside for a bird-brain, not enough for Einstein!" We all laughed politely. But I was not convinced. Sure, the skull was small. The lower half was devoted to jaw and most of the upper half to beak and eyeholes. Yet enough neurons could be fitted into the remaining space to enable the barn owl to catch mice in total darkness. They can even snatch bats on the wing, these princes of nighttime stealth. We had to invent sonar for locating submarines, radar for locating airplanes; neither is much use with mice or bats. Barn owls can also see dead— and therefore silent—prey in light one-hundredth as bright as we would need. Like the ability to saw a board square or judge the consistency of bread dough, that might not amount to scholarship, but it is certainly a wisdom of the body. It has worked for some sixty million years. Farmers in Scandinavia, not caring about IQ, often build roosts and special doors near the peaks of their barns for these efficient rodent-killers.

I'm afraid we give owls credit for wisdom chiefly because they look like us. Behold the rounded head, the prominent eyes set in front, a disk of feathers radiating outward from each eye like cheeks, dark slashes across the forehead like eyebrows, the lethal beak protruding only far enough to resemble a nose. Aha, we think, here are feathered, midget versions of ourselves; they must be smart. I suppose the owls, noting the same resemblance, would assume we are expert killers, and they would be right.

You can't judge owls by appearance. Their daytime faces— glimpsed in zoos and museums and books, occasionally on birds I discover at their perches—don't match the nighttime voices Don and I were hearing. The face of a screech owl could belong to Cotton Mather or some other Puritan divine, full of wrath and fiery judgment; yet its whistle falls as forgivingly as rain. Round facial markings make the barred owl look like a pilot in goggles, jet-black eyes fresh from outer space, rotund head filled with unearthly lore. Yet when I hear the "Who cooks for you, who cooks for you all?" cry, I can only think of lovers yodeling beneath balconies or strangling from disappointment. Barn owls, with faces pale and heart-shaped as old valentines, look like sad elves. But their repertoire of cries includes a screech that will set your teeth on edge and stiffen your neck hairs.

One of these elfin-looking barn owls once scared me nearly witless. I was camping with some other boys on a ridge overlooking the Mahoning River in northern Ohio. The sun was down. We'd made a fire, the light splashing on the undersides of sycamore leaves, and while we sat with our backs toward the dark woods, my father was telling us a ghost story. I can't remember the gory details, but the story climaxed with a squadron of ghouls pouncing on some unsuspecting boys as they sat around a campfire. "And the blood-drinking ghosts hooked their claws in the sycamore bark," my father was whispering, "and they spied down on those poor boys, kind of sizing them up. And then the ghosts tilted forward just a little bit on the sycamore limbs, and they—JUMPED!" We jumped. Then *he* jumped, as a scream burst over our heads, so loud it seemed to crack the night open. My heart quit, lungs quit, brain played turtle in my skull. I was doing my best to imitate a rock, so the blood-sucking ghouls would nab the guy next to me. Only when the scream sounded again, farther away, down along the river, did I open my eyes. The other boys looked like prisoners of war, like pale stowaways who had just come blinking onto deck. My father's voice still shook as he explained, "It was just a barn owl. I expect we scared it off its roost."

Don and I heard no barn owls on the night of the winter solstice. Never common in the Middle West, this prowler has become even scarcer in recent years because of pesticide poisoning. Like all predators, owls are near the top of the food chain, and so they gobble toxins in concentrated doses. We're predators, too, feeding on the whole of nature. Although we don't eat owls, we poison them, with chemicals designed to protect our corn from worms, our apples from blemishes. One price of the perfection we expect on our dinner table is the death of night-hunters, the death of singers, the death of birds that impersonate ghosts.

We did hope to rouse a great-horned owl before daylight. Don knew a likely place, a hillside planted to sweetgum and pine, about a mile from the ridge where we had listened to the barred and screech owls. So we hiked the mile on ice-cake feet, scaring up a rabbit and meadowlark along the way. Although the sun was rising, the temperature wasn't. The messages coming from my hands and feet were as shrill as the static on a shortwave radio during electrical storms.

By the time we reached the hillside, both eastern and western horizons were glowing, with rising sun and setting moon. The tips of pines and cedars fretted the skyline like saw-teeth. It was a dangerous hour, this lull between night and day, for any beast small enough to become owl food. Rabbits, squirrels, porcupines, skunks, mice and rats, snakes and all manner of birds—any of these might provide breakfast for the great horned owl. Here is a formidable bird, growing to a height of two feet and a wingspan of nearly five, capable of killing (but not carrying) animals that outweigh it. Pound-for-pound—as announcers say about bantam-weight boxers—this character is fiercer than a mountain lion. Any sort of owl is likely to get mobbed in daytime if smaller birds find it roosting. But great horneds drive crows into a particular frenzy. I once saw fifteen of those braggart birds pestering a great horned owl, diving and jabbering at him until he suddenly lashed out with a taloned foot and set a ragged clump of feathers tumbling. Unenlightened, the fourteen survivors resumed their pestering, and the owl dispatched two more before they left. If you have the bad luck or bad judgment to climb into its nesting tree while the youngsters are about, the great horned will greet you with a wallop and give your head and arms a good raking.

A friend of mine, a gangling man who assembles color televisions for a living and who has lost two wives because of his passion for birding, told me about meeting a great horned owl in a tulip tree. He had climbed the tree before dawn to wait to photograph the sunrise over Lake Monroe. There he perched, on a morning warmer than the one Don and I had picked for owling, his legs straddling a limb and his back against the trunk. Presently, the branch just above his head shook, as if someone had given it a single karate chop. Looking up, he saw the solemn bird. It was scanning the territory, head tilted forward and slowly pivoting, ear-tufts raised like twin antennae, saucer eyes making a murderous survey of the lakeside. When it spied my friend, the owl glanced casually away, and then did a comical double-take. For a moment the two perchers stared eye-to-eye, the man calculating whether there was light enough for a photo, the bird probably calculating whether this gawky beast would do for breakfast. Evidently deciding no, the owl gave a noncommittal hoot and flew away. My friend was lucky this was a hunting rather than a nesting tree, for had he approached the nest, the bird would probably have mauled him.

The great horned owl typically gives a gurgling call of one, two, and then three notes, as if it were learning to count. Don, as you might have predicted, can gurgle convincingly, and did so on that brightening hillside. No answer. He tried again and again, pausing between calls, but the great horned owls had apparently clocked out for the night. I was so ecstatic with sunrise and moonset, so intoxicated with the night-voices we had already heard, that I would have turned entirely to ice before giving up on this last of our neighborhood owls. Don patiently crowed, I rocked on numb legs, the sun opened in the east like the mouth of a furnace. At last a gurgling voice answered from the woods. When I finally distinguished the sound, I realized I had been hearing it for several minutes, but had not recognized it amid the wind noises and the chatter of awakening songbirds. Guessing the direction, I peered intently, hoping to catch a glimpse of the bird. The song unraveled for five minutes or more, and then came to an abrupt end. In the first moment of quiet I saw a huge shadow rise above the treetops, wings large enough for an angel. It flapped once, twice, and then swerved and was gone. I blinked, wondering if I had really seen it, or had only conjured it out of the dawn sky. But Don had seen it, too. Beside me he was murmuring, "Wonderful, wonderful!"

When I try to explain to friends why I rise so early on a December day to go shiver in the owl-haunted woods, I find that those who have to ask my reasons cannot be made to understand them. When you sit near a waterfall, with the mist playing over your skin and the roar shaking your spine, you either realize that this is one of the authentic experiences, one of the touchstones for all living, or you don't. If you don't feel that thrill in the presence of a waterfall, or a stand of virgin timber, or a mountain peak, or a calling owl, then no explanation on earth will make you feel it.

Think of it, carrying on half of a love-duet with a bird. There you stand in your human shape, flightless and nightblind, conversing with a killer that navigates through darkness. Our literature and film are crowded with aliens from outer space, tentacled and bug-eyed, possessed of mysterious powers. But is any of these extraterrestrials stranger than an owl? Until visitors actually arrive from some remote planet, let me talk with owls or whales or even Sufis, and I will find my conversation alien enough. Such talk makes *us* the visitors, the invaders from ultima Thule. The owl cannot speak in our tongue, but we can speak in his. The creation lures us out of ourselves, while the owl remains tucked snugly in the pouch of his instincts. He only speaks to us because we have entered his precinct, gone out to met him, put off for a while our human garments and assumed his.

Chilled and triumphant, Don and I hiked back toward the car, neither of us speaking, as if we had tacitly agreed to keep the owls in our ears as long as possible. Our path took us along the shore of the lake, where cattails and reeds stood rigid in a frozen border of ice. In the deeper parts, waves lapped against the hem of ice with the sound of polite applause. In the shallow bays, where ice glinted like gunmetal from shore to shore, steam rising from the surface turned rose and violet in the early sunlight. It was like the smoke from incense, an offering fit for owl-gods or any other deities. Here and there a whirlwind lifted columns of steam twenty or thirty feet into the air. The spouts trailed across the ice, sinuous as snakes, and then collapsed back into the lower mists.

As the light grew stronger, I noticed that near the lake's edge the black ice was covered with a rough white fur. Bending closer, I could see that the fur was really a miniature forest of ice crystals, each crystal fern-shaped, a tiny glistening lattice. The boughs of this frozen forest were so delicate that they swayed when I breathed on them. The tallest thicket of crystals was no higher than the knuckle on a flattened hand, yet within those pygmy thickets was more intricacy than the eye could follow.

Every weed and twig on the shore was covered with the same fragile wafers of ice. I plucked a stem of foxtail grass and held it between me and the sun. The light shattered on the crystals as I gently twirled the stem; a sliver of ice, thinner than an eyelash, broke the glow from a hydrogen explosion into rainbows. Soon the frost on my foxtail melted. Before my very eyes the ice forest was evaporating from the margins of the lake, a disappearing trick more astonishing than any Saturday-afternoon magic. The mists and spouts over the frozen bays were thinning away. I wanted to seize this moment of ice-beauty, hold it still for my perpetual delight. But it would not linger, anymore than the owls would.

All the way up the hillside, whenever I turned to face the sun, I saw ice crystals needling through the air. Blown or shaken loose from trees, they drifted slantwise like silver seeds, like migrating sparks.

We heard, arising from somewhere near the car, the raucous scolding of blue jays. "They're pestering something," said Don.

"A hawk?" I guessed.

"Or an owl, maybe."

Putting off our weariness, we clumped on numb legs toward the noise. There were six or eight jays swooping and squawking about the hollow crown of a dead beech.

"That's got to be an owl tree," Don whispered.

At our approach, the jays spiraled away, screeching indignantly. Don and I circled the beech in opposite directions, eyes alert for any movement in the tree's rot-blackened top. But we met on the far side of the circle without having spied anything.

"You go beat on the trunk with a stick," Don suggested, "and I'll keep watch."

"How would a great horned owl, say, feel about somebody come knocking on his tree?" I asked.

"He wouldn't like it one bit," Don allowed.

"What's he likely to do about it?"

The creases about Don's eyes deepened. "He's likely to come out fast," he said, "too fast for messing with you or me, and then he's going to disappear in about half a blink."

Still wary, I picked up a thick branch from the ground, approached the hollow beech, and gave the trunk a polite thwack.

"Hit it hard," Don urged.

So I grasped the stick with both hands and slammed the tree a few home-run blows. Between strokes I glanced up, to catch a glimpse of anything that might fly from the rotten peak. Or anything that might come plummeting down on me, talons lowered for the kill. Nothing flew, nothing plummeted.

After a few more thumps, Don called, "It's no use. If the jays had an owl in there, it was gone before we got here."

I dropped the stick, feeling a little ashamed, as if, in the daylight, I had tried to summon up by brute force what only patience and stillness had been able to summon up in the darkness. The hollow beech was a reminder, if I needed a reminder, that owls will not be bullied. You can hoot at them until you're blue in the face, but they will only answer when they please, if they please. Talking with them is like soliciting a word from the gods. There are rituals to be observed, such as choosing the right season of year and time of day. Certain owl-callers, like certain priests, enjoy better luck than others. But after you have made all your preparations, you can only wait. If the owls choose to remain invisible and silent, then, like the gods, silent and invisible they will remain. There are no switches you can throw to make them perform. They fly their own missions, speak their own messages, with no more regard for us than the moon has.

From the car, I turned to look back down at the lake. The mists had now almost all dissolved away into daylight. The whirlwinds of steam had ceased their revels. In the ragged patches of open water near the middle of the lake, a few ducks and geese congregated. The two bald eagles spotted here this season would find the hunting poor. Another week of freezing weather would close the lake entirely, driving water birds south and the eagles after them. But the owls would stay on. Adaptable, stealthy, expert at killing and not overly particular about what they eat, they would endure. By keeping to the night-side, owls avoid their one dangerous enemy—us, lords of the dayside. So long as there are woods, and not too many poisons, there will be owls. So long as there are owls, we can hear night-voices and remain humble.

"I rejoice that there are owls," says Thoreau. "Let them do the idiotic and maniacal hooting for men. It is a sound admirably suited to swamps and woods which no day illustrates, suggesting a vast and undeveloped nature which men have not recognized." Most of us still don't recognize that "undeveloped nature," that nature which dances and unfurls its life without regard to human purposes. We can't hear the earth sing above all the racket our species makes. Listening to owls is a remedy for such deafness.

Analyzing and Discussing the Text

1. Examine the overall structure of Sanders's essay on owls, noting the individual sections and how they fit into the whole of the essay. What overall structural pattern, if any, emerges as he moves from section to section? Examine the shifting tones in the essay. Explain where and why these shifts back and forth between sober wonderment and humor occur.
2. Do you feel a sense of discovery on the part of the narrator? If so, how does Sanders convey this process of exploration?
3. Is the second section of the essay, the very brief summary of evolution, effective? Support your judgment with an analysis of how Sanders uses word choice and sentence structure to make his points.
4. The tenth section of the essay concerns the futile attempt to roust a great horned owl. Is this failure, in the context of this essay, a surprise? A disappointment? Explain your response.
5. By the conclusion of this essay, "listening to owls" has become a symbol for human attitudes toward wilderness. Summarize what is involved in this symbol—what the owl, in Sanders's essay, has come to represent.

Experiencing and Writing About the World

1. Activity in the natural world is frequently, as in this essay, associated with physical hardship. Write a short essay conveying one of your own experiences in the natural world; its focus can be either hardship or perhaps its opposite, the delight and physical pleasure connected with the experience.
2. Like Peter Matthiessen in *The Snow Leopard,* Sanders and his night-time companion in "Listening to Owls" make only limited contact with the animals they seek to encounter. Write an essay on the idea of elusiveness and wild animals. Is this elusiveness part of the mystery that attracts people to such animals in the first place? Does the experience of elusiveness constitute a triumph in its own right? You might wish to support your explanation of this phenomenon with anecdotes of your own adventures in pursuit of wild animals.
3. Write an essay that compares and contrasts the attitudes and the narrative strategies displayed by Sally Carrighar and Scott Russell Sanders in writing about birds.

SUE HUBBELL

From A Country Year

Sue Hubbell (1935–   ) was born in Kalamazoo, Michigan. She attended Swarthmore College and the University of Michigan before graduating from the University of Southern California in 1956. In 1963 Hubbell completed an M.S. at Drexel Institute. She worked as a bookstore manager and a librarian in New Jersey and Rhode Island before moving to a farm in the Ozark Mountains of Missouri and starting a commercial beekeeping business in 1973. She now divides her time between the farm, which provides the setting for the following essay, and Washington, D.C., where her second husband lives. About her beekeeping work, Hubbell says: "My bees cover a thousand miles of land which I do not own in their foraging flights, flying from flower to flower for which I pay no rent, stealing nectar but pollinating plants in return. It is an unruly, benign kind of agriculture, and making a living by it has such a wild, anarchistic, raffish appeal that it unsuits me for any other, except possibly robbing banks." And possibly writing, too, for this "raffish" playfulness surfaces even in Hubbell's essays, which have been collected in two books so far: *A Country Year: Living the Questions* (1986) and *The Book of Bees: And How to Keep Them* (1988).

Hubbell's literary art is very much tied both to the natural world and to the process of self-discovery. As she states, "I am a beekeeper but I am also a writer, and some years ago I sat down at the typewriter to experiment with words, to try to tease out of the amorphous, chaotic and wordless part of myself the reason why I was staying on this hilltop in the Ozarks after my first husband with whom I had started a beekeeping business and I had divorced." Many of Hubbell's characteristic skills as an essayist—her humor; her sharp depictions of the differences between the sexes; her rhetorical control and precise language; and her continual, determined discovery of self—are prominent in "Becoming Feral," which comes from her first book.

[Becoming Feral]

Hoohoo-hoohoo . . . hoohoo-hoohooaww. My neighbor across the river is doing his barred owl imitation in hopes of rousing a turkey from the roost. It is turkey-hunting season, and at dawn the hunters are trying to outwit wild turkeys and I listen to them as I drink my coffee under the oak trees.

133

Hoohoo-hoohoo . . . hoohoo-hoohooawww.

GahgahGAHgah replies an imitation turkey from another direction.
I know that neighbor, too. Yesterday he showed me the hand-held
wooden box with which he made the noise that is supposed to sound
like a turkey cock gobbling. It doesn't. After the turkey cocks are down
from their roosts, the hunters, by imitating hen turkeys, try to call
them close enough to shoot them. The barred owl across the river once
showed me his turkey caller. He held it in his mouth and made a soft
clucking noise with it.

"Now this is the really sexy one," he said, arching one eyebrow,
"*Putput . . . putterputput.*"

It is past dawn now, and I imagine both men are exasperated. I have
not heard one real turkey yet this morning. The hunting season is set by
the calendar but the turkeys breed by the weather, and the spring has
been so wet and cold that their mating has been delayed this year. In the
last few mornings I have started hearing turkeys gobbling occasionally,
and it will be another week or two before a wise and wary turkey cock
could be fooled by a man with a caller.

There are other birds out there this morning. The indigo buntings,
who will be the first birds to sing in the dawn later on, have not yet returned to the Ozarks, but I can hear cardinals and Carolina chickadees.
They wintered here, but today their songs are of springtime. There are
chipping sparrows above me in the oak trees and field sparrows nearby.
There are warblers, too; some of their songs are familiar, and others,
those of the migrators, are not. I hear one of the most beautiful of bird-
songs, that of the white-throated sparrow. He is supposed to sing "Old
Sam Peabody, Peabody, Peabody." This is the cadence, to be sure, but
it gives no hint of the lyrical clarity and sweetness of the descending
notes of his song.

I slept outdoors last night because I could not bear to go in. The
cabin, which only last winter seemed cozy and inviting, has begun to
seem stuffy and limiting, so I spread a piece of plastic on the ground
to keep off the damp, put my sleeping bag on it and dropped off to
sleep watching the stars. Tazzie likes to be near me, and with me on the
ground she could press right up to my back. But Andy is a conservative
dog who worries a lot, and he thought it was unsound to sleep outside
where there might be snakes and beetles. He whined uneasily as I
settled in, and once during the night he woke me up, nuzzling me and
whimpering, begging to be allowed to go inside to his rug. I think he
may be more domesticated than I am. I wonder if I am becoming feral.
Wild things and wild places pull me more strongly than they did a few
years ago, and domesticity, dusting and cookery interest me not at all.

Sometimes I wonder where we older women fit into the social
scheme of things once nest building has lost its charm. A generation
ago Margaret Mead, who had a good enough personal answer to this

question, wondered the same thing, and pointed out that in other times and other cultures we have had a role.

There are so many of us that it is tempting to think of us as a class. We are past our reproductive years. Men don't want us; they prefer younger women. It makes good biological sense for males to be attracted to females who are at an earlier point in their breeding years and who still want to build nests, and if that leaves us no longer able to lose ourselves in the pleasures and closeness of pairing, well, we have gained our Selves. We have another valuable thing, too. We have Time, or at least the awareness of it. We have lived long enough and seen enough to understand in a more than intellectual way that we will die, and so we have learned to live as though we are mortal, making our decisions with care and thought because we will not be able to make them again. Time for us will have an end; it is precious, and we have learned its value.

Yes, there are many of us, but we are all so different that I am uncomfortable with a sociobiological analysis, and I suspect that, as with Margaret Mead, the solution is a personal and individual one. Because our culture has assigned us no real role, we can make up our own. It is a good time to be a grown-up woman with individuality, strength and crotchets. We are wonderfully free. We live long. Our children are the independent adults we helped them to become, and though they may still want our love they do not need our care. Social rules are so flexible today that nothing we do is shocking. There are no political barriers to us anymore. Provided we stay healthy and can support ourselves, we can do anything, have anything and spend our talents any way that we please.

Hoohoo-hoohoo . . . hoohoo-hooaww.

The sun is up now, and it is too late for a barred owl. I know that man across the river, and I know he must be getting cross. He is probably sitting on a damp log, his feet and legs cold and cramped from keeping still. I also know the other hunter, the one with the wooden turkey caller. This week what both men want is a dead turkey.

I want a turkey too, but I want mine alive, and in a week I'll have my wish, hearing them gobbling at dawn. I want more, however. I want indigo buntings singing their couplets when I wake in the morning. I want to read *Joseph and His Brothers* again. I want oak leaves and dogwood blossoms and fireflies. I want to know how the land lies up Coon Hollow. I want Asher to find out what happens to moth-ear mites in the winter. I want to show Liddy and Brian the big rocks down in the creek hollow. I want to know much more about grand-daddy-longlegs. I want to write a novel. I want to go swimming naked in the hot sun down at the river.

That is why I have stopped sleeping inside. A house is too small, too confining. I want the whole world, and the stars too.

Analyzing and Discussing the Text

1. What are the implications of the scene sketched for us in the first paragraph of the essay? How does the humor of the two human neighbors trading bird calls with each other—rather than real birds—fit Hubbell's purpose? How do the birds in the sixth paragraph develop this idea?
2. What strategic point is served by the fourth paragraph's careful distinction between the calendar time used by the hunters and the actual progress of the seasons?
3. Paragraph 7 of this essay begins with a ringing declarative tone. Is that sense of a credo repeated elsewhere in the essay? Is it effective here? Why or why not?
4. The fourth and fifth paragraphs from the end of the essay set up a very explicit, precise sociological analysis and then quickly proceed to reject it. What effect does this kind of argument have on the reader?
5. What effect does the repetition of "I want" in the next-to-last paragraph achieve? What would change if these sentences appeared earlier in the essay?

Experiencing and Writing About the World

1. Hubbell's decision to sleep outdoors is her way of letting "wild things" and "wild places" exert their pull on her. If you were to enact your own version of "becoming feral," what actions would it entail? Would it (wildness) be a temporary or permanent state? Either enact or imagine enacting such a process, then describe your experiences in an essay called "Becoming Feral."
2. Write a long paragraph of "I want . . . " sentences like those in Hubbell's paragraph. Is it difficult to be as concrete and vivid as she is?
3. Develop a short essay from the point of view of one of Hubbell's male neighbors. Include his view of her activities and values, but do so in the humorous, indirect way that she employs here.
4. Write a persuasive essay arguing *against* the feral values expressed in this selection from *A Country Year*.
5. Write a comparative essay in which you examine the important connections and distinctions between Hubbell's essay and Annie Dillard's "Living Like Weasels," which expresses a very similar attraction to wildness.

ALICE WALKER

Am I Blue?

Alice Walker (1944–   ), the eighth child in a black sharecropping family, was born in Eatonton, Georgia. Along with her other childhood memories, she can still recall with pleasure the Georgia countryside where she "fished and swam and walked through fields of black-eyed Susans." She won a scholarship to Spelman College in Atlanta, then she transferred to Sarah Lawrence College outside of New York City in 1964. It was there that she started to write, and her first book of poems (called *Once*) was accepted for publication in 1965. In that year she also graduated from Sarah Lawrence and returned to Georgia to spend time registering black voters. Walker worked for the New York Welfare Department until 1967, when she won writing fellowships from the Merrill Foundation and the MacDowell Colony. That same year, Walker married Mel Leventhal, a civil rights lawyer, and they moved to Jackson, Mississippi, where he practiced civil rights law and Walker taught at Jackson State College and wrote. They moved to Brooklyn, New York, in 1973. During the early 1970s, Walker published her first novel, *The Third Life of Grange Copeland* (1970), a short story collection called *In Love and Trouble: Stories of Black Women* (1973), and another collection of poems, *Revolutionary Petunias & Other Poems* (1973). In 1976, Walker and Leventhal were divorced, and she published *Meridian*, a novel about the Civil Rights Movement that began to win a wider audience for her work. Walker moved to northern California in 1979; in this landscape, which reminded her of her childhood home, she began to write another novel. *The Color Purple* has become her best-known work, winning both the Pulitzer Prize and the American Book Award for fiction in 1983. Walker's most recent novel is *Possessing the Secret of Joy* (1992).

Walker also excels at the art of the essay, as her two collections, *In Search of Our Mothers' Gardens: Womanist Prose* (1983) and *Living by the Word* (1988), make clear. Much of her fiction has concentrated on feminist and black concerns, and she has been rightly viewed as an important spokesperson for both groups. As the following essay from *Living by the Word* demonstrates, Walker has also begun to express concern about the rights of nature, especially the rights of animals. In a piece called "The Universe Responds" from the same collection, she says that "Am I Blue?" is "about how humans treat horses and other animals, how hard it is for us to see them as the suffering, fully conscious, enslaved beings they are. It also marked the beginning of my effort to become non-meat-eating (fairly successful)." Thus in this essay we see how Walker's evolving sense of kinship with animals influences not only her beliefs, but also her outward behavior.

"Ain't these tears in these
eyes tellin' you?"*

For about three years my companion and I rented a small house in the country that stood on the edge of a large meadow that appeared to run from the end of our deck straight into the mountains. The mountains, however, were quite far away, and between us and them there was, in fact, a town. It was one of the many pleasant aspects of the house that you never really were aware of this.

It was a house of many windows, low, wide, nearly floor to ceiling in the living room, which faced the meadow, and it was from one of these that I first saw our closest neighbor, a large white horse, cropping grass, flipping its mane, and ambling about—not over the entire meadow, which stretched well out of sight of the house, but over the five or so fenced-in acres that were next to the twenty-odd that we had rented. I soon learned that the horse, whose name was Blue, belonged to a man who lived in another town, but was boarded by our neighbors next door. Occasionally, one of the children, usually a stocky teen-ager, but sometimes a much younger girl or boy, could be seen riding Blue. They would appear in the meadow, climb up on his back, ride furiously for ten or fifteen minutes, then get off, slap Blue on the flanks, and not be seen again for a month or more.

There were many apple trees in our yard, and one by the fence that Blue could almost reach. We were soon in the habit of feeding him apples, which he relished, especially because by the middle of summer the meadow grasses—so green and succulent since January—had dried out from lack of rain, and Blue stumbled about munching the dried stalks half-heartedly. Sometimes he would stand very still just by the apple tree, and when one of us came out he would whinny, snort loudly, or stamp the ground. This meant, of course: I want an apple.

It was quite wonderful to pick a few apples, or collect those that had fallen to the ground overnight, and patiently hold them, one by one, up to his large, toothy mouth. I remained as thrilled as a child by his flexible dark lips, huge, cubelike teeth that crunched the apples, core and all, with such finality, and his high, broad-breasted *enormity*; beside which, I felt small indeed. When I was a child, I used to ride horses, and was especially friendly with one named Nan until the day I was riding and my brother deliberately spooked her and I was thrown,

*©1929 Warner Bros., Inc. (renewed). By Grant Clarke and Harry Akst.

head first, against the trunk of a tree. When I came to, I was in bed and my mother was bending worriedly over me; we silently agreed that perhaps horseback riding was not the safest sport for me. Since then I have walked, and prefer walking to horseback riding—but I had forgotten the depth of feeling one could see in horses' eyes.

I was therefore unprepared for the expression in Blue's. Blue was lonely. Blue was horribly lonely and bored. I was not shocked that this should be the case; five acres to tramp by yourself, endlessly, even in the most beautiful of meadows—and his was—cannot provide many interesting events, and once rainy season turned to dry that was about it. No, I was shocked that I had forgotten that human animals and nonhuman animals can communicate quite well; if we are brought up around animals as children we take this for granted. By the time we are adults we no longer remember. However, the animals have not changed. They are in fact *completed* creations (at least they seem to be, so much more than we) who are not likely *to* change; it is their nature to express themselves. What else are they going to express? And they do. And, generally speaking, they are ignored.

After giving Blue the apples, I would wander back to the house, aware that he was observing me. Were more apples not forthcoming then? Was that to be his sole entertainment for the day? My partner's small son had decided he wanted to learn how to piece a quilt; we worked in silence on our respective squares as I thought. . . .

Well, about slavery: about white children, who were raised by black people, who knew their first all-accepting love from black women, and then, when they were twelve or so, were told they must "forget" the deep levels of communication between themselves and "mammy" that they knew. Later they would be able to relate quite calmly, "My old mammy was sold to another good family." "My old mammy was ____ ____." Fill in the blank. Many more years later a white woman would say: "I can't understand these Negroes, these blacks. What do they want? They're so different from us."

And about the Indians, considered to be "like animals" by the "settlers" (a very benign euphemism for what they actually were), who did not understand their description as a compliment.

And about the thousands of American men who marry Japanese, Korean, Filipina, and other non-English-speaking women and of how happy they report they are, "*blissfully*," until their brides learn to speak English, at which point the marriages tend to fall apart. What then did the men see, when they looked into the eyes of the women they married, before they could speak English? Apparently only their own reflections.

I thought of society's impatience with the young. "Why are they playing the music so loud?" Perhaps the children have listened to much of the music of oppressed people their parents danced to before they were born, with its passionate but soft cries for acceptance and love, and they have wondered why their parents failed to hear.

I do not know how long Blue had inhabited his five beautiful, boring acres before we moved into our house; a year after we had arrived—and had also traveled to other valleys, other cities, other worlds—he was still there.

But then, in our second year at the house, something happened in Blue's life. One morning, looking out the window at the fog that lay like a ribbon over the meadow, I saw another horse, a brown one, at the other end of Blue's field. Blue appeared to be afraid of it, and for several days made no attempt to go near. We went away for a week. When we returned, Blue had decided to make friends and the two horses ambled or galloped along together, and Blue did not come nearly as often to the fence underneath the apple tree.

When he did, bringing his new friend with him, there was a different look in his eyes. A look of independence, of self-possession, of inalienable *horse*ness. His friend eventually became pregnant. For months and months there was, it seemed to me, a mutual feeling between me and the horses of justice, of peace. I fed apples to them both. The look in Blue's eyes was one of unabashed "this is *it*ness."

It did not, however, last forever. One day, after a visit to the city, I went out to give Blue some apples. He stood waiting, or so I thought, though not beneath the tree. When I shook the tree and jumped back from the shower of apples, he made no move. I carried some over to him. He managed to half-crunch one. The rest he let fall to the ground. I dreaded looking into his eyes—because I had of course noticed that Brown, his partner, had gone—but I did look. If I had been born into slavery, and my partner had been sold or killed, my eyes would have looked like that. The children next door explained that Blue's partner had been "put with him" (the same expression that old people used, I had noticed, when speaking of an ancestor during slavery who had been impregnated by her owner) so that they could mate and she conceive. Since that was accomplished, she had been taken back by her owner, who lived somewhere else.

Will she be back? I asked.

They didn't know.

Blue was like a crazed person. Blue *was*, to me, a crazed person. He galloped furiously, as if he were being ridden, around and around his five beautiful acres. He whinnied until he couldn't. He tore at the ground with his hooves. He butted himself against his single shade tree. He looked always and always toward the road down which his partner had gone. And then, occasionally, when he came up for apples, or I took apples to him, he looked at me. It was a look so piercing, so full of grief, a look so *human*, I almost laughed (I felt too sad to cry) to think there are people who do not know that animals suffer. People like me who have forgotten, and daily forget, all that animals try to tell us.

"Everything you do to us will happen to you; we are your teachers, as you are ours. We are one lesson" is essentially it, I think. There are those who never once have even considered animals' rights: those who have been taught that animals actually want to be used and abused by us, as small children "love" to be frightened, or women "love" to be mutilated and raped. . . . They are the great-grandchildren of those who honestly thought, because someone taught them this: "Women can't think," and "niggers can't faint." But most disturbing of all, in Blue's large brown eyes was a new look, more painful than the look of despair: the look of disgust with human beings, with life; the look of hatred. And it was odd what the look of hatred did. It gave him, for the first time, the look of a beast. And what that meant was that he had put up a barrier within to protect himself from further violence; all the apples in the world wouldn't change that fact.

And so Blue remained, a beautiful part of our landscape, very peaceful to look at from the window, white against the grass. Once a friend came to visit and said, looking out on the soothing view: "And it *would* have to be a *white* horse; the very image of freedom." And I thought, yes, the animals are forced to become for us merely "images" of what they once so beautifully expressed. And we are used to drinking milk from containers showing "contented" cows, whose real lives we want to hear nothing about, eating eggs and drumsticks from "happy" hens, and munching hamburgers advertised by bulls of integrity who seem to command their fate.

As we talked of freedom and justice one day for all, we sat down to steaks. I am eating misery, I thought, as I took the first bite. And spit it out.

Analyzing and Discussing the Text

1. From her first reference to Blue as "our closest neighbor," Walker carefully chooses her words to establish a community that includes both "human animals and nonhuman animals." Look for other language in the essay that accomplishes this same purpose.
2. Why do you think Walker takes her title and her epigraph (introductory quotation) from an old blues song?
3. The extended commentary on slavery and oppression in paragraphs 7–10 occurs almost at the exact center of the essay. Is it essential to the essay's meaning? Why? Would it have worked as well elsewhere? How would the effect of the essay change if this commentary were omitted?

4. Explain how this essay uses comparison and contrast to develop a level of meaning beyond the story of the author's relationship with one particular horse.
5. Explain what Walker means when she says, "We are one lesson."
6. Does this essay conclude effectively? Explain why Walker ends her piece as she does and how this conclusion affects you.

Experiencing and Writing About the World

1. Select a single animal that was at one time an important part of your life and write a personal essay describing how your relationship to it was important to you. What attitudes determined your relationship with this animal? With the current attention focused on the ethics of human–animal relationships, do you feel that your attitudes are changing?
2. Walker's essay on Blue raises interesting larger questions about our relationship to animals, about the whole issue of the rights of animals. Choose a related topic—human use of animals as pets or as attractions in zoos—as the subject for an expository essay in which you first describe and then argue persuasively for or against society's current relationship with animals.
3. Find a copy of Walker's book *Living by the Word* and write an analytical essay on her attitude toward animals as developed throughout the essays included in the collection.
4. Several writers whose work appears in this anthology, including Stephen Harrigan and Sally Carrighar, display an occasional inclination to attribute humanlike consciousness to nonhuman animals. Compare Walker's anthropomorphic tendency with theirs and/or other examples among the essays in this book, analyzing and assessing this approach to animals as both a literary technique and a philosophical position.

Suggestions for Further Reading

Bass, Rick. *The Deer Pasture*. 1985. New York: Norton, 1989.
Bedichek, Roy. *Adventures with a Texas Naturalist*. Austin: U of Texas P, 1947.
Berger, Bruce. *The Telling Distance: Conversations with the American Desert*. 1990. New York: Doubleday, 1991.

Burroughs, Franklin. "A Snapping Turtle in June." *Georgia Review* 42.3 (1988): 511–30.

Burroughs, John. *Wake-Robin. The Writings of John Burroughs.* Vol. I. 1871. Boston: Houghton, 1913.

Byrd, William. "History of the Dividing Line." *The Prose Works of William Byrd of Westover.* 1841. Ed. Louis B. Wright. Cambridge: Harvard UP, 1966.

Dobie, J. Frank. *The Voice of the Coyote.* 1947. Lincoln: U of Nebraska P, 1949.

Douglas, William O. *My Wilderness: East to Katahdin.* 1961. New York: Pyramid, 1968.

Eiseley, Loren. *The Immense Journey.* New York: Random, 1957.

Ellis, Richard. *Men and Whales.* New York: Knopf, 1991.

Hansard, Peter, and Burton Silver. *What Bird Did That? A Driver's Guide to Some Common Birds of North America.* Berkeley, CA: Ten Speed, 1991.

Heinrich, Bernd. *Raven in Winter.* New York: Random, 1989.

Knowler, Donald. *The Falconer of Central Park.* Princeton: Karz-Cohl, 1984.

Kumin, Maxine. *In Deep: Country Essays.* Boston: Beacon, 1988.

Lopez, Barry. *Of Wolves and Men.* New York: Scribner's, 1978.

McNamee, Thomas. *The Grizzly Bear.* New York: Knopf, 1984.

Mowat, Farley. *Never Cry Wolf.* New York: Dell, 1963.

Palmer, Thomas. *Landscape with Reptile: Rattlesnakes in an Urban World.* Boston: Ticknor, 1992.

Peacock, Doug. *The Grizzly Years: Encounters with the Wilderness.* New York: Henry Holt, 1990.

Schaller, George. "The Snow Leopard." *Stones of Silence: Journeys in the Himalaya.* New York: Viking, 1980.

Wallace, David Rains. *Bulow Hammock: Mind in a Forest.* San Francisco: Sierra Club, 1988.

©Michal Heron, 1982/Woodfin Camp and Associates

CHAPTER FOUR

Weather and Seasons

In rural New Hampshire, Donald Hall writes in *Seasons at Eagle Pond* (1991), "we know ourselves by Winter—in snow, in cold, in darkness." However, this shaping of lives by the seasons seems less direct and noticeable for most city-bound Americans. We are as a society much closer to the kind of life Morris Longstreth described in *Knowing the Weather* (1943): "Weather was once a matter of life and death. The sailor, the hunter, and the herdsman had to read the skies aright or perish. Flood, drought, hurricane, and blizzard were not simply things that happened to somebody else's bank account. They were personal and deadly. Then came cities and steam heat. . . . An urban generation lost its feeling for weather and the old racial wisdom of the wind and the rain." In the fifty years following this observation, our assumption that we can separate ourselves from the effects of weather and the seasons has only increased. Except for major catastrophes such as blizzards, earthquakes, and droughts, we try not to think about weather as a major influence on our lives. Yet for all of our air conditioning and our wishful thinking about climate control, we receive continual reminders that people are, after all, part of the world of weather and seasons, and furthermore, that we ignore this membership and its reciprocal effects at our own peril. Acid rain, air pollution, and the depleted ozone layer tell us that the atmosphere is something more real than a satellite image on the nightly news, that it contains us and structures our existence just as we affect it.

The essayists in this chapter all acknowledge, rather than disregard, the correspondence between the patterns of weather and seasons and our human lives. May Sarton sees spring in New Hampshire in humorous—sometimes wildly humorous—terms, as she does battle with the forces that accompany the change in seasons. Joan Didion's vision of the Santa Ana wind's effect on the human inhabitants of Los Angeles is less benign and more deterministic; for her, this particular atmospheric phenomenon drives human behavior directly and demonically. In his essay, John Hay compares the seasonal movement of migratory birds with his own seasonal shifts in residence. Gretel Ehrlich's autumn experiences on a Wyoming ranch are precisely opposed to the modern changes described by Longstreth; life on the western range makes her acutely aware of both the threat of death and the generative pull of sexual desire. Chet Raymo, in his essay on the excesses of color, reads the sky from an aesthetic and seasonal perspective, while Annie Dillard recalls a down-to-earth and profoundly satisfying winter incident from her childhood. Dillard's chase narrative, which is set outdoors in snow-covered Pittsburgh, makes the important point that isolation from the forces of weather need not be the result of modern urban life.

MAY SARTON

Mud Season

May Sarton (1912–   ) was born in Belgium, the daughter of Mabel Elwes Sarton, an Englishwoman who was a talented artist and a devoted gardener, and George Sarton, a distinguished historian of science. When World War I drove the Sarton family out of Belgium in 1916, they settled in Cambridge, Massachusetts, where May Sarton became a naturalized U.S. citizen in 1924. Sarton's only formal education was in elementary and secondary schools there and in a year of study at the Institut Belge de Culture Française. She left for New York immediately after her graduation from high school in 1929 and began work as an apprentice theatre director at Eva Le Gallienne's Civic Repertory Theatre. In the 1930s, Sarton worked in the theatre in New York and in Hartford, Connecticut, where she founded the Associated Actors Theatre. During these years, Sarton also began her publishing career as a poet and fiction writer with two collections of poetry, *Encounter in April* (1937) and *Inner Landscape* (1939), and her first novel, *The Single Hound* (1938). These books launched her as a prolific writer of novels, poetry, children's books, and personal essays. During subsequent decades, Sarton became a widely read writer and a teacher of writing. She was the Briggs–Copeland Instructor in English composition at Harvard University between 1949 and 1952, and she taught creative writing at Wellesley College from 1960 to 1964. Sarton lectured at the Bread Loaf Writers' Conference in Middlebury, Vermont, from 1951 to 1954, and in 1954 she was awarded a Guggenheim Fellowship. Critics consider her most important novels to be *Faithful Are the Wounds* (1955) and *Mrs. Stevens Hears the Mermaids Singing* (1965). A collection selected from her many volumes of poetry was published as *The Selected Poems of May Sarton* (1978).

Sarton's publication of literary nonfiction began with *The Fur Person* (1957), a book about a pet tomcat that demonstrates her long-time fascination with and love for animals. In 1958, Sarton began renovation of an old farmhouse in rural Nelson, New Hampshire, a project that led to the publication of two memoirs, *Plant Dreaming Deep* (1968), the book in which "Mud Season" appears, and *Journal of a Solitude* (1973). Her later move to Wild Knoll, a house on the coast of Maine, also led to two books, *The House by the Sea* (1977) and *Recovering* (1980), a book that describes her recovery from a mastectomy. Sarton has characterized her own work as unsentimental and humorous, two qualities that are strongly present in the following essay about the mud, black flies, and destructive woodchucks she confronted during her first New Hampshire spring.

In most places spring begins in March, but in this ornery part of the country April finds us still bogged down in limbo. When crocuses are out in Cambridge, we may still have a blizzard. Extreme weather brings a certain exhilaration with it; what is harder to bear is the long wait in a soggy gray world. The rocks stand up, raw and desolate in the colorless meadow; the trees look thin and exhausted, and the longer days only accentuate the sour wilderness feel of it all, a meager wilderness, all stains and patches and broken stone walls. I have learned that April is a good time to go out lecturing, to go toward spring long before it reaches Nelson, when hepaticas are lifting their delicate blue and white heads in Indiana, and the Judas tree and white dogwood are in flower in Kentucky. Almost anywhere is better than here in "mud season." But that first year, full of expectation, exhilarated by having survived the winter, I did not know the ordeals to come.

In February I had pored, enchanted, over the seed catalogues and their glossy photographs, dreaming the still nonexistent garden. My idea was to combine vegetables and picking flowers in a plot just behind the house. Sitting at the kitchen table in a snowstorm I had joyously imagined Chinese peas (eaten pod and all), zucchini, cucumber, every kind of lettuce. I went wild on flowers—cosmos, zinnia, marigolds, elegant salpiglossis, annual phlox, delphinium, bachelor's-buttons—with a total disregard of how all this was to be fitted into one small patch. After all, one has to be allowed some extravagance in February. By April all those little packages of hope were stowed away in a big tin breadbox, in case a mouse decided on nasturtium (delicious!) as an aperitif before going on to candle ends, soap, and any crumbs I might have left lying about.

By April I wandered about outside, peering under the spruce and hemlock boughs I had strewn over the flower beds to see whether anything was coming up. Would the peonies, the phlox, have survived the winter? So far there was no sign.

Then one evening I heard a slight, shrill, continuous singing, a little like distant sleigh bells. And I suddenly remembered what Tink had said when we sat on a pile of lumber eating lunch that summer day—"The peepers! Wait till you hear them when it seems as if spring would never come!" The long wait was coming to an end. The brooks, unfrozen at last, rich in melted snow, ran impetuously over and around boulders, making pools of brown foam wherever they were impeded,

and tiny waterfalls and whirlpools. And I understood better than before Gerard Manley Hopkins's fascination with the patterns of moving
water as, remembering the exquisite drawings in his Notebooks, I myself bent to observe closely the rich flow of spirals and swirls, curling
themselves around a rock. What a thrill when the first skunk cabbage
came out, thrusting its baroque green through moldy old leaves! I was
starved for color as well as for motion in the static world, and that first
bright green of the skunk cabbage was a tonic. But the greatest change
was going on in the air overhead: skies were a gentler blue; soft white
clouds piled up into quick rainfall, and the sunsets lost their winter brilliance as bright gold changed to pale gold, crimson to pink, against a
hyacinthine sky. Best of all, one could smell earth again, after the long
frozen months when only woodsmoke sweetened the icy air. A pair
of phoebes appeared, flicking their tails on the telephone wires; they
were building a nest under the porch eaves, as they have every year
since. A bunch of snowdrops pushed up through the sodden grass by
the front step.

It was the beginning all right, but there was still a long way to go.
This brief explosion was followed by weeks when nothing happened.
It rained. I learned what mud season means when the car got stuck
again and again, making deep ruts in the driveway. The grass was still
gray. Since I could not reach the dump on wheels, I had to haul the
ash cans inch by inch up a steep incline slithery with mud. It snowed
again. It froze again. (At least once each spring, I see the daffodils and
crocuses completely covered by snow after they have flowered.) I was
to learn that the snow is kind—"poor man's fertilizer," they call it—but
that frost is the killer. And we have had frost in Nelson at one time or
another in every month except July. So through all of April and through
most of May we are still suspended.

The birds come before the leaves and flowers—warblers on their
way north, the first fat robins to stay, running and stopping, running
and stopping, to pull a worm with their knowing beaks. Swallows come
back, to fly restlessly in and out of the broken windowpane I have left
as a swallow door in the barn. And one morning that first spring I
looked out of the window and caught sight of a bluebird sitting on a
granite post just a few feet away!

I do not really mind the long wait, but I do mind the fact that when
spring finally comes, it comes with such a rush that one cannot keep
track of all that is happening. This swift change from not enough to too
much is disturbing. Where to look? What to do? Where to begin? Who
can keep up with a spring that comes and goes, it would seem, in the
space of a clap of thunder? that takes you by the throat, as it were? The
maples, which had looked so old and forlorn all winter, were suddenly
covered with small green umbrella-flowers. Shall I ever manage to be
present in the hour they open? Always they have just arrived while my
back was turned.

At last, when I tossed the hemlock branches onto a big pile for burning, I saw that everything I had planted was alive. The phlox was already there in green fleshed-out humps. Tulips and daffodils had pierced through, and the small red spears of the peonies were above ground. I went out on a warm day to measure off the picking garden to prepare for seed-planting, stopping to look at the apple tree by the barn, covered with bright pink buds, each branch as rich and stiff as coral. The sun was deliciously warm on my back; I worked so hard that I did not realize what was happening. It was only when I went in that I discovered large swollen red bites all over my neck, wrists, and ankles. Black flies!

The truth is that every season in the country has its special ordeals, but what made the first year both exhilarating and difficult was that I came on them unprepared. I had heard of black flies, of course, and that a seasoned tourist keeps away from New Hampshire in May and June, when they are at their worst. Now I understood why.

Whenever I went out, at whatever time of day, a black cloud hovered over my head, a cloud of flies that settled, one by one, in every exposed place, crept under my glasses to bite my eyelids, crept into my ears, under the cuffs of my shirt, and up the legs of my jeans. Years later I discovered a remedy only a little less disgusting than the bites. It is thick, brown, and smells of tar, and if I cover my face, neck, hands, and legs with this "Woodsman's Dope," I can work more or less in peace. But brief snatches of work out of doors, when the spirit moves, are out of the question, since I have to undress and have a bath after each expedition.

The black flies could be endured—I had not reckoned with the woodchucks! Visually speaking, a woodchuck, especially a baby woodchuck, is an endearing animal; round as a teddy bear, it sits up and hugs itself like a squirrel. My first emotion when I saw a mother with two babies playing in front of the barn was joyful surprise. The babies rolled over on their backs; the mother nibbled grass; it all seemed like a spring scherzo. But when I looked out the kitchen window the next morning and saw that all the new phlox had been eaten back to the root, the dear little creatures became deadly enemies.

Until then I thought I had learned that if I didn't panic I could handle any crisis that came up. This was different. I dashed out a hundred times a day, waving my arms and shouting, knowing perfectly well that the marauders would return as soon as my back was turned—and of course the stone wall was a perfect apartment house with many safe entrances and exits for them. I lay awake at night, wondering whether they were out or in. I was up at dawn.

But the phlox grew back, and by then there was a lot of green stuff in the woods; surely the animals would find something as good to eat elsewhere. I could not accept that my garden might be destroyed without ever having existed! That seemed to me preposterous, unfair, not to be borne.

Then the day came when I looked out and saw that the phlox had been eaten down a second time! I burst into tears of woe and frustration, and on an impulse called the Newt Tolmans. Janet recognized a note of desperation and assured me that Newt would be over with his gun within the hour.

I don't suppose I have ever seen a more welcome arrival than Newt in his jeep. He came up the porch steps with a gun in his hand and a twinkle in his eye.

"Here I am," he said. "What's up?"

I explained my ridiculous plight, of trying to make a garden against what appeared to be insuperable odds, and—God bless him—he didn't laugh. He said quite vehemently, "Why didn't you call for help, woman? That's what neighbors are for!"

We spent an hour drinking martinis and talking while we stood at the kitchen counter and watched and waited. Sure enough, a family of woodchucks appeared again, and Newt crept to the door like an Indian and got in a couple of shots, just too late to catch the wary and speedy creatures. How could I ever have dreamed that I would *want* an animal killed? But, after all, the phlox too was a live thing and had proved its resilience; the woodchuck had plenty to eat in the woods. Must they have caviar? Newt did kill one before he left, for Newt is a very good shot.

This visit did not dispose of the problem but it gave me new courage; in time of need help would be forthcoming. And from more than one direction. A few mornings later I heard secretive footsteps go by my bedroom window, and looked out, startled, to see Ted Murdough out in the field with his gun. He came by every morning for a week on his way to work, and after that the woodchuck got the message . . . or perhaps they found something in the woods that they liked better than delicate perennials.

The indomitable phlox came up a third time, and even flowered later on in the summer. So I have learned, through the years, to be more philosophical. I have also invested in a rifle. It has to be reloaded after every shot, so it is not a very effective weapon, but it makes a loud bang, and that is a comfort. It is more dignified to go out with a rifle than to rush out waving one's arms and screaming. I do not shoot to kill or wound but to scare, and repeated scaring does have an effect, so that rifle has added a good deal to my composure and self-reliance.

Self-reliance? Yes, but that first spring I had to learn dependency too. By crying for help and seeing help come from several directions, I began to learn what the village is all about: on the one hand, respect for privacy, and on the other, awareness of each other's needs. So, however solitary some of us may look to an outsider, we are in truth part of an invisible web and supported by its presence.

Help does materialize in a most astonishing way, as if some signal flashed off into space at a moment of need. Once one of my cats had been chased to the very top of a thin, tall locust. I had called myself hoarse, had pleaded in vain, had gone in to let her think things over, had come back hopefully only to be met by terrified mews but not the slightest attempt to come down. Just then a car stopped on the road. When a stranger got out and walked across the lawn toward me, I supposed that he wanted to ask directions. But he had seen what was happening and had taken the trouble to stop in order to offer his help.

"The darned cat won't come down," I said crossly. For what could *he* do about it?

"I used to be a fireman," he said, stripped off his coat, shinnied up thirty feet or more, caught the cat, and brought her down in a trice.

I stammered my thanks, still too much of a city person not to be wholly amazed by such unexpected kindness.

I can count on help in moments of real desperation, but for three years I had to rely on casual encounters or lucky chance to find a man to do this job or that which I could not manage alone. Most of the men around the village work on the roads, grading and cutting brush in summer, plowing in winter. They have their hands full just keeping us rolling. But I had not come to the country only to prove to myself that I could master various problems to do with cutting grass or pruning trees or making a garden where none had been before. I had come to write. There were times when I felt overwhelmed by these practical matters. But I always came back to the reality—that the problems or ordeals connected with life in the country are enriching in some way even when they seem like interruptions and bring frustration rather than fruition in their wake. Problems to do with climate, with snow or drought or high wind, problems to do with growing things, bring one right down to the marrow. They quickly become metaphor in the mind; they are the stuff of poetry. And there is never loss, the deadly dull loss that life in the city almost always means. The loss of time spent battling one's way home in an airless subway cannot be compared, for example, with the loss of time spent in getting a cat down out of a tree! And chasing a woodchuck is, on the whole, more fun than chasing a taxi.

But there were times that first spring—and have been since—when I asked myself whether I had undertaken more than I could manage. A place like this is more like a novel than a poem—complex, never quite "finished," operated on extended time, a balancing of many themes against each other. Work on it cannot be finished in one quick push. It must be resumed spring after spring, when black flies and wood-chucks come back. It cannot be neglected for long—or you find yourself back where you started. A place like this must be fashioned and re-fashioned inch by inch. You wait and see. You wait and hope. You wait and work.

What I needed, of course, was someone who would stay at my side, who would bring with him many kinds of lore that I do not possess, who would not panic as I sometimes do, a steady worker through all the seasons.

Analyzing and Discussing the Text

1. What tone does Sarton use to introduce her subject?
2. How does she build her description of the first signs of spring in paragraph 4? The next paragraph begins with the sentence, "It was the beginning all right, but there was still a long way to go." What is the effect of this sentence? How is it relevant to one of the main points Sarton tries to make about spring in New Hampshire?
3. In the final eight paragraphs of the essay, the writer's attention shifts to the idea of self-reliance. How does this issue tie in with the preceding discussion?
4. Explain what Sarton means when she says that the problems connected with life in the country are "the stuff of poetry."

Experiencing and Writing About the World

1. Choose one aspect—for instance, mud, dryness, flashfloods, fog, constant sunshine—of the weather or seasons where you are currently located and use it as the subject of an essay. What are its physical qualities? How do these physical qualities affect you? Have you observed their effects on others? If they create hardship, is it possible to be humorous about it, as Sarton is?
2. Write a paper in which you identify and analyze the humor in Sarton's essay. Is it primarily humor that stems from her situation? Does it come from her word choice, her sentence structure, and her arrangement of ideas? How does her humor compare with that of other writers in this collection? What effect would the omission of humor have on this essay?
3. Embedded in Sarton's essay are a series of contrasts between country life and city life. Write an essay detecting and explaining Sarton's views on this topic.

JOAN DIDION

Los Angeles Notebook

Joan Didion (1934–   ) was born in Sacramento, California, into a family that had lived in the area for five generations. She graduated from the University of California at Berkeley with an English B.A. in 1956 and then moved to New York City to become an associate feature editor for *Vogue* magazine. She worked there until her first book, *Run River* (1963), a novel set in the Sacramento Valley, was published. After her 1964 marriage to the novelist John Gregory Dunne, who was then an editor for *Time* magazine, they moved to Los Angeles. She wrote articles and feature magazine essays for national magazines, and her first collection of essays, *Slouching Towards Bethlehem*, was published in 1968. This book, from which "Los Angeles Notebook" was taken, first established the characteristic attitude of her work. Its title and its worldview echo the lines at the beginning of William Butler Yeats's poem "The Second Coming": "Things fall apart / The centre cannot hold." In the following essay, this bleak worldview is linked to the hot Santa Ana winds that bake and enervate southern California. This sense of intense uneasiness and impending disintegration also characterizes Didion's best-selling novels *Play It As It Lays* (1970) and *A Book of Common Prayer* (1977). She has also published such essay collections as *The White Album* (1979), *Salvador* (1983), and *Miami* (1987). A new collection *After Henry* appeared in 1992.

Didion's essays have won her a reputation as a master stylist. Her work has been widely praised for its use of precise, vivid details; for its employment of a lean style able to make its points without unnecessary elaboration; and for its powerful sense of drama, despite characteristic understatement. As this selection illustrates, her essays also emphasize dialogue, seeking to reproduce the sound and mood of everyday speech at the same time that they convey Didion's vision of the emptiness at the heart of the American Dream. Structurally, her nonfiction often builds meaning through a kind of collage effect, achieving range and intensity through the accumulation and juxtaposition of a series of short scenes.

There is something uneasy in the Los Angeles air this afternoon, some unnatural stillness, some tension. What it means is that tonight a Santa Ana will begin to blow, a hot wind from the northeast whining down through the Cajon and San Gorgonio Passes, blowing up sandstorms out along Route 66, drying the hills and the nerves to the flash point. For a few days now we will see smoke back in the canyons, and hear sirens in the night. I have neither heard nor read that a Santa Ana is due, but I know it, and almost everyone I have seen today knows it too. We know it because we feel it. The baby frets. The maid sulks. I rekindle a waning argument with the telephone company, then cut my losses and lie down, given over to whatever it is in the air. To live with the Santa Ana is to accept, consciously or unconsciously, a deeply mechanistic view of human behavior.

I recall being told, when I first moved to Los Angeles and was living on an isolated beach, that the Indians would throw themselves into the sea when the bad wind blew. I could see why. The Pacific turned ominously glossy during a Santa Ana period, and one woke in the night troubled not only by the peacocks screaming in the olive trees but by the eerie absence of surf. The heat was surreal. The sky had a yellow cast, the kind of light sometimes called "earthquake weather." My only neighbor would not come out of her house for days, and there were no lights at night, and her husband roamed the place with a machete. One day he would tell me that he had heard a trespasser, the next a rattlesnake.

"On nights like that," Raymond Chandler once wrote about the Santa Ana, "every booze party ends in a fight. Meek little wives feel the edge of the carving knife and study their husbands' necks. Anything can happen." That was the kind of wind it was. I did not know then that there was any basis for the effect it had on all of us, but it turns out to be another of those cases in which science bears out folk wisdom. The Santa Ana, which is named for one of the canyons it rushes through, is a *foehn* wind, like the *foehn* of Austria and Switzerland and the *hamsin* of Israel. There are a number of persistent malevolent winds, perhaps the best known of which are the mistral of France and the Mediterranean sirocco, but a *foehn* wind has distinct characteristics: it occurs on the leeward slope of a mountain range and, although the air begins as a cold mass, it is warmed as it comes down the mountain and appears as a hot dry wind. Whenever and wherever a *foehn* blows, doctors hear about headaches and nausea and allergies, about "nervousness," about "depression." In Los Angeles some teachers do not attempt to conduct formal classes during a Santa Ana, because the children become un-manageable. In Switzerland the suicide rate goes up during the *foehn*, and in the courts of some Swiss cantons the wind is considered a mit-igating circumstance for crime. Surgeons are said to watch the wind, because blood does not clot normally during a *foehn*. A few years ago an Israeli physicist discovered that not only during such winds, but for the ten or twelve hours which precede them, the air carries an unusually high ratio of positive to negative ions. No one seems to know exactly why that should be; some talk about friction and others suggest solar disturbances. In any case the positive ions are there, and what an excess of positive ions does, in the simplest terms, is make people unhappy. One cannot get much more mechanistic than that.

Easterners commonly complain that there is no "weather" at all in Southern California, that the days and the seasons slip by relentlessly, numbingly bland. That is quite misleading. In fact the climate is characterized by infrequent but violent extremes: two periods of torrential subtropical rains which continue for weeks and wash out the hills and send subdivisions sliding toward the sea; about twenty scattered days a year of the Santa Ana, which, with its incendiary dryness, invariably means fire. At the first prediction of a Santa Ana, the Forest Service flies men and equipment from northern California into the southern forests, and the Los Angeles Fire Department cancels its ordinary non-firefighting routines. The Santa Ana caused Malibu to burn the way it did in 1956, and Bel Air in 1961, and Santa Barbara in 1964. In the winter of 1966–67 eleven men were killed fighting a Santa Ana fire that spread through the San Gabriel Mountains.

Just to watch the front-page news out of Los Angeles during a Santa Ana is to get very close to what it is about the place. The longest Santa Ana period in recent years was in 1957, and it lasted not the usual three or four days but fourteen days, from November 21 until December 4. On the first day 25,000 acres of the San Gabriel Mountains were burning, with gusts reaching 100 miles an hour. In town, the wind reached Force 12, or hurricane force, on the Beaufort Scale; oil derricks were toppled and people ordered off the downtown streets to avoid injury from flying objects. On November 22 the fire in the San Gabriels was out of control. On November 24 six people were killed in automobile accidents, and by the end of the week the Los Angeles *Times* was keeping a box score of traffic deaths. On November 26 a prominent Pasadena attorney, depressed about money, shot and killed his wife, their two sons, and himself. On November 27 a South Gate divorcee, twenty-two, was murdered and thrown from a moving car. On November 30 the San Gabriel fire was still out of control, and the wind in town was blowing eighty miles an hour. On the first day of December four people died violently, and on the third the wind began to break.

It is hard for people who have not lived in Los Angeles to realize how radically the Santa Ana figures in the local imagination. The city burning is Los Angeles's deepest image of itself: Nathanael West perceived that, in *The Day of the Locust*; and at the time of the 1965 Watts riots what struck the imagination most indelibly were the fires. For days one could drive the Harbor Freeway and see the city on fire, just as we had always known it would be in the end. Los Angeles weather is the weather of catastrophe, of apocalypse, and, just as the reliably long and bitter winters of New England determine the way life is lived there, so the violence and the unpredictability of the Santa Ana affect the entire quality of life in Los Angeles, accentuate its impermanence, its unreliability. The wind shows us how close to the edge we are.

2

"Here's why I'm on the beeper, Ron," said the telephone voice on the all-night radio show. "I just want to say that this *Sex for the Secretary* creature—whatever her name is—certainly isn't contributing anything to the morals in this country. It's pathetic. Statistics *show*."

"It's *Sex and the Office*, honey," the disc jockey said. "That's the title. By Helen Gurley Brown. Statistics show what?"

"I haven't got them right here at my fingertips, naturally. But they *show*."

"I'd be interested in hearing them. Be constructive, you Night Owls."

"All right, let's take *one* statistic," the voice said, truculent now. "Maybe I haven't read the book, but what's this business she recommends about *going out with married men for lunch*?"

So it went, from midnight until 5 A.M., interrupted by records and by occasional calls debating whether or not a rattlesnake can swim. Misinformation about rattlesnakes is a leitmotiv of the insomniac imagination in Los Angeles. Toward 2 A.M. a man from "out Tarzana way" called to protest. "The Night Owls who called earlier must have been thinking about, uh, *The Man in the Grey Flannel Suit* or some other book," he said, "because Helen's one of the few authors trying to tell us what's really going *on*. Hefner's another, and he's also controversial, working in, uh, another area."

An old man, after testifying that he "personally" had seen a swimming rattlesnake, in the Delta-Mendota Canal, urged "moderation" on the Helen Gurley Brown question. "We shouldn't get on the beeper to call things pornographic before we've read them," he complained, pronouncing it porn-ee-oh-graphic. "I say, get the book. Give it a chance." The original *provocateur* called back to agree that she would get the book. "And then I'll burn it," she added.

"Book burner, eh?" laughed the disc jockey good-naturedly.

"I wish they still burned witches," she hissed.

3

It is three o'clock on a Sunday afternoon and 105° and the air so thick with smog that the dusty palm trees loom up with a sudden and rather attractive mystery. I have been playing in the sprinklers with the baby and I get in the car and go to Ralph's Market on the corner of Sunset and Fuller wearing an old bikini bathing suit. That is not a very good thing to wear to the market but neither is it, at Ralph's on the corner of Sunset and Fuller, an unusual costume. Nonetheless a large woman in a cotton muumuu jams her cart into mine at the butcher counter. "*What a thing to wear to the market*," she says in a loud but strangled voice. Everyone looks the other way and I study a plastic package of rib lamb chops and she repeats it. She follows me all over the store, to the Junior Food, to the Dairy Products, to the Mexican Delicacies, jamming my cart whenever she can. Her husband plucks at her sleeve. As I leave the checkout counter she raises her voice one last time: "*What a thing to wear to Ralph's,*" she says.

4

A party at someone's house in Beverly Hills: a pink tent, two orchestras, a couple of French Communist directors in Cardin evening jackets, chili and hamburgers from Chasen's. The wife of an English actor sits at a table alone; she visits California rarely although her husband works here a good deal. An American who knows her slightly comes over to the table.

"Marvelous to see you here," he says.

"Is it," she says.

"How long have you been here?"

"Too long."

She takes a fresh drink from a passing waiter and smiles at her husband, who is dancing.

The American tries again. He mentions her husband.

"I hear he's marvelous in this picture."

She looks at the American for the first time. When she finally speaks she enunciates every word very clearly. "He...is...also...a...fag," she says pleasantly.

5

The oral history of Los Angeles is written in piano bars. "Moon River," the piano player always plays, and "Mountain Greenery." "There's a Small Hotel" and "This Is Not the First Time." People talk to each other, tell each other about their first wives and last husbands. "Stay funny," they tell each other, and "This is to die over." A construction man talks to an unemployed screenwriter who is celebrating, along, his tenth wedding anniversary. The construction man is on a job in Montecito: "Up in Montecito," he says, "they got one square mile with 135 millionaires."

"Putrescence," the writer says.

"That's all you got to say about it?"

"Don't read me wrong, I think Santa Barbara's one of the most— Christ, *the* most—beautiful places in the world, but it's a beautiful place that contains a...*putrescence.* They just live on their putrescent millions."

"So give me putrescent."

"No, no," the writer says. "I just happen to think millionaires have some sort of lacking in their . . . in their elasticity."

A drunk requests "The Sweetheart of Sigma Chi." The piano player says he doesn't know it. "Where'd you learn to play the piano?" the drunk asks. "I got two degrees," the piano player says. "One in musical education." I go to a coin telephone and call a friend in New York. "Where are you?" he says. "In a piano bar in Encino," I say. "Why?" he says. "Why not," I say.

1965–1967

Analyzing and Discussing the Text

1. In her essay "Why I Write," Didion argues emphatically that "the arrangement of words matters." What evidence do you see here of that concern for the arrangement of words? Select two or three sections of the essay to show how she positions her words to achieve a desired result.

2. Discuss how sections 2 through 5 of the essay are connected to the essay's first section. Are they meant to be examples that support Didion's views about the Santa Ana, or do they make other points about contemporary life? Analyze the role of weather throughout the entire essay.

3. Why does Didion call this piece "Los Angeles Notebook"? In what sense is the essay structured like a notebook or focused on the kinds of experiences a writer might record in a notebook?

4. What is the thematic significance of the phone call that concludes the essay? How important is it that this is a call to New York?

Experiencing and Writing About the World

1. Select a kind of weather that has special importance for you and write a short essay about it. Be precise in your selection of details to describe this weather; try to have your sense of it emerge through careful use of narrative and descriptive details rather than direct statement.

2. Early in her essay, Didion claims to espouse "a deeply mechanistic view of behavior." Does her essay support this view? Write an essay, using examples from your own experience and observation,

that agrees or disagrees with the view that weather shapes human behavior.

3. Didion's view of California is in sharp contrast to the view that often emerges in the media depictions of life there. Write an essay analyzing how the world of advertising creates a sense of southern California as the embodiment of certain aspects of the American Dream; emphasize how the popular media view differs from or agrees with the one put forth by Didion.

JOHN HAY

A Season for Swallows

John Hay (1915–   ) was born in Ipswich, Massachusetts. His family ties to New England go very deep; his grandfather, also named John Hay, was Secretary of State for Theodore Roosevelt, and his father was the archaeological curator for the American Museum of Natural History. Hay graduated from Harvard in 1938, worked as a reporter for the *Charleston News and Courier*, then spent two months at Cape Cod studying with the poet Conrad Aiken before he was drafted into service in World War II. After the war, he moved back to the Cape and began his writing career with a volume of poems published in 1947. Soon afterwards, however, Hay turned to natural history writing, and he has gone on to produce a series of important books about the world of nature and our relationship to it. The first of these, *The Run* (1959), studies the spawning of the alewives—food fish of the herring family—in Stony Brook, a stream on the Cape. Like each of his later books, it engages and holds the reader through its mixture of careful observation and an excited sense of discovery about how the world works. *The Great Beach* (1963) came soon afterwards and won the John Burroughs Medal for outstanding natural history of writing. Hay's many books after that, which include *In Defense of Nature* (1970), *The Undiscovered Country* (1981), and *The Immortal Wilderness* (1987), have solidified his place as one of our foremost voices for nature. Through the years, Hay also has been an active worker for environmental education as well as a writer; he served for twenty years as president of the Cape Cod Museum of Natural History in Brewster, Massachusetts, and for fifteen years he taught classes at Dartmouth College in nature writing and in nature and human values. "A Season for Swallows" appeared in *The Undiscovered Country*; as this essay indicates, Hay now divides his time between Maine and Cape Cod.

One of the joys of reading Hay comes from his frankness about the way his own views on the environment have changed and developed. When, for example, he talks about his first readings in ecology, Hay says that "the idea that each life was so aptly fitted to its environment was a little difficult for me. Influenced by a world flung out in all directions, I must have had the notion that anything might be anywhere." Hay is also characteristically observant and candid about his own literary style. "I'm not a linear type," he says. "I circle like alewives and terns and herring gulls."

Any new arrival, any little bird landing in a tree at dusk, has come to seem immeasurably important to me because of the unknown dimensions it brings with it. Who know what it has seen, or what great risks it has taken? It is a true interpreter of the times. If I ignore or dismiss it, I may lose some of my own precarious footing in the hemisphere. In some of its attributes it is more sensitive to direct messages from the universe than I am. It may have experienced some major phenomenon, some change of global importance, while I was reading the newspaper.

I see no reason to suppose that in the life of my "sister swallow," to use Shelley's lovely phrase, there may not be any number of tangential lines to my own experience, any number of encounters I could share in. Though she lacks my language and my much advertised brain, she is a world being, tied to all worlds, and has as much right to center stage as any of us. The living earth honors its true receivers as much as those who attempt its mastery, and equips them accordingly. We do not live on a one-way street. (If the swallow, like the sparrow, is under the all-seeing eye of God, then neither of us can be said to suffer from neglect.)

So I have yearned impossibly to follow the far-flying swallows the year around, from South to North and back again, so as to see what exactions they have to endure, what hairbreadth hemispheric escapes they make, the degree to which their journeys relate to the constellations, the circulation of the atmosphere, earth's landmarks, and magnetism. This means flying with them, and clearly, I'll never make it, any more than I can get inside a bird's strange being; though it has to be said that if you don't trust some of your own impossible impulses you may never migrate very far yourself.

Before spending another summer in Maine, I went up early, toward the end of April, in order to dig a vegetable garden. There is a small barn close by the house where in previous years barn and cliff swallows had nested in the loft along the rafters, but they were past due when I arrived. Our neighbor told me that a few pair had been flying in and out of her toolshed, but were not satisfied with it as a place to nest. "Nervous about it" was the way she put it. Their problem was lack of access to the barn. They had been coming in each spring through some broken holes in the glass of two old window frames high on the north end, but I had boarded those up in the autumn.

So I climbed up into the loft and took out the boards, and almost at once, as I was climbing down again, four barn swallows flew in, filling the barn with their warbly chatter. A whole new realm of talk and feeling had moved in, a world that in spite of all the years I had watched the passing swallows was largely unknown to me. What were all these low buzzy sounds and higher twitterings all about? Did they have to do with claiming territory, urging each other on to nest, irritation at my presence, or simply the satisfaction of having arrived? In any case it was a pleasure to listen to, like the talk of some cheerful and urgent company moving in on a person who has been too long alone.

These four, with their tribal talk, were of a race that can travel all the way from the latitude of the Yukon to Brazil or Argentina. Their return to the nesting places where they grew up, or where they nested before, ties immense distances together. As it is with the terns, thousands of miles of directive knowledge and memory are in those little frames that can home in on a few yards of territory.

When I let the swallows in I felt as if I had let in earth's hunger. I had relieved some of the pressures of primary need, and at the same time I was struck with how much we block out. It is not only a matter of our overwhelming ability to destroy life, but the extent to which we do not allow it to materialize. The boards against the windows are of our manufacture, which may have all kinds of implications about the human dilemma and the pity of it, but, more important, we should not forget to take them off when it is time.

When we got back there, toward the end of June, the earth was burning. The days were loaded with magnificent African heat, making it close and humid along the Atlantic shore, the kind of weather that causes people to complain and threaten one another. This is natural enough. When the earth sweats, boils, and upheaves, should we not feel similar torment in ourselves? The fishing was poor, some said disastrous. It was reported that many dead warblers had been found in the month of June, probably because of an earlier period of unusually cold weather and a resulting lack of food. The heat was interrupted by periods of fog and drizzle. Hours without wind were filled with thousands of midges and mosquitoes. Local existence seemed punctuated by bursts of pent-up vitality, followed by exhaustion. I woke up, after a night of battling mosquitoes, to listen to the news—of plane crashes, economic failures, of the cheaters and the cheated, and dire predictions about the future. As a result of human tampering with the atmosphere, the glaciers were going to melt and flood our coastal cities. On the other hand there might be a new ice age. The doomsayers had only switched their time span, as a result of the awkward and untried use of geologic periods. We were as confirmed in our fears as we were two thousand years ago.

"Behold, the Lord maketh the earth empty, and maketh it waste, and turneth it upside down, and scattereth the inhabitants thereof." (The difference is that the Lord is no longer the chief culprit, which only adds to the common instinct for misfortune. We have altogether too much to be responsible for.)

By early July, some of the swallows were already fledged and flying outside or gathering on the wires to roost. They ordinarily have two broods, and an occasional pair may be attending to their young as late as the end of August, or even into September. I watched them close up from inside a window of the house as they lay along the sills in the summer heat, evidently enjoying it, though they panted with open beaks in the full glare of the sun's rays. They scratched and picked away at their feathers. I fancied a sort of glazed, grim look in their little brown eyes. This was a life directly engaged in the cosmic business. I was not altogether envious of swallows if they were as narrowly serious as they appeared to be. On the other hand, I watched a number of them playing with a feather as it drifted along the eaves of the barn, picking it up and passing it along in a way that charmed me. One day too I saw a dead swallow at the side of the road after it had been hit by a car. Its mate lingered by it, flying up and around and then alighting next to the dead one, time and time again, with obvious concern. So the elements of play, of love and mourning, entered in, and the birds went on conversing half the day, with their flickering, warbly, wawky phrases ending in little spitting sounds, a sort of "zzzzz."

They flew over land and water, continually darting and swiftly turning, bringing in a daily catch of vast numbers of insects to feed their young. They would occasionally swish by my head in a mild warning as I walked by the barn. Once I saw them fly out to attack a trim, silvery-feathered tern as it flew over the inlet, and it put on a fine show of aerial maneuvers to avoid them, dipping and rising, going into an almost corkscrew flight, spiraling down to the surface of the water.

"Keep in touch. Keep in touch," the swallows seemed to say. All summer long, through light and heavy weather, I heard their voices running on with minor comments of their own. There was a constant urgency to what they did, as there was with the tern colony, as if every passing hour were the last and first. We could empathize with them through the moods of the weather where we trailed along in our own fashion, moving in, staying out, obeying our impulses.

"I'll guess I'll go home now" drifted over from across the way, or "Come in out of the rain," which was a grandmother talking to her granddaughter, who did as she was told, though she felt that the rain admired her.

(A collaborative understanding runs through all of life's varied motions, which is never quite captured by the human ability to discriminate between its elements. Swallows and grandchildren share in this flowing tide. Knowing no better, they are centered in the earth's variety. On a more sophisticated level, a physicist might say that the innocent human eye only thinks it sees an unending diversity in the color, shape, and motion of things around it, whereas science knows that diversity can deceive. Through the study of orders and relationships, form and pattern can be resolved into elementary simplicities. So the mind seeks out final order, refining, whittling, getting rid of the superfluous, down to the last invisible "quark"; but since infinity remains, and with it our irreducible sense of diversity, so there is not only virtue but wisdom in innocence.)

Now and then a dense fog closed in along the shore. Like Beethoven's "Grosse Fuge," it was made up of the most complicated harmonies, and open to deep deliberations, near meetings, searchings, and interweavings. Over swirling, gushing tidewater sounds, I heard a single "tik" from a songbird. A swallow flitted out of the barn without a sound. There were droplets of water over the webs of spiders, over intricate twigs and branches, and on glass windows they made flowery blooms. Five people stepped into a boat down by the shore and started rowing off into the fog. They moved in one direction and then angled off on another, involved in the general caution and its major slows and complexities.

After they disappeared, I heard the sound of young eiders splashing in the waters of the inlet. The ducklings made high, warbling calls, which were interspersed with grunting, moaning sounds from their female escorts. They gradually moved out on the ebbing tide like little drifting engines, ducking under all the while into rocks and seaweed, probably picking off periwinkles. (The adults prefer larger food items such as mussels.) These sea ducks, nesting on offshore islands, have highly developed homing instincts. At this stage, the young may be getting further strengthened in their sense of locality, moving out some miles from where they were hatched. They are unable to fly until the end of summer, taking sixty days to fledge, after which they begin to move farther out again, among the seaward islands. Over open water a creche of ducklings looks like a brown, rounded clump of moss, and as a boat comes nearer to them they begin to separate, first in a line, if there is time, then scattered out, ducking under to reappear many yards away.

When a dog ran down to the water's edge and barked, one of the adults made a little snort of alarm. These females, some of them mothers, some nonbreeders, began to herd their charges further away from the shoreline. I could hear a satiny, ripping sound as they would occasionally lift and beat their wings.

Those swallows not already feeding their young were brooding their eggs, and finally I heard the chittering squeaks of more hatchlings demanding food, food, food, with wide open beaks and gullets like small pipes. The parents responded, untiringly.

One night a thunderstorm shook the house. I sat up in bed and was almost knocked back again by a tremendous flash of lightning and a cannonade of thunder. The screens fell off some of the windows. Fruit rolled off the shelf and was spread over the kitchen floor. The front door blew open and sheets of rain came in. The family dog was trembling, hearing the power and judgment of the wild. There was a continuous flickering outside, interrupted now and then by a white light that hit like sudden day, and the thunder and lightning struck the sheeted, tidal waters beyond us with a ponderous crash. The swallows too must have been listening to the gods.

Life's relationship to elemental expression escapes research. What is a thunderstorm, to a bird? During an afternoon of hard, driving showers and sudden gusts, with tumbling thunder and freakish lightning, two people were killed while walking out across a breakwater in Rockland. It was in the news the following day. About the time this tragedy occurred, I was listening to the liquid sound of a thrush, during a lull in the galloping storm, when the light had cleared a little. Then, after each cessation of hard rain, followed by an abrupt silence, white-throated sparrows, chickadees, warblers, and finches all sang together.

After mid-July many more swallows, trees as well as barn and cliff, than had been nesting in our barn began to gather on clothes-lines or electric wires, still communicating in their flickering voices. If their range of expression is limited, this only seems to add to its intensity. Their common messages have a vital content. Mutual insistence, when it has to do with food, alarm, or a time of migration, concentrates a thousand words.

The month of August wheeled around again. It is named for Caesar Augustus, rather than for some lowlier animal. But it was not so with the Mayans. For them this was the month of the frog, or Uo. The frog, being associated with water, was chosen for that part of the year which was the height of the rainy season; its first day corresponds to August 5 of our year. Water goes deeper than empire.

During a period of ferocious, record heat, the swallows raced outside, hunting insects. Inside the barn, twenty-five fledged young were lined up for shelter, while three others, less able to fly, had moved out of their nests and hopped down from the hayloft to the barn floor. Several days later and they were still there. When adult birds flew by they begged for food in their staccato tones, but they did not seem to be getting any attention. Possibly their parents had abandoned them because of an absence of food or had met with an accident. It was probably the former, because they had died in a day or two and I found several more dead ones on the floor of the loft.

August, a month when nothing succeeds like excess, began to merge and fall away with the night sky where Jupiter and its moons appeared over the horizon. The asters, deep rose, white, and violet, spun their wheels in the changing light, to which some of the salt-marsh plants also responded with cream-colored seeds, and a few maples began to turn red. There was a new quality to existence. During the divine relocation, the seals moved away from offshore rocks, flocks of shorebirds went racing by, egrets appeared to roost with gulls and cormorants, their plumage shining through water-gray light across the coves. Hard showers of white rain hit loping silver waters. Then the sunlight flooded in again, lying deftly over leaves and in long strips across the grass. Cloud banks lifted, and it turned cold and clear.

There was silence in the barn. Outside it, thirty to forty swallows were lined up, chattering in an agitated way like emigrants about to leave for a foreign land. The dark, temporary well of nurture was being left behind. They would flutter, veer, and bend away, leaping off into the circulation that bathed the globe, taking a header, unconscious of casualty, joined in the deeper unconscious of nature. No other event was more momentous.

Now when I look up at swallows, wherever I happen to be, I can locate myself there and in a wider world. And I know the eternally renewable is close by, no matter how far I go. I praise them for their accomplishment thus far, up to the minute. Birth is the thing, the first and lasting mystery. To be born as a small bird means fierce obedience to eternal process, life's conquest of oblivion. Swallows are lessons in supreme closeness, inescapable connections. Love and disaster begin at home.

How will we ever know the earth unless we listen to what these little ones tell us about inextricable ties? Wake up, somnambulists of the human world: you have a journey to take.

Analyzing and Discussing the Text

1. Hay asserts, in the second paragraph, that the swallow is a "world being" with "as much right to center stage as any of us." Is this the thesis of his essay? Examine how the rest of the essay develops support of this view.
2. In the seventh paragraph of the essay, Hay expands his action in boarding the barn windows used by the swallows into a metaphor for

our general human relationship to nature. Discuss the effectiveness of this paragraph and its placement in the essay.

3. What rhetorical purpose does the last paragraph of the essay serve? Why does Hay shift his pronoun here from "I" to "we"? What does he mean by the phrase "inextricable ties"?

4. Although Hay describes his writing style as circular, this narrative also works with a clear structural pattern of progression through the months of summer. Discuss the relationship between linear and circular organization in this piece.

Experiencing and Writing About the World

1. Research the migration patterns of a bird that lives in your region of the country, then write an essay presenting that information in ways designed to engage your reader.

2. Much of the recent decline in bird populations stems from habitat destruction. Write an essay in which you blend description of bird behavior in your region with an argument for the importance of birds and their habitat.

3. Hay marks the passing seasons by observing the comings and goings of the swallows. Notice how the other writers in this chapter tend to rely on observations of the external world rather than the abstract calendar in monitoring the seasons, the passage of time. Write a philosophical essay in which you consider the meaning of time, particularly the differences between clock-time/calendar-time and experiential time.

GRETEL EHRLICH

A Storm, the Cornfield, and Elk

Gretel Ehrlich (1946–   ) first went to Wyoming in 1976 to make a film about sheepherders. When her partner died that summer, she stayed on and has made Wyoming her home. In *The Solace of Open Spaces* (1985), her first book and the one from which the following essay

is taken, Ehrlich describes that time in her life: "I suspect that my original motive for coming here was to 'lose myself' in new and unpopulated
territory." Instead, as she tells us in the essays that make up this book,
Ehrlich grieved for her lost partner, learned to love the vast landscapes
of Wyoming and the ranch life there, met a rancher who became her
husband, and settled down with him on a ranch near the Big Horn
Mountains in northern Wyoming. For Gretel Ehrlich, who was born in
Santa Barbara, California, and who studied at Bennington, the U.C.L.A.
film school, and the New School for Social Research in New York City,
this shift to a rural western landscape was a dramatic change, and it became an impetus to her creative life. As she learned about the work that
went into ranch life and the personalities involved in it, Ehrlich also began, one piece at a time, to formulate the essays that would eventually
make up *The Solace of Open Spaces*. That first book was very well received; it won an award from the American Academy of Arts and Letters.
Ehrlich has since been honored with both a Whiting Award (1988) and
a Guggenheim Fellowship (1989). She has also published two books
of poetry; a book of stories (with Edward Hoagland) called *City Tales,
Wyoming Stories* (1986); a novel about the Japanese-American internment camps in Wyoming during World War II called *Heart Mountain*
(1988); a collection of short stories set in Wyoming called *Drinking Dry
Clouds* (1991); and, most recently, another book of personal essays,
Islands, the Universe, Home (1991).

Throughout her work, Ehrlich meditates on the relation between
place and art, between landscape and the printed page; "The truest
art," she says in her preface to *The Solace of Open Spaces*, "would be
to give the page the same qualities as earth." In the following essay,
as elsewhere, Ehrlich conveys a complex sense of autumn in Wyoming
through her keen eye for paradox, her use of dramatic metaphor, and
her finely tuned sense for arranging the individual pieces of an essay
into a richly varied whole.

Last week a bank of clouds lowered itself down summer's green
ladder and let loose with a storm. A heavy snow can act like fists: trees
are pummeled, hay- and grainfields are flattened, splayed out like deer
beds; field corn, jackknifed and bleached blond by the freeze, is bedraggled by the brawl. All night we heard groans and crashes of cottonwood
trunks snapping. "I slept under the damned kitchen table," one rancher
told me. "I've already had one of them trees come through my roof."
Along the highway electric lines were looped to the ground like dropped
reins.

As the storm blows east toward the Dakotas, the blue of the sky
intensifies. It inks dry washes and broad grasslands with quiet. In their
most complete gesture of restraint, cottonwoods, willows, and wild rose

engorge themselves with every hue of ruddiness—russet, puce, umber, gold, musteline—whose spectral repletion we know also to be an agony, riding oncoming waves of cold.

The French call the autumn leaf *feuille morte*. When the leaves are finally corrupted by frost they rain down into themselves until the tree, disowning itself, goes bald.

All through autumn we hear a double voice: one says everything is ripe; the other says everything is dying. The paradox is exquisite. We feel what the Japanese call "aware"—an almost untranslatable word meaning something like "beauty tinged with sadness." Some days we have to shoulder against a marauding melancholy. Dreams have a hallucinatory effect: in one, a man who is dying watches from inside a huge cocoon while stud colts run through deep mud, their balls bursting open, their seed spilling into the black ground. My reading brings me this thought from the mad Zen priest Ikkyu: "Remember that under the skin you fondle lie the bones, waiting to reveal themselves." But another day, I ride in the mountains. Against rimrock, tall aspens have the graceful bearing of giraffes, and another small grove, not yet turned, gives off a virginal limelight that transpierces everything heavy.

Fall is the end of a rancher's year. Third and fourth cuttings of hay are stacked; cattle and sheep are gathered, weaned, and shipped; yearlings bulls and horse colts are sold. "We always like this time of year, but it's a lot more fun when the cattle prices are up!" a third-generation rancher tells me.

This week I help round up their cows and calves on the Big Horns. The storm system that brought three feet of snow at the beginning of the month now brings intense and continual rain. Riding for cows resembles a wild game of touch football played on skis: cows and cowboys bang into each other, or else, as the calves run back, the horse just slides. Twice today my buckskin falls with me, crushing my leg against a steep sidehill, but the mud and snow, now trampled into a gruel, is so deep it's almost impossible to get bruised.

When the cattle are finally gathered, we wean the calves from the cows in portable corrals by the road. Here, black mud reaches our shins. The stock dogs have to swim in order to move. Once, while trying to dodge a cow, my feet stuck, and losing both boots in the effort to get out of the way, I had to climb the fence barefooted. Weaning is noisy; cows don't hide their grief. As calves are loaded into semis and stock trucks, their mothers—five or six hundred of them at a time—crowd around the sorting alleys with outstretched necks, their squared-off faces all opened in a collective bellowing.

On the way home a neighboring rancher who trails his steers down the mountain highway loses one as they ride through town. There's a high-speed chase across lawns and flower beds, around the general store and the fire station. Going at a full lope, the steer ducks behind the fire truck just as Mike tries to rope him. "Missing something?" a friend yells out her window as the second loop sails like a burning hoop to the ground.

"That's nothing," one onlooker remarks. "When we brought our cattle through Kaycee one year, the minister opened the church door to see what all the noise was about and one old cow just ran in past him. He had a hell of a time getting her out."

In the valley, harvest is on but it's soggy. The pinto bean crops are sprouting, and the sugar beets are balled up with mud so that one is indistinguishable from the other. Now I can only think of mud as being sweet. At night the moon makes a brief appearance between storms and laces mud with a confectionary light. Farmers whose last cutting of hay is still on the ground turn windrows to dry as if they were limp, bedridden bodies. The hay that has already been baled is damp, and after four inches of rain (in a county where there's never more than eight inches a year) mold eats its way to the top again.

The morning sky looks like cheese. Its cobalt wheel has been cut down and all the richness of the season is at our feet. The quick-blanch of frost stings autumn's rouge into a skin that is tawny. At dawn, mowed hay meadows are the color of pumpkins, and the willows, leafless now, are pink and silver batons conducting inaudible river music. When I dress for the day, my body, white and suddenly numb, looks like dead coral.

After breakfast there are autumn chores to finish. We grease head gates on irrigation ditches, roll up tarp dams, pull horseshoes, and truck horses to their winter pasture. The harvest moon gives way to the hunter's moon. Elk, deer, and moose hunters repopulate the mountains now that the livestock is gone. One young hunting guide has already been hurt. While he was alone at camp, his horse kicked him in the spleen. Immobilized, he scratched an SOS with the sharp point of a bullet on a piece of leather he cut from his chaps. "Hurt bad. In pain. Bring doctor with painkiller," it read. Then he tied the note to the horse's halter and threw rocks at the horse until it trotted out of camp. When the horse wandered into a ranch yard down the mountain, the note was quickly discovered and a doctor was helicoptered to camp. Amid orgiastic gunfire, sometimes lives are saved.

October lifts over our heads whatever river noise is left. Long carrier waves of clouds seem to emanate from hidden reefs. There's a logjam of them around the mountains, and the horizon appears to drop seven thousand feet. Though the rain has stopped, the road ruts are filled to the brim. I saw a frog jump cheerfully into one of them. Once in a while the mist clears and we can see the dark edge of a canyon or an island of vertical rimrock in the white bulk of snow. Up there, bulk elk have been fighting all fall over harems. They charge with antlered heads, scraping the last of the life-giving velvet off, until one bull wins and trots into the private timber to mount his prize, standing almost humanly erect on hind legs while holding a cow elk's hips with his hooves.

In the fall, my life, too, is timbered, an unaccountably libidinous place: damp, overripe, and fading. The sky's congestion allows the eye's iris to open wider. The cornfield in front of me is torn parchment paper, as brittle as bougainvillea leaves whose tropical color has somehow climbed these northern stalks. I zigzag through the rows as if they were city streets. Now I want to lie down in the muddy furrows, under the frictional sawing of stalks, under corncobs which look like erections, and out of whose loose husks sprays of bronze silk dangle down.

Autumn teaches us that fruition is also death; that ripeness is a form of decay. The willows, having stood for so long near water, begin to rust. Leaves are verbs that conjugate the seasons.

Today the sky is a wafer. Placed on my tongue, it is a wholeness that has already disintegrated; placed under the tongue, it makes my heart beat strongly enough to stretch myself over the winter brilliances to come. Now I feel the tenderness to which this season rots. Its defenselessness can no longer be corrupted. Death is its purity, its sweet mud. The string of storms that came across Wyoming like elephants tied tail to trunk falters now and bleeds into a stillness.

There is neither sun, nor wind, nor snow falling. The hunters are gone; snow geese waddle in grainfields. Already, the elk have started moving out of the mountains toward sheltered feed-grounds. Their great antlers will soon fall off like chandeliers shaken from ballroom ceilings. With them the light of these autumn days, bathed in what Tennyson called "a mockery of sunshine," will go completely out.

Analyzing and Discussing the Text

1. The first paragraph of this essay provides a dramatic introduction to the end of summer in the mountains. Analyze the ways in which Ehrlich makes this introduction so forceful.
2. The fourth paragraph completes the introductory section with its emphasis on the double character of fall. What is the "exquisite" paradox developed in paragraph 4? What other dimensions are added to this sense of paradox in the rest of the second section? In the rest of the essay?

3. How would you describe the change in tone that occurs in the essay's second section? Discuss whether the whole essay would change in character if that section were placed first.
4. The second paragraph of the third section describes a harvest scene almost exclusively in terms of color. What purpose does this reliance on color serve? Is this description an effective part of Ehrlich's essay? Why?
5. Why does the narrator here use the word "timbered" to characterize herself in the final paragraph of the fourth section? Note other places in this essay where Ehrlich uses the repetition of words or phrases to make her point.
6. Characterize the tone of the final paragraph and describe precisely how Ehrlich's prose creates the mood that concludes her essay on fall.

Experiencing and Writing About the World

1. Think about the season that elicits the most complex emotional responses from you and write a short essay about it; use anecdotes, metaphor, and detailed description to convey your sense of this season.
2. One of the most important passages in Ehrlich's essay is her early explanation of the Japanese concept of *aware* ("ah-wah-ray"), which she translates as "beauty tinged with sadness." Write an analytical and reflective essay in which you explain how this idea, with its emphasis on the aesthetic dimension of transience, suits the seasonal subject matter in "A Storm, the Cornfield, and Elk." You might also wish to compare Ehrlich's depiction of autumn with John Nichols's meditations and photographs in *The Last Beautiful Days of Autumn* (1982).
3. Ehrlich's prose style has been called "poetic." Look carefully at her use of word choice, metaphor, and the sounds of words, and explain in an analytical essay just how her prose style could be called poetic.

CHET RAYMO

The Blandishments of Color

Chet Raymo (1936–   ) was born in Chattanooga, Tennessee. He received a B.S. in electrical engineering from the University of Notre Dame in 1958, an M.S. in physics from U.C.L.A. in 1960, and his Ph.D. in physics from Notre Dame in 1964. Raymo is now a professor of physics and descriptive astronomy at Stonehill College in North Easton, Massachusetts, where he has also taught courses in expository writing and literary nonfiction. In addition, he writes a weekly column for the *Boston Globe* that considers the human side of science. Raymo is probably best known for his books on astronomy, *365 Starry Nights* (1982) and *The Soul of the Night: An Astronomical Pilgrimage* (1985), but he has also written several books on geology—*A Geologic and Topographical Profile of the United States* (1981), *Biography of a Planet: Astronomy, Geology, and the Evolution of Life* (1984), and *Honey from Stone: A Naturalist's Search for God* (1987). In 1991 he published an essay collection, *The Virgin and the Mousetrap: Essays in Search of the Soul of Science*, and a novel, *In the Falcon's Claw: A Novel of the Year 1000.*

In his introduction to *The Soul of the Night*, the book from which the following essay is taken, Raymo describes his essays as "a personal pilgrimage into the darkness and the silence of the night sky in quest of a human meaning." These literary pilgrimages demonstrate the author's ability to bring together a wide range of knowledge from art and science, literature and the natural world. Raymo says, in fact, that he became a writer "because it is the connections in the world that really interest me"; like Susan Sontag, he feels that the great thing about being a writer is that "nothing is irrelevant." For all this range of knowledge, however, the unifying core of Raymo's quest is an aesthetic one. He makes the following declaration in his introduction to *365 Starry Nights*: "Let it be said at once that although I have been trained as a scientist and have taught courses in descriptive astronomy, my interest in the sky is primarily esthetic rather than scientific. If I were to be exiled on a desert island and allowed to take the traditional handful of books, they would not be works of science but of poetry and natural history. The night sky possesses an unparalleled power to excite the human imagination." In "The Blandishments of Color," Raymo teases out a subtle, multiple analogy between black-and-white photography, late autumn, and the night sky, finding that all three of these phenomena resist the aesthetic frivolity of color and require sophisticated awareness on the part of the human observer.

In her collection of critical essays *Diana and Nikon,* Janet Malcolm speaks of the difference between black-and-white and color photography. "It is black-and-white photography," she says, "that demands of the photographer close attention to the world of color, while color photography permits him to forget it." Of course, there are magnificent artists in the medium of color film, but it has traditionally been the rejection of color that separates the serious photographer from the snapshooter. The black-and-white medium is hard, says Malcolm, color easy. The former requires art, the latter doesn't.

As I write these lines the trees outside my window are gaudy with color. In New England in October anyone can take a pretty picture, and most do. The cerulean blue sky, the lead white of church spires, the bold brushstrokes of deciduous reds and golds . . . few places in the world can be more beautiful. Point your camera in any direction, snap the shutter, and the image cannot fail to please. Color does it for you. The eye gets lazy.

In a few weeks November comes and the leaves will be gone. Then begins the season when the eye must pay close attention, the season of black and white. Color in November is caught in brief, evasive glimpses. The tiny crimson berry of the Canada mayflower. The cap of the golden-crowned kinglet glittering in the branches of the spruce. A speckle of pink feldspar in the granite outcrop. The eye works hard for the color it finds in November.

The serious photographer, says Malcolm, resists "the blandishments of color." Walking the woods in November is like doing black-and-white photography. It is the eye that must compose nature's beauty. It is the eye that must frame the pale rose breast of the nuthatch against the crusty black skin of the pine. It is the eye's subtle chemistry that fixes in the curled leaves of the winter beech the color of freshly baked bread. "The beech is a bakeshop open all winter," writes the poet Maxine Kumin, and art has made of slight color a masterful image.

But today, ostentatious October fills my window, demanding attention, squeezing its energy into every inch of the frame. In a month, all of that technicolor razzle-dazzle will be gone. October's color redounds to nature's credit. Color in November is the work of art.

Like color in November, color in the night sky is the work of art. The night sky is November all year round. Night is the black-and-white print. The stars twinkle in a monochrome of pure silver chloride. The stars are resonantly colorless.

Or are they? A little artfulness will show that the stars are not mere points of white light. Many stars are indeed white. But others have tints of red, orange, yellow, or blue. Some, it is said, are green or purple. The reason the stars appear white to the impatient eye is an accident of the eye's chemistry.

There are two kinds of light receptors on the retina of the eye: the rods and the cones. The cones are the color sensors, but they do not respond to faint illumination. The rods are more finely attuned to dim light, but they do not discriminate colors. When we look at the stars, it is the sensitive but color-blind rods that do most of the work of seeing, and that is why the stars appear mostly white. But turn a telescope toward the stars, or take the time to look at the brighter stars with care, and they will take on the colors of the rainbow.

The color of a star is determined by the temperature of its surface. In this respect, a star is like any other incandescent object. An object just hot enough to reach incandescence glows with a dull red light. As the temperature goes up, the amount of energy radiated at the shorter (bluer) wavelengths increases relative to the longer (redder) wavelengths. As the object grows hotter, its appearance changes from red, to orange, to yellow, to white, and finally to blue. Or perhaps I should say from reddish, to orangish, to yellowish, to white, to bluish-white, for the colors of the stars are never pure but a mixture of all wavelengths; it is the dominance of a certain part of the spectrum that determines the color we perceive. The surface temperature of our sun is about 5800 degrees Centigrade, and like any incandescent object of that temperature it radiates a predominantly yellow light. No child fails to put a yellow face on the sun. The sun's yellow hue is apparent to the eye because that star is near and bright, and the cones of the retina go about their business of "seeing" color with efficiency. But put the sun at the distance of Alpha Centauri A, a yellow star that is the sun's exact twin, and you will see only a white dot on a black sky.

A careful observer can distinguish the colors of the brighter stars in the night sky. Often I have pointed to Antares and said "a red star," or to Vega and said "blue." That's a bit of an exaggeration. Antares is classified as a red giant star, but it will probably appear pale orange to the naked eye. Vega, if it looks blue at all, is white with a bluish cast. And the sun, in spite of the child's yellow face, is really more white than yellow. Perhaps the best way to see star colors is by contrast. Orion offers a vivid demonstration. Rigel, the star in the giant's forward foot, is decidedly blue. Betelgeuse, in the raised arm, is orange. The colors are most easily seen by glancing back and forth between the two stars. Star colors are more readily perceived if the intensity of the starlight is amplified with binoculars or a telescope. My favorite demonstration of star color is little Albireo, the star at the beak of Cygnus the Swan. Albireo is a binary star and appears double in a small instrument. One member of the pair is golden, the other a brilliant blue. Once you have seen the blue and gold of Albireo you will never again think of the stars as uniformly white.

The art of observing the night sky is 50 percent vision and 50 percent imagination. Nothing illustrates the truth of the saying better than the colors of the stars. Nineteenth-century observers seem to have had the best luck at seeing the colors of stars, no doubt because their observations included a larger dose of imagination relative to vision. Richard Hinckley Allen's book *Star Names: Their Lore and Meaning*, which came out just at the end of the century, calls Albireo "topaz yellow and sapphire blue." Antares, also double in fair-sized telescope, is referred to as "fiery red and emerald green." Allen describes other stars as *straw, rose, grape,* and *lilac,* and you would think you were in his garden rather than the sky. Allen's color descriptions were mostly borrowed from the celebrated British observer William Henry Smyth, whose eye was apparently refined enough to see a dozen shades of white, including *pearly, lucid, creamy, silvery,* and just plain *whitely white.*

The most elaborate nineteenth-century system of star colors was that of the Russian-German astronomer Wilhelm Struve. Struve's classification used Latin labels, and the words themselves have an exotic ring, like the Latin names of tropical birds. *Egregie albae, albaesubflavae, aureae, rubrae, caeruleae, virides, purpureae.* Sometimes these basic descriptions did not seem sufficiently accurate, so Struve invented new one, like *olivaceasubrubicunda* for pinkish-olive. Show me a star that is *olivaceasubrubicunda* and I'll show you imagination making art of thin stimulus.

Armed with cameras and electronics, the modern astronomer has reduced star color to objective number. Rigel in Orion has a color index of -0.04 and a spectral type of B8, and that says it all to the professional. But the amateur stargazer needs only a little imagination to see that Rigel is blue and Betelgeuse is orange. With Smyth's level of imagination he might even see the "pale rose" of Aldebaran or the "golden yellow" of Arcturus. Allen's book describes the stars of binary Regulus as "flushed white and ultramarine." These are colors no camera can catch.

Stargazing, like black-and-white photography, demands close attention to color. There are no ravishing sunsets in the midnight sky, no deciduous riots of red and gold in the forest of the night. The snapshooter turns from the telescope in despair, but the artful observer will take the hint and let his imagination enrich the palette. William Henry Smyth fixed his telescope on the stars and saw "'crocus," "damson," "sardonyx," and "smalt." This is the kind of imagination that labels paint chips. Smyth's descriptions of star colors reminds me of the experience of the artist Vasili Kandinsky when he bought his first box of tubed pigments at the age of thirteen. Kandinsky tells how at the slightest pressure of his fingers on the open tubes the colors slipped out like animate beings, some cheerful and jubilant, others meditative and dreamy. Some colors seemed to emerge "self-absorbed." Others slid from the tubes with "bubbling roguishness," some with a "sigh of relief," still others with a "deep sound of sorrow." Some of Kandin-sky's colors were "obstinate," others "soft" and "resilient." The artist's almost mystical experience with colored oils evokes stars of damson and smalt.

It is just as well that the colors of the stars are not easily seen. As John Burroughs said, if the deep night were revealed to us in all its naked grandeur, it would perhaps be more than we could bear. But half of infinity is still infinite. A hint of infinity is infinite too—if we can take the hint. A trait here, a trait there, Burroughs said. Of hints and traits we make our way.

On a night that is perfectly dark and perfectly clear, the naked eye can just discern the Great Orion Nebula as a patch of fuzzy white light in the sword of Orion. In a moderate-sized instrument, the nebula glows with an eerie green light, and the eye sees hints of shape—a shape like a curled hand with the palm aflame. Long time-exposure photographs of the Orion nebula reveal a stunning complex of stars in the trauma of birth, swaddled in vortices and streamers of collapsing luminous gas, a star-cradle measured by light-years and charged with the energy of Creation. The colors of the nebula are as various as the photographs. On Kodacolor 400 film Orion's great cloud is plum and lilac, cerulean blue and milky white. On Ektachrome 400 the nebula is apricot and red, tinted with deep ochers and browns. On Kodacolor 1000 film Orion's nebula is mauve and amethyst, blushed with rose. But all of these colors are artifacts of the film; they are not what the eye would see if we could approach the nebula and stand in its awesome light.

Here on my desk is a photograph of the Great Orion Nebula that was made with a special care to reproduce the color sensitivity of the human eye. The colors of the print were created with three black-and-white time exposures taken in twilight with the 3.9-meter Anglo-Australian telescope. The plates were made with a combination of emulsions and filters that gave a uniform response across the en-tire visual spectrum. Masking techniques were used to accentuate the delicate structure of the nebula. The Orion nebula is more than 20,000 times larger than our solar system. There is enough hydrogen, helium, and other materials in the cloud to form 10,000 stars like our sun. The light of the nebula comes mostly from the radiation of doubly ionized oxygen (green) and the alpha radiation of ionized hydrogen (deep red). The gas is made to glow by the energy of hot young stars embedded in the nebula, stars only recently born of the stuff of the nebula itself. The Anglo-Australian photograph shows the nebula feathered with filaments of gas like a great bird of prey. In the bird's knarry talons are gripped a dozen intensely white stars. The green oxygen light available in the moderate-sized instrument unites with the reds and blues of the traditional Kodacolor photographs to brown and yellow the light. There are olives and khakis in the composite print, and the reds and oranges of a log fire. There are ominous browns and grays, banked against the black of space like ash and cinder. There is movement and violence; the nebula seems charged with a terrible malevolent power. It is not a pretty picture. This carefully contrived photograph is not a drugstore snapshot of a pretty Vermont village steeped in the colors of October. It is the face of Leviathan, wrenching us into a space as deep and as terrible as the bowels of the sea. It is God's sturdy hand, the fist that grips us in its clinched infinities. The is the power that hides in the colorless night like the rocks in foaming breakers that crack a ship, or the white whale that drags all who seek him to black oblivion.

It would be impossible to end this meditation on the blandishments of color without rereading Melville's chapter on the whiteness of Moby Dick. Ishmael rehearses for us the way in which white stands for what is good and true. He parades for our attention snow-white chargers, the ermines of Justice, the white-robed four-and-twenty Elders before the great white Throne, and Jove in the guise of the snow-white bull. But all of these he dismisses when he turns to Moby Dick. It is the whiteness of the whale, he says, that above all else appalls him. In spite of the associations of whiteness with "whatever is sweet and honorable, and sublime," there yet lurks an elusive something in the innermost idea of white that strikes "more of panic to the soul than that redness which affrights the blood." When coupled with any object terrible in itself, concludes Ishmael, whiteness heightens the terror to the furthest bounds.

If the retina of the human eye had only rods, and those with the sensitivity of cones, then the stars would shine with October's reds and golds, and Orion's nebula would unfold like a flower of ocher and green at the hunter's knee. If that had been so, then perhaps we would never have sought divinities in the sky. Then perhaps ours would have been a snapshooter's theology, a philosophy of the drugstore print, a metaphysics all prettified and simple. But the night, like Ahab's whale, cloaks its immensity in whiteness. *The great principle of light touches all objects in the night sky, stars and nebulae, with its own blank tinge, and the palsied universe lies before us like a leper* (the words are Ishmael's). We gaze ourself blind at the monumental shroud that wraps our brightly colored planet. The pilgrim who would find his way to the edge of the galaxies and to the beginning of time must forgo daylight's easy color and launch himself upon the black-and-white sea of the night and in those huge spaces find stars the colors of damson, crocus, grape, and straw. The quest will perhaps require more courage than you or I can bear, and there is the possibility that we will be drawn, like Ahab, into the starry deep, lashed to the object of our search with the lines of the chase. "Of all these things," says Ishmael, "the Albino whale was the symbol. Wonder ye then at the fiery hunt?"

Analyzing and Discussing the Text

1. Why does Raymo use the word "blandishments" here? How does this word in the title shape the meaning of the essay?
2. Explain the connections between the seasons and the stars. Why does Raymo so consciously emphasize the time of year in this essay? Is it merely coincidental that it happens to be autumn?
3. The third and fourth sections discuss some imaginative descriptions of the colors of stars in a way that is often humorous. Identify the humorous passages and analyze the kind of humor they use. Is this humor mixed with other attitudes?
4. The last paragraph in the third section is a view of the Orion nebula without the blandishments of color. What worldview comes into the essay with this description?
5. Observe how Raymo brings the views of other writers and scientists into this essay. Do they help him establish the authority of his essay? Does he give equal weight to scientific knowledge and literary insights?

Experiencing and Writing About the World

1. The first section of this essay ends with the assertion that "Like color in November, color in the night sky is the work of art." Explain precisely what Raymo means by that statement in an expository paragraph summarizing the meaning of the first section.
2. Given Raymo's sense of October and November in New England, how might he describe the dead of winter? Write a paragraph in which you, using his aesthetic framework, argue for the values that might come with December and January.
3. Write an essay that opposes Raymo's claims for the aesthetic superiority of November's subtle coloration. You can argue for the colors of October or the green of springtime, but your essay should incorporate the kind of aesthetic value that Raymo assigns to seasons. Or, if you wish, write a more general essay in which you argue for the integrity and worth of color in tying us to the external world, as opposed to its misleading seductiveness ("blandishments").
4. Take some factual, scientific knowledge that has personal meaning for you (this can be material from geology, biology, chemistry, or any other scientific discipline) and write an essay in which you convey both that knowledge and its importance in shaping your larger quest for meaning.

ANNIE DILLARD

From An American Childhood

For biographical information, see the headnote for "Living Like Weasels" in Part One, Chapter One.

In her book *The Writing Life* (1989), Annie Dillard asks herself the rhetorical question, "Why would anyone read a book instead of watching big people move on a screen?" Her answer is both simple and complex: "a book can be literature." She explains that "the more literary the book—the more purely verbal, crafted sentence by sentence, the more imaginative, reasoned, and deep—the more likely people are to read it." The essay below, which is a self-contained section from Dillard's memoir about growing up in Pittsburgh, *An American Childhood* (1987), acquires these literary qualities from the way Dillard develops her story of the chase through the snow-covered city. In her narrative, what could have been a simple stereotypical anecdote about rebellious children, an angry adult, and a winter confrontation comes to symbolize the idea of living, even as an adult, with weasel-like (and childlike) intensity. In a talk called "To Fashion a Text" at the New York Public Library the year before *An American Childhood* appeared, Dillard explained that her forthcoming book was "about two things: a child's interior life—vivid, superstitious and timeless—and a child's growing awareness of the world." This fascination with "waking up," with the mysterious workings of the human mind, guides virtually all of Dillard's work.

[Winter Chase]

Some boys taught me to play football. This was fine sport. You thought up a new strategy for every play and whispered it to the others. You went out for a pass, fooling everyone. Best, you got to throw yourself mightily at someone's running legs. Either you brought him down or you hit the ground flat out on your chin, with your arms empty before you. It was all or nothing. If you hesitated in fear, you would miss and get hurt: you would take a hard fall while the kid got away, or you would get kicked in the face while the kid got away. But if you flung yourself wholeheartedly at the back of his knees—if you gathered and joined body and soul and pointed them diving fearlessly—then you likely wouldn't get hurt, and you'd stop the ball. Your fate, and your team's score, depended on your concentration and courage. Nothing girls did could compare with it.

Boys welcomed me at baseball, too, for I had, through enthusiastic practice, what was weirdly known as a boy's arm. In winter, in the snow, there was neither baseball nor football, so the boys and I threw snowballs at passing cars. I got in trouble throwing snowballs, and have seldom been happier since.

On one weekday morning after Christmas, six inches of new snow had just fallen. We were standing up to our boot tops in snow on a front yard on trafficked Reynolds Street, waiting for cars. The cars traveled Reynolds Street slowly and evenly; they were targets all but wrapped in red ribbons, cream puffs. We couldn't miss.

I was seven; the boys were eight, nine, and ten. The oldest two Fahey boys were there—Mikey and Peter—polite blond boys who lived near me on Lloyd Street, and who already had four brothers and sisters. My parents approved Mikey and Peter Fahey. Chickie McBride was there, a tough kid, and Billy Paul and Mackie Kean too, from across Reynolds, where the boys grew up dark and furious, grew up skinny, knowing, and skilled. We had all drifted from our houses that morning looking for action, and had found it here on Reynolds Street.

It was cloudy but cold. The cars' tires laid behind them on the snowy street a complex trail of beige chunks like the crenellated castle walls. I had stepped on some earlier; they squeaked. We could have wished for more traffic. When a car came, we all popped it one. In the intervals between cars we reverted to the natural solitude of children.

I started making an iceball—a perfect iceball, from perfectly white snow, perfectly spherical, and squeezed perfectly translucent so no snow remained all the way through. (The Fahey boys and I considered it unfair actually to throw an iceball at somebody, but it had been known to happen.)

I had just embarked on the iceball project when we heard tire chains come clanking from afar. A black Buick was moving toward us down the street. We all spread out, banged together some regular snowballs, took aim, and, when the Buick drew nigh, fired.

A soft snowball hit the driver's windshield right before the driver's face. It made a smashed star with a hump in the middle.

Often, of course, we hit our target, but this time, the only time in all of life, the car pulled over and stopped. Its wide black door opened; a man got out of it, running. He didn't even close the car door.

He ran after us, and we ran away from him, up the snowy Reynolds sidewalk. At the corner, I looked back; incredibly, he was still after us. He was in city clothes: a suit and tie, street shoes. Any normal adult would have quit, having sprung us into flight and made his point. This man was gaining on us. He was a thin man, all action. All of a sudden, we were running for our lives.

Wordless, we split up. We were on our turf; we could lose ourselves in the neighborhood backyards, everyone for himself. I paused and considered. Everyone had vanished except Mikey Fahey, who was just rounding the corner of a yellow brick house. Poor Mikey, I trailed him. The driver of the Buick sensibly picked the two of us to follow. The man apparently had all day.

He chased Mikey and me around the yellow house and up a back-yard path we knew by heart: under a low tree, up a bank, through a hedge, down some snowy steps, and across the grocery store's delivery driveway. We smashed through a gap in another hedge, entered a scruffy backyard and ran around its back porch and tight between houses to Edgerton Avenue; we ran across Edgerton to an alley and up our own sliding woodpile to the Halls' front yard; he kept coming. We ran up Lloyd Street and wound through mazy backyards toward the steep hilltop at Willard and Lang.

He chased us silently, block after block. He chased us silently over picket fences, through thorny hedges, between houses, around garbage cans, and across streets. Every time I glanced back, choking for breath, I expected he would have quit. He must have been as breathless as we were. His jacket strained over his body. It was an immense discovery, pounding into my hot head with every sliding, joyous step, that this ordinary adult evidently knew what I thought only children who trained at football knew: that you have to fling yourself at what you're doing, you have to point yourself, forget yourself, aim, dive.

Mikey and I had nowhere to go, in our neighborhood or out of it, but away from this man who was chasing us. He impelled us forward; we compelled him to follow our route. The air was cold; every breath tore my throat. We kept running, block after block; we kept improvising, backyard after backyard, running a frantic course and choosing it simul-taneously, failing always to find small places or hard places to slow him down, and discovering always, exhilarated, dismayed, that only bare speed could save us—for he would never give up, this man—and we were losing speed.

He chased us through the backyard labyrinths of ten blocks before he caught us by our jackets. He caught us and we all stopped.

We three stood staggering, half blinded, coughing, in an obscure hilltop backyard: a man in his twenties, a boy, a girl. He had released our jackets, our pursuer, our captor, our hero: he knew we weren't going anywhere. We all played by the rules. Mikey and I unzipped our jackets. I pulled off my sopping mittens. Our tracks multiplied in the backyard's new snow. We had been breaking new snow all morning. We didn't look at each other. I was cherishing my excitement. The man's lower pants legs were wet; his cuffs were full of snow, and there was a prow of snow beneath them on his shoes and socks. Some trees bordered the little flat backyard, some messy winter trees. There was no one around: a clearing in a grove, and we the only players.

It was a long time before he could speak. I had some difficulty at first recalling why we were there. My lips felt swollen; I couldn't see out of the sides of my eyes; I kept coughing.

"You stupid kids," he began perfunctorily.

We listened perfunctorily indeed, if we listened at all, for the chewing out was redundant, a mere formality, and beside the point. The point was that he had chased us passionately without giving up, and so he had caught us. Now he came down to earth. I wanted the glory to last forever.

But how could the glory have lasted forever? We could have run through every backyard in North America until we got to Panama. But when he trapped us at the lip of the Panama Canal, what precisely could he have done to prolong the drama of the chase and cap its glory? I brooded about this for the next few years. He could only have fried Mikey Fahey and me in boiling oil, say, or dismembered us piecemeal, or staked us to anthills. None of which I really wanted, and none of which any adult was likely to do, even in the spirit of fun. He could only chew us out there in the Panamanian jungle, after months or years of exalting pursuit. He could only begin, "You stupid kids," and continue in his ordinary Pittsburgh accent with his normal righteous anger and the usual common sense.

If in that snowy backyard the driver of the black Buick had cut off our heads, Mikey's and mine, I would have died happy, for nothing has required so much of me since as being chased all over Pittsburgh in the middle of winter—running terrified, exhausted—by this sainted, skinny, furious red-headed man who wished to have a word with us. I don't know how he found his way back to his car.

Analyzing and Discussing the Text

1. In what ways do the first two paragraphs connect to the rest of the essay? Is it important that the other two people involved in the chase are male?

2. Annie Dillard, like Gretel Ehrlich, is fond of paradox. How does she make use of it in this essay? Does she employ it in ways that are reminiscent of or different from Ehrlich's use of it in her essays?

3. Find and discuss instances where Dillard's own careful efforts in the crafting of this narrative—especially in word choice and sentence structure—are evident.

4. What does the essay suggest as the real reason that the man chases the children? Is this point related to Dillard's statement late in the essay that "We all played by the rules"?

Experiencing and Writing About the World

1. Describe an outdoor adventure from your childhood that is as charged with adventure and meaning as this chase was for Annie Dillard. Pay special attention to how you tie together your narrative of the events and your sense of what those events mean so that the significance does not overwhelm the drama of the actual event. Consider the role that the time of year (for instance, winter) had in at least providing the opportunity for adventure and make a point of using vivid seasonal references throughout your account.
2. Write a version of Dillard's narrative from the viewpoint of the man whose car was hit by the snowball. This version can emphasize values similar to Dillard's, but from the adult's different perspective.
3. Compare the excerpt from *An American Childhood* to Dillard's essay "Living Like Weasels." Do the two pieces focus on similar aspects of human psychology? Are the essays written similarly or are there interesting differences?

Suggestions for Further Reading

Bass, Rick. *Winter: Notes from Montana.* Boston: Houghton, 1991.

Bly, Carol. *Letters from the Country.* New York: Harper, 1981.

Finch, Robert. "A Summer Place." *Outlands: Journeys to the Outer Edges of Cape Cod.* Boston: Godine, 1986.

Hall, Donald. *Seasons at Eagle Pond.* Boston: Ticknor, 1991.

Hubbell, Sue. *A Country Year: Living the Questions.* New York: Random, 1986.

Hurston, Zora Neale. Chapter 18. *Their Eyes Were Watching God.* 1937. Urbana: U of Illinois P, 1978.

Jerome, John. *Stone Work: Reflections on Serious Play & Other Aspects of Country Life.* New York: Viking, 1989.

Kittredge, William. "Yellowstone in Winter." *Owning It All.* St. Paul, MN: Graywolf, 1987.

Madson, John. "North Again." *Audubon* 79.2 (1977): 18–29.

Nichols, John. *The Last Beautiful Days of Autumn.* New York: Holt, 1982.

Saint Exupéry, Antoine de. "The Elements." *Wind, Sand and Stars.* 1939. New York: Harcourt, 1967.

PART TWO

Human Visitors

Roger B. Chapman/PhotoWorld/Freelance Photographer's Guild

CHAPTER ONE

Walking: On the Trail and Off

Most people learn to walk at a very early age, and with this simple means of locomotion comes the possibility of entering the natural world as a visitor, a temporary but attentive passerby. Walking requires no special equipment or surroundings—no rafts or climbing ropes, no rivers or mountains. We can walk as easily in our own backyards or in city parks as we can in national parks or along ocean beaches. Sometimes we don't even need shoes. Because most of us walk so routinely in our lives—from dorms to classrooms, from libraries to parking lots— we may hardly consider it an activity worth reflecting on and recording. But the following writers will show, in a wide range of prose styles and geographical settings, the possibility of deriving pleasure, insight, and even wonderment from the mere process of putting one foot in front of the other, as long as the senses and the mind are kept open to experience.

Walking is not always such fun. The wilderness hiker must experience fear, fatigue, and nagging blisters just as often as the delights of beautiful views, freedom, solitude, and self-discovery. The following essays, however, will emphasize the more positive aspects of walking, beginning with Henry David Thoreau's famous proclamation that the person who truly understands "the art of Walking" must be " 'a Sainte-Terrer,' a Saunterer, a Holy-Lander," appreciating every stretch of ground he or she covers. Likewise, Linda Hogan considers the process of walking, of moving through the world at a leisurely, meditative pace, an opportunity to become splendidly attentive—not only to move from one place to another, but to watch and listen. David Black and

Barry Lopez also attend closely to the landscapes they pass through, the Great Beach of Cape Cod and the frozen terrain of the Arctic, respectively. But for them, the walk also becomes a literary device, a means of unifying intricate meditations on the human mind and natural history. Black devotes as much space in "Walking the Cape" to personal and historical recollections as he does to his actual walks from Eastham to Provincetown. In his study of narwhals, Lopez often explains at length the biological and mythological qualities of the animal, but he always returns to the narrative thread, to the image of himself walking near the Arctic sea. For Betsy Hilbert, a walk along the beach in Miami means not merely pleasant exercise, but also the opportunity to involve herself in the natural order of things—to "disturb" nature or contribute to the survival of a species. David Brendan Hopes turns from the physical activity of walking to its social implications, speculating about differences between men and women in the wilderness and about the various advantages of hiking alone versus those of hiking with a partner.

HENRY DAVID THOREAU

From **Walking**

For Henry David Thoreau (1817–1862), the goal of life was to perceive the world with freshness and intensity, to "suck out all the marrow
of life" rather than merely plodding through a life of "quiet desperа-
tion," as he puts it in his most famous book, *Walden* (1854), a complex,
meditative account of his two-year stay (1845–1847) in a small house he
built of scrap lumber in the woods near Walden Pond on the outskirts of
his hometown of Concord, Massachusetts. One of Thoreau's principal
metaphors for the enriched or "awakened" experience of life is the process of traveling, for to the eye of the genuine traveler the world always
seems new and full of surprises. As he says in the following excerpt from
the essay "Walking" (1862), the best walker is the *saunterer*, the person
who appreciates his or her surroundings as if he or she were crossing
holy land—indeed, Thoreau suggests that the very word "saunterer"
derives from the phrase "sainte terre," or holyland. But this holiness is in
the mind of the individual, not the place itself. This appreciative attitude
toward the world affects more than the person's physical movement in
the world—one's senses and one's language, too, must "saunter," he
suggests. Indeed, in an 1852 journal entry, he urges himself to "walk
with more free senses." "What I need is not to look at all," he writes,
"but a true sauntering of the eye."

Thoreau performed most of his mental and physical sauntering in
the town of Concord or in the surrounding fields and woods. He attended nearby Harvard College, graduating in 1837, and later lived
briefly (at the suggestion of Ralph Waldo Emerson) in Staten Island,
New York. But otherwise he spent his entire life in Concord, taking occasional excursions to Cape Cod, the woods of Maine, and Minnesota.
He published his first book, *A Week on the Concord and Merrimack
Rivers*, in 1849, and *Walden* appeared several years later; his essays
about Maine were published as *The Maine Woods* two years after his
death. *Cape Cod*, another collection of essays, was also published in
1864. At the time of his death, Thoreau was virtually unknown and his
books had sold poorly. He had supported himself after college by working as an occasional surveyor and handyman and by helping out in
his family's pencil factory in Concord. But his main activity, it now seems,

was roaming the nearby countryside, recording observations in his journal. Never a permanent inhabitor of the genuine wilderness, Thoreau
preferred to live what he calls in "Walking" a "sort of border life, on the
confines of a world into which I make occasional and transient forays
only." When he celebrates "wildness" in this essay ("in wildness is the
preservation of the world"), he refers not only to the wildness of external
nature, but also to the potential wildness of the human being. This idea
emerges in his comments about writing; as he says in his journal, "we
cannot write well or truly but what we write with gusto. . . . It is always
essential that we love to do what we are doing, do it with a heart."

I wish to speak a word for Nature, for absolute freedom and wildness, as contrasted with a freedom and culture merely civil,—to regard
man as an inhabitant, or a part and parcel of Nature, rather than a
member of society. I wish to make an extreme statement, if so I may
make an emphatic one, for there are enough champions of civilization:
the minister and the school committee and every one of you will take
care of that.

I have met with but one or two persons in the course of my life
who understood the art of Walking, that is, of taking walks,—who had
a genius, so to speak, for *sauntering*, which word is beautifully derived
"from idle people who roved about the country, in the Middle Ages,
and asked charity, under pretense of going *à la Sainte Terre*," to the
Holy Land, till the children exclaimed, "There goes a *Sainte-Terrer*," a
Saunterer, a Holy-Lander. They who never go to the Holy Land in
their walks, as they pretend, are indeed mere idlers and vagabonds;
but they who do go there are saunterers in the good sense, such as I
mean. Some, however, would derive the word from *sans terre*, without
land or a home, which, therefore, in the good sense, will mean, having
no particular home, but equally at home everywhere. For this is the
secret of successful sauntering. He who sits still in a house all the time
may be the greatest vagrant of all; but the saunterer, in the good sense,
is no more vagrant than the meandering river, which is all the while
sedulously seeking the shortest course to the sea. But I prefer the first,
which, indeed, is the most probable derivation. For every walk is a sort
of crusade, preached by some Peter the Hermit in us, to go forth and
reconquer this Holy Land from the hands of the Infidels.

It is true, we are but faint-hearted crusaders, even the walkers,
nowadays, who undertake no persevering, never-ending enterprises.
Our expeditions are but tours, and come round again at evening to the
old hearth-side from which we set out. Half the walk is but retracing
our steps. We should go forth on the shortest walk, perchance, in the
spirit of undying adventure, never to return,—prepared to send back

our embalmed hearts only as relics to our desolate kingdoms. If you are ready to leave father and mother, and brother and sister, and wife and child and friends, and never see them again,—if you have paid your debts, and made your will, and settled all your affairs, and are a free man, then you are ready for a walk.

Analyzing and Discussing the Text

1. What kind of audience do you think Thoreau anticipated when he prepared "Walking"? Was he writing for a group of environmentalists? Are there any clues in the text that indicate who the intended readers are?
2. Explain Thoreau's definition of *sauntering*. Look *saunter* up in the *Oxford English Dictionary (OED)*—does the etymological explanation match Thoreau's?
3. What is the connection between "walking" and "sauntering"?
4. Do Thoreau's ideas about walking seem to apply only to excursions into the natural world? Could you, according to Thoreau, saunter through *town*?

Experiencing and Writing About the World

1. Think of an activity that, for you, defines the essence of a worthwhile existence: running, eating, thinking, singing, talking, or something else. Then write a precise, sentence-by-sentence imitation of Thoreau's statement on sauntering, modifying his sentence patterns slightly to fit the meaning of your own topic. Look up your favorite activity in the *OED* and present, like Thoreau, an explanatory and celebratory etymology.
2. Take another approach to Thoreau's subject. Can you write a brief celebration of walking in a way other than the etymological breakdown of a specific type of walking?
3. Examine one or more of the other essays in this anthology with Thoreau's notion of sauntering in mind. Do the other writers seem to understand the idea (perhaps an oxymoron) of "intense leisure" suggested by Thoreau? In particular, you might want to analyze one of the other walking essays and then explain in a paper how the essay succeeds or fails in living up to Thoreau's notion of the ideal way to experience the world.

4. Read Thoreau's statement about "home-cosmography" later in this anthology (excerpted from *Walden*) and then write an analytical essay in which you explain the connections between sauntering and home-cosmography. You might extend this analysis further by considering whether the entries we have selected from Thoreau's journal (see the chapter on "Wilderness Journals") effectively demonstrate these fundamental concepts and processes.

DAVID BLACK

Walking the Cape: A Distance Measured in Time

David Black (1945–   ), a 1967 graduate of Amherst College and the author of such books as the novel *Like Father* (1978), a biography of a prominent nineteenth-century New York social and political figure called *The King of Fifth Avenue: The Fortunes of August Belmont* (1981), and the mystery *Murder at the Met* (1984), is not usually included in the ranks of important nature writers. But the following article, which first appeared in *Harper's* (1985), provides a fascinating alternative to the less explicit self-absorption of such writers as Rachel Carson, Lewis Thomas, Edward Hoagland, and John Hay. A walk along the Great Beach of Cape Cod, the stretch of sand, surf, and dune between Eastham and Provincetown, Massachusetts, becomes, for Black, a movement through time as well as space. Each observation in the present triggers a memory of something the author has read or experienced. "We use the past— stories about the past—to nourish us," says Black.

Whereas other writers of walking narratives suggest that the act of moving through the natural world absorbs them wholly in the experience of the present moment, Black seems to take the opposite perspective, concluding that any author must become the "measure" of what he or she experiences, that "on the outside, enclosing everything, is ourselves." This unabashed egoism, this willing internalization of the past, other people, and the natural world, sharply distinguishes Black from most of the other writers in this anthology. Or perhaps Black is simply more candid about his egoism than the others. This candor occurs throughout the essay; for instance, when he describes the nearly erotic pleasure he derives from writing: "I delight in the attempt to translate the physical details of the world into art—whether the art is deliberate, an artifact like a story or a painting, or only a stray thought, a narrative moment. We live in our heads; no wonder we enjoy the intellectual equivalent of a hard-on, pleasure at the fact of creation, even if the act of creation is merely identifying—recognizing—what we are experiencing." Critics have praised Black's nonfiction, particularly *The King of Fifth Avenue*, for its engaging, fictionlike qualities. The following essay, too, catches and keeps our attention—or at least aims to do so—by way of the author's inventiveness and verbal flair.

Cape Cod is an arm flexing into the Atlantic, an ambiguous gesture: America summoning Europe, showing its muscle, or giving the Italian equivalent of the finger. In 1849 and in 1857, Henry David Thoreau walked from Eastham to Provincetown, a distance of about twenty-eight miles. Since then the dunes haven't changed much, but Provincetown has been transformed from a fishing village into a capital of honky-tonk. So walking from Eastham to Provincetown, which I do each summer, is like hiking through time, from 1849 to the present, from a landscape that is not too different from what Thoreau saw to one that is very different. And comparing Thoreau's Cape with the Cape today is a means of measuring some of the ways in which our country has changed in the past century and a third. Or so I, at first, thought.

> On reaching Boston . . . we noticed in the streets a handbill headed "Death! one hundred and forty-five lives lost at Cohasset." . . . The brig *St. John*, from Galway, Ireland, laden with emigrants, was wrecked on Sunday morning.

The first time I walked up the Cape, in the summer of 1974, when I was twenty-nine, the body of a woman had just been found in a secluded spot in the dunes near Provincetown. She had been sexually assaulted, and her hands had been chopped off. At the time, it had seemed a neat, if melodramatic counterpart to the shipwreck that had greeted Thoreau on his first walk up the Cape.

Thoreau's egoism—the selfishness that led him to seek at Walden Pond a life in which any dealing with others could be on his terms—had found in the wreck an excuse to turn life into a pageant staged for his benefit. "If I had found one body cast upon the beach in some lonely place, it would have affected me more," he wrote. "I sympathized rather with the winds and waves. . . . " One hundred and forty-five dead, and

Thoreau sympathized with the forces that killed them. It is unpopular to suggest that Thoreau's self-reliance—which in our time has been reinterpreted to mean *self-service*—might be rooted in narcissism, the theatrical pride of a spoiled kid who retreats to his bedroom, slamming the door to keep out the adults. But throughout his book *Cape Cod*, Thoreau makes himself the measure of what he hears and sees—which is, of course, exactly what any author must do. Literature is full of the sound of slamming doors.

The 1974 dune murder was so barbarous that it stirred elemental fears. People in bars were sure the killing had been part of a satanic ritual. A garage mechanic claimed he'd heard that the body had been drained of blood; the killing was an act of vampirism, although he took comfort in his conviction that the vampire wasn't a supernatural creature. It was merely a man with a taste for blood.

In a restaurant in Hyannis, a local lawyer who sat next to me at the counter said he was sure the murder had been done by hippies—this was 1974, remember, not long after the height of what was then called the counterculture. He'd just seen a science fiction movie about the end of the world. Reveling in the apocalypse, people went crazy, he told me; had sex in the streets, broke windows, trampled one another. It was the same up there in Provincetown, he said. They—he jabbed his thumb over his shoulder as though *they* followed him around, a ghost chorus—lived as if the world were about to end. That's how *they* could do such ghastly things.

The crime became a promiscuous symbol, representing whatever evils an outraged citizen felt threatened by. The breakdown of the family. The sexual revolution. The decline in respect for property.

For years—this is my own door slamming—whenever I walked up the Cape, I took smug satisfaction in believing that the woman-in-the-dunes murder fixed the present in the same way that the wreck of the *St. John* fixed the past. It betrayed the barbarism of our age. There is something seductive about living through what we convince ourselves is a crisis in civilization; it gives us the illusion that everything we do is important because the times are so extraordinary.

A few years later, on the way to make my annual walk, I stopped for lunch in Fall River, Massachusetts, and overheard two other out-of-towners discussing Lizzie Borden, who was accused of hacking her father and stepmother to death in that town in the summer of 1892. Violence, even meaningless violence, is a constant in human nature, as unchanging as the dunes.

Last year, I took my walk late, the week after Labor Day. I arrived on the beach near Eastham at dawn, about two hours before high tide. The wind was blowing from the southeast. There was a drizzle pockmarking the sand. The sea and sky were gray, and a mist smudged out the horizon, so looking at the ocean was like staring at the inside of an egg, which—as the mist lifted—seemed to be cracking along its middle as though the world were about to hatch.

The Nauset Light, on the cliff to my left, was a squat tower, like a chess rook: white on the bottom, red on the top. Its searchlight, pale yellow, getting paler as the sky brightened, turned off as I passed below on the beach. The three lighthouses Thoreau had seen were destroyed in 1892, the same year Lizzie Borden was accused of her crime.

Two surf-casters were walking back and forth along the shore, checking their rods, which they'd stuck upright in metal tubes jammed into the sand. They were serious fishermen, one in an orange wind-breaker, the other in a blue-hooded sweatshirt, who except for their costumes could have been on the beach when Thoreau walked up the Cape. As I passed, the three of us nodded as solemnly as if we'd been in church.

Once I was far enough along the shore so that they were out of sight, I sat in the shelter of the high cliff that ran along the length of the beach all the way to Provincetown. I unpacked a thermos of coffee and a doughnut from the rucksack I was carrying (Thoreau had walked with an umbrella) and had breakfast. The surf sounded like a stereo demonstration record: soft off to my right, getting louder as the breakers rolled along the beach, cracking like a gunshot right in front of me, and getting softer as they rolled farther along the beach to my left. The waves as they slid up the sand, foamed and hissed like butter sizzling in a frying pan.

The noise the surf made would have been the same 135 years ago, but Thoreau would have heard it differently. It is not just that I use a simile he would not have used, but that because I live in a time in which stereos exist, I actually hear the noise of the surf differently. Figures of speech are not decorations, but clues to how our minds interpret the world.

Sitting there, I had my first suspicion that my thesis about walking forward through time might be arbitrary. I could just as easily have been walking backward through time—from a landscape very different from the one Thoreau had seen to a town that, for all its modern honky-tonk, was closer to the village he'd visited than I had at first assumed.

Because it was harder to get to, the beach seemed far more savage to Thoreau than it did to me. For him, it was "a wild, rank place" with "no flattery in it." For me, it was a park, protected by the federal government, subject to regulations, planted with Erosion Control Area signs.

For Thoreau, Provincetown was "a flourishing town" that looked forward to a prosperous future. For me, it was a city that looked back-ward to its past. Its history was the central fact of its life, the thing that heightened its value as a tourist attraction. As for the town's notoriety as a sinkhole of vice, Provincetown had a bad reputation as far back as 1727. The Devil, according to Mary Heaton Vorse, chased a ship's captain named Jeremiah Snaggs all over the Cape, from Barnstable to Orleans to Wellfleet, finally catching him in Provincetown.

> "Well," said Captain Jeremiah, "you caught me fair and squar'. Whar do we go from here?"
> "Go?" said the devil. "Nowhar. Ain't we to Provincetown?"

When I started walking again, the last of the mist was rolling in big balls off the cliffs and spreading along the beach. The sun broke through. A man in a red plaid shirt and chinos, another beach hiker, appeared up the shore about 200 feet ahead of me, his long-legged shadow stretched out on the sand. I was to see him off and on all day.

By the time I reached Marconi Beach, the sun was out for good. Where the water retreated on the sand, it left a silvery luster like the sheen of a dead fish. Styrofoam egg cartons, plastic six-pack holders, and empty bleach bottles washed up with the waves. The debris Thoreau found, the remains of wrecked ships and their cargo, seemed more heroic—ships breaking up in storms instead of bathers tossing beer cans into the surf. But, of course, littering doesn't lead to loss of life; shipwrecks do.

At various secluded spots, the garbage had been turned into art. In one place, driftwood, colored cloth, crab shells, plastic containers, and yellow rope had been used to build the skeleton of a boat. At another spot garbage had been organized into an antic house, something out of an Edward Lear poem, flying half-deflated balloons and raggedy pennants made of old T-shirts.

> There is usually, as I have said, no bathing on the backside of the Cape, on account of the undertow.

On Marconi Beach, three white lifeguard towers stood empty, facing the sea. It was still before seven o'clock in the morning, almost an hour before high tide, and there were no bathers in sight, although farther along the shore I found an elderly man dressed in white slacks, a shirt the pale yellow of the Nauset Light, a blue blazer, and a white visored cap with an emblem of a jumping marlin stitched to the front. He sat in a low beach chair on the very edge of the dry sand, his polished loafers planted as though, like King Canute, he were daring the sea to advance.

By the time I reached the Wellfleet beaches, a few late-season bathers were sitting on towels, waiting to get warm enough to dash into the water; and some scavengers were wandering along the shore, looking not for firewood or valuable cargo from shipwrecks (like the scavengers Thoreau met), but for shells and stones and pieces of smooth colored glass. I'd been filling my pockets with souvenirs, too: rocks shaped as perfectly as eggs, clam shells, ark shells, periwinkles, and translucent gray stones that looked like solidified smoke.

A few hundred feet from the crowded part of the beach, naked bathers lay, working on tans. The adults were nude, and the kids were clothed. In 1954, before I'd ever heard of Thoreau, my family visited one of my father's cronies—let's call him Ernst Weibeck—who had a summer place in Wellfleet, a large Queen Anne house with double doors that opened onto a strip of sand. Beyond, framed by the door's arch, the ocean gleamed like black plastic.

There were a few other families down for the day. It was mid-May, so no one had thought to bring a bathing suit; but it was unseasonably warm, so the younger kids had stripped and were playing at the water's edge, naked.

"Go on in," my father told me.

I'd just turned nine and was too old, I thought, to swim naked.

My father kept goading me, and I kept refusing—much to the amusement of the other adults.

"It's too babyish," I said.

"Balls," said Weibeck, who in Germany in the early 1930s had been a member of the Verband Volksgesundheit, a socialist nudist organization. In the middle of the living room, he stripped; and he ran through the double doors down to the water—followed by the other men, who also stripped and who, cavorting in the sand, looked as goatish as figures in a late Picasso print.

As I passed a nude woman, stretched out on her back, she opened her eyes, started—as a token of modesty—to raise one knee so she wouldn't be caught spread-eagled, then resisted the impulse, staying defiantly as she was.

I like nudity, but I've never been able—as friends of mine claim they have—to find it innocent. When I used to camp on these dunes with the couples with whom my wife and I were sharing a house, I was never able to pretend that skinny-dipping was an act of liberation—which meant I found it hard to counterfeit a disinterested gaze at the bodies of the women as they proved how free they were by wandering around the campsite naked. I'm sure it is a character flaw. But my response to seeing an attractive woman undressed is nearly always lewd.

Even in a museum, when I come upon a nude—whether it is an obviously pornographic Boucher or a matter-of-fact Manet—I take pleasure as much in the sexual tension as in the solution to the formal artistic problem. Like Miles, the writer in John Fowles's novel *Mantissa*, I look forward to the "sexy parts." Which doesn't mean that I like only erotica. It does mean that I delight in the attempt to translate the physical details of the world into art—whether the art is deliberate, an artifact like a story or a painting, or only a stray thought, a narrative moment.

We live in our heads; no wonder we enjoy the intellectual equivalent of a hard-on, pleasure at the fact of creation, even if the act of creation is merely identifying—recognizing—what we are experiencing.

One the other hand, I know it is possible to look on even the most obscene image with innocent eyes. Once, as I drove through Times Square, my daughter, who was then five years old, gazed through the window at a marquee cutout of the porno star Vanessa Del Rio, twelve feet high and shamelessly draped—or rather undraped—in transparent scarves, and cried, "Look. Tinker Bell!"

The tide was now going out. A dead sand shark, about two feet long, was washed up on the beach. Its belly was very white and streaked with blood, which looked like water stains on wallpaper. The gills and eye sockets were filled with sand. The dorsal fin fluttered in the breeze. A little beyond the shark were the remains of what must have been a skate, although part of the tail and most of the body had been eaten away. The chunks of flesh that still stuck to the bones looked like clumps of tapioca pudding.

Thoreau called the beach a vast morgue. That hasn't changed. Between Wellfleet and Provincetown I saw half a dozen more dead sand sharks, the stinking carcass of an animal that could have been a dog, the remains of a seagull covered with flies that buzzed away in a cloud when I approached, small dead fish that looked like spilled exclamation points, and, of course, shells, all that remained of clams, scallops, cockles, and limpets.

I walked through patches of dried kelp that rustled like autumn leaves. For a while, I strolled along popping the little air bladders in the strands of rockweed. Where the beach was deserted, gulls stood in crowds, each gazing over the heads of the others, like guests at a chic party on the lookout for celebrities. Later, I noticed crowds of gulls that all faced the same way, south, into the breeze. Their footprints looked like wishbones, or photographs of chromosomes.

I sat on the beach, drank some more coffee, ate a gritty blueberry muffin, and, having stripped, ran through the chilly air into the waves. I came out, dried myself, dressed, and drank some warm whiskey out of a pint bottle I'd been carrying in my back pocket.

By two in the afternoon I had reached the Truro shore, more than halfway from Eastham to Provincetown. The day after I graduated from Amherst College, in 1967, I headed—as I did after school ended every year—for the Cape, detouring by way of Providence, Rhode Island, to visit my grandparents. That morning, my grandfather had awakened hardly able to breathe. The doctor was there when I arrived, examining him. My grandfather gazed up at me mildly, unable to speak, smiling over the doctor's shoulder. Six and a half feet tall, broad as a refrigerator, white hair like hot phosphorous, he had loomed over me in my childhood, not only because of the foreshortening with which kids view adults—looking up from below as if at skyscrapers—but also because he seemed, with his pawlike fists and booming laugh, an elemental force, a hurricane or an earthquake. He had always been a heroic and comic figure, like Gargantua, Falstaff, or Paul Bunyan. On his back, in bed, he looked shrunken, defeated, apologetic. By the time I left the room he had become—in the story I told myself about his life—a tragic figure: perhaps still Falstaff, but the Falstaff at the end of *Henry IV, Part 2.* Even his hair, once as fiery as a halo, was now the dingy yellow of old teeth.

My grandmother had called my parents, who were on their way from their home in Springfield, Massachusetts. She took me into the living room, where we sat, made formal by death, before glass-fronted bookcases filled with Hebrew prayer books and a set of Dickens. These were the only volumes she'd kept from a collection she had saved up for when she first came to America and was sewing dresses in a sweat-shop in New York City. The rest of the collection, about 500 books, was intended to form the core of a library for the children of the village in Lithuania where she had been born; but when she took the books to Europe shortly before World War I, the wooden trunks in which they were packed were stolen at a railway terminal in Poland. Having come so far, she didn't want to cancel her trip, so she continued on her way, carrying the stories in her head. Surrounded by the children of her village, she recited what she could remember of *Oliver Twist, David Copperfield,* and *Great Expectations,* placing the events in twentieth-century New York City, not nineteenth-century London, to make them more immediate, as though they were true tales she was importing from her experience in the New World, tales in which—out of tribal loyalty—Riah (the Jew in *Our Mutual Friend*) became the hero and Fagin a ruined Cossack. In my grandmother's America, Cossacks drove through the Lower East Side in jalopies.

Despite how fast and loose she played with Dickens's plots, my grandmother worshiped books and felt unworthy of them. The one time she visited me at college, she refused to go into the library—a great campus attraction, which JFK had dedicated a few weeks before he'd been shot—because (she said) she wasn't dressed properly. As I tried to convince her that she was dressed just fine, the bells of Johnson Chapel tolled the hour, and my grandmother turned white. I loved the sound of the bells. For me, they evoked a sense of community; they transformed the landscape into a Norman Rockwell painting. For my grandmother, the sound was murderous. In the village in which she was born, Christians rang church bells as they rode through the Jewish quarter, killing and burning. In us, the bells set off clashing stories; and the stories kept us apart.

Trying to distract me—and herself—from my grandfather's illness, my grandmother asked, now that I had graduated, what I intended to do.

"I'm going to be a writer," I said.

She grabbed my hands and squeezed them as though I'd blasphemed.

"That's not something we do," she said. "That's for the gentry."

I pulled away. Furious—maybe because I half believed her—I grabbed my rucksack, slammed from the house, and, when I got to the corner of the block, stuck out my thumb and hitched to the Cape. When I got to Truro, I called Providence to apologize. My mother told me my grandfather had died that afternoon. I said I'd hitch back the next morning. I spent the night in a shack I'd rented, an abandoned gas station with a huge plate-glass window facing the highway. There were no curtains. In full view of the passing cars, on my old portable typewriter, I wrote about how my grandmother had refused to enter the Amherst College library and how terrified she'd been of the Johnson Chapel bells, trying to reduce the distance between us by making her story part of my story.

North of Truro, a surfer in a black wet suit flopped in flippers down to the ocean. He looked like a great lizard that had learned to walk erect, one of the creatures from Karel Čapek's novel *War with the Newts*. A woman, bundled in a parka and with a plaid blanket wrapped around her legs, waited for him on-shore, fiddling with a portable radio. When Thoreau arrived on the Cape, he saw two organ grinders on their way to Provincetown, who, he thought, would provide the only music to be found in the towns he would be passing.

I had become a human sundial. At the beginning of my hike, my shadow had been behind me and to my left. As I walked up the Cape, my shadow had moved clockwise around me until at noon it had been right in front. By the time I reached the Highland Light, about five o'clock, my shadow was behind me and to my right.

Thoreau had stayed overnight at the Highland Light and had talked at length with the lighthouse keeper. I scrambled up the cliff, grabbing on to the beach grass. At the top was a field. The breakers, below, were abruptly softer, as if someone had turned the volume down. Crickets chirruped in the bushes. A bobwhite called off to the left. It was idyllic. The wind had changed, coming now from the southwest. All the stalks of grass leaned over in the light breeze and pointed the same way.

Beyond the field were radar domes, dimpled like golf balls. To the right was the lighthouse with a high fence around it. When Thoreau walked up the Cape, he had been a welcome distraction to the lighthouse keeper. Now, the lighthouse was off-limits to hikers.

I slid back down the cliff and headed up the beach to Provincetown. For a while, I was kept company by a woman riding a horse along the sand. She would trot beside me, then suddenly canter into the waves, which would splash up and make the horse toss its head.

Another dead shark, dried, gutted, and collapsed like a punctured inflatable toy, lay nearby. Beyond that I found the arm of a doll, a rubber snake, a toy horse, and a plastic dinosaur scattered over the sand, looking like the failed attempts of a bungling god to populate a dead planet.

Outside of Provincetown, I passed a section of beach that had been fenced off as a tern colony: a separate site set apart for birds—it seemed the most alien thing to Thoreau's world that I had seen. I climbed the cliff and followed a footpath through the dunes.

The obvious difference between Thoreau's Provincetown and ours lies in a reversal of the public and private.

> The outward aspect of the houses and shops frequently suggested a poverty which their interior comfort and even richness disproved.

Provincetown now presents a rich mask, hiding an impoverished life. During the summer, Commercial Street, Provincetown's main thoroughfare, becomes a carnival. Shops sell candied applies, spun sugar, saltwater taffy, fudge, hot dogs, hamburgers, ice cream, fried clams, portraits in chalk, tintypes (customers dress up in clothes from Thoreau's time and have their pictures taken so they'll look in the photos like their own great-grandparents, so they'll become their own ancestors), ceramics, "Poetic Impressions: original pen and ink prints and poetry, personalized for you by the poet, $1.50 matted, $1.00 unmatted," trinkets. The music from one bar merges with the music from another bar up the street. People lounge at outdoor cafes, watching the passing circus.

In the late summer, the town seemed as deserted as an off-season amusement park. In a bar, a man was sipping a drink, apparently oblivious to the blond girl holding him around the waist and resting her cheek against his shoulder. At a table in the back of the room sat the man in the red plaid shirt I'd been shadowing all day. I wanted to ask him why he'd hiked up the Cape, but by the time I'd ordered my drink he was gone.

Later, I walked out along the pier. Mist was coming off the water in strands like cigarette smoke. At the end of the dock, a man was urinating into the harbor.

When I look at old photographs of the Cape—or of New York City, or of anyplace—I rarely try to imagine what life was like then. Instead, I try to fit the past into the present. I like to go to the location where the picture was snapped and try to conjure the image up, so I can see how it would look on that spot now. When I was writing a biography of August Belmont, a nineteenth-century financier and sportsman, I used to walk up Broadway from the Battery to Prince Street, where Niblo's Garden used to stand, superimposing old New York on the present city.

The past has its own geography, crosshatched with emotional longitudes and latitudes. It is no longer a physical place, but a series of overlapping stories. We use the past—the stories about the past—to nourish us. And we need nourishment. We are hungry as Saturn. But, unlike Saturn, we devour not our own children, but those who lived before us. We are continually doing what I did with my grandmother's memories of tolling church bells, what I do with Thoreau's *Cape Cod* every time I repeat his walk: making the past part of the present, and making of the present one more story that will feed us in the future.

Every day, we turn life's Chinese boxes inside out. At the center is the infinite universe; then, each a little larger and enclosing the last, come successive realities—all the way down to our country, our city, our community, our family, until, on the outside, enclosing everything, is ourselves.

In Islamic legend, a king sewed up a peacock's head in a bag so there would be nothing to distract from the beauty of its tail. The bird forgot what the world was like, assumed that all existence was encompassed within the limits of the bag. Its beauty was beyond its comprehension.

The stories we tell ourselves are a way of seeing through the bag, a way of making the Chinese boxes transparent, so that we can see through our own lives into the infinite heart of the puzzle. The stories help us comprehend whatever beauty our lives accidentally make as we blindly move through time.

I returned to the bar. The man with the girl draped over him was still sipping his drink. He muttered, "Unreal, unreal, unreal."

Analyzing and Discussing the Text

1. What does the subtitle of this essay—"A Distance Measured in Time"—mean?
2. Black claims that "throughout his book *Cape Cod,* Thoreau makes himself the measure of what he hears and sees—which is, of course, exactly what any author must do." What does this mean? Does Black believe that even a walk through the natural world, such as the hike from Eastham to Provincetown on Cape Cod, is merely an excuse for egocentrism or narcissism? Can you think of any writing about nature that is not so self-centered?
3. "Figures of speech are not decorations," writes Black, "but clues to how our minds interpret the world." Explain this idea, and then, using examples of Black's figures of speech, explain how *his* mind works.

4. Early in this essay Black refers to a famous Cape Cod murder as a sign of "the barbarism of our age," but he proceeds to describe the human debris on the beach nonchalantly, as if it were of no consequence. "[L]ittering doesn't lead to loss of life," he claims. What can we infer about Black's worldview from these comments?

5. Black talks about filling his pockets with souvenirs from the beach, various shells and stones and pieces of worn glass. What kind of attitude toward the natural world does this imply? Is it somehow related to Abbey's idea about naming and possessing (see Part Two, Chapter Two)?

6. "We live in our heads," asserts Black. Discuss the section of his essay concerning the nudist beach. Is this a realistic version of the way the human mind works? Is Black's self-absorption any more exaggerated than that of the average person? Connect Black's statement to his later description of the dead animals on the beach and his grandmother's horrified response to the bells at Amherst.

7. At the end of Black's essay, a man utters "Unreal, unreal, unreal." Does Black's narrative—his interwoven "stories"—help to make life's "Chinese boxes transparent"? In what sense does Black seem "nourished" by his walk, by his reflections?

Experiencing and Writing About the World

1. Tell the story of one of your own excursions, allowing your narrative to digress as you recall personal experiences or things you've read that are somehow linked to what you see. Make a point of emphasizing the digressions rather than the current experience; does this enable *you* to "measure the distance in time"?

2. Describe one or more specific scenes with exaggeratedly artificial language—multiple similes, metaphors, unusual adjectives. Then describe the same scenes more directly, more plainly, but with similar detail. Explain in a paragraph or two the different attitudes toward the world implied by the two types of description.

3. Prepare an analytical essay in which you explain Black's use of figurative language. How do his frequent metaphors and similes contribute to the essay and how do they detract from it? You might wish to compare Black's figures of speech with those of another essayist from this anthology, such as Susan Mitchell (see Part Three, Chapter Three).

4. Write an analysis of "Walking the Cape" in which you explain the author's use of autobiographical material. Why does he say so much about himself? Is this essay about David Black, Cape Cod, or the process of writing? Explain how the three are interconnected.

BARRY LOPEZ

The Image of the Unicorn

Barry Lopez (1945–   ), who was born in Port Chester, New York, grew up in southern California before attending a Jesuit high school in New York and then the University of Notre Dame, where he received a B.A. in 1966 and an M.A. in teaching in 1968. He briefly attended graduate school at the University of Oregon (1969–1970), but quit to devote himself to writing for magazines. For many years Lopez has been a contributing editor for the *North American Review* and *Harper's*. He has also served as Distinguished Visiting Writer at Eastern Washington University (1985), as Ida Beam Visiting Professor at the University of Iowa (1985), and as Distinguished Visiting Naturalist at Carleton College (1986). His first collection of essaylike fiction, *Desert Notes: Reflections in the Eye of a Raven*, appeared in 1976. Since then Lopez has published several collections of short fiction. His first book of nonfiction, *Of Wolves and Men*, won the John Burroughs Medal for outstanding natural history writing in 1978. In 1986 Lopez received an award from the American Academy and Institute of Arts and Letters for his many important works, and the following year he held a Guggenheim Fellowship. The parable *Crow and Weasel*, which contemplates Lopez's favorite motifs of travel and storytelling, came out in 1990. Although Lopez himself travels frequently to such distant regions as the Arctic, Japan, the Galápagos Islands, Africa, and, most recently, Antarctica to conduct his research, he returns to his home in the woods near the McKenzie River, east of Eugene, Oregon, to write.

Lopez received the American Book Award in 1986 for his collection of essays *Arctic Dreams: Imagination and Desire in a Northern Landscape*. In his acceptance speech, he referred to the Japanese principle of *kotodama*, which suggests that writers have a responsibility to "take care for the spiritual quality, the holy quality, the serious quality of language." Lopez's own writing demonstrates an explicit respect not only for language itself, but also for his subject matter and his readers. As he once told an interviewer, "The bow of respect toward the material means try to understand what's coming from it, not what you are trying to impose on it. Listen. Pay attention. Do your research. Don't presume." The following essay, initially published in the *North American Review* and then reprinted as the chapter called "Lancaster Sound: *Monodon monoceros*" in *Arctic Dreams*, demonstrates Lopez's multiple approaches to the task of "paying attention," his alternating use of scholarly and experiential information regarding his subject: the natural world in general; the Arctic region; the region's human visitors and inhabitants; and, in this case, chiefly the unicornlike sea animal known in English as the "narwhal." The essay appears in this section of the anthology, although it could easily have fit elsewhere (for instance, in "Birds and Beasts"), because of the way Lopez uses a lengthy, interrupted walking narrative as a strand to tie together the whole essay, beginning and ending with the concrete, the particular. For Lopez, though, this is more than an artistic ploy, a way of engaging the reader. In the prologue of *Arctic Dreams*, Lopez writes that "if we are to devise an enlightened plan for human activity in the Arctic, we need a more particularized understanding of the land itself—not a more refined mathematical knowledge, but a deeper understanding of its nature, as if it were, itself, another sort of civilization we had to reach some agreement with." This walking narrative attempts to particularize the reader's understanding of the world.

I am standing at the margin of the sea ice called the floe edge at the mouth of Admiralty Inlet, northern Baffin Island, three or four miles out to sea. The firmness beneath my feet belies the ordinary sense of the phrase "out to sea." Several Eskimo camps stand here along the white and black edge of ice and water. All of us have come from another place—Nuvua, 30 miles to the south at the tip of Uluksan Peninsula. We are here to hunt narwhals. They are out there in the open water of Lancaster Sound somewhere, waiting for this last ice barrier to break up so they can enter their summer feeding grounds in Admiralty Inlet.

As I walk along the floe edge—the light is brilliant, the ceaseless light of July; but after so many weeks I am weary of it; I stare at the few shadows on the ice with a kind of hunger—as I walk along here I am aware of both fear and elation, a mix that comes in remote regions with the realization that you are exposed and the weather can be capricious, and fatal. The wind is light and from the north—I can see its corrugation on the surface of the water. Should it swing around and come from the south, the ice behind us would begin to open up. Traverse cracks across the inlet, only a few inches wide yesterday, would begin to widen. We would have difficulty getting back to Nuvua, even if we left at the first sign of a wind shift.

A few days ago one of these men was caught like that. A distant explosion, like dynamite, told him what a compass bearing he quickly took on Borden Peninsula confirmed—that the five-square-mile sheet of floe ice he had camped on was being swept out of Admiralty Inlet toward open water in Lancaster Sound. He and his companion, knowing the set of local currents, struck out immediately to the east. Twelve hours later, near exhaustion, they came to a place where the ice floe was grounded in shallow coastal water, making a huge, slow turn in the current before breaking loose into Lancaster Sound. They leaped and plunged across broken ice cakes for the firm shore.

I am not so much thinking of these things, however, as I am feeling the exuberance of birds around me. Black-legged kittiwakes, northern fulmars, and black guillemots are wheeling and hovering in weightless acrobatics over the streams and lenses of life in the water—zooplankton and arctic cod—into which they plunge repeatedly for their sustenance. Out on the ice, at piles of offal from the narwhal hunt, glaucous and Thayer's gulls stake a rough-tempered claim to some piece of flesh, brash, shouldering birds alongside the more reticent and rarer ivory gulls.

Birds fly across these waters in numbers that encourage you to simply flip your pencil in the air. Certain species end their northward migration here and nest. Others fly on to Devon and Ellesmere islands or to northwest Greenland. From where I now stand I can study some that stay, nesting in an unbroken line for 10 miles on a cliff between Baillarge Bay and Elwin Inlet, a rugged wall of sedimentary and volcanic rock pocked with indentations and ledges, rising at an angle of 80° from the water. More than 50,000 northern fulmars. At other such rookeries around Lancaster Sound, guillemots, murres, and kittiwakes congregate in tens and even hundreds of thousands to nest and feed during the short summer. Gulls, arctic terns, snow geese, eiders, red-breasted mergansers, and dovekies have passed through in droves already. Of the dovekies—a small, stocky seabird with a black head and bright white underside—something on the order of a third of the northwest Greenland population of 30 *million* passes over Lancaster Sound in May and June.

On the white-as-eggshell ice plain where we are camped, with the mottled browns and ochers of Borden Peninsula to the east and the dark cliffs of Brodeur Peninsula obscured in haze to the west, the adroit movements of the birds above the water give the landscape an immediate, vivid dimension: the eye, drawn far out to pale hues on the horizon, comes back smartly to the black water, where, *plunk,* a guillemot disappears in a dive.

The outcry of birds, the bullet-whirr of their passing wings, the splashing of water, is, like the falling light, unending. Lancaster Sound is a rare arctic marine sanctuary, a place where creatures are concentrated in the sort of densities one finds in the Antarctic Ocean, the richest sea waters in the world. Marine ecologists are not certain why Lancaster Sound teems so with life, but local upwelling currents and a supply of nutrients from glacial runoff on Devon Island seem critical.[1]

[1]Lancaster Sound has been proposed as a world biological reserve by the International Biological Programme and singled out by the United Nations as a Natural Site of World Heritage Quality. The stability of this ecosystem is currently threatened by offshore oil development and increased shipping traffic. David Nettleship, an arctic ornithologist with preeminent experience here, has written that such economic development "should be strictly controlled in order to prevent the destruction of a uniquely rich high arctic oasis. To harm it would go far towards making a desert of arctic waters." —Author's note.

Three million colonial seabirds, mostly northern fulmars, kitti-wakes, and guillemots, nest and feed here in the summer. It is no longer the haunt of 10,000 or so bowhead whales, but it remains a summering ground for more than 30 percent of the belukha whale pop-ulation of North America, and more than three-quarters of the world's population of narwhals. No one is sure how many harp, bearded, and ringed seals are here—probably more than a quarter of a million. In addition there are thousands of Atlantic walrus. The coastal regions are a denning area for polar bear and home to thousands of arctic fox in the summer.

I am concerned, as I walk, however, more with what is immediate to my senses—the ternlike whiffle and spin of birds over the water, the chicken-cackling of northern fulmars, and cool air full of the breath of sea life. This community of creatures, including all those invisible in the water, constitutes a unique overlap of land, water, and air. This is a special meeting ground, like that of a forest's edge with a clearing; or where the fresh waters of an estuary meet the saline tides of the sea; or at a river's riparian edge. The mingling of animals from different ecosystems charges such border zones with evolutionary potential. Fly-ing creatures here at Admiralty Inlet walk on ice. They break the pane of water with their dives to feed. Marine mammals break the pane of water coming the other way to breathe.

The edges of any landscape—horizons, the lip of a valley, the bend of a river around a canyon wall—quicken an observer's expectations. That attraction to borders, to the earth's twilit places, is part of the shape of human curiosity. And the edges that cause excitement are like these where I now walk, sensing the birds toying with gravity; or like those in quantum mechanics, where what is critical straddles a border between being a wave and being a particle, between being what it is and becoming something else, occupying an edge of time that defeats our geometries. In biology these transitional areas between two different communities are called ecotones.

The ecotone at the Admiralty Inlet floe edge extends in two planes. In order to pass under the ice from the open sea, an animal must be free of a need for atmospheric oxygen; the floe edge, therefore, is a barrier to the horizontal migration of whales. In the vertical plane, no bird can penetrate the ice and birds like gulls can't go below water with guillemots to feed on schools of fish. Sunlight, too, is halted at these borders.

To stand at the edge of this four-foot-thick ice platform, however, is to find yourself in a rich biological crease. Species of alga grow on the bottom of the sea ice, turning it golden brown with a patchwork of life. These tiny diatoms feed zooplankton moving through the upper layers of water in vast clouds—underwater galaxies of copepods, amphipods, and mysids. These in turn feed the streaming schools of cod. The cod feed the birds. And the narwhals. And also the ringed seal, which feeds the polar bear, and eventually the fox. The algae at the bottom of this food web are called "epontic" algae, the algae of the sea ice. (Ringed seals, ivory gulls, and other birds and mammals whose lives are ice-oriented are called "pagophylic.") It is the ice, however, that holds this life together. For ice-associated seals, vulnerable on a beach, it is a place offshore to rest, directly over their feeding grounds. It provides algae with a surface to grow on. It shelters arctic cod from hunting seabirds and herds of narwhals, and it shelters the narwhal from the predatory orca. It is the bear's highway over the sea. And it gives me a place to stand on the ocean, and wonder.

I walk here intent on the birds, half aware of the biological mysteries in these placid, depthless waters in which I catch fleeting silver glimpses of cod. I feel blessed. I draw in the salt air and feel the warmth of sunlight on my face. I recall a childhood of summer days on the beaches of California. I feel the wealth to be had in life in an aimless walk like this, through woods or over a prairie or down a beach.

It is not all benign and ethereal at the ice edge, however. You cannot—I cannot—lose completely the sense of how far from land this is. And I am wary of walrus. A male walrus is a huge animal, approaching the size of a small car. At close range in the water its agility and speed are intimidating. Walruses normally eat only bottom-dwelling organisms like clams, worms, and crabs, but there is an unusual sort of walrus—almost always a male, a loner, that deliberately hunts and kills seals. Its ivory tusks are crosshatched with the claw marks of seals fighting for their lives. (It is called *angeyeghaq* by the Eskimos on Saint Lawrence Island, who are familiar with its unusual behavior.) This rare carnivore will charge off an ice floe to attack a small boat, and actively pursue and try to kill people in the water. A friend of mine was once standing with an Eskimo friend at an ice edge when the man cautioned him to step back. They retreated 15 or 20 feet. Less than a minute later a walrus surfaced in an explosion of water where they had been standing. A polar bear trick.

When I walk along the floe edge I think of that story. I have no ear educated as was his companion's to anticipate the arrival of the walrus. A native ear. Experience. I walk here susceptible as any traveler to the unknown.

I stood still occasionally to listen. I heard only the claver of birds. Then there was something else. I had never heard the sound before, but when it came, plosive and gurgling, I knew instinctively what it was, even as everyone in camp jumped. I strained to see them, to spot the vapor of their breath, a warm mist against the soft horizon, or the white tip of a tusk breaking the surface of the water, a dark pattern that retained its shape against the dark, shifting patterns of the water. Somewhere out there in the ice fragments. Gone. Gone now. Others had heard the breathing. Human figures in a camp off to the west, dark lines on the blinding white ice, gesture toward us with upraised arms.

The first narwhals I ever saw lived far from here, in Bering Strait. The day I saw them I knew that no element of the earth's natural history had ever before brought me so far, so suddenly. It was as though something from a bestiary had taken shape, a creature strange as a giraffe. It was as if the testimony of someone I had no reason to doubt, yet could not quite believe, a story too farfetched, had been verified at a glance.

I was with a bowhead whale biologist named Don Ljungblad, flying search transects over Bering Sea. It was May, and the first bowheads of spring were slowly working their way north through Bering Strait toward their summer feeding grounds in the Chukchi and Beaufort seas. Each day as we flew these transects we would pass over belukha whale and walrus, ringed, spotted, and ribbon seals, bearded seals, and flocks of birds migrating to Siberia. I know of no other region in North America where animals can be met with in such numbers. Bering Sea itself is probably the richest of all the northern seas, as rich as Chesapeake Bay or the Grand Banks at the time of their discovery. Its bounty of crabs, pollock, cod, sole, herring, clams, and salmon is set down in wild numbers, the rambling digits of guesswork. The numbers of birds and marine mammals feeding here, to a person familiar with anything but the Serengeti or life at the Antarctic convergence, are magical. At the height of migration in the spring, the testament of life in Bering Sea is absolutely stilling in its dimensions.

The two weeks I spent flying with Ljungblad, with so many thousands of creatures moving through the water and the air, were a heady experience. Herds of belukha whale glided in silent shoals beneath transparent sheets of young ice. Squadrons of fast-flying sea ducks flashed beneath us as they banked away. We passed ice floes stained red in a hundred places with the afterbirths of walrus. Staring all day into the bright light reflected from the ice and water, however, and the compression in time of these extraordinary events, left me dazed some evenings.

Aspects of the arctic landscape that had become salient for me— its real and temporal borders; a rare, rich oasis of life surrounded by vast stretches of deserted land; the upending of conventional kinds of time; biological vulnerability made poignant by the forgiving light of summer—all of this was evoked over Bering Sea.

The day we saw the narwhals we were flying south, low over Bering Strait. The ice in Chukchi Sea behind us was so close it did not seem possible that bowheads could have penetrated this far; but it is good to check, because they can make headway in ice as heavy as this and they are able to come a long way north undetected in lighter ice on the Russian side. I was daydreaming about two bowheads we had seen that morning. They had been floating side by side in a broad lane of unusually clear water between a shelf of shorefast ice and the pack ice—the flaw lead. As we passed over, they made a single movement together, a slow, rolling turn and graceful glide, like figure skaters pushing off, these 50-ton leviathans. Ljungblad shouted in my earphones: "Waiting." They were waiting for the ice in the strait to open up. Ljungblad saw nearly 300 bowheads waiting calmly like this one year, some on their backs, some with their chins resting on the ice.

The narwhals appeared in the middle of this reverie. Two males, with ivory tusks spiraling out of their foreheads, the image of the unicorn with which history has confused them. They were close to the same size and light-colored, and were lying parallel and motionless in a long, straight lead in the ice. My eye was drawn to them before my conscious mind, let alone my voice, could catch up. I stared dumbfounded while someone else shouted. Not just to see the narwhals, but *here*, a few miles northwest of King Island in Bering Sea. In all the years scientists have kept records for these waters, no one had ever seen a narwhal alive in Bering Sea. Judging from the heaviness of the ice around them, they must have spent the winter here.[2] They were either residents, a wondrous thought, or they had come from the nearest population centers the previous fall, from waters north of Siberia or from northeastern Canada.

The appearance of these animals was highly provocative. We made circle after circle above them, until they swam away under the ice and were gone. Then we looked at each other. Who could say what this was, really?

Because you have seen something doesn't mean you can explain it. Differing interpretations will always abound, even when good minds come to bear. The kernel of indisputable information is a dot in space; interpretations grow out of the desire to make this point a line, to give it a direction. The directions in which it can be sent, the uses to which it can be put by a culturally, professionally, and geographically diverse society, are almost without limit. The possibilities make good scientists chary. In a region like the Arctic, tense with a hunger for wealth, with fears of plunder, interpretation can quickly get beyond a scientist's control. When asked to assess the meaning of a biological event—What were those animals doing out there? Where do they belong?—they hedge. They are sometimes reluctant to elaborate on what they saw, because they cannot say what it means, and they are suspicious of those who say they know. Some even distrust the motives behind the questions.

I think along these lines in this instance because of the animal. No large mammal in the Northern Hemisphere comes as close as the narwhal to having its very existence doubted. For some, the possibility that this creature might actually live in the threatened waters of Bering Sea is portentous, a significant apparition on the eve of an era of disruptive oil exploration there. For others, those with the leases to search for

[2]The narwhal is not nearly as forceful in the ice as the bowhead. It can break through only about 6 inches of ice with its head. A bowhead, using its brow or on occasion its more formidable chin, can break through as much as 18 inches of sea ice.—Author's note.

oil and gas in Navarin and Norton basins, the possibility that narwhals may live there is a complicating environmental nuisance. Hardly anyone marvels solely at the fact that on the afternoon of April 16, 1982, five people saw two narwhals in a place so unexpected that they were flabbergasted. They remained speechless, circling over the animals in a state of wonder. In those moments the animals did not have to mean anything at all.

We know more about the rings of Saturn than we know about the narwhal. Where do they go and what do they eat in the winter, when it is too dark and cold for us to find them? The Chilean poet and essayist Pablo Neruda wonders in his memoirs how an animal this large can have remained so obscure and uncelebrated. Its name, he thought, was "the most beautiful of undersea names, the name of a sea chalice that sings, the name of a crystal spur." Why, he wondered, had no one taken Narwhal for a last name, or built "a beautiful Narwhal Building?"

Part of the answer lies with a regrettable connotation of death in the animal's name. The pallid color of the narwhal's skin has been likened to that of a drowned human corpse, and it is widely thought that its name came from the Old Norse for "corpse" and "whale," *nár+hvalr*. A medieval belief that the narwhal's flesh was poisonous has been offered in support of this interpretation, as well as the belief that its "horn" was proof at that time against being poisoned. The eighteenth-century naturalist Buffon characterized the animal for all the generations that would read him as one that "revels in carnage, attacks without provocation, and kills without need." Among its associations with human enterprise in the inhospitable north is the following grim incident. In 1126, Arnhald, first bishop of Iceland, was shipwrecked off the Icelandic coast. Drowned men and part of the contents of the ship's hold washed up in a marsh, a place afterward called the Pool of Corpses. Conspicuous among the items of salvage were a number of narwhal tusks, "with runic letters upon them in an indelible red gum so that each sailor might know his own at the end of the voyage."

W. P. Lehmann, a professor of Germanic languages, believes the association with death is a linguistic accident. The Old Norse *nárhvalr* (whence the English *narwhal*, the French *narval*, the German *Narwal*, etc.), he says, was a vernacular play on the word *nahvalr*—the way *high-bred corn* is used in place of *hybrid corn*, or *sparrowgrass* is used for *asparagus*. According to Lehmann, *nahvalr* is an earlier, West Norse term meaning a "whale distinguished by a long, narrow projection" (the tusk).

Some, nevertheless, still call the narwhal "the corpse whale," and the unfounded belief that it is a cause of human death, or an omen or symbol to be associated with human death, remains intact to this day in some quarters. Animals are often fixed like this in history, bearing an unwarranted association derived from notions or surmise having no connection at all with their real life. The fuller explanations of modern field biology are an antidote, in part, to this tendency to name an animal carelessly. But it is also, as Neruda suggests, a task of literature to take animals regularly from the shelves where we have stored them, like charms or the most intricate of watches, and to bring them to life.

The obscurity of narwhals is not easily breeched by science. To begin with, they live underwater. And they live year-round in the polar ice, where the logistics and expense involved in approaching them are formidable barriers to field research, even in summer. Scientists have largely been limited to watching what takes place at the surface of the water in the open sea adjacent to observation points high on coastal bluffs. And to putting hydrophones in the water with them, and to making comparisons with the belukha whale, a close and better-known relative. About the regular periodic events of their lives, such as migration, breeding, and calving, in relation to climatic changes and fluctuations in the size of the population, we know next to nothing.[3]

Scientists can speak with precision only about the physical animal, not the ecology or behavior of this social and gregarious small whale. (It is the latter, not the former, unfortunately, that is most crucial to an understanding of how industrial development might affect narwhals.) Adult males, 16 feet long and weighing upwards of 3300 pounds, are about a quarter again as large as adult females. Males are also distinguished by an ivory tusk that pierces the upper lip on the left side and extends forward as much as 10 feet. Rarely, a female is found with a tusk, and, more rarely still, males and females with tusks on both sides of the upper jaw.

From the side, compared with the rest of its body, the narwhal's head seems small and blunt. It is dominated by a high, rounded forehead filled with bioacoustical lipids—special fats that allow the narwhal to use sound waves to communicate with other whales and to locate itself and other objects in its three-dimensional world. Its short front flippers function as little more than diving planes. The cone-shaped body tapers from just behind these flippers—where its girth is greatest, as much as eight feet—to a vertical ellipse at the tail. In place of a dorsal fin, a low dorsal ridge about five feet long extends in an irregular crenulation down the back. The tail flukes are unique. Seen from above, they appear heartshaped, like a ginkgo leaf, with a deep-notched center and trailing edges that curve far forward.

Viewed from the front, the head seems somewhat squarish and asymmetrical, and oddly small against the deep chest. The mouth, too,

---

[3]The knowledge and insight of Eskimos on these points, unfortunately, are of little help. Of all the areas of natural history in which they show expertise, native hunters are weakest in their understanding of the population dynamics of migratory animals. The reason is straightforward. Too much of the animal's life is lived "outside the community," beyond the geographic and phenomenological landscape the Eskimos share with them.—Author's note.

seems small for such a large animal, with the upper lip just covering the edge of a short, wedge-shaped jaw. The eyes are located just above and behind the upturned corners of the mouth, which give the animal a bemused expression. (The evolutionary loss of facial muscles, naturalist Peter Warshall has noted, means no quizzical wrinkling of the forehead, no raised eyebrow of disbelief, no pursed lip of determination). A single, crescent-shaped blowhole on top of the head is in a transverse line with the eyes.

Narwhal calves are almost uniformly gray. Young adults show spreading patches and streaks of white on the belly and marbling on the flanks. Adults are dark gray across the top of the head and down the back. Lighter grays predominate on top of the flippers and flukes, whites and light yellow-whites underneath. The back and flanks are marbled with blackish grays. Older animals, especially males, may be almost entirely white. Females, say some, are always lighter-colored on their flanks.

The marbled quality of the skin, which feels like smooth, oiled stone, is mesmerizing. On the flukes especially, where curvilinear streaks of dark gray overlap whitish-gray tones, the effect could not be more painterly. Elsewhere on the body, spots dominate. "These spots," writes William Scoresby, "are of a roundish or oblong form: on the back, where they seldom exceed two inches in diameter, they are the darkest and most crowded together, yet with intervals of pure white among them. On the side the spots are fainter, smaller, and more open. On the belly, they become extremely faint and few, and in considerable surfaces are not to be seen." These patterns completely penetrate the skin, which is a half-inch thick.

In the water, depending on sunlight and the color of the water itself, narwhals, according to British whaling historian Basil Lubbock, take on "many hues, from deep sea green to even an intense lake [blue] colour."

Narwhals are strong swimmers, with the ability to alter the contours of their body very slightly to reduce turbulence. Their speed and maneuverability are sufficient to hunt down swift prey—arctic cod, Greenland halibut, redfish—and to avoid their enemies, the orca and the Greenland shark.

Narwhals live in close association with ice margins and are sometimes found far inside heavy pack ice, miles from open water. (How they determine whether the lead systems they follow into the ice will stay open behind them, ensuring their safe return, is not known.) They manage to survive in areas of strong currents and wind where the movement of ice on the surface is violent and where leads open and close, or freeze over, very quickly. (Like seabirds, they seem to have an uncanny sense of when a particular lead is going to close in on them, and they leave.) That they are not infallible in anticipating the movement and formation of ice, which seals them off from the open air and oxygen, is attested to by a relatively unusual and often fatal event called a savssat.

Savssats are most commonly observed on the west coast of Greenland. Late in the fall, while narwhals are still feeding deep in a coastal fiord, a band of ice may form in calm water across the fiord's mouth. The ice sheet may then expand toward the head of the fiord. At some point the distance from its landward to its seaward edge exceeds the distance a narwhal can travel on a single breath. By this time, too, shorefast ice may have formed at the head of the fiord, and it may grow out to meet the sea ice. The narwhals are thus crowded into a smaller and smaller patch of open water. Their bellowing and gurgling, their bovinelike moans and the plosive screech of their breathing, can sometimes be heard at a great distance.

The Danish scientist Christian Vibe visited a savssat on March 16, 1943, on the west coast of central Greenland. Hundreds of narwhals and belukhas were trapped in an opening less than 20 feet square. The black surface of the water was utterly "calm and still," writes Vibe. "Then the smooth surface was suddenly broken by black shadows and white animals which in elegant curves came up and disappeared—narwhals and white whales by the score. Side by side they emerged so close to each other that some of them would be lifted on the backs of the others and turn a somersault with the handsome tail waving in the air. First rows of narwhal, then white whales and then again narwhals—each species separately. It seethed, bobbed, and splashed in the opening. With a hollow, whistling sound they inhaled the air as if sucking it in through long iron tubes. The water was greatly disturbed... and the waves washed far in over the ice." The splashed water froze to the rim of the breathing hole, as did the moisture from their exhalations, further reducing the size of the savssat. In spite of the frenzy, not a single animal that Vibe saw was wounded by the huge tusks of the narwhal.[4]

The narwhal is classed in the suborder Odontoceti, with toothed whales such as the sperm whale, in the superfamily Delphinoidea, along with porpoises and dolphins, and in the family Monodontidae with a single companion, the belukha. In contrast to the apparently coastally-adapted belukha, biologists believe the narwhal is a pelagic or open-ocean species, that it is more ice-adapted, and that it winters farther to the north. Extrapolating on the basis of what is known of the belukha, it is thought that narwhals breed in April and give birth to a single, five-foot, 170-pound calf about fourteen months later, in June or

---

[4]Eskimo hunters killed 340 narwhals and belukhas at this savssat in a week, before the ice fractured and the rest escaped. In the spring of 1915, Eskimos at Disko Bay took more than a thousand narwhals and belukhas at two savssats over a period of several months. Inattentive birds, especially thick-billed murres and dovekies which require a lot of open water to take off, may also suddenly find themselves with insufficient room and may be trapped.

July. Calves carry an inch-thick layer of blubber at birth to protect them against the cold water. They appear to nurse for about two years and may stay with their mothers for three years, or more. Extrapolating once again from the belukha, it is thought that females reach sexual maturity between four and seven years of age, males between eight and nine years.

Narwhals are usually seen in small groups of two to eight animals, frequently of the same sex and age. In the summer, female groups, which include calves, are sometimes smaller or more loosely knit than male groups. During spring migration, herds may consist of 300 or more animals.

Narwhals feed largely on arctic and polar cod, Greenland halibut, redfish, sculpins, and other fish, on squid and to some extent on shrimps of several kinds, and on octopus and crustaceans. They have a complex, five-chambered stomach that processes food quickly, leaving undigested the chitonous beaks of squid and octopus, the carapaces of crustaceans, and the ear bones and eye lenses of fish, from which biologists can piece together knowledge of their diets.

Two types of "whale lice" (actually minute crustaceans) cling to their skin, in the cavity where the tusk passes through the lip, in the tail notch in the flukes, and in wounds (all places where they are least likely to be swept off by the flow of water past the narwhal's body). The tracks of the sharp, hooked legs of these tiny creatures are sometimes very clear on a narwhal's skin. Older animals may carry such infestations of these parasites as to cause an observer to wince.

If you were to stand at the edge of a sea cliff on the north coast of Borden Peninsula, Baffin Island, you could watch narwhals migrating past more or less continuously for several weeks in the twenty-four-hour light of June. You would be struck by their agility and swiftness, by the synchronicity of their movements as they swam and dived in unison, and by a quality of alert composure in them, of capability in the face of whatever might happen. Their attractiveness lies partly with their strong, graceful movements in three dimensions, like gliding birds on an airless day. An impressive form of their synchronous behavior is their ability to deep-dive in groups. They disappear as a single diminishing shape, gray fading to darkness. They reach depths of 1000 feet or more, and their intent, often, is then to drive schools of polar cod toward the surface at such a rate that the fish lose consciousness from the too-rapid expansion of their swim bladders. At the surface, thousands of these stunned fish feed narwhals and harp seals, and rafts of excited northern fulmars and kittiwakes.

Watching from high above, one is also struck by the social interactions of narwhals, which are extensive and appear to be well organized according to hierarchies of age and sex. The socializing of males frequently involves the use of their tusks. They cross them like swords above the water, or one forces another down by pressing his tusk across the other's back, or they face each other head-on, their tusks side by side.

Helen Silverman, whose graduate work included a study of the social organization and behavior of narwhals, describes as typical the following scene, from her observations in Lancaster Sound. "On one occasion a group of five narwhals consisting of two adult males, one adult female, one [calf] and one juvenile were moving west with the males in the lead. The group stopped and remained on the surface for about 30 [seconds]. One male turned, moved under the [calf], and lifted it out of the water twice. There was no apparent reaction from the mother. The male then touched the side of the female with the tip of its tusk and the group continued westward."

Sitting high on a sea cliff in sunny, blustery weather in late June—the familiar sense of expansiveness, of deep exhilaration such weather brings over one, combined with the opportunity to watch animals, is summed up in a single Eskimo word: *quviannikumut*, "to feel deeply happy"—sitting here like this, it is easy to fall into speculation about the obscure narwhal. From the time I first looked into a narwhal's mouth, past the accordian pleats of its tongue, at the soft white interior splashed with Tyrian purple, I have thought of their affinity with sperm whales, whose mouths are similarly colored. Like the sperm whale, the narwhal is a deep diver. No other whales but the narwhal and the sperm whale are known to sleep on the surface for hours at a time. And when the narwhal lies at the surface, it lies like a sperm whale, with the section of its back from blowhole to dorsal ridge exposed, and the rest of its back and tail hanging down in the water. Like the sperm whale, it is renowned for its teeth; and it has been pursued, though briefly, for the fine oils in its forehead.

Like all whales, the narwhal's evolutionary roots are in the Cretaceous, with insect-eating carnivores that we, too, are descended from. Its line of development through the Cretaceous and into the Paleocene follows that of artiodactyls like the hippopotamus and the antelope— and then it takes a radical turn. After some 330 million years on dry land, since it emerged from the sea during the Devonian period 380 million years ago, the line of genetic development that will produce whales returns to the world's oceans. The first proto-whales turn up in the Eocene, 45 million years ago, the first toothed whales 18 million years later, in the Oligocene. By then, the extraordinary adjustments that had to take place to permit air-breathing mammals to live in the sea were largely complete.

Looking down from the sea cliffs at a lone whale floating peacefully in the blue-green water, it is possible to meditate on these evolutionary changes in the mammalian line, to imagine this creature brought forward in time to this moment. What were once its rear legs have disappeared, though the skeleton still shows the trace of a pelvis. Sea water gave it such buoyancy that it required little in the way of a skeletal structure; it therefore has achieved a large size without loss of agility. It left behind it a world of oscillating temperatures (temperatures on the arctic headland from which I gaze may span a range of 120° F over twelve months) for a world where the temperature barely fluctuates. It did not relinquish its warm-blooded way of life, however; it is insulated against the cold with a layer of blubber two to four inches thick.

The two greatest changes in its body have been in the way it now stores and uses oxygen, and in a rearrangement of its senses to suit a world that is largely acoustical, not visual or olfactory, in its stimulations.

When I breathe this arctic air, 34 percent of the oxygen is briefly stored in my lungs, 41 percent in my blood, 13 percent in my muscles, and 12 percent in the tissues of other of my organs. I take a deep breath only when I am winded or in a state of emotion; the narwhal always takes a deep breath—its draft of this same air fills its small lungs completely. And it stores the oxygen differently, so it can draw on it steadily during a fifteen-minute dive. Only about 9 percent stays in its lungs, while 41 percent goes into the blood, another 41 percent into the muscles, and about 9 percent into other tissues. The oxygen is bound to hemoglobin molecules in its blood (no different from my own), and to myoglobin molecules in its muscles. (The high proportion of myoglobin in its muscles makes the narwhal's muscle meat dark maroon, like the flesh of all marine mammals.)

Changes in the narwhal's circulatory system—the evolution of *rete mirabile*, "wonder nets" of blood vessels; an enlargement of its hepatic veins; a reversible flow of blood at certain places—have allowed it to adapt comfortably to the great pressures it experiences during deep dives.

There is too little nitrogen in its blood for "the bends" to occur when it surfaces. Carbon dioxide, the by-product of respiration, is effectively stored until it can be explosively expelled with a rapid flushing of the lungs.

It is only with an elaborate apparatus of scuba gear, decompression tanks, wet suits, weight belts, and swim fins that we can explore these changes. Even then it is hard to appreciate the radical alteration of mammalian development that the narwhal represents. First, ours is largely a two-dimensional world. We are not creatures who look up often. We are used to exploring "the length and breadth" of issues, not their "height." For the narwhal there are very few two-dimensional experiences—the sense of the water it feels at the surface of its skin, and that plane it must break in order to breathe.

The second constraint on our appreciation of the narwhal's world is that it "knows" according to a different hierarchy of senses than the one we are accustomed to. Its chemical senses of taste and smell are all but gone, as far as we know, though narwhals probably retain an ability to determine salinity. Its tactile sense remains acute. Its sensitivity to pressure is elevated—it has a highly discriminating feeling for depth and a hunter's sensitivity to the slight turbulence created by a school of cod cruising ahead of it in its dimly lit world. The sense of sight is atrophied, because of a lack of light. The eye, in fact, has changed in order to accommodate itself to high pressures, the chemical irritation of salt, a constant rush of water past it, and the different angle of refraction of light underwater. (The narwhal sees the world above water with an eye that does not move in its socket, with astigmatic vision and a limited ability to change the distance at which it can focus.)

How different must be "the world" for such a creature, for whom sight is but a peripheral sense, who occupies, instead, a three-dimensional acoustical space. Perhaps only musicians have some inkling of the formal shape of emotions and motivation that might define such a sensibility.

The Arctic Ocean can seem utterly silent on a summer day to an observer standing far above. If you lowered a hydrophone, however, you would discover a sphere of "noise" that only spectrum analyzers and tape recorders could unravel. The tremolo moans of bearded seals. The electric crackling of shrimp. The baritone boom of walrus. The high-pitched bark and yelp of ringed seals. The clicks, pure tones, birdlike trills, and harmonics of belukhas and narwhals. The elephantine trumpeting of bowhead whales. Added to these animal noises would be the sounds of shifting sediments on the sea floor, the whine and fracture of sea ice, and the sound of deep-keeled ice grounding in shallow water.

The narwhal is not only at home in this "cacophony," as possessed of the sense of a neighborhood as we might conceivably be on an evening stroll, but it manages to appear "asleep," oblivious at the surface of the water on a summer day in Lancaster Sound.

The single most important change that took place in the whale's acoustical system to permit it to live in this world was the isolation of its auditory canals from each other. It could then receive waterborne sound independently on each side of its head and so determine the direction from which a sound was coming. (We can do this only in the open air; underwater, sound vibrates evenly through the bones of our head.) The narwhal, of course, receives many sounds; we can only speculate about what it pays attention to, or what information it may obtain from all that it hears. Conversely, narwhals also emit many sounds important, presumably, to narwhals and to other animals too.

Acoustical scientists divide narwhal sound into two categories. Respiratory sounds are audible to us as wheezes, moans, whistles, and gurgles of various sorts. The second group of sounds, those associated with, presumably, echolocation and communication, scientists divide into three categories: clicking, generated at rates as high as 500 clicks per second; pulsed tones; and pure tones. (Certain of these sounds are audible to someone in a boat in the open air, like an effervescence rising from the surface of the water.)

Narwhals, it is believed, use clicking sounds to locate themselves, their companions, their prey, and such things as floe edges and the trend of leads. Pulsed tones are thought to be social in nature and susceptible to individual modification, so each narwhal has a "signature" tone or call of its own. Pure-tone signals, too, are thought to be social or communicative in function. According to several scientists writing in the *Journal of the Acoustical Society of America,* the narwhal "seems much less noisy [than the belukha], appears to have a smaller variety of sounds, and produces many that are outside the limits of human hearing." A later study, however, found narwhals "extremely loquacious underwater," and noted that tape recordings were "almost saturated with acoustic signals of highly variable duration and frequency composition." The same study concluded, too, that much of the narwhal's acoustically related behavior "remains a matter of conjecture."

I dwell on all this because of a routine presumption—that the whale's ability to receive and generate sound indicates it is an "intelligent" creature—and an opposite presumption, evident in a Canadian government report, that the continuous racket of a subsea drilling operation, with the attendant din of ship and air traffic operations, "would not be expected to be a hazard [to narwhals] because of . . . the assumed high levels of ambient underwater noise in Lancaster Sound."

It is hard to believe in an imagination so narrow in its scope, so calloused toward life, that it could write these last words. Cetaceans may well be less "intelligent," less defined by will, imagination, and forms of logic, than we are. But the *idea* that they are intelligent, and that they would be affected by such man-made noise, is not so much presumption as an expression of a possibility, the taking of a respectful attitude toward a mystery we can do no better than name "narwhal." Standing at the edge of a cliff, studying the sea-washed back of such a creature far below, as still as a cenobite in prayer, the urge to communicate, the upwelling desire, is momentarily sublime.

I stare out into Lancaster Sound. Four or five narwhals sleep on the flat calm sea, as faint on the surface as the first stars emerging in an evening sky. Birds in the middle and far distance slide through the air, bits of life that dwindle and vanish. Below, underneath the sleeping narwhal, fish surge and glide in the currents, and the light dwindles and is quenched.

The first description of a unicorn, according to British scholar Odell Shepard, appears in the writings of Ctesias, a Greek physician living in Persia in the fifth century B.C., who had heard reports of its existence from India. The existence of such an animal, a fierce, horselike creature of courageous temperament, with a single horn on its forehead, gained credibility later through the writings of Aristotle and Pliny and, later still, in the work of Isidore of Seville, an encyclopedist. The Bible became an unwitting and ironic authority for the unicorn's existence when Greek translators of the Septuagint rendered the Hebraic term *re'em* (meaning, probably, the now extinct aurochs, *Bos primigenius*) as "the unicorn."

The legend of the unicorn, and the subsequent involvement of the narwhal, is a story intriguing at many levels. Until well into the Middle Ages the legend passed only from one book to another, from one learned individual to another; it was not a part of the folk culture of Europe. During the Renaissance, scientists, scholars, and theologians put forth various learned "explanations" for the unicorn's existence. However farfetched these explanations might have seemed to skeptics, the concrete evidence of a narwhal's tusk to hand seemed irrefutable. Furthermore, no Christian could deny the unicorn's existence without contradicting the Bible.

Scholars argue that the animal in Ctesias' original report from Persia represents the transposed idea of an oryx or a rhinoceros. It went unquestioned, they speculate, because Greeks such as Ctesias took "the grotesque monstrosities of Indian religious art" rendered in the Persian tapestries they saw for real animals. In medieval Europe, trade in rare narwhal and walrus tusks, confusion with the mythical animals of Zoroastrian as well as Christian tradition, and the bucolic practice of making bizarre alterations in the horns of domestic animals, all lent credence to the legend. The interest of the wealthy and learned in this regal animal, moreover, went beyond mere fascination; it was also practical. European royalty was besieged with politically motivated poisonings in the fourteenth and fifteenth centuries, and the unicorn's horn was reputedly the greatest proof against them.

In *The Lore of the Unicorn*, Odell Shepard writes of the great range of appreciation of Renaissance people for the unicorn's horn; it was "their companion on dark nights and in perilous places, and they held it near their hearts, handling it tenderly, as they would a treasure. For indeed it was exactly that. It preserved a man from the arrow that flieth by day and the pestilence that walketh in darkness, from the craft of the poisoner, from epilepsy, and from several less dignified ills of the flesh not to be named in so distinguished a connection. In short it was an amulet, a talisman, a weapon, and a medicine chest all in one."

The narwhal's tusk, traded in bits and pieces as the unicorn's horn, sold for a fortune in the Middle Ages, for twenty times its weight in gold. Shepard estimates that in mid-sixteenth-century Europe there were no more than fifty whole tusks to be seen, each with a detailed provenance. They were gifted upon royalty and the church and sought as booty by expeditionary forces who knew of their existence. Two tusks stolen from Constantinople in 1204 were delivered by Crusaders to the Cathedral of Saint Mark in Venice, where they may be seen to this day.

The presence of these tusks in Europe depended upon Greenlandic and Icelandic trade. The oddity was that they were delivered to Europe by men like those who drowned with the Bishop of Iceland, sailors with no notion of unicorns and no knowledge of the value of the tusk to those who did know. On the other hand, the tusk was frequently bought by people who had not the remotest notion of the existence of such an animal as the narwhal.

The first European to bring these disparate perceptions together, it seems, was the cartographer Gerhard Mercator, who clearly identified the narwhal as the source of the unicorn's horn in 1621. In 1638, Ole Wurm, a Danish professor and a "zoologist and antiquarian of high attainment," delivered a speech in Copenhagen in which he made the same connection. But by then the story of the unicorn was simply too firmly entrenched at too many levels of European society to be easily dispelled, and the horn itself was too dear an item of commerce to be declared suddenly worthless. Besides, it was argued, was not the tusk simply the horn of the unicorn of the sea? Why shouldn't it have the same power as the horn of the land unicorn?

Over time the narwhal's tusk lost its influence in medical circles, trade dwindled, and the legend itself passed out of the hands of ecclesiastics and scholars to the general populace, where it became dear to the hearts of romantics, artists, and poets. It was passed on, however, in a form quite different from the secular tradition in Ctesias. In its secular rendering the unicorn was a creature of nobility and awesome though benign power. It was a creature of compassion, though solitary, and indomitably fierce. It became, as such, the heraldic symbol of knights errant and of kings. It was incorporated into the British coat of arms by James I in 1424, and in 1671 Christian V became the first Danish king to be crowned in a coronation chair made entirely of narwhal tusks.

Under Christian influence, the story of the unicorn became the story of a captured and tamed beast. The animal lost its robust, independent qualities, that aloofness of the wild horse, and was presented as a small, goatlike animal subdued by a maiden in a pastoral garden. The central episode of its fabulous life, its power to turn a poisonous river into pure water so that other creatures might drink, as Moses had done with his staff at the waters of Marah, passed into oblivion. The creature of whom it was once written in Solinus' *Polyhistoria*, "It is an animal never to be taken alive—killed possibly, but not captured," became a symbol of domestic virginity and obeisance.

One winter afternoon in Vancouver, British Columbia, I spoke with the only person ever to have succeeded in putting an adult narwhal, briefly, on display. (The six animals, brought back from northern Canada in 1970, all died of pneumonia within a few months.) Murray Newman, director of the British Columbia Aquarium, explained the great difficulties inherent in capturing such animals and later of maintaining them in captivity, especially the male, with its huge tusk. He doubted any aquarium would ever manage it successfully. The description from Solinus' *Polyhistoria* seemed at that moment, as we gazed across the aquarium's trimmed lawns toward Vancouver's harbor, oddly apt and prophetic.

A narwhal's tusk, hefted in the hands, feels stout but resilient. It is a round, evenly tapered shaft of ivory, hollow for most of its length. (The cavity is filled with dental pulp in the living animal.) A large tusk might weigh 20 pounds, be eight or nine feet long, and taper from a diameter of four inches at the socket down to a half-inch at the tip. The smooth, polished tip, two to three inches long, is roundly blunt or sometimes wedge-shaped. The rest of the tusk is striated in a regular pattern that spirals from right to left and may make five or six turns around the shaft before fading out. Often a single groove parallel to the spiraling striations is apparent. The tusk also shows a slight, very shallow ripple from end to end in many specimens.

The striated portion is rough to the touch, and its shallow grooves are frequently encrusted with algae. These microorganisms give the tusk a brindled greenish or maroon cast, contrasting with the white tip and with the 10 to 12 inches of yellower ivory normally embedded in the upper left side of the animal's skull.

Well into the nineteenth century there was a question about which of the sexes carried the tusk (or whether it might be both). Although many thought it was only the males, a clear understanding was confounded by authenticated reports of females with tusks (a female skull with *two* large tusks, in fact, was given to a Hamburg museum in 1684 by a German sea captain), and an announcement in 1700 by a German scientist, Solomon Reisel, that some narwhals carried "milk tusks." It did not help matters, either, that there was much conjecture but no agreement on the function of the tusk. (A more prosaic error further confused things — printers sometimes inadvertently reversed drawings, making it seem that the tusk came out of the right side of the head instead of the left, and that it spiraled from left to right.)

Several certainties eventually emerged. The tusk spirals from right to left. In normal development, two incipient tusks form as "teeth" in the upper jaw of both sexes, one on each side. In the female, both teeth usually harden into solid ivory rods with a protuberance at one end, like a meerschaum pipe (these were Reisel's "milk tusks"). In males, the tusk on the right remains undeveloped, "a miniature piece of pig iron," while the one on the left almost always develops into a living organ, a continually growing, fully vascularized tooth. On very rare occasions, both tusks develop like this, in both sexes. And both tusks spiral from right to left (i.e., they are not symmetrical like the tusks of an elephant or a walrus). Viewed from above, twin tusks diverge slightly from each other. In some males the left tusk never develops (nor does the right in these instances). In perhaps 3 percent of females a single tusk develops on the left.

Solving this problem in sexual systematics and physiology proved simpler than determining the tusk's purpose. It was proposed as a rake, to stir up fish on the seabed floor; as a spear to impale prey; and as a defensive weapon. All three speculations ignored the needs of narwhals without tusks. In addition, Robin Best, a Canadian biologist with a long-standing interest in the question, has argued that the tusk is too brittle to stand repeated use as a rake or probe; that attacking the sorts of fish narwhals habitually eat with the tusk would be difficult and unnecessary and getting large fish off the tusk problematic; and that there are no records of narwhals attacking other animals or defending themselves with their tusks.

The fact that narwhals frequently cross their tusks out of water and that the base of the tusk is located in the sound-producing region of the narwhal's skull led to speculation that it might serve some role in sound reception or propagation (again ignoring the female component of the population). Oral surgeons determined that the tooth's pulp does not contain the bioacoustical lipids necessary for echolocation, but this does not mean that the narwhal can't in some way direct sound with it and, as some have suggested, "sound-joust" with other males. (On their own, the oral surgeons speculated that because the tooth was so highly vascularized, the narwhal could get rid of a significant amount of body heat this way, which would presumably allow males to hunt more energetically. The biologists said no.)

William Scoresby, as bright and keen-eyed an observer as ever went to sea, speculated in 1820 that the tusk was only a secondary sexual characteristic, like a beard in humans, and was perhaps used to fracture light ice when narwhals of both sexes needed to breathe. Scientists say narwhals are too careful with their tusks to subject them to such impact, but on the first point Scoresby was correct.

Male narwhals engage in comparative displays of their tusks, like the males of other species, but they also appear to make some kind of violent physical contact with each other occasionally. The heads of many sexually mature males are variously scarred, and scientists have even found the broken tips of tusks in wounded narwhals. (A scientist who made a detailed examination of the narwhal's musculature said the muscles are not there in the neck to allow the animals to parry and thrust with rapierlike movements. Indeed, males appear always to move their tusks with deliberation, and dexterously, as at savssats.) The circumstances under which head scarring might occur—the establishment and continual testing of a male social hierarchy, especially during the breeding season—are known; but how these wounds are suffered or how frequently they are inflicted is still widely debated. One plausible thought is that males align their tusks head-on and that the animal with the shorter tusk is grazed or sometimes severely poked in the process.

A significant number of narwhals, 20 to 30 percent, have broken tusks. Some broken tusks have a curious filling that effectively seals off the exposed pulp cavity. Oral surgeons say this rod-shaped plug is simply a normal deposition of "reparative dentine," but others have long insisted it is actually the tip of another narwhal's tusk, to which it bears an undeniable resemblance. (The broken tips of other narwhals' tusks are filled with stones and sediment.)

Exposed tooth pulp creates a site for infection, not to mention pain. That animals would try to fill the cavity (if "reparative dentine" didn't) makes sense. That one narwhal entices another into this ministration is as intriguing a notion as the thought that males put the tips of their tusks on the opposite male's sound-sensitive melon and generate a "message" in sound-jousting. It would be rash to insist categorically that narwhals don't do *something* odd with the tusk on occasion, like prodding a flatfish off the sea bottom. (Herman Melville drolly suggested they used it as a letter opener.) But it seems clear that its principal, and perhaps only, use is social. Robin Best argues, further, that because of its brittleness, its length, and the high proportion of broken tusks, the organ may have reached an evolutionary end point.

A remaining question is, Why is the tusk twisted? D'Arcy Wentworth Thompson, a renowned English biologist who died in 1948, offered a brilliant and cogent answer. He argued that the thrust of a narwhal's tail applied a very slight torque to its body. The tusk, suspended tightly but not rigidly in its socket in the upper jaw, resisted this force with a very slight degree of success. In effect, throughout its life, the narwhal revolved slowly around its own tusk, and over the years irregularities of the socket gouged the characteristic striations in the surface of the tooth.

Thompson pointed out that the tooth itself is not twisted—it is straight-grained ivory, engraved with a series of low-pitched threads. No one has disproved, proved, or improved upon Thompson's argument since he set it forth in 1942.

Because the ivory itself dried out and became brittle and hard to work, the greatest virtue of a narwhal tusk to the Eskimos who traditionally hunted the animal was its likeness to a wood timber. Some of the regions where narwhals were most intensively hunted were without either trees or supplies of driftwood. The tusk served in those places as a spear shaft, a tent pole, a sledge thwart, a cross brace—wherever something straight and long was required.

Narwhals were most often hunted by Eskimos during their nearshore migration in spring, and in bays and fiords during the summer. To my knowledge, Eskimos attach no great spiritual importance to the narwhal. Like the caribou, it is a migratory food animal whose spirit (*kirnniq*) is easily propitiated. The narwhal does not have the intercessionary powers or innate authority of the polar bear, the wolf, the walrus, or the raven.

Beyond its tusk, Greenlanders valued the narwhal's skin above all other leathers for dog harnesses, because it remained supple in very cold weather and did not stretch when it became wet. The sinews of the back were prized as thread not only for their durability but also for their great length. The outside layer of the skin was an important source of vitamin C, as rich in this essential vitamin as raw seal liver. The blubber, which burned with a bright, clean yellow flame, gave light and warmth that were utilized to carve a fishhook or sew a mitten inside the iglu in winter. A single narwhal, too, might feed a dog team for a month.

It is different now. The hunter's utilitarian appreciation of this animal is an attitude some now find offensive; and his considerable skills, based on an accurate and detailed understanding of the animal and its environment, no longer arouse the sympathetic admiration of very many people.

In the time I spent watching narwhals along the floe edge at Lancaster Sound in 1982 no whale was butchered for dog food. The dogs have been replaced by snow machines. No sinews were removed for sewing. Only the tusk was taken, to be traded in the village for cash. And muktuk, the skin with a thin layer of blubber attached, which was brought back to the hunting camp at Nuvua. (This delicacy is keenly anticipated each spring and eaten with pleasure. It tastes like hazelnuts.)

The narwhal's fate in Lancaster Sound is clearly linked with plans to develop oil and gas wells there, but current hunting pressure against them is proving to be as important a factor. In recent years Eskimo hunters on northern Baffin Island have exhibited some lack of discipline during the spring narwhal hunt. They have made hasty, long-range, or otherwise poorly considered shots and used calibers of gun and types of bullets that were inadequate to kill, all of which left animals wounded. And they have sometimes exceeded the quotas set by Department of Fisheries and Oceans Canada and monitored by the International Whaling Commission.[5] On the other side, Eskimos have routinely been excluded from the upper levels of decision-making by the Canadian government in these matters and have been offered no help in devising a kind of hunting behavior more consistent with the power and reach of modern weapons. For the Eskimos, there is a

[5]These charges are detailed in K. J. Finley, R. A. Davis, and H. B. Silverman, "Aspects of the Narwhal Hunt in the Eastern Canadian Arctic," *Report of the International Whaling Commission* 30 (1980): 459–464; and K. J. Finley and G. W. Miller, "The 1979 Hunt for Narwhals (*Monodon monoceros*) and an Examination of Harpoon Gun Technology Near Pond Inlet, Northern Baffin Island," *Report of the International Whaling Commission* 32 (1982): 449–460.

relentless, sometimes condescending scrutiny of every attempt they make to adjust their culture, to "catch up" with the other culture brought up from the south. It is easy to understand why the men sometimes lose their accustomed composure.

In the view of Kerry Finley, a marine mammal biologist closely associated with the Baffin Island narwhal hunts, "It is critical [to the survival of narwhals] that Inuit become involved in meaningful positions in the management of marine resources." The other problems, he believes, cannot be solved until this obligation is met.

I would walk along the floe edge, then, in those days, hoping to hear narwhals, for the wonder of their company; and hoping, too, that they would not come. The narwhal is a great fighter for its life, and it is painful to watch its struggle. When they were killed, I ate their flesh as a guest of the people I was among, out of respect for distant ancestors, and something older than myself.

I watched closely the ivory gull, a small bird with a high, whistly voice. It has a remarkable ability to appear suddenly in the landscape, seemingly from nowhere. I have scanned tens of square miles of open blue sky, determined it was empty of birds, and then thrown a scrap of seal meat into a lead, where it would float. In a few minutes an ivory gull would be overhead. It is hard to say even from what direction it has come. It is just suddenly there.

So I would watch them in ones and twos. Like any animal seen undisturbed in its own environment, the ivory gull seems wondrously adapted. To conserve heat, its black legs are shorter in proportion to its body than the legs of other gulls, its feet less webbed. Its claws are longer and sharper, to give it a better grip of frozen carrion and on the ice. It uses seaweed in its nest to trap the sun's energy, to help with the incubation of its eggs. To avoid water in winter, which might freeze to its legs, it has become deft at picking things up without landing. In winter it follows the polar bear. When no carrion turns up in the polar bear's wake, it eats the polar bear's droppings. It winters on the pack ice. Of the genus *Pagophila*. Ice lover.

And I would think as I walked of what I had read of a creature of legend in China, an animal similar in its habits to the unicorn but abstemious, like the ivory gull. It is called the *ki-lin*. The *ki-lin* has the compassion of the unicorn but also the air of a spiritual warrior, or monk. Odell Shepard has written that "[u]nlike the western unicorn, the *ki-lin* has never had commercial value; no drug is made of any part of his body; he exists for his own sake and not for the medication, enrichment, entertainment, or even edification of mankind." He embodied all that was admirable and ideal.

With our own Aristotelian and Cartesian sense of animals as objects, our religious sense of them as mere receptacles for human symbology, our single-mindedness in unraveling their workings, we are not the kind of culture to take the *ki-lin* very seriously. We are another culture, and these other times. The *ki-lin*, too, is no longer as highly regarded among modern Chinese as it was in the days of the Sung dynasty. But the idea of the *ki-lin*, the mere fact of its having taken shape, is, well, gratifying. It appeared after men had triumphed over both their fear and distrust of nature and their desire to control it completely for their own ends.

The history of the intermingling of human cultures is a history of trade—in objects like the narwhal's tusk, in ideas, and in great narratives. We appropriate when possible the best we can find in all of this. The *ki-lin*, I think, embodies a fine and pertinent idea—an unpossessible being who serves humans when they have need of its wisdom, a creature who abets dignity and respect in human dealings, who underlines the fundamental mystery with which all life meets analysis.

I do not mean to suggest that the narwhal should be made into some sort of symbolic *ki-lin*. Or that buried in the more primitive appreciation of life that some Eskimos retain is an "answer" to our endless misgivings about the propriety of our invasions of landscapes where we have no history, or our impositions on other cultures. But that in the simple appreciation of a world not our own to define, that poised arctic landscape, we might find some solace by discovering the *ki-lin* hidden within ourselves, like a shaft of light.

Analyzing and Discussing the Text

1. Discuss the significance of the opening narrative. Why does Lopez begin the essay like this? What do we learn about the place and the speaker's state of mind? How does it prepare you for the later, non-narrative sections?
2. Edges, ecotones, and borders of any kind are, according to Lopez, especially attractive to the human mind. Why? Do you feel this attraction, too? Try to recall some of your own experiences with edges.
3. "I walk here susceptible as any traveler to the unknown," writes Lopez. Where in the essay does he manage to convey a sense of the Arctic's exoticness, of his own vulnerability?
4. When Lopez suggests that "Because you have seen something doesn't mean you can explain it," does he mean humans should not *try* to understand the natural world? What exactly is his point?
5. Explain the information Lopez presents in the third section of the essay. How does this section differ stylistically from the first two?

What is the connection between this material and the title of the essay, "The Image of the Unicorn"?

6. Why does Lopez shift into the second person ("you") at the beginning of the fourth section? How does he use visual perspective in this section?

7. Where in the essay do narrative and exposition begin to merge? What is the significance of this?

8. Explain Lopez's critique of the "imagination so narrow in scope," evident in a Canadian government report that downplays the possible effects of a subsea drilling operation on intelligent underwater wildlife.

9. What is the point of devoting an entire section of the essay to a study of the narwhal's tusk?

10. Explain the concept of the *ki-lin*. What does Lopez mean when he concludes that we "might find some solace by discovering the *ki-lin* hidden within ourselves"?

Experiencing and Writing About the World

1. Using one particular excursion as a "structural guide," prepare an in-depth study of an unusual animal. Do research in the library (in the field, too, if possible) to gather information about your subject, but organize your essay by returning intermittently from the "learned information" to the "experiential information," to the excursion that brought you into contact with this animal or during which you at least meditated on the animal while in contact with the sensory world. What does such an approach imply about the hierarchy of knowledge?

2. Write a brief narrative in which you consider the world from the perspective of another animal. For instance, concerning the narwhal, Lopez writes, "How different must be 'the world' for such a creature, for whom sight is but a peripheral sense, who occupies, instead, a three-dimensional acoustical space." You might describe the world from a narwhal's point of view.

3. Lopez relies on the structural technique of digression in "The Image of the Unicorn." In an analytical essay, compare Lopez's digressive style with another essayist who employs this device—for instance, Scott Russell Sanders, David Black, or David Brendan Hopes (all represented in this anthology). What seem to be the main goals of each writer? Does digression serve the same purpose in each text?

BETSY HILBERT

Disturbing the Universe

A native of Brooklyn, New York, Betsy Hilbert (1941–   ) has lived in Miami, Florida, since she was five years old. She earned her B.A. and M.A. at the University of Miami and in the mid-1960s began teaching in the English Department at Miami–Dade Community College, where she is now the chair of the Independent Studies Department. Hilbert received her Ph.D. from the Union Graduate School in 1976. Her interest in nature writing began in the late 1970s, when she encountered Peter Matthiessen's *The Snow Leopard*. Since then she has specialized in scholarship on women's nature writing and has strongly advocated the inclusion of environmental studies in the humanities curriculum at the college level. Hilbert's 1990 bibliography of American women nature writers (published in the *American Nature Writing Newsletter*) brought to light many previously neglected authors. In 1991 she served as editor of the *CEA Critic's* special issue entitled "The Literature of Nature."

In addition to her scholarly work, Hilbert has published numerous literary essays about the natural world, essays on such topics as alligators making love (*North American Review*, 1986). The following essay, "Disturbing the Universe," concerns her work as part of the Tropical Audubon Society's sea-turtle rescue effort during the 1980s. Although she has not had time recently to carry turtle eggs to safety, she still feels "connected to the universe" through the study of ecological thought and environmental literature. Her essay on turtles considers the possibility that human efforts to intervene in the natural world, even if well-intentioned, may be ineffective and perhaps harmful. Still, she concludes her essay by asserting, "While the choice is mine, I choose to walk." It's better to care and to try to preserve the natural world, she suggests, than to do nothing. However, she urges students to realize that they need not participate in "direct action" in order to contribute to the environment. Such work is lifelong, and even if one never contributes through environmental activism, other ways are possible—for example, the study of environmental texts, she says, "is an important and vital activity." In her Editor's Introduction to the special issue of the *CEA Critic*, Hilbert rejoices that "an amazing number of people are out there, all across the landscape, thinking and teaching and writing about the literature of nature."

Five thirty A.M.; the parking lot of Crandon Park is deserted. An empty plastic drinking cup crunches under the tires as we pull in. Nothing seems worth doing in the world this early. Ute and I climb groggily out of the car. Then the dawn blazes up out over the ocean, rose and gold across the sky. Everything has its compensations.

The beach is still in shadow under the brightening sky, and the dim figures of the morning cleanup crew make a clatter among the trash bins. The two of us are on a cleanup of a different kind this morning, amid the beachwrack and the crumpled potato-chip bags.

"Seen anything?" my partner calls to one of the crew further down the beach, who is slamming a trash can with particular vengeance.

"No, Señora," a voice drifts back, in the soft, mixed-ethnic accents of Miami. "No tortugas today."

Actually, we don't want the turtles themselves; it is turtle eggs we're looking for, in their night-laid nests along this populous beach. Our job is to find and rescue the eggs of endangered loggerhead turtles, and to move them to a fenced area nearby maintained by the local Audubon Society, where the hatchlings can be safe from the picnickers and the beach-cleaning machines, and other dangers inherent on a public beach.

We begin our long walk south, where miles ahead the condominiums of Key Biscayne loom in the pale light. Pity the sea turtle who tries to climb their seawalls, or dig her nest in a carefully landscaped patch of St. Augustine grass. A series of grunts and swishes erupts behind us, as an early-morning beach jogger huffs past.

Ute's practiced strides take her up the beach almost faster than I can follow, distracted as I am by the pelican practicing hang-gliding in the morning air and the rippled sand in the tidal shallows. She stops suddenly, taking a soft breath, and I rush up to look. Leading upward from the high-water mark is a long, two-ridged scrape, balanced on either side by the zig-zag series of close, rounded alternating prints. Turtle crawl. Has she nested? Like all good predators, we sniff around a bit before deciding where to dig.

Just below the high dunes, in a circular patch about six feet across, the sand has been conspicuously flailed around. She has tried to discourage nest-robbers not by camouflage or hiding, but by leaving too much notice; the disturbed area is so big, and digging in the packed sand so difficult, that the attempt would discourage hunters with less sense of mission than we have. We could poke a sharp stick into the sand until it came up sticky with egg white, as is the traditional technique throughout the Caribbean, but that would damage eggs we are trying to protect. Nothing to do but start digging.

Beneath the turbulence of the dry top sand, the rough, damp subsurface scrapes against the skin of our hands. We run our fingers across the hard sand, hoping to find a soft spot. When no depression becomes apparent—this time it isn't going to be easy—we hand-dig trenches at intervals across the area. Sometimes it takes an hour or more of digging before the nest is found; sometimes there are no eggs at all.

In my third trench, about four inches down, there is a lump that doesn't feel like rock or shell. A smooth white surface appears, and another next to it and slightly lower. The eggs look exactly like ping-pong balls, little white spheres, but the shell is soft and flexible. With infinite care, I lift the little balls out as Ute counts them, then place them in a plastic container, trying always to keep them in the same position they were laid. Turtle embryos bond to the shells, and turning the eggs as we rebury them might put the infants in the wrong position, with catastrophic results.

One hundred fourteen little worlds come out of their flask-shaped, smooth-sided nest. The eggs are spattered lightly with sand, and my probing fingers hit patches of sticky wetness among them, apparently some kind of lubricating fluid from the mother. The surprising softness of the shells makes sense to me as I dig deeper; hard shells might have cracked as the eggs dropped onto one another.

Carrying the egg container to the reburying place, I am glowing like the sunrise with self-satisfaction. Savior of sea turtles, that's me. Defender of the endangered. Momma turtle would be very pleased that her babies were receiving such good care.

Or would she? I look down at the eggs in their plastic box, and realize that she'd regard me as just another predator, if she regarded me at all. That turtle, if we ever met, would be much more concerned about my species' taste for turtle meat than about my professed interest in her offspring. What would I be to her except another kind of nuisance? Perhaps the Mother of Turtles might respond as the Pigeon in *Alice in Wonderland* does when Alice tries to explain that she's not a snake, but a little girl: "No, no! You're a serpent; and there's no use denying it. I suppose you'll be telling me next that you never tasted an egg!"

What was I to these eggs but just another nest-robber? Did I really know the impact of my actions, the extended chain of events I was setting in motion? With present scientific knowledge, no human alive could chart the course of that one loggerhead as she found her way across the seas. Where she bred and slept, where her food came from, are still mysteries. Not only are there too few scientists searching for the answers, too little money for research, but ultimately there are "answers" we can probably never have. Our ways of knowing are species-locked, our understandings limited by human perceptual processes. I was a shadow on a dusky beach, groping in the dark for more than turtle eggs, digging, shoulder-deep, in holes not of my making.

Suppose we save these eggs, and the turtles that hatch return years later as hoped, to nest on this beach? This land will never be wild any more; the skyscrapers that rise across Biscayne Bay bear megalithic testimony that the future of South Florida is written in concrete. The beach, if preserved, will continue public, and pressured, one of a small number of recreation areas for an ever-growing number of people. So there will never be a time when these animals can live out their lives without the intervention of people like Ute and me. Like so much else of nature now, the turtles of Crandon Park will be forever dependent on human action. Thanks to us, they are surviving; but thanks to us, they are also less than self-sufficient.

And why am I so convinced I'm actually doing good, anyway? Suppose more babies survive than can be supported by their environment, and next year there is a crash in their food supply, or that something we do, entirely unknowing, weakens the hatchlings so that their survival rate is actually lowered? Maybe we should just leave them alone. Maybe they would be better off taking their chances where their mothers first laid them, risking the raccoons and the beach parties.

None of us knows the final outcome of any action, the endless chain of ripples that we start with every movement. We walk in the world blindly, crashing into unidentified objects and tripping over rough edges. We human beings are too big for our spaces, too powerful for our understanding. What I do today will wash up somewhere far beyond my ability to know about it.

And yet, last year, five thousand new turtles were released from the Audubon compound, five thousand members of a threatened species, which would almost certainly not have been hatched otherwise. A friend who urged me to join the turtle project said that on a recent trip to Cape Sable in the Everglades he found at last fifteen nests on a short walk, every one of them dug up and destroyed by raccoons. Whatever chance these hundred fourteen embryos have, nestled inside their shells in the styrofoam cradle, is what we give them.

In *The Encantadas,* his description of what are now called the Galápagos Islands, Herman Melville depicted the sea tortoises of "dateless, indefinite endurance" which the crew of the whaling ship takes aboard. Melville pointed out that those who see only the bright undersides of the tortoises might swear the animal has no dark side, while those who have never turned the tortoise over would swear it is entirely "one total inky blot." "The tortoise is both black and bright," Melville cautioned. So, too, my morning beach walk has two sides, one purposeful, the other full of doubt.

Whatever my ambivalences may be, the eggs are still in my hands. Ute and I reach the hatchery enclosure and unlock the chain-link fence. We dig another hole as close in size and shape to the original as we can imitate, and then rebury our babies, brushing our doubts back into the hole with the sand. As we mark the location of the new nest with a circle of wire fencing, I am reminded that in the world today there is no way, any more, not to do something. Even if despite our best efforts there will never again be any loggerhead turtles, even if the numbers of the people concerned are few and our knowledge pitifully limited, even if we sometimes do unconscious harm in trying to do good, we no longer have the option of inaction. The universe is already disturbed, disturbed by more than my presence on an early-morning beach, with the sunlight glinting off the blue-tiled hotel swimming pools. While the choice is mine, I choose to walk.

Analyzing and Discussing the Text

1. Hilbert compares herself and her companion to predators as they walk up the beach looking for turtle eggs to rescue. What do you think of this analogy? Why does the author emphasize it?
2. Does the author's participation in the sea-turtle rescue effort seem totally selfless, totally altruistic? What are the compensations she receives for her work?
3. "We walk in the world blindly, crashing into unidentified objects and tripping over rough edges," writes Hilbert. What are the implications of this sentence and of the essay as a whole? Does this writer come across as a clumsy, blundering sort of person? Why such dire statements?
4. "While the choice is mine," concludes Hilbert, "I choose to walk." Does "walking" here come to symbolize something more than physical movement? Do you think the author is merely voicing her personal choice or attempting to encourage others to "walk"? Explain your answer.

Experiencing and Writing About the World

1. Find out what programs are going on in your area to study and/or rescue endangered species of wildlife. Participate, if possible, in some of their activities and write a narrative of your experiences, including Hilbert-like meditations on the meaning of the activities.
2. Gather information about endangered species in your area and prepare an impersonal expository analysis of the problems and likely solutions. How does such a report compare in vividness to Hilbert's narrative? Could there be appropriate audiences for such writing?
3. Borrow Hilbert's title, "Disturbing the Universe," and write a brief essay in which you contemplate the impact one of your own activities might have on the external world. Can we ever fully gauge such

impact? How do we decide whether to act or not, if the results of our behavior are uncertain?

4. Find one or two additional essays in this collection that combine narratives of personal experience with discussions of more abstract environmental issues, such as Edward Abbey's "Floating" and John Daniel's "The Impoverishment of Sightseeing." Write an analytical essay in which you compare these authors' techniques for merging or alternating narrative and analytical/argumentative prose with Hilbert's approach. What seem to be the principal uses of narrative in essays that ultimately seek to address important environmental issues?

DAVID BRENDAN HOPES

Crossings

David Brendan Hopes (1953–   ), born in Akron, Ohio, grew up in the vacant lots and public schools of Akron before entering Hiram College, also in Ohio. He began graduate school at Johns Hopkins University, dropped out and "bummed around" for a few years, then completed an M.A. in creative writing and a Ph.D. in British and American literature at Syracuse University. Hopes taught at Syracuse and Hiram, serving in between as Writer in Residence at Phillips Exeter Academy in New Hampshire. In 1983 he began teaching at the University of North Carolina at Asheville, where he is now a professor of literature and humanities, coordinator of the creative writing program, and director of Pisgah Players, a theater group dedicated to the production of original plays. Hopes's work, which covers an extraordinary range of genres, includes a poetry collection called The Glacier's Daughters (winner of the University of Massachusetts Press's Juniper Prize in 1981); the play Timothy Liberty (winner of the North Carolina Playwrights' Prize in 1986); and the collection of nature essays, A Sense of the Morning (1988), from which the following piece was selected. Immediately forthcoming are the novel A Book of Songs and a collection of essays about childhood called A Childhood in the Milky Way. His play The Christmas Count appeared at Broadway's Nat Horne Theater in the fall of 1991.

Hopes developed his unusually digressive and episodic essay style as a result of his initial concentration on writing poetry, moving on only later to literary nonfiction. "I developed the idea that the way the mind functions is to receive vivid images which it then weaves into a fabric of understanding," he writes. "Truth comes not from argument but from perception, and perception is not extruded like metal but blinding and instantaneous. If we discuss something and you make an unheard-of observation, I will know instantly whether it is true or not, though it may take me a while to *understand* it. That, I guess, is why I write the way I write. The discursive, systematic essay which we teach our freshmen is artificial and probably a calamity. It is hard to write and hard to read precisely because it is unnatural. The essayists we prize are tangential and digressive because the point of the essay is not its ostensible subject matter, but a process of the mind." The following essay, "Crossings," is a good example of this process of gathering moments of "blinding and instantaneous" perception—in this case, the episodes cohere because of the author's persistent contemplation of the social and solitary dimensions of hiking. Hopes begins by describing his "habit of hiking alone": "One on one with the wild: It's an obsession that comes to seem both shocking and inevitable, like a difficult love affair at once excluding the lover from the world and giving him a special place in it." Yet even the solitary hiker finds himself considering not just the world itself, but the attractions and difficulties of human companionship. This essay concludes with Hopes's reflections on experiences with a particularly good "hiking buddy" whom he calls simply "TE"; the presence of this and other friends in the wilderness intensifies the author's self-awareness, distracting him from the natural world.

The vernal equinox. It is at once the last day of winter and the first of spring. I've driven north up the Blue Ridge Parkway until the barrier at Craggy Garden. I get out of the car, fuss with my gear, put on an extra shirt, start walking. Beyond the barrier the Craggy Pinnacle Tunnel remains impassable. Two breast-shaped mounds of ice block the lanes. I run through, because of the cold, out the north entrance into a wall of light. It must have been as bright on the other side, but I didn't notice. I keep trotting, to get as deep into the light as I can. Blue, of course, though the word does not suffice. Living blue. Crystalline. I slow down, as though the light were a substance dragging at my clothes. Snow lies in ravines and on the north face of the mountains. Snow-colored clouds marble the horizon. I am walking in a sapphire whose few snowy imperfections intensify the universal blue.

Except for the prongs of the mountains, I walk atop everything. If I sailed off the road I'd hit nothing for 2,000 miles, 12,000 if I flew east.

A raven flaps over the valley, beating fast for so large a bird, chattering to himself like a sorcerer rehearsing spells. I am walking in a sapphire, utterly alone.

This is a crowded world, and yet I am perfectly, imperially alone. Houses visible under the raven's wings in the valley might as well be the moon. I walk out two hours, nap half an hour on a sunny bank, walk back two hours. In all that time the blue remains as changeless as a jewel in a pharoah's forehead. In all that time there has not been one other person. A feast, an orgy of solitude, and I gobble it down, with an orgiast's greed, and shame.

When I return, three boys bellow at and jostle one another at the tunnel's mouth. They take turns climbing down to a scenic place and having their photo taken. I should ask if they want me to take a picture of them all at once, but instead I try to pass by unseen, feeling I've arrogated something that belonged as much to them.

All that sapphire. All that solitude.

That they never wanted it is immaterial.

Long ago I acquired the habit of hiking alone.

On the mountain I'm a monster of shyness, backing like an animal from the sound of approaching humanity.

One on one with the wild: It's an obsession that comes to seem both shocking and inevitable, like a difficult love affair at once excluding the lover from the world and giving him a special place in it.

Another person on the trail distracts me. If I meet someone in the woods, I smile and say either "Hi" or "Hey," depending on how far south we are. But I consider turning back, knowing that the trail ahead contains none of the surprises available to the first soul passing. Like a Castilian husband, I treasure virginity. If the other person is *with* me, the distraction multiplies. I don't mean to imply an unpleasant distraction. Few experiences are not improved by sharing. Just different. More an encounter with the other soul than with the world. Fine.

But sometimes you leave before morning, tiptoeing in the dark, carrying your shoes to lace them on the doorstep, your companion sleeping, or maybe awake and knowing what you need today.

I'm very small, and sensible of the need to keep to the path, as otherwise the undergrowth waves above my head as surely as the trees. A man walks just ahead. I think he's my father, though the picture is unclear, and when I asked he had no such memory. He speaks. I don't recognize the words, and for a while I think he's jabbering on in the unfathomable way adults have. Suddenly I realize he's naming the trees. Oak. Maple. Dogwood. I run close, to miss nothing, touching their peculiar flesh as he calls the words out. *Dogwood? Why that?* I wonder without asking. The man is very tall, and I see he walks toward a sunny space where the trees end. I follow. It does not occur to me that I have another choice. Yet I long to turn back, to see these things that have just been named for me when it is they and I alone.

Great lovers know what merely obsessive lovers do not understand. In the highest love there is communion, but never identity. A perfect union of lovers is the end of love. The soul is always singular.

Mrs. Timberlake leads us through the great south field of the metropolitan park. She teaches kindergarten, and each day she draws a gaggle of neighborhood children to school in her wake. It's impossible for me to keep up. I try to run, but I slow after a few yards like a toy winding down. I don't know that I'm sick, so I believe that I lag farther and farther behind, in greater and greater discomfort, because I'm lazy or for some reason can't walk as well as the others. I decide I don't care, and I sit down. Grass leaps over my head, hiding me completely. Green, yellow, tawny, the blaze of sky above. I feel safe and enclosed. I tell myself they can pick me up on the way home. It's a ridiculous thought, and I begin to laugh. Just before Mrs. Timberlake's alarmed voice sings my name over the forest of grass, I focus on a stalk at eye level, where a praying mantis arranges herself for a better look at me, her saw-arms braced on grass as one leans against a fencepost to contemplate the two-headed calf.

Same field, two years later, in second grade. Our schedules no longer coincide with Mrs. Timberlake's, so we walk by ourselves. We're supposed to keep to the sidewalk, but we cut across the meadow because it's quick, beautiful, and forbidden. Also dangerous. We see him coming a long way off, Steve Benjamin, the school bully, older than we, and twice our size. He too has told us not to walk the meadow, claiming it as personal property. He leaps from the wood's edge when he sees us, like a young ram defending his mountainside. We scan, but there's no adult to whose protection we can appeal. Steve is yards away, so my companion takes the main chance and begins to run. With the head start, he'll probably be safe. I know I can't run. I plod along, conserving my energy. Steve pulls up beside me, panting and red in the face. He says, "I told you not to."
I keep plodding.
He says, "I want you to go all the way back and stay on the street."
I keep plodding, with my eyes thrown to the side, to watch his every move. I see him raise his arm to hit me. I turn, neither fast nor

slow, my own fists raised. Before he can recover from the shock, I've landed two blows in his stomach and one in his face. He holds his nose. Blood runs between his fingers. I turn back to my way, remembering I wanted only to be left alone. Then something odd happens. I think of the blood. I think of his stomach shrinking away from the blows of my fist. I whirl on my heels, run toward him, screaming. He turns, runs. I chase him until I'm out of breath, feeling an exhilaration unknown to me before.

Tall Kurt pauses over a cluster of ant hills in a sandy space beside the path. Sun's admitted into the forest by a fallen beech, but how the sand got here I don't know. Maybe the ants themselves hauled it up from the guts of the mountain. In dry country, the experienced fossil hunter checks anthills daily for stone teeth and exquisite bones of proto-mammals spat out by the labor of the colony. Kurt stands still, contemplating. Finally, with his toe he nicks the top of an anthill, sends a cascade of sand down the hole.

I say, "What are you doing?"

"History. I'm making history. I want them to remember today."

We kick in two of the dozen or so anthills, to give it the randomness of a real event. As we walk, we recite the chronicles by which the scribes of the Myrmidons memorialize our passing.

Mike Havens and I snowshoe the sheer cliffs of Clark Reservation, near Syracuse. He's been talking about Coleridge. I've been watching to my right, where the glacial cliffs tumble 400 feet into the plungepool, black and deep, unfrozen at the center though without detectable current. It's night and I'm frightened, never having walked farther than across a lawn on snowshoes before. Sweat freezes on my shirt, breath on my beard, so thick I have to pick it away to talk.

We come to a cliff. I've done this path a hundred times snowless, so I know the cliff is there, but somehow I believed it would vanish by the force of my willing it to. Michael says, "We have to climb."

"That's a lousy idea."

"Then we'll have to go back the way we came."

I think of the narrow rock path meandering the cliff, the star-filled freezing void above the water. I think of my propensity to tread on my own shoe and pitch sideways.

We climb. How we let it get dark I don't know. I'm cursing under my breath, blaspheming every fingerhold, every agonizing straddle around the shoes. Mike remains silent, his way of doing the same thing.

At the top, pouring sweat, breathless, we begin to run, legs spread like animals three times taller than we. We've said nothing to each other, never made a sign. Anything to put that cliff behind.

Nights later I dream of it, wake up sweating.

During college came the Year of the Female Hiking Companion. Three stand out.

Jane was good for long hauls over hills, through bogs, into the dangers of local farms with their dogs and wild-running, bad-tempered sows. Jane skipped class to hike with you and expected the same in return.

Toni wanted to hike—insisted on it—as a cure for a dramatic case of panphobia. I'm trying to think of something outside that she didn't fear. One was glad to be part of the therapy for a while, until—after the dozenth dog barked or pheasant exploded underfoot or other hiker appeared unanticipated on the trail and sent Toni screaming at prodigious pitch and duration, hands over her ears so she couldn't hear herself—one thought again of the pleasures of solitude.

Heather was the best of the lot. She could make a pun out of the name of any woodland creature. Gaudy birds—kingfishers, green herons, sun-struck warblers—hid themselves until her binoculars were raised. She homed in on salamander rocks with a hunter's sureness. With her unhurried doe-gait, she was tireless, ever ready for the next rise. It's a comfort to me in this changeable world that once every year or so we get to hike together again, in more exotic settings, but with the same sense of limitless expectancy.

A friend maintains that the one irreducible social, psychological, daily functional physiological difference between men and women is that men like to piss in the woods, prefer it even to the comforts of the modern bathroom, and women do not. I have considered this, and it seems sound.

First, let me say that hiking is, except under unusual circumstances, a single-sex activity. Women are better off hiking with women, men with men. This is almost entirely the fault of men, who get, for perfectly understandable evolutionary reasons, show-offy around women in the wild. We turn from doctors and cellists into bull bison, huffing and flaring our nostrils and hacking at innocent vegetation and losing the way because looking at the map is not a masculine activity. Nor is listening to someone who *has* looked at the map.

Women on the trail remain calm, uncomplaining, collected. This in itself can be a provocation to the male, who secretly longs for some calamity by which he can put his woodcraft and his courage on display. Women out for a hike are twentieth-century individuals who like Bach and fine wines and anticipate returning to them, nerves smoothed and palates cleaned by the mountain trail. They carry civilization with them. Men blank out the memory of anything Before, the car we came in, the polyresins swathing our bodies, the traffic sixty feet below on the Parkway. Our ears cock for the stirring of panthers, the tread of the enemy's moccasin on dry sticks. Listen to boys play army or space adventure and you'll know where exclusive imaginative involvement with the imperiling moment comes from.

I don't know what women think of this. I hope they find it endearing.

No matter how enlightened otherwise, we men secretly feel that the ease of our micturition is somehow a mark of superiority, if only in matters connected to that activity. For men hiking together this is not an issue, nor I imagine for women hiking together. But when men and women mix, a little voice at the back of his mind will wonder every mile or so, "When will she have to do it?" relishing the opportunity to stop, wait ostentatiously, heave great and patient sighs.

The same friend mentioned above—a woman—goes on to speculate that the relative ease of men in relieving themselves in the forest is proof that civilization was made by women.

I buy this too. The reason that the intelligent porpoise doesn't really *achieve* anything is that he's just too comfortable doing what comes naturally. I speculate that the human male was in the same condition, hunting with his buddies, pissing luxuriously, trailing home to brag about it all. Woman, on the other hand, was uncomfortable. Build her a room. Line it with tiles. Paint the tiles with leaping dolphins. Put in plumbing. Presto: civilization.

I don't hike so much to cover ground or get away from it all as to look at things. This proves to be surprisingly idiosyncratic. I would have thought flat-out eyes-forward walking could be accomplished anywhere, yet I must be mistaken, for I drive hiking companions berserk with my endless stooping and poking and turning over stones. For this reason too I go alone.

But for a while I had a good hiking buddy.

Accepting a hiking buddy is as particular and personal an activity as choosing a career, or a lover. It informs you about yourself. It tells you what you need from someone when it will be you and he against the illimitable world. Sometimes it's enough that he'll carry his half of the gear, or that he has a special stove that weighs nothing and tans you at fifty paces.

TE was better than that. Of course he carried his half. He didn't mention it when I wadded the maps instead of rolling them with the Eleusian immaculateness affected by some outdoorsy types. He didn't exhaust one by telling of past adventures in the wildwood. Though accustomed to the outdoors, he was a virgin when it came to paying attention to it. I could say anything, and he'd let on it was news to him. TE endured calm and delightable; he let me do the talking when the subject was the wild, talked for me when the subject was the world we'd left behind. Whether writing these things about him is a gift or a violation, I don't know. Gift is what I mean.

I wrote about us in my journal:

Footsore from hiking the bare heights. Brought TE here for a nightcap—probably a bad idea, since our bellies were empty and our muscles worn out. Still, the moon hung bright, clusters of starfire like clouds over the mountain, Orion three tight diamonds beyond my fingertips. From the valley bottom the frog-chorus already began, that ecstatic sound, next to thunder the loveliest song of earth. I knew great peace in the moment before I unlocked the door and entered the house.

I said, meaning the frogs, "They are early."

TE answered, "They are always on time."

As I walked out of the laundry room this afternoon, through the trees came fluttering a sharp-shinned hawk, his striped tail dragging like a spear in the air behind. Light stood so bright around him, the forest radiant, still all the mountain a stage set and ready, and he the single dancer. As I watched I heard my inner voice turn it into narrative, to pass to TE sometime when we hear a hawk scream over the trees.

Rose at 6 o'clock to go birding. The best we saw were green heron, yellow-breasted vireo, myrtle warbler, thrasher, towhee. The sky was raging sapphire. Necks sore from craning up into hundred-foot tulips. TE waits for a bird book to come out that features birds' rumps, as that's what you mostly see.

Frogs call in the darkness under a hand of white stars. I walk to the mailbox in the terrific dark of a cloudy mountain night. A creature stirs in the trees as I pass. My heart leaps when I hear it, hoping it is formidable, even dangerous, hoping it comes near me in the black. I hear the footsteps run, pause, then proceed calmly away, sure now I will not follow.

Ate at a despicable restaurant, drove the Parkway in blazing spring light. Day after day of this blue.

Because I'm driving and refuse to go farther without touching my toes to dirt, we stop along the roadside, penetrate a few hundred yards into the blossoming forest, never so deep that we can't hear the highway.

TE asks, "Why here?" and I glance around for a reason. "Ferns," I say. "Look at all the ferns." I lift the fronds to display the sori. The seeds of fern confer invisibility. I brush my finger along the frond's underside, touch it to my tongue. Still, there's my shadow on the ground. Another tale shot to hell.

We listen for birds. Woodpeckers, crows, too early for the full tide of warblers. I chatter the whole time, as though the forest creatures are my family and I'm introducing them, longing for him to think well of them.

I pull up a log, hoping to find a salamander. I do, a lovely green-gold one, the color of an old coin or an autumn leaf. I bear it to TE, holding it in my hand the way you must, half between crushing and escape. He shrinks back. I think he must believe it's a snake. I say, amazed at his hesitation, "It's a *salamander.*"

"Doesn't it bite?"

I touch its nose with the tip of my little finger. "You see it doesn't."

I push it at him until he takes it in his hand, but he's uneasy. I say, "Okay," and take it back. "Didn't you ever play with salamanders when you were little?"

"No. Gators. Looks like a gator to me."

We have our little lecture on the difference between reptiles and amphibians. The whole time, the 'mander rests on my palm. How cold the little creature is, how small, its claws, though I feel them, exquisite to the point of invisibility. I don't understand how anything so small and cold can live.

Prionosuchus plummeri roamed the Brazilian river bottoms 230 million years ago. Thirty feet long, with the tapering needle jaws of a crocodile, it was the largest land animal and most formidable predator of the Permian age. Also, it was an amphibian, a protosalamander. I cradle ghosts of those terrible genes in my hand with the two inches of cold wood creature, whose skull I could crush now with a breath. I hope TE sees the immensity of it, for it cannot be said.

Exhaustion like intoxication, dreamlike, license to indulge myself in cold drinks flavored with lime. Yesterday I came down with a debilitating, muscle-aching-sore-throat-and-headache flu. Walking was an effort. My voice dropped a sixth. Sickness is part of the exhaustion, but the larger part is TE and I having hiked the Joyce Kilmer Memorial Forest, where we saw the largest hemlock on the surface of the Earth. So the withered lady with the anemone in her buttonhole told us in the parking lot.

Drove through mountains darkened with storm and cloud, dazzled with escaping spears of light. The forest itself is lovely, though with a different feel. What? TE calls it "eerie," and that will do. Too alive, maybe: like finding yourself in a terrarium.

The air is so moist as to be visible, especially over the little rocketing streams. To breath is to feel swathed and healed. The lungs pull at their own corners, trying to get bigger.

I don't remember richer forest: life upon life, life under life, golden fungus gnawed by black-and-gold beetles, snow-colored anemone backed by wood of lustrous absolute black, the red of shattered hemlock, the silver of mist, orange and pale of fungus, rust-backed toads, gigantic millipedes of elegant dust-rose and pewter, blood-red wake-robin. Over all, of course, green, green, green, green. Dazzling green. Electric green. Moss green. Mist-green. Hemlock silver-green. Gold-green of tulip poplars diffused from 200 feet over our heads. TE fits in, like a young trunk pushing up in the forest. He catches me looking at him and says, "What?"

I say, "Behind you" and leave him looking at the green drapery.

A Blackburnian warbler harvests the path at our feet. We stand like latter-day Moseses, awestruck by a Burning Bird. Bird takes his time. Finally, impatient, we brush past, he yielding the path barely long enough for the seams of our jeans to get by.

It rains. It leaves off raining. We are damp and as indifferent as the trees.

I regret being ill, for no forest has rung such a chord of *belonging,* as though I had dwelt there primevally and must return. If one lay down on the venereal soil one would before a week was out sprout ferns and fronds. One would harbor salamanders in the creases of one's clothes.

Stay a fortnight and transfigure to an animal.

Stay a month and be a god.

Deep crying of frogs in the night. Somewhere I picked up the notion that things must be mine before I can love them.

TE and I met for breakfast Friday. In some ways he is very young. He sings to himself when he rides, carrying on private dramas and dialogues—not oblivious to me but comfortable with me—in a way I do only when alone and perhaps not at all anymore.

He wanted a long ride, so we drove to Mount Mitchell. I don't know what his drama turned to, but I was Shelley balanced on the rim of Arve, the blasts and mists of Blanc raging around. A poet who knew his business could make this the axis of the world.

Mist ripped upward through the firs, meeting cloud in whirling air above the mountain. Ravens flew low in the mist, sorcerers in bird-shape, appearing and disappearing as they wove the thicknesses, their harsh voices like damaged voices of men.

We climbed the cement tower, left coins at all four corners for the gods of the mountain. Cold and beautiful. Clouds shifted over.

We ate in the little restaurant on the edge of the mountain, seeing nothing for the blank of the mist. We drove down again into Asheville, like prophets descended from the face of God.

TE listens. Nothing seems to be lost. He quotes what I have said. I think back, back, to an offhand comment weeks before that I had forgotten itself. It's a burden. I will have to say what I mean.

Pouring sweat as I write, as though it were a matter of honor not to turn on the air conditioner before morning. Sky a raging turquoise, punched at the top with stars.

When I returned, two huge dogs and a little toad were seated on my doorstep. I am trying to hammer them into images of grace. TE says I hoard all these things for weapons, to wield them when the time is ripe. It sounds violent and calculating, but I suppose it's right.

Night heat. Chirring of cicadae. A mockingbird sang; I looked to see what disturbed him, but universal darkness took the mountain away. Perhaps he was singing out his dream.

I quote poetry at TE as we go. If it's funny, he laughs. If it's serious, he keeps silent, keeps walking. Whether this is awe or admonition I don't know. Maybe he senses that the words stand outside the things they mean, like a tree beside another tree. I want them to be the same thing— the word and the object it signals. I say so, He keeps walking.

TE says. "You're different in the woods." I accept that as a statement of fact, until I realize he's almost never known me elsewhere. He must be right, though; we all are.

If you hike alone you see the world. If you hike with an acquaintance you see him. If you hike with a friend you see yourself. You must decide what is necessary.

He won't hike in the snow, not that there's much around here anyway. I prepare to accuse him of being afraid, then realize I want to put myself into that danger and discomfort because I too am afraid. Old bravado. Handy sometimes, but not now.

I should remember, too, the odd shape of his stockinged feet, blunted on the left foot where he lost the second and third toes to frostbite. A spring rain soaking through whitens his face with pain.

Thank God, I say secretly, put down my boots, take up the cocoa tin.

Holly and I hike in the shadow of Pisgah one morning late this winter. We come across the purple knit hat I know is TE's. I smell his smell on it, at once comforting and lonely, though whether the loneliness is his or mine I don't know. I should think first of danger, that he may be lost or hurt in the woods, but it doesn't seem very likely. It crosses my mind that he has foreseen we would pass this way and left us a memento.

Holly reads my mind. She says, "Somebody you know?"

Inexplicably, I answer, "No."

A mile or so farther along, I take my hat off, put his on. I give Holly my hat, and the circle stands complete.

Analyzing and Discussing the Text

1. Why does Hopes treasure solitude so much while hiking in the mountains? How does his language emphasize the extremity of his pleasure?
2. What happens to one's experience of the world when one is not alone, according to the author? Does this make sense to you or do you feel differently? Explain your response.
3. Describe the structure of Hopes's essay. What is the effect of this form? Does it seem constrained by specific examples or do they resonate beyond the specific?
4. Examine Hopes's explanation of the differences between male and female behavior in the woods. Is there any validity to his observa-

tions or are they purely humorous? What is it that *makes* this writing funny (if it seems so to you)?

5. Why does Hopes set apart the lengthy section about hiking with TE? Why is this material different from descriptions of the other hiking episodes?
6. "If you hike alone you see the world. If you hike with an acquaintance you see him. If you hike with a friend you see yourself. You must decide what is necessary." What does "necessary" mean? Does Hopes imply that one type of experience is better than the others or does he leave the decision up to the individual? What is "necessary" for you?
7. Why does Hopes put on TE's hat at the end of the essay and give his own to Holly? What does "the circle stands complete" mean?

Experiencing and Writing About the World

1. Consider the connection between social experience and environmental experience. Does an activity like walking/hiking enable one to merge the two? Write a manifesto in which you proclaim your own preference for solitude or society—devote approximately 500 words to explaining the issue and your particular stance.
2. Write an essay on "men, women, and wilderness." How does gender determine our behavior in the outdoors? Are gender-based explanations old-fashioned? What happens when men and women are together in the woods? Do you agree with Hopes's scenarios?
3. Attempt your own version of Hopes's thoroughly episodic writing technique. Use numerous specific scenes to create a matrix of meaning, a set of illustrations so vividly etched that they require minimal abstract explanation. Apply this technique to one of the two topics above or to another topic.

LINDA HOGAN

Walking

Linda Hogan (1947–   ), a Native American poet, fiction writer, and essayist of Chickasaw descent, was born in Denver, Colorado, and currently teaches at the University of Colorado, where she received her M.A. in 1978. She formerly taught at Colorado College (1981–1984) and then served as associate professor of American studies and American Indian studies at the University of Minnesota before returning to Colorado in the late 1980s. Her books include four collections of poetry— *Calling Myself Home* (1978), *Daughters, I Love You* (1981), *Eclipse* (1983), and *Seeing Through the Sun* (1985)—and two collections of short fiction— *That Horse* (1985) and *The Big Woman* (1987). In 1990 she published a novel called *Mean Spirit*. For the past several years, she has been working on nonfiction essays about animals and humans. As she told one interviewer, "I am interested in the deepest questions, those of spirit, of shelter, of growth and movement toward peace and liberation, inner and outer. My main interest at the moment is in wildlife rehabilitation and studying the relationship between humans and other species, and trying to create world survival skills out of what I learn from this."

In her essay "The Two Lives" (1987), Hogan recalls, "When I began to write, I wrote partly to put this life in order, partly because I was too shy to speak. I was silent and the poems spoke first. I was ignorant and the poems educated me. When I realized that people were going to read the poems, I thought of the best way to use words, how great was my responsibility to transmit words, ideas, and acts by which we could live with liberation, love, self-respect, good humor, and joy." Hogan shows this sense of responsibility in her prose—her fiction and nonfiction—as well as her poetry. The following essay called "Walking" was first published in 1990 and explicitly echoes Thoreau's famous title; this piece is about perceiving the natural world in a deeper way, and to this end Hogan's language is detailed, nuanced, and respectful of her own potential to pay attention and of the world's intrinsic meaning. "Walking," for Hogan, involves more than putting one foot in front of the other—walking is a state of mind.

It began in dark and underground weather, a slow hunger moving toward light. It grew in a dry gully beside the road where I live, a place where entire hillsides are sometimes yellow, windblown tides of sunflower plants. But this one was different. It was alone, and larger than the countless others who had established their lives further up the hill. This one was a traveler, a settler, and like a dream beginning in conflict, it grew where the land had been disturbed.

I saw it first in early summer. It was a green and sleeping bud, raising itself toward the sun. Ants worked around the unopened bloom, gathering aphids and sap. A few days later, it was a tender young flower, soft and new, with a pale green center and a troop of silver gray insects climbing up and down the stalk.

Over the summer this sunflower grew into a plant of incredible beauty, turning its face daily toward the sun in the most subtle of ways, the black center of it dark and alive with a deep blue light, as if flint had sparked an elemental fire there, in community with rain, mineral, mountain air, and sand.

As summer changed from green to yellow there were new visitors daily: the lace-winged insects, the bees whose legs were fat with pollen, and grasshoppers with their clattering wings and desperate hunger. There were other lives I missed, lives too small or hidden to see. It was as if this plant with its host of lives was a society, one in which moment by moment, depending on light and moisture, there was great and diverse change.

There were changes in the next larger world around the plant as well. One day I rounded a bend in the road to find the disturbing sight of a dead horse, black and still against a hillside, eyes rolled back. Another day I was nearly lifted by a wind and sandstorm so fierce and hot that I had to wait for it to pass before I could return home. On this day the faded dry petals of the sunflower were swept across the land. That was when the birds arrived to carry the new seeds to another future.

In this one plant, in one summer season, a drama of need and survival took place. Hungers were filled. Insects coupled. There was escape, exhaustion, and death. Lives touched down a moment and were gone.

I was an outsider. I only watched. I never learned the sunflower's golden language or the tongues of its citizens. I had a small understanding, nothing more than a shallow observation of the flower, insects, and birds. But they knew what to do, how to live. An old voice from somewhere, gene or cell, told the plant how to evade the pull of gravity and find its way upward, how to open. It was instinct, intuition, necessity. A certain knowing directed the seed-bearing birds on paths to ancestral homelands they had never seen. They believed it. They followed.

There are other summons and calls, some even more mysterious than those commandments to birds or those survival journeys of insects.

In bamboo plants, for instance, with their thin green canopy of light and golden stalks that creak in the wind. Once a century, all of a certain kind of bamboo flower on the same day. Whether they are in Malaysia or in a greenhouse in Minnesota makes no difference, nor does the age or size of the plant. They flower. Some current of an inner language passes between them, through space and separation, in ways we cannot explain in our language. They are all, somehow, one plant, each with a share of communal knowledge.

John Hay, in *The Immortal Wilderness*, has written: "There are occasions when you can hear the mysterious language of the Earth, in water, or coming through the trees, emanating from the mosses, seeping through the undercurrents of the soil, but you have to be willing to wait and receive."

Sometimes I hear it talking. The light of the sunflower was one language, but there are others, more audible. Once, in the redwood forest, I heard a beat, something like a drum or heart coming from the ground and trees and wind. That underground current stirred a kind of knowing inside me, a kinship and longing, a dream barely remembered that disappeared back to the body.

Another time, there was the booming voice of an ocean storm thundering from far out at sea, telling about what lived in the distance, about the rough water that would arrive, wave after wave revealing the disturbance at center.

Tonight I walk. I am watching the sky. I think of the people who came before me and how they knew the placement of stars in the sky, watched the moving sun long and hard enough to witness how a certain angle of light touched a stone only once a year. Without written records, they knew the gods of every night, the small, fine details of the world around them and of immensity above them.

Walking, I can almost hear the redwoods beating. And the oceans are above me here, rolling clouds, heavy and dark, considering snow. On the dry, red road, I pass the place of the sunflower, that dark and secret location where creation took place. I wonder if it will return this summer, if it will multiply and move up to the other stand of flowers in a territorial struggle.

It's winter and there is smoke from the fires. The square, lighted windows of houses are fogging over. It is a world of elemental attention, of all things working together, listening to what speaks in the blood. Whichever road I follow, I walk in the land of many gods, and they love and eat one another.

Walking, I am listening to a deeper way. Suddenly all my ancestors are behind me. Be still, they say. Watch and listen. You are the result of the love of thousands.

Analyzing and Discussing the Text

1. This essay initially appeared in a special issue of *Parabola: The Magazine of Myth and Tradition* devoted to "attention." Explain how Hogan's essay seems to fit this topic and this magazine.
2. Have you ever heard the earth "talking"? When Hogan refers to the language of birds and sunflowers, what does she mean? How does the earth's language relate to human language?
3. Discuss the shift in tense between the second and third sections of the essay—how does this change mirror the change in the narrator's relationship to the world? When exactly does the speaker cease to be an outsider?
4. What other activities is Hogan engaged in *while* walking? How does her walking resemble Thoreau's sauntering?

Experiencing and Writing About the World

1. Write an account of one of your own recent walks in which you attempt to describe the natural world in a rhapsodic, spiritually elevated way, imitating Hogan's style at the end of her essay. Can you actually *feel* this way toward the world or does it seem artificial?
2. Write your own contribution to a special issue of a magazine devoted to "attention." What does the concept mean to you? Is it consequential or insignificant? Include one or more experiences from your own life that demonstrate extraordinary attentiveness or inattentiveness.
3. Prepare a brief critical analysis of Hogan's "Walking," explaining the evolution of her persona. What subtle clues in the text indicate the narrator's changes? What are the broader implications of the essay and how are they related to the changes in the first-person narrator?
4. Compare the heightened attentiveness described in Hogan's essay to the psychological condition depicted in one of the essays in the chapter called "Spiritual and Aesthetic Responses to Nature" (Chapter Three in Part Three). Write an essay in which you carefully explain not only the mental states of the two authors, but also their literary strategies in representing these ways of viewing the world.

Suggestions for Further Reading

Abbey, Edward. "Terra Incognita: Into the Maze." *Desert Solitaire: A Season in the Wilderness.* New York: McGraw, 1968.

——. "Walking." *The Journey Home: Some Words in Defense of the American West.* New York: Dutton, 1977.

Bashō, Matsuo. *The Narrow Road to the Deep North and other Travel Sketches.* 1671–94. Trans. Nobuyuki Yuasa. New York: Penguin, 1966.

Berry, Wendell. "An Entrance to the Woods." *The Unforeseen Wilderness.* UP of Kentucky, 1977.

Fletcher, Colin. *The Man Who Walked Through Time.* New York: Knopf, 1967.

Gruchow, Paul. *The Necessity of Empty Places.* New York: St. Martin's, 1988.

Jenkins, Peter. *A Walk Across America.* New York: Fawcett, 1979.

McPhee, John. *Encounters with the Archdruid.* New York: Farrar, 1971.

Muir, John. *A Thousand-Mile Walk to the Gulf.* Ed. William F. Badè. Boston: Houghton, 1917.

Roberts, David. "Burnout in the Maze." *Moments of Doubt and Other Essays.* Seattle: Mountaineers, 1986.

CHAPTER TWO

Floating: Water Narratives

"The river is very deep, the canyon very narrow, . . . the waters reel and roll and boil, and we are scarcely able to determine where we can go." These words, from the nineteenth-century journal of the famous one-armed explorer John Wesley Powell as he and his crew worked their way down the unknown canyons of the Colorado River, capture an important aspect of the floating experience: the physical adventure. Although there are fewer unknown rivers and routes today, the danger, the sense of challenge, and the thrill of negotiating white water remain. Floating can be a way to test and measure oneself and one's knowledge of the world's rivers, lakes, and oceans. It also enables us to develop and express a sense of community; when survival depends on successful teamwork on a raft or when travel together promotes the exchange of ideas and stories, floating fosters meaningful companionship. Other forms of floating offer quieter and more solitary kinds of adventure. A journey by water can be a way to learn about nature, to observe closely the life in, above, and next to the water, or to listen to the quieter voices of the self. Suspended in slower, less dangerous currents, the mind itself floats freely. While drifting alone on a still lake or pond, increased receptiveness to creative contemplation can generate new perspectives and make new connections.

The essays in this chapter reflect both extremes of water experiences—the adventurous and the meditative. Edward Abbey's trip down the Rio Dolores in Colorado offers the opportunity for some adventure and companionship, but, because this river has been dammed like so many others, the contemplative moments of the journey are tinged with sadness and anger rather than the thrill of discovery. The artist Ann Zwinger's trip offers the chance to observe very closely the Green River, to meditate on its history, and finally to immerse herself in the physical place as a way of joining with nature. For John Tallmadge, learning is also the focus, but he is less concerned with the precise natural history of the boundary waters in Ontario's Quetico Provincial Park than with the lessons canoe travel can offer him and his students about differences between the activities of climbing and floating. With a group of friends on the crowded Nantahala River in North Carolina, Rick Bass experiences first the crisp thrill of white water, wildness, and freedom, and later the tranquil happiness of a riverside picnic. Eddy Harris, setting out on his solo adventure down the Mississippi River, hopes for adventure, for the chance to test and prove himself; yet the early passage from this river narrative also becomes a forum to express misgivings and uncertainties about the author's place in the world. Gretel Ehrlich, crossing a small pond with little effort on her part, floats in a different realm. The experience of being aimlessly adrift frees Ehrlich to reflect on such cosmic questions as the creation of life in the universe and the mutually shaping powers of landscape and mind.

EDWARD ABBEY

Floating

Edward Abbey (1927–1989), a self-designated "agrarian anarchist" and advocate for American wilderness, was born on a farm in western Pennsylvania. He studied philosophy at the University of New Mexico, receiving his B.A. in 1951 and his M.A. in 1956; he was also a Fulbright Scholar at the University of Edinburgh (Scotland) and a Wallace Stegner Fellow in creative writing at Stanford University. Abbey spent his life working as a seasonal park ranger, a fire-lookout, a writer, and a professor (at the University of Arizona), always fighting humorously, bitterly, and irreverently for American wilderness, especially for the desert country and rivers of the American West. Abbey's goals, according to his long-time friend Doug Peacock, were simple: he sought to "save the world but not allow it to become more than a part-time job." His best-known book is the contemporary classic of American nature writing, *Desert Solitaire: A Season in the Wilderness* (1968), which is based on Abbey's experiences as a park ranger in what is now Arches National Monument (Utah) before it had paved roads, an influx of tourists, and all the other ills of what Abbey calls "Industrial Tourism." He also published a number of other important works of nonfiction, such as *The Journey Home* (1977), *Abbey's Road* (1979), *Down the River* (1981), and *One Life at a Time, Please* (1987). His many novels include *The Brave Cowboy* (1960); *The Monkey Wrench Gang* (1975), an influential novel of "ecotage" or sabotage on behalf of the environment; and *Hayduke Lives!* (1991), a posthumously published sequel to *The Monkey Wrench Gang*.

Describing his own style of writing, Abbey stated: "I write in a deliberately outrageous or provocative manner because I like to startle people. I like to wake up people." Yet he also said that he wrote in order "to give pleasure and promote esthetic bliss" and "to honor life and praise the divine beauty of the world." Abbey wrote a number of river narratives, several of which, including "Floating," appeared in the collection *Down the River*. Unlike the other authors whose work is collected in this chapter, Abbey cannot separate his own experiences on the river from broader—and often disturbing—issues concerning people and their effect on the natural world. This narrative of Abbey's trip down the Rio Dolores in southwestern Colorado moves between the author's two characteristic modes—the provocative and the pleasurable.

Each precious moment entails every other. Each sacred place suggests the immanent presence of all places. Each man, each woman, exemplifies all humans. The bright faces of my companions, here, now, on this Rio Dolores, this River of Sorrows, somewhere in the melodramatic landscape of southwest Colorado, break my heart—for in their faces, eyes, vivid bodies in action, I see the hope and joy and tragedy of humanity everywhere. Just as the hermit thrush, singing its threnody back in the piney gloom of the forest, speaks for the lost and voiceless everywhere.

What am I trying to say? The same as before—everything. Nothing more than that. Everything implied by water, motion, rivers, boats. By the flowing . . .

What the hell. Here we go again, down one more condemned river. Our foolish rubber rafts nose into the channel and bob on the current. Brown waves glitter in the sunlight. The long oars of the boatpeople—young women, young men—bite into the heavy water. Snow melt from the San Juan Mountains creates a river in flood, and the cold waters slide past the willows, hiss upon the gravel bars, thunder and roar among the rocks in a foaming chaos of exaltation.

Call me Jonah. I should have been a condor, sailing high above the gray deserts of the Atacama. I should have stayed in Hoboken when I had the chance. Every river I touch turns to heartbreak. Floating down a portion of Rio Colorado in Utah on a rare month in spring, twenty-two years ago, a friend and I found ourselves passing through a world so beautiful it seemed and had to be—eternal. Such perfection of being, we thought—these glens of sandstone, these winding corridors of mystery, leading each to its solitary revelation—could not possibly be changed. The philosophers and the theologians have agreed, for three thousand years, that the perfect is immutable—that which cannot alter and cannot ever be altered. They were wrong. We were wrong. Glen Canyon was destroyed. Everything changes, and nothing is more vulnerable than the beautiful.

Why yes, the Dolores, too, is scheduled for damnation. Only a little dam, say the politicians, one little earth-fill dam to irrigate the sorghum and alfalfa plantations, and then, most likely, to supply the industrial parks and syn-fuel factories of Cortez, Shithead Capital of Dipstick County, Colorado. True, only a little dam. But dammit, it's only a little river.

Forget it. Write it off. Fix your mind on the feel of the oars in your hands, observe with care the gay ripples that lead to the next riffle, watch out for that waterlogged fir tree there, clinging to the left bank, its trunk beneath the surface, one sharp snag like a claw carving the flow, ready to rip your tender raft from stem to stern. Follow that young lady boatman ahead, she knows what she's doing, she's been down this one before, several times. Admire her bare arms, glistening with wetness, and the deep-breathing surge of her splendid breasts— better fasten that life jacket, honey!—as she takes a deep stroke with the oars and tugs her boat, ferrywise, across the current and past the danger. Her passengers groan with delight.

Women and rivers. Rivers and men. Boys and girls against United Power & Gas. Concentrating too hard, I miss the snag but pivot off the submerged rock beyond, turning my boat backward into the rapids. My two passengers look anxious—

"For godsake, Ed, didn't you see that rock?"

"What rock?"

—but I have no fear. Hardly know the meaning of the word. God will carry us through. God loves fools, finds a need for us, how otherwise could we survive? Through all the perilous millennia? Fools, little children, drunks, and concupiscent scriveners play a useful function, its precise nature not yet determined, in the intricate operations of evolution. Furthermore, I reflect—

"Watch out!"

"What?"

"Rock!"

"Where?"

—as we do another graceful pivot turn off a second rock, straightening my boat to face downstream again, furthermore, it seems clear at last that our love for the natural world—Nature—is the only means by which we can requite God's obvious love for it. Else why create Nature? Is God immune to the pangs of unreciprocated love? I doubt it. Does God love *us*? Well, that's another question. Does God exist? If perfect, He must. But nobody's perfect. I ponder the ontological dilemma.

"Watch it!"

"Who?"

"The wall!"

The strong current bears us toward the overhanging wall on the outside bend of the river. A sure deathtrap. Wrapped on stone by a liquid hand with the force of a mountain in its pressure, we would drown like rats in a rainbarrel pushed under by wanton boys with brooms. ("We are as boys to wanton sports. . . . ") Panic, terror, suffocation—not even our life jackets could save us there. Something to think about, I think, as I contemplate the imminent danger, and meditate upon possible alternatives to a sudden, sodden, personal extinction. Walt Blackadar, I remember, world's greatest kayaker, died in similar fashion beneath a jammed half-sunken tree on the Payette River in Idaho.

"Jesus!"

"What?"

"Good Christ!"

God's love. God's elbow. We graze the wall and spin out into the sun. Not much damage: a slightly bent oarlock, a smear of powdery sandstone on the left gunwale, and my old straw hat left behind forever, snared on the branch of a shrub of some kind protruding from the rock. A last-minute pull with my oars—good reflexes here—has saved us from the deepest part of the overhang and propelled us into safety. I've said it before: Faith alone is not enough. Thou must know what thou art doing. *His Brother* sayeth it: "Good works is the key to Heaven . . . be ye doers of the Word, and not hearers only . . . " (James 1:22).

Yes, sir.

Flat water lies ahead. Our River of Sorrows, bound for a sea it will never reach, rolls for a while into a stretch of relative peace.

A good boatman must know when to act, when to react, and when to rest. I lean on the oars, lifting them like bony wings from the water, and ignore the whining and mewling from the two passengers seated behind me. Will probably be free of them after lunch; they'll find another boat. Nothing more tiresome to a thoughtful oarsman than critics.

I think of lunch: tuna from a tin, beslobbered with mayonnaise. Fig Newtons and Oreo cookies. A thick-skin Sunkist orange peeled in a crafty way to reveal a manikin in a state of urgent priapism. Salami and cheese and purple-peeled onions. Our world is so full of beautiful things: fruit and ideas and women and good men and banjo music and onions with purple skins. A virtual Paradise. But even Paradise can be damned, flooded, overrun, generally mucked up by fools in pursuit of paper profits and plastic happiness.

My thoughts wander to Mark Dubois. Talk about the *right stuff.* That young man chained himself to a rock, in a hidden place known only to a single friend, in order to save—if only for the time being— a river he had learned to know and love too much: the Stanislaus in northern California. Mark Dubois put his life on the rock, below high-water line, and drove half the officialdom of California and the Army Corps of Engineers into exasperated response, forcing them to halt the filling of what they call the New Melones Dam. For a time.

In comparing the government functionaries of the United States to those of such states as the Soviet Union, or China, or Brazil or Argentina, we are obliged to give our own a certain degree of credit: they are still reluctant to sacrifice human lives to industrial purposes in the full glare of publicity. (Why we need a free press.) But I prefer to give my thanks direct to people like Mark Dubois, whose courage, in serving a cause worthy of service, seems to me of much more value than that of our astronauts and cosmonauts and other assorted technetronic whatnots: dropouts, all of them, from the real world of earth, rivers, life.

One river gained a reprieve; another goes under. Somebody recently sent me a newspaper clipping from Nashville, in which I read this story:

> Loudon, Tenn. (AP)—Forty years of dreams and sweat have died beneath a bulldozer's blade as the Tennessee Valley Authority crushed the last two homes standing in the way of its Tellico Dam.
>
> The bulldozers arrived Tuesday hours after federal marshals evicted the last two of 341 farmers whose land was taken for the 38,000-acre, $130-million federal project.
>
> By nightfall the barn and white frame house that the late Asa McCall had built for his wife in 1939 and the home where postman Beryl Moser was born 46 years ago had been demolished. . . .
>
> "It looks like this is about the end of it," Moser said, as three carloads of marshals escorted him from his home. "I still feel the same way about it I did ten years ago; to hell with the TVA. . . . "
>
> The W. B. Ritcheys, the other holdouts, packed their furniture Monday. . . . All three families had refused government checks totaling $216,000 mailed to them when their land was condemned. . . .
>
> Supreme Court Justice William Brennan on Tuesday rejected a plea by Cherokee Indians for an injunction to prevent TVA from closing the dam gates. Justice Potter Stewart and the 6th U.S. Circuit Court of Appeals in Cincinnati rejected the same request last Friday.
>
> The Cherokee contend that a lake over their ancient capital and burial grounds violates their First Amendment rights of religious freedom. . . .

Sandstone walls tower on the left, five hundred feet above this Dolores River. The walls are the color of sliced ham, with slick, concave surfaces. Streaks of organic matter trail like draperies across the face of the cliff. Desert varnish, a patina of blue-black oxidized iron and manganese, gleams on the rock. A forest of yellow pine glides by on our right, so that we appear to be still in high mountain country while descending into the canyonlands. Bald eagles and great blue herons follow this river. A redtail hawk screams in the sky, its voice as wild and yet familiar as the croak and clack of ravens. The windhover bird, riding the airstream. Staring up at the great hawk, I hear human voices fretting and fussing behind my back, urging caution. A glance at the river. I miss the next rock. Can't hit them all. And bounce safely off the one beyond.

"Don't tell Preston," I suggest to my passengers. Preston—Preston Ellsworth—leader of this expedition, veteran river guide, owner and operator of Colorado River Tours, Inc., is one of the best in a difficult business. At the moment he is somewhere ahead, out of sight around the next bend. Though a sturdy and generous fellow, he might be disturbed by my indolent style of boatmanship. This sixteen-foot neoprene raft I am piloting from rock to rock belongs to him, and a new one would cost $2,300. And the rapid called Snaggletooth lies ahead, day after next.

Be of good cheer. All may yet be well. There's many a fork, I think, in the road from here to destruction. Despite the jet-set androids who visit our mountain West on their cyclic tours from St. Tropez to Key West to Vail to Acapulco to Santa Fe, where they buy their hobby ranches, ski-town condos, adobe villas, and settle in, telling us how much they love the West. But will not lift a finger to help defend it. Will not lend a hand or grab ahold. Dante had a special place for these ESTers, esthetes, temporizers, and castrate fence-straddlers; he locked them in the vestibule of Hell. They're worse than the simple industrial developer, whose only objective, while pretending to "create jobs," is to create for himself a fortune in paper money. The developer is what he is; no further punishment is necessary.

As for politicians, those lambs and rabbits—

"Watch it!"

Missed that one by a cat hair. As for the politicians—forget them. We scrape by the next on the portside, a fang of limestone under a furl of glossy water. Fatal loveliness, murmuring at my ear. I glide into a trough between two petrified crocodiles and slide down the rapid's glassy tongue into a moderate maelstrom. I center my attention on the huge waves walloping toward us. We ride them out in good form, bow foremost, with only a stroke now on one oar, now on the other, to keep the raft straight.

We leave the forest, descending mile after mile through a winding slickrock canyon toward tableland country. It is like Glen Canyon once again, in miniature, submerged but not forgotten Glen Canyon. The old grief will not go away. Like the loss of a wife, brother, sister, the ache in the heart dulls with time but never dissolves entirely.

We camp one night at a place called Coyote Wash, a broad opening—almost a valley—in the canyon world. After dark one member of the crew, a deadly pyromantic, climbs a thousand-foot bluff above camp and builds a bonfire of old juniper and piñon pine. He is joined by a second dark figure, dancing around the flames. As the flames die the two shove the mound of glowing coals over the edge. A cascade of fire streams down the face of the cliff. Clouds of sparks float on the darkness, flickering out as they sink into oblivion. A few spot fires burn among the boulders at the base of the cliff, then fade. The end of something. A gesture—but symbolizing what?

Maybe we should all stay home for a season, give our little Western wilderness some relief from Vibram soles, rubber boats, hang gliders, deer rifles, and fly rods. But where is home? Surely not the walled-in prison of the cities, under that low ceiling of carbon monoxide and nitrogen oxides and acid rain—the leaky malaise of an overdeveloped, overcrowded, self-destroying civilization—where most people are compelled to serve their time and please the wardens if they can. For many, for more and more of us, the out-of-doors is our true ancestral estate.

For a mere five thousand years we have grubbed in the soil and laid brick upon brick to build the cities; but for a million years before that we lived the leisurely, free, and adventurous life of hunters and gatherers, warriors and tamers of horses. How can we pluck *that* deep root of feeling from the racial consciousness? Impossible. When in doubt, jump out.

Ah yes, you say, but what about Mozart? Punk Rock? Astrophysics? Flush toilets? Potato chips? Silicon chips? Oral surgery? The Super Bowl and the World Series? Our coming journey to the stars? Vital projects, I agree, and I support them all. (On a voluntary basis only.) But why not a compromise? Why not—both? Why can't we have a moderate number of small cities, bright islands of electricity and kultur and industry surrounded by shoals of farmland, cow range, and timberland, set in the midst of a great unbounded sea of primitive forest, unbroken mountains, virgin desert? The human reason can conceive of such a free and spacious world; why can't we allow it to become—again—our home?

The American Indians had a word for what we call "wilderness." For them the wilderness was home.

Another day, another dolor. The dampness of the river has soaked into my brain, giving it the consistency of tapioca. My crackpot dreams fade with the dawn. Too many questions, not enough answers.

We are approaching Snaggletooth Rapid at last. A steady roar fills the canyon. My passengers, a new set today, life jackets snug to their chins, cling with white knuckles to the lashings of our baggage as I steer my ponderous craft down the tongue of the rapid, into the maw of the mad waters. I try to remember Preston's instructions: ferry to the right, avoiding that boat-eating Hole beyond the giant waves; then a quick pull to the left to avoid wrapping the boat upon Snaggletooth itself, an ugly talon of rock that splits and divides the main force of the river.

I grip the oars and shut my eyes. For a moment. The shock of cold water in the face recalls me to duty. A huge wave is rising over the port bow, about to topple. Pull to the right. The wave crashes, half-filling the boat. We ride down past the side of the Hole, carried through by momentum. The Tooth looms beyond my starboard bow, an ugly shark's fin of immovable stone. Pull to the left. We slip by it, barely *touching*—dumb luck combined with blind atavistic natural talent. The boat wallows over the vigorous vee-waves beyond. Wake up. I'm drifting beyond the beaching point. I strain at the oars—oh, it's hard, it's hard—and tug this lumpen-bourgeois river rig through the water and into the safety of an eddy. My swamper jumps ashore, bowline in hand. We drag the raft onto the sand and tie up to a willow tree.

Safely on the beach I watch (with secret satisfaction) the mishaps of the other oarsmen. And oarswomen. Nobody loses or overturns a boat, but several hit the Tooth, hang there for awesome seconds, minutes, while tons of water beat upon their backs. They struggle. Hesitation: then the boats slide off, some into the current on the wrong side of the rock to go ashore on the wrong side of the canyon. No matter; nobody is hurt, or even dumped in the river, and no baggage is lost.

Recovered, reassembled, we eat lunch. We stare at the mighty rapids. We talk, meditate, reload the boats and push out, once again, onto the river.

Quietly exultant, we drift on together, not a team but a family, a human family bound by human love, through the golden canyons of the River of Sorrows. So named, it appears, by a Spanish priest three centuries ago, a man of God who saw in our physical world (is there another?) only a theater of suffering. He was right! He was wrong! Love can defeat that nameless terror. Loving one another, we take the sting from death. Loving our mysterious blue planet, we resolve riddles and dissolve all enigmas in contingent bliss.

On and on and on we float, down the river, day after day, down to the trip's end, to our takeout point, a lonely place in far western Colorado called Bedrock. Next door to Paradox. There is nothing here but a few small alfalfa farms and one gaunt, weathered, bleak old country store. The store is well stocked, though, with Michelob beer, and Budweiser (next morning we'll find among us a number of sadder Budweiser men), and also a regional brew known as—Cures? Yes, Cures beer, a weak, pallid provincial liquescence brewed, they say, from pure Rocky Mountain spigot water. Take a twelve-pack home tonight. Those who drink from these poptop tins will be, in the words of B. Traven, America's greatest writer, "forever freed from pain."

Three of the boat people are going on down the Dolores to its junction with the Colorado, and from there to the Land of Moab in Darkest Utah. My heart breaks to see them go without me. But I have a promise to keep. Preston Ellsworth has business waiting in Durango; the others elsewhere. Must all voyages end in separation? Powell lost three of his men at Separation Rapids, far down there in *The* Canyon. And Christopher Columbus, after his third voyage to the Indies, got in trouble with his royal masters and was sent back to Spain in chains, leaving his men behind on Hispaniola.

Which made no difference. There will always be a 1492. There will always be a Grand Canyon. There will always be a Rio Dolores, dam or no dam. There will always be one more voyage down the river to Bedrock, Colorado, in that high lonesome valley the pioneers named Paradox. A paradox because—anomaly—the river flows across, not through, the valley, apparently violating both geo-logic and common sense. Not even a plateau could stop the river. Their dams will go down like dominoes. And another river be reborn.

There will always be one more river, not to cross but to follow. The journey goes on forever, and we are fellow voyagers on our little living ship of stone and soil and water and vapor, this delicate planet circling round the sun, which humankind call Earth.

Analyzing and Discussing the Text

1. Why does Abbey begin with the comment "Each precious moment entails every other"? Is this idea developed elsewhere in the essay?
2. In the fourth paragraph from the end of his essay, Abbey talks about Bedrock and Paradox and Cures. Do you think these are actual names? Why does Abbey use them here?
3. What does Abbey seem to mean when he says that "There will always be a 1492"? Would this phrase have a different meaning for present-day readers than it did for readers in the 1980s, when his essay was published?
4. Identify the multiple forms of humor that Abbey employs in this essay. Does any one kind of humor dominate the tone of "Floating"? What does Abbey gain by mixing humor with his anger about "this Rio Dolores, this River of Sorrows"?
5. Abbey carefully modulates the moods of his prose; observe the shifts in this essay from internal reflection to external action, from history to description, and from pessimism to hope for the land. How do these tonal shifts fit together in the overall pattern of his narrative?

Experiencing and Writing About the World

1. Consider something in the world—an environmental issue, a social issue, or whatever comes to mind—that makes you feel outraged. Write an essay on this subject in which you combine (or alternate) the tone of anger with rhapsodic appreciation for something you value deeply and wish to preserve.
2. Why are dams useful and why are they troubling? Read some articles about dams. Visit one in your community, speaking to the officials in charge and the people who live nearby. Then write a paper taking a stand for or against this dam in your community.
3. Abbey writes that "Every river I touch turns to heartbreak" and "Their dams will go down like dominoes." Write an essay analyzing his views on the environment in which you explain how these two apparently opposing views fit together in his work.
4. Abbey's humor and anger are so powerfully expressed in his prose that we can sometimes overlook his effort to "promote esthetic bliss." Look at this essay and Abbey's "The Great American Desert," later in this anthology; write an essay about Abbey's descriptions of the natural world and his methods of conveying to readers his own sense of nature's beauty.

ANN ZWINGER

Fort Bottom to Turks Head

Ann Zwinger (1925–   ) was born in Muncie, Indiana, where she grew up with the White River "across the street and down the bank." As she suggests in her introduction to *Run, River, Run: A Naturalist's Journey Down One of the Great Rivers of the West* (1975), the influence of those early years on the river is still with her: "When there is a river in your growing up, you probably always hear it." Zwinger went on to earn a B.A. (1946) in art history at Wellesley College and an M.A. (1950) at Indiana University; she also studied at Radcliffe College in 1951–1952 and at Colorado College in 1963–1964 and 1978–1980. After a series of frequent moves occasioned by her husband's air force career, the couple and their three daughters bought land near Colorado Springs, Colorado, in 1960. Zwinger's observations of nature on these forty acres at an elevation of eight thousand feet became the subject for her first book, *Beyond the Aspen Grove* (1970). Her subsequent writings include *Land Above the Trees: A Guide to American Alpine Tundra* (1972); *Wind in the Rock: The Canyonlands of Southeastern Utah* (1978); *A Conscious Stillness: Two Naturalists on Thoreau's Rivers* (1982), co-authored with Edwin Way Teale; *A Desert Country near the Sea* (1983); and *The Mysterious Lands: The Four Deserts of the United States* (1989). Between 1973 and 1990, she served as a visiting lecturer at Colorado College, and she spent part of 1987 at the University of Arizona. In 1990 she was named the first holder of the Hulbert Center Endowed Chair in Southwestern Studies at Colorado College. To the beginning writer, Zwinger advises: "Think about what gets *you* interested. Your interest in a subject is infectious. . . . If you're intrigued by the mating habits of damsel flies, you'll make that interesting to others. Take the reader with you on a walk. If you can get others to look at a damsel fly, it will become part of their world and they will begin to care about it. When people care *about* something, they will take care *of* it. That's why I write."

Considering her artistic background, it is not surprising that Zwinger's books view the natural world through an artist's eye. Zwinger's descriptions reveal her careful attention to color and texture, and she often accompanies the text with her own pencil drawings of plants, fossils, geological formations, and topographical patterns. The following essay is a chapter from *Run, River, Run*, Zwinger's book about her trip down the Green River of Wyoming, Colorado, and Utah, which won the John

Burroughs Medal for natural history writing in 1976. Zwinger shapes the narrative to involve her reader in the all-important process of really seeing the Green River and the landscape through which it flows, making us aware of the way humans and nature interact.

Of all the places on the Green River that have their own character, Stillwater Canyon is the one that remains in the back of my mind as a measure of the meaning of the river. Many sections of the river have, by pure chance, come to be associated in my mind with particular times of the year or day: Lodore will be forever, to me, a foreboding, sense-of-winter canyon; Split Mountain's rapids are always those of a spring morning, even though I have run them more often in the fall. But Stillwater has no temporal annotations. When I think about the river I always come back to Stillwater, my place of *déjà vu*.

Part of the enchantment of Stillwater Canyon lies in its name. Stillwater remains one of the most mellifluous names with which Powell endowed this river, an almost onomatopoetic balancing of syllables, a word of peaceful sound and rhythm, definitive, just as the skyline itself is, defined by White Rim Sandstone. In all its separate parts, it always conveys the same meaning, in a summation that means more than the simple sum of its individual parts.

The surface excitement of rapids does not exist in Stillwater. Those who come to the river only for rapids and who must pass through the slows of Labyrinth and Stillwater to reach Cataract Canyon must find it a nuisance. But those who go on the river just for rapids miss the totality of the river. Rapids are only a part, a very small part of the river. The high of running rapids can remain for a long time, but Stillwater remains longer, the measure behind the running, the peace of the river.

The White Rim rises out of the river at an angle of intent and authority, an angle of progression, sloping upward like the corner angle of the pediment of a Greek temple allotted to a river deity. It is so reminiscent of that pediment angle that the formation might be an old river god fused back into stone, before it was carved into personification. This time the White Rim appears at noon and the day stretches loose on either side, warm, somnolent, walled-in noontime.

The name White Rim derives from local usage; it is a prominent rim visible from land or river or air, a clear, light color against the darker lower beds, the topmost of the formations—White Rim Sandstone, Organ Rock Shale, Cedar Mesa Sandstone—that form the Cutler Group. The White Rim records a persistent quiet marine current that left sand bars built up by offshore currents moving down from the northwest some 225 to 275 million years ago. White Rim Sandstone differs from the wind-laid Navajo Sandstone, for sands laid underwater usually lie at a lower angle of bedding since the angle of repose for water-laid sands is less than that for wind-laid. Wind deposits are also likely to be more multidirectional because of the greater variety of surface winds. White Rim Sandstone also bears symmetrical ripple marks characteristic of those scooped out by oscillating ocean waves rather than the symmetrical ones formed by the wind.

In Labyrinth Canyon, cliffs of Wingate Sandstone darkly define the skyline, and one can see little behind or above them while on the river. In Stillwater, the White Rim is a lower rimrock, variegated with high mesas and buttes. Some bear fanciful names, like Butte of the Cross and Cleopatra's Chair, witness to the sentimental side of Powell's nomenclature. The names are forgettable; it is the changing aspect of the skyline, as one floats downriver, that is memorable—the convexity of rock, the concavity of sky, a view that spills open to high buttes beyond and around, and between which distant storms pace stately pavanes, a panorama constantly rearranged and reunderstood as one drifts downriver. The relationship of one solid to another, seen from passing angles, creates an explanatory landscape of great clarity, and floating through Stillwater Canyon is the same privilege as walking around a piece of great sculpture.

On shore the White Rim shelves down to the river. Each shelf drops off to the next in a series of broad gentle steps. One shelf is contoured, pitted with shallow holes. Another resembles San Blas Indian embroidery, each thin lamina cut through to a new layer beneath. A scattering of cobbles down a gully look ready to roll at the first wind; in reality they are stable, each firmly mounted on top of a quarter-inch pedestal built by washed-in sand. I pick one up. Its impression in the sand is clear and smooth. A river rock is a work of art in itself, containing the elegant curve of a Brancusi sculpture, the curve of satisfaction, the weight of meaning, the shape of river. I scrupulously replace it as it was.

Farther downriver, the thin beds of the White Rim show edge on. Embedded in the rock are spheres of iron concretions, many haloed by a five-inch brilliant red disk that fades to rust, sometimes enclosed with a thin charcoal-gray line. Although minor features of most sedimentary rocks, nodules are common. They form from materials within the rock, generally after the rock has hardened. They are dense, often precipitating around a nucleus; the most frequent ones are formed of those minerals most common in the rocks in which they occur: silica, calcite, iron oxide. Nodules are often round or oval, and when several form close together they may coalesce into knobs or even into layers.

There are many nodules here, some lying loose to be picked up and weighed in the hand, heavy, dark rust-brown iron pellets the size of hazelnuts and larger. Sometimes the spheres stand above the eroded surface, and sometimes the rock is pegged with nodules that weather out to cylinders pointing toward the river like two-inch sundial handles. Or protrude, like ancient clamps, awaiting a façade not yet carved.

When I am on the river I feel the necessity to check with it before I go to bed, some primeval necessity, I suppose, of obeisance to the river gods. At the river's edge, reedgrass stridulates two feet over my head, dried stalks rattling in the evening wind. The whole patch is restive, passing on the sound. Some are weathered to gray and darker; last year's stalks are Naples yellow, lined dark at the joints. They are surprisingly tough—years ago they were used by Indians for arrow shafts.

The stars emerge, remote, cool. The night sounds begin, the aural warnings and announcements, the statements and challenges, floating upvalley, across canyon, dimming with distance but not blurred, for the fragile clarity holds in this dry air. The rocks are moon bright. The White Rim glows. It is light enough to write without a flashlight. My sleeve sibilates across the paper, pen making ink sounds, words made audible, loud enough to mask the river's flowing. The river goes so quietly that I hear it only when I stop writing and listen. The big open W of Cassiopeia reflects in the water. I feel caught in some ancient spell, listening to the river, held by some demonic sign of stone and water and approaching solstice.

Anderson's Ferry is one of the few crossings on the lower river. Cattle were once ferried back and forth to Anderson's Bottom across the river, wintering in Moab, brought back each spring. The flotsam of civilization infests the place: a decrepit truck, a disheveled fence, a disintegrating mattress and bedsprings, an ancient refrigerator, the last three in a cave where six of us once sat out an afternoon storm.

A rancher can run cattle and sheep in this country, but there is neither enough grass nor enough moisture, and the land becomes over-grazed so quickly that it soon turns to dust and blows away. The good natural grasses that make nourishing feed are insufficient to support large herds, and now that this is a national park, grazing has been ter-minated. Anderson's Bottom has fertile alluvial soil, for it is a cutoff meander, a horseshoe of land around which the river once flowed, and then broke through the narrow neck, abandoning its former course but leaving an enriched soil.

Below Anderson's Bottom the White Rim rises farther above the river to become the rimrock of Stillwater Canyon. Within a few miles the next-lower formation of the Cutler Group emerges, deep maroon infused with brown: Organ Rock Shale. Almost as if in response, the character of the White Rim solidifies into an impassable cliff. Where it meets the Organ Rock Shale it becomes concave, scooped back, a *cavetto* arched with shadow, full of seepage lines defined by inky streaks, flanked by white stripes. Spalling leaves fresh areas that are paler still, creamy white tinged with apricot. Fremont Indian structures are often found in the contact between the two formations, storage cists mostly, tucked into the overhangs, approached by an almost impossible slope of loose, sliding rock. The overhangs are narrow, the structures small, a few dozen pieces of rock, unshaped and rough. Most are windowless, so close to the spirit of the rock that one is looking at them before one registers that they are there, so well protected from weather and sight are they.

The White Rim holds a near-uniform cliff; the dark strata below present a steep slope, striped with broad white panels of talus slumped from the White Rim. This combination of vertical and diagonal produces the particular steplike profile characteristic of arid lands: hard rock verticals, soft rock diagonals. As the softer rock falls away beneath, the undermined harder rock breaks away above, usually on vertical planes of weakness along joints, repeating the configuration of the previous cliff.

At Valentine Bottom, the rain begins in isolated circles on the water, and then it comes more quickly and the circles interlock, and then it rains hard and each white drop is answered by a dark peak of water, a constant staccato alternation of dark and light. Everything drips. The wind kicks up a chop that curls on top, contemptuously going against the current. It is November cold, settling down around the head, enshrouding the shoulders. It rains all afternoon and into the evening, darkening the sky by five in the afternoon. Rain firehoses off the cliffs as the notches of dry washes on top of the cliff fill with water and turn into drain spouts. The jets shoot out almost horizontally before they fall. In this climate these dry washes do not carry water often enough to cut canyons to the river level, so they come in high off the cliff, draining the roof of rock that catches the main brunt of the storm.

On shore, the bank is sodden. Looking for a place to stow notebook and sketch pad, I find a few dry inches under a sandstone shelf. Rain drips off its edges and makes rosettes in the sand. The rain has an incessant feel, as if it had rained yesterday and will rain tomorrow. I feel encapsulated in a shimmering wetness that drips off my eyelashes and nose. The sandstone smells dank. It crumbles underfoot, granular, disintegrating, leaving a red residue on my sneakers. It rains even harder and the whole terrace shimmers with a sheet of water. Even as I watch, the trickle of running sand at my feet swirls and feathers into the river, staining it red, creating minuscule vortices opening downstream, the arterial blood of the mesas going downriver.

The storm passes slowly. A double rainbow illumines the still-smoky sky. A last flare from the clearing sky to the west kindles the cliffs. The White Rim is wet and darkened across its entire face except for one illuminated prow that is tender, creamy salmon in the afterglow, a diaphanous, transitory moment. Watching the light, I find the visual experience so intense that I forget about the rain and the chill, about cold, wet sneakers and dissonant voices complaining about wet gear, and concentrate upon locking the resonance of the color in my mind.

The river pulsates all night. At dawn it runs deep terra cotta, rufous. The sky is only faintly blue at first light, creamy on the horizon; the land lies in amorphous shadow. Last evening's storm must have cleared off the mesas and scoured the sandstones, for there is a great deal of flotsam on the surface. Debris brocades the water. Islands of foam four and five inches across saucer and wheel in the current. Brief rainstorms such as these transport most of the sediment into the lower river; they pull away more sediment over a period of time than the rare major storms that occur infrequently and, while torrential, last only a short time. These summer storms that come frequently are responsible for the main erosion on this semiarid and arid land; they need not even be massive cloudbursts—a large proportion of the sediments are picked up by rainfalls of less than one inch.

Sunlight begins to pick out forms, to light patches of green. Distant mesas are still cool and flat. Water vapor coming off the warm river condenses into opaline mists. By the time the raft is loaded and we are ready to leave, the sun is well up, the mists gone. A hot stillness settles on the river. The chill and rain are but a memory. Only the color of the river, like a slashed jugular, tells of swift runoff and gnawing erosion, and a rainstorm that pared off the mesas and buttes.

By Turks Head, Cedar Mesa Sandstone flanks the river, and Fremont petroglyphs have been cut into a wall of it set above a mud-caked alluvial flat. This is one of the fertile places on the river. Perhaps a little corn or squash was grown here, seeds poked into the ground with a planting stick. In other settlements places of habitation were quite separate from rock art, and there is no reason to think otherwise here. On the east side of the Green River, where Fremont Indians did not live, their pictographs and petroglyphs have been found in situations that suggest that they might have been used as trail markers on migration routes.

The petroglyphs here are almost hidden behind a slab of outcrop, shadowed in the wall. Cedar Mesa Sandstone is a very hard rock; to chip out such symbols takes time and effort, and this implies intent. One may doodle with a pencil and paper or a stick in the dirt, but this is not true of a near-perfect circle, ten inches in diameter, with four others laid inside, each a finger width wide, pecked a quarter inch deep into the sandstone. The circles appear again, like pebbles dropped into the water: a smaller and two larger ones, the latter all chipped out in the center, the first elaborated with ten, the second with nine spokes radiating outward. The third circle is quartered, with only some of the rays completed.

When I recall Fremont drawings, it is these circles that I remember. A circle is the first shape perceived, depending upon the way in which neurological reactions take place in the brain. It has nothing to do with culture or heredity. It is simply the expression of brain structure. The simplest arm movement is a rotational one, out of the ball and socket of the shoulder, and circles are the first shapes drawn by children. A circle is perfect and complete, therefore a shape that attracts the eye, but it is also ambiguous: is it a hollow ring, a flat disk, or a round sphere? Overcoming that ambiguity is the next step, and this is also a universal one, that of combination, such as the addition of radiating lines—the repetition of sunwheels in many cultures, like those of children's drawings, reflects a basic human expression using pictorial forms. Shields, a more sophisticated use of the circle, are often represented in Fremont drawings, shown covering all but rudimentary head and stick limbs. Huge shields, which would have covered most of the body, have been found and identified as Fremont, giving these drawings a strong realistic flavor. Although only a few basic lines are used in all these representations, the conception has reached a high level of complexity, based on acute observation.

Some anthropologists feel that these drawings have little symbolic or narrative significance for the modern observer, and, from a Renaissance fixed-point-perspective outlook, which puts heavy emphasis upon naturalism, this may be so. But this kind of observation has profitably been ignored by many cultures, such as that of ancient Egypt, and by modern artists, such as Paul Klee and Marc Chagall, who enrich ordinary visual experiences by just such free-wheeling conceptions of spatial relationships. Fremont petroglyphs are remarkable. A few selected lines are able to conjure up a recollection of complex objects and ideas; a keen eye and a disciplined hand are coupled to present a fresh view of reality, fulfilling one of the criteria of a work of art.

With the river so high this spring, and level sleeping space at a premium, a leaf-covered triangle seems like very good luck. A thatch of dead branches still attached to the sheltering scrub oak needs to be put aside. I pull each branch back, one by one, beside a big boulder. After I have nearly finished I realize that on top of that boulder is a coiled piece of diamond-patterned rosy-brown rope that has two eyes. It has given no warning, no sound; its head is turned slightly away, but it watches. I am amazed to find that I am neither afraid nor repelled, only extremely curious and exceedingly cautious.

The paucity of sleeping places decides me. I pitch my tent as planned and keep it zipped tight. We do not disturb each other. When I get up in the morning it is still here, whirring softly at a hand shadow passed in front of it. It is gone by the time we leave.

Under the spire of Turks Head, in the Organ Rock Shale, there is a splendid two-foot-thick seam of jasper. Indians were known to travel many miles to areas where superior flint could be collected or quarried; these areas may well have been neutral grounds. Shattered pieces of jasper lie in the sun, hot in the hand. Jasper is almost pure silica, mineral matter precipitated out after the sandstone formed. This vein is brick-red, subtly mottled with other warm colors—Indian red fused with liver, pale salmon shading to warm gray.

Although it was valuable as a utilitarian rock, in this land of abrasive granular sandstones and unreliable sliding shales, it is somehow also a sensuous stone. It has a soft peculiar smell from lying in the dirt. Jasper does not change color, like so many rocks, when wet or weathered. A piece of jasper in the hand is a talisman, and with skill, the flaking is predictable, leaving conchoidal fractures and a knife edge. On the other side of the river, a ledge of White Rim Sandstone slopes into the sandy ground, and I found, at its base, a handful of similar jasper chips, tomato red, scattered in the sand. The sandstone lay at a good slant for pressure flaking; it would have been impossible to break off such uniformly small bits without control. The color of the chips was beautiful and pure. And a point made from such perfection of material must have been exquisite, translucent on the moon-shaped edges, rich red in the center.

One of the delights of a river evening, especially after chinning up sandstone and shale ledges and poking around dry, silty terraces, is a rinse in the river. There is a place below Turks Head which, at high water, fulfills the requirements of privacy and a safe place out of the current. The water temperature in May is hardly tepid, at 62°F., but the air is warm. There are two table rocks, firm sandstones, upon which I can stand and safely submerge, letting the water swirl around me. In water that is so opaque, it is a matter of some faith to sit down. The current nudges but little in this back eddy, yet it is still easy to feel the erosive power of a big springtime river. The river sounds ear close. Seated eye level with the surface, I feel like an apprentice Lorelei, learning the siren sounds of the river.

The silt wells and fumes, voluminous and soft, just beneath the surface. It is fascinating to discover that by moving a hand just under water I can evoke all kinds of kaleidoscopic patterns. This silt settles out of a container of river water within twenty-four hours, but the remaining water looks like clam juice, colored by finer particles that do not precipitate as quickly in response to gravity. These extremely small particles are colloidal; since they have more surface compared to their volume, and so a specific gravity less than that of water, they remain in suspension almost indefinitely, settling out only if they cluster together to form larger particles. Gravels in a stream may fall out in less than a second when the velocity drops; colloidal particles may remain for decades.

The Green River, at this time of moderately heavy runoff, is probably carrying more than half its silt load for the year. The average load held in suspension by the river is estimated at 19 tons a year, plus 2.5 million tons dissolved. The silt content near the mouth of the Green, by volume, was once estimated at 0.5 percent; it seems a minute amount, but evenly distributed by the current it forms an effective screen, creating the year-round turbidity in the river from the Gates of Lodore south.

The sandpaper surface of the rock, unslicked by algae, provides a sense of stability in a flowing, swirling, moving world. How to explain the pure delight of being here—some of it no doubt stems from the fact that, after a day of unrelenting sunshine, almost any kind of ablution feels welcome. But there is an ineffable sybaritic pleasure beyond the necessity. The cool slide of water slips down the back of my neck, down my arm, drips off my elbow, picks patterns on the river's surface. The water that tugs around my ankles is pure hedonistic enticement, issuing a reminder of downriver delights in a branch that bobs by, on its way to other appointments.

After seeing ruins all day, I am extremely conscious of those who came here before me. So too, on a warm spring evening, a thousand years ago, someone must have stood like this, soothing calloused feet, cactus-scratched legs. I feel no time interval, no difference in flesh between who stood here then and who stands here now. The same need exists for the essentials of food and shelter, the same need to communicate and to put down symbols for someone else to see, and, so I cannot help but believe, the same response to cool water and warm sun and heated rock and sandstone on bare feet.

The last rays of the sun keep it warm enough to air dry. The sun hangs for a moment above the cliff. As it disappears behind the rim, the air cools. And yet it is not cold; maybe time to robe and leave, but not yet, not cold yet. As long as I can stand, ankle deep, without civilization, without defense, going back to self, as long as there is yet enough warmth in the air to respect needful body temperature, so long as possible I stand here, submerged physically only to the ankles, psychologically to the base of being.

Analyzing and Discussing the Text

1. Zwinger uses the word "enchantment" to describe Stillwater Canyon. What is it about this section of the Green River that warrants this word? How does Zwinger go about conveying this to us?
2. Designate where in this essay we see the influence of Zwinger's artistic background at work. Is there subtle as well as obvious evidence of this training and interest?
3. The first paragraph in the essay's second section mentions how "The flotsam of civilization infests the place." Is this infestation visible anywhere other than Anderson's Ferry?
4. The third section of this essay describes in careful detail the progress of a rainstorm passing over the river. Analyze the way Zwinger merges narration and description here. Does her use of detail help to create the sense of how that particular storm in that particular place felt? What sets this section apart from other portions of the chapter?
5. The fifth section relates an important river encounter in two brief, but important, paragraphs. Why does Zwinger not name directly the creature that she meets? Do the quiet tone and understatement of this whole section help her make a point about our relationship to a frequently feared part of nature? Explain.

Experiencing and Writing About the World

1. Write a thorough description (500–750 words) of a physical landscape in which you are present but not conspicuous. Use occasional references to yourself as a way of focusing your readers' attention on the place without making yourself the subject of the paper. Consider supplementing your written description with one or two pencil sketches; how will you decide which details in your environment to draw? Will your use of drawings change the way you describe the landscape in words?
2. The final three paragraphs of Zwinger's essay resonate with thematic importance. Analyze the ideas that Zwinger foregrounds in this section of her narrative and explain how they fit together to suggest what is central in her relationship to the natural world.
3. Zwinger's background and her essay itself serve to raise important questions about the relationship between art and nature. Write an essay in which you discuss what she is saying about "the Fremont petroglyphs," the "river rock" that she sees as "a work of art in itself, containing the elegant curve of a Brancusi sculpture," and her own

essay on nature. How do beautiful parts of nature fit together with human artworks depicting nature and, in the case of the petroglyphs, also interacting with it?

4. Zwinger's piece and Abbey's essay "Floating" each chronicle trips down western rivers. Within this broad common framework, isolate two other important and specific areas of relationship between the essays and explore them in a comparative essay.

JOHN TALLMADGE

In the Mazes of Quetico

John Tallmadge (1947–   ) was born in Orange, New Jersey. He graduated from Dartmouth College in 1969 and received his Ph.D. from Yale University in comparative literature in 1977. He has taught American literature and environmental education at the University of Utah, at Carleton College, and most recently at the Union Institute in Cincinnati, Ohio, where he also served as associate dean of the graduate school and where he founded the Environmental Studies Institute. Tallmadge has also worked as a wilderness guide, and he frequently—as described in the following essay—brings together his interests in leading wilderness trips, in natural history, and in environmental education by incorporating educational wilderness trips as part of his university courses. His scholarship includes essays on Charles Darwin, Henry David Thoreau, Ralph Waldo Emerson, John Muir, Aldo Leopold, environmental ethics, the spiritual dimensions of backpacking, and teaching wilderness values to undergraduates. He is also an accomplished personal essayist, whose pieces, like the next one (which originally appeared in *Orion Nature Quarterly*), move beyond his own specific experiences with environmental education to explore broad questions about human relationships to nature.

Throughout his writing, Tallmadge grapples with the tension between the American tradition of seeing wilderness as a source of adventure—"a scene for heroic action"—and the urgent need to end our century's "warfare against nature," to "achieve a healthy and mutually nourishing relationship to the earth." "In the Mazes of Quetico," a narrative about the field-trip portion of a class on American wilderness literature, becomes an essay of ethical exploration; "To launch canoes," as Tallmadge states elsewhere, is "to begin a study in ethics." The setting for this particular exploration differs strikingly from the flowing rivers of many canoe adventures. Tallmadge tells us that "Quetico is a vast system of baffles, chambers, and catch basins; it has no slope, no axis, and no geometry. Everything is contorted, looped, knotted, and twisted together. A cup of water poured in at one end might take a thousand years to get to the other side."

> "My indirection found direction out."
> Theodore Roethke

Northwest of Lake Superior, in Ontario's Quetico Provincial Park, there is a lake called Kahshahpiwi. To get there you have to paddle five days from the nearest road and pack your gear over a dozen portages, six of which are among the longest and swampiest anywhere. On the fourth day you start at a lake with the ominous name of Silence and begin working your way through a chain of nameless ponds, gradually losing patience and dry clothes, until at last you slide your canoe into a bay crooked like a bent finger. Choked with rushes and lily pads, it does not look promising, but soon you round a point and Kahshahpiwi unrolls at last, like a long temple corridor paved with blue stone.

I have a good view of the lake from where I sit now, on the tip of an island not far from its center. Kahshahpiwi is narrow here, barely a quarter of a mile wide, and lies in a trough between high forested ridges. At regular intervals the bedrock swells into bluffs a hundred feet high which plunge straight into the water. Up close, they reveal the striations of glaciers; from a distance, they look like the stumps of ruined columns. The water is exceptionally clear, with no trace of the tannin that turns some lakes the color of tea.

Canoeists talk a lot about Kahshahpiwi, and most emphasize the difficulty of access, the beauty of the scenery, the depth and clarity of the water, or the good fishing. But many will also mention the abandoned fire tower on the western ridge, which you can reach by taking a trail that starts at an old ranger cabin on the shore. Apparently, this is the only place in Quetico where you can get an overview of the country, and for that reason, I suppose, many consider it the climax of their trip.

This fire tower has also attracted us—myself, that is, and four students from the Wilderness Field Station operated by the Associated Colleges of the Midwest near Ely, Minnesota. They are taking my course on American wilderness literature and, after a week and a half of classes, they are out for a ten-day field trip. Their assignment is to imitate the life of travel, observation, and meditation described by our nature writers while keeping what Thoreau called "a meteorological journal of the mind." Quetico is supposed to act as an intellectual and psychological laboratory, and the trip is meant to be more than just a vacation. But so far no one seems to be writing much, and, after five straight days of canoeing, tempers are getting short all around. No one objected when I proposed that we stop for a day on Kahshahpiwi to write, relax, and visit the fire tower.

This morning, after a breakfast of wild blueberry pancakes, we dispersed with our journals to different parts of the island. The students looked preoccupied, with what I suspect were personal questions. Two, Cindi and Jon, have extensive outdoor experience, while the others, Sara and Chris, are making their first canoe trip. Quiet, strong, and immensely competent in the woods, Cindi has emerged as a sort of mainstay, tireless on portages and cheerful in any weather. She has a naturalist's eye and a real affection for wildlife. Jon, on the other hand, is quite concerned about the spiritual aspects of wilderness travel. A serious vegetarian and an aspiring writer, he canoes in a purple longjohn shirt and cut-off fatigues, with his Dionysian curls held back by a rolled bandana, but his rustic appearance and easy manner belie an intense, almost driven intellect.

Cindi and Jon have clearly won the admiration of the novices. Sarah, who is stylish and suburban, feels out of place and worries about slowing us down on portages. We have been kidding her about her "designer equipment," all of which bears the Eddie Bauer label, and about her remarkable talent for looking well-groomed under any conditions. For her, this trip is a rite of initiation, but she has kept her sense of humor and so far has been writing more than anyone. Chris, the other novice, is also a child of suburbia. He seems to have memorized every Beatles song and Monty Python comedy routine, not to mention a large number of recent TV commercials, and keeps us entertained with a stream of media chatter. Yet he often notices things the others miss, like the gray water spiders that spin hidden webs among shoreline rocks. He is quick, surprisingly intuitive, and enthusiastic about everything.

Fortunately, this island has enough solitude for all of us. So, while the students are off collecting their thoughts, I've decided to collect some of mine. Like Jon, I am interested in the larger implications of wilderness travel, and, after many trips to the West, I have thought a good deal about how mountaineering relates to our literary and philosophical traditions. But even after five trips to Quetico, I am still not sure what to think about canoeing.

First of all, I still sometimes feel out of place and even disoriented, as if I were entering the country for the first time. The arts of mountain travel do not seem as effective here, and I wonder what it is that makes canoeing so different. Second, I've noticed that my slides of canoe trips never seem to fit very well with my memories. Everyone agrees that each lake, portage, or campsite has a distinctive character, but it never seems to come out on film. How, then, do I recognize it when I travel here, and what is the best way to respond? Finally, I wonder whether one really can speak of spiritual values in canoeing. Certainly the mountains have always drawn people on vision quests, but no such imagery clings to the lakes of Quetico. Canoeing is a much humbler form of travel than mountaineering, and its literature consists of a few Indian myths, a handful of voyageurs' songs, and the vignettes of a small group of nature writers. Who ever heard of a mystic in a canoe? It seems quixotic to look for spiritual dimensions here, and yet the possibility nags me like a child's riddle.

Well, the sun is already lifting above the trees, and mare's tail clouds are breezing in from the west. If these questions have any answers at all, Kahshahpiwi ought to provide some clues. With its granite bluffs and glaciated shores, it reminds me more of the mountains than any other lake in Quetico. Today it seems pristine, fresh, vibrant, cleansed, and charged with the energy of light and wind.

I certainly never expected to find such a place up here, and, as usual, the long interstate journey north from Minneapolis did nothing to prepare me for it. The first time I made that drive I eagerly watched for signs of approaching wilderness, but the canoe country had no clear borders like the foothills that mark the gates of the mountains. I and my companions noticed only a gradual change in the vegetation from grassland to hardwoods to northern mixed forest. The towns grew scattered, and the farms thinned out into derelict pastures invaded by sumac and juniper, with gray sagging barns and tin roofs streaked with rust. The road sometimes crossed a brushed-in stream or passed a lakeshore clotted with cabins, but otherwise it just bored for hours through undifferentiated woods. I did not know I had entered the canoe country until the road turned suddenly to dirt and ended, ten miles later, at the opening of a lake. It was like being jolted awake in a strange house. This, I knew, was the jumping-off place. Yet, though I could see far across the water, I had no idea which way to go in order to begin a journey.

But we launched canoes all the same, and the first thing I learned was that travel in Quetico depends on finding the campsites and portages. They are the only fixed points on your journey, and they are easy to miss. For camping you need a place close to shore with enough dry, level ground for a couple of tents. But surprisingly few such places exist in these tangled, rocky forests. There may be only two or three on a given lake, and they are not shown on the maps. If you have not been told where they are, you may have to spend several hours exploring before you can settle down for the night.

It is much the same with portages, which connect lakes by the shortest and most practical routes. They are not visible from a distance, and without maps you could never tell where they were. On a lake with twenty-two inlets (not an extravagant number for Quetico), only three or four may lead to portages, while the others may end surrounded by hills or marshes. You soon learn to travel in small, straight lines from point to point, avoiding broad stretches of open water and referring constantly to your maps. You cannot afford to lose track of your position, for all lakes look pretty much the same from a canoe: islands blend into the shoreline, bays remain hidden until you round a point, and portages and campsites appear only when you are just about to land, as faint anomalies in the forest wall. So canoe travel keeps you constantly on the alert. Once you misjudge a position, you're lost.

I've often wondered what you could do if something happened to your maps. In the mountains, it would be easy to circle back to the trail, but here there are no trails apart from the portages, and those only lead to another lake, thus leaving you, so to speak, in the same boat. You could try retracing your steps, but you leave no tracks on a lake, and everything looks different when seen from the other side. You could take a compass bearing and strike out across country, but bushwhacking with a canoe is not much fun, particularly over terrain as wet and tangled as this. You could abandon your canoe and try walking out, but you'd soon hit another lake—maybe one of the long, narrow ones—and have to hike twenty miles around to gain one mile on your bearing. In the mountains, it would be easy to climb for an overview of the country, but Quetico has no summits and no obvious landmarks on which to take a bearing. As a last resort you might try going downstream till you struck a road or a dam, but here the land is so flat that the water, when it flows at all, may flow in any conceivable direction. Quetico is a vast system of baffles, chambers, and catchbasins: it has no slope, no axis, and no geometry. Everything is contorted, looped, knotted, and twisted together. A cup of water poured in at one end might take a thousand years to get to the other side.

Consider also the sense of progress you get in the mountains, where your trip proceeds by a series of minor climaxes. Passes and river crossings add up to a good story organized by adventures and culminating at a point of extreme consciousness from which you can see the whole world spread out like a map at your feet. With the vast geometry of the landscape converging upon the peak where you stand, you feel a wonderful power and a weightlessness in your limbs, as if you could go on hiking and climbing forever.

But no such ecstasies reward the canoeist, whose path twists and turns on itself, following crooked streams, or threads its way among islands scattered like rocky crumbs on the flat, deceptive lakes. Nowhere does his journey culminate in a godlike view, nor does it resolve into adventures shaped by topography. Instead it unfolds gradually, almost organically. The canoeist remains connected to home by a long, thin thread of memory, but while he is traveling he feels little sense of progress. If the mountains present themselves dramatically, as a setting for heroic action, the canoe country presents itself problematically, as a maze where all journeys proceed by feints and starts and all progress is by indirection.

Fortunately, aerial photography has given us excellent maps which clearly indicate where the portages ought to be. When we get there, we find them trodden bare from centuries of use. Who first discovered them? I suspect it was the Indians, who came into this country soon after the ice had melted. Think how many thousands of hours they must have spent poking into every channel and inlet, looking for the shortest distance between lakes. How could they know if the trees on shore were hiding only a low rock ridge or three miles of black spruce and alder? Those native explorers must have paid close attention, remembering every detail of every lake until they were able to perfect in their minds a map of this country as precise as the ones we carried.

In those days, every traveler needed a guide, someone who had explored until the land was imprinted in his nerves. No maps existed apart from human beings, and to pass on their knowledge the guides would have to go with the young people on initiatory journeys. We have found their markings on certain cliffs, dull figures of moose, canoes, or human hands, in rusty pigment, protected by overhangs, and hardly visible at thirty yards. Even today you have to know precisely where to look for them. As with campsites, you still need someone to tell you where they are.

For thousands of years there was only one way to thread the mazes of Quetico: build a relationship to the old people as you learned the land by heart. My students and I have done neither. Instead, we have used our maps to cheat the maze. Because they present an artificial view of the land (as it might be seen from the top of a mountain), they enable us to navigate without relying on memory. Hence, they give us only a shallow sense of where we are. Our journey remains undisciplined; though we move freely, like tourists, we gain no strength. No wonder we still feel dependent and vulnerable: we know instinctively that without our maps we would be stranded.

I now see why we have been drawn to the fire tower. The view would validate the imagery of our maps, thus reducing to some extent our feelings of helpless dependency. It would also give us a sense of accomplishment and possession, revealing the shape of our journey in a moment of time. It would provide our trip with an obvious climax, thus making it easier to turn into a story. Best of all, it would imitate the summit experience of mountaineering, which is familiar to all of us in one form or another, and thereby disengage us momentarily from this probing and inconclusive mode of travel by canoe. But of course it would provide only a false sense of security. Rather than bringing us closer to the land, it would actually increase our distance from it.

The sun is high now, and the mare's tails have extended clear across the sky. Beneath them, small gray puffs have appeared in the west.

Time to think about getting some lunch. I put the journal away, stretch around, and am startled to see Jon squatting barefoot on a rock.

He laughs, "I've been watching for fifteen minutes. You were really concentrating."

"How did your writing go?" I ask, stammering a little.

"Pretty well," he says. "I got some good stuff about rocks. They must go deep into the earth, much deeper than the lakes. This is the Canadian Shield, four billion years old. There were mountains here once. This rock we're sitting on must have been inside a mountain."

"Does this remind you of places you've seen out West?"

"Partly, but the country up here is more mixed. The land and water sort of penetrate into each other. I always feel as if I'm walking *on* the mountains, but here I feel kind of sucked in. The whole place is like one giant sponge."

"What are the others up to?"

"Making lunch. They sent me to find you. They still want to go to the fire tower."

"Don't you?"

"I don't think so," he says. "This is a very beautiful lake, very pure. It bugs me that someone would put up a steel tower here. That's not what I came for."

"Then perhaps we shouldn't go." I suggest.

"No," he says. "I know how I feel about it, but I wouldn't want to speak for the others."

He's right, of course. We have been running the trip along more or less democratic lines.

As we start for camp, he says, "You ought to try taking off your shoes. This moss feels really good on the feet."

Back at camp we find the others busily gooping peanut butter on rounds of Cindi's homemade pita bread. Chris says he is "written out" and wants to take off for the fire tower right after lunch. "I've checked out this whole island," he says. "I feel like climbing something." Cindi and Sarah nod. When neither Jon nor I join in, Chris adds, "Besides, you're the only one who really knows where we are, because you've got the maps. It would be nice if the rest of us could see where we're going. We could see everything from up there. It could be the high point of the trip."

Jon cannot restrain himself. "It's ugly," he says. "It doesn't belong here. It isn't natural."

"Neither is this," says Chris defiantly, striking one of the canoes. It thuds like a trash can hitting the sidewalk.

Jon glances quickly at me, then backs off with a shrug. It appears that we will stick to the original plan. The sandwiches come around; we pick off the spots of mold and wash down the bread with instant lemonade. Meanwhile, the wind picks up and the gray puffs at the far end of the lake begin massing into a squall. By the time we have finished, barely half an hour later, the lake has taken on a sullen, oily hue and the wind comes sweet with the smell of rain. Even Chris has to agree that this is no time to be launching canoes.

We stash our firewood under the upturned boats and string a tarp over the packs and life jackets. Visibly disappointed, the students retreat into their tents, and soon I can hear the fluffing of sleeping bags, the flap of journal pages, and the grunts of someone getting a back rub. I am less disappointed than they are but still not eager to spend the afternoon in a tent. Besides, Chris's statement reminds me of one of the morning's questions. I decide to stay out under the tarp and watch the rain.

Chris had said, "You're the one who really knows where we are." In what sense is that true? Certainly not because of the maps, which now seem at best a cheap expedient. Certainly not because of my memory, which is only five journeys old. I wonder what it means to be somewhere in Quetico. How do we sense the character of its places, which are so memorable yet so difficult to photograph? If we can't see ahead, how do we know where we are? And, while we travel, how do we tell one place from another?

Predictably, the rain hits long before the answers. Driving like spray through every chink in the forest, it shrinks my visible world to a radius of a hundred yards. It even drifts in under the tarp, threatening to soak my journal. No point in sitting here, where it's almost as wet as outside. I wriggle into parka and rain pants. If I can't get any writing done, I might as well go for a walk.

Once out from under the tarp, I notice that while the rain has obscured everything at a distance, it has heightened the colors and textures of everything nearby. A colleague who had lived in Japan once told me that his hosts preferred to walk in their gardens after a rain, explaining that water brought out the hidden character of things. This rain, which denies us the fire tower, seems to have turned our wilderness into a garden. As I walk, I am forced to experience everything up close for the first time.

On its shoreward arm our island is rocky but thick with woods. The trees are jack pine, red pine, spruce, and fir, and the ground is covered with sphagnum, star moss, blueberries, and wintergreen. Today, every pine needle carries a drop of silver. The moss underfoot compresses soundlessly, like down. As I start to climb, the litter of twigs and pine cone scales creaks softly to my step, as rich and scratchy as Harris tweed. Dead leaves shine like polished leather. The seamless bark of a young balsam fir wraps tightly around its trunk. I touch it, and it feels as smooth as an apple skin, almost satiny, certainly alive. How could I have missed all these textures? On top of the island, fringing bare rock, the lichens grow bunched like cauliflower. I press them down and they spring back with wonderful resiliency. Two hours of sun would dry them to a crisp, but now I can work my fingers deep into them, feeling the gritty soil beneath and the obdurate, depthless bed-rock they eat.

A clean smell of earth comes up from the lichens, like the scent of an April garden. I close my eyes and feel the rain trickling down my fingers and into the soil. Suddenly the whole place seems to be pulsating! I open my eyes, and the world jumps back, quivering just a few yards away. There is water everywhere, streaming down twigs and branches, braiding the tree trunks, dancing in every crease of exposed rock. My parka and hands are soaked. The moss underfoot has swollen like a sponge. In fact, the whole country *is* a sponge! I can hardly tell land from water anymore. Things are getting mixed, ambiguous. Time to get up and go. But where to? I seem to be *in* the land rather than on it, more like a swimming fish than a human being. Maybe the shore, where land and water are more distinct, would give me a better perspective.

With all my senses so strongly engaged, it is hard to contemplate this powerful place. Because I cannot actually see it, that is, comprehend it in a single view, I have trouble conceptualizing it. I could not know, or recognize, it by visual signs alone. But mountain places appeal very strongly to vision: we easily recognize them from pictures because we usually remember them as *scenes.* Our culture has evolved a scheme of aesthetic categories for landscapes, and because some mountain ranges (like the High Sierra) fit more closely than others, we think of them as inherently more attractive. Their landscapes tend to be self-composing and therefore easy to capture on film. But places like this island forest are harder to photograph because we experience them largely through senses other than sight.

The distinctive spirit of a place can enter in many ways, through touch, for instance, or smell. Remember the silky rush of water against your skin, the chafing of stone against your palm, the lumpy ground massaging your back as you fall asleep after paddling all day. Think of the smells that surround and penetrate before you're even aware of them: the Christmas fragrance of balsam fir, the pepper of woodsmoke that stays in your sweater for days, or the oily scent of fish on your hands long after you've cleaned them. I love the stink of swamps as we push our way through: it's a blend of mud, fart, and rotting vegetables. And who can forget his companions after he's smelled them reeking of sweat, old woolens, insect repellent, and squashed mosquitoes?

Tastes linger too: the frosty tartness of wild blueberries, the deli-cate snowy flavor of smallmouth bass caught less than an hour before. Something about wild foods invites us to eat with a certain ceremony, as if we were absorbing into our bodies the condensed essences of their native ground. What sweetness the blueberry sucks from the ancient rocks of Quetico! And the white meat of the bass, as fresh as spring water or wilderness air, allows us to take on some of its pure, darting life and commune—not just in fancy—with the deepest waters of Kahshahpiwi, where it grew.

I move through the dripping forest toward the shore, comforted by the swish and slap of rain-slickened branches. It is a sound I know, and so loud as to deafen me to almost everything else. But here is a good flat rock where I can stand and listen for the hiss of raindrops striking the lake or the clop and chuckle of small waves breaking. I think of all the other sounds that water makes in this country: the ploosh of paddles dipping to their stroke, the rustle of water under the bow, the snore of rapids a long way off, the tap and tink of droplets in wet woods, or the sound of a lake at night, in dead calm, which is not a single sound but a magnification of every sound, as if the water had gradually tightened into one enormous resonant membrane.

It is easy to be overwhelmed by your sensations here, and because you experience places through all your senses, it is not easy to tell where one place begins and another ends; you feel only a rising or lessening intensity of character. In the mountains, you can know a place by the way it is framed, but here is no landscape in the usual sense, no scenery to label picturesque or sublime.

In Quetico, the sense of place seems to depend as much upon internal as upon external factors. It is, for example, as much a matter of time as of space. Take this island, which has become real to me only because I have spent time in its textured and dripping woods. No one told us about it, and if it had not been for the rain we would all have run off to the fire tower. No doubt others have passed it by, even on sunnier days. Seen from a distance, it looks like nothing special, but known with the intimacy of touch and smell, it leaps into vivid life.

I realize, therefore, that sensing a place in Quetico begins when you engage yourself with a part of the land. The deeper your investment of time and attention, the stronger the place will become. Conversely, the same spot might have a different character for someone else, or even for you, should you ever return. For where you are cannot be separated from who you are, and going from one place to another involves a process of growth. To travel, therefore, is to be changed. Perhaps this is another reason why the land resists tourism and photography: because it cannot be known easily or quickly, it is hard to package or anthologize. It is too complicated and spreads too far. To know it you have to let it absorb you, entering, like a symbiotic microbe, into the tissues of a larger, more intricate being.

I walk back toward camp, reaching every now and then for a hand-ful of blueberries. (Man shall not live by truth alone.) I wonder what the students are doing. Though the rain has stopped, clouds still hide the southern shore, and the wind has churned the lake into jagged waves the color of wet cement. Chris will be disappointed, but now I am glad we won't be climbing the fire tower. It seems not only a cheat but an actual threat to the intimacy we ought to be seeking. I imagine it standing against the sky with a kind of imperial insolence, stark and aggressive, like the watchtowers along the East German frontier. But the threat here is more subtle. Jon was right to suspect the fire tower: it would seduce us into accepting a superficial knowledge of the land. Instead of a living relation, it would give us a visual image, falsely separating the place from the person. Thus, while making us feel in control, it would actually leave us weaker and more dependent.

Back at camp I find a crackling driftwood fire, built by Sarah using one match and a roll of birchbark. Jon stirs a pot of macaroni and cheese made with five kinds of vegetable pasta. Cindi has been watching gulls all afternoon, correlating their behavior with the phases of the storm. Chris comes in with a bucket of blueberries. "I found the lunker!" he grins, showing me one as big as the end of my thumb. "I came out to talk with you but you were gone, so I went for a walk. I got some great sensations for the journal."

"Sorry about the rain," I say, not meaning it.

"Couldn't we go up the fire tower tomorrow?" Sarah asks.

"Why not?" says Chris, turning to me. "It's on our way, isn't it?"

I turn to Jon, who shrugs, "I'm easy." And Cindi says, "If we get off early, I wouldn't mind." What now? I do not want these people seduced into tourism: it would go against everything I am trying to teach them. And yet, if I step in to prevent them from going, I risk splitting the group and alienating the beginners. The moment lengthens uncomfortably. Finally, I say, "Let's get up early and see how we feel. We can decide when we get under way."

This seems to work for everyone but me, and we gather around the fire as Jon loads our plates with steaming, adhesive macaroni. Cindi tells a few mountain stories, and Chris winds up with vignettes from Monty Python. By the time we have finished, it is well after dark, and all we can hear is the sigh of wind and the clatter of wavelets on the shore.

Chris goes off to wash the dishes while the others crawl into their tents. I stay up to douse the fire and check the canoes and gear. When I finish, Chris has still not returned. I eventually find him at the south end of the island, watching stars appear and disappear through the streaming clouds.

"I'm going to be sorry to leave this place," he says. "I had a great walk this afternoon. It was the best day yet."

Later, when everyone is in bed, I lie awake wondering what will happen tomorrow. If the group insists on climbing the fire tower, perhaps I can use it as a scene of instruction. The moment of greatest temptation might be the best time to reveal this afternoon's ideas. But if I am going to criticize my students for wanting that artificial view, I'll have to present a good argument for the virtues of canoeing. I know how to thread the mazes of Quetico and how to appreciate the character of its places. But what spiritual values inhere in canoeing, and how can I get them across? Outside, rain taps like fingers on the tent. The wind smells of water and broken evergreens. The hard ground kneads my back as I fall asleep, still wondering.

Next morning the sun is out and the lake is calm. We will have easy paddling to the south end, where a mile-long portage will take us away from Kahshahpiwi. As people mill around the campsite, cleaning up and packing their gear, I sense a real change in the mood of the group. Surprisingly, no one seems in much of a hurry, except for the gulls, who want to scavenge our camp. They float a few yards offshore, fluffing their wings and squawking in our direction.

As we launch canoes, a gentle breeze rises from the north, blowing our way. The woods smell fragrant and newly washed. It feels good to be moving again, after a whole day in one place. Chris and Sarah take the lead, with Jon in his purple shirt duffing between them. Cindi and I follow, carrying the rest of the gear. Our paddles knife through the waves, and the canoes leap forward, trailing a wake that fizzes, swirls, and closes without a trace. Our island drops away to the stern, and fifteen minutes later I can hardly distinguish it from the dark, crowding forest of the shore.

As I relax into the rhythm of paddling, my mind drifts back to the last unanswered question. The fire tower is still a few miles away, and perhaps before we get there I can find something to tell my students. If canoeing has any spiritual values, they must be quite different from those of mountaineering, and it would be foolish to seek one in country appropriate for the other. Yet this, apparently, is what we have been trying to do. Perhaps I can distinguish these two modes of travel by thinking about the elements that most define them: rock for the mountains, and for the canoe country, water.

The mountains present themselves as a series of obstacles, where you travel by fixed landmarks and focus your mind on tangible goals. You struggle against the massive impenetrability of rock, forcing a way upward against gravity. Success requires an inflexible, almost crystalline strength of will. Often you have to take desperate risks, but the mountains promise immediate rewards. You gain strength from overcoming your mental and physical limitations, and the summit euphoria frees you from all self-doubt. Moreover, your identity is confirmed through opposition to something monumental. Mountaineering thus appeals to the romantic and the young, for whom self-definition is a primary concern. It is fitting that their symbol should be a high peak standing in splendid isolation, enduring with the intense, geometric fixity of rock.

Canoe country, on the other hand, presents itself as a maze. Though it has plenty of rock, its dominant element is water, which penetrates it on every level to link all animate and inanimate beings. This water runs in the sap of ferns, the resin of white pines, the urine of wolves, the juice of blueberries, the blood of herons, the slime of earthworms, and the sweat of human beings. It gathers in deep lake basins, braids into rivers and creeks, or stretches to hairline seeps that quicken the joints of the bedrock. It floats your canoe and makes travel possible, but by seeking its own level it withholds any sense of direction. Because of water the land presents itself as a series of choices and thereby forces you to create your own journey. It does not pose challenges but questions, and in so doing it absorbs you, almost without your knowing.

Successful canoeing requires you to give up the aims and skills of a mountaineer. In the first place, you must learn to travel without a goal, for Quetico has no center and promises no summit views. Borne on water, you move in a horizontal plane, probing the maze with close attention but always returning by kinked and knotted paths to the point where you first launched canoes. You must also renounce the desire for trophies, since Quetico has no passes or secondary peaks, and its places elude your efforts to capture them on film. Finally, you must give up the pleasures of storytelling, since travel here is very much a continuous process not easily broken into episodes. A canoe trip does not advance so much as it grows, unfolding gradually, like a bud, or pushing on like a root that follows a crack in the rock. Where is the heroism in such a process? Where does it climax? In Quetico, the land is hardly dramatic and will not let you define yourself by struggle, aggression, or mythmaking.

Yet I have found that this practice of renunciation provides appropriate rewards. Though goalless travel may create a sense of disorientation, it also frees your mind to receive unpredictable gifts. I remember, for instance, an extraordinary thing that happened on our way into Kahshahpiwi. We had come to a portage in the pouring rain and were standing, soaked and discouraged, under the dripping trees. Too tired to speak, we just stared at the gray lake, waiting for the rain to go away. Suddenly, two minks came slithering down the slope beside us, darted twice around my legs before realizing I wasn't a tree, stopped and stared up with what seemed the most flabbergasted expressions, and streaked off into the bushes. I had never seen wild animals playing before. They were beautiful with their bright black eyes and amber fur slickened to dark points by the rain. If we had not been standing utterly still, worn out and discouraged and wet to the skin, they would never have come so close. We looked at one another and broke into smiles. The minks were gone. Who could have found them by seeking?

Another reward of travel by canoe is an increasing familiarity with the land and a corresponding sense of inner strength. The more time and attention you give, the more you begin to feel at home here. You can spend a day on an island and leave with no remorse, for you carry its character impressed in your memory. The more you engage with the land, the more willing you are to let it change you, and the less eager you are to emerge with the same thoughts and feelings you had when you went in. Quetico purifies you, as a wetland cleanses the waters migrating through it. Canoeing teaches you to love deeply and let go, to accept disorientation as an opportunity to learn. Rather than confirming your self-image, it affirms your capacity to grow. It strengthens the gentle virtues of poise, self-effacement, intimacy, and faith.

The mountains draw you with their sublime landscapes, promising heroism and the power of godlike vision. You measure yourself against eternal rock, and you succeed by the energy of your aspiration. But here to be strong is to bend and flow, to launch yourself on this fluid medium with a willingness to set off in any direction. For there are numberless ways to thread the mazes of Quetico, and you will succeed only by imitating water, which overcomes all things by not resisting.

The end of canoeing as a spiritual discipline is to turn you from an explorer into a guide. In the beginning, you chafe against the sense of disorientation, yet as you extend yourself into the country over many trips, learning the campsites and portages, a map of the maze begins to grow in your memory. It is marked out with vivid places, but when you bring others here you may find that they see things differently. All you can do is to show them the way through. It is not important that they should all reach the same place, or that you should try always to control what they learn. They have their own journeys to make. Your job is to build their faith in the process of journeying itself, to put them in touch with Quetico and withdraw. You must believe that the land will teach them as it has taught you, and that one day they too will mature into guides, stewards and preservers of all things linked by water.

So I realize, with something like a laugh, that I should no longer worry about whether or not we climb the fire tower. I will neither forbid nor encourage it, since the process of decision is part of my students' personal growth. As young people, they have every reason to think in terms of a summit experience, just as I, a young teacher, have been all too eager to control what they learn. I watch them pulling rhythmically to their strokes, tanned and strong after a week on the trail, and suddenly I feel a great rush of affection. It's wonderful to be together here, on Kahshahpiwi Lake with a brisk north wind and the August sunlight tossing up from the waves.

As we round a point, a queer white shape appears in the woods, and I soon realize it's the abandoned ranger cabin. Though the fire tower is not visible, the trail starts there, and this morning we could have the place all to ourselves. Soon the cabin comes into plain view. And then an extraordinary thing happens. As we approach, still close to shore, the lead canoe shows no inclination to turn. We pass the cabin, and no one says anything. The only sound is water rustling under the bow of my canoe. Ahead the shore begins narrowing toward the portage. The wind brings a Christmas fragrance of balsam fir.

Analyzing and Discussing the Text

1. What functions do the character sketches of the four students at the start of the essay serve? Would the essay have been as effective if their different backgrounds and personalities had been less carefully sketched at the beginning and, instead, developed throughout the essay? Explain your response.
2. Much of this essay builds meaning through a comparison and contrast of mountaineering and canoeing. Why is the Quetico setting so well suited to such considerations? What values does Tallmadge ascribe to each form of wilderness travel? Do you agree? Does the contrast work with all forms of canoeing?
3. What does the Lake Kahshahpiwi firetower come to symbolize?
4. Why is it important that Jon goes barefoot and that he urges Tallmadge to try taking off his shoes?
5. Much of the focus on maps in the essay leads to the larger question of how we know, really know, where we are. Summarize what the reading says about how to attain such knowledge.
6. Why does the essay end with the wind bringing "a Christmas fragrance of balsam fir"?

Experiencing and Writing About the World

1. This essay illustrates the use of a nature journal as a way of spiritual questing, a way to test the actual value of one's experiences in nature. Keep a similar journal for a period of time. The experiences you ponder in it can be retrospective (your memories of significant outdoor excursions), or they can relate more to current, nearby nature. The crucial thing is that you meditate, through your writing, on what the experience with nature means.
2. Envision for yourself and your class an excursion into a local natural area and write it up as a persuasive proposal outlining an actual excursion for your college or university class.
3. Write an essay in which you classify and describe the major types of interaction between humans and nature in your everyday life.
4. Tallmadge's essay and the excerpt from Gretel Ehrlich's *Islands, the Universe, Home* are the only two lake narratives among the water essays in this anthology. Do the authors' experiences on lakes seem to determine the styles and themes of their narratives in any definable way? Are there any prominent differences between these two essays? Prepare a comparative essay in which you study these two literary responses to floating and paddling on lakes.

RICK BASS

From River People

By the age of thirty-three, Rick Bass (1958–   ) had already published five books. Bass grew up in Houston, Texas, then went west
to study wildlife management at Utah State University and eventually
switched to petroleum geology because it seemed more practical. After working for several years as a petroleum geologist in Mississippi,
Bass (then twenty-nine) quit his job and moved with his girlfriend (now
his wife), Elizabeth Hughes, to the remote Yaak Valley in Montana, not
far from the Canadian border, where a few people live scattered in the
mountains without paved roads or telephones, getting electricity only
from gasoline-powered generators. Bass's first book, *The Deer Pasture*
(1985), derives from the author's nostalgia for the Texas hill country, an
area where he and his family hunted for many years. Two years later
he published *Wild to the Heart*, a collection of essays about wilderness
experiences throughout the country, frequently desperate, marathon escapes to the mountains during brief vacations from his job in Jackson,
Mississippi. In 1989 Bass published an account of his work in the oil industry, *Oil Notes*, and his first collection of short fiction, called *The Watch*.
Winter: Notes from Montana appeared in 1991. His many literary awards
include the General Electric Younger Writers Award, a PEN/Nelson Al-
gren Award Special Citation for fiction, and a National Endowment for
the Arts fellowship.

As a writer Bass is most noticeably a rhapsodist, a celebrator. *The
Deer Pasture* celebrates a favorite little corner of Gillespie County in
Central Texas. The stories in *The Watch* celebrate a startling variety of
people and places, from the nouveau riche in Houston to an ambivalent
Mormon girl in Moab, Utah, and from the backwoods of Mississippi
to semiurban Jackson, where an aspiring student writer named Robby
is trying to write enough "good sentences" to burst the "confining,
restricting, elastic-like bubble" that surrounds him and taste the "clean
and crisp air" on the outside. In *Winter,* the rhapsodist expresses his love
for the beauty and quiet of Montana's mountain country, for the cantankerous people who live there, and for winter itself: "There are days,"
he tells us, "when I promise, when I swear, that as long as I can walk
up the trail behind my house, or as long as I can go out into the yard
and look up at the stars, I'll never be unhappy, never. Not just count my
blessings, but shout them." The following selection is an excerpt from
Bass's essay "River People" (*Wild to the Heart*), and in it we can see the

author's appreciation for moments of wildness and freedom, even on a crowded river during a holiday weekend in North Carolina. "If it's wild to your own heart," the longer essay concludes, "protect it. Preserve it. Love it."

[The Nantahala]

I'm up early, but so is Lucian. He's lifting a rather big rock up and down, repeatedly. I sit and watch for a while—neither of us says anything—until I tire of watching and go look for firewood. When I return he has finished his rock exercises and already has a fire going.

Breakfast is cooked; breakfast is eaten. It's a cool, almost cold, foggy morning down in the Nantahala Gorge; it's often like that, even in summer, because the gorge walls are so steep and high. Water trickles down the cliffs from a hundred different little seeps above our tents; gentle ferns and wildflowers are everywhere this time of year. Jim squats by the fire and flips another blueberry pancake; the sun rises, and filters down through twenty different stages of hardwood to land with a golden glow on our campsite. It's a fuzzy sort of morning, slow and sleepy. Everything seems to be either green or gold, soft looking, like a pastel. It's beautiful, and above all, relaxing.

Campers (fellow river people) walk down the road past our camp, headed for the river, walking downhill in lazy-legged plod-strides that belie their eagerness to get to the water. They pretend to be drinking in and basking in the beauty of the North Carolina summer morning, but I know they are faking it—I know what they're really thinking about is the rage of the river. Jim flips another blueberry pancake, and then puts another skillet on the fire and begins frying some sausage patties. Winfred E. drives up, bleary-eyed but smiling. He's short, and wiry, not at all like his brother. He shouts and whoops and gets out and dances around in the road when he sees us.

At this point in time, he'd been away from a river for almost two solid months. He had broken his arm over on the Chattooga earlier in the spring.

There are hugs, and handshakes, and backs are slapped. The pastel aura lifts; everything seems suddenly sharper. A thrush sings from the cliff; a blue jay flies through the trees. Winfred E. sits down and asks if breakfast is ready.

It's a funny river, I suppose. It's a little sad, really—it reminds me of watching a great powerful dog being chained to a pole, or something like that. It's a release-and-flow river. It's been dammed, for power, but each day it's released for twelve hours to keep the lake behind the dam from flooding, and to send power and water on down the road to others. It's a Jekyll-and-Hyde existence. For twelve hours, it's a meek and mild trickle; sportsmen fish in the little riffles, and you can see the stony bottom all the way across. It's a creek, not a river. It's like looking at it without its clothes on; it embarrasses us, as well as the river.

It makes up for it the other twelve hours. It's a wild thing, much wilder than it would be if it were free all the time instead of being cooped up half the day. It is this wildness that makes river people appreciate it so. They can, as the phrase goes, relate.

The water is usually turned on around nine o'clock in the morning. It's as cold as winter, coming out of the bottom of the deep lake, and it races down the gorge like it has something to prove, like it's afraid that each day might be its last. From put-in to take-out it is an eight-mile run, and is one of the finest in the East. It's good whitewater river; it's technical, and it's high volume, but it is also pretty clean. There aren't any sunken trees and limbs to snag and drown capsized boaters as they tumble downstream.

We wait around camp for a while, and watch the morning grow warmer—the fog lifts, leaving everything crisp looking and dripping—and then, when we feel that the first-rush crowd waiting for the release up at the put-in has gotten started, we too get in our cars and head north. We leave Win's car at the bottom, at the take-out; we all five ride in the Volvo up to the put-in. The road follows the river. Halfway there, we notice a change in the volume of the river noise. It is much louder. We pull over and peer down into the gorge. The river has changed.

For twelve hours, it is free. We get back in Lucian's car and continue. We reach the put-in, unload the boats, and blow up the inflation bags. Ramona says nothing. I catch her adjusting her life jacket on seven different occasions. Even after she finally has it the way she wants it, she nervously continues to finger it up around the throat, like a woman feeling a pearl necklace to make sure it's still there. Her eyes are glassy, we can tell they're not seeing the soft green mountains and rocks and sky or the excitement of all the other paddlers—jeeps and trucks and cars and vans of every possible description, and people too—and Lucian pinches her behind to make her jump. She does, and yips too, and turns in outrage to see who did it. We all laugh. It wasn't that funny, but we're so excited, so tense, that we'd have laughed at anything. We carry the boats down to the water. I notice that Lucian is carrying Winfred E.'s as well as his own. I help Ramona tote hers down, then we come back for mine. Winfred E. has wandered over to a little gazebo-like stand the Forest Service has set up and is leaning against it, saying something to a rather attractive girl in blue-jean cutoffs and a halter top. She has long white hair, hair down to her shorts: not good canoeing material. We turn away for a moment, and when we look back, she is coming with us. Or rather, with Winfred E. Her name is Allison. She's from Missouri, we find out. No, she's never canoed before. Yes, she'd like very much to try—is Winfred sure there's enough room? Winfred says he guesses there is.

We're in the water. Those first few cold splashes as you run out into the shallows, push off, and then jump in; the first couple of paddle strokes where it feels like you're not doing any good, like you're paddling in molasses, and then they begin to catch, and the canoe starts to move forward, quickly, strongly . . . the canoe itself sings down the river, like a thing released from a dam too.

We feel the same.

One of the best things about the Nantahala is this: there is a good set of rapids right around the corner from the first put-in. It's called Patton's Run, and it's a good idea not to dump in it, because it'll be a long day. The sun never strikes the river straight-on for very long; it's always at least partially in the shadows, and the water's very cold. Also, it is a very long stretch of whitewater—you'll probably be washed down for as far as a quarter of a mile before it flattens out enough for you to crawl out and empty your boat.

But Ramona handles it perfectly; so do Winfred E. and Allison, and the rest of us. It's over incredibly quickly, in just a few seconds it seems, and we eddy out into a still place and gasp and pant and all try to talk at once. Our hearts race.

It's not the best stretch of rapids on the river, but it's one of my favorites. It's sure a nice way to start a Memorial Day weekend.

We're in the shadows; we're wet from the spray, and shivering. Also, we're pumped with adrenalin. We wheel out into the mainstream and push on. We race down the river like snow skiers coming down a mountain. The boats rise and chop and crash against the waves; we scream and shout and laugh and dodge through the rocks; the boats and the river are holding a wild and joyfully angry communion together, and we're lucky enough to be caught in the middle. Lucian shouts out instructions from time to time to Ramona, but most of the time, I can tell, she does not hear them; the river is too loud, too jealous. No matter—she appears to be holding her own. Jim races past me, stroking hard. His red beard is soaked with river spray, and he is grinning madly. He does not notice me. There is an odd shine in his eyes.

I fall in a good distance behind him; I try to follow his turns, to avoid the rocks and really bad waves, but it is not until the second stretch of hard rapids that I begin to suspect he is aiming into the tallest waves on purpose rather than trying to avoid them. I draw out to one side and strike out on my own.

That's another good thing about the Nantahala: there's always plenty of people, yes, but there's also plenty of room. And traffic is fast: if you don't like it, just wait, and it will blow past you in a second. You can go where you want to, do what you want; the bank on either side, and the fact that you can't go back upstream, are your only boundaries.

Actually, when you analyze it, it's a little surprising. You really only have one choice of where to go, and that's downstream. And yet it seems like you've got more freedom than you've ever had in your life: those banks on either side, and that wall of water pushing down on you from behind are so far from your mind that they're not even comprehensible—all you can think about is the wild joy of going down, down, down the river, hard out, all the way to the end.

If you focus on the right things, and ignore the others, you can find wildness and freedom anywhere, I am convinced.

I did not notice the road that ran above us a few hundred feet, following the river; I did not notice the awesome rock quarry we passed, cut into the side of a mountain, with tiny yellow cranes scratching weakly at its base while it waited patiently for them to finish and go away with whatever it was they came for. I did not notice the rafts and inner tubes and sometimes overall carnival-like atmosphere of all the river people on the slower stretches. I focused instead on the stretch and pull of my muscles and the paddle pulling water, and the sleek way the canoe carried itself downstream, and the caddisfly larvae in the shallow pools, and the wonderfully shocking coldness and cleanness of the water, and the green and pink of the mountain laurels, and the cold clean smell that all river canyons have in their shadowy parts, and I saw not one person go by that I didn't honestly like.

In Jackson, sometimes, I'll walk an entire city block, to the bank and back, and never smile at anyone.

In some places, it is true, it is easier to focus than in others.

We had lunch in a meadow, up off the river in a wide spot where the gorge stretches to a width of perhaps five miles. There were a few other people up in the meadow picnicking also, looking down on the river, but most of them were continuing to bomb on down the river; most of them probably didn't even see the meadow.

It's good to bomb down the river, that's the best way, but for sure if you take little breaks then inevitably they'll help you rest up so when you do get back on the river you can go one hundred percent again.

Bombing is fine, but if you're going to do it, you need to do it right. You need to go one hundred percent. Even if this means doing something as sinfully pleasurable as taking a break to picnic in a North Carolina riverside meadow. There was dark beer, and potato chips, and a semidamp blanket to sit on. There were avocado sandwiches. I ate three of them, and lay back in the warm sun and felt my stomach. I felt happy.

You would not believe what a wizard Trunz is when it comes to food. The sun was warm on my face. There wasn't any wind. I closed my eyes. Everything seemed to hang suspended, frozen: crouched and ready to go, yet also motionless, like a child playing red-light green-light. Even sounds seemed frozen; it was as if Everything was waiting for Something. The moment hung heavy as ore for a few seconds, then sighed and moved on. I sat up and watched it leave. I was ready to go one hundred percent down the river again. I looked at my fellow river people and could tell they were too.

Also, I could tell this: that they too had felt the odd moment. It wasn't eerie, it was just puzzling, like a phenomenon, like one of those secrets of nature that you glimpse only every so often—a north-flowing river, an anomaly of gravity, an albino elk—little things She shows you only so often, just to keep you in awe, or maybe just to reward you. We chose to view it as a reward. We grinned but said nothing of it; that would have spoiled it. We pretended we hadn't seen it, so as not to startle it.

Beautiful things like that frozen-time moment embarrass easily; startle them, or study them too closely, and they might not come back. We chose just to appreciate it, not analyze it, and then we cleaned up our avocado peelings and folded the blanket and went back down to the river.

Campfire. Much like the one so many years ago (was it only seven?) around which I first heard stories about Jim Bridger, about Jed Smith. I'm in the mountains again, oddly so, though who'd ever have dreamed then they'd be the tame mountains of the East? Not I, I'd have said, had someone seen into the future.

The sparks don't pop the same, the forests don't smell the same, even the pull of gravity and sigh of the wind doesn't feel and sound the same, but the camaraderie is exactly identical, almost eerily so. This puzzles me; I muse on it at length as the others toast and cheer Ramona, who successfully and even aggressively ran Lesser Wesser with grace and beauty.

Analyzing and Discussing the Text

1. How does Bass's language in the opening section of this essay seek to recreate the "pastel aura" of a spring morning on the Nantahala?
2. Closely examine the sentence patterns in this essay. Do they change from section to section? Does the abruptness of the style seem analogous to the intensity of the river itself? Explain your response.
3. Does the Nantahala seem to have a personality of its own in Bass's narrative? What would be the point of personifying the river?
4. When the river changes in volume, the moods of the "river people" change, too. How does Bass describe this change? Why is mood or atmosphere important in this narrative?
5. "[T]he canoe itself sings down the river, like a thing released from a dam, too. We feel the same," writes Bass. Explain the significance of these lines.

6. At the end of the second section of the essay, the author explains how being on the river helps him "focus." Explain this state of mind and its connection with floating.
7. When Bass and his companions experience the "beautiful" moment of "suspended" time as they eat after running the river, he says, "We chose just to appreciate it, not to analyze it. . . . " Is Bass's own description of the scene appreciative or analytical? How so? Why did the group resist intellectualizing the experience?

Experiencing and Writing About the World

1. Choose any three consecutive paragraphs from this essay and imitate their sentence patterns as precisely as possible while telling a story of some particularly intense personal experience (on a river or elsewhere). Attempt to use the exact sentence lengths and punctuation that you see in Bass's writing, but change the words to fit your own narrative.
2. Describe a perfect moment: a meal, a campfire scene, the view from a mountain summit, a quiet pause in the heart of an old-growth forest, or another example that comes to mind. Try to capture (and even exult in) the mood of the actual experience without resorting to clichés and beer-commercial slogans. The challenge in this assignment is to invent a fresh, vigorous language of appreciation—of rhapsody.
3. Analyze the two meal scenes in this narrative. How can you explain the different atmospheres and prose styles of the two passages? Write a short (250–500 words) critical essay on this topic.
4. "If you focus on the right things, and ignore the others," Bass writes, "you can find wilderness and freedom anywhere, I am convinced." Explain the implications of this idea both within the context of "The Nantahala" and more broadly. How could you interpret this sentence so that it would be of significance to your own life?
5. Write an analytical essay in which you compare and contrast the narrative style of Bass's essay with that of one of the lake narratives in this anthology. How does the river experience differ fundamentally from the experience of merely floating (or even paddling) on a lake? For a more ambitious writing project, study the interesting similarities and differences between river and lake narratives in general, using all of the examples in this book.

EDDY L. HARRIS

From Mississippi Solo: A River Quest

Eddy L. Harris (1955–   ) was born in St. Louis, Missouri, and he says that as he grew up the Mississippi River "captured my imagination when I was young and never let go." He graduated from Stanford University in 1977, and he now makes his home near the banks of the Mississippi in Kirkwood, Missouri. After traveling throughout South America and Europe and after working as a journalist and screenwriter, Harris decided that he wanted to know the Mississippi in a deeper way—to experience the river firsthand—and through that experience to be fully *in* the world. This, for Harris, meant going down the Mississippi in a canoe, solo. He approached the trip with powerful ambivalence, knowing that "you don't find many blacks canoeing solo down the Mississippi River and camping out every night" and that he was not a great canoeist. On the other hand, Harris told himself that he was thirty years old, an age when he had come to the painful realization that "there will be no Yankee try-out." Besides, he writes, "I've never minded looking stupid and I have no fear of failure." When Harris did choose to go, the result was an eventful, successful journey. His adventures and reflections on this trip form the basis for his first book, *Mississippi Solo: A River Quest* (1988). A second book, *Native Stranger: A Black American's Journey into the Heart of Africa*, was published in early 1992.

In this excerpt from *Mississippi Solo,* which emphasizes the question "What in the world am I doing out here?," Harris records his fearful night thoughts shortly after beginning the trip. His mood during the early days on the river alternates between a developing self-confidence and an eagerness to know when the search party will be sent out after him, between his delight in the beauty of the river and the wildlife—the herons, ducks, and deer—along the way and his sense that the river is an adversary to be conquered. In this passage, he carefully and rationally explains away his fears by sorting through all of the reasons that he, a self-described "city fellow, urbane and civilized," has for being on the river.

[What in the World Am I Doing Out Here?]

In the night the mind voices what was only a creepy suspicion during the day. *What in the world am I doing out here?*

I'm a city fellow, urbane and civilized. I always use the correct fork. I keep my napkin in my lap. And like a good little boy who does what

296

his mommy tells him, I chew my food fifty-six times before swallowing. My idea of travel and good fun is shooting craps in Las Vegas or playing roulette in the Grand Casino at Monte Carlo, fishing for marlin off Bimini, scuba diving the reefs of the Caribbean, hiking the Swiss Alps and skiing the Austrian, dining and wining in Paris, bicycling through Scotland. I see myself wearing tuxedoes and drinking champagne, not eating beans and weenies and wearing the same smelly clothes for weeks.

And I'm no expert in a canoe. That much is evident now. I think I'd been in a canoe maybe five times before. Floating the Black River a couple of times—mostly just an easy stream but I still managed to tip over and fall in. One time canoeing leisurely in the summer sun on the Thames not far from London. Once on a lake just drifting lazily with a fishing rod in hand but not even a nibble to worry about, only the weeds and the marsh and the water lilies snagging the canoe and forcing me to work. And once on the Severàn, a lazy little river in the north of Sweden. Not exactly training for the proving ground of the Mississippi.

Nor was I any more experienced as a camper. Not an outdoorsman at all. Cleaning fish is not one of my favorite things. I don't like snakes, can't stand mosquitoes, and creatures that growl in the night scare me.

And yet. . . .

I'm haunted by the ghost of Ernest Hemingway. All writers—American male—probably are. His style of writing, sure, but mostly his zesty style of living—big-game hunter, deep-sea fisher, hard drinker. Lover of man and women and good times and travel to exotic locales. A courter of danger.

It was a different world then, though. Everything wasn't taken so much for granted. A punch in the nose risked a return punch in the nose, a few moments' sweat and adrenaline, not a lawsuit. Air travel was an adventure. Getting there—anywhere—was as thrilling as being there. Skiing was not chic, the thing to do, but rather hard work down the mountain, harder work back up, an exhilaration, an exotic adventure. Your tales had zing in those days because everyone you know hadn't already been to Europe. Living was an adventure. And Paris was really Paris.

It was a different world all right.

Now life is a media event. Well publicized, well sign-posted, the paths well worn and all the right things to do and places to go marked out. And absolutely everyone has a ticket to watch.

Is that what we've become? Mere spectators at a zoo? With real living removed from us and kept safely behind bars?

I hope to God I'm not out here because I miss the Good Old Days.

What good old days? Twenty years from now, these will be the good old days.

And not because I wanted to be Ernest Hemingway.

I want to be Eddy Harris. I want to live a life of my own adventures, my own tryings, triumphs—even failures.

I look at the Mississippi and I see a symbol of America, the spine of the nation, a symbol of strength and freedom and pride, wanderlust and history and imagination. The river is also a symbol of our times, for the river fights in a desperate battle against the US Army Corps of Engineers who refuse to let the river find its own way. The Corps of Engineers fights the river with technology and brute brain power to bend the river, make it conform to the needs of society in order to save homes that would otherwise be flooded, to aid shipping, to strip the river of its power and its will and its natural dignity. Nobody has asked the river. The river which yearns to be free, rages for it.

Alas! Time runs out—for the river, for me, for us all. The world around closes in.

Computerized, mechanized, itemized, formalized, and most dangerously, standardized. Laws hemming us in and fencing us out, stripping us down and standardizing behavior. Hotel chains and fast food joints standardize travel and eating. Dallas looks like Denver looks like Tacoma looks like Tallahassee. Traveling is truly home away from home. No surprises, no disasters at mealtime, no disappointments, no thrills. Just a steady heartbeat and a blank look.

Doesn't it make you mad enough to holler and spit?

Taking chances. Isn't that what life is all about? Sometimes you come up winners, sometimes you lose. But without the risk of defeat, where is the triumph? Without death hanging over the head, what value is life?

And *that* is why I wanted to do this foolish thing. If I were expert with canoe, fishing gear, bow and arrow and rifle, if I were the Daniel Boone type used to spending weeks at a time in the same clothes, in the woods, if I loved gutting rabbits and sleeping out in the rain, a trip down the big river would have been a simple thing. Fun, but little more than routine. Only half an adventure.

This voyage, on the other hand, was a true adventure. Looking back on all I had to go through just to get here to Lake Itasca, it was no wonder I said to Robinovich:

"I don't really have to go now. The climax was getting the canoe." (And canoeing out of Lake Itasca, of course.)

And in a way, it was. I had spent so much energy and emotion trying to put this expedition together that once it was done and everything had finally slipped into place, it felt as though I had already succeeded. I didn't need to go on. Much the same as the seducer who gets the one desired moves on once he's won. The thrill is in the hunt.

I had decided on August 18 that I would do this thing and would leave October 1. I thought a month and a half would be plenty of time to prepare. Even three weeks beyond the target date I barely had enough gear, and I did *not* have the canoe.

Canoes are very personal, like toothbrushes, and people who have them do not lend them out. I thought I would have to buy one. But I had no money. Not for the canoe, not for good warm clothing, not for a telephoto lens for the camera and a mountain of film. Not for lanterns and a sleeping bag, life jacket, knives, axes, cooking and eating equipment and all sorts of other junk I considered necessary if I was going to do this right: safely and as comfortably as possible.

It soon became clear that if I was going at all, I would not be going in style. I cut my list to the bone, to the barest essentials, and I borrowed most of those. I managed to buy a handgun for small game—rabbits and squirrels for Daniel Boone dinners—and for protection, as it turned out. But I took nothing fancy and nothing for comfort.

Just before it would have been too late, a friend of Robinovich's came up with the canoe. I was going, but not in grand style.

And by then, despite the lateness of the season and the advancing winter, despite the fear which mounted now that the dream had become as real as surgery, despite the drain and the strain and the low energy, I had to go.

This river trip would be different. So deep inside me would this thing reside that it would be a part of my soul, and yet with a spirit of its own that would leap to mind of its own accord, being such a part of me that it would enter my marrow and alter the way I think and feel and walk, leaving me with more than memories and smiles, leaving me changed in a deep and abiding way. Rather like love that defies explanation, deep and passionate and affecting even long after the object of that love has vanished. In the heart it remains.

The Mississippi offered this to me, promising that if I gave her a try she would be a part of me forever. It wouldn't matter if I finished, if I went for twenty-five miles or twenty-five hundred, six days or six weeks. The desire and the intention were what really mattered. (I learned this along the way.) A marriage. You enter it, if it's real, with every intention of seeing it through to the end, *till death do us part.* You plan to weather the storms and the cold nights, enjoy the sunshine and the warmth and have plenty to look back on when you're old and finished. But sometimes, try as you might, work hard as you can at it, fighting with all the strength that's in you, it just is not to be and you're forced out. Sad and painful but even after it's long over it remains a part of you.

An adventure, a challenge, no tuxedoes, no ties, no uniforms. Not civilized and no rules apply. Just very basic: hard work and dirty hands. You don't need a diploma. No experience is necessary. Just common sense and guts. Anyone can do it. *Just put in and see if you can handle it, see how far you can get.* That's what the river said to me in the night, daring me to succeed the same as my father used to bait me when I was a kid, daring me to try something new, pushing me to be strong and courageous, preparing me for life. I accepted his challenges; I accepted the river's.

But I was still scared.

Analyzing and Discussing the Text

1. What purpose does the elaborate list serve in the second paragraph of this essay? Is this purpose furthered by mixing humor in with the list of glamorous outdoor experiences? How do all of these contrast with the reality of this river adventure?
2. Elaborate on the values suggested by Harris's reference to "the ghost of Ernest Hemingway." What are Hemingway's attitudes toward nature and toward defining oneself as a male?
3. What relationship between the river and the individual in contemporary society does Harris set up in paragraphs 14 through 16?
4. What precisely defines this journey for Harris as a "true adventure"?
5. Can you explain what Harris means when he says that "the dream had become as real as surgery"?
6. How does the final line work with the rest of the essay?

Experiencing and Writing About the World

1. Write a short personal essay in which you identify your fear of some aspect of the natural world and then elaborate on all the reasons not to be afraid.
2. Harris writes that this journey altered him, leaving him "changed in a deep and abiding way." Have you experienced such an event, especially some encounter with nature, that has changed you in such a profound way? If so, write an essay in which you convey how this process occurred.
3. Do you agree with Harris's statement "Now life is a media event"? Write an essay designed to persuade your reader to accept your own views on this subject.
4. Write an essay in which you further explore the parallels Harris suggests between the attempts to subdue nature and the conforming pressures of society.

GRETEL EHRLICH

From Islands, the Universe, Home

For biographical information, see the headnote for "A Storm, the Cornfield, and Elk" in Part One, Chapter Four.

This passage from *Islands, the Universe, Home* (1991) recounts Ehrlich's experience floating on a human-made, nine-acre, "nothing-fancy" pond on the Wyoming ranch where she and her husband live. These trips, made in a beat-up blue canoe that cost eight dollars at a local thrift store and was given to her by a friend, are a new experience for her. Ehrlich says that she remembers how to row from her childhood days on the Pacific Ocean, but she feels that she does not really know how to paddle. Instead, she often chooses to let her canoe and her thoughts float free. By thus surrendering her own will and letting the water take her where it will, Ehrlich lets herself engage in a lyrical meditation on the creation of life in the universe, on the inseparability of the human and the natural world, and on the power of both the mind and the external landscape to influence each other.

[On the Pond Again]

Now it's October. On the pond again, I hear water clank against the patched hull. It is my favorite music, like that made by halyards against aluminum masts. It is the music emptiness would compose if emptiness could change into something. The seat of my pants is wet because the broken seat in the canoe is a sponge holding last week's rainwater. All around me sun-parched meadows are green again.

In the evening the face of the mountain looks like a ruined city. Branches stripped bare of leaves are skeletons hung from a gray sky, and next to them are tall buildings of trees still on fire. Bands and bars of color are like layers of thought, moving the way stream water does, bending at point bars, eroding cutbanks. I lay my paddle down, letting the canoe drift. I can't help wondering how many ways water shapes the body, how the body shapes desire, how desire moves water, how water stirs color, how thought rises from land, how wind polishes thought, how spirit shapes matter, how a stream that carves through rock is shaped by rock.

Now the lake is flat, but the boat's wake—such as it is—pushes water into a confusion of changing patterns, new creations: black ink shifting to silver, and tiny riptides breaking forward-moving swells.

I glide across rolling clouds and ponder what my astronomer friend told me: that in those mysterious moments before the Big Bang there was no beginning, no tuning up of the orchestra, only a featureless simplicity, a stretch of emptiness more vast than a hundred billion Wyoming skies. By chance this quantum vacuum blipped as if a bar towel had been snapped, and resulted in a cosmic plasma that fluctuated into and out of existence, finally moving in the direction of life.

"But where did the bar towel come from?" I asked my friend. He laughed. No answer. Somehow life proceeded from artlessness and instability, burping into a wild diversity that follows no linear rules. Yet in all this indeterminacy, life keeps opting for life. Galactic clouds show a propensity to become organic, not inorganic, matter; carbon-rich meteorites have seeded our earthly oasis with rich carbon-based compounds; sea vents let out juvenile water warm enough to generate growth, and sea meadows brew up a marine plasma—matter that is a thousandth of a millimeter wide—and thus give rise to all plant life and the fish, insects, and animals with which it coevolved.

I dip my paddle. The canoe pivots around. Somewhere out there in the cosmos, shock waves collapsed gas and dust into a swirl of matter made of star grains so delicate as to resemble smoke, slowly aggregating, gradually sweeping up and colliding with enough material to become a planet like ours.

Dusk. A bubble of cloud rises over the mountain. It looks like the moon, then a rock tooth pierces it, and wind burnishes the pieces into soft puffs of mist. Forms dissolve into other forms: a horsehead becomes a frog; the frog becomes three stick figures scrawled across the sky. I watch our single sun drop. Beyond the water, a tree's yellow leaves are hung like butter lamps high up near the trunk. As the sun sinks, the tree appears to be lit from the inside.

Analyzing and Discussing the Text

1. Why does Ehrlich compare the sound of water against the hull to the music "made by halyards against aluminum masts"? How does this analogy tie in with the themes of her meditation?
2. Explain what is meant by the sentence: "It is the music emptiness would compose if emptiness could change into something." How does it connect with other parts of the essay?

3. Is Ehrlich's summary of "the Big Bang" theory of creation effective? What is gained and what is lost by this kind of rendering of scientific theory?
4. What are the connotations in Ehrlich's description of creation as "burping into a wild diversity that follows no linear rules"?
5. Why does she describe the sunset with the words "our single sun"? How does this fit in with the previous emphasis on the "wild diversity" of creation and with her assertion that "life keeps opting for life"?
6. How and why do the rhetorical patterns in the last paragraph echo those of the earlier descriptions of creation in the fourth and fifth paragraphs? Do they differ in any significant way?

Experiencing and Writing About the World

1. Write several paragraphs in which you recall some personal moment of will-lessness and immersion in the flow of nature. Where did such floating lead you? Did it cause a kind of metaphysical musing like that described by Ehrlich, or did it have some other kind of effect on you?
2. Get a canoe, a raft, an inner tube, or an air mattress—some sort of water vehicle or flotation device that you can either control manually or set adrift. Go to a nearby body of water—a river, pond, swimming pool, or whatever seems safe and accessible—and set yourself afloat on it. Try alternately paddling and merely drifting. Carefully monitor both types of floating, then eventually go ashore and write a detailed account of the physical sensations you experienced while on the water. Attempt to record a variety of sensory experiences, including sounds, sights, smells, and the feel of being afloat.
3. Choose an important scientific theory, review its main features, and, like Ehrlich, try to summarize it in a very brief and engaging way. Test your summary with a friend for readability and accuracy. Is such as task harder than you thought when you read the Ehrlich essay?

Suggestions for Further Reading

Abbey, Edward. "Down the River with Henry Thoreau," "Notes from a Cold River," "Running the San Juan," and "River Rats." *Down the River.* New York: Dutton, 1982.
Bartram, William. *Travels.* 1791. New York: Dover, 1955.

Brooks, Paul. "The Uses of a Canoe." *Roadless Area*. New York: Knopf, 1964.

Brower, Kenneth. *The Starship & the Canoe*. New York: Harper, 1978.

Graves, John. *Goodbye to a River*. New York: Knopf, 1960.

Hemingway, Ernest. *The Old Man and the Sea*. New York: Scribner's, 1950.

LaBastille, Anne. *Beyond Black Bear Lake*. New York: Norton, 1987.

McPhee, John. *The Survival of the Bark Canoe*. New York: Farrar, 1975.

Nelson, Richard. "The Forest of Eyes." *The Island Within*. San Francisco: North Point, 1989.

Powell, John Wesley. *The Exploration of the Colorado River and Its Canyons*. 1895. New York: Penguin, 1987.

Slocum, Joshua. *Sailing Alone Around the World*. 1900. New York: Dover, 1956.

Thoreau, Henry David. *A Week on the Concord and Merrimack Rivers*. Ed. Carl Hovde. 1849. Princeton: Princeton UP, 1980.

Twain, Mark. *Life on the Mississippi*. 1896. New York: Bantam, 1985.

Galen Rowell/Mountain Light Photography

CHAPTER THREE

——————————— ▬▬▬ ———————————

Climbing: Mountain Narratives

Scholars credit Petrarch, the poet and scholar of the Italian Renaissance, with changing European attitudes toward mountains by writing so rhapsodically about his ascent of Mount Ventoux in France in the year 1336. Nearly four centuries later, the English theologian John Ray sought to prove the "great Use, Benefit, and Necessity" of mountains, despite the fact that many of his contemporaries still viewed them as the earth's "Warts and superfluous Excrescencies." The aesthetician John Ruskin, working in England and continental Europe in the mid-nineteenth century, strongly supported the growing appreciation of picturesque mountain vistas, viewed safely from the lowlands; but Ruskin harshly criticized the aesthetic insensitivity of mountain climbers and he detected in mountain-dwelling people "that gloomy foulness that is suffered only by torpor, or by anguish of soul," as he put it in the chapter of *Modern Painters* called "Mountain Gloom." Yet today people commonly enjoy not only the distant appearance of mountains, but also the experience of climbing them, straining against gravity, geological and climatic obstacles, and often social tensions. Although Edward Abbey is not typically considered a mountaineering writer, even he has attempted in an essay titled "Mountain Music" (collected in *The Journey Home* in 1977) to answer the age-old question, Why climb mountains? "Even a simple hike up Whitney... involves that element of risk and effort which compensates for the usual banality of our lives," writes Abbey. "*We love the taste of freedom. We enjoy the smell of danger.* We take pleasure in the consummation of mental, spiritual, and physical effort; it is the achievement of a summit that brings the three together, stamps them with the harmony and unity of a point. Of a meaning."

This yearning for freedom, danger, and ultimately meaning has inspired extraordinarily dramatic writing about experiences on mountains large and small. Isabella Bird's account of her 1879 ascent of Long's Peak in Colorado combines her descriptions of mountain sublimity with a provocative rendering of the tensions between her and several male climbing companions. John Muir, climbing alone as usual, uses his rambles in the Sierra Nevadas as a source of both spiritual and scientific insight. Unlike the other mountaineering writers in this chapter, Jack Kerouac is a reluctant outdoorsman, tentative and even terrified as he clings to the slopes of the Matterhorn (also in the Sierra Nevadas) before experiencing a revelation about his relationship to the mountain by watching his climbing partner dance fearlessly down a slope of scree. Both the glory and the gloom of climbing emerge in David Roberts's account of a major ascent that he and several college friends accomplished in Alaska. Arlene Blum emphasizes the human dimensions, both private and social, of a major climbing expedition in the Himalayas—the particular narrative anthologized here shows the decision-making process involved in selecting a small team to try for the summit of Annapurna. Scott Russell Sanders's only companion as he hikes up modest Hardesty Mountain in Oregon is his infant son, who rides on his back; but the mountain, the process of hiking, and the behavior of "Baby Jesse" inspire the writer's reflection on basic issues of human existence.

ISABELLA BIRD

A Lady's Life in the Rocky Mountains: Letter VII

Like Matthew Henson in his description of the Arctic, Isabella Bird (1831–1904) begins the account of her 1873 ascent of 14,255-foot Long's Peak in the Rocky Mountains of Colorado with an apology for her inability to capture "the unspeakable awfulness and fascination" of the landscape in her prose. And yet, like Henson, she succeeds nonetheless in crafting a wonderfully evocative narrative of adventure and aesthetic engagement with the natural world. Bird first left her native England in the 1850s, undertaking a voyage to Canada and the United States as a cure for depression, neuralgia, and a chronic spinal problem; but she continued traveling for the rest of her life, even journeying to Hawaii and Asia. Although she did not consider herself a scientist, her writing demonstrates precise knowledge of geography and botany, and for this reason she was inducted as a Fellow in the Royal Geographical Society, the first woman ever to receive this honor.

In the following narrative, originally written as a letter to her sister and later published as part of the volume *A Lady's Life in the Rocky Mountains* (1879), Bird repeatedly uses language in a way that suggests both fear and pleasure, physical discomfort and genuine enjoyment of the scenery and the rough company. There is also a curious mixture of pride and humility in her narrative: "You know I have no head and no ankles, and never ought to dream of mountaineering," she writes to her sister, "and had I known that the ascent was a real mountaineering feat I should not have felt the slightest ambition to perform it." But once the "feat" has been accomplished, she writes with delight that her guide "must be grievously disappointed, both in my courage and strength." Repeatedly Bird relies on what we might call "the strategy of surpassed expectation" to emphasize the wonders of the Rocky Mountains: her "shocking" one-eyed guide, Jim, "as awful looking a ruffian as one could see," suddenly exclaims as they look out over the Colorado Plains while making their way up the mountain, "I believe there is a God!" And Bird herself, although she claims that she "usually dislike[s] bird's-eye and panoramic views," allows herself to be overcome by the beauties of the mountains, reveling hyperbolically in nature's "grandeur, solitude, sublimity, beauty, and infinity" — a string of superlatives to rival any of John Muir's. But throughout this tale of adventure we encounter the author's intensely conflicting moods, the highs and the lows. "Never-to-be-forgotten glories they were," Bird reminds us, "burnt in upon my memory by six succeeding hours of terror." This combination of exaltation and terror is inherent in the activity of mountain climbing, regardless of one's gender, one's historical milieu, and one's experience at high altitudes.

Estes Park, Colorado, *October*

As this account of the ascent of Long's Peak could not be written at the time, I am much disinclined to write it, especially as no sort of description within my powers could enable another to realise the glorious sublimity, the majestic solitude, and the unspeakable awfulness and fascination of the scenes in which I spent Monday, Tuesday, and Wednesday.

Long's Peak, 14,700 feet high, blocks up one end of Estes Park, and dwarfs all the surrounding mountains. From it on this side rise, snow-born, the bright St Vrain, and the Big and Little Thompson. By sunlight or moonlight its splintered grey crest is the one object which, in spite of wapiti and bighorn, skunk and grizzly, unfailingly arrests the eye. From it come all storms of snow and wind, and the forked lightnings play round its head like a glory. It is one of the noblest of mountains, but in one's imagination it grows to be much more than a mountain. It becomes invested with a personality. In its caverns and abysses one comes to fancy that it generates and chains the strong winds, to let them loose in its fury. The thunder becomes its voice, and the lightnings do it homage. Other summits blush under the morning kiss of the sun, and turn pale the next moment; but it detains the first sunlight and holds it round its head for an hour at least, till it pleases to change from rosy red to deep blue; and the sunset, as if spell-bound, lingers latest on its crest. The soft winds which hardly rustle the pine needles down here are raging rudely up there round its motionless summit. The mark of fire is upon it; and though it has passed into a grim repose, it tells of fire and upheaval as truly, though not as eloquently, as the living volcanoes of Hawaii. Here under its shadow one learns how naturally nature worship, and the propitiation of the forces of nature arose in minds which had no better light.

Long's Peak, 'the American Matterhorn', as some call it, was ascended five years ago for the first time. I thought I should like to attempt it, but up to Monday, when Evans left for Denver, cold water was thrown upon the project. It was too late in the season, the winds were likely to be strong, etc.; but just before leaving, Evans said that the weather was looking more settled, and if I did not get farther than the timber line it would be worth going. Soon after he left, 'Mountain Jim' came in, and said he would go up as guide, and the two youths who rode here with me from Longmount and I caught at the proposal. Mrs Edwards at once baked bread for three days, steaks were cut from the steer which hangs up conveniently, and tea, sugar, and butter were benevolently added. Our picnic was not to be a luxurious or 'well-found' one, for, in order to avoid the expense of a pack mule, we limited our luggage to what our saddle horses could carry. Behind my saddle I carried three pair of camping blankets and a quilt, which reached to my shoulders. My own boots were so much worn that it was painful to walk, even about the park, in them, so Evans had lent me a pair of his hunting boots, which hung to the horn of my saddle. The horses of the two young men were equally loaded, for we had to prepare for many degrees of frost. 'Jim' was a shocking figure; he had on an old pair of high boots, with a baggy pair of old trousers made of deer hide, held on by an old scarf tucked into them; a leather shirt, with three or four ragged unbuttoned waistcoats over it; an old smashed wideawake from under which his tawny, neglected ringlets hung; and with his one eye, his one long spur, his knife in his belt, his revolver in his waistcoat pocket, his saddle covered with an old beaver-skin, from which the paws hung down; his camping blankets behind him, his rifle laid across the saddle in front of him, and his axe, canteen, and other gear hanging to the horn, he was as awful looking a ruffian as one could see. By way of contrast he rode a small Arab mare, of exquisite beauty, skittish, high-spirited, gentle, but altogether too light for him, and he fretted her incessantly to make her display herself.

Heavily loaded as all our horses were, 'Jim' started over the half-mile of level grass at a hand-gallop, and then throwing his mare on her haunches, pulled up alongside of me, and with a grace of manner which soon made me forget his appearance, entered into a conversation which lasted for more than three hours, in spite of the manifold checks of fording streams, single file, abrupt ascents and descents, and other incidents of mountain travel. The ride was one series of glories and surprises, of 'park' and glade, of lake and stream, of mountains on mountains, culminating in the rent pinnacles of Long's Peak, which looked yet grander and ghastlier as we crossed an attendant mountain 11,000 feet high. The slanting sun added fresh beauty every hour. There were dark pines against a lemon sky, grey peaks reddening and etherealising, gorges of deep and infinite blue, floods of golden glory pouring through canyons of enormous depth, an atmosphere of absolute purity, an occasional foreground of cottonwood and aspen flaunting in red and gold to intensify the blue gloom of the pines, the trickle and murmur of streams fringed with icicles, the strange *sough* of gusts moving among the pine tops—sights and sounds not of the lower earth, but of the solitary, beast-haunted, frozen upper altitudes. From the dry, buff grass of Estes Park we turned off up a trail on the side of a pine-hung gorge, up a steep pine-clothed hill, down to a small valley, rich in fine, sun-cured hay about eighteen inches high, and enclosed by high mountains whose deepest hollow contains a lily-covered lake, fitly named 'The Lake of the Lilies'. Ah, how magical its beauty was, as it slept in silence, while *there* the dark pines were mirrored motionless in its pale gold, and *here* the great white lily cups and dark green leaves rested on amethyst-coloured water!

From this we ascended into the purple gloom of great pine forests which clothe the skirts of the mountains up to a height of about 11,000 feet, and from their chill and solitary depths we had glimpses of golden atmosphere and rose-lit summits, not of 'the land very far off', but of the land nearer now in all its grandeur, gaining in sublimity by nearness—glimpses, too, through a broken vista of purple gorges, of the illimitable Plains lying idealised in the late sunlight, their baked, brown expanse transfigured into the likeness of a sunset sea rolling infinitely in waves of misty gold.

We rode upwards through the gloom on a steep trail blazed through the forest, all my intellect concentrated on avoiding being dragged off my horse by impending branches, or having the blankets badly torn, as those of my companions were, by sharp dead limbs, between which there was hardly room to pass—the horses breathless, and requiring to stop every few yards, though their riders, except myself, were afoot. The gloom of the dense, ancient, silent forest is to me awe-inspiring. On such an evening it is soundless, except for the branches creaking in the soft wind, the frequent snap of decayed timber, and a murmur in the pine tops as of a not distant waterfall, all tending to produce *eeriness* and a sadness 'hardly akin to pain'. There no lumberer's axe has ever rung. The trees die when they have attained their prime, and stand there, dead and bare, till the fierce mountain winds lay them prostrate. The pines grew smaller and more sparse as we ascended, and the last stragglers wore a tortured, warring look. The timber line was passed, but yet a little higher a slope of mountain meadow dipped to the south-west towards a bright stream trickling under ice and icicles, and there a grove of the beautiful silver spruce marked our camping ground. The trees were in miniature, but so exquisitely arranged that one might well ask what artist's hand had planted them, scattering them here, clumping them there, and training their slim spires towards heaven. Hereafter, when I call up memories of the glorious, the view from this camping ground will come up. Looking east, gorges opened to the distant Plains, then fading into purple grey. Mountains with pine-clothed skirts rose in ranges, or, solitary, uplifted their grey summits, while close behind, but nearly 3000 feet above us, towered the bald white crest of Long's Peak, its huge precipices red with the light of a sun long lost to our eyes.

Close to us, in the caverned side of the Peak, was snow that, owing to its position, is eternal. Soon the afterglow came on, and before it faded a big half-moon hung out of the heavens, shining through the silver blue foliage of the pines on the frigid background of snow, and turning the whole into fairyland. The 'photo' which accompanies this letter is by a courageous Denver artist who attempted the ascent just before I arrived, but, after camping out at the timber line for a week, was foiled by the perpetual storms, and was driven down again, leaving some very valuable apparatus about 3000 feet from the summit.

Unsaddling and picketing the horses securely, making the beds of pine shoots, and dragging up logs for fuel, warmed us all. 'Jim' built up a great fire, and before long we were all sitting round it at supper. It didn't matter much that we had to drink our tea out of the battered meat-tins in which it was boiled, and eat strips of beef reeking with pine smoke without plates or forks.

'Treat Jim as a gentleman and you'll find him one,' I had been told; and though his manner was certainly bolder and freer than that of gentlemen generally, no imaginary fault could be found. He was very agreeable as a man of culture as well as a child of nature; the desperado was altogether out of sight. He was very courteous and even kind to me, which was fortunate, as the young men had little idea of showing even ordinary civilities. That night I made the acquaintance of his dog 'Ring', said to be the best hunting-dog in Colorado, with the body and legs of a collie, but a head approaching that of a mastiff, a noble face with a wistful human expression, and the most truthful eyes I ever saw in an animal. His master loves him if he loves anything, but in his savage moods ill-treats him. Ring's devotion never swerves, and his truthful eyes are rarely taken off his master's face. He is almost human in his intelligence, and, unless he is told to do so, he never takes notice of anyone but 'Jim.' In a tone as if speaking to a human being, his master, pointing to me, said, 'Ring, go to that lady, and don't leave her again tonight.' Ring at once came to me, looked into my face, laid his head on my shoulder, and then lay down beside me with his head on my lap, but never taking his eyes from 'Jim's' face.

The long shadows of the pines lay upon the frosted grass, an aurora leaped fitfully, and the moonlight, though intensely bright, was pale beside the red, leaping flames of our pine logs and their red glow on our gear, ourselves, and Ring's truthful face. One of the young men sang a Latin student's song and two negro melodies; the other, 'Sweet Spirit, Hear my Prayer'. 'Jim' sang one of Moore's melodies in a singular falsetto, and all together sang 'The Star-spangled Banner' and 'The Red, White, and Blue.' Then 'Jim' recited a very clever poem of his own composition, and told some fearful Indian stories. A group of small silver spruces away from the fire was my sleeping-place. The artist who had been up there had so woven and interlaced their lower branches as to form a bower, affording at once shelter from the wind and a most agreeable privacy. It was thickly strewn with young pine shoots, and these, when covered with a blanket, with an inverted saddle for a pillow, made a luxurious bed. The mercury at 9 P.M. was 12 degrees below the freezing point. 'Jim', after a last look at the horses, made a huge fire, and stretched himself out beside it, but Ring lay at my back to keep me warm. I could not sleep, but the night passed rapidly. I was anxious about the ascent, for gusts of ominous sound swept through the pines at intervals. Then wild animals howled, and Ring was perturbed in spirit about them. Then it was strange to see the notorious desperado, a red-handed man, sleeping as quietly as innocence sleeps. But, above all, it was exciting to lie there, with no better shelter than a bower of pines, on a mountain 11,000 feet high, in the very heart of the Rocky Range, under twelve degrees of frost, hearing sounds of wolves, with shivering stars looking through the fragrant canopy, with arrowy pines for bed-posts, and for a night lamp the red flames of a camp fire.

Day dawned long before the sun rose, pure and lemon-coloured. The rest were looking after the horses, when one of the students came running to tell me that I must come farther down the slope, for 'Jim' said he had never seen such a sunrise. From the chill, grey Peak above, from the everlasting snows, from the silvered pines, down through mountain ranges with their depths of Tyrian purple, we looked to where the Plains lay cold, in blue grey, like a morning sea against a far horizon. Suddenly, as a dazzling streak at first, but enlarging rapidly into a dazzling sphere, the sun wheeled above the grey line, a light and glory as when it was first created. 'Jim' involuntarily and reverently uncovered his head, and exclaimed, 'I believe there is a God!' I felt as if, Parsee-like, I must worship. The grey of the Plains changed to purple, the sky was all one rose-red flush, on which vermilion cloud-streaks rested; the ghastly peaks gleamed like rubies, the earth and heavens were new-created. Surely 'the Most High dwelleth not in temples made with hands'! For a full hour those Plains simulated the ocean, down to whose limitless expanse of purple, cliffs, rocks, and promontories swept down.

By 7 we had finished breakfast, and passed into the ghastlier solitudes above, I riding as far as what, rightly or wrongly, are called the 'Lava Beds', an expanse of large and small boulders, with snow in their crevices. It was very cold; some water which we crossed was frozen hard enough to bear the horse. 'Jim' had advised me against taking any wraps, and my thin Hawaiian riding-dress, only fit for the tropics, was penetrated by the keen air. The rarefied atmosphere soon began to oppress our breathing, and I found that Evans's boots were so large that I had no foothold. Fortunately, before the real difficulty of the ascent began, we found, under a rock, a pair of small over-shoes, probably left by the Hayden exploring expedition, which just lasted for the day. As we were leaping from rock to rock, 'Jim' said, 'I was thinking in the night about your travelling alone, and wondering where you carried your Derringer, for I could see no signs of it.' On my telling him that I travelled unarmed, he could hardly believe it, and adjured me to get a revolver at once.

On arriving at the 'Notch' (a literal gate of rock), we found ourselves absolutely on the knife-like ridge or backbone of Long's Peak, only a few feet wide, covered with colossal boulders and fragments, and on the other side shelving in one precipitous, snow-patched sweep of 3000 feet to a picturesque hollow, containing a lake of pure green water. Other lakes, hidden among dense pine woods, were farther off, while close above us rose the Peak, which, for about 500 feet, is a smooth, gaunt, inaccessible-looking pile of granite. Passing through the Notch, we looked along the nearly inaccessible side of the Peak, composed of boulders and débris of all shapes and sizes, through which appeared broad, smooth ribs of reddish-coloured granite, looking as if they upheld the towering rock-mass above. I usually dislike bird's-eye and panoramic views, but, though from a mountain, this was not one. Serrated ridges, not much lower than that on which we stood, rose, one beyond another, far as that pure atmosphere could carry the vision, broken into awful chasms deep with ice and snow, rising into pinnacles piercing the heavenly blue with their cold, barren grey, on, on for ever, till the most distant range upbore unsullied snow alone. There were fair lakes mirroring the dark pine woods, canyons dark and blue-black with unbroken expanses of pines, snow-slashed pinnacles, wintry heights frowning upon lovely parks, watered and wooded, lying in the lap of summer; North Park floating off into the blue distance, Middle Park closed till another season, the sunny slopes of Estes Park, and winding down among the mountains the snowy ridge of the Divide, whose bright waters seek both the Atlantic and Pacific Oceans. There, far below, links of diamonds showed where the Grand River takes its rise to seek the mysterious Colorado, with its still unsolved enigma, and lose itself in the waters of the Pacific; and nearer the snow-born Thompson bursts forth from the ice to begin its journey to the Gulf of Mexico. Nature, rioting in her grandest mood, exclaimed with voices of grandeur, solitude, sublimity, beauty, and infinity, 'Lord, what is man, that Thou art mindful of him? or the son of man, that Thou visitest him?' Never-to-be-forgotten glories they were, burnt in upon my memory by six succeeding hours of terror. You know I have no head and no ankles, and never ought to dream of mountaineering; and had I known that the ascent was a real mountaineering feat I should not have felt the slightest ambition to perform it. As it is, I am only humiliated by my success, for 'Jim' dragged me up, like a bale of goods, by sheer force of muscle. At the Notch the real business of the ascent began. 2000 feet of solid rock towered above us, 4000 feet of broken rock shelved precipitously below; smooth granite ribs, with barely foothold, stood out here and there; melted snow, refrozen several times, presented a more serious obstacle; many of the rocks were loose, and tumbled down when touched. To me it was a time of extreme terror. I was roped to 'Jim', but it was of no use, my feet were paralysed and slipped on the bare rock, and he said it was useless to try to go that way, and we retraced our steps. I wanted to return to the Notch, knowing that my incompetence would detain the party, and one of the young men said almost plainly that a woman was a dangerous encumbrance, but the trapper replied shortly that if it were not to take a lady up he would not go up at all. He went on to explore, and reported that further progress on the correct line of ascent was blocked by ice; and then for two hours we descended, lowering ourselves by our hands from rock to rock along a boulder-strewn sweep of 4000 feet, patched with ice and snow, and perilous from rolling stones. My fatigue, giddiness, and pain from bruised ankles, and arms half pulled out of their sockets, were so great that I should never have gone half-way had not 'Jim', *nolens volens*, dragged me along with a patience and skill, and withal a determination that I should ascend the Peak, which never failed. After descending about 2000 feet to avoid the ice, we got into a deep ravine with inaccessible sides, partly filled with ice and snow and partly with large and small fragments of rock, which were constantly giving way, rendering the footing very insecure. That part to me was two hours of painful and unwilling submission to the inevitable; if trembling, slipping, straining, of smooth ice appearing when it was least expected, and of weak entreaties to be left behind while the others went on. 'Jim' always said that there was no danger, that there was only a short bad bit ahead, and that I should go up even if he carried me!

Slipping, faltering, gasping from the exhausting toil in the rarefied air, with throbbing hearts and panting lungs, we reached the top of the gorge and squeezed ourselves between two gigantic fragments of rock by a passage called the 'Dog's Lift', when I climbed on the shoulders of one man and then was hauled up. This introduced us by an abrupt turn round the south-west angle of the Peak to a narrow shelf of considerable length, rugged, uneven, and so overhung by the cliff in some places that it is necessary to crouch to pass at all. Above, the Peak looks nearly vertical for 400 feet; and below, the most tremendous precipice I have ever seen descends in one unbroken fall. This is usually considered the most dangerous part of the ascent, but it does not seem so to me, for such foothold as there is is secure, and one fancies that it is possible to hold on with the hands. But there, and on the final, and, to my thinking, the worst part of the climb, one slip, and a breathing, thinking, human being would lie 3000 feet below, a shapeless, bloody heap! Ring refused to traverse the Ledge, and remained at the 'Lift' howling piteously.

From thence the view is more magnificent even than that from the Notch. At the foot of the precipice below us lay a lovely lake, woodembosomed, from or near which the bright St Vrain and other streams take their rise. I thought how their clear cold waters, growing turbid in the affluent flats, would heat under the tropic sun, and eventually form part of that great ocean river which renders our far-off islands habitable by impinging on their shores. Snowy ranges, one behind the other, extended to the distant horizon, folding in their wintry embrace the beauties of Middle Park. Pike's Peak, more than one hundred miles off, lifted that vast but shapeless summit which is the landmark of Southern Colorado. There were snow patches, snow slashes, snow abysses, snow forlorn and soiled-looking, snow pure and dazzling, snow glistening above the purple robe of pine worn by all the mountains; while away to the east, in limitless breadth, stretched the green-grey of the endless Plains. Giants everywhere reared their splintered crests. From thence, with a single sweep, the eye takes in a distance of 300 miles—that distance to the west, north, and south being made up of mountains 10, 11, 12, and 13,000 feet in height, dominated by Long's Peak, Gray's Peak, and Pike's Peak, all nearly the height of Mont Blanc! On the Plains we traced the rivers by their fringe of cottonwoods to the distant Platte, and between us and them lay glories of mountain, canyon, and lake, sleeping in depths of blue and purple most ravishing to the eye.

As we crept from the lodge round a horn of rock, I beheld what made me perfectly sick and dizzy to look at—the terminal Peak itself—a smooth, cracked face or wall of pink granite, as nearly perpendicular as anything could well be up which it was possible to climb, well deserving the name of the 'American Matterhorn'.[1]

Scaling, not climbing, is the correct term for this last ascent. It took one hour to accomplish 500 feet, pausing for breath every minute or two. The only foothold was in narrow cracks or on minute projections on the granite. To get a toe in these cracks, or here and there on a scarcely obvious projection, while crawling on hands and knees, all the while tortured with thirst and gasping and struggling for breath, this was the climb; but at last the Peak was won. A grand, well-defined mountain-top it is, a nearly level acre of boulders, with precipitous sides all round, the one we came up being the only accessible one.

It was not possible to remain long. One of the young men was seriously alarmed by bleeding from the lungs, and the intense dryness of the day and the rarefaction of the air, at a height of nearly 15,000 feet, made respiration very painful. There is always water on the Peak, but it was frozen as hard as a rock, and the sucking of ice and snow increases thirst. We all suffered severely from the want of water, and the gasping for breath made our mouths and tongues so dry that articulation was difficult, and the speech of all unnatural.

---

[1]Let no practical mountaineer be allured by my description into the ascent of Long's Peak. Truly terrible as it was to me, to a member of the Alpine Club it would not be a feat worth performing.—Author's note.

From the summit were seen in unrivalled combination all the views which had rejoiced our eyes during the ascent. It was something at last to stand upon the storm-rent crown of this lonely sentinel of the Rocky Range, on one of the mightiest of the vertebrae of the backbone of the North American continent, and to see the waters start for both oceans. Uplifted above love and hate and storms of passion, calm amidst the eternal silences, fanned by zephyrs and bathed in living blue, peace rested for that one bright day on the Peak, as if it were some region

> Where falls not rain, or hail, or any snow,
> Or ever wind blows loudly.

We placed our names, with the date of ascent, in a tin within a crevice, and descended to the Ledge, sitting on the smooth granite, getting our feet into cracks and against projections, and letting ourselves down by our hands, 'Jim' going before me, so that I might steady my feet against his powerful shoulders. I was no longer giddy, and faced the precipice of 3500 feet without a shiver. Repassing the Ledge and Lift, we accomplished the descent through 1500 feet of ice and snow, with many falls and bruises, but no worse mishap, and there separated, the young men taking the steepest but most direct way to the Notch, with the intention of getting ready for the march home, and 'Jim' and I taking what he thought the safer route for me—a descent over boulders for 2000 feet, and then a tremendous ascent to the Notch. I had various falls, and once hung by my frock, which caught on a rock, and 'Jim' severed it with his hunting-knife, upon which I fell into a crevice full of soft snow. We were driven lower down the mountains than he had intended by impassable tracts of ice, and the ascent was tremendous. For the last 200 feet the boulders were of enormous size, and the steepness fearful. Sometimes I drew myself up on hands and knees, sometimes crawled; sometimes 'Jim' pulled me up by my arms or a lariat, and sometimes I stood on his shoulders, or he made steps for me of his feet and hands, but at six we stood on the Notch in the splendour of the sinking sun, all colour deepening, all peaks glorifying, all shadows purpling, all peril past.

'Jim' had parted with his *brusquerie* when we parted from the students, and was gentle and considerate beyond anything, though I knew that he must be grievously disappointed, both in my courage and strength. Water was an object of earnest desire. My tongue rattled in my mouth, and I could hardly articulate. It is good for one's sympathies to have for once a severe experience of thirst. Truly, there was

> Water, water, everywhere,
> But not a drop to drink.

Three times its apparent gleam deceived even the mountaineer's practised eye, but we found only a foot of 'glare ice'. At last, in a deep hole, he succeeded in breaking the ice, and by putting one's arm far down one could scoop up a little water in one's hand, but it was tormentingly insufficient. With great difficulty and much assistance I recrossed the Lava Beds, was carried to the horse and lifted upon him, and when we reached the camping ground I was lifted off him, and laid on the ground wrapped up in blankets, a humiliating termination of a great exploit. The horses were saddled, and the young men were all ready to start, but 'Jim' quietly said, 'Now, gentlemen, I want a good night's rest, and we shan't stir from here tonight.' I believe they were really glad to have it so, as one of them was quite 'finished'. I retired to my arbour, wrapped myself in a roll of blankets, and was soon asleep. When I woke, the moon was high shining through the silvery branches, whitening the bald Peak above, and glittering on the great abyss of snow behind, and pine logs were blazing like a bonfire in the cold still air. My feet were so icy cold that I could not sleep again, and getting some blankets to sit in, and making a roll of them for my back, I sat for two hours by the camp fire. It was weird and gloriously beautiful. The students were asleep not far off in their blankets with their feet towards the fire. Ring lay on one side of me with his fine head on my arm, and his master sat smoking, with the fire lighting up the handsome side of his face, and except for the tones of our voices, and an occasional crackle and splutter, as a pine-knot blazed up, there was no sound on the mountain side. The beloved stars of my far-off home were overhead, the Plough and Pole Star, with their steady light; the glittering Pleiades, looking larger than I ever saw them, and 'Orion's studded belt' shining gloriously. Once only some wild animals prowled near the camp, when Ring, with one bound, disappeared from my side; and the horses, which were picketed by the stream, broke their lariats, stampeded, and came rushing wildly towards the fire, and it was fully half an hour before they were caught and quiet was restored. 'Jim', or Mr Nugent, as I always scrupulously called him, told stories of his early youth, and of a great sorrow which had led him to embark on a lawless and desperate life. His voice trembled, and tears rolled down his cheek. Was it semi-conscious acting, I wondered, or was his dark soul really stirred to its depths by the silence, the beauty, and the memories of youth?

We reached Estes Park at noon of the following day. A more successful ascent of the Peak was never made, and I would not now exchange my memories of its perfect beauty and extraordinary sublimity for any other experience of mountaineering in any part of the world. Yesterday snow fell on the summit, and it will be inaccessible for eight months to come.

I. L. B.

Analyzing and Discussing the Text

1. What is Bird's attitude toward Long's Peak in the introduction of her essay? How does her description of the mountain as the object of attention, as the *objective*, make her narrative different from the hiking/walking narratives earlier in this anthology?
2. How does the description of "Mountain Jim" contribute to our sense of Bird's expedition up the mountain? What is Jim's role throughout the narrative? Why, for instance, does she mention that Jim urged her to get a revolver?
3. As Bird came closer to Long's Peak, it seemed "yet grander and ghastlier" to her. How do such adjectives affect our feelings about the adventure?
4. How explicitly does Bird present her own emotions in the narrative? Look for expressions of emotion: rapture, distaste, fear, excitement. What would the story be like without them?
5. Does Bird take exaggerated pride in climbing the mountain? Does she exaggerate her humility?
6. What is the structure of the narrative? Are the various sections of the essay somehow determined by the contours of the landscape Bird is experiencing?
7. Is there anything about Bird's narrative or behavior during the climb that seems noticeably feminine? Do we, as readers, need to pay any attention to the gender of the author? What does Bird mean when she says that Jim "must be grievously disappointed, both in my courage and strength"?
8. How does Bird's final remark about the newfallen snow on the summit of the mountain contribute to the artistry of the essay?

Experiencing and Writing About the World

1. Describe an experience of your own in which the feelings of excitement and horror were closely intertwined. Attempt, like Bird, to attach your feelings to precise external observations and concrete physical experiences.
2. If you have ever been in a situation where your companions (friends, parents, coaches, teachers) expected you to fail, explain how you responded to these expectations. Did you somehow accept the expectations or, like Bird, did you take satisfaction in defying the odds? Tell your story and explain why you responded as you did.
3. Write an essay comparing Bird's nineteenth-century narrative of a woman in the mountains with Arlene Blum's account of a recent all-women's expedition to the Himalayas (later in this chapter). Have

changes occurred in the last century since Bird's climb that affect women's understanding of their potential as high-altitude climbers? How do the social tensions within Bird's climbing party differ from the relationships among the climbers on the Annapurna expedition?

JOHN MUIR

Prayers in Higher Mountain Temples, OR A Geologist's Winter Walk

John Muir (1838–1914), like Henry David Thoreau and Rachel Carson, is one of a handful of truly legendary figures in the tradition of American nature writing. Born in Dunbar, Scotland, Muir immigrated with his family to Wisconsin in 1849. In *The Story of My Boyhood and Youth* (1913), he recounts the tyranny of his devout father, who forced his young sons to run the family farm while he was off saving souls. Still, John had time to develop his natural mechanical talent, which eventually enabled him to create an assortment of ingenious wooden gadgets — clocks and thermometers — for display at the Wisconsin State Agricultural Fair in 1860. After this exposure brought him local acclaim, Muir studied for two years at the University of Wisconsin before leaving to devote the rest of his life to what he called the "University of the Wilderness." In March of 1868, after a thousand-mile walk from Indiana to the gulf coast of Florida (the journal that became a book in 1913), Muir arrived by boat in San Francisco. Supposedly, he asked one of the first people he saw the quickest way out of the city to "anywhere that is wild." Thus he made his way to the Yosemite Valley in eastern California, the region that is now permanently associated with Muir's sublimely rhapsodic narratives. At the urging of his friend Jeanne C. Carr, the wife of one of his professors from Wisconsin, Muir began publishing narratives of his excursions in the *Overland Monthly* in 1872; eventually, more than a dozen books appeared, primarily collections of essays and letters or editions of his journals. The best known of his books may be *The Mountains of California* (1894). But Muir always voiced reservations about his writing and about books in general: "I have a low opinion of books; they are but piles of stones set up to show coming travelers where other minds have been.... No amount of word-making will ever make a single soul to *know* these mountains.... One day's exposure to mountains is better than cartloads of books." Despite this disclaimer, Muir's own words have been tremendously influential in encouraging public enthusiasm for wild places. "I care to live only to entice people to look at Nature's loveliness," he wrote to Mrs. Carr in 1874.

The following essay, "Prayers in Higher Mountain Temples, OR A Geologist's Winter Walk," was written as a letter to Mrs. Carr in 1873, then published posthumously in the collection *Steep Trails* (1918). In this piece we can see Muir's characteristic enthusiasm and sense of at-homeness in the mountains of California. Like Thoreau, who once wrote that civilization made him feel "cheap and dissipated," Muir seeks out the wildest possible mountain terrain in order to shake off the effects of "the town fog." "A fast and a storm and a difficult cañon were just the medicine I needed," he writes. Beyond merely commenting on his own quest for mental and physical health, though, Muir subtly combines his celebration of the sacred wilderness with observations of the glacial sculpting that created the Yosemite Valley—thus the two parts of the essay's title, the spiritual and the scientific.

After reaching Turlock, I sped afoot over the stubble fields and through miles of brown hemizonia and purple erigeron, to Hopeton, conscious of little more than that the town was behind and beneath me, and the mountains above and before me; on through the oaks and chaparral of the foothills to Coulterville; and then ascended the first great mountain step upon which grows the sugar pine. Here I slackened pace, for I drank the spicy, resiny wind, and beneath the arms of this noble tree I felt that I was safely home. Never did pine trees seem so dear. How sweet was their breath and their song, and how grandly they winnowed the sky! I tingled my fingers among their tassels, and rustled my feet among their brown needles and burrs, and was exhilarated and joyful beyond all I can write.

When I reached Yosemite, all the rocks seemed talkative, and more telling and lovable then ever. They are dear friends, and seemed to have warm blood gushing through their granite flesh; and I love them with a love intensified by long and close companionship. After I had bathed in the bright river, sauntered over the meadows, conversed with the domes, and played with the pines, I still felt blurred and weary, as if tainted in some way with the sky of your streets. I determined, there-fore, to run out for a while to say my prayers in the higher mountain temples. "The days are sunful," I said, "and, though now winter, no greater danger need be encountered, and no sudden storm will block my return, if I am watchful."

The morning after this decision, I started up the cañon of Tenaya, caring little about the quantity of bread I carried; for, I thought, a fast and a storm and a difficult cañon were just the medicine I needed. When I passed Mirror Lake, I scarcely noticed it, for I was absorbed in the great Tissiack—her crown a mile away in the hushed azure; her purple granite drapery flowing in soft and graceful folds down to my feet, embroidered gloriously around with deep, shadowy forest. I have gazed on Tissiack a thousand times—in days of solemn storms, and when her form shone divine with the jewelry of winter, or was veiled in living clouds; and I have heard her voice of winds, and snowy, tuneful waters when floods were falling; yet never did her soul reveal itself more impressively than now. I hung about her skirts, lingering timidly, until the higher mountains and glaciers compelled me to push up the cañon.

This cañon is accessible only to mountaineers, and I was anxious to carry my barometer and clinometer through it, to obtain sections and altitudes, so I chose it as the most attractive highway. After I had passed the tall groves that stretch a mile above Mirror Lake, and scrambled around the Tenaya Fall, which is just at the head of the lake groves, I crept through the dense and spiny chaparral that plushes the roots of the mountains here for miles in warm green, and was ascending a precipitous rock-front, smoothed by glacial action, when I suddenly fell—for the first time since I touched foot to Sierra rocks. After several somersaults, I became insensible from the shock, and when consciousness returned I found myself wedged among short, stiff bushes, trembling as if cold, not injured in the slightest.

Judging by the sun, I could not have been insensible very long; probably not a minute, possibly an hour; and I could not remember what made me fall, or where I had fallen from; but I saw that if I had rolled a little further, my mountain-climbing would have been finished, for just beyond the bushes the cañon wall steepened and I might have fallen to the bottom. "There," said I, addressing my feet, to whose separate skill I had learned to trust night and day on any mountain, "that is what you get by intercourse with stupid town stairs, and dead pavements." I felt degraded and worthless. I had not yet reached the most difficult portion of the cañon, but I determined to guide my humbled body over the most nerve-trying places I could find; for I was now awake, and felt confident that the last of the town fog had been shaken from both head and feet.

I camped at the mouth of a narrow gorge which is cut into the bottom of the main cañon, determined to take earnest exercise next day. No plushy boughs did my ill-behaved bones enjoy that night, nor did my bumped head get a spicy cedar plume pillow mixed with flowers. I slept on a naked boulder, and when I awoke all my nervous trembling was gone.

The gorged portion of the cañon, in which I spent all the next day, is about a mile and a half in length; and I passed the time in tracing the action of the forces that determined this peculiar bottom gorge, which is an abrupt, ragged-walled, narrow-throated cañon, formed in the bottom of the wide-mouthed, smooth, and beveled main cañon. I will not stop now to tell you more; some day you may see it, like a shadowy line, from Cloud's Rest. In high water, the stream occupies all the bottom of the gorge, surging and chafing in glorious power from wall to wall. But the sound of the grinding was low as I entered the gorge, scarcely hoping to be able to pass through its entire length. By cool efforts, along glassy, ice-worn slopes, I reached the upper end in a little over a day, but was compelled to pass the second night in the gorge, and in the moonlight I wrote you this short pencil-letter in my notebook:—

The moon is looking down into the cañon, and how marvelously the great rocks kindle to her light! Every dome, and brow, and swelling boss touched by her white rays, glows as if lighted with snow. I am now only a mile from last night's camp; and have been climbing and sketching all day in this difficult but instructive gorge. It is formed in the bottom of the main cañon, among the roots of Cloud's Rest. It begins at the filled-up lake-basin where I camped last night, and ends a few hundred yards above, in another basin of the same kind. The walls everywhere are craggy and vertical, and in some places they overlean. It is only from twenty to sixty feet wide, and not, though black and broken enough, the thin, crooked mouth of some mysterious abyss; but it was eroded, for in many places I saw its solid, seamless floor.

I am sitting on a big stone, against which the stream divides, and goes brawling by in rapids on both sides; half of my rock is white in the light, half in shadow. As I look from the opening jaws of this shadowy gorge, South Dome is immediately in front—high in the stars, her face turned from the moon, with the rest of her body gloriously muffled in waved folds of granite. On the left, sculptured from the main Cloud's Rest ridge, are three magnificent rocks, sisters of the great South Dome. On the right is the massive, moonlit front of Mount Watkins, and between, low down in the furthest distance, is Sentinel Dome, girdled and darkened with forest. In the near foreground Tenaya Creek is singing against boulders that are white with snow and moonbeams. Now look back twenty yards, and you will see a waterfall fair as a spirit; the moonlight just touches it, bringing it into relief against a dark background of shadow. A little to the left, and a dozen steps this side of the fall, a flickering light marks my camp—and a precious camp it is. A huge, glacier-polished slab, falling from the smooth, glossy flank of Cloud's Rest, happened to settle on edge against the wall of the gorge. I did not know that this slab was glacier-polished until I lighted my fire. Judge of my delight. I think it was sent here by an earthquake. It is about twelve feet square. I wish I could take it home for a hearthstone. Beneath this slab is the only place in this torrent-swept gorge where I could find sand sufficient for a bed.

I expected to sleep on the boulders, for I spent most of the afternoon on the slippery wall of the cañon, endeavoring to get around this difficult part of the gorge, and was compelled to hasten down here for water before dark. I shall sleep soundly on this sand; half of it is mica. Here, wonderful to behold, are a few green stems of prickly rubus, and a tiny grass. They are here to meet us. Ay, even here in this darksome gorge, "frightened and tormented" with raging torrents and choking avalanches of snow. Can it be? As if rubus and the grass leaf were not enough of God's tender prattle words of love, which we so much need in these mighty temples of power, yonder in the "benmost bore" are two blessed adiantums. Listen to them! How wholly infused with God is this one big word of love that we call the world! Good-night. Do you see the fire-glow on my ice-smoothed slab, and on my two ferns and the rubus and grass panicles? And do you hear how sweet a sleep-song the fall and cascades are singing?

The water-ground chips and knots that I found fastened between the rocks kept my fire alive all through the night. Next morning I rose nerved and ready for another day of sketching and noting, and any form of climbing. I escaped from the gorge about noon, after accomplishing some of the most delicate feats of mountaineering I ever attempted; and here the cañon is all broadly open again—the floor luxuriantly forested with pine, and spruce, and silver fir, and brown-trunked librocedrus. The walls rise in Yosemite forms, and Tenaya Creek comes down seven hundred feet in a white brush of foam. This is a little Yosemite valley. It is about two thousand feet above the level of the main Yosemite, and about twenty-four hundred below Lake Tenaya.

I found the lake frozen, and the ice was so clear and unruffled that the surrounding mountains and the groves that look down upon it were reflected almost as perfectly as I ever beheld them in the calm evening mirrors of summer. At a little distance, it was difficult to believe the lake frozen at all; and when I walked out on it, cautiously stamping at short intervals to test the strength of the ice, I seemed to walk mysteriously, without adequate faith, on the surface of the water. The ice was so transparent that I could see through it the beautifully wave-rippled, sandy bottom, and the scales of mica glinting back the down-pouring light. When I knelt down with my face close to the ice, through which the sunbeams were pouring, I was delighted to discover myriads of Tyndall's six-rayed water flowers, magnificently colored.

A grand old mountain mansion is this Tenaya region! In the glacier period it was a *mer de glace*, far grander than the *mer de glace* of Switzerland, which is only about half a mile broad. The Tenaya *mer de glace* was not less than two miles broad, late in the glacier epoch, when all the principal dividing crests were bare; and its depth was not less than fifteen hundred feet. Ice-streams from Mounts Lyell and Dana, and all the mountains between, and from the nearer Cathedral Peak, flowed hither, welded into one, and worked together. After eroding this Tenaya Lake basin, and all the splendidly sculptured rocks and mountains that surround and adorn it, and the great Tenaya Cañon, with its wealth of all that makes mountains sublime, they were welded with the vast South, Lyell, and Illilouette glaciers on one side, and with those of

Hoffman on the other—thus forming a portion of a yet grander *mer de glace* in Yosemite Valley.

I reached the Tenaya Cañon, on my way home, by coming in from the northeast, rambling down over the shoulders of Mount Watkins, touching bottom a mile above Mirror Lake. From thence home was but a saunter in the moonlight.

After resting one day, and the weather continuing calm, I ran up over the left shoulder of South Dome and down in front of its grand split face to make some measurements, completed my work, climbed to the right shoulder, struck off along the ridge for Cloud's Rest, and reached the topmost heave of her sunny wave in ample time to see the sunset.

Cloud's Rest is a thousand feet higher than Tissiack. It is a wavelike crest upon a ridge, which begins at Yosemite with Tissiack, and runs continuously eastward to the thicket of peaks and crests around Lake Tenaya. This lofty granite wall is bent this way and that by the restless and weariless action of glaciers just as if it had been made of dough. But the grand circumference of mountains and forests are coming from far and near, densing into one close assemblage; for the sun, their god and father, with love ineffable, is glowing a sunset farewell. Not one of all the assembled rocks or trees seemed remote. How impressively their faces shone with responsive love!

I ran home in the moonlight with firm strides; for the sun-love made me strong. Down through the junipers; down through the firs; now in jet shadows, now in white light; over sandy moraines and bare, clanking rocks; past the huge ghost of South Dome rising weird through the firs; past the glorious fall of Nevada, the groves of Illilouette; through the pines of the valley; beneath the bright crystal sky blazing with stars. All of this mountain wealth in one day!—one of the rich ripe days that enlarge one's life; so much of the sun upon one side of it, so much of the moon and stars on the other.

Analyzing and Discussing the Test

1. "I felt that I was safely home," Muir writes in the opening paragraph of this essay. How does this attitude determine what the author says throughout the narrative?
2. Does the natural world seem inert and unconscious to Muir? Explain your response.
3. Explain the significance of Muir's fall after returning from civilization to the mountains. Does the mishap make Muir feel less at home in the mountains?

4. Why does Muir sleep "on a naked boulder"? What is the effect of this direct contact with the natural world?
5. Does Muir emphasize his climbing in this essay or do all of his movements seem to happen with ease? Does the narrative itself saunter, appreciative and without clear-cut destination? Compare this climbing essay with Bird's.
6. Why does Muir subtitle the essay "A Geologist's Winter Walk"? What aspects of geology seem to concern him?

Experiencing and Writing About the World

1. Muir describes his time spent roaming through Yosemite Valley as "one of the rich ripe days that enlarge one's life." Recount such a day in your own life, a day when you felt exhilarated, wholly alive. Call your essay "Prayers in _____." Does Muir mean the word "prayers" in a formal religious sense?
2. The landscape through which Muir was wandering when he prepared this essay is a spectacular but rugged one. Describe your own experiences in a similarly extraordinary place, human-made or natural, emphasizing your own sense of belonging. Try to display the feeling of absolute at-homeness.
3. Muir's narrative is the only account of a wholly solitary climbing excursion included in this anthology. Using this essay, one or two of the essays describing group excursions, and your own experiences on group or solo trips (in the mountains or elsewhere), write an essay on the value of each kind of experience. Why it is important for us to consider the social dimension of outdoor experience?

JACK KEROUAC

From The Dharma Bums

Jack Kerouac (1922–1969) was born and raised in the factory town of Lowell, Massachusetts. After graduating from Lowell High School, Kerouac spent a year at the Horace Mann Prep School in New York City and then enrolled as a freshman at Columbia University on a football scholarship in 1940. But Kerouac's football career was short-lived, as were his days as a student at Columbia. Even as a young child, Kerouac had amused himself by writing stories, and he devoted his time in New York to writing and hanging around with Allen Ginsberg, a fellow student who was to become one of the most famous twentieth-century American poets, and a growing circle of bohemian friends. In July of 1947, after a few years of traveling in the merchant marine, Kerouac made his way out to San Francisco by a combination of hitchhiking and riding on Greyhound buses, but this was just the first in a series of cross-country excursions—including later marathon drives with the legendary Neal Cassady and hobo rides aboard freight trains—to be etched in American literary history, and indeed in the nation's mythology, thanks to such books as *On the Road* (1957), *The Dharma Bums* (1958), and *Lonesome Traveler* (1960).

Kerouac spent much of 1955–1956 living in San Francisco and Berkeley, California, with Ginsberg, Gary Snyder, and an assortment of other writers and artists who would come to be known as "The Beat Generation." A year later Kerouac described his experiences when he wrote the self-mythologizing, slightly fictionalized book, *The Dharma Bums*. Although he is primarily remembered for his association with avant-garde, urban artists, saintly poor people, and experimenters with marijuana and other drugs, Kerouac writes in the following excerpt from *The Dharma Bums* about one of the more wholesome and rejuvenating experiences of his life, his ascent of the Matterhorn in the Sierra Nevada Mountains of California with Gary Snyder ("Japhy Ryder") and John Montgomery ("Henry Morley"); the author himself goes by the name "Ray Smith" in this book. Kerouac strove in his more adventurous writing to achieve what he called "spontaneous prose": "Time being of the essence in the purity of speech, sketching language is undisturbed flow from the mind of personal secret idea-words, *blowing* (as per jazz musician) on subject of image." The Matterhorn narrative shows a less extreme form of the wild, jazzlike style of composition Kerouac used in *Visions of Cody* (1959) and other books—*The Subterraneans*, for instance, was supposedly written in three intense nights in 1953. Kerouac claimed that he "learned all about natural storytelling" from his French-Canadian mother's long stories about Canada and New Hampshire. In this climbing narrative, the cool, world-weary outlook of the Beat Generation is replaced by feelings of terror, wonder, and delight—the mountain becomes a source of revelation and regeneration.

[Gonna Climb That Mountain]

At about noon we started out, leaving our big packs at the camp where nobody was likely to be till next year anyway, and went up the scree valley with just some food and first-aid kits. The valley was longer than it looked. In no time at all it was two o'clock in the afternoon and the sun was getting that later more golden look and a wind was rising and I began to think "By gosh how we ever gonna climb that mountain, tonight?"

I put it up to Japhy who said: "You're right, we'll have to hurry."

"Why don't we just forget it and go on home?"'

"Aw come on Tiger, we'll make a run up that hill and then we'll go home." The valley was long and long and long. And at the top end it got very steep and I began to be a little afraid of falling down, the rocks were small and it got slippery and my ankles were in pain from yesterday's muscle strain anyway. But Morley kept walking and talking and I noticed his tremendous endurance. Japhy took his pants off so he could look just like an Indian, I mean stark naked, except for a jockstrap, and hiked almost a quarter-mile ahead of us, sometimes waiting a while, to give us time to catch up, then went on, moving fast, wanting to climb the mountain today. Morley came second, about fifty yards ahead of me all the way. I was in no hurry. Then as it got later afternoon I went faster and decided to pass Morley and join Japhy. Now we were at about eleven thousand feet and it was cold and there was a lot of snow and to the east we could see immense snowcapped ranges and whooee levels of valleyland below them, we were already practically on top of California. At one point I had to scramble, like the others, on a narrow ledge, around a butte of rock, and it really scared me: the fall was a hundred feet, enough to break your neck, with another little ledge letting you bounce a minute preparatory to a nice goodbye one-thousand-foot drop. The wind was whipping now. Yet that whole afternoon, even more than the other, was filled with old premonitions or memories, as though I'd been there before, scrambling on these rocks, for other purposes more ancient, more serious, more simple. We finally got to the foot of Matterhorn where there was a most beautiful small lake unknown to the eyes of most men in this world, seen by only a handful of mountainclimbers, a small lake at eleven thousand some odd feet with snow on the edges of it and beautiful flowers and a beautiful meadow, an alpine meadow, flat and dreamy, upon which I immediately threw myself and took my shoes off. Japhy'd been there a half-hour when I made it, and it was cold now and his clothes were on again. Morley came up behind us smiling. We sat there looking up at the imminent steep scree slope of the final crag of Matterhorn.

"That don't look much, we can do it!" I said glad now.

"No, Ray, that's more than it looks. Do you realize that's a thousand feet more?"

"That much?"

"Unless we make a run up there, double-time, we'll never make it down again to our camp before nightfall and never make it down to the car at the lodge before tomorrow morning at, well at midnight."

"Phew."

"I'm tired," said Morley. "I don't think I'll try it."

"Well that's right," I said. "The whole purpose of mountainclimbing to me isn't just to show off you can get to the top, it's getting out to this wild country."

"Well I'm gonna go," said Japhy.

"Well if you're gonna go I'm goin with you."

"Morley?"

"I don't think I can make it. I'll wait here." And that wind was strong, too strong, I felt that as soon as we'd be a few hundred feet up the slope it might hamper our climbing.

Japhy took a small pack of peanuts and raisins and said "This'll be our gasoline, boy. You ready Ray to make a double-time run?"

"Ready. What would I say to the boys in The Place if I came all this way only to give up at the last minute?"

"It's late so let's hurry." Japhy started up walking very rapidly and then even running sometimes where the climb had to be to the right or left along ridges of scree. Scree is long landslides of rocks and sand, very difficult to scramble through, always little avalanches going on. At every few steps we took it seemed we were going higher and higher on a terrifying elevator, I gulped when I turned around to look back and see all of the state of California it would seem stretching out in three directions under huge blue skies with frightening planetary space clouds and immense vistas of distant valleys and even plateaus and for all I knew whole Nevadas out there. It was terrifying to look down and see Morley a dreaming spot by the little lake waiting for us. "Oh why didn't I stay with old Henry?" I thought. I now began to be afraid to go any higher from sheer fear of being too high. I began to be afraid of being blown away by the wind. All the nightmares I'd ever had about falling off mountains and precipitous buildings ran through my head in perfect clarity. Also with every twenty steps we took upward we both became completely exhausted.

"That's because of the high altitude now Ray," said Japhy sitting beside me panting. "So have raisins and peanuts and you'll see what kick it gives you." And each time it gave us such a tremendous kick we both jumped up without a word and climbed another twenty, thirty steps. Then sat down again, panting, sweating in the cold wind, high on top of the world our noses sniffling like the noses of little boys playing late Saturday afternoon their final little games in winter. Now the wind began to howl like the wind in movies about the Shroud of Tibet. The steepness began to be too much for me; I was afraid now to look back any more; I peeked: I couldn't even make out Morley by the tiny lake.

"Hurry it up," yelled Japhy from a hundred feet ahead. "It's getting awfully late." I looked up to the peak. It was right there, I'd be there in five minutes. "Only a half-hour to go!" yelled Japhy. I didn't believe it. In five minutes of scrambling angrily upward I fell down and looked up and it was still just as far away. What I didn't like about that peak-top was that the clouds of all the world were blowing right through it like fog.

"Wouldn't see anything up there anyway," I muttered. "Oh why did I ever let myself into this?" Japhy was way ahead of me now, he'd left the peanuts and raisins with me, it was with a kind of lonely solemnity now he had decided to rush to the top if it killed him. He didn't sit down any more. Soon he was a whole football field, a hundred yards ahead of me, getting smaller. I looked back and like Lot's wife that did it. *"This is too high!"* I yelled to Japhy in a panic. He didn't hear me. I raced a few more feet up and fell exhausted on my belly, slipping back just a little. *"This is too high!"* I yelled. I was really scared. Supposing I'd start to slip back for good, these screes might start sliding any time anyway. That damn mountain goat Japhy, I could see him jumping through the foggy air up ahead from rock to rock, up, up, just the flash of his boot bottoms. "How can I keep up with a maniac like that?" But with nutty desperation I followed him. Finally I came to a kind of ledge where I could sit at a level angle instead of having to cling not to slip, and I nudged my whole body inside the ledge just to hold me there tight, so the wind would not dislodge me, and I looked down and around and I had had it. *"I'm stayin here!"* I yelled to Japhy.

"Come on Smith, only another five minutes. I only got a hundred feet to go!"

"I'm staying right here! It's too high!"

He said nothing and went on. I saw him collapse and pant and get up and make his run again.

I nudged myself closer into the ledge and closed my eyes and thought "Oh what a life this is, why do we have to be born in the first place, and only so we can have our poor gentle flesh laid out to such impossible horrors as huge mountains and rock and empty space," and with horror I remembered the famous Zen saying, "When you get to the top of a mountain, keep climbing." The saying made my hair stand on end; it had been such cute poetry sitting on Alvah's straw mats.

Now it was enough to make my heart pound and my heart bleed for being born at all. "In fact when Japhy gets to the top of that crag he *will* keep climbing, the way the wind's blowing. Well this old philosopher is staying right here," and I closed my eyes. "Besides," I thought, "rest and be kind, you don't have to prove anything." Suddenly I heard a beautiful broken yodel of a strange musical and mystical intensity in the wind, and looked up, and it was Japhy standing on top of Matterhorn peak, letting out his triumphant mountain-conquering Buddha Mountain Smashing song of joy. It was beautiful. It was funny, too, up here on the not-so-funny top of California and in all that rushing fog. But I had to hand it to him, the guts, the endurance, the sweat, and now the crazy human singing: whipped cream on top of ice cream. I didn't have enough strength to answer his yodel. He ran around up there and went out of sight to investigate the little flat top of some kind (he said) that ran a few feet west and then dropped sheer back down maybe as far as I care to the sawdust floors of Virginia City. It was insane. I could hear him yelling at me but I just nudged farther in my protective nook, trembling. I looked down at the small lake where Morley was lying on his back with a blade of grass in his mouth and said out loud "Now there's the karma of these three men here: Japhy Ryder gets to his triumphant mountaintop and makes it, I almost make it and have to give up and huddle in a bloody cave, but the smartest of them all is that poet's poet lyin down there with his knees crossed to the sky chewing on a flower dreaming by a gurgling *plage,* goddammit they'll never get me up here again."

I really was amazed by the wisdom of Morley now: "Him with all his goddamn pictures of snowcapped Swiss Alps" I thought.

Then suddenly everything was just like jazz: it happened in one insane second or so: I looked up and saw Japhy *running down the mountain* in huge twenty-foot leaps, running, leaping, landing with a great drive of his booted heels, bouncing five feet or so, running, then taking another long crazy yelling yodelaying sail down the sides of the world and in that flash I realized *it's impossible to fall off mountains you fool* and with a yodel of my own I suddenly got up and began running down the mountain after him doing exactly the same huge leaps, the same fantastic runs and jumps, and in the space of about five minutes I'd guess Japhy Ryder and I (in my sneakers, driving the heels of my sneakers right into sand, rock, boulders, I didn't care any more I was so anxious to get down out of there) came leaping and yelling like mountain goats or I'd say like Chinese lunatics of a thousand years ago, enough to raise the hair on the head of the meditating Morley by the lake, who said he looked up and saw us flying down and couldn't believe it. In fact with one of my greatest leaps and loudest screams of joy I came flying right down to the edge of the lake and dug my sneakered heels into the mud and just fell sitting there, glad. Japhy was already taking his shoes off and pouring sand and pebbles out. It was great. I took off my sneakers and poured out a couple of buckets of lava dust and said "Ah Japhy you taught me the final lesson of them all, you can't fall off a mountain."

"And that's what they mean by the saying, When you get to the top of a mountain keep climbing, Smith."

"Dammit that yodel of triumph of yours was the most beautiful thing I ever heard in my life. I wish I'd had a tape recorder to take it down."

"Those things aren't made to be heard by the people below," says Japhy dead serious.

"By God you're right, all those sedentary bums sitting around on pillows hearing the cry of the triumphant mountain smasher, they don't deserve it. But when I looked up and saw you running down that mountain I suddenly understood everything."

"Ah a little satori for Smith today," says Morley.

"What were you doing down here?"

"Sleeping, mostly."

"Well dammit I didn't get to the top. Now I'm ashamed of myself because now that I know how to come *down* a mountain I know how to go *up* and that I can't fall off, but now it's too late."

"We'll come back next summer Ray and climb it. Do you realize that this is the first time you've been mountainclimbin and you left old veteran Morley here way behind you?"

"Sure," said Morley. "Do you think, Japhy, they would assign Smith the title of Tiger for what he done today?"

"Oh sure," says Japhy, and I really felt proud. I was a Tiger.

"Well dammit I'll be a lion next time we get up here."

"Let's go men, now we've got a long long way to go back down this scree to our camp and down that valley of boulders and then down that lake trail, wow, I doubt if we can make it before pitch dark."

"It'll be mostly okay." Morley pointed to the sliver of moon in the pinkening deepening blue sky. "That oughta light us a way."

"Let's go." We all got up and started back. Now when I went around that ledge that had scared me it was just fun and a lark, I just skipped and jumped and danced along and I had really learned that you can't fall off a mountain. Whether you *can* off a mountain or not I don't know, but I had learned that you can't. That was the way it struck me.

It was a joy, though, to get down into the valley and lose sight of all that open sky space underneath everything and finally, as it got graying five o'clock, about a hundred yards from the other boys and walking alone, to just pick my way singing and thinking along the little black cruds of a deer trail through the rocks, no call to think or look ahead or worry, just follow the little balls of deer crud with your eyes cast down and enjoy life. At one point I looked and saw crazy Japhy who'd climbed for fun to the top of a snow slope and skied right down to the bottom, about a hundred yards, on his boots and the final few yards on his back, yippeeing and glad. Not only that but he'd taken off his pants again and wrapped them around his neck. This pants bit of his was simply he said for comfort, which is true, besides nobody around to see him anyway, though I figured that when he went mountainclimbing with girls it didn't make any difference to him. I could hear Morley talking to him in the great lonely valley: even across the rocks you could tell it was his voice. Finally I followed my deer trail so assiduously I was by myself going along ridges and down across creekbottoms completely out of sight of them, though I could hear them, but I trusted the instinct of my sweet little millennial deer and true enough, just as it was getting dark their ancient trail took me right to the edges of the familiar shallow creek (where they stopped to drink for the last five thousand years) and there was the glow of Japhy's bonfire making the side of the big rock orange and gay. The moon was bright high in the sky. "Well that moon's gonna save our ass, we got eight miles to go downtrail boys."

We ate a little and drank a lot of tea and arranged all our stuff. I had never had a happier moment in my life than those lonely moments coming down that little deer trace and when we hiked off with our packs I turned to take a final look up that way, it was dark now, hoping to see a few dear little deer, nothing in sight, and I thanked everything up that way. It had been like when you're a little boy and have spent a whole day rambling alone in the woods and fields and on the dusk homeward walk you did it all with your eyes to the ground, scuffling, thinking, whistling, like little Indian boys must feel when they follow their striding fathers from Russian River to Shasta two hundred years ago, like little Arab boys following their fathers, their fathers' trails; that singsong little joyful solitude, nose sniffling, like a little girl pulling her little brother home on the sled and they're both singing little ditties of their imagination and making faces at the ground and just being themselves before they have to go in the kitchen and put on a straight face again for the world of seriousness. "Yet what could be more serious than to follow a deer trace to get to your water?" I thought. We got to the cliff and started down the five-mile valley of boulders, in clear moonlight now, it was quite easy to dance down from boulder to boulder, the boulders were snow white, with patches of deep black shadow. Everything was cleanly whitely beautiful in the moonlight. Sometimes you could see the silver flash of the creek. Far down were the pines of the meadow park and the pool of the pond.

At this point my feet were unable to go on. I called Japhy and apologized. I couldn't take any more jumps. There were blisters not only on the bottoms but on the sides of my feet, from there having been no protection all yesterday and today. So Japhy swapped and let me wear his boots.

With these big lightweight protective boots on I knew I could go on fine. It was a great new feeling to be able to jump from rock to rock without having to feel the pain through the thin sneakers. On the other hand, for Japhy, it was also a relief to be suddenly lightfooted and he enjoyed it. We made double-time down the valley. But every step was getting us bent, now, we were all really tired. With the heavy packs it was difficult to control those thigh muscles that you need to go *down* a mountain, which is sometimes harder than going up. And there were all those boulders to surmount, for sometimes we'd be walking in sand awhile and our path would be blocked by boulders and we had to climb them and jump from one to the other then suddenly no more boulders and we had to jump down to the sand. Then we'd be trapped in impassable thickets and had to go around them or try to crash through and sometimes I'd get stuck in a thicket with my rucksack, standing there cursing in the impossible moonlight. None of us were talking. I was angry too because Japhy and Morley were afraid to stop and rest, they said it was dangerous at this point to stop.

"What's the difference the moon's shining, we can even sleep."

"No, we've got to get down to that car tonight."

"Well let's stop a minute here. My legs can't take it."

"Okay, only a minute."

But they never rested long enough to suit me and it seemed to me they were getting hysterical. I even began to curse them and at one point I even gave Japhy hell: "What's the sense of killing yourself like this, you call this fun? Phooey." (Your ideas are a crock, I added to myself.) A little weariness'll change a lot of things. Eternities of moonlight rock and thickets and boulders and ducks and that horrifying valley with the two rim walls and finally it seemed we were almost out of there, but nope, not quite yet, and my legs screaming to stop, and me cursing and smashing at twigs and throwing myself on the ground to rest a minute.

"Come on Ray, everything comes to an end." In fact I realized I had no guts anyway, which I've long known. But I have joy. When we got to the alpine meadow I stretched out on my belly and drank water and enjoyed myself peacefully in silence while they talked and worried about getting down the rest of the trail in time.

"Ah don't worry, it's a beautiful night, you've driven yourself too hard. Drink some water and lie down here for about five even ten minutes, everything takes care of itself." Now I was being the philosopher. In fact Japhy agreed with me and we rested peacefully. That good long rest assured my bones I could make it down to the lake okay. It was beautiful going down the trail. The moonlight poured through thick foliage and made dapples on the backs of Morley and Japhy as they walked in front of me. With our packs we got into a good rhythmic walk and enjoying going "Hup hup" as we came to switchbacks and swiveled around, always down, down, the pleasant downgoing swinging rhythm trail. And that roaring creek was a beauty by moonlight, those flashes of flying moon water, that snow white foam, those black-as-pitch trees, regular elfin paradises of shadow and moon. The air began to get warmer and nicer and in fact I thought I could begin to smell people again. We could smell the nice raunchy tidesmell of the lake water, and flowers, and softer dust of down below. Everything up there had smelled of ice and snow and heartless spine rock. Here there was the smell of sun-heated wood; sunny dust resting in the moonlight, lake mud, flowers, straw, all those good things of the earth. The trail was fun coming down and yet at one point I was as tired as ever, more than in that endless valley of boulders, but you could see the lake lodge down below now, a sweet little lamp of light and so it didn't matter. Morley and Japhy were talking a blue streak and all we had to do was roll on down to the car. In fact suddenly, as in a happy dream, with the suddenness of waking up from an endless nightmare and it's all over, we were striding across the road and there were houses and there were automobiles parked under trees and Morley's car was sitting right there.

"From what I can tell by feeling this air," said Morley, leaning on the car as we slung our packs to the ground, "it mustn't have froze at all last night, I went back and drained the crankcase for nothing."

"Well maybe it did freeze." Morley went over and got motor oil at the lodge store and they told him it hadn't been freezing at all, but one of the warmest nights of the year.

"All that mad trouble for nothing," I said. But we didn't care. We were famished. I said "Let's go to Bridgeport and go in one of those lunchcarts there boy and eat hamburg and potatoes and hot coffee." We drove down the lakeside dirt road in the moonlight, stopped at the inn where Morley returned the blankets, and drove on into the little town and parked on the highway. Poor Japhy, it was here finally I found out his Achilles heel. This little tough guy who wasn't afraid of anything and could ramble around mountains for weeks alone and run down mountains, was afraid of going into a restaurant because the people in it were too well dressed. Morley and I laughed and said "What's the difference? We'll just go in and eat." But Japhy thought the place I chose looked too bourgeois and insisted on going to a more workingman-looking restaurant across the highway. We went in there and it was a desultory place with lazy waitresses letting us sit there five minutes without even bringing a menu. I got mad and said "Let's go to that other place. What you afraid of, Japhy, what's the difference? You may know all about mountains but I know about where to eat." In fact we got a little miffed at each other and I felt bad. But he came to the other place, which was the better restaurant of the two, with a bar on one side, many hunters drinking in the dim cocktail-lounge light, and the restaurant itself a long counter and a lot of tables with whole gay families eating from a very considerable selection. The menu was huge and good: mountain trout and everything. Japhy, I found, was also afraid of spending ten cents more for a good dinner. I went to the bar and bought a glass of port and brought it to our stool seats at the counter (Japhy: "You sure you can do that?") and I kidded Japhy awhile. He felt better now. "That's what's the trouble with you Japhy, you're just an old anarchist scared of society. What difference does it make? Comparisons are odious."

"Well Smith it just looked to me like this place was full of old rich farts and the prices would be too high, I admit it, I'm scared of all this American wealth, I'm just an old bhikku and I got nothin to do with all this high standard of living, goddammit, I've been a poor guy all my life and I can't get used to some things."

"Well your weaknesses are admirable. I'll buy 'em." And we had a raving great dinner of baked potatoes and porkchops and salad and hot buns and blueberry pie and the works. We were so honestly hungry it wasn't funny and it was honest. After dinner we went into a liquor store where I bought a bottle of muscatel and the old proprietor and his old fat buddy looked at us and said "Where you boys been?"

"Climbin Matterhorn out there," I said proudly. They only stared at us, gaping. But I felt great and bought a cigar and lit up and said "Twelve thousand feet and we come down outa there with such an appetite and feelin so good that now this wine is gonna hit us just right." The old men gaped. We were all sunburned and dirty and wildlooking, too. They didn't say anything. They thought we were crazy.

We got in the car and drove back to San Francisco drinking and laughing and telling long stories and Morley really drove beautifully that night and wheeled us silently through the graying dawn streets of Berkeley as Japhy and I slept dead to the world in the seats. At some point or other I woke up like a little child and was told I was home and staggered out of the car and went across the grass into the cottage and opened my blankets and curled up and slept till late the next afternoon a completely dreamless beautiful sleep. When I woke up the next day the veins in my feet were all cleared. I had worked the blood clots right out of existence. I felt very happy.

Analyzing and Discussing the Text

1. Closely analyze the prose style of this narrative. How does Kerouac use language to achieve intimacy with his readers?
2. What is the narrator's initial attitude toward the mountain? Is he especially brave or strong? Is Ray Smith, like Muir, blissfully at-home? Why is this attitude important to our understanding of the narrative?

3. Discuss the relationship between Ray and his two companions, Japhy Ryder and Henry Morley. Why are these relationships important to our understanding of Ray's experience on the mountain?
4. How does the danger of the climb affect Ray's mind? What kinds of thoughts does he have?
5. Explain the Zen saying, "When you get to the top of a mountain, keep climbing."
6. "Then suddenly everything was just like jazz," writes Kerouac. What does Ray Smith realize in this instant?
7. What, according to this narrative, is the value of mountaineering?

Experiencing and Writing About the World

1. Using rambling, informal, unselective, conversational language, tell the story of an experience you once had when you were first too scared to do something, but then went ahead with it and made a psychological breakthrough.
2. Even good friends experience friction and disagreements. Recall a time when you and one or two friends had an argument of some kind. Try to recreate the dialogue and explain how the dispute was eventually resolved. What did you learn from the experience?
3. Consider the implications of Kerouac's comparison of mountain climbing (or mountain *descending*) to jazz. Is it true that you can't fall off a mountain? Write a five-hundred-word meditation on this feeling of indomitability and belonging. Analyze Kerouac's jazz analogy and add to it any other analogies that occur to you.
4. The Matterhorn climb is an unusual experience for Ray Smith, who (in Kerouac's autobiographical novel, *The Dharma Bums*) spends most of his time poesizing and drinking with bohemian Berkeley friends. Consider, in an essay of 500–750 words, the significance of temporarily visiting the mountains and then returning to an urban life-style.

DAVID ROBERTS

Five Days on Mount Huntington

David Roberts (1943–   ), although born in Denver, Colorado, was raised until the age of five in the town of Climax at 11,300 feet, where his father, an astronomer, worked with the world's highest coronograph. Later Roberts's family moved to Boulder, and he developed such varied enthusiasms as baseball, music (playing the cello), and mathematics—not until the end of high school, though, did he become involved in mountain climbing. Yet this interest in climbing grew into a passion at Harvard University, where Roberts majored in math and was an active member of the Harvard Mountaineering Club (HMC). After graduating from Harvard in 1965, Roberts attended graduate school in English at the University of Denver (Ph.D., 1970) before becoming an English professor and director of the outdoors program at Hampshire College (Massachusetts). In 1979 he quit his job at Hampshire and discovered he could make a living as a freelance writer of adventure articles for various national magazines, chiefly *Outside*.

Roberts wrote his first book, *The Mountain of My Fear* (1968), in nine days during spring break of his first year of graduate school—he was twenty-three years old. This book presents a complete account of the 1965 expedition Roberts and three of his HMC friends took to the spectacularly beautiful and dangerous Mount Huntington in Alaska. The following article, first published in *Harvard Mountaineering* in 1967, is one of four articles Roberts wrote about the climb before writing the book. Roberts has since claimed that his "younger mountain writing... was suffused with a romantic intensity that was crucially inarticulate. I felt so keen about the sport that when I tried to communicate the feeling, it came out as forced lyricism." Despite his own critique, Roberts clearly manages even in his early work to capture the emotional turbulence of mountaineering. This essay was reprinted in the collection *Moments of Doubt and Other Mountaineering Essays of David Roberts* (1986). His other books include *Deborah: A Wilderness Narrative* (1970), *Jean Stafford* (1989), *Iceland: Land of the Sagas* (1990), and *The Early Climbs: Deborah & the Mountain of My Fear* (1991).

On July 29, 1965, it dawned perfectly clear again, the fifth such day in a row. In the small tent pitched on a three-foot ledge of ice beneath the huge granite overhang, Don Jensen and Ed Bernd prepared for an early start. They were tired from the strenuous pace of the last few days, but with the weather holding so remarkably, they knew they shouldn't waste an hour. By 7:30 A.M. they had begun climbing up the line of stirrups fixed on the overhang, the crux of the whole west face, which Matt Hale had skillfully led three days before. They were short on pitons and fixed ropes, but they were carrying the bivouac tent, in hopes of a chance to reach the summit of Mount Huntington. They knew that Matt and I would be bringing up equipment from our lower camp that day, but they couldn't afford to wait for it.

It took only a short while for both of them to top the overhang; but as soon as they had, Ed realized he'd forgotten his ice axe. A moment's pause—then they decided to go on without it. They alternated pitches, the leader using Don's axe, the second only a long ice piton. They were on a sixty-degree ice slope, patched with small rock outcroppings. They climbed well, chopping small steps, using only a belay piton at the top of each pitch. On the second, Don could place nothing better than a short soft-iron knife-blade, which he had to tie off. They left fixed ropes on the first three pitches, then saved their last one for the final cliff. Almost before they expected it, they were at the foot of it. Don took the lead. As Ed belayed, facing out, he could survey the throng of unnamed peaks to the south, and look almost straight down to the floor of the Tokositna Glacier, 5000 feet below his feet. Don started up the pitch boldly, swinging on his hands around a corner of the rough, solid granite, and placed a good piton. He used only two more above that, both for aid: the first, a shaky stirrup on a blank spot; the second, a hundred feet above Ed, a tiny knife-blade as a handhold by which he pulled himself up to the top of the cliff. Ed knew it was a magnificent lead, and he must have thrilled at Don's competence. In his turn he led up a steep snow fluting, and suddenly emerged on the bare, sweeping summit icefield. It rose, completely smooth, at a fifty-degree angle toward the mountain's summit. Quickly they climbed four pitches, but the ice was already starting to melt in the early afternoon sun. They stopped at the only rock outcrop in the whole expanse, and pitched the bivouac tent on a tiny ledge. There they sat, cooking a pot of soup on their laps, as the sun slanted toward the western horizon, toward Mounts Hunter and Foraker. As accustomed as they were by now to that sight, it must have seemed almost new this time, with the summit in reach for the first time in a month. After sunset they would start out for it, as soon as the snow had begun to freeze again.

Meanwhile, Matt and I had reached the high tent with supplies. We decided to go on above. Even if we couldn't catch up with Don and Ed, we thought we might safeguard the route for their descent. Matt noticed Ed's axe outside the tent. For a moment we were disturbed; then we decided he had simply forgotten it, so we packed it up to take with us.

Above the big overhang, we could follow the fixed ropes and the steps chopped in the ice. When I reached the top of the second pitch, I could see the anchor piton was poor. I tried to get a new one in, but there were no cracks. At last I clipped in to the eye of the bad piton— a mistake, for the fixed ropes were tied to the hero loop, not to the piton—and belayed Matt up. Matt led on. A few feet above me, he stopped to adjust his crampon. Suddenly he slipped, falling on top of me. Not very alarmed, I put up a hand to ward off his crampons and take the impact. I felt the snow ledge I was standing on break under my feet; then, abruptly, we were both falling. I was still holding Matt on belay; vaguely I realized the piton had probably pulled, but I couldn't understand why the fixed ropes weren't holding us. We gathered speed and began to bounce. Somehow I thought I was being hurt, without pain; and somehow, without fear, I anticipated the fatal plunge. But suddenly we stopped. Matt was still on top of me. Shakily we got to our feet. Now the fear came in little waves of panic. I said, almost hysterically, "We've got to get in a piton." We were standing on little knobs of rock in the middle of the clean, steep slope. Quickly I hammered in three or four pitons, none of them any good, and clipped us in. We were bruised, but not seriously hurt. However, Matt had lost one crampon and both his mittens. One of my crampons had been knocked off, but dangled from my ankle. My glasses had caught on the toe of my boot. Matt thought he had lost his axe, too, but we looked up and saw it planted in the ice where he had stopped to fix the crampon. We also saw the fixed ropes, still intact, even though the piton dangled near my feet. Then what had stopped our fall? Simultaneously we saw, almost unbelieving, that the climbing rope, dragging behind us, had snagged on one of the little knobs of rock, a rounded nubbin about the size of one's knuckle.

The discovery made us almost giddy, with a mixture of fear and astonishment at our luck. We discussed whether we should continue or descend. After a little while we decided to go on. Matt, with only one crampon, couldn't lead; but if I enlarged the right-foot steps for him, he could second. We felt very nervous as we climbed. I deliberately overprotected the route, putting in solid pitons wherever I could. We marvelled at the pitches Don and Ed had led with so few pitons, but began to worry about them a little. We climbed the last cliff as the sun, low in the sky, turned the rock golden brown. The world seemed achingly beautiful, now that we had been reprieved to see it a while longer. The hard climbing seemed to stimulate us to a breathless exhilaration, the obverse face of the panic we had just felt.

As we emerged on the summit icefield, Ed saw us from their bivouac ledge. He let out a shout. Quickly we joined them, though the slope was in dangerously bad shape, and I had to use two rock pitons in the ice for anchors. Our reunion was poignant. We kidded Ed about leaving his axe; but when we told them about our near-accident, they seemed genuinely upset. Don was confident the summit could be reached that night. For weeks we had climbed, even camped, in separate pairs, meeting only as our ropes occasionally crossed while we switched leaders. Now we might climb toward the summit together; it would be a perfect finale.

Around 10 P.M. we roped together and started up. Don led in the almost pitch-dark; I came second; Matt followed me; and Ed brought up the rear. We were inexpressibly happy to be together. This silent climb in the night to the top of the mountain seemed a superb way to share our friendship. Our excitement was contagious. We were very tired, and yet the sky was full of stars, and the air was breathlessly still. Silhouetted in the constellation Cassiopeia, Don was leading; below me, Matt and Ed competently paced their movement to fit Don's.

Shortly after midnight we reached the summit ridge. Here we could walk continuously, but only with great care, for on one hand in the eerie darkness the drop was 5000 feet, 6000 feet on the other. Don could not be sure how large the cornices were that overlooked the Ruth Glacier; not, that is, until he stuck his foot through one. He pulled it back and retreated to my ice axe belay. He was near exhaustion from a long day of leading; I took over from him.

There remained only two vertical snow cliffs, precariously carved by a year's winds. I attacked them right on the cornice, reassured by the weight of the other three belaying me. The hollow snow required brutal efforts, and took almost the last of my strength. But finally I got up them both. Then it was only three easy pitches to the summit. The light was returning; in the northeast an orange rim of flame was sweeping the tundra. As we reached the very top, the sun rose.

We were extremely tired. We sat, listless, just below the summit, full of a dazed sense of well-being, but too tired for any celebration. Ed had brought a firecracker all the way to the top from some roadside stand in Wyoming; but we urged him not to set it off for fear it would knock the cornices loose.

It had taken us more than a month to climb Huntington's west face, a route some people had said was impossible. But people have always said things like that—our achievement had a much higher personal importance to us. It had been very difficult; the climbing had been spectacular; we had grown so discouraged that we almost abandoned the effort. But now this perfect finish, at dawn on a splendid day, together! I remember thinking even then that this was probably the best climb I could ever do, because things work out that well so rarely.

We talked to each other there, but the summit was for each of us a private experience. I do not know what Don, or Matt, or Ed felt. After an hour and a half, we started down. All the descent was anticlimactic. We wanted to hurry before the sun could melt the snow on the summit icefield. Below the bivouac tent we split again into two ropes of two. I realized how fatigued I was when I found it nearly impossible to swing out on rappel to retrieve some pitons. Finally, on the edge of exhaustion, we rappelled the overhang into our highest camp.

The four of us crowded into the two-man tent, pitched narrow to fit on its ledge of ice. There were still thirty-five pitches below us, sixteen to our other tent. At last we could relax, but we were terribly cramped and uncomfortable. We laughed and cheered and ate all the delicacies from our food box. We even managed to sleep a bit. But the weather was deteriorating, after five perfect days. In the late afternoon Ed suggested that he and I descend to the other tent that night. I agreed.

We were off by 9:40 P.M. A storm was evidently on its way in, and the air was relatively warm. The snow, consequently, was not in very good condition. As it grew dark, I occasionally shouted directions to Ed, who had been over these pitches only once, compared to my five times. I still felt tired, but Ed was in an exuberant mood. He said he felt he "could climb all night." We were being extra-cautious, it seemed, but this was easy going with the fixed ropes; it was even fun. We unroped to set up a rappel on the twenty-sixth pitch, a fine lead up a vertical inside corner that Don had made about two weeks before. Just before midnight on this last day of July, we chatted as Ed placed the carabiner and wound the rope around his body. We were talking about other rappels, about the first ones he had done at the Quincy Quarries back in Boston.

I said, "Just this pitch, and it's practically walking to camp."

"Yeah," he answered.

He leaned back. I heard an abrupt, jerking sound, and saw Ed's crampons spark the rock. Suddenly he was falling free below me. Without a word he fell, hit the ice fifty feet below, slid and bounced out of sight over a cliff. I shouted, but I doubt he even heard me. Suddenly he was gone. I knew he must have fallen 4000 feet, to the upper basin of the Tokositna, where no one had ever been.

I was alone. The night was empty. I shouted for Ed, but all that answered me was a mindless trickle of water near my face. I shouted for help to Don and Matt, then listened to more silence: they were too far above to hear me. I could not believe Ed was gone, and yet I could not believe anything else. I could feel the sense of shock wrapping me, like a blanket; I was seized with an urgency to do something. My first thought was to go down to look for Ed, but I put it out of my mind at once. For a moment I thought only of going up. Then it struck me that Ed was undeniably dead; therefore there was no emergency and I had to continue down.

I was without a rope, but I cut off a hank of fixed rope to tie in to the ropes below, and managed to climb down the vertical pitch. From there it was easy—but I went too fast, despite telling myself to slow down.

I reached the tent within twenty minutes after the accident. The sense of shock seemed to gather and hit me as I arrived. The tent was full of water (Matt and I had left the back door open!) Numbly I sponged it out and got in my sleeping bag. I took two sleeping pills. I could not figure out what had happened. Somehow the carabiner had come loose, for both it and the rope had disappeared with Ed. But no piton had pulled, no jerk had come on the fixed ropes. Out of all the mechanical explanations, all implausible, all irrelevant to our loss, emerged only the fact that it had happened. Ed was gone.

The pills and my tiredness put me to sleep. In the morning I woke with a dull sense of dread. The storm was continuing, and it had begun to snow. All that day I anticipated the arrival of Matt and Don, though I knew they would be taking their time. I became constantly nervous—what if something had happened to them, too? The minutes passed with agonizing slowness. I caught myself holding my breath, listening for a sound from them. When nightfall on August 1 came without their arrival, I was terribly disappointed. Again I took sleeping pills. Again I slept in a drugged stupor. The next day was the same; the same white-out and lightly falling snow. I grew afraid of the 3000-foot drop beyond the door of the tent. I tied myself in each time I had to go outside the tent. My balance seemed poor, my hearing painfully acute. I simply waited.

Meanwhile, Don and Matt had relaxed, slept well, eaten well. They had talked about the wonderful summit day while they waited for the weather to break clear again. At last, in the afternoon of August 2, they decided to pack up and descend. The pitches were in bad shape, and their heavy packs made for awkward climbing. In places the fixed ropes were coated with a solid sheath of ice.

They could see Ed's and my tracks below; and, though they could not see the tent itself, they could see that there were no tracks below it. This vaguely disturbed them, but they could think of no real cause for worry. Don noticed on the twenty-sixth pitch that some of the fixed rope had been cut off; this seemed very strange to him, but there were tracks below the pitch. . . . They were getting down with reasonable speed. Matt was going first. As he rounded a corner of the rock and looked down, all his fears dissolved: he saw the familiar orange tent and my head sticking out of it. He shouted a cheery hello, but I seemed not to have heard it in the wind. Don came in sight, then, and shouted another greeting. Again, I didn't answer. Matt was almost down to the tent. My silence seemed a bit peculiar, but surely—then he looked at the snow platform beside the tent, and saw that there was only one pack.

They took it bravely. They could understand the accident even less well than I. I had been afraid to tell them, but I leaned on them now, and they took the weight of my shock and helped me hold it.

We crowded together again and spent the night in the tent. The next day the storm increased. Around 7 P.M. we decided to complete the descent. We thought it should take about two more hours. It actually took eight.

The moment we got outside the tent, the whipping wind numbed us. We had a great deal of trouble chopping out the tent, and at last ripped out the corner of it. We had only one rope for the three of us, which made using the fixed ropes terribly clumsy. Matt had only one crampon, so he went in the middle. We tried placing him at various places along the rope, but none worked smoothly.

The conditions were hideous. A layer of new snow slid treacherously off the old ice. It grew dark quickly. We were shivering constantly, and had to shout at the tops of our voices to hear each other. Soon we couldn't even see the slope at our feet. We had to follow the ice-coated fixed ropes by feel, pulling them out of the crusted snow. I felt a continual dread of the sheer drop beneath us. We had three falls on the way down, but managed to catch each one with the fixed ropes.

It was the worst, most frightening climbing I have ever done. At last, in the early morning, we reached the last rappel. We slid down the ropes, out of the fierce gale to the blessedly flat, safe glacier below. Then we pulled down the rappel rope, cutting ourselves off for good from our route, from the summit, from the long, wonderful days of climbing, from Ed. We trudged back to our snow cave. Five days later Don Sheldon flew us out.

Thus an accident that made no sense, except in some trivial, mechanical way, robbed us suddenly of Ed, and of most of the joy of our accomplishment. Don, Matt, and I are left instead with a wilderness of emotions, with memories that blur too quickly of a friend who died too young. The shock and fear we lived with during the last days of our expedition all too easily now obscure the bright image of one perfect day—the summit day—when we seemed to work flawlessly together. Should we have found a safer way to become friends? Perhaps we could not. Perhaps the risk itself was what it took to bind us.

Analyzing and Discussing the Text

1. This essay begins *in medias res*—in the middle of things. How does this affect your response to the narrative? What "blanks" do you have to fill in? Does this serve to focus your attention?
2. Do the early climbing scenes resemble the climbing passages in Blum's essay? Roberts seems to place special emphasis on safety precautions; why is this significant in light of the rest of the essay?

3. Roberts recalls after the first accident that "The world seemed achingly beautiful, now that we had been reprieved to see it a while longer." Why does the accident accent the beauty of the place? Can you relate this to Sanders's point in "Cloud Crossings" (later in this chapter)?

4. As the four climbers near the summit of Mount Huntington, Roberts writes, "We were inexpressibly happy to be together." Explain how the sense of achievement contributes to the feeling of friendship. How does this passage also set up the emotional blow that would occur during the descent?

5. "All the descent was anticlimactic," writes Roberts as the climbers leave the summit. Explain the irony of this statement.

6. Does Roberts manage to capture the suddenness of Ed's accident, the ache of loss that he felt? Examine this passage. How does Roberts describe his own emotions?

Experiencing and Writing About the World

1. Roberts concludes his essay with the statement: "Should we have found a safer way to become friends? Perhaps we could not. Perhaps the risk itself was what it took to bind us." Have you ever done something risky, something dangerous, that ended up creating a deep bond between you and another person? Recount this experience and explore the connection between the risk itself and the human bond that resulted from it.

2. Consider some of the experiences in your life that have entailed a certain degree of risk, perhaps even the possibility of death. Was it worth the risk just to have the experience of skiing down a dangerous slope, scaling an exposed cliff, or hiking solo for a week? What about walking through a city park at night or, in the era of AIDS, neglecting "safe sex" procedures? How do we even begin to assess the risks and benefits of our various activities, either in daily life or in pursuit of adventure? Tell the story of a time when something went wrong during a risky activity (mountaineering, hang-gliding, hitchhiking, motorcycle riding) and present this story (perhaps with additional generalized commentary) as an explanation of the activity to someone who cares about your well-being but is likely to have trouble understanding why you did what you did.

3. Analyze Roberts's exposure to death on Mount Huntington in light of one or more of the essays on death in the "Fecundity and Mortality" chapter of this anthology. In particular, consider in an analytical essay how writers like Lewis Thomas and John Daniel would response to Roberts's account of disaster and loss.

ARLENE BLUM

From Annapurna: A Woman's Place

Arlene Blum (1945–   ) was born in Davenport, Iowa, and grew up mostly in Chicago, Illinois. She began climbing as a student at Reed College in Portland, Oregon, when she took mountain climbing to fulfill her physical education requirement; as a chemistry major at Reed (B.A., 1966), she wrote her senior thesis on "fumarole emanations" (volcanic gases) from Mount Hood, east of Portland. After a year at the Massachusetts Institute of Technology, she went on to earn a doctorate in biophysical chemistry from the University of California at Berkeley in 1971 and to teach and do research at Stanford, Wellesley, and Berkeley. Blum's research helped to ban tris, a cancer-causing chemical that was used in children's sleepwear. Her interest in mountain climbing has frequently led her beyond the continental United States: in 1970, Blum served as deputy leader of the first all-women's expedition to Mount McKinley (in Alaska); in 1971–1972, she organized and led "Endless Winter," a fifteen-month, round-the-world mountaineering trip that included major ascents throughout Africa and Asia; in 1976, she participated in the American Bicentennial Expedition to Mount Everest; and in 1981–1982, she was the coleader of the Great Himalayan Traverse, which covered a stretch of 2,400 miles from Bhutan to Ladakh. From 1983 to 1988, Blum organized and taught a Himalayan travel and trekking course through the Center for South Asian Studies at Berkeley. She went on a three-hundred-mile trek across the Alps in 1987 with her infant daughter. Blum devotes much of her time now to presenting motivational lectures and leadership workshops, and she serves on the board of directors of the Earth Island Institute. Her second book, *Women in High Places: A History of Women in Mountaineering*, is currently in progress. In 1984 she became one of only eight members (including Amelia Earhart, Margaret Mead, and Mary Leakey) to receive the Society of Women Geographer's Gold Medal for Outstanding Achievement.

The following narrative is a chapter from Blum's 1980 book, *Annapurna: A Woman's Place*, an account of the American Women's Himalayan Expedition, which resulted, on October 15, 1978, in the first successful ascent by women of one of the highest mountains in the world; two of the women climbers and two sherpas (Nepalese climbing guides) made it to the summit. This particular section of the narrative discusses a crucial moment in the expedition: the selection of a small group of climbers to make the final push to the top. Blum's account shows the uniquely democratic approach to this decision taken by the expedition members. In fact, the very style of the narrative, the mixture of Blum's authorial voice with excerpts from the other climbers' diaries, suggests that the expedition was a cooperative effort, markedly different from traditional, all-male expeditions that were run like military procedures with a single "general" making most decisions himself. The use of diary entries also allows the powerful emotions and the physical conditions on the mountain to emerge prominently in the text; the narratives of Bird, Muir, Kerouac, Sanders, and Roberts, for all of their energy and drama, seem detached and luxuriously reflective by comparison. Blum says that her focus in *Annapurna* was on the climbers' motivations and interactions: "the people story is more important than the mountain story."

[Plans and Changes]

October 3–8

Arriving back up at Camp II, I was greeted with the welcome news that Irene and Piro, rather than the Sherpas, had taken over the lead above Camp III. They were making good progress on the 400-foot ice step which was the first major obstacle on the route to Camp IV.

Piro's diary records the details:

> Irene and I sat in our little tent at IIIa for four days waiting for the storm to end. When it finally cleared, we spent the next day breaking trail through thigh-deep powder up to Camp III, planning to move up and start leading the next day. Then Ang and Mingma came up the trail we had broken and announced that they were going to stay at Camp III. "Sherpa lead. Climb mountain. In three days summit."
>
> We tried to explain to them that the steep ice above Camp III was ours, that we had been waiting for five days to lead it. No luck. They just smiled at us and settled in for the night up there. We stomped back down to Camp IIIa, showering blessings on all Sherpas, their mothers, nannies, grandmothers, and unborn children.
>
> So we weren't too sad when Ang Pemba got altitude sick the next day, and he and Mingma had to come down. The lead of the ice step was to be ours after all.
>
> October 4: Morning windy and incredibly cold. Irene led out on a nasty, steep traverse on rotten snow, and came to a very awkward corner of steep ice deeply covered with powder. She spent a long time getting protection in, finally managed to place a small deadman high up on the left, then oozed around the corner onto more stable snow. Every once in a while her ice axe would disappear into a hole—better you than me, I thought. She brought me up, and I had a chance to lead a short, steep pitch on ice, then an easy slog to the mouth of a steep rock and ice chimney. At first I was nice and warm, even though I was out of the sun by a few yards. When Irene climbed up to me and took the gear for the

next lead, she looked up into the chimney and grunted. I was grinning the grin of the righteous because I had done my bit for a while.

The chimney had vertical walls of hard blue ice and a sloping back. Irene put her crampons into the back and used her hands on the sides to jam and slither up to the top. She tried to put in an ice screw, but the ice was too brittle. Finally she got a sling around an icicle for protection.

The grin froze on my face as I stood there belaying Irene. After fifteen minutes I was barely comfortable, then cold and finally shivering and shaking. I didn't dare make a move to put on more clothes. I was thinking about death by hypothermia when Irene gave her "belay on" call. I tried to move fast to get warm and scrambled up the chimney admiring Irene's lead. As I poked my head out at the other end, the sun hit my face and my belayer took a casual picture of my arrival. We both felt good until we looked at the next ice pitch—not too steep but apparently very rotten.

I started out and found that the ice was easier than I had feared—I actually had more trouble with deep snow on the steep upper part just under the rim of the plateau. The usually uncomplaining Irene yelled plaintively up to me, "What's taking you so long?" After considerable floundering in the deep snow, even using the dog-paddle technique to get ahead, I got a picket in and brought Irene up. She led off to the plateau. No sooner had she disappeared than I found that I was getting hypoglycemic. Boy, P. K., I thought, what a winner. First you get cold, then hungry—next thing you know, you'll be calling for your mommy. I felt disgusted with myself and almost oblivious to some of the most spectacular scenery I'd ever seen. Then I saw Irene poke her nose over the edge of the plateau. The ice step had been climbed.

The next day Piro went down to Camp II, and Annie and Vera K. joined Irene in the lead on the plateau. The three of them put in a long, strenuous day plowing through very deep snow and finally reached the foot of another, shorter ice step where fixed lines were needed again. The next day Irene descended, and Mingma and Chewang came up to help lead the terrain beyond the plateau—short, steep ice pitches alternating with deep snow.

Annie, Vera K., Chewang, and Mingma put in two long hard days of climbing to establish Camp IV. Vera K. described the first day in her diary:

> We start early, have a long way to go with heavy packs. Annie and I carry the wands—a particularly awkward load. We pass the site of the Dutch Camp IV which is too low—we want to put our Camp IV much higher. At about 3:30 in the afternoon we have used up all our fixed rope, and Chewang in particular is disappointed because he wants so badly to get there today. I explain it is too late, but he is inconsolable. Finally, we give up and go down, knowing we'll reach the camp tomorrow for sure. Back at Camp III the four of us cook dinner together and talk until very late. We make ice cream and set it outside to cool, and we joke forever about how a baby yeti is going to come and eat it.

The next day Mingma easily and elegantly led a nearly vertical 40-foot ice wall, and the four climbers reached Camp IV at 23,000 feet early in the afternoon. The campsite was a small platform in the shadow of an enormous serac. It was a cold, cramped place but with a spectacular view. Once there, they found they had used up all of their anchors, so Annie contributed her ice axe for the last fixed anchor, and she had to descend the plateau without an axe.

With Camp IV established, the question of the day at Camp II was: "Who's going to be on the summit teams?" I invariably answered that the final decision would best be made at the last minute, because circumstances often change summit plans right up to the end. I told the story of our Everest climb, on which the two climbers who reached the summit on the first team had originally been slated for later teams. In fact, one of them had been so discouraged by his exclusion from the first team that he had almost given up and gone home.

I had assumed all along that by the time we were ready for the summit push, natural selection would make the choice of the summit teams obvious. On many expeditions, after months of hard work at high altitude, some climbers are too tired physically or psychologically to try for the top. But there had been little attrition on this climb. Indeed, most of the members were growing stronger and more determined by the day.

Physiology may have been a factor in this. The average woman's body is 25 percent fat, while an average man's is only 15 percent fat. This extra fat is an energy reserve that can help women to remain strong and healthy under the most severe conditions; it is said to give women a higher tolerance for cold, exposure, and starvation. Joan Ullyot, in her book *Women's Running*, notes, "Among the survivors of shipwrecks, mountaineering, and similar disasters, women generally outnumber men . . . endurance rather than power seems to be their natural strength." Women excel in athletic activities such as long-distance swimming in cold water, where their fat provides insulation and can also be mobilized for energy. It has been suggested that women may have superior ability to utilize fat for energy and consequently do relatively better at events that demand stamina more than sheer power.

Whatever the explanation, after forty days on Annapurna, seven of the ten members—everyone but Joan, Liz, and me—were still eager to try for the top. Though I was delighted that we had such depth on the team, it did mean that the summit decision would not be made by attrition, and I spent hours considering how two or three summit teams could best be made up of the seven eager climbers.

The women could be grouped in pairs: Margi and Annie, Vera W. and Alison, Vera K. and Irene were natural combinations since they had climbed together, were close friends, and had told me they hoped to be on a summit team with the other. This left only Piro, who got along with everyone and could climb with any of the three pairs. No one could be eliminated from consideration on the basis of not being fit. What Vera W. might lack in speed, for example, she certainly compensated for in determination.

The vital psychological factors were harder to assess. No one was clearly unfit for the top, although Margi had been severely shaken by the avalanches. She had quickly recovered from the illness that stopped her from continuing to lead the rib with Liz and joined Vera W. and Alison to carry a load to Camp III. But a few days later, when it was her turn to carry a second load to the camp, Margi was very uncertain about crossing the avalanche slope another time. She left with a load but was back after a few minutes, saying she had forgotten her toothbrush and had returned for it. It took me a while to realize that she was joking to cover her nervousness. She had walked up, taken a look at the avalanche chute, and turned around. Margi and I discussed her misgivings about continuing to climb.

"Remember how before the trip you told us that expedition climbing was boring?" she asked. "You said the hardest thing is going over the same dull slopes day after day carrying heavy loads? But this trip is a thrill a minute. It's certainly not monotonous with that ice hanging over us all the time. I think I've had enough. I want to go down and take a break, think about whether I really want to climb this thing. I'd rather carry loads between Camps I and II for a few days than face the avalanches."

"Fine, Margi," I agreed. "Go down and make up your mind about whether you want to keep climbing."

"But I don't feel comfortable doing that either," she went on. "Alison thinks it's not fair for me to get out of carrying my share of the loads to Camp III. She says she's doing carries to Camp III every other day, even though she's afraid, and that if I want to climb the mountain, I should too. She says that I should do things in the proper way."

"There's no 'proper way,' " I reassured her, "You should do what you feel comfortable doing. It doesn't matter that much if you don't carry one of your loads to Camp III. Now go on down and relax and try not to worry."

Three days later Margi was back up from Camp I looking calm and confident. She had made her decision.

"I want to go on up," she told me, "even though I'm terrified of the avalanches, I can't resist. I want to climb this mountain, see the view, and find out how I feel up there."

I had to give Margi credit for a lot of courage. On other trips I had seen climbers pass their fears on to others in the party and so undermine group morale. Margi admitted she was frightened but went on anyway.

Margi's friend, Annie, was climbing strongly and accepting the avalanches without complaint. I wondered if part of her calm was based on Yeshi's support. Annie had taken to helping him cook our meals, and we could hear them talking together in the cook tent until all hours of the night. They made an attractive couple, but I was concerned that their romance might strain relations between members and Sherpas. The Sherpas were very conscious of the relationship between Annie and Yeshi and apparently couldn't understand why the rest of us were not similarly inclined. Marie complained that the Sherpas kept looking at her in a way that made her feel very uncomfortable.

I had asked Annie several times to wait until we got back to Kathmandu to be with Yeshi, but she was noncommittal. Otherwise, she was proving to be an ideal expedition member: unselfish, uncomplaining, strong, and hard-working.

Vera K. was another member whose strengths were becoming more evident the higher we climbed. Annie told me that when they were together at Camp III, Vera K. made sure that she and Annie put in four consecutive days of hard work. After a grueling day Annie would sometimes just want to go to sleep, but Vera would insist that they melt snow and eat dinner. The peculiar mannerisms we had all noticed in Vera K. at lower altitudes faded away higher up, where she was solid and amiable.

Irene, too, had shed her self-doubt and was certain she wanted to try for the top. After all her agonizing about the risk and about her own abilities, she and Piro had spent five days sitting out a storm at Camp IIIa and then several more leading the steep terrain above the rib. Both had come back full of enthusiasm for the summit.

Piro returned to Camp II a day before Irene, who stayed up at Camp III to film. Generally Piro worked hard and talked little, but coming down from the rib, she was positively voluble.

"It's fantastic up there," she beamed. "Leading that steep ice step was one of the best things I've ever done. I'm so glad Irene and I got the lead from the Sherpas. It was everything climbing should be—just two climbers working out a route, good weather, solid ice, spectacular surroundings. The pleasure was so intense that it more than made up for all those days of waiting out the storm."

I asked Piro how she and Irene had managed during their long confinement.

"No problem. We decided early on that we were only going to have what we were wearing and the two sleeping bags inside the tent, and we didn't cook much. We just melted snow whenever there was a break in the storm. For entertainment we had ice avalanches, powder avalanches, and rockfalls. And Christy's fine jokes.

"Things would have been better with more to eat, though. On the third day we had to go out and repitch the tent. By that time our body heat had melted the snow beneath us, and the tent floor was like two bathtubs. We began shoveling snow to level the surface underneath the tent, but a couple of strokes sent us sprawling into the snow gasping. That pushed the panic button. Those three days of lying around not eating must have weakened us. We dove back into the tent and started scarfing those terrible candy bars; then we cooked up the last tuna dinner. After we ate all that stuff, we went back out to repitch the tent. Damn hard work in thigh-deep powder."

Piro coughed deeply. "And we both had these high-altitude coughs most of the time and had to take codeine to sleep. Then, of course, we had to deal with the side effects of codeine, like constipation. Trying to contend with that at 21,000 feet with a fresh wind whipping the new snow around wasn't fun. But it was all worth it."

Physiological studies have shown that climbers deteriorate physically and mentally when they spend prolonged periods above 19,000 feet, but Piro and Irene didn't seem to have suffered unduly. They were obviously strong contenders for the first summit team.

Vera W. and Alison were less happy about the way the climb was progressing. Vera W. had not led as much as she had hoped to and was very conscious of being somewhat slower than most of the others. Alison had done some of the best leading but was still dissatisfied with the style of the climb and extremely concerned about the avalanche danger. In a letter to Janusz, her husband, she wrote:

> Life here is a constant game of Russian roulette. It's the most dangerous mountain I've been on. Between Camp II (a relatively safe site, although we sometimes get shaken by avalanche winds) and the foot of the Dutch Rib, you have to "run the gauntlet" for over an hour on the way up. Each side of the rib is a great gully topped by ice cliffs, and the floor of each gully is polished green ice with some bare rocks, testifying to the frequency with which they are swept from above. Threatening our route is the great Sickle couloir above.
>
> Vera W. and I are carrying to III again tomorrow, a prospect I don't enjoy. It's a hard day. Yesterday we left at 7:00 A.M. and got back at 6:00 P.M., and the worst thing is the continual avalanche fear. Hopefully, if we survive tomorrow, it's the last time we'll have to go up and back. Next time we'll go to stay at III and carry to IV and on to V and the summit. If the weather holds.

With dogged persistence, if little pleasure, Vera and Alison made the dangerous carry to Camp III every other day. Besides aiding the progress of the climb, their hard work was a means to a personal end: they were counting on being chosen for summit teams.

Eventually I worked out what I considered a fair and flexible strategy for the summit attempts, though I had not yet decided who should be on the teams. During the 6:00 P.M. radio call on October 8, the day Camp IV was established, I presented the general plan to the members and Sherpas at all the camps.

"The first summit team will consist of three members using oxygen," I began. "The second will be two members and two Sherpas, but there may not be oxygen available for them. A third team is a possibility if anyone else still wants to try for the top. The first team will make their attempt between October 14 and 16; the second, two days later; and the third, two days after that. Of course, this plan may have to be changed in case of further storms or other problems."

At Camp II the reactions were varied. Alison, for one, was not pleased. "I think all the members of the team—all nine of us now that Liz has left—should have a reasonable chance for the summit. Your plan gives only five members positions in the first and second teams. And I doubt there will be a third. What about the rest of us? Everyone should have some guarantee of being on a summit team after they've risked their lives doing carries to Camp III."

"I can't guarantee anyone that they will be on a summit team," I responded. "If you feel you need that promise to do carries to Camp III, then you shouldn't do them."

Margi said, "If anyone gets to the summit, even if it's not me, I'll be really happy."

"Of course, so will I," Alison agreed. "I just want everyone to feel they have a chance for the top. I think we ought to have three members and one Sherpa on the second attempt. Members deserve places much more than Sherpas. We've invested so much more in this expedition than they have. And there should definitely be a third team so everyone gets a chance."

"I'm sorry," I said, "but there's no way all nine of us are going to try for the top. Joan isn't acclimatized enough after her illness, and ever since the avalanche at Camp I, I haven't cared to try. That leaves seven at the very most."

The other members seemed willing to go along with my plan. But Lopsang, who was feeling better and had come up to Camp II to discuss the matter with me, objected strongly.

"No, bara memsahib, bad plan. Too many people going to summit. Annapurna is very dangerous. When one member and one Sherpa reach summit, then we all are very happy and go home. Everything okay."

"No, Lopsang. All the members want to climb to the top, and many Sherpas do also. They've all worked very hard. Before we go home, we must give them a chance."

"No, bara memsahib, one member, one Sherpa enough. You are leader. You are responsible for what your members do. You must tell members that everyone cannot climb mountain. They will do what you say."

I smiled, thinking of the problems Lopsang had in controlling the Sherpas. "Lopsang, you cannot make Sherpas do what you want. I cannot make members do what I want." We both laughed.

I could see Lopsang's point of view, though, just as I could see Alison's. Lopsang was sick and tired of this climb and wanted to go home before anyone was hurt. I was inclined to agree with him but respected the team's request that everyone who wanted to would get a chance for the summit. The weather was stable, and snow conditions were getting better daily; it was beginning to seem possible that everybody might get that chance.

The climbers contending for summit teams were not the only ones who were adapting well to the altitude. Joan, Christy, and the film crew were also getting stronger all the time. Since that morning at Camp II when, with tears in their eyes, they had filmed the emotional scene around the breakfast table, it was clear that Dyanna and Marie were truly part of the team. Subsequently they had also managed to shoot some excellent climbing footage. The first time they had ventured onto the ice by Base Camp, they had been very nervous—it was their first glacier after all. But now they were walking confidently among the enormous crevasses of the Annapurna North Glacier. After the avalanche above Camp I that had nearly buried them, they had naturally been afraid. But they were professionals and needed climbing footage high on the mountain; they particularly wanted to film us climbing the steep slopes of the Dutch Rib. So they suppressed their fear of avalanches and climbed up to and above Camp II to film. For these two young women who had never climbed before, this achievement was as great as reaching the summit would be for the rest of us.

Marie and Dyanna had already tried unsuccessfully to get up to Camp II a few days earlier. When they finally made it, after dragging their unwilling bodies through the deep snow and the heat, they were ecstatic. "We did the hardest things we've ever done today—to think we were dragged through it all by women!" Dyanna marveled. "And I just love being roped," she continued.

It had never occurred to me that being on a rope represented anything more than security, so I asked her why.

"Well, even though it's awkward for everyone to have to move at the same pace, your energies are linked. You're 75 feet apart, but you're connected. You have to be sensitive to the movement of the others on your rope and notice when someone is slowing down because of a hill or difficult part. The movement of the line in the snow tells you about your partners and their movements, and that makes me feel good."

"I can't decide whether I love climbing or hate it," Marie commented. "I'm in ecstacy over the beauty but exhausted by the hard work, and I'm terrified of the avalanches."

"Those five hours slogging up here were like the five-hour drive to our summer vacation when I was a little kid—endless." Dyanna sighed. "But we're here now, and we'll stay and do what we have to. But, God, am I afraid of the avalanches."

Dyanna's diary reflects how she and Marie reacted to being high up on Annapurna.

> I was exhausted and weak and afraid. But when you must you must. Learn not to resist the inevitable, not to bitch and moan, just to start the works rolling. We got all our gear ready, and by 3:30 in the afternoon the brave but humble film crew made it to its goal—19,000 feet. I was glad I wasn't expected to go any higher or farther. We felt great pride in having made it, despite exhaustion.
>
> Got one mag of Irene and Piro on the steepest part of the ice wall, and then we hustled down before frostbite set in. Being up there made me want to yell. It was so stunning. Coming down I noticed how colorful Camp II is: orange and blue dome tents, bird-shaped yellow and blue tents, the green mess tent, brightly colored sleeping bags draped everywhere.
>
> We slept in mounds of fiberfill and down that night. Nothing was familiar like at Camp I, our cozy home. New tent, new tent-door zippers, no flashlight, where on earth is the pee bottle, how to avoid stepping on someone's head, endless coughing, claustrophobia, tossing Marie, and the dreaded snow falling thicker and thicker all night. But morning finally came and the snow stopped and an avalanche hadn't swept us away.

Even after their miserable night, Marie and Dyanna decided to go up to 19,000 feet a second time to get more footage of the climbers on the rib. Dyanna wrote:

> Vera K. and Annie were anxious to get across the chute before it got too late. By sheer will I tore up the ridge the last 500 feet and managed to delay them until I got the rig set up.
>
> Damned if we didn't shoot synch at 19,000 feet in this incredible place. We really did it—our very best.

They certainly did. Many people were incredulous that these two nonclimbers were able to become part of the expedition, climb to 19,000 feet, and shoot synchronized film and sound the whole time. Their success reinforced my belief that mountain climbing is not just the province of a few superb athletes, but can be enjoyed by anyone for whom the mountains hold an attraction.

Joan had recovered from her pneumonia and pleurisy and had been slowly but persistently conditioning. Although she would not be strong enough for the summit, she was diligently carrying loads to Camps I and II, helping to manage the lower camps, and generally doing whatever she could to make the climb run smoothly.

And Christy was another success story. It was hard to imagine that she was the same woman who had been so grumpy on the steaming trek. Up here in the snow she was in her element, eyes shining and cheeks rosy. I don't know how, living on the plains of Kansas and Iowa for most of her life, she had discovered her love for high places. Four years ago Christy had never set foot on a mountain. Now here she was at 19,000 feet on Annapurna in Nepal, and couldn't have been happier.

Joan, who had just turned fifty, and Christy, now thirty-eight, were striking demonstrations that age was no barrier to achievement. Many women have told me they felt they were too old to take up a strenuous activity like climbing. These women are probably unduly influenced by the competitive versions of sports like swimming and gymnastics, in which the participants are in their early teens. But women of all ages can enjoy these sports, if they can avoid becoming intimidated by the media's emphasis on youth. Mountaineering and hiking, too, can be enjoyed at any age. The Mazamas, a Portland-based climbing club, have sponsored well-attended climbs of Mount Hood in Oregon for people sixty years and older. Climbers tend to keep active all their lives and to be more alive because of it.

Both physically and psychologically, then, all the members had adapted well to life high on Annapurna. This was, in itself, an achievement, and I wondered again why more women did not have the opportunity to climb the highest mountains. Clearly, the reasons for the paucity of women on expeditions are more psychological than physical. What are considered admirable traits in men—assertiveness, independence, ambition, competitiveness—are still often seen as undesirable in women. Yet most successful climbers, male or female, possess these characteristics.

Our leadership qualities need to be developed as well. For example, it was difficult for me to go against my upbringing, which taught me to be accommodating, soothing, and likable, when I had to be a strong leader. Until there are confident women leaders, women will have to depend on men to invite them on expeditions—and this is unfortunately rare. So a major requirement is to believe in ourselves and in other women.

What we had already accomplished on Annapurna, both individually and as a team, was an example we could point to with pride. I remembered Liz's words at breakfast on the morning after the flag raising: "In my mind this expedition has been a success even if we don't get any higher."

Analyzing and Discussing the Text

1. Explain the competition (recorded in Piro's diary) between the women climbers and their Sherpa guides.
2. Compare Piro's description of Annapurna with Isabella Bird's description of Long's Peak. Does Piro find Annapurna "sublime"? What aspects of the mountain does her account emphasize?
3. What is the effect on the narrative as a whole when Blum quotes lengthy passages from her companions' diaries?
4. How do the members of the expedition decide who will make the final ascent to the top of Annapurna? Do the women interact with each other differently from the way you would expect male climbers to behave?
5. Blum devotes considerable attention to describing the human relationships during the expedition. How does this affect the climbing narrative? Does it significantly alter the grim, summit-oriented focus that we have encountered so far in some of the other mountaineering narratives?
6. Blum quotes Alison's letter to her husband, in which she says, "Life here is a constant game of Russian roulette. It's the most dangerous mountain I've been on." Does the climb strike you as an enriching experience? What are the benefits and drawbacks of such rigorous, life-threatening climbing at high altitudes?
7. Discuss the significance of Dyanna's comments on "being roped." Compare this to Jack Kerouac's jazz analogy.
8. Discuss the ideological conclusions of this essay. Do they follow convincingly from the narrative?

Experiencing and Writing About the World

1. Have you ever attempted an excursion with a large group of people? Perhaps a school trip or a family vacation? What about an Outward Bound course? Recount this experience and pay particular attention to the way group members behaved toward each other and to the group's approach to making decisions.
2. If possible, take a new climbing or backpacking trip with a group of students. Encourage everyone to keep a diary of some kind during the trip. Afterwards collect the diaries and use them to produce a collagelike, multiperspective account of the excursion.
3. Write an essay analyzing Blum's performance as both leader and chronicler of the expedition, based on this excerpt from the book *Annapurna: A Woman's Place*. What are her attitudes and strategies, and how effective are the latter?

4. Do men and women have similar or different ways of responding to nature in general or to dangerous natural situations in particular? Using Blum's essay and several others (by both men and women), prepare an essay of your own in which you argue either for or against the idea of gender-linked responses.

SCOTT RUSSELL SANDERS

Cloud Crossing

For biographical information, see the headnote for "Listening to Owls" in Part One, Chapter Three.

Scott Russell Sanders writes in "Cloud Crossing" (collected in *The Paradise of Bombs*, 1987) about neither a large expedition nor a major mountain. Instead, he tells the story of an afternoon's excursion to the 4,237-foot top of Hardesty Mountain in Oregon—parking the car at approximately 3,600 feet. The mountain, for Sanders, is less a source of adventure or spiritual enrichment than an opportunity to observe and experience the psychological process of wonderment. In many of the other mountain narratives in this collection, the natural terrain—the ups and downs of the mountains themselves—determines the forms and moods of the texts. However, in "Cloud Crossing," Sanders's baby son Jesse controls the author's experience of the mountain and the structure of the narrative; each time Sanders's attention drifts away to the trees or the rocks or the clouds, Jesse does something to place himself once again at the front of his father's mind. "No peace for meditation with an eleven-month-old on your back," sighs the author with mock resignation. But important meditations occur nonetheless. The natural setting very quickly gets the author thinking of other things—the sight of mountains poking above the clouds reminds him of leaping porpoises, and the clouds themselves, with their temporary shapes, inspire thoughts of change, of the author's own impermanence. Jesse himself seems to take the mountain's mass into himself (or so it seems to the pack mule father), and in the end his "babbling oration" changes in accordance with shifts in "internal weather." Loren Eiseley, taking a geological view of time, writes in "The Flow of the River" (Part Three, Chapter Three) of "the eternal pulse that lifts Himalayas and which, in the following systole, will carry them away." But for Sanders, viewing time and change from a minute human perspective, it seems that "except for [distant peaks] and the rocks where I stand, everything is cotton." He looks at his child and thinks: "Even while I peek at him over my shoulder he is changing, neurons hooking up secret connections in his brain, calcium swelling his bones as mud gathers in river deltas." This narrative thus demonstrates the tendency David Black describes in "Walking the Cape" (Part Two, Chapter One), the use of an encounter with external nature to refine self-understanding.

Clouds are temporary creatures. So is the Milky Way, for that matter, if you take the long entropic view of things. I awake on a Saturday in mid-October with the ache of nightmares in my brain, as if I have strained a muscle in my head. Just a week before I turn thirty-three, just a month before my son turns one, I do not need physics or nightmares to remind me that we also are temporary creatures.

Baby Jesse is changing cloud-fast before my eyes. His perky voice begins pinning labels on dogs and bathtubs and sun. When I say, "Want to go for a walk?" on this morning that began with nightmares of entropy, he does not crawl towards me as he would have done only a few days ago. He tugs himself upright with the help of a chair, then staggers toward me like a refugee crossing the border, arms outstretched, crowing, "Wa! Wa!"

So I pack baby and water and graham crackers into the car, and drive thirty miles southeast of Eugene, Oregon, to a trailhead on Hardesty Mountain. There are several hiking paths to the top, ranging in length from one mile to six. I choose the shortest, because I will be carrying Jesse's twenty-two pounds on my back. I have not come here to labor, to be reminded of my hustling heart. I have come to watch clouds.

Markers on the logging road tell us when we drive up past 2,500 feet, then 2,750 and 3,000. Around 3,250 the Fiat noses through the first vapors, great wrinkled slabs of clouds that thicken on the windshield. In the back seat Jesse strains against his safety harness, his hands fisted on the window, hungry to get out there into that white stuff. I drive the last few hundred yards to the trailhead with lights on, in case we meet a car groping its way down the mountain.

Beside a wooden sign carved to announce HARDESTY MOUNTAIN TRAIL, I park the Fiat with its muzzle downhill, so we can coast back to the highway after our walk in case the weary machine refuses to start. I lean the backpack against the bumper and guide Jesse's excited feet through the leg-holes, one of his calves in each of my hands. "Wa! Wa!" he cries, and almost tips the pack over into the sorrel dust of the logging road. Shouldering the pack requires acrobatic balancing, to keep him from tumbling out while I snake my arms through the straps. Once safely aloft, assured of a ride, he jounces so hard in the seat that I stagger a few paces with the same drunken uncertainty he shows in his own walking.

Clouds embrace us. Far overhead, between the fretted crowns of the Douglas fir, I see hints of blue. Down here among the roots and matted needles, the air is mist. My beard soon grows damp; beads glisten on my eyelashes. A few yards along the trail a Forest Service board, with miniature roof to protect its messages, informs us we are at 3,600 feet and must hike to 4,237 in order to reach the top of Hardesty. Since I came to see the clouds, not to swim in them, I hope we are able to climb above them into that tantalizing blue.

On my back Jesse carries on a fierce indecipherable oration concerning the wonders of this ghostly forest. Giddy with being outside and aloft, he drums on my head, yanks fistfuls of my hair. Every trunk we pass tempts him more strongly than the apple tree could ever have tempted Eve and Adam. He lurches from side to side, outstretched fingers desperate to feel the bark. I pause at a mammoth stump to let him touch. Viewed up close, the bark looks like a contour map of the Badlands, an eroded landscape where you might expect to uncover fossils. While Jesse traces the awesome ridges and fissures, I squint to read another Forest Service sign. No motorized vehicles, it warns, and no pack animals.

I surely qualify as a pack animal. For long spells in my adult life, while moving house or humping rucksacks onto trains or hauling firewood, I have felt more like a donkey than anything else. I have felt most like a beast of burden when hauling my two children, first Eva and now Jesse. My neck and shoulders never forget their weight from one portage to another. And I realize that carrying Jesse up the mountain to see clouds is a penance as well as a pleasure—penance for the hours I have sat glaring at my typewriter while he scrabbled mewing outside my door, penance for the thousands of things my wife has not been able to do on account of my word mania, penance for all the countless times I have told daughter Eva "no, I can't; I am writing." I know the rangers did not have human beasts in mind when they posted their sign, yet I am content to be a pack animal, saddled with my crowing son.

As I resume walking, I feel a tug. Jesse snaps a chunk of bark from the stump and carries it with him, to examine at leisure. Beneath one of the rare cottonwoods I pick up a leathery golden leaf, which I hand over my shoulder to the baby, who clutches it by the stem and turns it slowly around, tickling his nose with the starpoints. The leaf is a wonder to him, and therefore also to me. Everything he notices, every pebble, every layered slab of bark, is renewed for me. Once I carried Eva outside, in the first spring of her life, and a gust of wind caught her full in the face. She blinked, and then gazed at the invisible breath as if it were a flight of angels streaming past. Holding her in the crook of my arm that day, I rediscovered wind.

Fascinated by his leaf, Jesse snuggles down in the pack and rides quietly. My heart begins to dance faster as the trail zigzags up the mountain through a series of switchbacks. Autumn has been dry in Oregon, so the dirt underfoot is powdery. Someone has been along here inspecting mushrooms. The discarded ones litter the trail like blackening pancakes. Except for the path, worn raw by deer and hikers, the floor of the woods is covered with moss. Fallen wood is soon hidden by the creeping emerald carpet, the land burying its own dead. Limegreen moss clings fuzzily to the upright trunks and dangles in fluffy hanks from limbs, like freshly dyed wool hung out to dry. A wad of it caught in the fist squeezes down to nothing.

A lurch from the backpack tells me that Jesse has spied some new temptation in the forest. Craning around, I see his spidery little hands reaching for the sky. Then I also look up, and notice the shafts of light slanting down through the treetops. The light seems substantial, as if made of glass, like the rays of searchlights that carve up the night sky to celebrate a store's opening or a war's end. "Light," I say to Jesse. "Sunlight. We're almost above the clouds." Wherever the beams strike, they turn cobwebs into jeweled diagrams, bracelet limbs with rhinestones of dew. Cloud vapors turn to smoke.

The blue glimpsed between trees gradually thickens, turns solid, and we emerge onto a treeless stony ridge. Clear sky above, flotillas of clouds below, mountains humping their dark green backs as far as I can see. The sight of so many slick backs arching above the clouds reminds me of watching porpoises from a ship in the Gulf of Mexico. Vapors spiral up and down between cloud layers as if on escalators. Entire continents and hemispheres and galaxies of mist drift by. I sit on the trail with backpack propped against a stone ledge, to watch this migration.

No peace for meditation with an eleven-month-old on your back. An ache in my shoulders signals that Jesse, so near the ground, is leaning out of the pack to capture something. A pebble or beetle to swallow? A stick to gnaw? Moss, it turns out, an emerald hunk of it ripped from the rockface. "Moss," I tell him, as he rotates this treasure about three inches in front of his eyes. "Here, feel," and I stroke one of his palms across the velvety clump. He tugs the hand free and resumes his private exploration. This independence grows on him these days faster than his hair.

"Clouds," I tell him, pointing out into the gulf of air. Jesse glances up, sees only vagueness where I see a ballet of shapes, and so he resumes his scrutiny of the moss. "Not to eat," I warn him. When I check on him again half a minute later, the moss is half its former size and his lips are powdered with green. Nothing to do but hoist him out of the pack, dig what I can from his mouth, then plop him back in, meanwhile risking spilling both of us down the mountainside. A glance down the dizzying slope reminds me of my wife's warning, that I have no business climbing this mountain alone with a baby. She's right, of course. But guilt, like the grace of God, works in strange ways, and guilt drives me up here among the skittery rocks to watch clouds with my son.

"Let Daddy have it," I say, teasing the hunk of moss from his hand. "Have a stick, pretty stick." While he imprints the stick with the marks of his teeth, four above and two below, I spit on the underside of the moss and glue it back down to the rock. Grow, I urge it. Looking more closely at the rockface, I see that it is crumbling beneath roots and weather, sloughing away like old skin. The entire mountain is migrating, not so swiftly as the clouds, but just as surely, heading grain by grain to the sea.

Jesse seems to have acquired some of the mountain's mass as I stand upright again and hoist his full weight. With the stick he idly swats me on the ear.

The trail carries us through woods again, then up along a ridge to the clearing at the top of Hardesty Mountain. There is no dramatic feeling of expansiveness, as there is on some peaks, because here the view is divvied up into modest sweeps by Douglas firs, cottonwoods, great gangling heaps of briars. The forest has laid siege to the rocky crest, and will abolish the view altogether before Jesse is old enough to carry his own baby up here. For now, by moving from spot to spot on the summit, I can see in all directions. What I see mostly are a few thousand square miles of humpbacked mountains looming through the clouds. Once in Ohio I lived in a valley which the Army Corps of Engineers thought would make a convenient bed for a reservoir. So the Mahoning River was dammed, and as the waters backed up in that valley, covering everything but the highest ridges, drowning my childhood, they looked very much like these clouds poured among the mountains.

"Ba! Ba!" Jesse suddenly bellows, leaping in his saddle like a bronco rider.

Bath, I wonder? Bed? Bottle? Ball? He has been prolific of B-words lately, and their tail-ends are hard to tell apart. Ball, I finally decide, for there at the end of the arrow made by his arm is the moon, a chalky peachpit hanging down near the horizon. "Moon," I say.

"Ba! Ba!" he insists.

Let it stay a ball for awhile, something to play catch with, roll across the linoleum. His sister's first sentence was, "There's the moon." Her second was, "Want it, Daddy." So began her astronomical yearnings, my astronomical failures. She has the itch for space flight in her, my daughter does. Jesse is still too much of a pup for me to say whether he has caught it.

We explore the mountaintop while the ocean of cloud gradually rises. There are charred rings from old campfires. In a sandy patch, red-painted bricks are laid in the shape of a letter A. Not large enough to be visible from airplanes. If Hardesty Mountain were in a story by Hawthorne, of course, I could use the scarlet A to accuse it of some vast geological harlotry. If this were a folklore mountain, I could explain the letter as an alphabetical inscription left by giants. But since this is no literary landscape, I decide that the bricks formed the foundation for some telescope or radio transmitter or other gizmo back in the days when this summit had a lookout tower.

Nearby is another remnant from those days, a square plank cover for a cistern. The boards are weathered to a silvery sheen, with rows of rustblackened nailheads marking the joints. Through a square opening at the center of the planks I catch a glint. Water? Still gathering here after all these years? Leaning over the hole, one boot on the brittle planks, I see that the glint is from a tin can. The cistern is choked with trash.

At the very peak, amid a jumble of rocks, we find nine concrete piers that once supported the fire tower. By squatting down beside one of those piers I can rest Jesse's weight on the concrete, and relieve the throb in my neck. I imagine the effort of hauling enough materials up this mountain to build a tower. Surely they used horses, or mules. Not men with backpacks. So what became of the tower when the Forest Service, graduated to spotter planes, no longer needed it? Did they pry out every nail and carry the boards back down again? A glance at the ground between my feet supplies the answer. Wedged among the rocks, where rains cannot wash them away, are chunks of glass, some of them an inch thick. I pick up one that resembles a tongue, about the size for a cocker spaniel. Another one, a wad of convolutions, might be a crystalline brain. Peering up through it at the sun, I see fracture lines and tiny bubbles. Frozen in the seams where one molten layer lapped onto another there are ashes. Of course they didn't dismantle the tower and lug its skeleton down the mountain. They waited for a windless day after a drenching rain and they burned it.

The spectacle fills me: the mountain peak like a great torch, a volcano, the tower heaving on its nine legs, the windows bursting from the heat, tumbling among the rocks, fusing into molten blobs, the glass taking on whatever shape it cooled against.

There should be nails. Looking closer I find them among the shards of glass, sixteen-penny nails mostly, what we called spikes when I was building houses. Each one is somber with rust, but perfectly straight, never having been pried from wood. I think of the men who drove those nails—the way sweat stung in their eyes, the way their forearms clenched with every stroke of the hammer—and I wonder if any of them were still around when the tower burned. The Geological Survey marker, a round lead disk driven into a rock beside one of the piers, is dated 1916. Most likely the tower already stood atop the mountain in that year. Most likely the builders are all dead by now.

So on its last day the Hardesty fire tower became a fire tower in earnest. Yesterday I read that two American physicists shared the Nobel Prize for discovering the background radiation left over from the Big Bang, which set our universe in motion some fifteen billion years ago. Some things last—not forever, of course; but for a long time—things like radiation, like bits of glass. I gather a few of the nails, some lumps of glass, a screw. Stuffing these shreds of evidence in my pocket, I discover the graham cracker in its wrapping of cellophane, and I realize I have not thought of Jesse for some minutes, have forgotten that he is riding me. That can mean only one thing. Sure enough, he is asleep, head scrunched down into the pack. Even while I peek at him over my shoulder he is changing, neurons hooking up secret connections in his brain, calcium swelling his bones as mud gathers in river deltas.

Smell warns me that the clouds have reached us. Looking out, the only peaks I can see are the Three Sisters, each of them a shade over 10,000 feet. Except for those peaks and the rocks where I stand, everything is cotton. There are no more clouds to watch, only Cloud, unanimous whiteness, an utter absence of shape. A panic seizes me—the same panic I used to feel as a child crossing the street when approaching cars seemed to have my name written on their grills. Suddenly the morning's nightmare comes back to me: everything I know is chalked upon a blackboard, and, while I watch, a hand erases every last mark.

Terror drives me down the Hardesty trail, down through vapors that leach color from the ferns, past trees that are dissolving. Stumps and downed logs lose their shape, merge into the clouds. The last hundred yards of the trail I jog. Yet Jesse never wakes until I haul him out of the pack and wrestle him into the car harness. His bellowing defies the clouds, the creeping emptiness. I bribe him with sips of water, a graham cracker, a song. But nothing comforts him, or comforts me, as we drive down the seven graveled miles of logging road to the highway. There we sink into open space again. The clouds are a featureless gray overhead.

As soon as the wheels are ringing beneath us on the blacktop, Jesse's internal weather shifts, and he begins one of his calm babbling orations, contentedly munching his cracker. The thread of his voice slowly draws me out of the annihilating ocean of whiteness. "Moon," he is piping from the back seat, "moon, moon!"

Analyzing and Discussing the Text

1. What is the attraction of clouds? What language does Sanders use to describe the clouds? How is this related to the central themes of the essay? In this study of change—both growth and decay—what do clouds and mountains come to symbolize?
2. Discuss Jesse's role in the narrative. How does his presence affect the author's experience of the clouds, the mountain, and the rest of the world? What does Sanders suggest about the relationship between children and adults while in the woods?
3. Explain the humor in Sanders's essay. Identify the use of gestures, analogies, and specific words to create humorous effects. Is humor the primary mood of the piece?
4. "I have no business climbing this mountain alone with a baby," admits Sanders. So why *does* he? Try to explain his motivation.
5. What compels Sanders to investigate the destruction of the fire-tower, to gather nails and glass fragments and bring them home? How does this section of the essay tie in with the opening paragraph of the piece?
6. When Jesse's "internal weather" shifts and he babbles "Moon...moon, moon" at the end of the essay, what does this suggest about human responses to the natural world? Can you associate Jesse's utterances with his sister Eva's first sentences (mentioned earlier in the essay)?

Experiencing and Writing About the World

1. "[E]verything I know is chalked upon a blackboard," writes Sanders, "and, while I watch, a hand erases every last mark." Write a brief analytical essay in which you explain this "nightmare" and elaborate on its connection with the rest of Sanders's article.
2. Using observations of nature as examples and stimuli of your own feelings, write an essay on the issue of transience and mortality. Clearly define the sections of your essay that express lamentation and celebration.
3. Have you ever spent time outdoors (mountain climbing?) with a small child? Write an essay to explain how the child's (or children's) interaction with the world contributed to your own awareness of the environment. If possible, try to combine serious reflection with humorous anecdote.

4. In his essay "Children in the Woods" (Part Four, Chapter One), Barry Lopez considers how adults can guide children to appreciate the world more deeply. How in "Cloud Crossing" does Sanders suggest the opposite idea? Write an essay explaining what the adult author learns from watching his infant son.

Suggestions for Further Reading

Abbey, Edward. "Mountain Music." *The Journey Home: Some Words in Defense of the American West.* New York: Dutton, 1977.

————. "Tukuhnikivats, the Island in the Desert." *Desert Solitaire: A Season in the Wilderness.* New York: McGraw, 1968.

Alvarez, A. *Feeding the Rat: Profile of a Climber.* New York: Atlantic Monthly P, 1988.

Bernstein, Jerome. *Mountain Passages.* Lincoln: U of Nebraska P, 1978.

Herzog, Maurice. *Annapurna: First Conquest of an 8000-Meter Peak.* Trans. Nea Morin and Janet Adam Smith. New York: Dutton, 1952.

Kerouac, Jack. "Alone on a Mountaintop." *Lonesome Traveler.* New York: Grove, 1960.

King, Clarence. *Mountaineering in the Sierra Nevada.* 1872. Lincoln: U of Nebraska P, 1970.

LaChapelle, Delores. "The Mountains Are Calling Me, and I Must Go." *Earth Wisdom.* Silverton, CO: Finn Hill Arts, 1978.

Long, Jeff. *Angels of Light: A Novel.* New York: Morrow, 1987.

Muir, John. *Mountaineering Essays.* Salt Lake City: Gibbs M. Smith, 1984.

————. *The Mountains of California.* 1894. New York: Penguin, 1985.

Nelson, Richard. "A Mountain in My Hand." *The Island Within.* New York: Random, 1989.

Pilley, Dorothy. *Climbing Days.* 1935. London: Hogarth, 1989.

Rukkila, Jean. "Mountain Flashes." *Quarterly West* 27 (Summer/Fall 1988): 80–89.

Salkeld, Audrey, and Rosie Smith, eds. *One Step in the Clouds: The Sierra Club Omnibus of Mountaineering Novels and Short Stories.* San Francisco: Sierra Club Books, 1990.

Stephen, Leslie. *The Playground of Europe.* 1871. New York: Longman, 1895.

Thoreau, Henry David. "Ktaadn." *The Maine Woods.* 1864. Ed. Joseph J. Moldenhauer. Princeton: Princeton UP, 1972.

Whymper, Edward. *Scrambles Amongst the Alps.* 1871. Berkeley, CA: Ten Speed P, 1981.

David Robertson

CHAPTER FOUR

—————————— ▬▬▬ ——————————

Wilderness Journals

The most obvious reasons for people to visit wild places may include such activities as walking, floating, and climbing, but many people view outdoor experiences as an ideal opportunity to record their observations and reflections through some form of writing and sketching, often a combination of the two. The wilderness journal is a means of informally joining raw experience with the clarity and concreteness of language. Using language can help us to see the world better. As Annie Dillard once put it, "Seeing is of course very much a matter of verbalization. Unless I call my attention to what passes before my eyes, I simply won't see it." The problem with describing one's experiences as they happen or immediately afterwards is that one lacks the distance, the perspective, necessary to understand the larger context and implications of an event; this can frustrate the writer who feels that the journal account is necessarily incomplete. Robert Finch, in his 1986 essay "North Beach Journal," admits that "it is hard writing about the life one is actually living. I came out here to put some distance between it and me, but I find that I carry it around with me, unfinished."

When reading published journals, it is important to keep in mind the difference between truly private journals (those written without publication in mind) and essays that merely adopt the journal as a structural technique and as a way of suggesting the writer's actual presence in the natural world. The following examples of journal writing include both kinds, private and public. The entries from Henry David Thoreau's 1853 journal were not published during his lifetime and demonstrate his inclination, as a journal-keeper, to record natural observations and everyday experiences. Three different versions of John Muir's famous narrative of an "unexpected adventure" behind Yosemite Falls show how the writer alters his account in turning a journal entry into a letter to a personal friend, and then further alters it many years later in producing a public version of the event. Edwin Way Teale published his 1953 book, *Circle of the Seasons,* with twelve months' worth of daily journal-like entries, but although the entire book may be based on Teale's actual journals, the published entries have clearly been refined and expanded. Ursula K. Le Guin and Stephen J. Pyne wrote their "journals" for the 1988 special issue of *Antaeus* devoted to journals, diaries, and notebooks. As in the case of Teale, these writers have sought to retain the structure, informality, and observational vividness of their original journals, while refining their phrasing and smoothing some of the transitions between ideas in order to make their pieces accessible to readers.

HENRY DAVID THOREAU
October 1–20, 1853

For biographical information, see the headnote for "Walking" in Part Two, Chapter One.

Henry David Thoreau, although almost unknown during his lifetime beyond the circle of Massachusetts intellectuals known as the "Transcendentalists," is now widely regarded as the father of the modern environmental movement, the writer whose words and ideas echo throughout twentieth-century nature writing. But Thoreau's own writing began in a rather private way when, on October 22, 1837, during the fall after his graduation from Harvard, the philosopher Ralph Waldo Emerson asked him, "What are you doing now? Do you keep a journal?" From this journal of daily thoughts and observations, begun at the age of twenty and continued until 1861 (shortly before his death at the age of forty-five), grew several books and a number of important essays, including *Walden* (1854), now considered masterpieces. But many readers have come to regard the journal itself (published in fourteen volumes in 1906) as Thoreau's primary activity as a writer. The following entries from October 1853 demonstrate Thoreau's increasing interest in raw observation (as opposed to imaginative reflection on observed phenomena) after 1850. The underlying purpose of his own seasonal observations was to test the correspondence and disjunction between the rhythms and moods of the world and his own inner life. But even for the less mystical writer, the keeping of a daily journal of observations has the potential to enhance attentiveness to and understanding of the world.

October, 1853

Oct. 1. Saturday. Went a-barberrying by boat to Conantum, carrying Ellen, Edith, and Eddie. Grapevines, curled, crisped, and browned by the frosts, are now more conspicuous than ever. Some grapes still hang on the vines. Got three pecks of barberries. Huckleberries begin to redden. Robins and bluebirds collect and flit about. Flowers are scarce.

Oct. 2. Sunday. The gentian in Hubbard's Close is frost-bitten extensively. As the [witch-] hazel is raised above frost and can afford to be later, for this reason also I think it is so. The white pines have scarcely begun at all to change here, though a week ago last Wednesday they were fully changed at Bangor. There is fully a fortnight's difference, and methinks more. The [witch-] hazel, too, was more forward there. There are but few and faint autumnal tints about Walden yet. The smooth sumach is but a dull red.

Oct. 3. Viola lanceolata in Moore's Swamp.

Oct. 4. The maples are reddening, and birches yellowing. The mouse-ear in the shade in the middle of the day, so hoary, looks as if the frost still lay on it. Well it wears the frost. Bumblebees are on the *Aster undulatus,* and gnats are dancing in the air.

Oct. 5. The howling of the wind about the house just before a storm to-night sounds extremely like a loon on the pond. How fit!

Oct. 6 and 7. Windy. Elms bare.

Oct. 8. Found a bird's nest (?) converted into a mouse's nest in the prinos swamp, while surveying on the new Bedford road to-day, topped over with moss, and a hole on one side, like a squirrel-nest.

Oct. 9. Sunday. A high wind south of westerly. Set sail with W. E. C. down the river.

The red maples are now red and also yellow and reddening. The white maples are green and silvery, also yellowing and blushing. The birch is yellow; the black willow brown; the elms sere, brown, and thin; the bass bare. The button-bush, which was so late, is already mostly bare except the lower part, protected. The swamp white oak is green with a brownish tinge; the white ash turned mulberry. The white maples toward Ball's Hill have a burnt white appearance; the white oak a salmon-color and also red. Is that scarlet oak rosed? Huckleberries and blackberries are red. Leaves are falling; apples more distinctly seen on the trees; muskrat-houses not quite done.

This wind carried us along glibly, I think six miles an hour, till we stopped in Billerica, just below the first bridge beyond the Carlisle Bridge,—at the Hibiscus Shore. I collected some hibiscus seeds and swamp white oak acorns, and we walked on thence, a mile or more further, over scrubby hills which with a rocky core border the western shore, still in Billerica, at last not far above the mills. At one place, opposite what I once called Grape Island (still unchanged), I smelled grapes, and though I saw no vines at first, they being bare of leaves, at last found the grapes quite plenty and ripe and fresh enough on the ground under my feet. Ah! their scent is very penetrating and memorable. Did we not see a fish hawk? We found ourselves in an extensive wood there, which we did not get out of. It took the rest of the day to row back against the wind.

Oct. 10. This morning it is very pleasant and warm. There are many small birds in flocks on the elms in Cheney's field, faintly warbling, — robins and purple finches and especially large flocks of small sparrows, which make a business of washing and pruning themselves in the puddles in the road, as if cleaning up after a long flight and the wind of yesterday. The faint suppressed warbling of the robins sounds like a reminiscence of the spring.

Cooler and windy at sunset, and the elm leaves come down again.

Oct. 11. Sassafras leaves are a rich yellow now and falling fast. They come down in showers on the least touching of the tree. I was obliged to cut a small one while surveying the Bedford road to-day. What singularly and variously formed leaves! For the most part three very regular long lobes, but also some simple leaves; but here is one shaped just like a hand or a mitten with a thumb. They next turn a dark cream-color.

Father saw to-day in the end of a red oak stick in his wood-shed, three and a half inches in diameter, which was sawed yesterday, something shining. It is lead, either the side of a bullet or a large buckshot just a quarter of an inch in diameter. It came from the Ministerial Lot in the southwest part of the town, and we bought the wood of Martial Miles. It is completely and snugly buried under some twelve or fifteen layers of the wood, and it appears not to have penetrated originally more than its own thickness, for there is a very close fit all around it, and the wood has closed over it very snugly and soundly, while on every other side it is killed, though snug for an eighth of an inch around it.

Oct. 12. To-day I have had the experience of borrowing money for a poor Irishman who wishes to get his family to this country. One will never know his neighbors till he has carried a subscription paper among them. Ah! it reveals many and sad facts to stand in this relation to them. To hear the selfish and cowardly excuses some make, — that *if* they help any they must help the Irishman who lives with them, — and him they are sure never to help! Others, with whom public opinion weighs, will think of it, trusting you never will raise the sum and so they will not be called on again; who give stingily after all. What a satire in the fact that you are much more inclined to call on a certain slighted and so-called crazy woman in moderate circumstances rather than on the president of the bank! But some are generous and save the town from the distinction which threatened it, and *some* even who do not lend, plainly would if they could.

Oct. 14. Friday. A Mr. Farquhar of Maryland came to see me; spent the day and the night. Fine, clear Indian-summer weather.

Oct. 15. Saturday. Last night the first smart frost that I have witnessed. Ice formed under the pump, and the ground was white long after sunrise. And now, when the morning wind rises, how the leaves come down in showers after this touch of the frost! They suddenly form thick beds or carpets on the ground in this gentle air, —or without wind, —just the size and form of the tree above. Silvery cinquefoil.

Oct. 16. Sunday. The third pleasant day. Hunter's Moon. Walked to White Pond. The *Polygonum dumetorum* in Tarbell's Swamp lies thick and twisted, rolled together, over the loose raised twigs on the ground, as if woven over basketwork, though it is now all sere. The *Marchantia polymorpha* is still erect there. *Viola ovata* out. The *Lysimachia stricta,* with its long bulblets in the axils, how green and fresh by the shore of the pond!

Oct. 18. P.M.—With Sophia boated to Fair Haven, where she made a sketch.

The red maples have been bare a good while. In the sun and this clear air, their bare ashy branches even sparkle like silver. The woods are losing their bright colors. The muskrat-houses are more sharpened now. I find my boat all covered—the bottom and seats—with the yellow leaves of the golden willow under which it is moored, and if I empty it, it is full again to-morrow. Some white oaks are salmon-red, some lighter and drier. The black oaks are a greenish yellow. Poplars (*grandidentata*) clear, rich yellow. How like some black rocks that stand in the river are these muskrat-houses! They are singularly conspicuous for the dwellings of animals.

The river is quite low now, lower than for many weeks, and accordingly the white lily pads have their stems too long, and they rise above the water four or five inches and are looped over and downward to the sunken pad with its face down. They make a singular appearance. Returning late, we see a double shadow of ourselves and boat, one, the true, quite black, the other directly above it and very faint, on the willows and high bank.

Oct. 19. Wednesday. Paddled E. Hoar and Mrs. King up the North Branch.

A seed of wild oat left on.

The leaves have fallen so plentifully that they quite conceal the water along the shore, and rustle pleasantly when the wave which the boat creates strikes them. On Sunday last, I could hardly find the Corner Spring, and suspected even it had dried up, for it was completely concealed by fresh-fallen leaves, and when I swept them aside and revealed it, it was like striking the earth for a new spring. At Beck Stow's, surveying, thinking to step upon a leafy shore from a rail, I got into water more than a foot deep and had to wring my stockings out; but this is anticipating.

Oct. 20. How pleasant to walk over beds of these fresh, crisp, and rustling fallen leaves,—young hyson, green tea, clean, crisp, and wholesome! How beautiful they go to their graves! how gently lay themselves down and turn to mould!—painted of a thousand hues and fit to make the beds of us living. So they troop to their graves, light and frisky. They put on no weeds. Merrily they go scampering over the earth, selecting their graves, whispering all through the woods about it. They that waved so loftily, how contentedly they return to dust again and are laid low, resigned to lie and decay at the foot of the tree and afford nourishment to new generations of their kind, as well as to flutter on high! How they are mixed up, all species,—oak and maple and chestnut and birch! They are about to add a leaf's breadth to the depth of the soil. We are all the richer for their decay. Nature is not cluttered with them. She is a perfect husbandman; she stores them all.

While I was wringing my wet stockings (*vide* last page), sitting by the side of Beck Stow's, I heard a rush of wings, looked up, and saw three dusky ducks swiftly circling over the small water. They rounded far away, but soon returned and settled within about four rods. They first survey the spot. Wonder they did not see me. At first they are suspicious, hold up their heads and sail about. Do they not see me through the thin border of leafless bushes? At last one dips his bill, and they begin to feed amid the pads. I suddenly rise, and [they] instantly dive as at a flash, then at once rise again and all go off, with a low wiry note.

Analyzing and Discussing the Text

1. How does Thoreau's language in the journal differ from that of "Walking" or *Walden*?
2. What aspects of the natural world seem to be of primary interest to Thoreau? Can you explain the purpose of such observations?
3. What kinds of details does Thoreau include in his journal entries? Do his comments seem concerned with how nature works or with its beauty? Does he devote much space to abstract reflection?

Experiencing and Writing About the World

1. Keep daily journal entries for a week (or longer), aiming for at least a page of natural description per day. The goal is descriptive detail, perhaps stylistic experimentation as well. Imitate the language and focus of Thoreau's journal at first, then allow your own voice and perspective to take over.
2. Keep an intermittent seasonal journal throughout the semester by making detailed observations of seasonal changes for three days or so every other week. When you read through the completed journal, does it present a discernible record of change, something like the verbal analogue of time-lapse photography?
3. Write an essay comparing the sections from Thoreau's journal and Edwin Way Teale's book *Circle of the Seasons* anthologized in this chapter. How do their writing styles and thematic interests overlap and deviate from each other? Which style of journal writing seems to take the most advantage of the journal as a literary genre?

JOHN MUIR

Yosemite Falls:
Journal Entry (April 3, 1871)
Letter to Mrs. Ezra S. Carr (April 3, 1871)
An Unexpected Adventure (1912)

For biographical information, see the headnote for "Prayers in Higher Mountain Temples" in Part Two, Chapter Three.

John Muir left behind sixty journals and an assortment of notes on loose sheets of paper when he died in 1914. These journals span the years from 1867 to 1911 and combine scientific records, narratives of his many excursions, and reflections on the meaning of wilderness. Muir's first journal was published in 1913 as *A Thousand-Mile Walk to the Gulf*; it describes his experiences during his 1867 trip on foot from Indianapolis, Indiana—where he had been blinded temporarily in a factory accident—through Kentucky, Tennessee, Georgia, and Florida. Muir continued keeping journals after he arrived in California in 1868, often carrying two or more notebooks with him on his trips in the mountains. Even while climbing, he would attach a notebook to his belt for scribbling pencil entries later on by the light of his campfire. Muir's journals are predominantly impersonal descriptions of the outside world; he once wrote, "As to putting more of myself into these sketches, I never had the heart to spoil their symmetry with mere personal trials and adventures." Nevertheless, the following entry from April 3, 1871, depicts one of his more dramatic moments in the mountains. We have reprinted this private account of his adventure behind upper Yosemite Falls together with the version he wrote shortly afterwards in a letter to his friend Mrs. Ezra S. (Jeanne C.) Carr and the version he eventually published in *The Yosemite* (1912); thus we can see the author's subtle shifts in style as he attempts to appeal to different audiences, or no audience at all. On April 5, 1871, he also wrote a brief account of the experience for his sister Sarah, noting simply that he "got drenched and had to go home"; "My wetting was received in a way that I scarcely care to tell," he told her, leaving out the harrowing—and sublime—details offered in the other narratives.

Many of Muir's journal entries are available in *John of the Mountains: The Unpublished Journals of John Muir*, edited by Linnie Marsh Wolfe and first published in 1938. Some scholars consider *My First Summer in the Sierra* (1911), the published version of Muir's 1869 Yosemite journal, his freshest, most inspiring account of wilderness adventure.

Journal Entry

Midnight, April 3.

At night, the lunar bows in the spray make a most impressive picture. There was the huge dark cavern of the gorge filled with tempestuous foam and scud and roar of many storms. The fall above hung white, ghostlike, and indistinct. Slowly the moon coming round the domes sent her white beams into the wild uproar, and lo, among the tremendous blasts and surges at the foot of the pit, five hundred feet below the ledge on which I stood, there appeared a rainbow set on end, colored like the solar bow only fainter, strangely peaceful and still, in the midst of roaring, surging, tempestuous power. Also a still fainter secondary bow.

I had intended to stay all night, but an hour ago I crept out on a narrow ledge that extends back of the fall, and as the wind swayed the mighty column at times a little forward from the face of the precipice, I thought it would be a fine thing to get back of the down-rushing waters and see them in all their glory with the moonlight sifting through them. I got out safely, though the ledge is only about six inches wide in one place, and was gazing up and out through the thin half-translucent edge of the fall, when some heavy plashes striking the wall above me caught my attention; then suddenly all was dark, and down came a dash of outside gauze tissue made of spent comets, thin and harmless to look at a mile off, but desperately solid and stony when they strike one's shoulders. It seemed as if I was being pelted with a mixture of choking spray and gravel. I grasped an angle of the ledge and held hard with my knees, and submitted to my frightful baptism with but little faith. When I dared to look up after the pelting had nearly ceased, and the column swaying back admitted the light, I hastily pounced back of a block of ice that was frozen to the ledge, squeezing myself in between the ice and the wall, and no longer feared being washed off.

When the moonbeams again slanted past the ever-changing edge of the torrent, I took courage to make a dash for freedom and escaped, made a fire and partially warmed my benumbed limbs, then ran down home to my cabin, reached it sometime towards morning, changed my clothing, got an hour or two of sleep, and awoke sane and comfortable, some of the earthiness washed out of me and Yosemite virtue washed in, better, not worse, for my wild bath in lunar bows, spent comet-tails, ice, drizzle, and moonshine. . . . Wonderful that Nature can do such wild passionate work without seeming extravagant, or that she will allow poor mortals so near her while doing it.

Letter to Mrs. Ezra S. Carr

Midnight [Yosemite, April 3, 1871]

Oh, Mrs. Carr, that you could be here to mingle in this night-noon glory! I am in the upper Yosemite Falls and can hardly calm to write, but from my first baptism hours ago, you have been so present that I must try to fix you a written thought.

In the afternoon I came up the mountain here with a blanket and a piece of bread to spend the night in prayer among the spouts of this fall. But what can I say more than wish again that you might expose your soul to the rays of this heaven?

Silver from the moon illumines this glorious creation which we term "falls," and has laid a magnificent double prismatic bow at its base. The tissue of the fall is delicately filmed on the outside like the substance of spent clouds, and the stars shine dimly through it. In the solid shafted body of the fall is a vast number of passing caves, black and deep, with close white convolving spray for sills and shooting comet sheaves above and down their sides, like lime crystals in a cave. And every atom of the magnificent being, from the thin silvery crest that does not dim the stars to the inner arrowy hardened shafts that strike onward like thunderbolts in sound and energy, all is life and spirit: every bolt and spray feels the hand of God. Oh, the music that is blessing me now! The sun of last week has given the grandest notes of all the yearly anthem.

I said that I was going to stop here until morning and pray a whole blessed night with the falls and the moon, but I am too wet and must go down. An hour or two ago I went out somehow on a little seam that extends along the wall behind the falls. I suppose I was in a trance, but I can positively say that I was in the body, for it is sorely battered and wetted. As I was gazing past the thin edge of the fall and away beneath the column to the brow of the rock, some heavy splashes of water struck me, driven hard against the wall. Suddenly I was darkened, down came a section of the outside tissue composed of spent comets. I crouched low, holding my breath, and anchored to some angular flakes of rock, took my baptism with moderately good faith.

When I dared to look up after the swaying column admitted light, I·pounced behind a piece of ice and the wall which was wedging tight, and I no longer feared being washed off, and steady moonbeams slanting past the arching meteors gave me confidence to escape to this snug place where McChesney and I slept one night, where I have a fire to dry my socks. This rock shelf, extending behind the falls, is about five hundred feet above the base of the fall on the perpendicular rock face.

How little do we know of ourselves, of our profoundest attractions and repulsions, of our spiritual affinities! How interesting does man become considered in his relations to the spirit of this rock and water! How significant does every atom of our world become amid the influences of those beings unseen, spiritual, angelic mountaineers that so throng these pure mansions of crystal foam and purple granite.

I cannot refrain from speaking to this little bush at my side and to the spray drops that come to my paper and to the individual sands of the slopelet I am sitting upon. Ruskin says that the idea of foulness is essentially connected with what he calls dead unorganized matter. How cordially I disbelieve him to-night, and were he to dwell a while among the powers of these mountains he would forget all dictionary differences betwixt the clean and the unclean, and he would lose all memory and meaning of the diabolical sin-begotten term *foulness*.

Well, I must go down. I am disregarding all of the doctors' physiology in sitting here in this universal moisture. Farewell to you, and to all the beings about us. I shall have a glorious walk down the mountain in this thin white light, over the open brows grayed with Selaginella and through the thick black shadow caves in the live oaks, all stuck full of snowy lances of moonlight.

[John Muir]

An Unexpected Adventure

A wild scene, but not a safe one, is made by the moon as it appears through the edge of the Yosemite Fall when one is behind it. Once, after enjoying the night-song of the waters and watching the formation of the colored bow as the moon came round the domes and sent her beams into the wild uproar, I ventured out on the narrow bench that extends back of the fall from Fern Ledge and began to admire the dim-veiled grandeur of the view. I could see the fine gauzy threads of the fall's filmy border by having the light in front; and wishing to look at the moon through the meshes of some of the denser portions of the fall, I ventured to creep farther behind it while it was gently wind-swayed, without taking sufficient thought about the consequences of its swaying back to its natural position after the wind-pressure should be removed. The effect was enchanting: fine, savage music sounding above, beneath, around me; while the moon, apparently in the very midst of the rushing waters, seemed to be struggling to keep her place, on account of the every-varying form and density of the water masses through which she was seen, now darkly veiled or eclipsed by a rush of thick-headed comets, now flashing out through openings between their tails. I was in fairyland between the dark wall and the wild throng of illumined waters, but suffered sudden disenchantment; for, like the witch-scene in Alloway Kirk, "in an instant all was dark." Down came a dash of spent comets, thin and harmless-looking in the distance, but they felt desperately solid and stony when they struck my shoulders, like a mixture of choking spray and gravel and big hailstones. Instinctively dropping on my knees, I gripped an angle of the rock, curled up like a young fern frond with my face pressed against my breast, and in this attitude submitted as best I could to my thundering bath. The heavier masses seemed to strike like cobblestones, and there was a confused noise of many waters about my ears—hissing, gurgling, clashing sounds that were not heard as music. The situation was quickly realized. How fast one's thoughts burn in such times of stress! I was weighing chances of escape. Would the column be swayed a few inches away from the wall, or would it come yet closer? The fall was in flood and not so lightly would its ponderous mass be swayed. My fate seemed to depend on a breath of the "idle wind." It was moved gently forward, the pounding ceased, and I was once more visited by glimpses of the moon. But fearing I might be caught at a disadvantage in making too hasty a retreat, I moved only a few feet along the bench to where a block of ice lay. I wedged myself between the ice and the wall, and lay face downwards, until the steadiness of the light gave encouragement to rise and get away. Somewhat nerve-shaken, drenched, and benumbed, I made out to build a fire, warmed myself, ran home, reached my cabin[1] before daylight, got an hour or two of sleep, and awoke sound and comfortable, better, not worse, for my hard midnight bath.

Analyzing and Discussing the Texts

1. You have just read three accounts of the same "unexpected adventure." Why does Muir record in his journal that he "submitted to [his] frightful baptism with but little faith," then tell his confidante Jeanne C. Carr in a letter written that same evening that he "took [his] baptism with moderately good faith"? Why does he replace the word "baptism" with "thundering bath" in the account he published forty-one years later in *The Yosemite*? Explain how the language in each version suits the intended audience. Can you pick out other ways in which Muir's language changes to suit his apparent goals in each of the narratives?
2. Discuss Muir's adventure behind the waterfall. Why did he venture out onto the ledge? Does this seem like a reasonable thing to do? What does the action imply about the way Muir felt at Yosemite?
3. Muir suggests that he began describing the experience in his journal and in the letter to Mrs. Carr immediately after it happened. Does this freshness come through in his writing? Does the freshness suffer when he revises the account for publication many years later?

Experiencing and Writing About the World

1. Thoreau's journal entries tend to be less emotional than Muir's. Try keeping a week-long journal in which you record *any* contact you have with the natural world—even just looking out the window of your dorm room or getting rained on while walking to class—but write the first half of the journal with Thoreauvian spareness and unexpressed emotion and the second half with Muir-like outbursts of glee, shock, horror, and any other extreme feelings that fit your experiences.

[1]Presumably his first Yosemite cabin, "a little shanty made of sugar pine shingles" which he built in 1869 and occupied until January, 1871. It was located on Yosemite Creek near the foot of the Lower Fall. —Editor's note.

2. Have you, in your own explorations of the world, ever experienced a combination of excitement, fear, and discomfort resembling Muir's intense mixture of feelings as he crouched on the ledge behind Yosemite Falls? Record the experience in a private journal entry (even if it happened some time ago). Then rewrite your narrative in the form of letters to someone concerned about your safety (a sibling? your parents?) and to someone you want to impress with your bravery, your wildness, or (as in Muir's letter to Mrs. Carr) your piety. Finally, write a brief essay on this experience for a more general audience, emphasizing the sublimity and danger of the natural world.

3. Do research on an environmental issue of special urgency in your local area. Record information and your personal response in a journal-like note to yourself. Then write two letters about the problem, one to a friend and another to a public official. Finally, write a statement on this issue for publication—consider this "public" version a potential editorial for either the university newspaper or one of the papers in your town. Using Muir's revisions as a model, make a point of changing your language in each version of this statement, so as to suit the specific audiences for each.

EDWIN WAY TEALE

From October

Edwin Way Teale (1899–1980), although a native of Joliet, Illinois, made a name for himself as a natural historian because of his journeys around the country. He covered twenty thousand miles, roaming from Cape Cod to California, in recording the natural history of a season in his book *Autumn Across America* (1956). After completing his master's degree at Columbia University, Teale worked as a teacher, writer, and editor, establishing himself as an important nature writer in the 1930s with descriptions and photographs of insects. In 1966, Teale received a Pulitzer Prize for *Wandering Through Winter*. His other major works include *North with the Spring* (1951), *A Walk Through the Year* (1978), and (with Ann Zwinger) *A Conscious Stillness; Two Naturalists on Thoreau's Rivers* (1982). He lived for many years in Hampton, Connecticut.

In her preface to *A Conscious Stillness*, written after Teale's death, Zwinger recalls several things Teale mentioned to her about the craft of writing. Both writers disliked writing first drafts, confining the dreams of a particular book to actual words on a page. "The reason revision is so fine," suggested Teale, "is that little by little, day by day, we feel we are lifting the book back nearer the original goal." Zwinger claims that one of Teale's strongest attributes as a natural history writer was his ability to take excellent notes while out in the field. When she once complimented him on his note-taking, he responded as follows in a letter:

> Speaking of journal-keeping, William Beebe once told me of something Ernest Thompson Seton said to him. I have thought of it innumerable times since. Seton advised Beebe to stop, when he was making notes in the jungle about something he planned to write about later, and imagine himself back at his desk at home, asking himself what else he would like to know. I have often done this and been thankful for the additional specific sights and sounds and smells recorded that helped bring the scene to life later on.

The following entries from the October chapter in Teale's *Circle of the Seasons: The Journal of a Naturalist's Year* (1953) are more crafted than the writer's actual field notebook would be, and yet in the precision of words and observations we can see the achievement of the skilled journal-keeper. Teale's entries, primed for publication as they are, seem strangely elaborate and orderly when compared to Thoreau's entries from October 1853—exactly a century earlier.

October 12

October Mist   A luminous, misty dawn. And, all down the hillside, the spider webs shining with dew. Like the stars, the webs have been there all time; moisture is the night that makes them visible. On such October days as this, we look about us as though in some new and magic land. The mystical draws close behind the luminous veil. We see the things about us and sense larger meanings just beyond our grasp. Looking back on such a time, we add—as Thoreau did one autumn day—"And something more I saw which cannot easily be described."

October 13

The Territory of the Mantis   All day long, on summer days, I have watched a praying mantis cling near a buddleia bloom, never varying its position more than a few inches from morning until night. An explorer friend of mine, at the American Museum of Natural History, once told me of a mantis he watched on a bush in the tropics. It came to the same spot day after day. So closely did it resemble a leaf in form and coloration that it virtually disappeared when it settled down among the foliage. Only when it remained still and the leaves around it were stirred by a breeze did it become apparent. But this was at rare intervals for, as soon as a breeze sprang up and the leaves stirred, the insect would begin bending its knees and swaying from side to side, moving like the moving leaves around it.

Remembering the mantis of this tropical bush and of my buddleia bloom, recently, I began to wonder to what extent a mantis has a definite territory of its own. Is the mantis I see today among the rose bushes the same individual I saw there yesterday and the day before and last week? The only way to tell is by marking the insect. So I got out my fine brush and white enamel and placed little distinguishing dots on various parts of the bodies of twelve praying mantes I found in the yard. Six were males, six females. I drew a little map and noted down where each mantis was hunting when it was marked. In the days that have followed, I have been keeping track of the movements of these branded insects.

One has a white spot on the tip of a wing, another a spot on the top of its abdomen, a third on its thorax, a fourth on its right foreleg, and so on. Exactly half of the twelve wandered away or were killed by birds. I never saw them again after the day I marked them. Among the other six, the most consistent was the fifth one I marked. It remained on or around a small yew for more than two weeks. Here I saw it with captured prey. Here I saw it mating. Here I saw it forming the froth oötheca that holds its eggs. Of the other marked insects, one remained for the better part of a week near a clump of pokeberries close to the kitchen window; another spent four days in a high, plumy clump of grass; a third kept reappearing among the rose bushes. The most surprising thing to me was that four out of the six mantes that remained in the yard were males. My impression is that it is the smaller, lighter males that do the most flying and moving about in the fall. I had expected that all of the more sedentary of the marked mantes would be females. Another time this might be so. For this one test is what a careful scientist might mark: "A Note Preliminary to Investigation." Another summer will see more marked mantes in my yard. That is something to look forward to.

October 14

The Habits of Trees   Three clumps of arrowwood rise by the path at the foot of the Insect Garden. One is brilliant red; another part red, part green; the third entirely green. On the slope, one of the wild cherry trees turned red long before its fellows. I recall this same tree was first to be clad in autumn foliage a year ago. Within sight of my study window, at home, there are a number of Norway maples. One tree, year after year, stands out because of the brilliance of its autumn leaves. Even trees are creatures of habit. The one that has the most color in its leaves this autumn is likely to have the most color next autumn. It is a part of the characteristics, or "habits," of the tree.

In the sunset, I walk home along the hillside. More and more, as the days of fall advance, the quiet of the garden at sundown will suggest the empty stage and wings of a theater. The lights are dimming; the audience has left; the actors are trooping away.

October 15

The Silent Battle   Again, the dawn mist is smoky gray beneath the trees, shining, silver gray in the open. As I wander through the Insect Garden, I come upon a woolly bear spangled and starred with droplets of moisture. A little wild cherry beside the trail is adorned like a Christmas tree. Its dead branches are spider-trimmed with ropes and webs and dew-decorated spangles. Above me, a cheery "perchicory!" call marks the passage of a goldfinch, invisible in the vapor. As I approach the swamp stream, out of the autumn fog phragmites and cattails suddenly seem to step forward.

For a decade and a half now, I have watched the silent battle between these two. Slowly the phragmites have extended their foothold. These high, plumed reeds have less food value for wildlife than the cattails. But around the world, where they are found near the coasts in temperate zones, they have many uses. The old masters used to shape their drawing pens from the stems of phragmites. Today, in the south of France, along the Mediterranean, the slender reeds are used for thatching houses. In Milburn Swamp, their chief value is as a shelter for blackbirds, grackles and starlings. Each day, at sunset, I see the great starling flocks come in to roost for the night. As I stand in the chill morning vapor, looking into the phragmites—gray and wavering in the gray mist—I begin to imagine what it must be like within that dense stand of canes when the starling hosts pour down from the sky. An adventure in viewpoint takes shape in my mind. Tomorrow, before sunset, I will return and secrete myself in the heart of the phragmites and watch homecoming birds descend around me.

October 16

In the Phragmites   A little before five P.M., wearing long boots, old army pants, a leather jacket and an ancient felt hat, I push my way into the jungle of the phragmites. The day has been warm for mid-October. But a chill rises early from the swamp. In the heart of the stand, I tramp out a little hollow. Here I await the returning birds and here I set down the following notes:

5:01 P.M.   I can see only four or five feet, at most, into the tangle around me. Here and there, by the laws of chance, the stems are arranged into corridors that open for several feet—high, thin corridors barred at the end by a maze of upright stems. The interior of the canebrake is so like pictures of bamboo jungles of the Orient that a tiger or cobra would hardly seem out of place. Over my head, eight or nine feet above the floor of the swamp, wave the plumes of the phragmites. Each stem is hardly thicker than my little finger.

5:05 P.M.   Each time a breeze sweeps across the swamp, there is a creaking of stems and a dry rustle of leaves. The fall is a time of growing brittleness.

5:07 P.M.   The first bird to arrive is a redwing. I hear its monosyllabic "Check! Check!" as it alights in the willow and then flies down to the far side of the phragmites.

5:09 P.M.   Birds are assembling in the swampside maples. The sun is going down and the flocks are coming in. I can hear the mingled calling of many birds.

5:12 P.M.   The clamor increases. The trees are thronging with new arrivals. Seeing little, I depend upon my ears for news. Suddenly there is the airy sound of great numbers of birds taking off, coming nearer. A cloud of redwings, grackles and starlings engulfs the phragmites. The flapping of wings is like a wind. Black shapes go hurtling across the tiny cope of my sky where the phragmites part slightly above my head. The reeds seem shaken by great gusts as birds pitch down from the air among them. The calling of redwings, the metallic voices of the grackles, the whistling of starlings blend into a medley that is almost deafening—the confused clamor of the great flock.

5:15 P.M.   After three minutes of this bird bedlam, my ears feel weary and battered and deafened. There are alarm notes, quarreling notes, excitement, discontent, gossiping, the hubbub of the hundreds of birds around me.

5:20 P.M.   The uproar reaches a crescendo. Then there is, suddenly, silence. A perfect hush falls on the multitude of birds. It is followed by a silken whirring, a mighty fluttering, and the plumes of the phragmites wave in the wing-formed wind as the birds rise in unison into the air. For a moment, all the stems around me rock as in a breeze.

5:22 P.M.   Beyond the swamp stream, the birds have alighted in another and larger stand of phragmites where they will spend the night. I hear their confused clamor muted by distance. I also hear the voices of a new concentration of starlings building up in the maples.

5:31 P.M.   The chill is growing. Shadows have engulfed the phragmites.

5:42 P.M.   Now the second wave breaks over the plumed reeds. The deserted phragmites are again filled with life. The concentration and the vast tumult builds up with each new addition to the flock. A redwing—one of those still to migrate—alights close behind my head. Its surprised "Check!" rings loud in my ears. There are little pauses, from time to time, in the vast tumult of bird voices beating against my ears. And in one of them a single starling, almost overhead, imitates a snatch of the sweet, plaintive song of the white-throat.

5:51 P.M.   Again there is the sudden hushing of the din, the sudden mounting "Wooosh!" of wings, the swaying of the plumes above my head. These birds, too, cross the stream to the larger stand of phragmites for the night.

6:07 P.M.   The individual reed stems are merging together in the gloom. The chill of the night, the smell of the swamp, the feel of mist is in the air.

6:39 P.M.   No more birds have come. Outside I hear the flutter and splash of two ducks alighting on the swamp stream. The thronging birds in the far phragmites have fallen quiet. Now, even the steely hum of a mosquito sounds large in my ears. I flounder out of the phragmites, feeling my way, and ascend the garden slope. Darkness is all around. The homecoming of the birds is over.

October 17

Spider Songs   For a long time now I have been listening for spider songs. But I have never heard one. Spiders are considered stealthy and silent creatures. Stealthy they may be; but they are not always silent. A number of species produce sounds audible to the human ear. John Burroughs was once sitting among fallen leaves in the autumn when he was attracted by a low, purring sound. He was amazed to find it was produced by a spider. All spider songs are instrumental. They are produced by spines that rub together. Most spider music is low and difficult to catch, but I have heard of one species that will stand its ground when disturbed and buzz loudly like an angry bee.

October 18

The Swinging Leaf   For five minutes this morning, I watched a mantis held prisoner by a swinging leaf. The insect clung to a rose bush just outside the kitchen window. Near it, a dry leaf dangled at the end of a thread of spider silk. The breeze swung the leaf back and forth pendulumwise, and the head of the mantis turned from side to side, like the head of a spectator at a tennis match, as it followed its movements. Anything that moves is of interest to the praying mantis. It is through movement that it is attracted to its prey.

A Blackbird Tries to Catch a Mantis   At the edge of the swamp, this afternoon, a praying mantis launched itself from a dry grass clump and fluttered away along the hillside. I watched a red-winged blackbird take after it, dive under it, come up from below and try to pick the slow-flying insect from the air. But the mantis landed among cattails unharmed and uncaptured. Perhaps its bizarre appearance turned the redwing aside at the last moment.

On a number of occasions, I have seen birds bluffed out by these fearless insects. A few days ago, a bluejay alighted near a mantis in our backyard. It hopped toward the reared insect. The mantis gave no ground. It lashed out with its spined forelegs whenever the bird came near. It turned to face the bluejay each time it approached from a different direction. In the end, the jay flew off. For minutes afterward, the aroused mantis remained erect, reared and ready for another attack.

October 19

The Gift of Wonder   What a natural wellspring—cooling and refreshing the years—is the gift of wonder! It removes the dryness from life and keeps our days fresh and expanding.

October 20

The Mighty Mites   I came upon a beetle this morning, one of the ground beetles, perhaps half an inch long, laboring across the driveway. It carried with it a bizarre, living cargo. Massed on the underside of its body and overflowing onto its back was a solid mass of mites. There seemed to be literally hundreds of them, crowded and clinging together, several deep. The mass was constantly in motion. The miserable beetle, supporting this parasitic host, moved slowly, painfully, with difficulty. Mites are everywhere in nature. They ride on birds and they travel pickaback on snakes and they invade stored foods and they produce minute galls in plants. There is a red mite that lives on dragonflies, a mite that preys on mosquitoes, even an almost-microscope white mite that is found on *Drosophila* fruit flies. Among the "littler fleas" of Swift's immortal jingle, mites are the *ad infinitum.* The mighty mites!

October 21

Sound of the Falling Leaves   Chill rain in the night has stripped down the leaves and I walk for the morning papers along a path paved with maple gold. The gray and white cat that, a few months ago, ran to meet me over the green of fallen maple keys, now runs over the yellow of fallen maple leaves. As I come home, I hear the wild clamor of geese in the sky and see the first arrowhead of autumn heading south.

By afternoon, the day has cleared. Sunshine streams through the threadbare clumps of wild cherries at the garden. I walk about, taking stock of the innumerable changes on the hillside. The clump of golden asters is now dry and brown, the milkweeds, stripped of their leaves, are straight spikes thrusting up from the ground and holding the browning seed pods. Seeds are everywhere. I find them between my fingers when I run my hands through the grass tops. Autumn is a time of accounting, summing up, harvest and inventory.

How small are the sounds produced by the death of a leaf! I see the maple leaves and the wild cherry leaves and the apple leaves lose their grip and descend through the air. I catch faint tappings and flutterings as they hit or rub against the twigs. Some leaves swoop and whirl and scud, others descend slowly, directly like the fall of a snowflake. But each breeze that sweeps through the branches overhead today, brings a rain of leaves descending around me. Each hour brings its visible changes to the garden. Change is a measure of time and, in the autumn, time seems speeded up. What was, is not, and never again will be; what is, is change.

Analyzing and Discussing the Text

1. Describe the differences between Thoreau's "raw" journal and Teale's "crafted" journal.
2. Which *specific* aspects of his environment does Teale examine in order to learn about autumn?
3. Teale usually begins his journal entries with his own natural observations, but these quickly evolve into meditations or accounts of related events. What is the point of structuring the writing with dates if each entry is actually a mini-essay and not a "true" journal entry? Is it possible to read the whole chapter as a unified essay? What kind of cohesiveness is there?
4. Why does Teale note the precise passage of time in his October 16 entry?
5. Explain what Teale means by "the gift of wonder" in the October 19 entry. Does his writing display this "gift"?

Experiencing and Writing About the World

1. "We see things about us," writes Teale, "and sense larger meanings just beyond our grasp." Spend a week jotting down daily observations and stretching to explain the deeper significance of what you perceive. Make a real effort to speculate about "larger meanings," not merely to accept phenomena at face value.

2. Keep your own "October Journal." Make some of your entries terse and Thoreauvian and others meditative and explanatory like Teale's. You might even devote a few entries to considering the differences between these two styles of observation and expression. Which one seems most natural to you?

3. Write an analytical essay in which you evaluate Teale's use of the journal format as a stylistic device. What seem to be the author's reasons for using the journal-like style in a book prepared for other readers? In what ways do the entries fall short of the valuable qualities— fresh emotion, informal language, observational detail—that emerge in other examples of genuinely private journal writing? Use as many specific examples from the text as possible, and attempt to note both the failures and the successes of this published journal.

URSULA K. LE GUIN

Riding Shotgun

Ursula K. Le Guin (1929–   ) was born in Berkeley, California, the daughter of the distinguished anthropologist Alfred L. Kroeber and the writer Theodora Kroeber (*Ishi: The Last of His Tribe*). Le Guin attended Radcliffe College (A.B., 1951) and Columbia University (A.M., 1952), and has since become a prominent novelist, poet, and essayist in her own right. In addition to her writing, she has served as a visiting lecturer and writer in residence at such institutions as Portland State University, the University of California at San Diego, the University of Reading in England, Kenyon College, and Tulane University. With the publication of *The Earthsea Trilogy* in 1977, she began to catch the eye of major literary scholars; this series of novels, influenced by Taoist philosophy, conceptualizes the universe as a vast equilibrium, a self-regulating ecological system. Le Guin's science fiction (or "speculative fiction") novel *The Left Hand of Darkness* (1969) received both the Hugo and the Nebula awards, as did her 1975 novel *The Dispossessed*. Her 1985 book *Always Coming Home* was nominated for the American Book Award. She has described her own speculative fiction as "thought experiments," asserting that she tends to describe "certain aspects of psychological reality in the novelist's way, which is by inventing elaborately circumstantial lies."

The following journal excerpt, published as part of the 1988 special issue of *Antaeus* devoted to journals, diaries, and notebooks, begins factually enough, noting speed, location, and precise physical observations as Le Guin rides in the passenger seat of a "diesel VW" en route from Oregon (she lives in Portland) to Georgia in June 1981. But she can't keep out her imagination. The entries become increasingly crafted, metaphorical — "The sky," she notes at one point, "is as blue as fire." Throughout the piece, however, the language remains notebook-like: terse, fragmented, undeveloped. In Le Guin's hands, raw information (names of places, bits of natural observation) assumes the intensity of poetry, as in the comment, "The rosepink shadowless mountains of dawn are now daylit, deep-shadowed, and the moon has lost her dominion." This journal demonstrates the power of the raw fact, when recorded in careful language, to "flower out into a truth," as Thoreau put it in one of his early journal entries.

From a diary written in the right front seat of a diesel VW on the way east from Oregon to Georgia in June of 1981, and on the way west from Georgia to California in July.

Indiana and Points East
We're doing 55 on Indiana 65.
> Jasper County.
> Flooded fields.
> Iroquois River spread way out, wide and brown as a Hershey
>> bar.
> Distances in this glacier-flattened, planed-down ground-level
>> ground aren't blue, but whitish, and the sky is whitish-blue.
> It's in the eighties at 9:30 in the morning, the air is soft and
> humid, and the wind darkens the flooded fields between rows of
>> oaks.
> Watch Your Speed — We Are.
Severely clean white farmhouses inside square white fences painted by
> Tom Sawyer yesterday produce
a smell of dung. A rich and heavy smell of dung on the southwest wind.
Can shit be heady?
La merde majestueuse.
> This is the "Old Northwest."
Not very old, not very north, not very west. And in Indiana
there are no Indians.
> Wabash River

right up to the road and the oaks are standing
ten feet out in the brown shadowmottled flood,
but the man at the diesel station just says:
You should of seen her yesterday.

The essence is motion being in motion moving on not resting at a point:
and so by catching at points and letting them go again without recur-
rence or rhyme or rhythm I attempt to suggest or imitate that essence
the essence of which is that you cannot catch it.
Of course there are continuities:
the other aspect of the essence of moving on.

The country courthouses.
Kids on bikes.
White frame houses with high sashed windows.
Dipping telephone wires, telephone poles.
The names of the dispossessed.
The redwing blackbird singing to you from fencepost to fencepost.
Dave and Shelley singing "You're the Reason God Made
    Oklahoma" on the radio.
The yellow weedy clover by the road.
The flowering grasses.
And the crow, not the Indian, the bird, you seen one crow you seen
    'em all, kronk kronk.

CHEW MAIL POUCH TOBACCO
TREAT YOURSELF TO THE BEST

on an old plank barn, the letters half-worn off, and that's a continuity,
not only in space but time: my California in the thirties, & I at
six years old would read the sign and imagine a Pony Express rider at
full gallop eating a candy cigarette.

Lafayette
Greencastle
And the roadsign points: Left to Indianapolis
                         Right to Brazil.

                    Now there's some choice.

Another day
Ohio, south Ohio, Clermont County.
Cloudpuffs repeat roundtop treeshapes.
Under the grass you see the limestone layers, as if you drove on the
ramparts of a fallen castle the size of Clermont County.

Ohio 50, following Stonelick Creek.
Daylilies dayglow orange in dark roadside woods
Brick farmhouses painted white, small, solid, far between.

Owensville founded 1839
Monterey
Milford
Marathon   Little towns beads on a string
Brown Country
Vera Cruz   A Spaniard in the works?
Fayetteville   founded 1818 by Cornelion MacGroarty
     on the Little Miami River
Nite Crawlers 65 cents a dozen

     There's a continuity, though the prices change:
     Nite Crawlers crawling clear across the continent.

Highland County
Dodsonville
Allenburg   The road dips up and down in great swells like the
     sea
Hoagland
The Mad River, about one and one-half foot wide
Hillsboro, home of Eliza Jane Thompson, Early Temperance
     Crusader
Clearcreek
   Boston
     Rainsboro
Ross County
   Bainbridge
     Paint Creek
Seip—

But Seip is older than Eliza Jane, and older than Ohio.
Seip is a village twenty centuries old.
Posts mark the postholes of the houses within the encircling wall; all
walls are air, now; you rebuild them in your mind.
Beyond the little houses stands the long, steepsided mound, silent in
the sunlight, except for the bumblebee of a power mower circling it,
performing the clockwise spiral rites of the god Technology, the god
that cuts the grass; the long, sweet grass on the enormous, ancient altar.
A church half the age of Stonehenge and twice the age of Chartres. A
country church.

Onward past Bourneville, Slate Mill, North Fork Farm, to Chillicothe.
   At Chillicothe, the Hopewell Burial Mounds.

The people whom the white invaders dispossessed had been living here
for several hundred years; they called the ones who built these mounds
the Old Ones.
Walk in the silence of the vast sacred enclosure among the green mounds
built above the bones and ashes of the illustrious dead
laid between levels of mica, sheets of mica
transparent and glittering as eyes, as souls.
The pipes are stolen
The sacred pipes are broken
The beautiful carvings of Bobcat, Prairie-hen, Raven, Turtle, Owl
The sheets of pure thin copper cut in the shape of the Bear,
    of the Falcon, the soul-falcon,
    of the falcon's foot
    and the human hand.

So, back to the New World, the thin, sick skin we laid on this land,
    the white skin. And onward past Londonderry, Salt Creek,
    Ratcliffburg, Allensville, Zaleski Freewill Baptist Church, Lump
    Coal for Sale,
and you can see the streaks of coal in the shaley yellow soil. Prattsville.
Dingers Motel in Prattsville. Athens County. Greysville. Coolville.
Hey man I come from Coolville. And cross the brown Ohio
into WEST VIRGINIA.

And another day
Now here are Allegheny names as we went in the early morning
with the red sun rising over the misty heads and chill fog-filled
hollers of the hills:

    Buky Run
    Ellenboro
    Pennboro
    Burnells Run
    Spring Run

The sun is robed in a glory of mist enrayed by tree-branch shadows
shooting like arrows down.

    Snow Bird Road
    Smithburg
    Englands Run
    Morgans Run
    Buckeye Run
    Dark Hollow
    Fort New Salem

Dog Run
Cherry Camp
Raccoon Run
Salem Fork
Flinderation.

After breakfast at Lums', the Entire Lums Family Thanks You,
comes the Child Evangelism Camp, and Harmony Grove,
and Pruntytown, 1798, Founded by John Prunty.
And we come over Laurel Mountain and from the top see all the misty
   ridges
and coming down we're into the Eastern Seabord smog, that yellow bile
that you see from airplanes, the yellow breath of our god.
Nite Crawlers 75 cents a dozen,
beside the Cheat River, a misty mirror for the hills.
Into Maryland at Backbone Mountain
and then right back into West Virginia, a state all backbone, loyal to
   the union.

Mineral County.
Mount Storm.
The Knobley Farm, 1766, on knobbly hills
Ridgeville village on the hogback ridge
Hampshire County, 1754, we keep going back
The Stone House
Little Cacapon River
Paw Paw, on Short Mountain. Where ye bin, honey?
            I bin to Paw Paw, maw.

WELCOME TO VIRGINIA!   *Jesus is coming ready or not*

And it's left one mile to Mecca, and right one mile to Gore.
We'd better go straight on.
So we went on to Georgia.

Far West Going West
WELCOME TO UTAH early in the morning.
The sunflowers are confused, haven't got turned sunwards yet, face
   every which way.
Juniper. A good, strong, catspray smell of juniper in the high dry air.
Sagebrush, chamiso, the little yellow-flowered clover that's been along
   our way from Oregon to Georgia and back. And crows.
Suddenly we descend from mountains into desert
where there are monsters.
A potbellied Mexican waterjug two hundred feet high
turns into a sphinx as you pass it.

A throne of red rock with no seat, a hundred feet high.
Red lumps and knobs and kneecaps and one-eyed skulls the size of a
    house.

The sunflowers now are all staring East like Parsees,
except a couple in the shadow of the roadcut, which haven't got the
news or received orders yet.
        There aren't a whole lot of names, in Utah,
        but here's one: Hole in the Rock:
                big white letters on a big red bluff with a hole in it, yessir,
                and also Paintings of Christ and Taxidermy.

A lone and conceivably insurgent but probably uninformed sunflower
stands in the shadow of a cliff, facing southwest, at 7:41 A.M.
Well the last time *I* saw the sun it was over *there* and how do I know
where the damn thing's got to?
        Arches National Monument, near Moab. Red stone arches. Red stone
        lingams, copulating alligators, camels, triceratops, keyholes,
        elephants, pillows, towers, leaves, fins of the Ouroboros, lizard's
        heads. A woman of red stone and a man of red stone, very tall,
        stand facing the falcon-faced god of the red stone. Many tall,
        strange stone people standing on the red sand under the red cliffs;
        and the sand dunes have turned to stone, and the Jurassic sea that
        lapped on these red beaches dried and dried and dried away and
        shrank to the Mormons' bitter lake. The sky is as blue as fire.
Northward, stone dunes in white terraces and stairways pile up to the
violet-red turrets and buttresses of a most terrible city inhabited
by the Wind. A purple fortress stands before the gates, and in front
of it, four tall, shapeless kings of stone stand guard.

Next morning
Heading out of green and gentle Delta to the Nevada line, early, to get
across the desert in the cool.
        Jackrabbits flit
        on the moonlit salt pans
        to the left of the mountains of dawn.
        Jackrabbits dance
        in the moonlit sagebrush
        to the left of the mountains of dawn.

        Four pronghorn drift
        from the road into the sage
        in the twilight of morning
        to the left of the mountains of dawn.

Nevada
There are no names here.
    The rosepink shadowless mountains of dawn now are daylit,
    deep-shadowed, and the moon has lost her dominion.
    In this long first sunlight the desert is grayish-gold.
By the road as straight as an imaginary canal on Mars are flowers:
    Michaelmas daisies, Matiliha poppies white as the moon up there,
    milkweed, blue chicory. The green lush South was flowerless.
There are
five fenceposts
    in the middle of a vast sagebrush flat of which the middle
    is everywhere and the circumference nowhere.
Five crows
one crow per post
soak up the morning sun.
      Only Crow's been with us all the way,
    north, middle, south, and west. Even the redwing blackbird
    gave out in Nevada, but Crow's here, Crow of the Six Directions.
Jackrabbits go lolloping off like wallabies
    with magnificent blacktipped ears.
    Gabbs Luning. There's a name for you!
    At Gabbs Luning there's a Schneelite Mine.
    I don't believe anything in Nevada. This is pure Coyote country.
A vast lake that holds no water
is full to the brim of glittering light.
Far out, toward the center of the lake,
lie the bones of a wrecked ship
that struck on the reef of the mirage
and sank through heatwaves down and down
to lie now bleaching fathoms deep in blinding light,
all souls aboard her drowned in air.
Probably a potash mine. Who knows? We drive on West.

Analyzing and Discussing the Text

1. Describe Le Guin's style in this "diary." Do these seem like casual
   notes or are they artful in some way?
2. Does this travel diary manage to capture the "essence of motion"? If
   so, how?
3. What use does Le Guin make of names in this diary?

4. Instead of giving dates, Le Guin merely writes "And another day" or "Next morning" or notes the general location, such as "Far West Going West." What is the effect of such divisions within the diary?
5. Examine Le Guin's descriptions of nature. Does she use any peculiar images or phrases? Give examples.

Experiencing and Writing About the World

1. Attempt to keep a Le Guin-like, freewheeling travel notebook, either during an extended trip or during a series of short drives through town. Imitate the disjointedness, efficiency, and eccentricity of Le Guin's entries—few words, no particular flow of ideas, and avoidance of clichés.
2. Notice how Le Guin makes artful use—or perhaps simply takes advantage of the inherent artfulness—of place names in this diary. Keep a diary of your own, even if you don't do any major traveling, in which you conspicuously record names of things and places. If yours is a diary of nearby travels, then simply record names of people, streets, neighborhoods, stores, and other local landmarks. As you do so, consider how knowing names contributes to our appreciation of places.
3. Write an analysis of the wide range of journal-writing styles in the examples selected for this anthology. What are the similarities between Le Guin's prose style and Thoreau's? How do the sparer styles contrast with those of Muir, Teale, and even Pyne (the final selection in this chapter)? What seem to be the particular advantages of each style?

STEPHEN J. PYNE

Monsoon Lightning

Born in San Francisco, Stephen J. Pyne (1949–   ) moved to Phoenix, Arizona, at an early age and has lived there for most of his life. At the age of eighteen, fresh out of high school, Pyne joined a forest fire crew at the North Rim of the Grand Canyon, thus launching an "obsession with fire" that brought him back to the North Rim to fight fires for fifteen summers. Pyne attended Stanford University, graduating in 1971 with a B.A. in English and a minor in geology. Five years later he completed his Ph.D. in American civilization at the University of Texas at Austin. He continued to fight forest fires in Grand Canyon National Park until 1981, but he gradually came to realize that fire fighting was "a young person's job." In 1981, after waiting five years simply to get an interview for an academic job, Pyne was hired to teach history at the University of Iowa, where he remained until 1986. He later taught briefly at the University of Arizona and at Arizona State University before joining the new American studies program at Arizona State University West in Phoenix. As a scholar, Pyne has forged a discipline out of his private passion, demonstrating in several major books that fire can serve as a paradigm for all environmental relationships. In 1982 the first volume of his planned five-book study of the history of fire throughout the world appeared—*Fire in America: A Cultural History of Wildland and Rural Fire.* *The Ice: A Journey to Antarctica* was published in 1986, adding to the series (which Pyne calls "the cycle of fire") a glimpse of the alternative to fire: a land of white ice. In 1989 Pyne published an account of his personal experience with fire called *Fire on the Rim. A Firefighter's Season at the Grand Canyon;* "Monsoon Lightning" is derived from the same notebooks that became this book. A five-year MacArthur Fellowship (1988–1992) enabled Pyne to prepare his next book, *Burning Bush: A Fire History of Australia* (1992). He is currently writing a "Eurasian" history on the same subject. This work all began with a question Pyne posed to himself more than a decade ago: "Could I imagine a world that was organized around fire?"

The following "journal of daily life" began in the terse, telegraphic notes of Pyne's actual fire-fighting journals. When approached by Daniel Halpern, the editor of *Antaeus,* about contributing to the journal's special issue on journals, diaries, and notebooks, Pyne set about the task of organizing his stray journal notes into a coherent article without altogether losing the immediacy and authenticity of the original language.

Unlike some of the other journal writers in this anthology, Pyne is not out to record the minute details of his environment; he focuses his attention instead on the issues and experiences related to his job on a forest fire crew. The irony of his effort to record his life as a fire fighter is that he has either "Lots of time to write, not much to write about," or so much work to do that there is no opportunity to write about it. Writing and living, Pyne quickly learns, are not especially compatible for the person who works every day—from reading Thoreau, Muir, Teale, and Le Guin, one could forget that many people don't have the luxury of casual observation and journal writing. In fact, Pyne's notebook serves two purposes: it is a record of his experiences as a fire fighter, but even more important, it is a log of the time he has put in on each fire, providing information needed for him to get paid. The title "Monsoon Lightning," suggesting intermittent torrents of activity, aptly describes Pyne's experience as he attempts to record what happens between June 26 and July 10: "First there is nothing to write about, then there is too much," he says. But in an essential way, writing is bound up with the activity of fire fighting, as shown in the formula "No report, no pay." The idea of a payoff for writing is seldom so concrete, but even the naturalist acknowledges the same connection between making a living and recording experiences as precisely and as thoroughly as possible.

> For fifteen summers I worked on a forest fire crew at the North Rim of Grand Canyon, and from time to time I kept a journal of daily life. What follows is a distillation of that experience. Some terms will be unfamiliar: "The Area" refers to the Park Service–developed "area" at Bright Angel Point; "fire cache" is what forest firefighters call their fire station; "fedco" is the tradename for a five-gallon backpack pump; "Affirms" is the acronym for a computer-based information system which also calculates fire-danger ratings; "SWFF" stands for Southwest Forest Firefighters—in this instance, a squad of Navajos. "Rim" of course refers to the North Rim.

The Area / June 26

Another day in the cache. SWFFS sent with Stieg to repair fence. *T'oo bah'ih,* they call it; "no good." Dry, hot, windy. Fire weather great: fires lousy.

Fires everywhere but on the Rim. Took coffee break at the Lodge and watched the smokes on the Hualapai Reservation. Joe says they burn to clear off the chained juniper and the hotter the fire the better. Everything smoked in to the southwest. Kent sighted what looked like a smoke to the south of Kendricks Peak, on the Coconino; Forest Service action. When he took the situation report on Affirms this morning, Joe says, half the national forests in Arizona have a project fire. Kent and The Kid drove to North Rim Tower for lunch and a look and found nothing.

Ran heliport—routine shuttle flights between rims. Mostly just moved in and out of the fire cache, painting and sharpening tools and wrestling with the saws; the Big Mac is the only one that works, which Joe says is about normal. Later The Kid attacked Joe with a fedco and we nearly had an all-out water brawl. If Kent hadn't sabotaged the pumper, Joe would have retaliated by flooding The Kid out of the cache.

Listened to Uncle Jimmy reminisce about the Old Days—lots of fires, no jerry jobs, no idiot bosses. B.S., no doubt. Says we have to wait for the monsoon. Says that all the fires we see around the Rim have been set by people, but almost all our fires are set by lightning. Says we have to wait for the monsoon lightning.

After everyone had left for Lodge, I walked to the helispot and watched stars over the Canyon. Strong, crazy winds along Rim. There are always winds along the Rim. You can hear it from the cabin. The Rim is a strange, violent place: it simply, directly joins Plateau and Canyon, and there is nothing to grade between them; a kind of geographic rite of passage. I guess that is why the winds are so busy there. But the Rim is where we live and work. Our cabin is right along Rim. Joe says most of our fires occur along the Rim, which figures. Uncle Jimmy says the Rim is a time as much as a place. Whatever that means.

Read, and wrote in journal. Lots of time to write, not much to write about. Have entered nothing for several days. Glad I didn't join the rest of crew at the Lodge. Things got pretty rowdy in the saloon and the rangers had to shut it down. Uncle Jimmy says that's what happens when there aren't enough fires.

The Area / June 29

It seems crazy to live on the North Rim and not see the Grand Canyon the tourists see, so yesterday—my lieu day—I left the Area for the scenic drive. When I got back Stieg told me about the fire at Ribbons Falls, along the Kaibab Trail.

Everyone went save him and me. Had I been here, he says, I would have gone too. I may be happy I missed it. Joe says that it was a typical Canyon fire—most of it burned out before anyone arrived (a bitch of a hike, too: everyone had to jog down with packs in noon heat). Joe and The Kid followed the flames up some talus slopes and chased them into pack-rat middens. Winds were too squirrely to fly in or out so they had to hike back up. Waited for the shadows. Too bad they didn't have any fishing tackle. I watched some of the fire from Bright Angel Point. Joe says I can go by myself next time.

This afternoon the Forest Service had a big fire break out in Moquitch Canyon. We hung around the cache, sort of waiting for a call as backup. But nothing came through. The Kid climbed the tree-tower by the office and watched the smoke billow skyward. He says he could see clouds building up on the Peaks, too. Uncle Jimmy said, yes, he thinks the monsoon is coming. Then tonight we all went to the Lodge (I was more or less told I was going) and sat on the veranda and watched the storms plaster the San Francisco Peaks with lightning. Everything was pitch-black—cloudy overhead, no moon, just lightning silhouetting the Peaks in orange and yellow. Joe said it's converging on us, it'll be our turn soon. As we left I thought I could hear thunder rumble through Bright Angel Canyon.

Walked home; the others drove.

Cape Final / June 30

Fire at Cape Final. Everyone went—SWFFS too. Fire was along Rim: Joe and The Kid had to go into the Canyon to catch part of the fire that slopped over into Canyon brush; the rest of us stayed on Rim, hotspotting; still don't have a complete line around fire. Got the blue pumper in. McLaren (Park fire officer) called for slurry and a plane (B-17?) from South Rim airport made two passes. Hard time finding fire until it flared up. Lots of confusion. Uncle Jimmy disgusted. Joe says it's about time; says we ought to name it the Finally fire.

Cape Final: furtherest point east on Rim. Sticks out like a sore thumb. Near nothing else. Kent says we may might as well be in Chuar Amphitheater. No source tree, and may not be lightning-caused. Fireroad E-7 not far from here, so a tourist might have walked out this far. No one knows.

Using pocket notebook. Will transfer notes to journal later. Rations at 21:00 hrs. Mopped up until midnight. Kent and The Kid sent back to the Area for sleeping bags and headlamps and more rations.

Cape Final / July 1

Mopped up all day. Worked in early dawn, then had breakfast. Kent found a swath of white ash and thinks fire started there. Two crews working pumpers, and we have lots of water, though Uncle Jimmy and a SWFF (Henry John) stayed with shovels and fedcos; says too much water is bad for your technique. Says we still don't know how to fight fire. We had some snag fires early in the season, but not everyone had arrived and the rookies like me hadn't even gone through fire school and we haven't really worked together since then. Joe told me to put down my pulaski and take care of the real mopup. He meant my times.

Keep track of every hour, he said. Nothing fancy, just the fires and times. Don't trust them to do it for you. They never make mistakes in your favor. Better yet, he said, fill out the report yourself. No report, no pay. Yes, I told him. I have my pocket notebook in my firepack.

Broke for dinner around sunset and sat on Rim. Not a great view—the Kaibab puts the Canyon into shadow, but sky colors wonderful. Took half-hour dinner so we could claim another hour of O.T. Left some handtools and a couple of canteens and a fedco in case more smokes show up after we leave. The Kid says he'll return tomorrow to check and pull up the flagging. We should make it back to the Area by 23:00.

The Area / July 2

Spent day in cache. The Kid and Uncle Jimmy checked the Finally fire and declared it out. Fixing tools and re-outfitting pumpers. Hot, cloudless.

Filled out a time report for the first time. This would normally be done by the fire boss, but I figured it would be good practice and that way Uncle Jimmy could make sure my times agreed with his. He spent day in Fire Pit completing the report. Every so often he would emerge and shout obscenities about the idiotic codes that you have to use to record everything and how he couldn't find the right code and what the hell difference did it make if the fire burned in fuel model C or U because it burned on the Rim which meant it burned in every kind of fuel. Then he would get a cup of coffee or fuss with the saws or pumpers before going back to the Pit.

Heard an incredible rumor. The rangers have coveted some Pivetta boots for their uniforms but haven't had any way to pay for them, so Kent says they told Uncle Jimmy to give them some overtime—charge it to the fire—enough to cover the costs. They say the fire was so disorganized, so many folks came and went, that no one would know. Uncle Jimmy refused. He says if they had any sense they would connive to get to the fires rather than to the money. But Kent thinks the reports were doctored after Uncle Jimmy sent them on.

A couple of the SWFFS came by looking for rides to the Lodge. Everyone else had gone, so I said I would drive them. Stayed for a couple of hours.

Copied jottings from notebook into log pretty much as is. I had thought that I could make it into a story. Now I find that there isn't much else to say. Can't write and fight both.

Swamp Ridge / July 4

Monsoon lightning. Fantastic storm throughout afternoon—bolts every few seconds, lights in cache and Pit blinking with each flash, rain and hail piling up on asphalt. Dispatched in pairs, one fire crew regular and one SWFF. Five fires so far. Sent out with Tommie Begaye to fire on Swamp Ridge.

Long drive, through national forest, then back into Park. Recon 1 gave us a bearing of 172°, corrected; snag fire; about half mile from Swamp Point road. Flagged our route in. Tommie spotted smoke, about forty yards from compass line. Gigantic ponderosa, base half-rotten. Cleared out swath along lean, then dropped tree. Put in a line. Bucked up and split open bole and scraped embers out and cooled with dirt and water. Little surface spread: needles and duff still wet from rains. Both of us made an extra trip back to pumper for fedcos and rations (only brought in one pack initially: took saw and fedco and handtools instead); dark when we left fire for vehicle. Mopped until now, around 23:00. Tommie has gone back for sleeping bags. Should finish in morning. Decided to name it the Independence fire. Listening to radio.

Half of crew on the Grail fire at Lancelot Point. Drier there and a patch of bug-killed snags, and fire got caught in strong winds along Rim and downdrafts from thunderheads. Uncle Jimmy says it's probably an acre, with maybe a dozen snags that need to be dropped. Lots of mopup. Reinforcements came in by helicopter—found old helispot not far from fire. Other fires about like ours. No one can raise Joe, somewhere in Kanabownits Canyon, and Chuck may send out a search party. Plan to go to Grail fire and help mop tomorrow. Uncle Jimmy says more fires will probably show up in morning. Got Joe on radio: says his fire was too easy and there won't be enough overtime and he wants another.

Twilight Zone, north of Point Sublime Road / July 5

Six fires this morning. Everyone dispatched from their fire to another except for the Grail fire, where two were left to drop snags and baby-sit. Recon 1 discovered smoke not far from us along Swamp Ridge, and we not only arrived there early but got pumper in (only couple hundred yards from W-4B fireroad). Green ponderosa, little spread by ground fire, fire mostly confined to lightning scar. Dropped and hosed down tree, then scratched a line. Over by noon. Sent to make initial attack on larger smoke in Twilight Zone—that's what Joe calls it. No fireroads here. Long hike on compass bearing (22°, corrected) from pumper. Joe and Henry John followed our flagging in. Tommie and I already had one small snag down and were ready to fell another. Joe said to finish it off. He said he and Henry would help clear a drop site, then dig line while Tommie and I bucked up the trunk. Took all afternoon. The Kid and two SWFFS joined us after dinner; brought in some fedcos and rations and canteens. All other fires out except Grail fire. Everyone else will go there tomorrow, and looks like they will call for Forest Service assistance—we're spread too thin. Uncle Jimmy wants to sling in some cubitainers of water and fedcos by helo to speed along the mopup at Grail. No storms today, but Uncle Jimmy thinks there may be more fires—sleepers, he calls them. Monsoon only starting.

Need to get new pocket notebook. This one nearly filled. Joe was right: if I hadn't kept score, I wouldn't remember which times went with which fire.

The Area / July 6

Grail fire still being mopped up, but everyone else back in Area; one FS tanker crew at Grail. Cache in uproar. Spent morning putting everything back in order—saws, pumpers, firepacks, times. Have to be ready for next bust. In afternoon, after Recon 1 gave us an all-clear, we returned to check old fires. Found a few smokes on Independence fire and dumped rest of canteens on them and worked the duff with shovels. Mopup—it's like proofing, it never ends. Waiting twenty minutes; no smokes, so left and pulled flags. The tough fires are on the Rim.

The Area / July 7
Rechecked Twilight fire—one small smoke in duff. Spent afternoon extracting a fire report from my notebook. As fire boss I have to submit reports (times) for both Independence and Twilight fires. Much more fun to fight fires than report them. The Kid says it's indecent to make fires continue by having to write them up. Joe says it's like double mopup. Affirms calls for drying spell over next few days, then new surge of monsoon moisture. Everyone back tonight, and I joined them at Lodge, but too tired for more than a couple of beers.

The Dragon / July 10
Big smoke reported on The Dragon around 16:00 two days ago. Chuck called for a helo, and Uncle Jimmy and I and Henry Goldtooth flew for initial attack. Winds too strong and squirrely to land; backed off on full power. Returned to Harvey Meadow and dropped Henry off and went back to Dragon and landed this time. Kent told to round up some reserves and drive them to the Dragon trailhead and hike in. Rest of regular crew and SWFFS to be flown in until dark. Uncle Jimmy and I flagged route from helispot to fire. Fire on Rim, a few acres in size.

Winds blustery. We jogged around fire with shovels and canteens. Lots of surface fire, whipped into red whitecaps by winds. Some fire apparently spilled over Rim into Canyon. Rim fire burning in a shallow basin, so we began lining it along the flanking ridges. Joe and Henry arrived. Sounds of helo overhead, the scrape and thunk of handtools on rock and duff and root, the whoosh and snap of flame. Work slow but heart fast: adrenalin flashed like lightning. More arrivals. Kent reached trailhead, but still had a couple-hour hike ahead of him; would arrive after dark. Sunset painted sky on fire.

Uncle Jimmy organized us into two squads—regular fire crew and SWFFS. Almost lost line at one point (flame advancing like a surf), but Henry John rallied SWFFS and they cut a scratch line and burned out and held. Joe found a good fire burning over Rim; but Uncle Jimmy wanted nothing to do with it at night. Kent and his mob arrived, and one fee collector crashed beneath a pine, and a thirsty ranger from the inner Canyon grabbed a quart canteen filled with chain oil, thinking it was water, and took a big swallow of thirty-weight; pretty well lubed for the night. Last helo flight brought in hot meal from Lodge. The Kid and

Tommie Begaye sent back to the helispot to get it. Very dark: only light comes from fire, boiling like lava. Cold. Sweat congealed. Joints stiff. Hungry. Can hear winds over and around Rim.

Ate late and by headlamp. Quiet; everyone tired. Joe and I sent on patrol. Kent told to take his mob and find a place to bed down; they'll begin mopping up in morning. Uncle Jimmy sat down on a small rise, with his back to the Rim—probably trying to take notes, get our times straight. Joe says we'll have to write a narrative for the fire because it is big and will cost more. We hiked around the perimeter, knocked fire out of the base of one snag, then lined it, and located a large flat rock that overlooked most of fire. Stars thick as embers.

The Dragon is a curious place, a peninsula that thrusts south into Canyon, nearly segregated from the Kaibab by erosion. It is all Rim: Canyon and Plateau nearly perfectly balanced, so that you are never far from either. Lots of fires. Fire signs everywhere. Lightning scars on many trees. Charred bark, scabs of brush where ponderosa burned out, bare limestone paves ground. Eerie, yet compelling. Joe says The Dragon has the highest fire load on North Rim. He says no one can be on the crew long and not experience a fire on Dragon, and no one can claim to have fought fire without coming here. No one else comes here; no rangers, no tourists, no one except the fire crew. Uncle Jimmy said in fire school that The Dragon was located at the apex of the Rim's fire triangle. Cute phrase, I thought. But The Dragon isn't cute: it's all fire and all Rim.

Listened to radio. Stieg didn't come. Suddenly refused to get into helo, and Kent had already departed, so he was left behind. Another fire was located just before sunset, however—small snag fire on Crystal Ridge. Stieg took Bundy (garbage collector), and our helo, on a return flight, helped guide him into smoke. Now his radio was stuck on broadcast, and we listened as he explained to a skeptical Bundy how they would drop the tree. Bundy didn't want to spot for Stieg under the tree, wanted to stand back with a fedco and squirt water on him if any branches fell; hilarious. Joe said that Stieg told him he planned to transfer to the rangers soon. Said it was too bad he froze up about flying because he had never been to a Dragon fire before. I guess he had had enough without The Dragon. Joe said Stieg deserved what was happening to him. Finally whatever jammed Stieg's radio open broke free. Joe called him and kidded him about not coming to a real fire. Then I saw it.

It was just a glow at first, an orange specter over the Rim. I saw tongues of flame and then Joe and I both heard it and we stared as the whole Canyon flank seemed to erupt into fire and Joe grabbed his radio and warned Uncle Jimmy who ran to the Rim in time to watch a thin stream of flame rush up to the Rim, then Uncle Jimmy shouted for the rest of the crew to get their asses out of their sleeping bags and get some tools because the whole fucking Canyon was on fire and if we didn't hold it at the Rim we would lose everything. Then it got really interesting.

A wild, true Rim fire. For half an hour everything was a frenzy of men and noise; saws whined and coughed, trees fell in crashes, handtools scraped and chipped in atonal splendor, radios and voices shouted over the roar of flames. Not once but several times long strips of flame rushed out of the Canyon. We stood on the Rim, our faces flushed with firelight, our backs in darkness. Uncle Jimmy was everywhere, shouting and cutting. But the line held. By the time we crawled back into our bags, a false dawn edged into view.

The fire went on for two more days. We dropped retardant from a PB4Y2 for several hours in that first morning to prevent another blowup. Uncle Jimmy reasoned that the fire had slopped over the Rim then crept along the surface downslope, drying out the brush above it, then caught some updrafts and swept up through the dessicated crowns. He didn't want that to happen again. Then mopup. All day. Sent Kent and the irregulars home; fire was lost on them. Joe and I donned fedcos and plunged down the slope into the scene of the night burn, the rocks slippery with slurry, careful to stay in the burned-out zones. Mopped up along slopes. Hot. Crummy night, slept only from exhaustion. Then another day of the same. Joe and I again had to go over the Rim and mop up. But that evening we were all flown home. Uncle Jimmy declared the fire out. He told me that Stieg would transfer soon and I could take over the blue pumper if I wanted.

Nothing left but the paperwork. Glad I took notes. Things were so confused that no one could agree on exactly what happened or to whom or when. Uncle Jimmy looked at my notes and gave me his and told me to write up a narrative. For a fire like this, he explained, you have to have a narrative as well as the coded report. You can't leave it in your pocket, he said. It has to be a public document. I hardly knew where to begin. First there is nothing to write about, then there is too much. It was as though a whole season had to be distilled into one bust, one fire. No report, no pay, Uncle Jimmy reminded me. All flame and no fortune. Write it.

Everyone planned to meet at the saloon and talk about The Dragon and fire and what a great time we had. The Kid suggested someone ought to write it up, and Joe said I was, and everyone laughed because they knew no one would read the narrative, only the times, and a real smokechaser would only want to go to another fire, not write up an old one. Sitting in the Pits, Joe calls it. Uncle Jimmy told everyone to go home and get ready for some serious drinking. Then he asked if I felt any different. Yeah, I said. I feel richer.

Walking to the Lodge tonight I saw Tommie Begaye on the other side of the road, mad that he had missed a ride and that I had chosen to walk rather than drive. This road *t'oo bah'ih*, he yelled. He ran over and then ahead of me. I ran past him. The pavement glistened like black scales. Then we both ran, shoulder-to-shoulder along the Rim, all the rest of the way.

Analyzing and Discussing the Text

1. What is the effect of Pyne's fire-fighter slang?
2. Why do the fire fighters have to wait for "monsoon lightning"? What does this phrase mean? Are the fire crews actually looking forward to fires?
3. How exactly does Pyne record his experiences? Does his language seem to have been written in the field? Does the language vary from entry to entry? Is there anything interesting about the way he describes fire itself?
4. Do you get a sense of the fire fighters as a "community"? How much does Pyne tell us about his co-workers?
5. Jimmy tells Pyne "the Rim is a time as much as a place." Why is there so much emphasis on time throughout the journal?
6. What, for Pyne, are the connections between writing and fire fighting?

Experiencing and Writing About the World

1. Have you ever had an outdoor job? Create a mock journal in which you describe several days' worth of typical experiences. Keep your writing clipped and hurried, notelike rather than in complete sentences. Try to use "authentic" language.
2. Keep a notebook about your current job, whether or not it is outdoors; if your job is being a student, then keep a notebook about your classes. Don't summarize complete days, though. Just record major or unusual events, comments people make, and interesting things you notice. Keep your writing trim. "Can't write and fight both," claims Pyne. Do you also find it hard to juggle writing and working?
3. Keep a journal strictly devoted to your leisure activities. How would it differ from a job-related notebook? After keeping this journal for a week or so, begin using occasional entries to contemplate the difference between leisure and work. Is there a fundamental difference

between doing something solely for pleasure or recreation and doing something to earn money? How would your outlook toward the natural world change if your income came directly from some sort of outdoor activity?

Suggestions for Further Reading

Bass, Rick. "On Camp Robbers, Rock Swifts, and Other Things Wild to the Heart." *Wild to the Heart*. New York: Norton, 1987.

Berry, Wendell. "Notes from an Absence and a Return." *A Continuous Harmony: Essays Cultural and Agricultural*. New York: Harcourt, 1972.

Deming, Alison. "An Island Notebook." *Georgia Review* 45.4 (1991): 747–59.

DeVoto, Bernard A. *Journals of Lewis & Clark*. Boston: Houghton Mifflin, 1973.

Durant, Mary, and Michael Harwood. *On the Road with John James Audubon*. New York: Dodd, 1980.

Finch, Robert. "North Beach Journal." *Outlands: Journeys to the Outer Edges of Cape Cod*. Boston: Godine, 1986.

Gruchow, Paul. *Journal of a Prairie Year*. Minneapolis: U of Minnesota P, 1985.

Kolodny, Annette, ed. "The Travel Diary of Elizabeth House Trist: Philadelphia to Natchez, 1783–84." *Journeys in New Worlds: Early American Women's Narratives*. Ed. William L. Andrews. Madison: U of Wisconsin P, 1990.

Muir, John. *My First Summer in the Sierra*. Boston: Houghton, 1911.

Peattie, Donald Culross. *An Almanac for Moderns*. 1935. Boston: Godine, 1980.

Prishvin, Mikhail. *Nature's Diary*. 1958. New York: Penguin, 1987.

Sarton, May. *Journal of a Solitude*. New York: Norton, 1973.

Schlissel, Lillian. *Women's Diaries of the Westward Journey*. New York: Schocken, 1982.

Snyder, Gary. *Earth House Hold*. New York: New Directions, 1969.

Wolfe, Thomas. *A Western Journal: A Daily Log of the Great Parks Trip, June 20–July 2, 1938*. 1939. Pittsburgh: U of Pittsburgh P, 1967.

PART THREE

Belonging to the World

©Katrina Thomas, 1968/Photo Researchers, Inc.

CHAPTER ONE

Nearby Nature

"Awareness," wrote Sigurd Olson, "is becoming acquainted with the environment no matter where one happens to be." If there is the danger, at one end of the spectrum, that we have become so separate from the natural world as to feel that nature is "alien" and "out there," then there is also a corresponding danger at the other end: the sense that there is no nature near us. We sometimes assume that nature is not really nature unless it is on a grand scale, located far away from our daily life and, preferably, featured on a television special. Like the explorers in Henry David Thoreau's time (and in earlier centuries) who sailed the world in search of treasure, we tend to feel that only what is distant is worthy of our attention, our investigation. Even a little observation and awareness remind us, however, that nature is also nearby. Thoreau himself insists that our most crucial knowledge of the world often comes from "home-cosmography." If we are aware of ourselves and of those aspects of nature that we, even the most thoroughly urbanized of us, encounter every day (such as the air, trees, lawns, and gardens), there is less chance that our society will continue seeing nature as something that exists only for us to manage, control, and exploit. Developing awareness of nearby nature may well be the best way to begin changing how we perceive and interact with the natural world.

Thoreau's exhortation to become "expert in home-cosmography" appears in the concluding chapter of *Walden*, and it is with this excerpt that we begin the following group of reflections on nearby nature. Sandra Cisnero's "Four Skinny Trees" shows that the local, the mundane, can be a source of inspiration and courage; the persistence of trees in the face of powerful, almost overwhelming urbanization, offers hope for a young woman who feels herself threatened in the city. In Maxine Kumin's essay, involvement with the tasks necessary to run her New Hampshire farm becomes intertwined with her sense of well-being and her poetic inspiration. For John Elder and Michael Pollan, the consideration of nearby nature leads directly to questions of environmental ethics. Elder sees the land near his Vermont home returning to wilderness, which raises the possibility that our society can get a second chance at increasing, rather than steadily depleting, wilderness land. For Pollan, on the other hand, the key ethical question is whether we should use our suburban land for gardens or for lawns. Each way of using the land involves a necessary battle with wild nature, but the values and goals associated with each approach are so different that the choice is critical. David Quammen voices ethical concerns about wild animals and what we do to them when we capture or breed them for our zoos, thus trying to make them a part of nearby nature.

HENRY DAVID THOREAU

From **Walden**

For biographical information, see the headnote for "Walking" in Part Two, Chapter One.

Thoreau's injunction to be "expert in home-cosmography" occurs in the concluding chapter of *Walden* (1854), marking his return to a central theme of the book—we do not need to leave our home place in order to "begin to find ourselves, and realize where we are and the infinite extent of our relations." In the following selection, however, the focus differs from the famous line in the book's first chapter: "I have travelled a good deal in Concord." Whereas the emphasis in the early line is on knowing one's surrounding areas—walking the woods near home rather than traveling abroad—he urges his reader in the following passage to "be a Columbus to whole new continents and worlds within you." For Thoreau, then, nearby nature offers the opportunity for both exploration of the external world and self-discovery. Thoreau sets his exhortation to "explore thyself" within a long catalogue of contemporary explorers who were much admired by his age but whom he finds wanting, and thus he serves as a social critic in this passage. His emblem for such false popular idols of his time is the famous British mariner, Sir John Franklin, an Arctic explorer who became lost and died while seeking a new Northwest trade route and whose wife achieved a kind of fame for herself by imploring other explorers to voyage in search of her lost husband. External voyaging thus offers only the lostness of "great circle-sailing"; for Thoreau, unlike most of his contemporaries, the crucial new channels are internal.

[Home-Cosmography]

To the sick the doctors wisely recommend a change of air and scenery. Thank Heaven, here is not all the world. The buck-eye does not grow in New England, and the mocking-bird is rarely heard here. The wild-goose is more of a cosmopolite than we; he breaks his fast in Canada, takes a luncheon in the Ohio, and plumes himself for the night in a southern bayou. Even the bison, to some extent, keeps pace with the seasons, cropping the pastures of the Colorado only till a greener and sweeter grass awaits him by the Yellowstone. Yet we think that if rail-fences are pulled down, and stone-walls piled up on our farms, bounds are henceforth set to our lives and our fates decided. If you are chosen town-clerk, forsooth, you cannot go to Tierra del Fuego this summer: but you may go to the land of infernal fire nevertheless. The universe is wider than our views of it.

Yet we should oftener look over the tafferel of our craft, like curious passengers, and not make the voyage like stupid sailors picking oakum. The other side of the globe is but the home of our correspondent. Our voyaging is only great-circle sailing, and the doctors prescribe for diseases of the skin merely. One hastens to Southern Africa to chase the giraffe; but surely that is not the game he would be after. How long, pray, would a man hunt giraffes if he could? Snipes and woodcocks also may afford rare sport; but I trust it would be nobler game to shoot one's self. —

> "Direct your eye sight inward, and you'll find
> A thousand regions in your mind
> Yet undiscovered. Travel them, and be
> Expert in home-cosmography."

What does Africa, —what does the West stand for? Is not our own interior white on the chart? black though it may prove, like the coast, when discovered. Is it the source of the Nile, or the Niger, or the Mississippi, or a North-West Passage around this continent, that we would find? Are these the problems which most concern mankind? Is Franklin the only man who is lost, that his wife should be so earnest to find him? Does Mr. Grinnell know where he himself is? Be rather the Mungo Park, the Lewis and Clarke and Frobisher, of your own streams and oceans; explore your own higher latitudes, —with shiploads of preserved meats to support you, if they be necessary; and pile the empty cans sky-high for a sign. Were preserved meats invented to preserve meat merely? Nay, be a Columbus to whole new continents and worlds within you, opening new channels, not of trade, but of thought. Every man is the lord of a realm beside which the earthly empire of the Czar is but a petty state, a hummock left by the ice. Yet some can be patriotic who have no *self*-respect, and sacrifice the greater to the less. They love the soil which makes their graves, but have no sympathy with the spirit which may still animate their clay. Patriotism is a maggot in their heads. What was the meaning of that South-Sea Exploring Expedition, with all its parade and expense, but an indirect recognition of the fact, that there are continents and seas in the moral world, to which every man is an isthmus or an inlet, yet unexplored by him, but that it is easier to sail many thousand miles through cold and storm and cannibals, in a government ship, with five hundred men and boys to assist one, than it is to explore the private sea, the Atlantic and Pacific Ocean of one's being alone. —

> "Erret, et extremos alter scrutetur Iberos.
> Plus habet hic vitæ, plus habet ille viæ."

> Let them wander and scrutinize the outlandish
>   Australians.
> I have more of God, they more of the road.

It is not worth the while to go round the world to count the cats in Zanzibar. Yet do this even till you can do better, and you may perhaps find some "Symmes' Hole" by which to get at the inside at last. England and France, Spain and Portugal, Gold Coast and Slave Coast, all front on this private sea; but no bark from them has ventured out of sight of land, though it is without doubt the direct way to India. If you would learn to speak all tongues and conform to the customs of all nations, if you would travel farther than all travellers, be naturalized in all climes, and cause the Sphinx to dash her head against a stone, even obey the precept of the old philosopher, and Explore thyself. Herein are demanded the eye and the nerve. Only the defeated and deserters go to the wars, cowards that run away and enlist. Start now on that farthest western way, which does not pause at the Mississippi or the Pacific, nor conduct toward a worn-out China or Japan, but leads on direct a tangent to this sphere, summer and winter, day and night, sun down, moon down, and at last earth down too.

Analyzing and Discussing the Text

1. Look closely at the first paragraph in this passage. Is its meaning and its place in the excerpt's overall argument readily apparent? Notice that the final sentence, with its references to a wider universe, might at first be misread as supportive of the kind of travel Thoreau opposes. What stylistic and teaching function might such a sentence finally serve for Thoreau?
2. What does Thoreau mean when he says of some people that "Patriotism is a maggot in their heads"?
3. Thoreau says that "it is easier to sail many thousand miles through cold and storm and cannibals . . . than it is to explore the private sea, the Atlantic and Pacific Ocean of one's being alone." Why might this be the case?

4. This excerpt demonstrates the rhetorical strategy of comparison and contrast, both linking and distinguishing between geographical travel and inner travel ("soul searching"). Analyze Thoreau's technique of comparison. If it is sometimes difficult to detect which two processes are being compared, try to explain (as a fellow writer) why he might have wanted to keep the comparison subtle rather than making the connection too directly.

Experiencing and Writing About the World

1. Imagine Thoreau as a social critic commenting on present-day society. Posing as a "latter-day Thoreau," write a short essay in which you speculate about what he might say about such features of contemporary culture as our efforts at space exploration, the adventure travel industry, or other examples of the modern interest in geographical travel.
2. Some social critics would argue that one of the perils in our own age is a kind of easy, even narcissistic, self-absorption. Write an essay in which you distinguish between the serious self-discovery advocated by Thoreau and this kind of bogus overinvolvement with oneself. What are the key features that distinguish them?
3. Select two or three essays from this anthology that demonstrate to some degree a belief in the importance of "home-cosmography." Write a careful analysis of these essays in which you explain precisely how they embody or deviate from the Thoreauvian ideals. A few pieces that might work well for this topic are Robert Finch's "Very Like a Whale," Annie Dillard's "Living Like Weasels," and Scott Russell Sanders's "Listening to Owls."
4. Do any of the essays in this anthology implicitly rebut Thoreau's critique of travel to geographically distant places by showing that such travel also can facilitate self-discovery? Write a critique of Thoreau's argument, using specific passages from such pieces as the excerpts from Peter Matthiessen's *The Snow Leopard*, Barry Lopez's "The Image of the Unicorn," Eddy Harris's remarks from the beginning of *Mississippi Solo*, and David Roberts's "Five Days on Mount Huntington" to support your ideas.

SANDRA CISNEROS

Four Skinny Trees

Sandra Cisneros (1954–   ) was born in Chicago, Illinois, the daughter of a Mexican father and a Mexican-American mother. She graduated from Loyola University in Chicago and from the University of Iowa Writers Workshop, and since then she has taught creative writing at an alternative school for high school drop-outs and as a visiting professor at a number of universities around the country. She has also worked as a college recruiter and an arts administrator. Cisneros, who has received two National Endowment for the Arts awards, has published one book of poetry, *My Wicked Wicked Ways* (1987); a collection of short stories called *Woman Hollering Creek and Other Stories* (1991); and a widely acclaimed novel entitled *The House on Mango Street* (1983), from which the following chapter is taken. She has said that she writes by obsession, not inspiration: "If I were asked what it is that I write about, I would have to say that I write about those ghosts inside who haunt me... of that which even memory does not like to mention."

In the "Four Skinny Trees" chapter from *The House on Mango Street*, however, Cisneros combats the ghosts of an inner-city childhood—the poverty, the sense of powerlessness, the loneliness, and the alienation—by depicting her narrator's strong kinship with nearby nature. From the character Esperanza's perspective, the four struggling young children in her family—herself, her sister Nenny, and her two brothers—are like the four skinny trees in their city neighborhood. Esperanza takes heart from these trees, which "grew despite concrete." When she feels herself to be only "a tiny thing against so many bricks," she sees in them a secret, but ferocious, strength that gives her inspiration and hope.

They are the only ones who understand me. I am the only one who understands them. Four skinny trees with skinny necks and pointy elbows like mine. Four who do not belong here but are here. Four raggedy excuses planted by the city. From our room we can hear them, but Nenny just sleeps and doesn't appreciate these things.

Their strength is secret. They send ferocious roots beneath the ground. They grow up and they grow down and grab the earth between their hairy toes and bite the sky with violent teeth and never quit their anger. This is how they keep.

Let one forget his reason for being, they'd all droop like tulips in a glass, each with their arms around the other. Keep, keep, keep, trees say when I sleep. They teach.

When I am too sad and too skinny to keep keeping, when I am a tiny thing against so many bricks, then it is I look at trees. When there is nothing left to look at on this street. Four who grew despite concrete. Four who reach and do not forget to reach. Four whose only reason is to be and be.

Analyzing and Discussing the Text

1. What kind of relationship between Esperanza and the trees is set up by the first two sentences? Why is "only" used twice? How does this word help to depict her character?
2. How are the trees described in the second paragraph? Does this run counter to the usual way we think about trees, as they appear in literature?
3. Define "keep" as Cisneros uses it here.
4. Explain precisely what it is that the trees "teach" in the third paragraph.
5. Analyze the thematic importance of the fourth paragraph. What does it add to the chapter? Why is this material at the end?

Experiencing and Writing About the World

1. Based on your own experience, write a short essay in which you describe some aspect of nature that you know survives despite the pressures of civilization. Note that this persistence need not necessarily be inspirational; weeds, for example, might provoke another response. Be sure to discuss the attitude that such persistence elicits from you.
2. Choose one national environmental issue—for instance, water quality or ozone depletion—as the subject for an essay in which you argue either for our need to intervene on behalf of nature or for nature's power to sustain itself.
3. Children may be especially susceptible to the psychological influences of nature, both reassuring and frightening. Write a comparative analysis of two or more essays/stories from this anthology in which the authors somehow reveal the effects of nature on children.

In addition to Cisneros's story, you might wish to consider Annie Dillard's winter chase narrative from *An American Childhood*, Scott Russell Sanders's "Cloud Crossing," Terry Tempest Williams's "Yucca," the golden carp scene from Rudolfo Anaya's *Bless Me, Ultima*, Larry Littlebird's "The Hunter," Barry Lopez's "Children in the Woods," Gary Soto's "Blue," and/or Randall Kenan's "A Visitation of Spirits."

MAXINE KUMIN

Menial Labor and the Muse

Maxine Kumin (1925–   ) was born in Philadelphia, Pennsylvania. She received both her B.A. (1946) and her M.A. (1948) from Radcliffe College, and she has taught creative writing at a number of institutions, including Radcliffe; the University of Massachusetts at Amherst; Tufts, Columbia, Princeton, Brandeis, Washington, and Bucknell Universities; and the Massachusetts Institute of Technology. Her books of poetry include *Halfway* (1961), *The Privilege* (1965), *The Nightmare Factory* (1970), *House, Bridge, Fountain, Gate* (1975), *The Retrieval System* (1978), *Our Ground Time Here Will Be Brief: New and Selected Poems* (1987), *The Long Approach* (1988), and *Nurture* (1989). Kumin's 1972 collection, *Up Country: Poems of New England, New and Selected*, won the Pulitzer Prize. She has also published more than twenty children's books, several novels, and two essay collections, *To Make a Prairie: Essays on Poets, Poetry, and Country Living* (1979) and *In Deep: Country Essays* (1987). She and her husband have raised three children, and they now live on a farm near Warner, New Hampshire, where she breeds horses and grows vegetables.

Kumin's writings are notable for their specificity, their careful attention to the details of farm work and natural processes, especially the lives of animals. She has said that because she is "without religious faith and without the sense of primal certitude that faith brings," she takes "her only comfort from the natural order of things." In fact, in *In Deep: Country Essays*, Kumin links her poetic inspiration to "the quiet, primitive satisfaction of putting up vegetables and fruits, gathering wild nuts and mushrooms, raising meat for the table, collecting sap for sweetening." "Menial Labor and the Muse," first published in *TriQuarterly* in 1989, explores the relationship between the process of literary creation and the satisfactions of farm work, an essential connection for a writer like Kumin who lives in constant proximity to nature.

An all-day rain of the mizzly seductive sort, compounded by snow fog; twilight began this day and will mediate it until fully dark.

Before settling in at my desk I've distributed an extra bale of hay to the horses, making a quick trip from house to barn in my slicker and muck boots. The whole main floor of the barn is packed, this time of year, with last August's second cutting, a mix of timothy and brome grass, mostly without the seed heads. The bales are still green, so sweet it makes me salivate as I inhale their aroma which cries *summer!* on the winter air. I have never understood why some entrepreneur has yet to capture the scent and market it as a perfume. Doesn't everyone melt, smelling new hay? I must have been a horse in the last incarnation or had a profound love affair in some sixteenth-century hayloft.

A perspicacious student once pointed out to me that it rains or snows in a large percentage of my poems. She's right, of course, though I hadn't ever thought of the connection.

Stormy days are my best writing days. The weather relieves me of my Jewish-Calvinist urgency to do something useful with one or another of the young stock, to longe or drive or ride the current two-, three- or four-year-old. Or, in season, to cut around the perimeters of the pastures, work that's known as *brushing out*. Or clean out and re-bed the run-in sheds and the central area under the barn my friend Robin calls the motel lobby. No need to bring the vegetable garden into this, or the sugar bush of a hundred maple trees. We probably won't be setting any taps this March. Acid rain and the depredations of the pear thrip that followed have weakened the trees to a possibly fatal point.

This year's wood is in, all split and stacked. Next year's is already on the ground, split in four-foot lengths to dry. It snowed before we could get two truckloads of manure on the garden, though. Victor says we'll have a thaw, that there is still time. He's still puttying and caulking as we button up for the hard months. *Still* is the wrong word, as there is no beginning and no apparent end. Outside water faucets are drained and closed off, heating element installed in the watering trough, and so on.

Writing and well-being. In the most direct, overt and uncomplicated way, my writing depends on the well-being that devolves from this abbreviated list of chores undertaken and completed.

One set of self-imposed deadlines nurtures the other: something harshly physical each day, the reward being a bone-tired sense of equipoise at nightfall. A daily session at the desk even when, as Rilke warned, nothing comes. I must keep holy even disappointment, even desertion. The leaven of the next day's chores will redeem the failed writing, infuse it with new energy or at the very least allow me to shred it while I await the Rilkean birth-hour of a new clarity.

The well-being of solitude is a necessary component of this equation. A "Good! No visitors today" mentality isn't limited to snowstorms or Monday mornings. On the contrary, this feeling of contentment in isolation pervades every good working day. My writing time needs to surround itself with empty stretches, or at least unpeopled ones, for the writing takes place in an area of suspension as in a hanging nest that is almost entirely encapsulated. I think of the oriole's graceful construction.

This is why poems may frequently begin for me in the suspended cocoon of the airplane, or even in the airport lounge during those dreary hours of layovers. There's the same anonymity, the same empty but enclosed space, paradoxical in view of the thousands of other travelers pulsing past. But I have no responsibility here. I am uncalled upon and can go inward.

My best ruminations take place in the barn while my hands (and back) are busy doing something else. Again, there's the haunting appeal of enclosure, the mindless suspension of doing simple, repetitive tasks—mucking out, refilling water buckets, raking sawdust—that allows those free-associative leaps out of which a poem may occasionally come. And if not, reasons the Calvinist, a clean barn is surely a sign of the attained state of grace. Thus I am saved. And if the Muse descends, my androgynous pagan Muse, I will have the best of both worlds.

Analyzing and Discussing the Text

1. Paragraphs 4, 6, and 10 of this essay play off each other in an interesting way. How would you describe the relationship between Kumin's "Jewish-Calvinist urgency to do something useful" and her poetic muse as it is developed in paragraph 4? In paragraph 6? In the tenth and final paragraph? Does she seem to be changing her ideas as she composes the essay, refining what she thinks on this set of questions? If so, explain how and why these changes occur. What other features of the essay contribute to this sense of ideas in progress?

2. What, according to Kumin, are the virtues of manual labor? How does it feed Kumin's creativity? Are such benefits of physical activity available only in the country?

3. The comparison of Kumin's "writing time" to an oriole's nest in the eighth paragraph stands out in the essay. Can you analyze what factors contribute to its prominence? Is it an effective simile? What is the effect on the reader when she promptly moves on to compare the solitude of airplane travel to being in a cocoon? Try to explain how the similes and metaphors throughout the essay contribute in an essential way to the discussion of menial labor.
4. Why is the Muse in the final paragraph "pagan"? How does this tie in with the rest of the essay? Why is the Muse "androgynous"? What are the two worlds?
5. How would you characterize the tone of this essay? Does it read like a journal with notations jotted down, like a more formal revised statement, or like a mixture of both?

Experiencing and Writing About the World

1. How do your daily nonacademic activities contribute to your writing or to your academic work in general? Write a paper in which you reflect on the relationship between "menial labor" (or physical activities of any kind) and your own "muse"—your intellectual life.
2. What is your own typical process of writing? Do you write by hand or type everything directly into the computer? Do you like working at home; in crowded public places; outside sitting under trees; or perhaps, like Kumin, in airplanes? Imitate Kumin's process of self-description by characterizing and explaining the way your own mind works in a descriptive paper.
3. Does Kumin's essay suggest that good writing must, in some fundamental way, be associated with physical activity and the natural world? Is her piece an implicit critique of urban writers who stay inside and do nothing but think and write, or is it simply a description of her own experience, which happens to be mostly rural? Although this essay appears to be a personal statement, write a paper of your own in which you explore the broader implications of Kumin's ideas. Could "Menial Labor and the Muse" serve as the basis for a manifesto supporting place-oriented writing?

JOHN ELDER

The Plane on South Mountain

John Elder (1947–   ) was born in Kentucky, but he grew up in Mill Valley, California, where his environmental interests were fostered by the natural beauty of the San Francisco Bay Area; by the high level of awareness in northern California; and especially by his exposure to Gary Snyder's writings, which emphasized his interest in Eastern philosophy. Elder graduated from Pomona College in 1969 with a degree in English, and he received his Ph.D. in English from Yale University in 1973. Since then he has lived in Vermont, continuing his studies of natural history in the New England countryside. Elder teaches both at Middlebury College, where he is Professor of English and Environmental Studies and Director of the Environmental Studies Program, and at the Bread Loaf Writers' Conference, where he leads workshops for nature writers. He is the author of a number of personal essays about nature and a book on twentieth-century nature poetry called *Imagining the Earth: Poetry and the Vision of Nature* (1985). He and Robert Finch co-edited *The Norton Book of Nature Writing* (1990). His latest book is *Following the Brush: American Encounters with Japanese Culture* (1992).

In the following essay, Elder's search for a downed World War II fighter plane in the Bristol Cliffs Wilderness Area near his home leads him to the recognition that this region, which was "among the first parts of the country to be heavily settled, is now growing wild." In this re-emergence of wilderness, as in the vegetation growing over the wrecked fighter plane, he comes to see the possibility of a "kind of redemptive grace." Through his interpretation of the experience of finding the wreckage of a human machine, Elder argues that we must work to move beyond an environmental philosophy that suggests that wilderness can never grow, but only diminish, to a new, more hopeful belief that we get a second chance, that wilderness can be regained.

Last August I followed an abandoned logging road up into the Bristol Cliffs Wilderness Area, looking for the hulk of a World War II fighter plane that crashed into South Mountain on October 24, 1945. I had learned about this old catastrophe when my next-door neighbor showed me the clippings about it in her scrapbook. A Curtiss Hell-diver with two Navy pilots aboard was returning to its base in Rhode Island after having taken part in a military air show in Burlington. But the clearance was low that afternoon, and the pilots somehow lost track

425

of their altitude. My neighbor Audrey told me that when the stocky, single-prop plane sheared through the trees and met the ground an explosion rattled windows in the village of Bristol.

I wanted to see beech trees reaching through those broken wings, shuffling history back into the forest's fluttering deck. But there was no plane to be found on this summer afternoon, despite the fact that I'd gotten directions from two people in town who had seen it for themselves. One had said to turn straight up the main ridge from the outlet of North Pond, then walk due south for twenty minutes. The other said to strike a line at southwest 220 from the pond; I would find myself climbing up a cut to the mountain's highest bog. There, amid hemlocks and spruce, I would discover the wreck. Neither of these routes worked for me, though. Hardwoods and puckerbrush grew so thickly in that season that it was hard to follow any line, while the corrugated terrain left me uncertain where the actual ridge was.

I soon realized that my directions would never bring me to the plane, so I began simply to criss-cross the mountain's eastern face where it went down. Sometimes I would spot the bluish needles of a hemlock, spruce, or white pine and stumble toward them, looking down with every other step because of toppled trees and branches littering that wind-torn slope. My heart lifted whenever a patch of sunlight made a granite slab or a beech tree gleam like alloy. But I soon lost hope each time, perceiving that I was not, after all, at the scene of a disaster.

I walked for six hours, up hill and down, looking for this human incident with which to punctuate the narrative of nature. The missing plane was so much in my eyes that I registered little of what I actually saw. My hearing was sharpest to the buzz of small craft passing overhead. "They're leading me," I thought, or more ambivalently, "What if they should crash at the exact spot?"

I never found the plane on that August hike. A broader circle through the woods, and through the seasons, was required before I reached the spot. One clear morning in early December of this year, our family's retriever, Maple, and I set out on a new expedition into Bristol Cliffs. It was a bright day, holding at around 30 degrees, and the roads in our village were bare. So I wore my running shoes in order to get up to the ridge faster, and to have more time before dark to comb that hummocky slope for the wreckage that eluded me on the previous attempt.

Just the couple of hundred feet in elevation between my house and the Cliffs turned the ground white. At the trail's beginning, frost coated the twig-strewn track so heavily that it formed a frozen lattice. As I jogged uphill the interstices filled in, smoothing the grid into a blank new page. Soon after that I slowed to a walk, as the snow reached ankle deep. But Maple continued to career over logs, her reddish golden fur looking warm and alive against that glinting world.

When the last tracing of those ancient log trucks disappeared, I followed an outlet creek uphill. It trickled from the stump-surrounded stockade of a beaver dam. The beavers' pond, brought into focus by a thatchy, conical lodge, extended north-south in a little valley of its own. Maple and I slid along the ice until it led us to North Pond itself— a perfect oval set among steeply surrounding hills. Blueberries grew thickly along the western side, their tough leaves leathery and purple at this season.

I clambered up the slope, heading for the "heighth" of land where one man had told me the plane would lie. But, as Maple and I climbed up and down during the next two and a half hours, I realized once again how hard it was to tell which portion of the broken and interfolded range was actually the ridge.

I was just about to give up once more, so as to make it back down to my car before darkness came to this short day, when I spotted the hub of one of the plane's wheels. It rose against the gray-white background in an arc of patchy blue metal, its curve highlighted by a ring of ice within the hub. I scrambled down into a little swale to take a look at this wreck so little like what I had imagined. In my mind's eye, there had been a largely intact fuselage of silvery aluminum, with the wings still attached though perforated by straight young beeches. Actually, there were large hunks of green or blue metal scattered around a circle almost thirty yards in diameter. It looked as if a plane made of blue ice had struck a rock and shattered.

The biggest remnant was the engine block. Huge, finned cylinders rotated out from the block proper, with a massive shaft showing where the single propeller was attached. In addition to the engine and the single wheel, I found part of the tail assembly, as well as pieces of the wings and belly. Only the wing flaps remained totally undamaged. Curved sheets of metal perforated with circular holes an inch in diameter, they would have slid out to slow the plane when it went into a dive—delivering the thousand-pound bomb carried internally in a Helldiver.

Explosion and decay have obviously been helped out, in the demolition of this plane, by souvenir hunters. No insignia remained, though on one scrap I did see the single tip of a white star, shining from what was once the rim of a painted blue circle. The tail itself, the propellers, the windows, the landing gear, the control panel, and the seats have all been carried away. I've heard that two machine guns originally mounted on the wings were skidded down to North Pond and sunk out of harm's way. And I have to admit that I carried one relic away with me too—a twisted piece of olive-drab aluminum the size of a fallen leaf. It's here beside me as I write, on the table by my wordprocessor.

It figures that I found the plane in early winter. The bewildering foliage of those hardwood groves had all rotated underfoot, and much

of the brush had been knocked down by the early storms. In his entry
for January in *A Sand County Almanac*, Aldo Leopold wrote,

> The months of the year, from January up to June, are a geometric pro-
> gression in the abundance of distractions. In January one may follow a
> skunk track, or search for bands on the chickadees, or see what young
> pines the deer have browsed, or what muskrat houses the mink have dug,
> with only an occasional and mild digression into other doings. January
> observation can be almost as simple and peaceful as snow, and almost as
> continuous as cold. There is time not only to see who has done what, but
> to speculate why.

Like all people who live in snowy regions, Vermonters are familiar
with this process of reduction and focus. The cold months settle into
our state as a gradual clarification. Winter holds up objects in high
relief—boulders sealed in globes of ice, strawberry-colored blades of
grass twisted through the frozen lacework at a pond's edge—for our
most careful regard. It invites us to be still and cool, to let one curve,
one color truly enter the mind.

Winter is just one of the erasures through which Vermont has
come into its own. Leopold had originally planned to call his book
A Sauk County Almanac, after the Wisconsin country where he worked
at reclaiming a worn-out farm. But "Sand County" is inclusive of a
broader locale—any of the districts across the United States where erosion, drought, deforestation, or just plain bad soil uprooted farming
communities and replanted the fields with a second growth of trees.
Much of northern New England and upstate New York belongs in Sand
County, a landscape in which loss and gain are inextricable.

Although Vermont was the fastest-growing state right before the
War of 1812, two of every five Vermonters departed in the period between 1850 and 1900. The untilled slopes that were such a draw to
immigrants after the Revolution often turned out to be so flinty that
the hill farmers' yields could not repay their labor. With the opening of
Iowa Territory, many Vermont farmers decided that they would rather
sail their plows across a sea of topsoil than break them on a boulder
shoal. I read in Charles Morrissey's history of the state that 75 percent
of Vermont had been cleared by 1850, as dairy farming and sheep raising prevailed. But unprofitable farms soon began to be abandoned and
forests reclaimed the mountains. Today, 75 percent of our state is once
more woodland. During the decades in which many parts of the country were ravaged by the mandates of prosperity, Vermont grew wilder
and greener every year.

Economic stagnation protected the unspoiled countryside, with its
network of villages. But there was too much suffering in these failed
homesteads to allow for easy celebration, and a legacy of poverty re-

mains in many of the hill-towns like Bristol. What's more, the pleasant stability of Vermont is being pressed hard today. The telecommunications revolution, with the decentralized way of doing business it makes possible, turns quiet little worlds like this into targets for settlement and exploitation more abrupt than anything Vermont saw in its heyday a century and a half ago. I expect the next subdivision between Bristol and Burlington to be called "Sand County Estates." This winter, as snow briefly muffles the sounds of construction along Routes 7 and 100, offers a chance to re-tell the story of Vermont, in preparation for the coming season of distraction.

The wilderness areas designated in Vermont during the past fourteen years are the climax of a century of enhancement through impoverishment. The Eastern Wilderness Act of 1974 (inspired in large part by Vermont's George Aiken) set aside lands that, while not pristine or vast like wilderness in the West and Alaska, still possessed natural qualities worthy of preservation. The Bristol Cliffs Wilderness behind my house was both farmed and thoroughly cut over, and it still turns up the stone and metal testaments of previous owners. This is no "virgin wilderness." Looking at the USDA *Soil Survey of Addison County,* it's also not too hard to see why our little ridge of wilderness was abandoned in the first place, allowing it to grow wild for this moment. While the fat soil to the west is identified on the survey maps by codes such as *Cw* and *VgB*—"Covington and Panton silty clays" and "Vergennes clay, 2 to 6 percent slopes"—Bristol Cliffs is scarified by labels like *LxE*—"Lyman-Berkshire very rocky complex, 20 to 50 percent slopes"—or simply *Rk.*

Such bony land along the heights is from one view just a discarded scrap. But a map of the state shows that our six wilderness areas— a total of 58,000 acres distributed along the Green Mountains' north-south axis—are also Vermont's green heart. Bristol cliffs, Bread Loaf, Big Branch, Peru Peak, Lye Brook, and the George D. Aikens Wilderness (east of Bennington) focus a landscape where nature and culture have circled toward balance in a surprising, retrograde progression. By statute, wilderness areas cannot be logged or built in. No new roads will be added, while existing ones will be allowed to fade away. As politicians consider plans for developing industry and broadening the tax base, these covenanted acres acknowledge a connection between Vermont's natural beauty and its century outside the mainstream. Just as valuable to me is the fact that the dense forests along these tracts are often fairly new, and that they are littered with reminders of previous chapters. They show that wildness can grow out of, and transform, the clearings of society. We don't always have to travel to Glacier National Monument or the Gates of the Arctic to find wilderness; under certain circumstances, it can come home to where we live.

These are the ironies of wilderness in many parts of the Northeast. This region, which was among the first parts of the country to be heavily settled, is now growing wild. Failing enterprises clear the ground for a new attempt at balance with the natural environment. And the abundant rainfall here allows the landscape to reassert its own agenda with a quickness unimaginable in states west of the hundredth meridian.

During this past December's hike into Bristol Cliffs, when I finally found the place, I kept thinking about Ron LaRose's word "heighth," in his description of where to search for the wreck. It reminded me of some lines in Frost's poem "Directive": "The height of the adventure is the height / Of country where two village cultures faded / Into each other. Both of them are lost." New York's shut down mine, the failed homesteads of Vermont, and the wreckage of the Helldiver all show where lives, and whole communities, have been lost. But they also point to places where human vestiges and the region's non-human life have begun to fade together, lost in an emerging balance of wilderness and culture.

For the past couple of years I have been playing weekly games of *go* with my friend Pete Schumer. Invented in China and refined in Japan, *go* is a board game in which opponents alternate placing round, flattened stones on 361 intersections. White and black stones swirl around each other as the players contend for dominance over territory in various portions of the board. A pattern emerges in which the stones of both colors combine—a beautiful, intricate design beyond competition or intention.

Aji is a concept in *go* that helps me understand the swirl of nature and wildness in Vermont. Sometimes a player turns away from an area of the board where the opponent's position has become dominant. But the seemingly abandoned stones retain *aji* within the opposing color's sphere of influence. This word, which comes from the Japanese term for a lingering "taste," describes the fact that a minimal presence can suddenly "come alive." Scattered, discounted stones are empowered, combining with new ones of the same color when the action spills back into that sphere after an engagement elsewhere.

The little patches of wilderness in our state have functioned as a kind of *aji*. Wildness spreads back down into the Champlain Valley from rugged heights like Bristol Cliffs—which were the first places abandoned by the farmers and loggers. The forests have been waiting to return, and with them, animals we had almost forgotten. Moose, whose population dwindled to a small group in the northeast corner of Vermont, are now appearing more frequently in Addison County, here at the western portion of mid-state. Harold Hitchcock, a retired professor of biology at Middlebury College, feels that even the panthers, as mountain lions are called in this region, have begun to reappear. He has made a hobby of interviewing everyone who claims to have seen a panther. Some of them, he feels, have only seen deer in the twilit woods. But others have described details which make him believe in what they say. The mountains come alive for me in a new way now—I know that I will probably never spot one of these keen-eyed shadows for myself, but one of them may at least sometime watch me.

Go, with its circularity and suspension, reflects my vision of wilderness and culture in New England. What began as an opposition has slowly turned into a balance. When I was in high school, living in California and paying my dues to Friends of the Earth, I played a lot of chess. That's how the wilderness movement felt then, too. Double ranks of chessmen squared off for an apocalyptic encounter. Black and white lines clashed at the center of the board, and the number of pieces diminished until one side obtained the leverage to force checkmate. But the number of stones in *go* increase steadily in a game. When all portions of a board have been tested and claimed or relinquished, the players decide that the game is at an end; there is no checkmate and, if the proper number of handicap stones were placed down at the beginning, the game is often within a couple of points of being a tie.

One reason why this Japanese metaphor for New England wilderness appeals to me is that both regions would be called the East in California. Thoreau pointed out this paradox of directions on a round planet when he wrote in *Walden* that he would only join the migration west if he could continue far enough to arrive at the East. This goes along for me with another ancient symbol originating in China. The emblem of yin-yang, in which the swimming curves of dark and light bend around to form one circle. At the heart of the circle's darker side is a white dot, while a seed of blackness nestles in the light. *Aji*, an intricate pattern of complementarity and balance.

Just as Bristol Cliffs has been a saving remnant in Vermont, a little patch from which the heights could once more grow towards wilderness, the plane on South Mountain is a different kind of redemptive trace. This wilderness will never be pristine again, anymore than the shattered Helldiver will ever fly. The machine guns will not be dredged up from the muddy margins of the pond. But a dialogue between wilderness and culture is what we need now anyway, not a resolution. It may keep us from drawing our boundaries too straight, and remind us that sometimes we must go down before we find our second chance. The western-based environmental movement has often asserted the value of "virgin wilderness." But Vermont's return to wildness around the wreck offers, instead, the image of a marriage. Not a dichotomy of male and female, public and private, but an ongoing process of accommodation between the many necessities of growth.

When I first hiked up into Bristol Cliffs last August, my image of the fallen plane screened out the world that I passed by. This morning, though, when what I see is the luminous green-on-black of my computer's screen, and when what I hear is the steady current of its fan, I recall the world I waded through, looking for something else.

Leaves were thick and dark overhead, making the forest a cool, flickering place. The warmth of decay had coaxed out mushrooms everywhere—dimpled and white, day-glo orange, spotted tan ones scattered around the stumps like toads. Stands of goldenrod and blackeyed susans grew in the clearings. But most of the woodland wildflowers were already gone by. In the dim light of the woods, only the whorled wood aster was blooming, and that in profusion. Vigorous whirls of foliage lifted up limp white petals that swirled, in their turn, round the loose-packed yellow of the central disk—elegant late bloomers, lingering among the berries.

And berries there were: baneberries like little clusters of white pop beads, trilliums with their single, maraschino-bright fruit, clintonia, with their pairs and triplets of purple berries turning black. Wildflowers lingered in their progeny, the consummation of their moving on. The August woods retained a memory of July. And now, as the earth undertakes its cold passage through December, orbiting back toward June, I return in writing to the scene of my reiterated hike. Memory compounds and thickens like the second growth woods above my Bristol home.

Analyzing and Discussing the Text

1. When Elder finally finds the wrecked plane, it differs greatly from the largely intact fuselage that he imagined. How precisely is it different? How does this difference set in motion the central themes of his essay?

2. What are the differences that Elder sees between the eastern part of the United States and the western region? Explain how these differences in environmental outlook are linked to topographical differences.

3. Paragraphs 22 through 26 develop the *aji* concept in the oriental game of *go* as a metaphor for a new "emerging balance between wilderness and culture." Summarize how this concept works and how it contrasts with what Elder sees as the previous cultural metaphor for wilderness protection. What exactly is meant by "an ongoing process of accommodation between the many necessities of growth"? How does this idea connect with Elder's interest in Eastern thought?

4. Why does Elder develop the analogy between the compounding effects of memory and the second growth wilderness woods near his house that concludes the essay? What does this add to the essay's themes and structure?

Experiencing and Writing About the World

1. Have you ever encountered human "ruins" of some kind during a walk through a wild or semiwild area? Make an effort to recall and describe in writing any previous experiences of this kind and take a few new excursions with an attentiveness to the rusted and crumbling remains of cars, houses, or other once useful things that you come across. Write an essay that incorporates both detailed descriptions of these ruins and thorough reflections on the implications of what you see. You can either agree with Elder's hopeful notion of wilderness reclaiming once civilized regions or explain the garbage you encounter as a sign of humanity's wastefulness. What other possible interpretations come to mind?

2. If we return to the beginning of the essay after reading and thinking about the whole piece, we see that the first sentence clearly introduces a variety of key themes. Write a paragraph in which you discuss how the details of Elder's first sentence set up what follows.

3. Elder's essay ties environmental progress to a period of economic impoverishment. Write an essay in which you depart from the prospects for renewed economic development outlined in paragraph 16 and develop in detail a way in which economic health and environmental growth can be sustained simultaneously.

MICHAEL POLLAN

Why Mow? The Case Against Lawns

Michael Pollan (1955–   ) was born in Farmingdale, New York, and grew up in a suburban subdivision on the north shore of Long Island, where he came by most of his knowledge about the American lawn. He earned his B.A. at Bennington College, attended Oxford University, and received his M.A. in English Literature from Columbia University with a thesis on Henry David Thoreau. Pollan has written for *Harper's*, *The New York Times Magazine*, *Orion Nature Quarterly*, and many other publications. He is currently executive editor for *Harper's*. His essay "Why Mow? The Case Against Lawns" was chosen for *Best American Essays 1990*, and his book *Second Nature: A Gardener's Education* was published in 1991. Pollan describes this book as being, in some ways, an extended argument with Thoreau's *Walden*, one of the key books in his own early reading.

In "Why Mow?" Pollan constructs an often humorously stated case against the distinguishing feature of our suburban landscape: the American lawn. Using cultural and family history, he seeks to persuade us that it is "a symptom of, and a metaphor for our skewed relationship to the land." Pollan bases this view on the argument, which he develops elsewhere, that any attempts to formulate an environmental philosophy solely in terms of a wilderness ethic are wrongheaded. Because wilderness accounts for only eight percent of American land, only a small part of the human relationship to nature consists of interaction with genuinely "wild" places. Pollan believes that we need to find a new, more comprehensive ethic and metaphor that will help us acknowledge "the indissoluble mixture of our culture and whatever it is that's really out there." In the following essay, he argues that the American garden—not the lawn—is our best hope for this.

Anyone new to the experience of owning a lawn, as I am, soon figures out that there is more at stake here than a patch of grass. A lawn immediately establishes a certain relationship with one's neighbors and, by extension, the larger American landscape. Mowing the lawn, I realized the first time I gazed into my neighbor's yard and imagined him gazing back into mine, is a civic responsibility.

For no lawn is an island, at least in America. Starting at my front stoop, this scruffy green carpet tumbles down a hill and leaps across a one-lane road into my neighbor's yard. From there it skips over some wooded patches and stone walls before finding its way across a dozen other unfenced properties that lead down into the Housatonic Valley, there to begin its march south to the metropolitan area. Once below Danbury, the lawn—now purged of weeds and meticulously coiffed—races up and down the suburban lanes, heedless of property lines. It then heads west, crossing the New York border; moving now at a more stately pace, it strolls beneath the maples of Scarsdale, unfurls across a dozen golf courses, and wraps itself around the pale blue pools of Bronxville before pressing on toward the Hudson. New Jersey next is covered, an emerald postage stamp laid down front and back of ten thousand split levels, before the broadening green river divides in two.

One tributary pushes south, and does not pause until it has colonized the thin, sandy soils of Florida. The other dilates and spreads west, easily overtaking the Midwest's vast grid before running up against the inhospitable western states. But neither flinty soil nor obdurate climate will impede the lawn's march to the Pacific: it vaults the Rockies and, abetted by a monumental irrigation network, proceeds to green great stretches of western desert.

Nowhere in the world are lawns as prized as in America. In little more than a century, we've rolled a green mantle of grass across the continent, with scarcely a thought to the local conditions or expense. America has more than fifty thousand square *miles* of lawn under cultivation, on which we spend an estimated $30 billion a year—this according to the Lawn Institute, a Pleasant Hill, Tennessee, outfit devoted to publicizing the benefits of turf to Americans (surely a case of preaching to the converted).

Like the interstate highway system, like fast-food chains, like television, the lawn has served to unify the American landscape; it is what makes the suburbs of Cleveland and Tucson, the streets of Eugene and Tampa, look more alike than not. According to Ann Leighton, the late historian of gardens, America has made essentially one important contribution to world garden design: the custom of "uniting the front lawns of however many houses there may be on both sides of a street to present an untroubled aspect of expansive green to the passer-by." France has its formal, geometric gardens, England its picturesque parks, and America this unbounded democratic river of manicured lawn along which we array our houses.

It is not easy to stand in the way of such a powerful current. Since we have traditionally eschewed fences and hedges in America (looking on these as Old World vestiges), the suburban vista can be marred by the negligence—or dissent—of a single property owner. This is why lawn care is regarded as such an important civic responsibility in the suburbs, and why the majority will not tolerate the laggard. I learned this at an early age, growing up in a cookie-cutter subdivision in Farmingdale, Long Island.

My father, you see, was a lawn dissident. Whether owing to laziness or contempt for his neighbors I was never sure, but he could not see much point in cranking up the Toro more than once a month or so. The grass on our quarter-acre plot towered over the crew-cut lawns on either side of us and soon disturbed the peace of the entire neighborhood.

That subtle yet unmistakable frontier, where the closely shaved lawn rubs up against a shaggy one, is a scar on the face of suburbia, an intolerable hint of trouble in paradise. The scar shows up in *The Great Gatsby,* when Nick Carraway rents the house next to Gatsby's and fails to maintain his lawn according to West Egg standards. The rift between the two lawns so troubles Gatsby that he dispatches his gardener to mow Nick's grass and thereby erase it.

Our neighbors in Farmingdale displayed somewhat less class. "Lawn mower on the fritz?" they'd ask. "Want to borrow mine?" But the more heavily they leaned on my father, the more recalcitrant he became, until one summer—probably 1959, or 1960—he let the lawn go altogether. The grass plants grew tall enough to flower and set seed; the lawn rippled in the breeze like a flag. There was beauty here, I'm sure, but it was not visible in this context. Stuck in the middle of a row of tract houses on Long Island, our lawn said *turpitude* rather than *meadow,* even though strictly speaking that is what it had become.

That summer I felt the hot breath of the majority's tyranny for the first time. No one said anything now, but you could hear it all the same: *Mow your lawn or get out.* Certain neighbors let it be known to my parents that I was not to play with their children. Cars would slow down as they drove by. Probably some of the drivers were merely curious: they saw the unmowed lawn and wondered if someone had left in a hurry, or perhaps died. But others drove by in a manner that was unmistakably expressive, slowing down as they drew near and then hitting the gas angrily as they passed—pithy driving, the sort of move that is second nature to a Klansman.

We got the message by other media, too. Our next-door neighbor, a mild engineer who was my father's last remaining friend in the development, was charged with the unpleasant task of conveying the sense of the community to my father. It was early on a summer evening that he came to deliver his message. I don't remember it all (I was only four or five at the time), but I can imagine him taking a highball glass from my mother, squeaking out what he had been told to say about the threat to property values, and then waiting for my father—who next to him was a bear—to respond.

My father's reply could not have been more eloquent. Without a word he strode out to the garage and cranked up the rusty old Toro for the first time since fall; it's a miracle the thing started. He pushed it out to the curb and then started back across the lawn to the house, but not in a straight line: he swerved right, then left, then right again. He had cut an S in the high grass. Then he made an M, and finally a P. These are his initials, and as soon as he finished writing them he wheeled the lawn mower back to the garage, never to start it up again.

I wasn't prepared to take such a hard line on my new lawn, at least not right off. So I bought a lawn mower, a Toro, and started mowing. Four hours every Saturday. At first I tried for a kind of Zen approach, clearing my mind of everything but the task at hand, immersing myself in the lawn-mowing here-and-now. I liked the idea that my weekly sessions with the grass would acquaint me with the minutest details of my yard. I soon knew by heart the exact location of every stump and stone, the tunnel route of each resident mole, the address of every anthill. I noticed that where rain collected white clover flourished, that it was on the drier rises that crabgrass thrived. After a few weekends I had a map of the lawn in my head as precise and comprehensive as the mental map one has of the back of one's hand.

The finished product pleased me too, the fine scent and the sense of order restored that a new-cut lawn exhales. My house abuts woods on two sides, and mowing the lawn is, in both a real and metaphorical sense, how I keep the forest at bay and preserve my place in this landscape. Much as we've come to distrust it, the urge to dominate nature is a deeply human one, and lawn mowing answers to it. I thought of the lawn mower as civilization's knife and my lawn as the hospitable plane it carved out of the wilderness. My lawn was a part of nature made fit for human habitation.

So perhaps the allure of lawns is in the genes. The sociobiologists think so: they've gone so far as to propose a "Savanna Syndrome" to explain our fondness for grass. Encoded in our DNA is a preference for an open grassy landscape resembling the short-grass savannas of Africa on which we evolved and spent our first few million years. This is said to explain why we have remade the wooded landscapes of Europe and North America in the image of East Africa.

Such theories go some way toward explaining the widespread appeal of grass, but they don't really account for the American Lawn. They don't, for instance, account for the keen interest Jay Gatsby takes in Nick Carraway's lawn, or the scandal my father's lawn sparked in Farmingdale. Or the fact that, in America, we have taken down our fences and hedges in order to combine our lawns. And they don't even begin to account for the unmistakable odor of virtue that hovers in this country over a scrupulously maintained lawn.

If any individual can be said to have invented the American lawn, it is Frederick Law Olmsted. In 1868, he received a commission to design Riverside, outside Chicago, one of the first planned suburban communities in America. Olmsted's design stipulated that each house be set back thirty feet from the road and it proscribed walls. He was reacting against the "high deadwalls" of England, which he felt made a row of homes there seem "as of a series of private madhouses." In Riverside, each owner would maintain one or two trees and a lawn that would flow seamlessly into his neighbors', creating the impression that all lived together in a single park.

Olmsted was part of a generation of American landscape designer-reformers who set out at midcentury to beautify the American landscape. That it needed beautification may seem surprising to us today, assuming as we do that the history of the landscape is a story of decline, but few at the time thought otherwise. William Cobbett, visiting from England, was struck at the "out-of-door slovenliness" of American homesteads. Each farmer, he wrote, was content with his "shell of boards, while all around him is as barren as the sea beach ... though there is no English shrub, or flower, which will not grow and flourish here."

The land looked as if it had been shaped and cleared in a great hurry—as indeed it had: the landscape largely denuded of trees, makeshift fences outlining badly plowed fields, tree stumps everywhere one looked. As Cobbett and many other nineteenth-century visitors noted, hardly anyone practiced ornamental gardening; the typical yard was "landscaped" in the style southerners would come to call "white trash"—a few chickens, some busted farm equipment, mud and weeds, an unkempt patch of vegetables.

This might do for farmers, but for the growing number of middle-class city people moving to the "borderland" in the years following the Civil War, something more respectable was called for. In 1870, Frank J. Scott, seeking to make Olmsted's ideas accessible to the middle class, published the first volume ever devoted to "suburban home embellishment": *The Art of Beautifying Suburban Home Grounds*, a book that probably did more than any other to determine the look of the suburban landscape in America. Like so many reformers of his time, Scott was nothing if not sure of himself: "A smooth, closely shaven surface of grass is by far the most essential element of beauty on the grounds of a suburban house."

Americans like Olmsted and Scott did not invent the lawn; lawns had been popular in England since Tudor times. But in England, lawns were usually found only on estates; the Americans democratized them, cutting the vast manorial greenswards into quarter-acre slices everyone could afford. Also, the English never considered the lawn an end in itself: it served as a setting for lawn games and as a backdrop for flower beds and trees. Scott subordinated all other elements of the landscape to the lawn; flowers were permissible, but only on the periphery of the grass: "Let your lawn be your home's velvet robe, and your flowers its not too promiscuous decoration."

But Scott's most radical departure from Old World practice was to dwell on the individual's responsibility to his neighbors. "It is unchristian," he declared, "to hedge from the sight of others the beauties of nature which it has been our good fortune to create or secure." One's lawn, Scott held, should contribute to the collective landscape. "The beauty obtained by throwing front grounds open together, is of that excellent quality which enriches all who take part in the exchange, and makes no man poorer." Like Olmsted before him, Scott sought to elevate an unassuming patch of turfgrass into an institution of democracy.

With our open-faced front lawns we declare our like-mindedness to our neighbors—and our distance from the English, who surround their yards with "inhospitable brick wall, topped with broken bottles," to thwart the envious gaze of the lower orders. The American lawn is an egalitarian conceit, implying that there is no reason to hide behind fence or hedge since we all occupy the same middle class. We are all property owners here, the lawn announces, and that suggests its other purpose: to provide a suitably grand stage for the proud display of one's own house. Noting that our yards were organized "to capture the admiration of the street," one garden writer in 1921 attributed the popularity of open lawns to our "infantile instinct to cry 'hello!' to the passer-by, to lift up our possessions to his gaze."

Of course the democratic front yard has its darker, more coercive side, as my family learned in Farmingdale. In specifying the "plain style" of an unembellished lawn for American front yards, the mid-century designer-reformers were, like Puritan ministers, laying down rigid conventions governing our relationship to the land, our observance of which would henceforth be taken as an index of our character. And just as the Puritans would not tolerate any individual who sought to establish his or her own back-channel relationship with the divinity, the members of the suburban utopia do not tolerate the homeowner who establishes a relationship with the land that is not mediated by the group's conventions.

The parallel is not as farfetched as it might sound, when you recall that nature in America has often been regarded as divine. Think of nature as Spirit, the collective suburban lawn as the Church, and lawn mowing as a kind of sacrament. You begin to see why ornamental gardening would take so long to catch on in America, and why my father might seem an antinomian in the eyes of his neighbors. Like Hester Prynne, he claimed not to need their consecration for his actions; perhaps his initials in the front lawn were a kind of Emerald Letter.

Possibly because it is this common land, rather than race or tribe, that makes us all Americans, we have developed a deep distrust of individualistic approaches to the landscape. The land is too important to our identity as Americans to simply allow everyone to have his own way with it. And once we decide that the land should serve as a vehicle of consensus, rather than an arena of self-expression, the American lawn—collective, national, ritualized, and plain—begins to look inevitable.

After my first season of lawn mowing, the Zen approach began to wear thin. I had taken up flower and vegetable gardening, and soon came to resent the four hours that my lawn demanded of me each week. I tired of the endless circuit, pushing the howling mower back and forth across the vast page of my yard, recopying the same green sentences over and over: "I am a conscientious homeowner. I share your middle-class values." Lawn care was gardening aimed at capturing "the admiration of the street," a ritual of consensus I did not have my heart in. I began to entertain idle fantasies of rebellion: Why couldn't I plant a hedge along the road, remove my property from the national stream of greensward and do something else with it?

The third spring I planted fruit trees in the front lawn, apple, peach, cherry, and plum, hoping these would relieve the monotony and begin to make the lawn productive. Behind the house, I put in a perennial border. I built three raised beds out of old chestnut barnboards and planted two dozen different vegetable varieties. Hard work though it was, removing the grass from the site of my new beds proved a keen pleasure. First I outlined the beds with string. Then I made an incision in the lawn with the sharp edge of a spade. Starting at one end, I pried the sod from the soil and slowly rolled it up like a carpet. The grass made a tearing sound as I broke its grip on the earth. I felt a little like a pioneer subduing the forest with his ax; I daydreamed of scalping the entire yard. But I didn't do it—I continued to observe front-yard conventions, mowing assiduously and locating all my new garden beds in the back yard.

The more serious about gardening I became, the more dubious lawns seemed. The problem for me was not, as it was for my father, the relation to my neighbors that a lawn implied; it was the lawn's relationship to nature. For however democratic a lawn may be with respect to one's neighbors, with respect to nature it is authoritarian. Under the mower's brutal indiscriminate rotor, the landscape is subdued, homogenized, dominated utterly. I became convinced that lawn care had about as much to do with gardening as floor waxing or road paving. Gardening was a subtle process of give and take with the landscape, a search for some middle ground between culture and nature. A lawn was nature under culture's boot.

Mowing the lawn, I felt that I was battling the earth rather than working it; each week it sent forth a green army and each week I beat it back with my infernal machine. Unlike every other plant in my garden, the grasses were anonymous, massified, deprived of any change or development whatsoever, not to mention any semblance of self-determination. I ruled a totalitarian landscape.

Hot, monotonous hours behind the mower gave rise to existential speculations. I spent part of one afternoon trying to decide who, in the absurdist drama of lawn mowing, was Sisyphus. Me? A case could certainly be made. Or was it the grass, pushing up through the soil every week, one layer of cells at a time, only to be cut down and then, perversely, encouraged (with fertilizer, lime, etc.) to start the whole doomed process over again? Another day it occurred to me that time as we know it doesn't exist in the lawn, since grass never dies or is allowed to flower and set seed. Lawns are nature purged of sex and death. No wonder Americans like them so much.

And just where *was* my lawn, anyway? The answer's not as obvious as it seems. Gardening, I had come to appreciate, is a painstaking exploration of place; everything that happens in my garden—the thriving and dying of particular plants, the maraudings of various insects and other pests—teaches me to know this patch of land intimately, its geology and microclimate, the particular ecology of its local weeds and animals and insects. My garden prospers to the extent I grasp these particularities and adapt to them.

Lawns work on the opposite principle. They depend for their success on the *overcoming* of local conditions. Like Jefferson superimposing one great grid over the infinitely various topography of the Northwest Territory, we superimpose our lawns on the land. And since the geography and climate of much of this country is poorly suited to turfgrasses (none of which are native), this can't be accomplished without the tools of twentieth-century industrial civilization—its chemical fertilizers, pesticides, herbicides, and machinery. For we won't settle for the lawn that will grow here; we want the one that grows *there,* that dense springy supergreen and weed-free carpet, that Platonic ideal of a lawn we glimpse in the ChemLawn commercials, the magazine spreads, the kitschy sitcom yards, the sublime links and pristine diamonds. Our lawns exist less here than there; they drink from the national stream of images, lift our gaze from the real places we live and fix it on unreal places elsewhere. Lawns are a form of television.

Need I point out that such an approach to "nature" is not likely to be environmentally sound? Lately we have begun to recognize that we are poisoning ourselves with our lawns, which receive, on average, more pesticide and herbicide per acre than just about any crop grown in this country. Suits fly against the national lawn-care companies, and interest is kindled in "organic" methods of lawn care. But the problem is larger than this. Lawns, I am convinced, are a symptom of, and a metaphor for, our skewed relationship to the land. They teach us that, with the help of petrochemicals and technology, we can bend nature to our will. Lawns stoke our hubris with regard to the land.

What is the alternative? To turn them into gardens. I'm not suggesting that there is no place for lawns *in* these gardens or that gardens by themselves will right our relationship to the land, but the habits of thought they foster can take us some way in that direction.

Gardening, as compared to lawn care, tutors us in nature's ways, fostering an ethic of give and take with respect to the land. Gardens instruct us in the particularities of place. They lessen our dependence on distant sources of energy, technology, food, and, for that matter, interest.

For if lawn mowing feels like copying the same sentence over and over, gardening is like writing out new ones, an infinitely variable process of invention and discovery. Gardens also teach the necessary if rather un-American lesson that nature and culture can be compromised, that there might be some middle ground between the lawn and the forest—between those who would complete the conquest of the planet in the name of progress and those who believe it's time we abdicated our rule and left the earth in the care of its more innocent species. The garden suggests there might be a place where we can meet nature halfway.

Probably you will want to know if I have begun to practice what I'm preaching. Well, I have not ripped out my lawn entirely. But each spring larger and larger tracts of it give way to garden. Last year I took a half acre and planted a meadow of black-eyed Susans and oxeye daisies. In return for a single annual scything, I am rewarded with a field of flowers from May until frost.

The lawn is shrinking, and I've hired a neighborhood kid to mow what's left of it. Any Saturday that Bon Jovi, Twisted Sister, or Van Halen isn't playing the Hartford Civic Center, this large blond teenaged being is apt to show up with a forty-eight-inch John Deere mower that shears the lawn in less than an hour. It's $30 a week, but he's freed me from my dark musings about the lawn and so given me more time in the garden.

Out in front, along the road where my lawn overlooks my neighbors', and in turn the rest of the country's, I have made my most radical move. I built a split rail fence and have begun to plant a hedge along it—a rough one made up of forsythia, lilac, bittersweet, and bridal wreath. As soon as this hedge grows tall and thick, my secession from the national lawn will be complete.

Anything then is possible. I *could* let it all revert to meadow, or even forest, except that I don't go in for that sort of self-effacement. I could put in a pumpkin patch, a lily pond, or maybe an apple orchard. And I could even leave an area of grass. But even if I did, this would be a very different lawn from the one I have now. For one thing, it would have a frame, which means it could accommodate plants more subtle and various than the screaming marigolds, fierce red salvias, and musclebound rhododendrons that people usually throw into the ring against a big unfenced lawn. Walled off from the neighbors, no longer a tributary of the national stream, my lawn would now form a distinct and private space—become part of a garden rather than a substitute for one.

Yes, there might well be a place for a small lawn in my new garden. But I think I'll wait until the hedge fills in before I make a decision. It's a private matter, and I'm trying to keep politics out of it.

Analyzing and Discussing the Text

1. What is the metaphor introduced in connection with Pollan's phrase, "no lawn is an island," and developed at length in the second and third paragraphs of the essay? How does this extended metaphor fit in with the rest of his essay? What role does it play in setting up Pollan's argument?
2. What other American institutions does Pollan compare to the lawn in the fifth paragraph? Why does Pollan choose these particular examples as points of comparison?
3. The second half of the second section of the essay is an entertaining narrative about Pollan's father as a "lawn dissident," fighting the tyranny of the majority. How does this narrative fit the rest of the essay? How is it related to Pollan's eventual dealings with his own lawn?
4. At the base of Pollan's argument is his belief that each type of landscape he discusses embodies a certain philosophy of nature. Take each of his major categories—lawn, garden, and forest—and summarize the values the author finds embodied in each. Are there other prominent types of American landscapes and value systems that come to mind but are not mentioned here?

Experiencing and Writing About the World

1. Write an essay in which you use arguments from your own observation and experience to oppose Pollan's view of the American lawn "as collective, national, ritualized, and plain" and as "laying down rigid conventions governing our relationship to the land."
2. Write an essay extending Pollan's arguments for gardens one step further to discuss and argue for one specific type of garden: vegetable garden, flower garden, mixed, and so forth. Why is this type more valuable than the others? You might consider exaggerating the value of your chosen garden type in order to achieve a humorous effect.
3. Choose a specific piece of public land near you—a park, a public square, or a golf course—then describe and analyze the philosophical values embodied in how we choose to deal with that public landscape. Refer to Pollan's essay for an example of how to classify vividly different forms of land use.

DAVID QUAMMEN

The White Tigers of Cincinnati: A Strabismic View of Zookeeping

For biographical information, see the headnote for "The Face of a Spider" in Part One, Chapter One.

In this essay, David Quammen once again leads his readers into the consideration of complex questions about how humans seek to know nature, how we currently undertake the process of learning about wildlife (or kid ourselves that we do), and where this process is flawed. This time the locus for his thoughts is the institution of the zoo, epitomized for him by the zoo in Cincinnati, which he visited as a child and has returned to as an adult. This zoo, in turn, and all the zoos it represents, are symbolized for him by the strikingly beautiful white tiger, an animal that has been "systematically bred at the Cincinnati Zoo, in roughly the same spirit as show-class dachshunds are bred elsewhere." Quammen's engaging blend of past and present personal experience, scientific information, and cultural criticism challenges us to rethink one of our culture's most common ways of interacting with "wild" nature.

When I was a boy, 38 years ago, the Cincinnati Zoo contained carnival rides. There was a low-amplitude and rather mild roller coaster, if I recall rightly, with a canopy top like on a Chevy convertible, which sprang up to wrap the riders in darkness. It moved ripplingly around on its circuit, this thing, a huge slinky tube of metal and cloth, and my dim recollection is that it may have been called The Caterpillar. Don't hold me to details, I was five. The Caterpillar loomed as a great wonder in five-year-old eyes, almost more thrilling to look at than to ride. I remember its astonishing wavy motion and its metallic roar; I remember the chatter of that wind-whipped canopy in duet with human squeals of glee. Eventually I was taken aboard it, no doubt, but what I mainly recall is my first distant glimpse. The other zoo rides haven't stayed with me so vividly. A miniature train. A merry-go-round, possibly. Coney Island (the Ohio version, not the New York) was a full-blown amusement park that offered more intricate and excessive forms of vertigo, but Coney Island was many miles east of the city, down on the river, a once-per-summer treat, and to a child greedy for thrills the zoo was a fair substitute. Also, of course, the zoo contained animals. I liked animals as much as the next five-year-old, and maybe more.

Stolid rhinos and giraffes stood around on bare dirt. Lions paced away their nervous boredom behind bars and glass. Big snakes slept coiled like tugboat rope but if I looked closely I could see them breathe. Elephants lived in an aromatic elephant house with a high domed roof, oddly resembling Monticello. Polar bears gasped from the midwestern July heat and swam in a pool of green water. They were, in their desolate extraction from context, a little greenish themselves. Sea lions performed on a wet stage at regular intervals, horn players without a string section, better musicians than I ever managed to become. Monkeys on an island. Crocodiles in a pit. There were tigers too, but in those days a tiger was black and orange.

It was an age of innocence. Tomatoes were juicy. Milk came in glass bottles. Tigers were colored to resemble the vertical patterns of a tropical woodland.

Times change. The Caterpillar is gone. Conservation and biodiversity are now watchwords at the Cincinnati Zoo. Endangered species are housed and bred there. Many of the outdoor displays are cleverly designed to suggest pockets of habitat rather than fenced compounds. You can walk through a hothouse approximation of rainforest. You can gawk at an ever-loving abundance of live invertebrate animals—spiders and scorpions and cockroaches and butterflies—finally given their place in the limelight. In many ways it's an exemplary institution, this zoo: scientific, well meaning, astute, and internationally recognized. Some things don't change, though, and the mandate of box-office appeal is one of them. In place of carnival rides, today, the Cincinnati Zoo contains white tigers.

White tigers are gorgeous creatures, and anyone who sets eyes on one will have a sense of witnessing something exceptional. Though that much is safely said, virtually everything else about them is controversial.

During the past 20 years, Cincinnati has been the birthplace of more white tigers than anywhere else in the world. It's no accident, and it's certainly no datum of biogeography. White tigers have been systematically bred at the Cincinnati Zoo, in roughly the same spirit as show-class dachshunds are bred elsewhere. The white tiger program is highly successful within its own terms, but not universally applauded; professional zoo people have argued about whether it's a triumph of wild-animal husbandry or a travesty. "White tigers are freaks," according to William Conway, general director of the New York Zoological Society, a famously harsh judgment from one of America's preeminent zoo-based conservationists, who adds: "It's not the role of a zoo to show two-headed calves and white tigers." Edward Maruska, director of the Cincinnati Zoo, objects to the term "freak" and prefers to consider them "off-tone genetic specimens" that occasionally turn up in the wild and therefore deserve also to be represented in zoos. Representing a certain mutational form, though, is not precisely the same as selectively breeding to proliferate that form.

Should these aberrant, handsome animals be propagated and protected in captivity? If so, why? Should it be done in the name of saving something natural and precious and wild—just as other zoos might propagate whooping cranes (*Grus americana*) or white rhinos (*Ceratotherium simum*) or the white starling (*Leucopsar rothschildi*) of Bali? Or are there other rationales, less lofty but more pragmatic? Do the lofty and the pragmatic rationales reinforce each other, or are they at cross-purposes?

Is white tiger propagation a legitimate enterprise in zookeeping? Or is it show business? Or is it perhaps both? The issue is complicated because those questions lead to others.

The easy questions are the scientific ones. For instance: What is a white tiger?

The hard questions involve social anthropology entangled with aesthetics and history and philosophy. For instance: What is a zoo?

The white tiger is not an endangered species. Nor is it even an endangered subspecies, like the Florida panther. Some people confuse white tigers with Siberian tigers, possibly on the sensible but erroneous grounds that a subspecies of tiger native to snowy country ought to be white. The Siberian tiger is yellowish in winter, orangish in summer, camouflage-relevant color shifts that are distinct from the phenomenon of whiteness. The Siberian tiger is an endangered subspecies, *Panthera tigris altaica*, native to northeastern Asia and larger-bodied than other tiger subspecies. A white tiger is a mutant.

More precisely, a white tiger is an individual animal endowed with a double genetic dose of a particular mutant gene (call it a recessive allele) that causes (only in the double-dose situation) partial albinism. A white tiger has blue eyes, a pink nose, and creamy white fur with chocolate stripes, all symptomatic of its inherited deficiency in pigment. Not uncommonly, a white tiger may be cross-eyed. Strabismus, the experts call it. This congenital malady, in which the two eyes can't be aimed at a single point, is related to an abnormal arrangement of visual pathways in the brain. Both the pathway disorder and the cross-eyed condition are often associated with albinism—in Siamese cats, ferrets, mink, and various other mammals, including white tigers. White tigers (or at least the males) also tend to be larger in body size than most other tigers, an accidental similarity to the Siberian subspecies. A mutation for partial albinism could potentially occur among any population, but the white tigers that have become zoo and circus celebrities during this century are descended mainly from the Bengal subspecies, *Panthera tigris tigris*.

A Bengal tiger with two normal alleles at the given gene site is colored normally. A Bengal with one normal allele and one "whiteness" allele also looks normal. Only a double dose of the mutant allele (the genetic equivalent of rolling snake-eyes) results in manifest whiteness. Since a mutant allele at any particular gene site tends to be only sparsely distributed among a wild population of animals, and since close relatives share more of the same alleles (even the rare ones) than strangers do, the surest way to produce a double dose in any newborn is by inbreeding.

The grand patriarch of white tiger collections in modern zoos was an animal known as Mohan, captured as a white cub in 1951 from a forest at Rewa in central India. Mohan spent his life in a palace as the exotic pet and genetic plaything of the last Maharaja of Rewa. Mohan's first offspring—fathered on an orange Bengal female—were as normally orange-colored as their mother. One of those cubs was Radha, a female who evidently carried (but didn't show) a single dose of the mutant gene. When Mohan was bred with Radha, his daughter, she gave birth to four white cubs, the first generation of captive-born white tigers in this century. Among the four was another female, Mohini, so named to echo the name of her father, who was also her grandfather. "Mohan" is Sanskrit for "one who charms." It seemed apt to the maharaja and it seems apt today. "Mohini" has been translated as "enchantress." True enough, there was something about these animals that would charm and enchant zookeepers and other folk to take leave of their common sense. Mohini and her lineage became renowned as the White Tigers of Rewa. In due time she was bred with an orange-colored male, Samson, who was both her uncle and her half-brother. As Mohan's son and Radha's brother, Samson was suspected to carry a dose of the "whiteness" mutation. He did, and together he and Mohini produced another white cub as well as some orange-colored carriers. The Maharaja of Rewa by this time had sold Mohini to the National Zoological Park in Washington, D.C. The NZP loaned two of Mohini's offspring to the Cincinnati Zoo, where they were bred with each other—brother with sister—and produced white cubs. The sister, named Kesari, stayed on in Cincinnati long enough to become founding matriarch of the white tiger collection there.

In Cincinnati, the inbreeding continued. Bhim, a white son of Kesari, was mated to his sister Kamala. Bhim was also mated to another sister, Sumita. This Sumita, a white daughter of Kesari, has been described by Edward Maruska as "one of our prime breeding females," an understated tribute to an animal who has delivered 25 live-born white cubs—almost certainly more than any other female tiger, wild or captive, in the history of the world. If she lived at large in a tropical forest, a white tiger would probably never experience the peculiar circumstances that have led Sumita to her record. Tiger territoriality and the dispersal of young males tend to discourage inbreeding in the wild. Sumita, by contrast, has produced all of her white cubs from matings with Bhim, her brother.

Inbreeding has its costs, and strabismus is only one of them. Among the others are susceptibility to disease, lowered fertility, raised incidence of stillbirths, reproductive deformities, skeletal deformities, and loss of adaptability to new circumstances. Inbreeding shrinks the gene pool of an animal population, and a shrunken gene pool is a form of demographic bad health. Sometimes the negative effects can be mitigated—for instance, by outbreeding occasionally with another family line—and sometimes a severely inbred population is lucky enough to survive for decades without showing evidence of its genetic impoverishment. Outbreeding whenever possible is a crucial part of most captive-propagation programs on behalf of endangered species. White tiger programs are run differently. These programs, including Cincinnati's, have tended to neglect outbreeding, because each outbreeding slows the rate of production of white cubs. Edward Maruska has argued emphatically that Cincinnati's white tigers have suffered little, at least so far, from the predictable problems of inbreeding. Possibly he's right. Possibly his program has been exceptionally skillful and exceptionally lucky. He can claim greater success at this peculiar task than any other zookeeper on the planet. But he can't change the laws of genetics.

What's the real purpose of inbreeding a family line to produce dozens of white tiger cubs? I carried that question back to the Cincinnati Zoo and knocked on an office door. I asked Bob Lotshaw, a curator of tigers, and he gave me an honest answer. "It's marketing. It's popularity. It's a major source of income for continuing other programs here at the zoo." White tigers boost zoo attendance in any city, but especially in Cincinnati, where even the football team is named after a subspecies of *Panthera tigris*. And in addition to gate receipts, there's the revenue from sale of excess animals. Cincinnati has sold its extra white tigers to zoos in Japan, South Korea, South Africa, Mexico, Canada, and Indonesia. It has also sold to Siegfried and Roy's Magic and Illusion Show, of Las Vegas, Nevada. Slightly defensive on this point, Bob Lotshaw assured me that Siegfried and Roy give their tigers high-quality care and affectionate training, and I have no reason to disbelieve him.

The going price for a white tiger is $60,000.

One of the sorry duties of a writer is to bite, every so often, the hand that has fed him. This is my relationship to the Cincinnati Zoo. I've returned there many times over the past 38 years, and most of those enjoyable hours did not involve carnival rides. I've gone there repeatedly with people I love and I've gone there alone when I needed a refuge. It's an enclave of great beauty and apparent tranquility. It wasn't the first place I experienced a sense of the wonders of nature, but it was certainly the first place I saw a bear or a tropical snake or a tiger. Maybe it played some sort of formative role in my life; or maybe not. Anyway, when I offer nasty cold judgments about this particular zoo, and about the dynamics of its appeal to the public, and for that matter about zoos generally, what I'm up to—in part—is an examination of conscience. Don't gag, we're not concerned here with my conscience, but I wanted to assure you that it's dirty.

Now to the larger question. What is a zoo?

How did these institutions come into being, and why do we continue to tolerate them? What logic can be offered for keeping tigers—white ones, orange ones, tigers of any subspecies or color or genetic persuasion—on a small patch of grass behind a high fence in a sycamore-shaded neighborhood of Cincinnati?

Zoos are educational, people say. Zoos represent the only glimpse of nature that many city-bound children, and their city-bound parents, will ever get. Zoos are the last refuge of certain endangered species. Zoos are a way to preserve a few tiny fragments of "the wild," whatever that is. The better zoos of today (including Cincinnati's) even play an important role in the captive propagation of rare and beleaguered animals that may eventually be released back into their native range, if by some miracle the habitat hasn't meanwhile been totally destroyed. People say each of these things. I'd like to agree, I try to agree, but in the back of my brain and the pit of my stomach I don't. To me it's all half-truth.

The pedagogic value of zoos is an afterthought, added on during the last century and a half to raise the intellectual and social tone of a much older tradition, the commercial menagerie. Even today, zoos aren't very educational. The white tiger exhibit in Cincinnati, for instance, is drastically coy on the subject of population genetics. Nor do zoos constitute fragments of "the wild." Wildness is precisely what's missing; the infinite intricacy of an ecosystem is missing; only the animate bodies of a few animals, stripped of their contexts and their community roles and therefore their living identities, some of them potentially dangerous to humans (which is not the same as wild), are present. Zoos do provide glimpses of biological exotica that can be taken to represent nature, it's true. But like many of the nature documentaries on public TV, I suspect, zoos may actually undermine the continued existence of what they purport to celebrate. People watch the films, they visit the zoos, and by the mesmeric power of these vicarious experiences they come carelessly to believe that the Bengal tiger (or the white rhino, or the giant panda, or the diademed sifaka) is alive and well because they have seen it. Well I'm sorry but they *haven't* seen it. They've seen images; they've seen taxidermy on the hoof. And the wellness, even the aliveness, is too often a theatrical illusion. Zoos are not fragments of the world of nature, no. They are substitutes.

That's why they're useful and that's why they're pernicious.

Let's start again. What is a zoo? Most essentially, it's an arena of the visual. It's a place to see wonders. The act of seeing is foremost—

whereas learning, thinking, emoting are dimensions of experience that come secondarily, if at all. We go there to *look*; in passing, we read a few labels and placards, of which the information content is low. William Conway, having made that remark about "freaks," continued with a statement that frames zoos (even great conservationist zoos, such as his) in visual terms: "We need to save our severely limited space for tiger subspecies that are close to totally disappearing in nature. If we choose to save the white tiger at the expense, say, of the Siberian tiger, it's like saving a copy of a Rembrandt painted in glitter on velvet and throwing out *The Man with the Golden Helmet*." A fellow named John Berger would take the argument still further.

Berger is a cantankerous British art critic who has written about the viewing experience of zoos. He's well qualified to address the subject because a zoo, after all, as William Conway implied, is more like an art museum than like a forest.

What we see in a zoo, according to John Berger, are creatures that have been rendered marginal. "The animals, isolated from each other and without interaction between species, have become utterly dependent upon their keepers." So they are no longer wild. They are no longer complete. Their responses, their behavior, probably even their sensory capacities, have changed. "Nothing surrounds them except their own lethargy or hyperactivity." Each has been separated, not just from its natural habitat, but from its identity. They are numbed; in some sense, as they stand or sleep or eat or pace the cage floor, they are already extinguished. To assume that they retain the capacity for seeing and experiencing us, while we are seeing and experiencing them, is recklessly hopeful. Some writers have argued that the value of a zoo visit comes when a human and another animal connect with each other through their eyes. Forget about that, says Berger, it doesn't happen. "At the most, the animal's gaze flickers and passes on. They look sideways. They look blindly beyond. They scan mechanically." They have been immunized against encounter, he says. When a human looks deep into the eyes of a zoo animal, according to John Berger, the human is alone.

I wasn't so sure. I wanted to look deep into the eyes of a white tiger. So, after talking with Bob Lotshaw, I walked back up to the compound in which four of the Cincinnati animals were basking beneath a wan winter sun.

They were confined to about a third of an acre of grassy slope, with a few rocks and bare trees, no prey, no competitors, no territorial structure, no forest, but they were making the best of it. Occasionally one would pounce on another playfully. Their noses were pink. Their fur was creamy, with umber stripes. They were impossibly, pathetically beautiful. If their eyes were blue, or otherwise remarkable, they didn't show me.

The fence was 18 feet high. Above was a wooden walkway, from which I and the few other visitors could look down. It was a quiet day in February—a day of low attendance, despite these box-office stars. Traffic sounds came from a distance, muffled by hills and trees. Suddenly a young boy on the walkway started screaming. The forced anger of his shrieks indicated a tantrum. He wanted his lunch, or an ice cream, or a Coke, or his nap, or simply his way on some other point. Maybe he wanted a carnival ride. He was about five. His squalling caught the attention of two tigers, below, and I watched as they stalked him along the fence. Their heads went low and they stepped carefully. They seemed to have come alive. Part of me hoped to see them snatch the little booger and eat him, of course. But I was divided.

Then the tigers remembered their own sad impotence, and they lost interest.

Analyzing and Discussing the Text

1. Why does Quammen juxtapose the Cincinnati Zoo and carnival rides in his first sentence? Try to explain why he waits until the final sentence of the introductory paragraph to bring up the subject of animals.
2. Analyze the tone of Quammen's descriptions of the animals in the second paragraph. Does the author pity the animals or admire them? How does the phrase "in those days the tigers were black and orange" convey Quammen's attitude toward zoo animals in general or toward white tigers in particular?
3. The scientific explanation of the inbreeding necessary to produce white tigers stresses that they are often cross-eyed. Explain how this ties in with the major themes of Quammen's essay, even with the title.
4. What rhetorical function does the discussion of conscience in paragraph 16 serve?
5. How does the essay's final anecdote—Quammen's watching the white tigers stalk another five-year-old boy—summarize his view of zoos? Would we read this incident differently if the essay had another focus in its introduction?
6. What are the implications of the full title of this essay? What would change if he called it simply "The White Tigers" without locating them geographically?

Experiencing and Writing About the World

1. Make a trip to a nearby zoo and record field notes on the animals; the visitors; and the interactions, if any, between them. What patterns emerge in your own observations? Would an essay about your local zoo lead you to differ with Quammen?
2. Write an essay in which you argue for zoos. Be sure that you take into account Quammen's arguments against them. In preparing this essay, do research either about a particular nearby zoo in your part of the country or about zoos in general. Use at least five printed sources to back up your argument.
3. Why do people like to have nature nearby, even if they seldom consciously analyze the philosophical and psychological implications of this desire? Using Quammen's study of zoos, other pieces from this chapter of the anthology, and even essays such as Edward Hoagland's "Dogs, and the Tug of Life" (in Part One, Chapter Three) to prompt and support your own reflections, write a meditation on the general idea of "nearby nature."

―――――――――――――――――――――

Suggestions for Further Reading

Berry, Wendell. "Getting Along with Nature." *Home Economics.* San Francisco: North Point, 1987.

Beston, Henry. *Northern Farm: A Chronicle of Maine.* New York: Ballantine, 1948.

Chavez, Denise. "Willow Game." *The Last of the Menu Girls.* Houston: Arte Publico, 1986.

Crawford, Stanley. *Mayordomo: Chronicle of an Acequia in Northern New Mexico.* 1988. New York: Doubleday, 1989.

Daniel, John. "The Garden and the Field." *North American Review* 274.3 (September 1989): 14–17.

Finch, Robert. *The Primal Place.* New York: Norton, 1983.

Jager, Ronald. *Eighty Acres: Elegy for a Family Farm.* Boston: Beacon, 1990.

Klinkenborg, Verlyn. *Making Hay.* New York: Vintage, 1986.

Middleton, Harry. *The Earth Is Enough: Growing Up in a World of Trout and Old Men.* New York: Simon, 1989.

Mitchell, John Hanson. *Living at the End of Time.* Boston: Houghton, 1990.

Naylor, Gloria. "Mattie Michael." *The Women of Brewster Place.* New York: Penguin, 1982.

Perrin, Noel. *First Person Rural: Essays of a Sometime Farmer.* New York: Penguin, 1980.

————.*Second Person Rural: More Essays of a Sometime Farmer.* Boston: Godine, 1980.

————.*Third Person Rural: Further Essays of a Sometime Farmer.* Boston: Godine, 1983.

Rhodes, Richard. *Farm: A Year in the Life of an American Farmer.* New York: Touchstone, 1989.

Siebert, Charles. "Where Have All the Animals Gone: The Lamentable Extinction of Zoos." *Harper's* May 1991: 49–58.

Ray Atkeson

CHAPTER TWO

A Sense of Place

Rick Bass's comment about his adopted home in Montana can help us apprehend how a sense of place evolves. "I don't know how to write about this country in an orderly fashion," he admits, "because I am just finding out about it. If a path develops, I'll be glad to see it—as with math, chemistry, genetics, and electricity, things with rules and borders—but for now it is all loose events, great mystery, random lives." Bass is explaining the difficulty of using words to convey a sense of place. To impose a pattern on a place, to draw the map before walking the terrain, is fatal to any attempt to describe it accurately. This is why the best descriptions and evocations of particular places are so often exploratory, groping efforts to find out about places by looking first at many disconnected events and phenomena, waiting to see if and how patterns and borders finally emerge. Such explorations of place are an art in themselves, a form of descriptive writing represented powerfully by such books as Edward Abbey's *Desert Solitaire: A Season in the Wilderness* (1968): "I wait and watch, guarding the desert, the arches, the sand and the barren rock, the isolated junipers and scattered clumps of sage surrounding me in stillness and simplicity under the starlight." Watching and learning about a place is, as Abbey continually reminds us, also a way to develop concern for it; to write lovingly and knowingly about a place initiates the process of protecting it.

Eudora Welty's history of the interaction between people and place in a particular region of Mississippi is cast carefully in the form of a walk through the place, her stories emerging as they actually happened, interwoven with landscape. Abbey's description of the desert place he loves is presented ironically in the form of a long catalogue of reasons for his readers not to experience the place for themselves; these very discomforts, however, help to sustain the isolation of the Great American Desert, the quality that so appeals to the author. Wendell Berry's native region, the Red River Gorge of Kentucky, comes alive to his readers through his use of different angles of vision, different forms of perception; by walking us through the gorge and later taking us through it by canoe, he leaves us feeling that we have experienced the place ourselves, somehow merging with the actual river to feel and shape the "country of edges." Terry Tempest Williams, Gloria Anzaldúa, and William Least Heat-Moon write about different regions of the country— Utah, New Mexico, South Texas, and Kansas—but they each convey a sense of place by presenting important cultural perspectives, intersections, and borders. By contrasting, linking, and explaining the diverse cultural traditions that predate and coexist with the attitudes of Anglo settlers and their descendants, these writers remind us that there are different ways to know a place, to understand our own connections with the land.

EUDORA WELTY

Some Notes on River Country

Eudora Welty (1909–   ), one of the most important Southern writers of the twentieth century, was born in Jackson, Mississippi, and she still lives there in the house built by her parents. She started college at the Mississippi State College for Women in 1925, then transferred to the University of Wisconsin in 1927 and graduated from there in 1929. Welty also studied advertising at the Columbia University School of Business for a brief period before returning in 1931 to live permanently in Jackson. Her short fiction has appeared in a variety of magazines, and it has been collected in *A Curtain of Green* (1941), *The Wide Net* (1943), *The Bride of the Innisfallen* (1946), and *The Golden Apples* (1949). Welty also has published five novels: *The Robber Bridegroom* (1942), *Delta Wedding* (1946), *The Ponder Heart* (1954), *Losing Battles* (1970), and *The Optimist's Daughter* (1972), which won the 1973 Pulitzer Prize in fiction. Her literary nonfiction has been collected in such books as *Place in Fiction* (1957) and *One Writer's Beginnings* (1984). Welty's writing has been honored by a Guggenheim Fellowship, the National Institute of Arts and Letters Gold Medal in 1972, and the National Book Foundation Medal for Distinguished Contribution to American Letters in 1991.

Throughout her work, Welty exhibits a deep awareness of the past and how it lives on in present times and places. In *One Writer's Beginnings,* she emphasizes that in writing, as in life, "the connections of all sorts of relationships and kinds lie in wait of discovery." In her concern, even preoccupation, with connections, the relationships between humans and nature play a central thematic role. In Welty's earliest stories, "the green curtain" symbolizes nature's fecund resistance to the human desire for control and order, and we see that same thematic concern figuring prominently in "Some Notes on River Country," with its emphasis on the tension between the wild country vegetation and human habitation. This essay, printed initially in 1944, was collected in *The Eye of the Story: Selected Essays and Reviews* (1977).

A place that ever was lived in is like a fire that never goes out. It flares up, it smolders for a time, it is fanned or smothered by circumstance, but its being is intact, forever fluttering within it, the result of some original ignition. Sometimes it gives out glory, sometimes its little light must be sought out to be seen, small and tender as a candle flame, but as certain.

I have never seen, in this small section of old Mississippi River country and its little chain of lost towns between Vicksburg and Natchez, anything so mundane as ghosts, but I have felt many times there a sense of place as powerful as if it were visible and walking and could touch me.

The clatter of hoofs and the bellow of boats have gone, all old communications. The Old Natchez Trace has sunk out of use; it is deep in leaves. The river has gone away and left the landings. Boats from Liverpool do not dock at these empty crags. The old deeds are done, old evil and old good have been made into stories, as plows turn up the river bottom, and the wild birds fly now at the level where people on boat deck once were strolling and talking of great expanding things, and of chance and money. Much beauty has gone, many little things of life. To light up the nights there are no mansions, no celebrations. Just as, when there were mansions and celebrations, there were no more festivals of an Indian tribe there; before the music, there were drums.

But life does not forsake any place. People live still in Rodney's Landing; flood drives them out and they return to it. Children are born there and find the day as inexhaustible and as abundant as they run and wander in their little hills as they, in innocence and rightness, would find it anywhere on earth. The seasons come as truly, and give gratefulness, though they bring little fruit. There is a sense of place there, to keep life from being extinguished, like a cup of the hands to hold a flame.

To go there, you start west from Port Gibson. This was the frontier of the Natchez country. Postmen would arrive here blowing their tin horns like Gabriel where the Old Natchez Trace crosses the Bayou Pierre, after riding three hundred wilderness miles from Tennessee, and would run in where the tavern used to be to deliver their mail, change their ponies, and warm their souls with grog. And up this now sand-barred bayou trading vessels would ply from the river. Port Gibson is on a highway and a railroad today, and lives on without its river life, though it is half diminished. It is still rather smug because General Grant said it was "too pretty to burn." Perhaps it was too pretty for any harsh fate, with its great mossy trees and old camellias, its exquisite little churches, and galleried houses back in the hills overlooking the cotton fields. It has escaped what happened to Grand Gulf and Bruinsburg and Rodney's Landing.

A narrow gravel road goes into the West. You have entered the loess country, and a gate might have been shut behind you for the difference in the world. All about are hills and chasms of cane, forests of cedar trees, and magnolia. Falling away from your road, at times merging with it, an old trail crosses and recrosses, like a tunnel through the dense brakes, under arches of branches, a narrow, cedar-smelling trace the width of a horseman. This road joined the Natchez Trace to the river. It, too, was made by buffaloes, then used by man, trodden lower and lower, a few inches every hundred years.

Loess has the beautiful definition of aeolian—wind-borne. The loess soil is like a mantle; the ridge was laid down here by the wind, the bottom land by the water. Deep under them both is solid blue clay, embalming the fossil horse and the fossil ox and the great mastodon, the same preserving blue clay that was dug up to wrap the head of the Big Harp in bandit days, no less a monstrous thing when it was carried in for reward.

Loess exists also in China, that land whose plants are so congenial to the South; there the bluffs rise vertically for five hundred feet in some places and contain cave dwellings without number. The Mississippi bluffs once served the same purpose; when Vicksburg was being shelled from the river during the year's siege there in the War Between the States, it was the daily habit of the three thousand women, children and old men who made up the wartime population to go on their all-fours into shelters they had tunneled into the loess bluffs. Mark Twain reports how the Federal soldiers would shout from the river in grim humor, "Rats, to your holes!"

Winding through this land unwarned, rounding to a valley, you will come on a startling thing. Set back in an old gray field, with horses grazing like small fairy animals beside it, is a vast ruin—twenty-two Corinthian columns in an empty oblong and an L. Almost seeming to float like lace, bits of wrought-iron balcony connect them here and there. Live cedar trees are growing from the iron black acanthus leaves, high in the empty air. This is the ruin of Windsor, long since burned. It used to have five stories and an observation tower—Mark Twain used the tower as a sight when he was pilot on the river.

Immediately the cane and the cedars become more impenetrable, the road ascends and descends, and rather slowly, because of the trees and shadows, you realize a little village is before you. Grand Gulf today looks like a scene in Haiti. Under enormous dense trees where the moss hangs long as ladders, there are hutlike buildings and pale whitewashed sheds; most of the faces under the straw hats are black, and only narrow jungly paths lead toward the river. Of course this is not Grand Gulf in the original, for the river undermined that and pulled it whole into the river—the opposite of what it did to Rodney's Landing. A little corner was left, which the Federals burned, all but a wall, on their way to Vicksburg. After the war the population built it back—and the river moved away. Grand Gulf was a British settlement before the Revolution and had close connection with England, whose ships traded here. It handled more cotton than any other port in Mississippi for about twenty years. The old cemetery is there still, like a roof of marble and moss overhanging the town and about to tip into it. Many names of British gentry stare out from the stones, and the biggest snakes in the world must have their kingdom in that dark-green tangle.

Two miles beyond, at the end of a dim jungle track where you can walk, is the river, immensely wide and vacant, its bluff occupied sometimes by a casual camp of fishermen under the willow trees, where dirty children playing about and nets drying have a look of timeless roaming and poverty and sameness. . . . By boat you can reach a permanent fishing camp, inaccessible now by land. Go till you can find the hazy shore where the Bayou Pierre, dividing in two, reaches around the swamp to meet the river. It is a gray-green land, softly flowered, hung with stillness. Houseboats will be tied there among the cypresses under falls of the long moss, all of a color. Aaron Burr's "flotilla" tied up there, too, for this is Bruinsburg Landing, where the boats were seized one wild day of apprehension. Bruinsburg grew to be a rich, gay place in cotton days. It is almost as if a wand had turned a noisy cotton port into a handful of shanty boats. Yet Bruinsburg Landing has not vanished: it is this.

Wonderful things have come down the current of this river, and more spectacular things were on the water than could ever have sprung up on shores then. Every kind of treasure, every kind of bearer of treasurer has come down, and armadas and flotillas, and the most frivolous of things, too, and the most pleasure-giving of people.

Natchez, downstream, had a regular season of drama from 1806 on, attended by the countryside—the only one in English in this part of the world. The plays would be given outdoors, on a strip of grass on the edge of the high bluff overlooking the landing. With the backdrop of the river and the endless low marsh of Louisiana beyond, some version of Elizabethan or Restoration comedy or tragedy would be given, followed by a short farcical afterpiece, and the traveling company would run through a little bird mimicry, ventriloquism and magical tricks inbetween. Natchez, until lately a bear-baiting crowd, watched eagerly "A Laughable Comedy in 3 Acts written by Shakespeare and Altered by Garrick called Catherine & Petrucio," followed by "A Pantomime Ballet Called a Trip through the Vauxhall Gardens into which is introduced the humorous song of Four and Twenty Fiddlers concluding with a dance by the characters." Or sometimes the troupe would arrive with a program of "divertisements"—recitations of Lochinvar, Alexander's Feast, Cato's Soliloquy of the Soul, and Clarence's Dream, interspersed with Irish songs by the boys sung to popular requests and concluding with "A Laughable Combat between Two Blind Fiddlers."

The Natchez country took all this omnivorously to its heart. There were rousing, splendid seasons, with a critic writing pieces in the newspaper to say that last night's Juliet spoke just a *bit* too loudly for a girl, though Tybalt kept in perfect character to delight all, even after he was dead—signed "X.Y.Z."

But when the natural vigor of the day gave clamorous birth to the minstrel show, the bastard Shakespeare went; and when the show-boat really rounded the bend, the theatre of that day, a child of the plantation and the river, came to its own. The next generation heard calliopes filling river and field with their sound, and saw the dazzling showboats come like enormous dreams up the bayous and the little streams at floodtime, with whole French Zouave troops aboard, whole circuses with horses jumping through paper hoops, and all the literal rites of the minstrel show, as ever true to expectations as a miracle play.

Now if you pick up the Rodney Road again, through twenty miles of wooded hills, you wind sharply round, the old sunken road ahead of you and following you. Then from a great height you descend suddenly through a rush of vines, down, down, deep into complete levelness, and there in a strip at the bluff's foot, at the road's end, is Rodney's Landing.

Though you walk through Rodney's Landing, it long remains a landscape, rather than a center of activity, and seems to exist altogether in the sight, like a vision. At first you think there is not even sound. The thick soft morning shadow of the bluff on the valley floor, and the rose-red color of the brick church which rises from this shadow, are its dominant notes—all else seems green. The red of the bricks defies their element; they were made of earth, but they glow as if to remind you that there is fire in earth. No one is in sight.

Eventually you see people, of course. Women have little errands, and the old men play checkers at a table in front of the one open store. And the people's faces are good. Theirs seem *actually* the faces your eyes look for in city streets and never see. There is a middle-aged man who always meets you when you come. He is like an embodiment of the simplicity and friendliness not of the mind—for his could not teach him—but of the open spirit. He never remembers you, but he speaks courteously. "I am Mr. John David's boy—where have you come from, and when will you have to go back?" He has what I have always imagined as a true Saxon face, like a shepherd boy's, light and shy and set in solitude. He carries a staff, too, and stands with it on the hill, where he will lead you—looking with care everywhere and far away, warning you of the steep stile. . . . The river is not even in sight here. It is three miles beyond, past the cotton fields of the bottom, through a dense miasma of swamp.

The houses merge into a shaggy fringe at the foot of the bluff. It is like a town some avenging angel has flown over, taking up every second or third house and leaving only this. There are more churches than houses now; the edge of town is marked by a little wooden Catholic church tiny as a matchbox, with twin steeples carved like icing, over a stile in a flowery pasture. The Negro Baptist church, weathered black with a snow-white door, has red hens in the yard. The old galleried stores are boarded up. The missing houses were burned—they were empty, and the little row of Negro inhabitants have carried them off for firewood.

You know instinctively as you stand here that this shelf of forest is the old town site, and you find that here, as in Grand Gulf, the cemetery has remained as the roof of the town. In a mossy wood the graves, gently tended here, send up mossy shafts, with lilies flowering in the gloom. Many of the tombstones are marked "A Native of Ireland," though there are German names and graves neatly bordered with sea shells and planted in spring-flowering bulbs. People in Rodney's Landing won silver prizes in the fairs for their horses; they planted all this land; some of them were killed in battle, some in duels fought on a Grand Gulf sand bar. The girls who died young of the fevers were some of them the famous "Rodney heiresses." All Mississippians know descendants of all the names. I looked for the grave of Dr. Nutt, the man who privately invented and used his cotton gin here, previous to the rest of the world. The Petit Gulf cotton was known in England better than any other as superior to all cotton, and was named for the little gulf in the river at this landing, and Rodney, too, was once called Petit Gulf.

Down below, Mr. John David's boy opens the wrought-iron gate to the churchyard of the rose-red church, and you go up the worn, concave steps. The door is never locked, the old silver knob is always the heat of the hand. It is a church, upon whose calm interior nothing seems to press from the outer world, which, though calm itself here, is still "outer." (Even cannonballs were stopped by its strong walls, and are in them yet.) It is the kind of little church in which you might instinctively say prayers for your friends; how is it that both danger and succor, both need and response, seem intimately near in little country churches?

Something always hangs imminent above all life—usually claims of daily need, daily action, a prescribed course of movement, a schedule of time. In Rodney, the imminent thing is a natural danger—the town may be flooded by the river, and every inhabitant must take to the hills. Every house wears a belt of ineradicable silt around its upper walls. I asked the storekeeper what his store would be like after the river had been over it, and he said, "You know the way a fish is?" Life threatened by nature is simplified, most peaceful in present peace, quiet in seasons of waiting and readiness. There are rowboats under all the houses.

Even the women in sunbonnets disappear and nothing moves at noon but butterflies, little white ones, large black ones, and they are like some flutter of heat, some dervishes of the midday hour, as in pairs they rotate about one another, ascending and descending, appearing to follow each other up and down some swaying spiral staircase invisible in the dense light. The heat moves. Its ripples can be seen, like the ripples in some vertical river running between earth and sky. It is so still at noon. I was never there before the river left, to hear the thousand swirling sounds it made for Rodney's Landing, but could it be that its absence is so much missed in the life of sound here that a stranger would feel it? The stillness seems absolute, as the brightness of noon seems to touch the point of saturation. Here the noon sun does make a trance; here indeed at its same zenith it looked down on life sacrificed to it and was worshipped.

It is not strange to think that a unique nation among Indians lived in this beautiful country. The origin of the Natchez is still in mystery. But their people, five villages in the seventeenth century, were unique in this country and they were envied by the other younger nations— the Choctaws helped the French in their final dissolution. In Mississippi they were remnants surely of medievalism. They were proud and cruel, gentle-mannered and ironic, handsome, extremely tall, intellectual, elegant, pacific and ruthless. Fire, death, sacrifice formed the spirit of the Natchez' worship. They did not now, however, make war.

The women—although all the power was in their blood, and a Sun woman by rigid system married a low-caste Stinkard and bore a Sun child by him—were the nation's laborers still. They planted and they spun, they baked their red jugs for the bear oil, and when the men came from the forests, they would throw at the feet of their wives the tongues of the beasts they had shot from their acacia bows—both as a tribute to womanhood and as a command to the wives to go out and hunt on the ground for what they had killed, and to drag it home.

The town of Natchez was named after this nation, although the French one day, in a massacre for a massacre, slew or sent into slavery at Santo Domingo every one of its namesakes, and the history of the nation was done in 1773. The French amusedly regarded the Natchez as either *"sauvages"* or *"naturels, innocents."* They made many notes of their dress and quaint habits, made engravings of them looking like Cupids and Psyches, and handed down to us their rites and customs with horrified withholdings or fascinated repetitions. The women fastened their knee-length hair in a net of mulberry threads, men singed theirs short into a crown except for a lock over the left ear. They loved vermilion and used it delicately, men and women, the women's breasts decorated in tattooed designs by whose geometrics they strangely match ancient Aztec bowls. *"En été"* male and female wore a draped garment from waist to knee. *"En hyver"* they threw about them swan-feather mantles, made as carefully as wigs. For the monthly festivals the men added bracelets of skin polished like ivory, and thin disks of feathers went in each hand. They were painted firecolor, white puffs of down decorated their shorn heads, the one lock left to support the whitest feathers. As children, the Natchez wore pearls handed down by their ancestors— pearls which they had ruined by piercing them with fire.

The Natchez also laughed gently at the French. (Also they massacred them when they were betrayed by them.) Once a Frenchman asked a Natchez noble why these Indians would laugh at them, and the noble replied that it was only because the French were like geese when they talked—all clamoring at once. The Natchez never spoke except one at a time; no one was ever interrupted or contradicted; a visitor was always allowed the opening speech, and that after a rest in silence of fifteen or twenty minutes, to allow him to get his breath and collect his thoughts. (Women murmured or whispered; their game after labor was a silent little guessing game played with three sticks that could not disturb anyone.) But this same nation, when any Sun died, strangled his wife and a great company of loyal friends and ambitious Stinkards to attend him in death, and walked bearing his body over the bodies of strangled infants laid before him by their parents. A Sun once expressed great though polite astonishment that a certain Frenchman declined the favor of dying with him.

Their own sacrifices were great among them. When Iberville came, the Natchez had diminished to twelve hundred. They laid it to the fact that the fire had once been allowed to go out and that a profane fire burned now in its place. Perhaps they had prescience of their end—the only bit of their history that we really know.

Today Rodney's Landing wears the cloak of vegetation which has caught up this whole land for the third time, or the fourth, or the hundredth. There is something Gothic about the vines, in their structure in the trees—there are arches, flying buttresses, towers of vines, with trumpet flowers swinging in them for bells and staining their walls. And there is something of a warmer grandeur in their very abundance—stairways and terraces and whole hanging gardens of green and flowering vines, with a Babylonian babel of hundreds of creature voices that make up the silence of Rodney's Landing. Here are nests for birds and thrones for owls and trapezes for snakes, every kind of bower in the world. From earliest spring there is something, when garlands of yellow jasmine swing from tree to tree, in the woods aglow with dogwood and redbud, when the green is only a floating veil in the hills.

And the vines make an endless flourish in summer and fall. There are wild vines of the grape family, with their lilac and turquoise fruits and their green, pink and white leaves. Muscadine vines along the stream banks grow a hundred feet high, mixing their dull, musky, delicious grapes among the bronze grapes of the scuppernong. All creepers with trumpets and panicles of scarlet and yellow cling to the treetops. On shady stream banks hang lady's eardrops, fruits and flowers dangling pale jade. The passionflower puts its tendrils where it can, its strange flowers of lilac rays with their little white towers shining out, or its fruit, the maypop, hanging. Wild wistaria hangs its flowers like flower-grapes above reach, and the sweetness of clematis, the virgin's-bower which grows in Rodney, and of honeysuckle, must fill even the highest air. There is a vine that grows to great heights, with heartshaped leaves as big and soft as summer hats, overlapping and shading everything to deepest jungle blue-green.

Ferns are the hidden floor of the forest, and they grow, too, in the trees, their roots in the deep of mossy branches.

All over the hills the beautiful white Cherokee rose trails its glossy dark-green leaves and its delicate luminous-white flowers. Foliage and flowers alike have a quality of light and dark as well as color in Southern sun, and sometimes a seeming motion like dancing due to the flicker of heat, and are luminous or opaque according to the time of day or the density of summer air. In early morning or in the light of evening they become translucent and ethereal, but at noon they blaze or darken opaquely, and the same flower may seem sultry or delicate in its being all according to when you see it.

It is not hard to follow one of the leapings of old John Law's mind, then, and remember how he displayed diamonds in the shop windows in France—during the organization of his Compagnie d'Occident— saying that they were produced in the cups of the wildflowers along the lower Mississippi. And the closer they grew to the river, the more nearly that might be true.

Deep in the swamps the water hyacinths make solid floors you could walk on over still black water, the Southern blue flag stands thick and sweet in the marsh. Lady's-tresses, greenish-white little orchids with spiral flowers and stems twisted like curls and braids, grow there, and so do nodding lady's-tresses. Water lilies float, and spider lilies rise up like little coral monsters.

The woods on the bluffs are the hardwood trees—dark and berried and flowered. The magnolia is the spectacular one with its heavy cups— they look as heavy as silver—weighing upon its aromatic, elliptical, black-green leaves, or when it bears its dense pink cones. I remember an old botany book, written long ago in England, reporting the magnolia by hearsay, as having blossoms "so large as to be distinctly visible a mile or more—seen in the mass, we presume." But I tested the visibility power of the magnolia, and the single flower can be seen for several miles on a clear day. One magnolia cousin, the cucumber tree, has long sleevelike leaves and pale-green flowers which smell strange and cooler than the grandiflora flower. Set here and there in this country will be a mimosa tree, with its smell in the rain like a cool melon cut, its puffs of pale flowers settled in its sensitive leaves.

Perhaps the live oaks are the most wonderful trees in this land. Their great girth and their great spread give far more feeling of history than any house or ruin left by man. Vast, very dark, proportioned as beautifully as a church, they stand majestically in the wild or line old sites, old academy grounds. The live oaks under which Aaron Burr was tried at Washington, Mississippi, in this section, must have been old and impressive then, to have been chosen for such a drama. Spanish moss invariably hangs from the live oak branches, moving with the wind and swaying its long beards, darkening the forests; it is an aerial plant and strangely enough is really a pineapple, and consists of very, very tiny leaves and flowers, springy and dustily fragrant to the touch; no child who has ever "dressed up" in it can forget the sweet dust of its smell. It would be hard to think of things that happened here without the presence of these live oaks, so old, so expansive, so wonderful, that they might be sentient beings. W. H. Hudson, in his autobiography, *Far Away and Long Ago*, tells of an old man who felt reverentially toward the ancient trees of his great country house, so that each night he walked around his park to visit them one by one, and rest his hand on its bark to bid it goodnight, for he believed in their knowing spirits.

Now and then comes a report that an ivory-billed woodpecker is seen here. Audubon in his diary says the Indians began the slaughter of this bird long before Columbus discovered America, for the Southern Indians would trade them to the Canadian Indians—four buckskins for an ivory bill. Audubon studied the woodpecker here when he was in the Natchez country, where it lived in the deepest mossy swamps along the windings of the river, and he called it "the greatest of all our American woodpeckers and probably the finest in the world." The advance of agriculture rather than slaughter has really driven it to death, for it will not live except in a wild country.

This woodpecker used to cross the river "in deep undulations." Its notes were "clear, loud, and rather plaintive . . . heard at a considerable distance . . . and resemble the false high note of a clarinet." "Pait, pait, pait," Audubon translates it into his Frenchlike sound. It made its nest in a hole dug with the ivory bill in a tree inclined in just a certain way— usually a black cherry. The holes went sometimes three feet deep, and some people thought they went spirally. The bird ate the grapes of the swampland. Audubon says it would hang by its claws like a titmouse on a grapevine and devour grapes by the bunch—which sounds curiously as though it knew it would be extinct before long. This woodpecker also would destroy any dead tree it saw standing—chipping it away "to an extent of twenty or thirty feet in a few hours, leaping downward with its body . . . tossing its head to the right and left, or leaning it against the bark to ascertain the precise spot where the grubs were concealed, and immediately renewing its blows with fresh vigor, all the while sounding its loud notes, as if highly delighted." The males had beautiful crimson crests, the females were "always the most clamorous and the least shy." When caught, the birds would fight bitterly, and "utter a mournful and very piteous cry." All vanished now from the earth—the piteous cry and all; unless where Rodney's swamps are wild enough still, perhaps it is true, the last of the ivory-billed woodpeckers still exist in the world, in this safe spot, inaccessible to man.

Indians, Mike Fink the flatboatman, Burr, and Blennerhassett, John James Audubon, the bandits of the Trace, planters, and preachers—the horse fairs, the great fires—the battles of war, the arrivals of foreign ships, and the coming of floods: could not all these things still move with their true stature into the mind here, and their beauty still work upon the heart? Perhaps it is the sense of place that gives us the belief that passionate things, in some essence, endure. Whatever is significant and whatever is tragic in its story live as long as the place does, though they are unseen, and the new life will be built upon these things—regardless of commerce and the way of rivers and roads, and other vagrancies.

Analyzing and Discussing the Text

1. "A place that ever was lived in is like a fire that never goes out"—this sentence provides a dramatic and effective introduction to Welty's essay. How do word choice and arrangement in this sentence contribute to its effectiveness?
2. What role does the reference to "wild birds" flying now where people once talked of "great expanding things" play in this essay's themes? How does it tie in specifically with the essay's conclusion?
3. In the sixth paragraph, the author imagines a gate between two different kinds of country. What kind of country lies on either side of this gate?
4. What sense of history do we get from the essay's presentation of the ruin of Windsor, the little village of Grand Gulf, and the remnants of Bruinsburg landing, at the same time that it refers to fields and to the "dark green tangle" of vegetation?
5. The last twelve paragraphs form a second section of the essay. What is the subject of this section and how is it connected to the first half of the essay? Is this second half also governed by the first sentence?
6. What is the thematic role of the discussion of the ivory-billed woodpecker in the second and third paragraphs from the end?

Experiencing and Writing About the World

1. Where in your own area do you see this ongoing tension between the fecundity and force of the natural world and human habitation? Write a short essay describing the struggle as it appears in nature near you. Your essay should suggest, rather than state directly, your sense of how this battle is going.
2. Think about particular places that have a strong hold on your memory and imagination. Choose one such place to emphasize in a short

essay conveying the power of this sense of place. Is the place you chose part of the natural world or part of civilization, or does it have elements of both?

3. Write an essay in which you analyze the structure of Welty's essay. Focus on the arrangement of individual sentences and paragraphs as well as the whole essay.

4. Like Welty, Wendell Berry is attuned to the history of the place he writes about in "A Country of Edges," but the history that concerns him is geological and has little to do with human beings. Write an analytical essay in which you explain, with as much detail and subtlety as possible, the concepts of history that guide these two authors in "Some Notes on River Country" and "A Country of Edges."

EDWARD ABBEY

The Great American Desert

For biographical information, see the headnote for "Floating" in Part Two, Chapter Two.

The bland title of this essay (from *The Journey Home*, 1977) suggests that it could be a newspaper piece for the Sunday magazine supplement or perhaps a standard-format essay for a travel or outdoor magazine. Here, however, the usual pattern for such pieces—persuasion through praise of the scenic attractions and the possibility of benign adventure—is turned upside down. When Abbey follows his injunction to "Stay out of there" with a listing and thorough discussion of the major hazards that befall visitors to the desert, ranging from kissing bugs, rattlesnakes, and other poisonous animals and plants to sunstroke and dehydration, it is clear that he at least begins his piece with another goal in mind. It is not until Abbey hits the conservationist core of his essay, the enlistment of his readers in the "Good Cause" of saving what remains of the American desert country, that he abandons his ironic approach and speaks more straightforwardly, at least for a while. In the last half of the essay, he mixes his mockery of the standard how-to-do-it travel article with the earnest expression of his own devotion to the arid Southwest.

In my case it was love at first sight. This desert, all deserts, any desert. No matter where my head and feet may go, my heart and my entrails stay behind, here on the clean, true, comfortable rock, under the black sun of God's forsaken country. When I take on my next incarnation, my bones will remain bleaching nicely in a stone gulch under the rim of some faraway plateau, way out there in the back of beyond. An unrequited and excessive love, inhuman no doubt but painful anyhow, especially when I see my desert under attack. "The one death I cannot bear," said the Sonoran-Arizonan poet Richard Shelton. The kind of love that makes a man selfish, possessive, irritable. If you're thinking of a visit, my natural reaction is like a rattlesnake's—to warn you off. What I want to say goes something like this.

Survival Hint #1: Stay out of there. Don't go. Stay home and read a good book, this one for example. The Great American Desert is an awful place. People get hurt, get sick, get lost out there. Even if you survive, which is not certain, you will have a miserable time. The desert is for movies and God-intoxicated mystics, not for family recreation.

Let me enumerate the hazards. First the Walapai tiger, also known as conenose kissing bug. *Triatoma protracta* is a true bug, black as sin, and it flies through the night quiet as an assassin. It does not attack directly like a mosquito or deerfly, but alights at a discreet distance, undetected, and creeps upon you, its hairy little feet making not the slightest noise. The kissing bug is fond of warmth and like Dracula requires mammalian blood for sustenance. When it reaches you the bug crawls onto your skin so gently, so softly that unless your senses are hyperacute you feel nothing. Selecting a tender point, the bug slips its conical proboscis into your flesh, injecting a poisonous anesthetic. If you are asleep you will feel nothing. If you happen to be awake you may notice the faintest of pinpricks, hardly more than a brief ticklish sensation, which you will probably disregard. But the bug is already at work. Having numbed the nerves near the point of entry the bug proceeds (with a sigh of satisfaction, no doubt) to withdraw blood. When its belly is filled, it pulls out, backs off, and waddles away, so drunk and gorged it cannot fly.

At about this time the victim awakes, scratching at a furious itch. If you recognize the symptoms at once, you can sometimes find the bug in your vicinity and destroy it. But revenge will be your only satisfaction. Your night is ruined. If you are of average sensitivity to a kissing bug's poison, your entire body breaks out in hives, skin aflame from head to toe. Some people become seriously ill, in many cases requiring hospitalization. Others recover fully after five or six hours except for a hard and itchy swelling, which may endure for a week.

After the kissing bug, you should beware of rattlesnakes; we have half a dozen species, all offensive and dangerous, plus centipedes, millipedes, tarantulas, black widows, brown recluses, Gila monsters, the deadly poisonous coral snakes, and giant hairy desert scorpions. Plus an immense variety and near-infinite number of ants, midges, gnats, bloodsucking flies, and blood-guzzling mosquitoes. (You might think the desert would be spared at least mosquitoes? Not so. Peer in any water hole by day: swarming with mosquito larvae. Venture out on a summer's eve: The air vibrates with their mournful keening.) Finally, where the desert meets the sea, as on the coasts of Sonora and Baja California, we have the usual assortment of obnoxious marine life: sandflies, ghost crabs, stingrays, electric jellyfish, spiny sea urchins, man-eating sharks, and other creatures so distasteful one prefers not even to name them.

It has been said, and truly, that everything in the desert either stings, stabs, stinks, or sticks. You will find the flora here as venomous, hooked, barbed, thorny, prickly, needled, saw-toothed, hairy, stickered, mean, bitter, sharp, wiry, and fierce as the animals. Something about the desert inclines all living things to harshness and acerbity. The soft evolve out. Except for sleek and oily growths like the poison ivy—oh yes, indeed—that flourish in sinister profusion on the dank walls above the quicksand down in those corridors of gloom and labyrinthine monotony that men call canyons.

We come now to the third major hazard, which is sunshine. Too much of a good thing can be fatal. Sunstroke, heatstroke, and dehydration are common misfortunes in the bright American Southwest. If you can avoid the insects, reptiles, and arachnids, the cactus and the ivy, the smog of the southwestern cities, and the lung fungus of the desert valleys (carried by dust in the air), you cannot escape the desert sun. Too much exposure to it eventually causes, quite literally, not merely sunburn but skin cancer.

Much sun, little rain also means an arid climate. Compared with the high humidity of more hospitable regions, the dry heat of the desert seems at first not terribly uncomfortable—sometimes even pleasant. But that sensation of comfort is false, a deception, and therefore all the more dangerous, for it induces overexertion and an insufficient consumption of water, even when water is available. This leads to various internal complications, some immediate—sunstroke, for example—and some not apparent until much later. Mild but prolonged dehydration, continued over a span of months or years, leads to the crystallization of mineral solutions in the urinary tract, that is, to what urologists call urinary calculi or kidney stones. A disability common in all the world's arid regions. Kidney stones, in case you haven't met one, come in many shapes and sizes, from pellets smooth as BB shot to highly irregular calcifications resembling asteroids, Vietcong shrapnel, and crown-of-thorns starfish. Some of these objects may be "passed" naturally; others can be removed only by means of the Davis stone basket or by surgery. Me—I was lucky; I passed mine with only a groan, my forehead pressed against the wall of a pissoir in the rear of a Tucson bar that I cannot recommend.

You may be getting the impression by now that the desert is not the most suitable of environments for human habitation. Correct. Of all the Earth's climatic zones, excepting only the Antarctic, the deserts are the least inhabited, the least "developed," for reasons that should now be clear.

You may wish to ask, Yes, okay, but among North American deserts which is the *worst?* A good question—and I am happy to attempt an answer.

Geographers generally divide the North American desert—what was once termed "the Great American Desert"—into four distinct regions or subdeserts. These are the Sonoran Desert, which comprises southern Arizona, Baja California, and the state of Sonora in Mexico; the Chihuahuan Desert, which includes west Texas, southern New Mexico, and the states of Chihuahua and Coahuila in Mexico; the Mojave Desert, which includes southeastern California and small portions of Nevada, Utah, and Arizona; and the Great Basin Desert, which includes most of Utah and Nevada, northern Arizona, northwestern New Mexico, and much of Idaho and eastern Oregon.

Privately, I prefer my own categories. Up north in Utah somewhere is the canyon country—places like Zeke's Hole, Death Hollow, Pucker Pass, Buckskin Gulch, Nausea Crick, Wolf Hole, Mollie's Nipple, Dirty Devil River, Horse Canyon, Horseshoe Canyon, Lost Horse Canyon, Horsethief Canyon, and Horseshit Canyon, to name only the more classic places. Down in Arizona and Sonora there's the cactus country; if you have nothing better to do, you might take a look at High Tanks, Salome Creek, Tortilla Flat, Esperero ("Hoper") Canyon, Holy Joe Peak, Depression Canyon, Painted Cave, Hell Hole Canyon, Hell's Half Acre, Iceberg Canyon, Tiburon (Shark) Island, Pinacate Peak, Infernal Valley, Sykes Crater, Montezuma's Head, Gu Oidak, Kuakatch, Pisinimo, and Baboquivari Mountain, for example.

Then there's The Canyon. *The* Canyon. The Grand. That's one world. And North Rim—that's another. And Death Valley, still another, where I lived one winter near Furnace Creek and climbed the Funeral Mountains, tasted Badwater, looked into the Devil's Hole, hollered up Echo Canyon, searched for and never did find Seldom Seen Slim. Looked for *satori* near Vana, Nevada, and found a ghost town named Bonnie Claire. Never made it to Winnemucca. Drove through the Smoke Creek Desert and down through Big Pine and Lone Pine and home across the Panamints to Death Valley again—home sweet home that winter.

And which of these deserts is the worst? I find it hard to judge. They're all bad—not half bad but all bad. In the Sonoran Desert, Phoenix will get you if the sun, snakes, bugs, and arthropods don't. In the

Mojave Desert, it's Las Vegas, more sickening by far than the Glauber's salt in the Death Valley sinkholes. Go to Chihuahua and you're liable to get busted in El Paso and sandbagged in Ciudad Juárez—where all old whores go to die. Up north in the Great Basin Desert, on the Plateau Province, in the canyon country, your heart will break, seeing the strip mines open up and the power plants rise where only cowboys and Indians and J. Wesley Powell ever roamed before.

Nevertheless, all is not lost; much remains, and I welcome the prospect of an army of lug-soled hiker's boots on the desert trails. To save what wilderness is left in the American Southwest—and in the American Southwest only the wilderness is worth saving—we are going to need all the recruits we can get. All the hands, heads, bodies, time, money, effort we can find. Presumably—and the Sierra Club, the Wilderness Society, the Friends of the Earth, the Audubon Society, the Defenders of Wildlife operate on this theory—those who learn to love what is spare, rough, wild, undeveloped, and unbroken will be willing to fight for it, will help resist the strip miners, highway builders, land developers, weapons testers, power producers, tree chainers, clear cutters, oil drillers, dam beavers, subdividers—the list goes on and on—before that zinc-hearted, termite-brained, squint-eyed, near-sighted, greedy crew succeeds in completely californicating what still survives of the Great American Desert.

So much for the Good Cause. Now what about desert hiking itself, you may ask. I'm glad you asked that question. I firmly believe that one should never—I repeat *never*—go out into that formidable wasteland of cactus, heat, serpents, rock, scrub, and thorn without careful planning, thorough and cautious preparation, and complete—never mind the expense!—*complete* equipment. My motto is: Be Prepared.

That is my belief and that is my motto. My practice, however, is a little different. I tend to go off in a more or less random direction myself, half-baked, half-assed, half-cocked, and half-ripped. Why? Well, because I have an indolent and melancholy nature and don't care to be bothered getting all those *things* together—all that bloody *gear*—maps, compass, binoculars, poncho, pup tent, shoes, first-aid kit, rope, flashlight, inspirational poetry, water, food—and because anyhow I approach nature with a certain surly ill-will, daring Her to make trouble. Later when I'm deep into Natural Bridges Natural Moneymint or Zion National Parkinglot or say General Shithead National Forest Land of Many Abuses why then, of course, when it's a bit late, then I may wish I had packed that something extra: matches perhaps, to mention one useful item, or maybe a spoon to eat my gruel with.

If I hike with another person it's usually the same; most of my friends have indolent and melancholy natures too. A cursed lot, all of them. I think of my comrade John De Puy, for example, sloping along for mile after mile like a god-damned camel—indefatigable—with those

J.C. Penney hightops on his feet and that plastic pack on his back he got with five books of Green Stamps and nothing inside it but a sketchbook, some homemade jerky and a few cans of green chiles. Or Douglas Peacock, ex-Green Beret, just the opposite. Built like a buffalo, he loads a ninety-pound canvas pannier on his back at trailhead, loaded with guns, ammunition, bayonet, pitons and carabiners, cameras, field books, a 150-foot rope, geologist's sledge, rock samples, assay kit, field glasses, two gallons of water in steel canteens, jungle boots, a case of C-rations, rope hammock, pharmaceuticals in a pig-iron box, raincoat, overcoat, two-man mountain tent, Dutch oven, hibachi, shovel, ax, inflatable boat, and near the top of the load and distributed through side and back pockets, easily accessible, a case of beer. Not because he enjoys or needs all that weight—he may never get to the bottom of that cargo on a ten-day outing—but simply because Douglas uses his packbag for general storage both at home and on the trail and prefers not to have to rearrange everything from time to time merely for the purposes of a hike. Thus my friends De Puy and Peacock; you may wish to avoid such extremes.

A few tips on desert etiquette:

1. Carry a cooking stove, if you must cook. Do not burn desert wood, which is rare and beautiful and required ages for its creation (an ironwood tree lives for over 1,000 years and juniper almost as long).

2. If you must, out of need, build a fire, then for God's sake allow it to burn itself out before you leave—do not bury it, as Boy Scouts and Campfire Girls do, under a heap of mud or sand. Scatter the ashes; replace any rocks you may have used in constructing a fireplace; do all you can to obliterate the evidence that you camped here. (The Search & Rescue Team may be looking for you.)

3. Do not bury garbage—the wildlife will only dig it up again. Burn what will burn and pack out the rest. The same goes for toilet paper: Don't bury it, *burn it.*

4. Do not bathe in desert pools, natural tanks, *tinajas,* potholes. Drink what water you need, take what you need, and leave the rest for the next hiker and more important for the bees, birds, and animals—bighorn sheep, coyotes, lions, foxes, badgers, deer, wild pigs, wild horses—whose *lives* depend on that water.

5. Always remove and destroy survey stakes, flagging, advertising signboards, mining claim markers, animal traps, poisoned bait, seismic exploration geophones, and other such artifacts of industrialism. The men who put those things there are up to

no good and it is our duty to confound them. Keep America Beautiful. Grow a Beard. Take a Bath. Burn a Billboard.

Anyway—why go into the desert? Really, why do it? That sun, roaring at you all day long. The fetid, tepid, vapid little water holes slowly evaporating under a scum of grease, full of cannibal beetles, spotted toads, horsehair worms, liver flukes and down at the bottom, inevitably, the pale cadaver of a ten-inch centipede. Those pink rattlesnakes down in The Canyon, those diamondback monsters thick as a truck driver's waist that lurk in shady places along the trail, those unpleasant solpugids and unnecessary Jerusalem crickets that scurry on dirty claws across your face at night. Why? The rain that comes down like lead shot and wrecks the trail, those sudden rockfalls of obscure origin that crash like thunder ten feet behind you in the heart of a dead-still afternoon. The ubiquitous buzzard, so patient—but only so patient. The sullen and hostile Indians, all on welfare. The ragweed, the tumbleweed, the Jimson weed, the snakeweed. The scorpion in your shoe at dawn. The dreary wind that blows all spring, the psychedelic Joshua trees waving their arms at you on moonlight nights. Sand in the soup du jour. Halazone tablets in your canteen. The barren hills that always go up, which is bad, or down, which is worse. Those canyons like catacombs with quicksand lapping at your crotch. Hollow, mummified horses with forelegs casually crossed, dead for ten years, leaning against the corner of a barbed-wire fence. Packhorses at night, ironshod, clattering over the slickrock through your camp. The last tin of tuna, two flat tires, not enough water and a forty-mile trek to Tule Well. An osprey on a cardón cactus, snatching the head off a living fish— always the best part first. The hawk sailing by at 200 feet, a squirming snake in its talons. Salt in the drinking water. Salt, selenium, arsenic, radon and radium in the water, in the gravel, in your bones. Water so hard it bends light, drills holes in rock and chokes up your radiator. Why go there? Those places with the hardcase names: Starvation Creek, Poverty Knoll, Hungry Valley, Bitter Springs, Last Chance Canyon, Dungeon Canyon, Whipsaw Flat, Dead Horse Point, Scorpion Flat, Dead Man Draw, Stinking Spring, Camino del Diablo, Jornado del Muerto . . . Death Valley.

Well then, why indeed go walking into the desert, that grim ground, that bleak and lonesome land where, as Genghis Khan said of India, "the heat is bad and the water makes men sick"?

Why the desert, when you could be strolling along the golden beaches of California? Camping by a stream of pure Rocky Mountain spring water in colorful Colorado? Loafing through a laurel slick in the misty hills of North Carolina? Or getting your head mashed in the greasy alley behind the Elysium Bar and Grill in Hoboken, New Jersey? Why the desert, given a world of such splendor and variety?

A friend and I took a walk around the base of a mountain up beyond Coconino County, Arizona. This was a mountain we'd been planning to circumambulate for years. Finally we put on our walking shoes and did it. About halfway around this mountain on the third or fourth day, we paused for a while—two days—by the side of a stream, which the Navajos call Nasja because of the amber color of the water. (Caused perhaps by juniper roots—the water seems safe enough to drink.) On our second day there I walked down the stream, alone, to look at the canyon beyond. I entered the canyon and followed it for half the afternoon, for three or four miles, maybe, until it became a gorge so deep, narrow and dark, full of water and the inevitable quagmires of quicksand, that I turned around and looked for a way out. A route other than the way I'd come, which was crooked and uncomfortable and buried—I wanted to see what was up on top of this world. I found a sort of chimney flue on the east wall, which looked plausible, and sweated and cursed my way up through that until I reached a point where I could walk upright, like a human being. Another 300 feet of scrambling brought me to the rim of the canyon. No one, I felt certain, had ever before departed Nasja Canyon by that route.

But someone had. Near the summit I found an arrow sign, three feet long, formed of stones and pointing off into the north toward those same old purple vistas, so grand, immense, and mysterious, of more canyons, more mesas and plateaus, more mountains, more cloud-dappled sun-spangled leagues of desert sand and desert rock, under the same old wide and aching sky.

The arrow pointed into the north. But what was it pointing *at?* I looked at the sign closely and saw that those dark, desert-varnished stones had been in place for a long, long, time; they rested in compacted dust. They must have been there for a century at least. I followed the direction indicated and came promptly to the rim of another canyon and a drop-off straight down of a good 500 feet. Not that way, surely. Across this canyon was nothing of any unusual interest that I could see—only the familiar sun-blasted sandstone, a few scrubby clumps of blackbrush and prickly pear, a few acres of nothing where only a lizard could graze, surrounded by a few square miles of more nothing-ness interesting chiefly to horned toads. I returned to the arrow and checked again, this time with field glasses, looking away for as far as my aided eyes could see toward the north, for ten, twenty, forty miles into the distance. I studied the scene with care, looking for an ancient Indian ruin, a significant cairn, perhaps an abandoned mine, a hidden treasure of some inconceivable wealth, the mother of all mother lodes. . . .

But there was nothing out there. Nothing at all. Nothing but the desert. Nothing but the silent world.

That's why.

Analyzing and Discussing the Text

1. Abbey begins his depiction of the desert country by placing himself "here on the clean, true, comfortable rock, under the black sun of God's forsaken country." What role do the paradoxical elements play in this description of the desert? Throughout the essay?
2. Abbey spends two complete paragraphs describing the "conenose kissing bug" and the effect it can have on humans. Why? How does he keep this extended description interesting?
3. In the sixth paragraph, Abbey states that "everything in the desert either stings, stabs, stinks, or sticks." What function is served by the sheer verbal energy and sense of play evident here and throughout the other lists of ills in this essay? What would change in the essay if these lists were not in themselves so exuberant and entertaining?
4. Notice how Abbey plays with the whole idea of classification in paragraphs 11 and 12. Why does he want to substitute his own categories for the standard geographical ones? Is he also mocking the whole notion of categories? If so, explain why he might want to do this.
5. How does the fifth section on desert etiquette differ from the first four? Why place it last on the list? How do the earlier sections prepare us for Abbey's brief first-person hiking narrative at the conclusion of the essay?
6. Why is it important to the point of Abbey's essay that the stone arrow he finds is an old one?

Experiencing and Writing About the World

1. Pick some aspect of your life that has the kind of gap between belief and practice that Abbey presents in paragraphs 17 and 18 and describe it in a brief essay. Try to make your description of this gap as humorous as Abbey's.
2. Write an essay about your own love for a dangerous place. Use this paper as a chance to experiment with a new prose style by closely imitating the precise sentence patterns in any three or more consecutive paragraphs from Abbey's essay. Choose model paragraphs that include unusual sentence patterns and types of punctuation that you normally don't use in your own writing.
3. Write a short essay telling why Abbey loves the desert. Your analysis should include material from all of the essay, not just the last section.
4. How do you think Abbey hoped to affect his readers with this essay? Write an analytical essay in which you try to gauge the intended "reader response." In particular, try to explain why Abbey begins the essay so emphatically with the statement: "If you're thinking of a

visit, my natural reaction is like a rattlesnake's—to warn you off. . . . Stay out of there. Don't go. . . . The Great American Desert is an awful place. People get hurt, get sick, get lost out there." Does he really expect to scare his readers away from the desert? Does he want to attract visitors? How does this essay attempt to protect and preserve the desert?

WENDELL BERRY

A Country of Edges

Wendell Berry (1934–   ) was born in Henry County, Kentucky. He attended the University of Kentucky, where he received his B.A. in 1956 and his M.A. a year later. The following year, Berry received a Wallace Stegner Fellowship at Stanford University, after which he stayed on an extra year as a lecturer in creative writing. After a year at home in Kentucky and another year on a Guggenheim Fellowship in Italy, he taught for three years at New York University before returning to the University of Kentucky in 1964, where he has remained for the rest of his teaching career, aside from another stint at Stanford in the late 1960s. In 1964, Berry made a deliberate choice to move back to the area of his birth and to run a small farm, raise his family, and write in that particular place. This move was, for him, a carefully considered, personal rejection of the "corporate revolution" that "has so determinedly invaded the farmland" and an affirmation of his notion of a true homeland, a place where individual farmers put the land to "kindly use." Berry argues in his 1977 collection of essays, *The Unsettling of America*, that "the first and greatest American revolution . . . was the coming of people who did not look upon the land as homeland." "Our industrial economy preys upon the native productivity of land and people," he believes, "and commercial conquest separates most Americans from the land and thus from direct access to the staples of life." Berry has articulated these convictions not only in many novels and collections of poetry, but in such books of literary nonfiction as *The Long-Legged House* (1969), *The Unforeseen Wilderness: An Essay on Kentucky's Red River Gorge* (1971), *A Continuous Harmony: Essays Cultural and Agricultural* (1972), *The Gift of*

Good Land (1981), *Home Economics* (1987), and *What Are People For?* (1990). His work has won major awards from the Rockefeller Foundation and the National Institute of Arts and Letters.

The following essay from *The Unforeseen Wilderness* describes an area near where Berry has chosen to live, and, although it is an early essay, the characteristically steady style of Berry's prose is very evident. Berry's language here, as elsewhere, is understated, seldom calling attention to its author or to the words themselves, but instead building our knowledge of the gorge by quietly describing the area from various angles of vision. This slow accumulation of knowledge involves all of the senses. When he sips water from a clear pool, he knows that "Looking and listening are as important as tasting. One drinks in the sense of being in a good place." Berry would argue that such "drinking" occurs only when one really knows a place and that such knowledge comes from patient watchfulness over time.

It is a country of overtowering edges. Again and again, walking down from the wooded ridgetops above the Red River Gorge one comes into the sound of water falling—the steady pouring and spattering of a tiny stream that has reached its grand occasion. And then one arrives at a great shady scoop in the cliff where the trail bends and steps and skids down to the foot of the fall. One looks up twenty or thirty or fifty or more feet to where the water leaps off the rock lip, catching the sunlight as it falls. Maybe there will be a rainbow in the spray. The trail may have passed through little shelves or terraces covered with wild iris in bloom. Or along the streamsides below the falls there may be pink lady's slippers. The slopes will be thickly shrubbed with rhododendron, darkened by the heavy green shade of hemlocks. And always on the wet faces of the rock there will be liverwort and meadow rue and mosses and ferns.

These places are as fresh, and they stay as fresh in the memory, as a clear, cold drink of water. They have a way of making me thirsty, whether I need a drink or not, and I like to hunt out a pool among the rocks and drink. The water is clean and cold. It is what water ought to be, for here one gets it "high and original," uncorrupted by any scientific miracle. There will be a clean gravelly bottom to the pool and its edges will bear the delicate garden-growth of the wet woods. There are the enclosing sounds of the water falling, and the voices of the phoebes and the Carolina wrens that nest in the sheltered places of the cliffs. Looking and listening are as important as tasting. One drinks in the sense of being in a good place.

The critical fact about water, wherever you find it in the Red River Gorge, is motion. Moving, it is gathering. All the little seeps and trickles of the slopes, the tiny streams heading up near the ridgetops and leaping and tumbling down the steep ravines—all are moving toward their union in the river.

And in the movement of its waters the place also is in motion; not to the human eye, nor to the collective vision of human history, but within the long gaze of geologic time the Gorge is moving within itself, deepening, changing the outline of its slopes; the river is growing into it like a great tree, steadily incising its branches into the land. For however gentle it may appear at certain seasons, this network of water known in sum as the Red River moves in its rocky notches as abrasive as a file.

How the river works as maker of the landscape, sculptor, arm of creation will always remain to some degree unknown, for it works with immeasurable leisure and patience, and often it works in turmoil. Although its processes may be hypothesized very convincingly, every vantage point of the country is also a point of speculation, a point of departure from the present surface into the shadowy questions of origin and of process.

By what complex interaction of flowing water, of weather, of growth and decay was that cliff given its shape? Where did this house-sized boulder fall from, what manner of sledging and breaking did it do coming down, what effect has it had on the course of the stream? What is happening now in all the swirling rapids and falls and eddies and pools of the river in flood? We know the results. But because we have not a thousand years to sit and watch, because our perspective is not that of birds or fish or of the lichens on the cliff face but only of men, because the life of the Gorge has larger boundaries than the life of a man, we know little of the processes.

To come to any understanding of the Red River one must consider how minute and manifold are its workings, how far beyond count its lives and aspects and manifestations. But one must also sense its great power and its vastness. One must see in it the motive force of a landscape, the formal energy of all the country that drains into it. And one must stand on its banks aware that its life and meaning are not merely local but are intricately involved in all life and all meaning. It belongs to a family of rivers whose gathering will finally bring its water to mingle with the waters of the Yellowstone and the Kanahwa and the ocean. Its life belongs within—is dependent upon and to some extent necessary to—the life of the planet.

And so in the aspect of the river, in any of its moods, there is always a residual mystery. In its being it is too small and too large, too complex and too simple, too powerful and too delicate, too transient and too ancient and durable ever to be comprehended within the limits of a human life.

On the last Saturday in March we set out from Fletcher Ridge to walk down Mariba Fork, Laurel Fork, and Gladie Creek to the river. Last weekend there was deep snow. This morning it is sunny and warm. We walk past an old house site on the ridge—the clearing now grown up in thicket, the ground still covered with the dooryard periwinkles—and then down a steep path through the cliffs. As we approach the stream at the foot of the slope we begin to find hepaticas in bloom. They are everywhere, standing up in bright jaunty clumps like Sunday bouquets beneath the big poplars and beeches and hemlocks, and on the tops of boulders.

The path fades out. We follow the rocky edges of the stream, descending with the water gradually deeper into the land. As along all the streams of the Gorge, the country is divided by stones or cliffs or trees into distinct enclosures, a series of rooms, each one different in light and look and feeling from all the rest.

We find other flowers in bloom: trout lilies, rue anemones, trailing arbutus with its delicately scented blossoms almost hidden among the dead leaves. But running through all that day like an insistent, endlessly varied theme in a piece of music are the little gardens of hepaticas. Climbing onto a streamside terrace or entering the mouth of a ravine, we find the ground suddenly rich with them, the flowers a deep blue or lavender or pink or white. They are like Easter gone wild and hiding in the woods.

Downstream from where we camp that night we can see the rocky point of a cliff, high up, with a dead tree standing alone on it. And at twilight a pair of pileated woodpeckers cast off from that tree and make a long steep descent into the woods below, their flight powerful and somehow abandoned, joyous, accepting of the night.

Our walk ends the next day in the midst of a violent downpour. We know that, behind us, the country we have passed through is changing. Its maker has returned to it yet again to do new work.

Flowing muddy and full, frothing over its rapids, its great sound filling the valley to the brim, the river is inscrutable and forbidding. The mind turns away from it, craving dry land like a frightened swimmer. The river will not stay still to be regarded or thought about. Its events are too much part of the flow, melting rapidly into one another, drawn on by the singular demand of the current.

Other times when the river is low, idling in its pools, its mysteries become inviting. One's thoughts eagerly leave solid ground then and take to the water. The current has ceased to be a threat and become an invitation. The thought of a boat comes to mind unasked and makes itself at home.

At such a time, a bright morning in early June, a canoe seems as satisfying and liberating as a pair of wings. One is empowered to pass beyond the shore, to follow the current that, other times, standing on the shore, one has merely wished to follow.

We wake at dawn, camped high on one of the ridges. Below us the hollows are drifted deep in white mist. While we eat breakfast and pack up we watch the mist shift with the stirrings of the air, rising, thickening and then thinning out, opening here and there so that we can see through to the treetops below, and closing again. It is as if the whole landscape is moving with a gentle dreaming motion. And then we drive down the windings of Highway 715, through the rapidly thinning mist, to the river. And now our canoe lies on the water in the shade-dappled weak light of the early morning. We have the day and the river before us.

Through the morning we paddle or drift through the long pools, idling with the river, stopping to look wherever our curiosity is tempted. We see a kingfisher, a water thrush, a Kentucky warbler, a muskrat, a snake asleep on an old tire caught on a snag, a lot of big, fat tadpoles three or four inches long, dragonflies with brilliant green bodies and black wings. In the clear shoals we see fish, and at intervals we pass the camps of fishermen, places their minds will turn back to, homesick, out of the confinement of winter and city and job. These are usually quiet and deserted; we have already passed the fishermen, fishing from the top of a boulder upstream, or we will find them in a boat a little way below.

On the bar at the mouth of Wolfpen Creek, where we stop for lunch, we watch several black and yellow swallowtail butterflies drinking together on a spot of damp sand. They are like a bouquet of flowers that occasionally fly away and return again.

Where the swift clear water of Wolfpen enters the river a school of minnows is feeding. They work up the current over a little shoal of rippled sand, and then release themselves into the flow, drifting down through the quick water shadows to start again.

And all along the stream are boulders as big as houses that have broken from the cliffs and tumbled down. They are splotched with gray lichens and with mosses and liverworts; where enough dirt has collected in cracks and depressions in the stone there will be clumps of ferns or meadow rue or little patches of bluets. Above the high water line, where the current cannot sweep them, the long drama of soil-building has taken place on the tops of some of these rocks, so that they are now covered with plants and trees, and their surfaces look much like the surrounding forest floor. Those within reach of the floods are cleaner and more stony looking. They are not to be imperceptibly eaten away by the acids of the decay of vegetation and by the prizing of root and frost; they are being hewed out like sculptures by the direct violence of the river. Those that stand in the stream have been undercut by the steady abrasion of the current so that they rise out of the water like mushrooms. Going by them, one thinks of the thousands of miles of water that have flowed past them, and of the generations of boatmen, Indians and white men, that have paddled around them or stopped to fish in their shadows—and one feels their great weight and their silence and endurance. In the slanting light of the early morning the reflections off the water waver and flicker along their sides, the light moving over them with the movement of water.

There is no river more intimate with its banks. Everywhere the shore rises up steeply from the water like a page offered to be read. Water-borne, one seems always within arm's reach of the land. One has a walker's intimacy with the animals and plants of the shore as well as a boatman's intimacy with the life of the water. Without rising from one's seat in the canoe one looks into the mossy cup of a phoebe's nest fastened to the rock and sees the five white eggs.

At intervals through the day we tense and focus ourselves as the river does, and move down into the head of a rapid. We pass through carefully, no longer paddling as we wish but as we must, following the main current as it bends through the rocks and the grassy shoals. And then we enter the quiet water of the pool below. Ahead of us a leaf falls from high up in a long gentle fall. In the water its reflection rises perfectly to meet it.

Analyzing and Discussing the Text

1. What does Berry mean when he says that the water there "is what water ought to be"?
2. Once we read it carefully, we see that the essay's second section is describing, without naming it, a process that we commonly call erosion. Why does Berry approach the topic in this way? How does this subject fit with the subjects and themes treated in the rest of the essay?
3. Why is there "residual mystery," which remains even after careful observation, about the Red River and its shaping of a landscape?
4. What changes in the fourth and fifth sections of this essay? How do these sections complement the earlier segments?
5. Why does Berry focus on the boulders and "the long drama of soil-building"? Is his vantage point, floating by in a canoe, of particular thematic relevance? Explain.
6. Does the end of this essay provide a sense of closure or progress? How does the tone of the essay's conclusion compare with that of other nature essays you have read?

Experiencing and Writing About the World

1. Choose a favorite place and write a brief (500–750 words) rhapsody about it, an expression of your appreciation. Feel free to choose any kind of place, urban or rural, such as your yard at home, a nearby alley, a bookstore, your dorm room, or a place in the mountains. Before you start writing, consciously plot out the pattern of your essay; plan a controlled discussion of your chosen place, moving, for instance, from the specific to the general or from the physical place to the way it makes you feel. Compose five sections, just as Berry does in "A Country of Edges"; the sections may vary from one to three paragraphs in length. If a pattern of organization springs to mind, go with it. Otherwise, imitate Berry's pattern: general but vivid description combined with identification of a few characteristics of the place, analysis of one characteristic, philosophical rumination, personal narrative, and renewed philosophizing framed in another narrative. Try to lure your reader, an innately sympathetic one, toward your perspective.

2. Choose a nearby landscape that you know has been shaped by natural forces and see if you can find some evidence of those forces at work now. Is the change you see slower or faster than the change Berry relates in his essay? Write a brief essay in which you bring together the visible agents of change and the larger picture.

3. The last segment of this essay could, with its description of a time when a "canoe seems as satisfying and liberating as a pair of wings," be included in the "Floating" chapter of this reader. Compare one essay from that chapter with this essay. What does each writer emphasize with the floating perspective? Are there common elements in the way each perceives the condition of being waterborne?

4. Carefully analyze Berry's apparent attitude toward the place described in this essay and compare this attitude—its emphasis on steadily increasing intimacy with the land—with the attitudes toward nature in the work of such writers as Annie Dillard, Edward Abbey, and Barry Lopez. Which of these writers resemble Berry in perspective and prose style, and which ones differ? Use specific textual examples to support your explanation. Also, try to discuss the significance of each way of approaching language and the natural world.

TERRY TEMPEST WILLIAMS

Yucca

Terry Tempest Williams (1955–   ) was born in the Salt Valley of Utah into a family that has deep roots in the area. Her ancestors arrived there almost 150 years ago, having moved West by pushing a small handcart filled with provisions over twelve hundred miles from Missouri. Their years of work laying pipe in the Utah substrate have given them what Williams calls "a fierce awareness of the forces outside of ourselves—call it a ditch-digging humility." She received a bachelor's degree in English and a master's in science education from the University of Utah, and she now teaches in the women's studies program there. She is also the curator of education and Naturalist-in-Residence at the Utah Museum of Natural History in Salt Lake City. Williams has written children's books with nature themes, including *The Secret Language of Snow* (1984), and a collection of stories set in southern Utah called *Coyote's Canyon* (1989). Her two nonfiction books, which blend natural history and personal experience, are *Pieces of White Shell: A Journey to Navajoland* (1984), the work from which "Yucca" is taken, and more recently *Refuge: An Unnatural History of Family & Place* (1991), a powerful study of landscape as refuge and the necessity of a mutually healing relationship between humans and nature. In all of her teaching and her writing, Williams seeks to help us become "bioregionally literate," to inculcate "an ethics of place."

Her work is also marked by a continuing concern with how the knowledge of nature can sustain a culture and how we can successfully go about sharing such knowledge, not only within cultures but also across cultures. In *Pieces of White Shell,* Williams draws on her experiences as a teacher on the Navajo reservation and her deep knowledge of Navajo tradition to give her readers a sense of the Navajos' healthy and intimate relationship to nature. The essays and stories become a way for her, with her Mormon background, and her readers, with their diverse backgrounds and traditions, to learn the "earth wisdom" embodied in Navajo culture. Such exchange, she feels, will help promote the healing of the earth and ourselves.

One night the stars pulled me into a dream. A basket sat before me, coiled: around and around and around and around. It was striped with persimmon. I should not touch it. This much I knew. I knelt down

484

closely and saw a woman's long black hair curled between stitches. I picked up a sprig of salt bush and rattled it above the hair strand. Suddenly, the woven bowl began to pulsate, writhe, until a snake uncoiled herself slowly. This is what I heard:

> Sha-woman, Sha-woman, hiss
> Sha-woman, Sha-woman, hiss
> Tongue, rattle, hiss
> Tongue, rattle, hiss
> Sha-woman, Sha-woman, hiss

She stopped. She raised her head and blew upward. I watched the breezes pull her vertically until she became a white desert torch. Yucca.

In the Navajo account of yucca's birth, Tracking Bear was a monster from whom there was no escape. He lived in a cave in the mountains. Monster Slayer, pursued by Tracking Bear, climbed a sheer wall. As he did so he grasped a fruit of the yucca in his left hand, and in his right a twig of hard oak. The monster feared these medicine rattles. Monster Slayer killed Tracking Bear and cut off his claws and large canine teeth, taking the gall and windpipe as trophies. He then cut the head into three pieces: One became the broad-leaved yucca, one the narrow-leaved yucca, and one the mescal.

And so yucca appears evenly spaced across the land. They stand as sentinels with their flowering stalks rising from vegetative swords. They are shields for creatures who live near. Sundown strikes yucca. Desert candles flame.

I remember peering into a yucca flower at dusk and seeing a tiny moth scraping pollen from within. The little white-robed pilgrim rolled the pollen into a tight ball and carried it to another blossom. There I watched her pierce the ovary wall with her long ovipositor and lay a clutch of eggs among the ovules, much as a farmer in the spring scatters seeds along his furrows. She packed the sticky mass of pollen through the openings of the stigma. Moth larvae and seeds would now develop simultaneously, with the larvae feeding on developing yucca. She walked to the edge of the petals. With her last bit of strength, she glided into the darkness, carried away by grace. The larvae would eventually gnaw their way through the ovary wall and lower themselves to the ground to pupate until the yuccas bloomed again. Circles. Cycles. Yucca and moth.

Perhaps the moth was on her way to pollinate the Navajo mind as well, for yucca and Navajo are relatives. Yucca is the single most important noncultivated plant to Indian peoples in the Southwest. It has been plaited into baskets, woven into mats, and wrapped around bundles. Early peoples walked with yucca bound around their feet.

Sandals. Imagine the care extended to plants when they mean your survival.

In days of painted language, yucca leaves were soaked in warm water to soften. They were then beaten against the rocks for further pliancy. Fibers finely peeled—like corn silk, only stronger—were twisted into cordage with organic tension. This same process can be tried today with patience.

The children know yucca, *tsá-ászi'*, intimately. On the banks of the San Juan River we stood in a circle with yucca at the center.

"What is this?" I asked.

"Yucca!" they sang out in unison.

"And what story does it tell?"

I heard as many responses as there are yucca blossoms. But one common strand connecting their stories was soap.

"We call it soapweed because there's soap under there. . . . "

"Yes?"

"Yes. You find the root under here—they pointed to the body of the plant—cut off a piece, and slice it into four strips. Then you pound it with your hands and add warm water until it lathers up."

"Then what do you do?"'

"We wash our hair with the suds."

Before I knew what was happening, two boys pulled the plant out from the sand. They cut off the root, sliced it into four strips, placed it on the sandstone, and began pounding it with a rock—just as they had said. It worked: The root was frothing with suds.

The boys didn't stop there. They moved to a desert pothole that was holding rainwater. Loren bent over the basin as Bryan washed his hair. The rest of the children gathered. This was a familiar sight and they laughed.

"Loren, you better watch out—tomorrow you'll come to school with hair hanging down your back!"

The lore of yucca supports this teasing. The Navajo say a yucca shampoo will make your hair long, shiny, and black. If there are doubts as to yucca magic, just look at the children.

On another occasion, the children warned me against using yucca.

"Why not?" I asked. My curiosity was up.

"Because it might give you warts." A wave of giggles rushed over them.

But on this day, things were different. After the boys had finished their demonstration, they handed me a fresh section of the root.

"Try it."

The girls disappeared and returned with a brush they had made from a bunch of rice grass. They began combing my hair. I sat toward the wind, unable to speak.

The ritual of bathing with yucca suds is woven into the Navajo Way. It has been said that the mound of earth upon which the basket for water and suds is placed commemorates the visit of two children to Changing Woman's home, where they witnessed her rejuvenation. Blessed yucca suds have the power to transform—to change the profane to sacred, the doubtful to controlled, the contaminated to the purified.

One of the Navajo ceremonies associated with yucca washings is *Kinaaldá*, Changing Woman's puberty rites. *Kinaaldá* is part of the Blessing Way, a Navajo rite that maintains harmony for the people by attracting the goodness and power of benevolent Holy People. Most Navajo use the word *kinaaldá* to refer to the "first menses," alluding to the ceremonial rather than the physical event.

Kinaaldá ushers the adolescent Navajo girl into womanhood and invokes blessings upon her, ensuring her health, prosperity, and well-being. It is a festive occasion where the accounts of Changing Woman and her *Kinaaldá* are retold and reenacted.

> The *Kinaaldá* started when White Shell Woman first menstruated. Nine days after her *Kinaaldá,* Changing Woman gave birth to twin boys: Monster Slayer and Child-of-the-waters. They were placed on the earth to kill the monsters. As soon as they had done this, their mother, Changing Woman, who was then living at Governador Knob, left and went to her home in the west, where she lives today.
>
> After she moved to her home in the west, she created the Navajo people. When she had done this, she told these human beings to go to their original home, which was Navajo country. Before they left, she said, "After this, all the girls born to you will have periods at certain times when they become women. When the time comes, you must set a day and fix the girl up to be *Kinaaldá;* you must have these songs sung and do whatever else needs to be done at that time. After this period, a girl is a woman and will start having children.
>
> That is what Changing Woman told the people she made in the west. She told them to go to their own country and do this.

And so *Kinaaldá* continues. A *Kinaaldá* may last anywhere from three to five days depending on the circumstances. Today, many families cannot afford this ceremony as it has become too expensive to hire a medicine man and provide food for friends and family. Even so, many young Navajo women have participated in this celebration. Traditionally, the singer or medicine man conducting the ceremony asks the mentoring woman, usually the girl's mother or aunt, to set out the basket containing the yucca roots. This is done usually before dawn of the last day of the ceremony. The roots have been carefully unearthed with two rocks found close by to aid in the crushing. The older woman ritualistically shreds the roots and pulverizes them. She then pours water into the basket, creating yucca suds so that the girl can bathe her hair. But first, the woman washes all the girl's jewelry—beads, bracelets, rings, and concha belt—and sets them on a blanket to dry. Then the girl kneels before the water, unfastens her hair tie, and begins to wash her hair with the same lather. The woman helps her, making certain she receives a good shampoo. All during the washing ritual "Songs of Dawn" are being sung and a ritual cake is being prepared.

The older woman takes the basket of soapweed water, *táláwosh*, to the west and empties it in a northerly direction. As soon as the singing stops, the young woman in *Kinaaldá* wrings out her hair and begins her last run to the east before dawn. Younger sisters and friends may follow her.

> The breeze coming from her as she runs
> The breeze coming from her as she runs
> The breeze coming from her as she runs is beautiful.
>
> The breeze coming from her as she runs
> The breeze coming from her as she runs
> The breeze coming from her as she runs is beautiful.

How many times have Navajo hands asked for the release of this root from the earth? How many times have these beaten roots been rubbed between flesh in warm water until heavy lather appeared? This source of soap, containing the compound saponin, has bathed skeins of yarn and skeins of hair, leaving both to glisten in desert sunlight.

Yucca is also edible. The children call yucca fruit "Navajo bananas." When boiled, it tastes much like summer squash, slightly sweet but with a twist of bitterness. But most of the yucca fruit is left in the heat to dry and wither. I have cut into its flesh many times and found exquisite symmetry. Six windows—once panes for seeds—become a chartreuse kaleidoscope.

The children look through yucca and see each other playing the ball and stick game, traditionally known as the "moccasin game."

"You play the game like this," they said. "You make a ball out of the yucca root with your hands, then everyone takes off their shoes and lines them up on either side of the yucca. One side takes the ball and hides it inside one of the shoes. The other team has to guess which shoe it's in. If they guess right it's their turn to hide the ball, but if they're wrong, the other side gets to cut off a yucca leaf. The side with the most yucca sticks at the end of the game wins."

Another story is told. A long, long time ago all creatures on earth, including insects, spoke as human beings. The Animal People gathered around the yucca and said, "Let's have a shoe game." A great hoopla rose from the crowd as everyone showed his favor for such an event.

"But how will we keep score?" asked a small beast.

"We will use the blades of yucca as counters," spoke another. And one hundred and two yucca sticks were pulled. A ball from the root of yucca was shaped, along with a stick for pointing.

"We will have the shoe game at a place called Tse'yaa Hodilhil," they said. And everyone ran, jumped, flew and crawled to the designated site.

Gopher dug two shallow furrows on either side. Four moccasins were placed in each groove and then covered with sand. Then it was asked among the herds, swarms, and flocks, "What shall we bet?"

A great stirring occurred in the animal assemblage as everyone offered opinions. Finally, all the diurnal beings said, "We will bet the earth to have continual sunlight."

The nocturnal beings stepped forward and said, "We will bet the sky to have perpetual darkness."

And so the bets were placed between day and night.

There were many, many Animal People on both sides. The diurnal creatures on the south, the nocturnal creatures on the north. Anticipation for the contest grew like midsummer corn.

The game began with one side hiding the ball in one of the four moccasins, then covering the moccasins up with sand. The other side began guessing with the indicator stick which shoe the ball was in. They were given three chances. If they guessed correctly it became their turn to hide the ball. If they were fooled, the opponents took a yucca counter. Back and forth, back and forth it went, with lots of laughter and singing.

The Animal People became so immersed in the shoe game that no one realized morning had come. They continued to play throughout the day and into the night placing their bets high, with neither side ever quite winning all one hundred and two yucca sticks.

They did things then just as people do today. Once they started something, they would not stop. The wager between day and night still continues.

The shoe game is played by Navajos with delight. Some call it Navajo gambling. But those who know the stories say it keeps Sun and Moon in balance.

After all the children have shared their own versions of the game, they are quick to tell you that "you must only play this game in winter." A botanist will tell you winter is the dormant season for yucca. Earth wisdom.

I brought out my pouch and took a slice, a circle of yucca. It had been aged by Sun. Once supple, now shriveled. Bitter, hard. What could this be? I mused over the possibilities. If I were home, it could be cucumber, zucchini, even eggplant. But here it could be peyote or datura, any number of powerful medicines. Where could they take me? I closed my eyes and slipped the yucca slice into my mouth. From a far-off place I could smell the smoke of piñyon.

Yucca. Plants. Navajo. Plants yield their secrets to those who know them. They can weep the colors of chokecherry tears, purplish-brown, into a weaver's hands. They can be backbones for baskets holding the blessings of *Kinaaldá*. Cedar bark and sage can purify; Indian paintbrush soothes an ailing stomach. Juniper ash water creates blue cornmeal. Petals of larkspur are sprinkled in ceremony. Native plants are a repository. They hold our health. A Navajo medicine man relies on plants as we rely on pharmacies.

Edward S. Ayensu, director of the Office of Biological Conservation at the Smithsonian Institution, tells a story about an African herbalist who told his students to pay attention to the natural world, to listen and observe the behavior of animals such as lizards, snakes, birds, rodents, and insects.

To stress his point, the herbalist narrated a fight between two chameleons. As Ayensu describes it:

> At the climax of the fight one of the chameleons passed out. The other quickly dashed into a thicket and came back with a piece of a leaf in its mouth. It forcibly pushed the leaf into the mouth of the unconscious lizard. In a matter of two or three minutes the defeated chameleon shook its body and took off.
>
> The specific plant that saved the life of the chameleon was not disclosed to me. When I insisted on knowing, the teacher smiled and said, "This is a trade secret. It is a plant that can spring a dying person to life. Unless you became one of us I cannot tell you."

This is earth medicine, and it is all around us, delivered into the hands that trust it. What do we know?

Yucca. The desert torch burns and returns its ashes to crimson sand. A snake slithers across the way and recoils itself under a slickrock slab. This is what I heard:

> Sha-woman, Sha-woman, hiss
> Sha-woman, Sha-woman, hiss
> Tongue, rattle, hiss
> Tongue, rattle, hiss
> Sha-woman, Sha-woman, hiss

Silence. A basket sits before me, coiled: around and around and around and around. It is striped with persimmon.

Analyzing and Discussing the Text

1. Why does Williams begin and end the essay with her dreams of the basket? How do the dreams tie in specifically with the essay's subject?
2. As Williams weaves together Navajo stories, field observations, her interactions with Navajo children, the rituals of the Navajo way, and the long story of the Animal People, does she arrange her material in any particular order? If so, how do the pieces fit together?
3. Why is the tiny moth in the fourth paragraph described as a "white-robed pilgrim"?
4. What does Williams mean when she refers to "days of painted language"?
5. Williams punctuates her recitation of stories and rituals with a paragraph that repeats the question "How many times...?" Does this paragraph constitute interpretive commentary as well as questioning? What is the function of this break in the stories?
6. What does she mean by "earth medicine"? How is it attained?

Experiencing and Writing About the World

1. Use this focus on Navajo stories to think about your own stories of the land. Are there tales, anecdotes, or pieces of your family history that talk about nature? Write down two or three of these stories in narrative form.
2. Write an essay on the topic of healing the earth. You will need to pick one specific area of healing and develop the theme of illness and plans for healing. Does your subject involve changes in attitudes as well as in behavior? If so, indicate how these changes will happen.
3. Search through this anthology for essays that represent three or more different cultural perspectives on the relationship between the human and the nonhuman world. Contemplate in writing not only the specific differences between these various perspectives, but also the benefits or problems that arise for you in attempting to understand (and perhaps embrace) such different values and viewpoints. Is it possible for one person to have or even tolerate more than one way of viewing the world at a time? Are we obligated to stick with the values with which we were raised, or are we entitled to adopt new philosophies, including philosophies or ideas from other cultures, if they seem especially meaningful to us?

GLORIA ANZALDÚA

El retorno

Gloria Anzaldúa (1942–   ) was born in Raymondville, Texas, and raised in the largely Hispanic town of Hargill. She remembers both her father's hard life as a Mexican farm laborer and the excesses of the area's agribusinesses, such as "the white feathers of three thousand Leghorn chickens blanketing the land for acres around." Anzaldúa went to Texas Women's University and then to the University of Texas–Pan American in Edinburg, where she received her B.A. in English, art, and education in 1969. She earned her M.A. in English and education in 1973 at the University of Texas, Austin, and she has done doctoral work in literature and in feminist literary theory at the University of California, Santa Cruz. She has taught Chicano studies, feminist studies, and creative writing at the University of Texas at Austin, Vermont College of Norwich University, and San Francisco State University. Anzaldúa is a co-editor of *This Bridge Called My Back: Writings by Radical Women of Color* (1983) and the author of *Borderlands/La Frontera: The New Mestiza* (1987), the book from which the following essay is taken.

When Anzaldúa asserts "I am a border woman," she refers in part to the physical borderland along Mexico and the southwestern United States. However, this geographic borderland of childhood and home also has its psychological, spiritual, and sexual equivalents in her life. As a self-described "Chicana *tejana* lesbian-feminist," she inhabits cultural, racial, class, and sexual borders as well. This life in the margins brings with it a complex mixture of emotions, including her hatred and anger toward exploitation and her joy in being "a participant in the further evolution of humankind." Throughout her writing, Anzaldúa consciously switches from English to Castilian Spanish to Mexican-American dialect, to Tex-Mex, to a sprinkling of Nahuatl. Such language she feels symbolizes her life at "the juncture of cultures," where languages cross-pollinate. In "El retorno" the author not only recalls a visit to her family and a return to the familiar mixture of human languages, but also contemplates the tragic devotion of the impoverished human inhabitants to the soil, plants, and unpredictable rain that offer sustenance. Hardship notwithstanding, Anzaldúa expresses a deep sense of belonging to this place, to the processes of "mother earth": "Growth, death, decay, birth. The soil prepared again and again, impregnated, worked on. A constant changing of forms, *renacimientos de la tierra madre.*"

All movements are accomplished in six stages,
and the seventh brings return.
                                    —I Ching[1]

Tanto tiempo sin verte casa mía,
mi cuna, mi hondo nido de la huerta.
                    —"Soledad"[2]

I stand at the river, watch the curving, twisting serpent, a serpent nailed to the fence where the mouth of the Rio Grande empties into the Gulf.

I have come back. *Tanto dolor me costó el alejamiento.* I shade my eyes and look up. The bone beak of a hawk slowly circling over me, checking me out as potential carrion. In its wake a little bird flickering its wings, swimming sporadically like a fish. In the distance the expressway and the slough of traffic like an irritated sow. The sudden pull in my gut, *la tierra, los aguaceros.* My land, *el viento soplando la arena, el lagartijo debajo de un nopalito. Me acuerdo como era antes. Una región desértica de vasta llanuras, costeras de baja altura, de escasa lluvia, de chaparrales formados por mesquites y huizaches.* If I look real hard I can almost see the Spanish fathers who were called "the cavalry of Christ" enter this valley riding their burros, see the clash of cultures commence.

Tierra natal. This is home, the small towns in the Valley, *los pueblitos* with chicken pens and goats picketed to mesquite shrubs. *En las colonias* on the other side of the tracks, junk cars line the front yards of hot pink and lavender-trimmed houses—Chicano architecture we call it, self-consciously. I have missed the TV shows where hosts speak in half and half, and where awards are given in the category of Tex-Mex music. I have missed the Mexican cemeteries blooming with artificial flowers, the fields of aloe vera and red pepper, rows of sugar cane, of corn hanging on the stalks, the cloud of *polvareda* in the dirt roads behind a speeding pickup truck, *el sabor de tamales de rez y venado.* I have missed *la yegua colorada* gnawing the wooden gate of her stall, the smell of horse flesh from Carito's corrals. *He hecho menos las noches calientes sin aire, noches de linternas y lechuzas* making holes in the night.

I still feel the old despair when I look at the unpainted, dilapidated, scrap lumber houses consisting mostly of corrugated aluminum. Some of the poorest people in the U.S. live in the Lower Rio Grande Valley, an arid and semi-arid land of irrigated farming, intense sunlight and

---

[1]Richard Wilhelm, *The I Ching or Book of Changes,* trans. Cary F. Baynes (Princeton, NJ: Princeton UP, 1950) 98.—Author's note.

[2]"*Soledad*" is sung by the group Haciendo Punto en Otro Son.—Author's note.

heat, citrus groves next to chaparral and cactus. I walk through the elementary school I attended so long ago, that remained segregated until recently. I remember how the white teachers used to punish us for being Mexican.

How I love this tragic valley of South Texas, as Ricardo Sánchez calls it; this borderland between the Nueces and the Rio Grande. This land has survived possession and ill-use by five countries: Spain, Mexico, the Republic of Texas, the U.S., the Confederacy, and the U.S. again. It has survived Anglo-Mexican blood feuds, lynchings, burnings, rapes, pillage.

Today I see the Valley still struggling to survive. Whether it does or not, it will never be as I remember it. The borderlands depression that was set off by the 1982 peso devaluation in Mexico resulted in the closure of hundreds of Valley businesses. Many people lost their homes, cars, land. Prior to 1982, U.S. store owners thrived on retail sales to Mexicans who came across the border for groceries and clothes and appliances. While goods on the U.S. side have become 10, 100, 1000 times more expensive for Mexican buyers, goods on the Mexican side have become 10, 100, 1000 times cheaper for Americans. Because the Valley is heavily dependent on agriculture and Mexican retail trade, it has the highest unemployment rates along the entire border region; it is the Valley that has been hardest hit.[3]

"It's been a bad year for corn," my brother, Nune, says. As he talks, I remember my father scanning the sky for a rain that would end the drought, looking up into the sky, day after day, while the corn withered on its stalk. My father has been dead for 29 years, having worked himself to death. The life span of a Mexican farm laborer is 56—he lived to be 38. It shocks me that I am older than he. I, too, search the sky for rain. Like the ancients, I worship the rain god and the maize goddess, but unlike my father I have recovered their names. Now for rain (irrigation) one offers not a sacrifice of blood, but of money.

"Farming is in a bad way," my brother says. "Two to three thousand small and big farmers went bankrupt in this country last year. Six years ago the price of corn was $8.00 per hundred pounds," he goes on. "This year it is $3.90 per hundred pounds." And, I think to myself, after taking inflation into account, not planting anything puts you ahead.

I walk out to the back yard, stare at *los rosales de mamá*. She wants me to help her prune the rose bushes, dig out the carpet grass that

---

[3]Out of the twenty-two border counties in the four border states, Hidalgo County . . . is the most poverty-stricken county in the nation as well as the largest home base (along with the Imperial in California) for migrant workers. It was here that I was born and raised. I am amazed that both it and I have survived.—Author's note.

is choking them. *Mamagrande Ramona también tenía rosales.* Here every Mexican grows flowers. If they don't have a piece of dirt, they use car tires, jars, cans, shoe boxes. Roses are the Mexican's favorite flower. I think, how symbolic—thorns and all.

Yes, the Chicano and Chicana have always taken care of growing things and the land. Again I see the four of us kids getting off the school bus, changing into our work clothes, walking into the field with Papí and Mamí, all six of us bending to the ground. Below our feet, under the earth lie the watermelon seeds. We cover them with paper plates, putting *terremotes* on top of the plates to keep them from being blown away by the wind. The paper plates keep the freeze away. Next day or the next, we remove the plates, bare the tiny green shoots to the elements. They survive and grow, give fruit hundreds of times the size of the seed. We water them and hoe them. We harvest them. The vines dry, rot, are plowed under. Growth, death, decay, birth. The soil prepared again and again, impregnated, worked on. A constant changing of forms, *renacimientos de la tierra madre.*

> This land was Mexican once
> was Indian always
> and is.
> And will be again.

Analyzing and Discussing the Text

1. Why does Anzaldúa use the word "serpent" to describe the river in the opening paragraph?
2. When the second paragraph switches from one language to another, it provides the reader with a forceful example of the border life that Anzaldúa wishes to depict. Do you find that even if you do not know the language, you can approximate the meaning—get a sense of what is happening—through the context? Explain your response.
3. What descriptive techniques does she use to convey what she has missed about her home in the third paragraph?
4. How are the examples of her causes for despair in the fourth paragraph tied to themes she develops in the fifth and sixth paragraphs?
5. The last four paragraphs of the essay focus on farming and gardening; discuss how the subject matter and the tone of the final two paragraphs fit with the previous two and their pessimistic discussion of farming.

6. Analyze the essay's closing paragraph in terms of how the subject changes and progresses and how the sentence structures and rhythms reinforce this thematic progression.
7. What basic process is Anzaldúa engaged in throughout this essay and how is this process related to the title of the piece?

Experiencing and Writing About the World

1. If there are moments in your own family history that demonstrate a kind of intimacy with the land or with some other aspect of nature like the childhood planting experience Anzaldúa develops in her final paragraph, choose one such time and describe it in a paragraph.
2. Write an essay on the role of agribusiness in contemporary life. Either your essay can be descriptive, conveying the changes that large-scale agriculture has caused and the pros and cons of this approach, or it can be persuasive, arguing for or against agribusiness and its effect on our lives.
3. Prepare a stylistic analysis of Anzaldúa's prose, particularly her alternating and mixing of languages and her poetic restatement of ideas. Attempt to establish essential connections between the prose style of the essay and the author's process of returning to her native place.

WILLIAM LEAST HEAT-MOON

Atop the Mound

William Least Heat-Moon (1939–   ) was born in Kansas City, Missouri. He now lives with his wife in a house that he built himself in Columbia, where he earned a bachelor's degree in photojournalism and a doctorate in English from the University of Missouri. He is of English-Irish and Osage descent, and his given name—William Trogdon—gives way to the pen name William Least Heat-Moon when he writes his books. This separation is not total, however, for Least Heat-Moon expresses both sides of himself—the European and the Native American—

in the process of writing his books. The nonlinear storytelling method at work in the overall arrangement of *PrairyErth: A Deep Map* (1992), the book from which "Atop the Mound" is taken, is an attempt to use "an American Indian approach of circling a subject, exploring facets of it, moving on and then later writing about another part of it." But if William Least Heat-Moon is "the architect" of the book, he sees William Trogdon as "the carpenter" executing those plans in an orderly fashion. William Least Heat-Moon's first book, *Blue Highways: A Journey into America* (1983), sold more than a million copies and has been compared by critics to such famous "road narratives" as Jack Kerouac's *On the Road* (1957) and John Steinbeck's *Travels with Charley* (1961). The *Blue Highways* project began in 1978 when Least Heat-Moon's part-time teaching job at Stephens College ended and he separated from his wife; he then packed up his van and spent three months traveling the backroads of America—the roads once colored blue on roadmaps—from Missouri to Georgia, then west to Oregon and Washington, and all the way back to the East Coast before circling home to Columbia. It then took him four years to write the book, which was named one of the five best nonfiction books of 1983 by *Time* magazine and won a Books-Across-the-Sea Award and a Christopher Award. Least Heat-Moon's second book, *The Red Couch*, appeared in 1984.

Unlike *Blue Highways*, which chronicled a thirteen-thousand-mile journey on the blue highways, or the backroads, of the United States, *PrairyErth* takes a very close look at one place on the Great Plains: Chase County in the Flint Hills of central Kansas. This region is at the geographic heart of the country, and it is also home to the last large area of tallgrass prairie in America. Least Heat-Moon's 624-page book takes a detailed look at the landscape, the history, and the 3,013 people in this 744-square-mile area as the author seeks to give us what he calls "a topographic map of words," a new way of seeing the plains country.

What I cherish I've come to slowly, usually blindly, not seeing it for some time, and that's just how I discovered Jacobs' Mound, a truncated cone sitting close to the center of the Gladstone quadrangle. This most obvious old travelers' marker shows up clearly from two of the three highways, yet I was here several days before I noticed it, this isolated frustum so distinct. I must have been looking too closely and narrowly, but once I saw its volcano-cone symmetry (at night in the fire season, its top can flame and smolder) I was drawn to it as western travelers have always been to lone protuberances—Independence Rock, Pompey's Pillar, Chimney Rock—and within a day I headed down the Bloody Creek Road until the lane played out in a grassed vale. Some two aerial miles west of the mound, I climbed a ridge and sat down and watched it as if it might disappear like a flock of rare birds. That morning four people told me four things, one of them, the last, accurate: the regular sides and flattened top of the knob prove Indians built it for a burial mound; Colorado prospectors hid gold in it; an oil dome lay beneath it; and, none of those notions was true.

I walked down the hawk-harried ridge and struck out toward the mound, seemingly near enough to reach before sunset. Its sea-level elevation is fifteen hundred feet, but it rises only about a hundred from its base and three hundred above the surrounding humped terrain. In places the October grasses, russet-colored like low flames as if revealing their union with fire, reached to my belt and stunted my strides, and there were also aromatic asters and false indigo, both now dried to scratching stiffness. From the tall heads of Indian grass and the brown stalks of gayfeather, gossamer strung out in the slow wind like pennants ten and twelve feet long and silver in the sun, and these web lines snagged my trousers and chest and head until, after a mile, I was bestrung and on my way to becoming cocooned. Gray flittings rose from the ground like winged stones and threw themselves immediately into invisibility—I think they were vesper sparrows. Twice, prairie chickens broke noisily and did their sweet, dihedral-winged glides to new cover (Audubon said their bent-down wings enable the birds to turn their heads to see behind as they fly). I stopped to watch small events but never for long because the mound was drawing me as if it were a stone vortex in a petrified sea.

There are several ways not to walk in the prairie, and one of them is with your eye on a far goal, because you then begin to believe you're not closing the distance any more than you would with a mirage. My woodland sense of scale and time didn't fit this country, and I started wondering whether I could reach the summit before dark. On the prairie, distance and the miles of air turn movement to stasis and openness to a wall, a thing as difficult to penetrate as dense forest. I was hiking in a chamber of absences where the near was the same as the far, and it seemed every time I raised a step the earth rotated under me so that my foot fell just where it had lifted from. Limits and markers make travel possible for people: circumscribe our lines of sight and we can really get somewhere. Before me lay the Kansas of popular conception from Coronado on—that place you have to get through, that purgatory of mileage.

But I kept walking, and, when I dropped into hollows and the mound disappeared, I focused on a rock or a tuft of grass to keep from convoluting my track. Hiking in woods allows a traveler to imagine comforting enclosures, one leading to the next, and the walker can possess those little encompassed spaces, but the prairie and plains permit no such possession. Whatever else prairie is—grass, sky, wind—it is most of all a paradigm of infinity, a clearing full of many things except boundaries, and its power comes from its apparent limitlessness; there is no such thing as a small prairie any more than there is a little ocean, and the consequence of both is this challenge: try to take yourself seriously out here, you bipedal plodder, you complacent cartoon.

I came up out of a hollow, Jacobs' Mound big now on the horizon, and I could feel its swell in my legs, and then I was in the steep climb up its slope, and: I was on top. From the highway I'd guessed the summit to be the size of a city block, but it was less than a baseball infield, its elliptical perimeter just a hundred strides. So, its power lay not in size but rather in shape and dominion and its thrust into the imagination.

I sat and looked. The thousands of acres that lay encircled around the knob I really didn't see, not at first. I saw air, and I said, good god, look at all this air, and I recalled a woman saying, *Seems the air here hasn't ever been used before.* From a plane you look down, and from a mountain you look down, but from Jacobs' Mound you look out, out into. You're not up in the sky and you're not on the ground: you're nicely in between, at the altitude of those who fly in their dreams and skim roofs and treetops. Jacobs' Mound is thrush-flight high.

And then I understood: I like this prairie county because of its illusion of being away, out of, and I like how its unpopulousness seems to isolate it. Seventy percent of Americans live on two percent of the land, but in front of me, no percentage of them lived. Yet, in the far southeast, I could see trucks inching out the turnpike miles, the turbulence of their passage silenced by distance. And I could see fence lines, transmission towers, and dug ponds, things the pioneers would have viewed as marks of a progressive civilization but which to me, a grousing neo-primitivist, were signs of the continuing onslaught. The view I had homesteaders would have loved, and the one they had of unbroken vegetation and its diversities I would cherish. On top of the mound, insects whirred steadily, and the wind blew in easy continuousness, a drone like that in a seashell at the ear. In the nineteenth century, the Kansas clergyman and author William Quayle (who once wrote, *In a purely metaphorical sense I am a turnip*) traded his autograph for an acre of prairie, and, yesterday, I thought him a thief, but now, seeing the paltriness of an acre, I figured he was the one swindled.

On his great western expedition of 1806, Zebulon Pike crossed the Flint Hills just south of this big knob, and he surely couldn't have resisted climbing this rise for a good look around. In later years, perpendicular to his course ran an old freighter road and stage line that cut between here and Phenis Mound across the county line and five miles east. Near its base, a century ago, farmer John Buckingham plowed up a small redwood chest, took it home, pried it open, and found some old parchments, one marked in crude characters of eccentric orthography advising that nearby a buried sword pointed to the spot on Phenis Mound where lay a cache of golden nuggets. Buckingham thought it a prank until he remembered plowing up a rusted saber the year before; but his and others' diggings yielded only what the inland sea put down a quarter billion years ago.

People connect themselves to the land as their imaginations allow. The links of Chase countians to Jacobs' Mound, at least in an earlier time, were more calligraphic than auricular, and at my feet lay proof: a piece of limestone, palm-sized and flattened like a slate and cut into it a reversed J surmounted by an upside-down V: perhaps a cattle brand. In the days of first white settlement, people rode out here in buggies and hayracks, filled their jugs at one of the springs below the mound, picnicked on the summit, and scratched their names into the broken stones. I looked for more: nothing. Then I turned over a small rock and there, in faint relief under the low sunlight, JOHNY, and on another, MAE, and then I began turning stones, their hardness against one another striking out a strange and musical ringing, and I found more intaglios weathered to near invisibility but the letters uncommonly adroit. The mound was so covered with bits of alphabet it was as if Moses had here thrown down his tablets.

And then from the dark, granular soil I turned one that froze me: WAKONDA. In several variants, Wakonda is a Plains Indian name for the Great Mysterious, the Four-Winds-Source-of-All. Then my sense returned: an ancient Indian writing in Roman characters? I looked closely and could barely make out W KENDA running to the fractured right edge. Perhaps once: W. KENDALL. I put it again face-down so that it might continue its transfer into the mound.

Across America, lone risings have been sacred places to tribal Americans, places to reach out for the infinite. Where whites saw this knob and dreamed gold, aboriginal peoples (it's my guess) found it and dreamed God, and it must have belonged to their legends and gramarye, and they surely came to this erosional ellipse as leaves to the eddy.

Analyzing and Discussing the Text

1. What does Least Heat-Moon mean by "the Kansas of popular conception"?
2. Why does he use such phrases as "bipedal plodder" and "complacent cartoon" to refer to the human race? Does the description of himself as "a grousing Neo-primitivist" serve a similar function?
3. How is the prairie a "paradigm of infinity"?
4. How does the emphasis on seeing in the sixth paragraph fit with the other paragraphs near the end of the essay?
5. Does the conclusion of the essay seem to embody the Osage or the English-Irish aspect of the author's heritage, or both?

6. Explain how Least Heat-Moon's discussion of the process of walking helps him to define an essential quality of the plains landscape. What other techniques could he have used to achieve this sort of regional definition or characterization?

Experiencing and Writing About the World

1. Least Heat-Moon sets up an intriguing contrast between prairie and woodland walking and describes how he had to adjust his sense of scale and time to fit the landscape. Write a paragraph about an experience of rescaling in your own life. Does something similar happen, for example, when we go to the ocean? When we enter an urban park?
2. Attempt to characterize your own region of the country by describing how people (or you, at least) must do some particular activity in a special way because of your location. Choose an activity like walking, dressing, bike riding, driving, or swimming—or anything else that would enable you to emphasize the distinctiveness of the area in which you live.
3. Do you agree with the statement that "People connect themselves to the land as their imaginations allow"? Write an essay in which you argue for or against the belief that people connect to the land primarily through their imaginative concepts of the country.

Suggestions for Further Reading

Conover, Ted. *Whiteout: Lost in Aspen.* New York: Random, 1991.

Ehrlich, Gretel. "The Solace of Open Spaces." *The Solace of Open Spaces.* New York: Penguin, 1985.

Finch, Robert. "The Tactile Land." *Outlands: Journeys to the Outer Edges of Cape Cod.* Boston: Godine, 1986.

Haines, John. "A Place of Sense." *Living Off the Country: Essays on Poetry and Place.* Ann Arbor: U of Michigan P, 1981.

Hiss, Tony. *The Experience of Place.* 1990. New York: Random, 1991.

Irving, Washington. "The Author's Account of Himself." *The Sketch Book.* 1820. New York: NAL, 1961.

Lawrence, D. H. "The Spirit of Place." *Studies in Classic American Literature.* New York: Viking, 1923.

McPhee, John. *Basin and Range.* New York: Farrar, 1980.

Madson, John. *Where the Sky Began: Land of the Tallgrass Prairie.* Boston: Houghton, 1982.

Nichols, John. *If Mountains Die: A New Mexico Memoir.* New York: Knopf, 1986.

Sanders, Scott Russell. *In Limestone Country.* Boston: Beacon, 1985.

Stafford, Kim. *Having Everything Right: Essays of Place.* Boise, ID: Confluence, 1986.

Stegner, Page. *Outposts of Eden: A Curmudgeon at Large in the American West.* San Francisco: Sierra Club, 1989.

Stegner, Wallace, and Page Stegner. *American Places.* New York: Greenwich House, 1983.

Tisdale, Sallie. *Stepping Westward.* New York: Henry Holt, 1992.

Turner, Frederick. *Spirit of Place: The Making of an American Literary Landscape.* San Francisco: Sierra Club, 1990.

Van Dyke, John C. *The Desert.* 1901. Salt Lake City, UT: Peregrine, 1980.

Wild, Peter, ed. *The Desert Reader: Descriptions of America's Arid Regions.* Salt Lake City: U of Utah P, 1991.

Visual Representations of Nature

Landscape Painting and Photograpy

Mt. Ktaadn (1853)

Yale University Art Gallery, New Haven, Connecticut; Stanley B. Resor, B.A. 1901, Fund.

Analyzing and Discussing the Painting

1. What are the principal natural elements in this painting? Explain the visual roles of Mt. Ktaadn itself (in the center of the painting), the clouds, the drinking cattle, and any other features of the landscape that seem important.
2. Are there any human elements in this painting? If so, what is their function? If not, why might the artist have wanted to exclude the human altogether?
3. When Henry David Thoreau climbed Mt. Ktaadn in September 1846, he was overwhelmed by the inhuman vastness of his surroundings. "*Contact! Contact!*" he exclaims in his account of how he felt on the summit: "*Who* are we? *where* are we?" (*The Maine Woods*, 1864). Compare Thoreau's response with the mood of Church's painting.
4. This is an example of a picturesque landscape. How would your experience of such a landscape differ if you were actually present in the scene? See John Daniel's essay "The Impoverishment of Sightseeing."

Writing About the Painting and the World

1. Attempt to describe this view of Mt. Ktaadn by using words only— "word-painting" is what literary critics often call such visually descriptive prose. Look at the mountain narratives of Isabella Bird and John Muir for models of picturesque mountain descriptions.
2. Church painted Mt. Ktaadn in 1853. Create a time-lapse narrative showing how this same scene might have changed in the past 140 years. Imagine the effect of both natural forces and the encroachment of human civilization.
3. Write an analytical essay comparing Church's painting with Julius Schrader's portrait of Alexander von Humboldt perched between Mount Chimborazo and Mount Cotopaxi in Ecuador (the following painting). How do the mountains in the two paintings differ? What is the effect of Humboldt's enormous presence in the foreground of Schrader's painting?
4. Do some research on the nineteenth-century artistic movement known as Luminism and write an essay explaining how Church's painting demonstrates the goals and stylistic strategies of the Luminist painters.

JULIUS SCHRADER

Baron Alexander von Humboldt (1859)

The Metropolitan Museum of Art, New York; Gift of H. O. Havemeyer, 1889.

Analyzing and Discussing the Painting

1. What is the human figure's relationship to nature in this painting?
2. Alexander von Humboldt (1769–1859) was a famous German explorer, scientist, and writer who spent five years (1799–1804) in South America during his best-known expedition. Schrader has painted him with the Ecuadoran peaks Mount Chimborazo and Mount Cotopaxi in the background. Knowing this, try to explain the symbolism in this painting. Does Humboldt actually seem present in the landscape? Why is he holding a pen and a book? How old does he appear in the painting?
3. Humboldt tried to climb Mount Chimborazo during his stay in Ecuador, but the difficulty of the climb and the inadequacy of his equipment foiled the attempt. Does Schrader's painting manage to convey the awesome size of this mountain? What can we tell about the South American landscape from this painting?

Writing About the Painting and the World

1. Do research on Humboldt's life and work, then construct the narrative that you imagine is going on inside his head at the time Schrader is painting his portrait. In other words, take the pen from Humboldt's hand and tell his story for him.
2. Compare Schrader's visual symbolism with the narrative symbolism in one or more of the essays in this anthology; for instance, Robert Finch's "Very Like a Whale," Barry Lopez's "The Image of the Unicorn," the excerpt from Henry David Thoreau's *Walden,* or Jeanne Wakatsuki Houston and James D. Houston's "Manzanar, U.S.A."
3. Look for instances of verbal portraiture among the readings in this anthology. Compare Jack Kerouac's Japhy Ryder, Susan Mitchell's Georgie, Randall Kenan's Horace, or any other interesting literary character descriptions with Schrader's depiction of Humboldt.

From the Plains (1919)

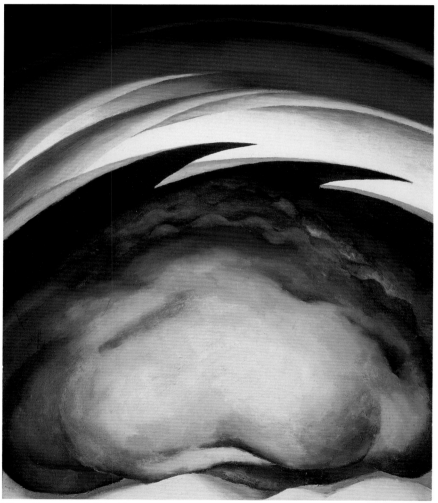

The Georgia O'Keeffe Foundation/ARS, New York. Photo by Malcolm Varon. Copyright© Malcolm Varon.

Analyzing and Discussing the Painting

1. What mood does this painting convey to you? How does O'Keeffe create this mood? Compare and contrast the mood of this painting with those of the other illustrations in this color insert.
2. Pick out the individual shapes in "From the Plains" and try to identify the natural phenomena they represent.
3. If Church's "Mt. Ktaadn" depicts a scene of tranquility, what kind of scene does O'Keeffe present? Is there any action suggested in this painting? How can a static, spatial work of art describe motion?
4. Have you ever seen a view like this one? What kinds of distortions does O'Keeffe create in order to communicate the impression of a storm without relying on realistic description?
5. Can we see the earth (the ground) in this painting or only the sky? What does this work imply about the relationship of the earth to the sky?

Writing About the Painting and the World

1. Produce a one-paragraph verbal version of O'Keeffe's painting. Describe the scene with similarly impressionistic imagery.
2. How do the three painters (Church, Schrader, and O'Keeffe) and the photographer Joel Meyerowitz use the sky in their work? Write a comparative analysis in which you seek to explain the goals and strategies of the artists' various skyscapes.
3. Compare O'Keeffe's September 11, 1916, letter to Anita Pollitzer (in the next chapter) with the painting "From the Plains," made three years later. Can you tell the same person constructed both renditions of evening lightning storms over the western plains? Try to compare O'Keeffe's prose style with her painting style during this early phase in her artistic career.

JOEL MEYEROWITZ

Porch, Provincetown, 1977

Cape Light. Color photograph by Joel Meyerowitz. Courtesy of James Danzinger Gallery, New York.

Analyzing and Discussing the Photograph

1. What is the visual relationship between the natural and the human-made in this photograph?
2. Explain the visual effect of the small boat near the lower left-hand corner of the photograph. How would the picture be different if the boat were absent?
3. Describe the use of color in this photograph. Does Meyerowitz emphasize "natural" or "unnatural" colors?
4. What is the effect of the skewed structure of the photograph? Does the picture seem weighted in one particular direction? Compare its structure with that of the three paintings—what organizing principles do the painters seem to use?

Writing About the Photograph and the World

1. Imagine what it would be like to have this view from the porch of your house. Recreate this scene in words, attempting to show how it affects your state of mind.
2. Create a written description of a water landscape (ocean, lake, or river) that you have actually experienced recently. As you write this description, pay close attention to such details as colors, shapes, spatial relationships, and combinations of human and nonhuman elements.
3. Analyze Meyerowitz's calculated juxtaposition of the porch, the ocean, and the sky, then compare his technique with the use of human/nature comparisons in a written text such as Annie Dillard's "Living Like Weasels" or John Elder's "The Plane on South Mountain."
4. In her essay "Dreaming in Public: A Provincetown Memoir," Susan Mitchell devotes considerable attention to describing sea- and skyscapes similar to the one depicted in Meyerowitz's photograph. In an analytical essay, study the similarities and differences between the two artists' representations of nature. How do their different media (photography and writing) seem to influence their aesthetic responses to the world?

Michael Goldman

CHAPTER THREE

Spiritual and Aesthetic
Responses to Nature

When Joyce Carol Oates criticized the "painfully limited set of responses" in nature writing, the overabundance of "REVERENCE, AWE, PIETY, MYSTICAL ONENESS" ("Against Nature," *Antaeus*, 1986), she was thinking of the kinds of writing that we have selected for this chapter. Although many of the other readings in this anthology display enthusiasm for the beauty and meaningfulness of nature, few dwell on these aspects to the same extent as the following texts. The extreme appreciation of nature demonstrated in these essays and stories may seem trite and predictable, but it is nonetheless an important type of response to the world. The painter Thomas Cole argued in 1836 that

> In this age, when a meager utilitarianism seems ready to absorb every feeling and sentiment, and what is sometimes called improvement in its march makes us fear that the bright and tender flowers of the imagination shall all be crushed beneath its iron tramp, it would be well to cultivate the oasis that yet remains to us, and thus preserve germs of a future and purer system. . . . The spirit of our society is to contrive but not to enjoy — toiling to produce more toil — accumulating in order to aggrandize. (570)[1]

Cole's critique of "meager utilitarianism" could be directed just as easily against our own eagerness to use natural resources merely for the pur-

---

[1] Cole, Thomas, "Essay on American Scenery," *The American Monthly Magazine* I (January 1836). Rpt. in *American Landscape: A Critical Anthology of Prose and Poetry.* Ed. John Conron. New York: Oxford UP, 1973: 568–78.

513

poses of human comfort and convenience as we approach the twenty-first century. The danger of spiritual and aesthetic responses, on the other hand, is that they will degenerate into clichéd, simple-minded, unfelt attitudes, just as rigid and unappreciative in their own way as the crassest utilitarianism.

Georgia O'Keeffe's 1916 letter describing the lightning flashes at evening over the Texas panhandle exemplifies the ideally unsentimental aesthetic appreciation of nature—her enthusiasm for the beauty of the sky is a genuine response to what she sees, not an utterance of preestablished visual taste and descriptive language. Loren Eiseley, too, manages to avoid crude clichés as he describes an experience of "cosmic consciousness," an intense convergence of his tiny self with the vast organic universe that occurs when he submits his body to the flow of the Platte River. Jeanne Wakatsuki Houston and James D. Houston show how the Japanese-American internees at Manzanar during World War II sustained themselves during the difficult war years both by enjoying the visual beauty of their mountainous surroundings and by grasping the lessons in endurance offered by the natural world. Rudolfo Anaya and Larry Littlebird, in their separate stories, show two different ways in which children come to appreciate the power and significance—the "sacredness"—of nature. Susan Mitchell, like O'Keeffe, demonstrates the artist's hyperaesthetic rendering of nature, alert to shape and color, less interested in the moral and conceptual implications of natural experience.

GEORGIA O'KEEFFE

Letter to Anita Pollitzer
(September 11, 1916)

Born in the small town of Sun Prairie, Wisconsin, Georgia O'Keeffe (1887–1986) eventually became famous for her paintings of landscapes, flowers, and bones and for her hermetic life-style in Abiquiu, New Mexico. O'Keeffe began her formal instruction as an artist at the School of the Chicago Art Institute (1905–1906) and continued the following year at the Art Students League of New York. Between 1911 and 1918, she worked as an art teacher in Virginia, Texas, and South Carolina, interrupting her own teaching with further studies at the University of Virginia and Columbia University's Teachers College. In 1918, the thirty-one-year-old O'Keeffe met Alfred Stieglitz (1864–1946), the important New York photographer, who was to support her dream of becoming an independent artist and who contributed to her eventual fame through his many distinctive portraits of her, often emphasizing her austere-looking face and expressive hands. O'Keeffe and Stieglitz were married in 1924. In 1949, three years after Stieglitz's death, O'Keeffe moved permanently from New York to New Mexico.

O'Keeffe's painting is known for its extreme simplification of shape and detail and its use of form and color as abstract symbols of the natural world. But her writing, too, provides powerful aesthetic responses to nature. O'Keeffe did not write for publication, but she maintained an active correspondence throughout her life with numerous friends and fellow artists, including such writers as Jean Toomer. The following letter to her friend Anita Pollitzer, whom she met when both were art students in New York in 1914, was written after O'Keeffe began teaching costume design and interior decoration at West Texas State Normal College in Canyon. The letter shows her fascination with the violence and variability of the plains sky, which is mimicked in the interruptive and explosively emotional prose style, including the frequent use of dashes in a manner reminiscent of the poet Emily Dickinson.

[Canyon, Texas, 11 September 1916]

Tonight I walked into the sunset—to mail some letters—the whole sky—and there is so much of it out here—was just blazing—and grey blue clouds were rioting all through the hotness of it—and the ugly little buildings and windmills looked great against it.

But some way or other I didn't seem to like the redness much so after I mailed the letters I walked home—and kept on walking—

The Eastern sky was all grey blue—bunches of clouds—different kinds of clouds—sticking around everywhere and the whole thing—lit up—first in one place—then in another with flashes of lightning—— sometimes just sheet lightning——and sometimes sheet lightning with a sharp bright zigzag flashing across it——.

I walked out past the last house—past the last locust tree——and sat on the fence for a long time—looking——just looking at the light-ning——you see there was nothing but sky and flat prairie land—land that seems more like the ocean than anything else I know—There was a wonderful moon——

Well I just sat there and had a great time all by myself—Not even many night noises—just the wind——

I wondered what you are doing——

It is absurd the way I love this country—Then when I came back—it was funny——roads just shoot across blocks anywhere— all the houses looked alike—and I almost got lost—I had to laugh at myself—I couldnt tell which house was home——

I am loving the plains more than ever it seems——and the SKY— Anita you have never seen SKY—it is wonderful—

Pat.

Analyzing and Discussing the Text

1. Explain O'Keeffe's style of punctuation—how does it affect the feeling of her prose?
2. In what sense does this letter present an aesthetic response to the sky? Can you tell by her language that O'Keeffe is a painter? What specific features of the plains sky does she mention?
3. Can you gauge O'Keeffe's relationship with Anita Pollitzer from the content of this letter? What is the purpose of writing such a letter?

Experiencing and Writing About the World

1. How does the language of this letter correspond to the visual representation of the sky in O'Keeffe's 1919 painting "From the Plains"? Write a comparative analysis of the two works, explaining the advantages of each medium (writing and painting).
2. Write a letter to one of *your* friends in which you recount a simple walk and provide a detailed, vividly visual description of the sky wherever *you* are. You might even imitate O'Keeffe's use of dashes in place of ordinary punctuation marks. Make a point of emphasizing your aesthetic response to the sky—exclude scientific, practical, and moral commentary. Instead, focus on the beauty of the natural subject, its visual appearance, its sounds, its feel (e.g., the feel of wind, humidity, or skin-cracking dryness).
3. Compare O'Keeffe's sky description with Susan Mitchell's "skying" in "Dreaming in Public." What are the precise linguistic differences between the two authors' prose styles? Does the fact that one was writing for publication and the other a personal letter have something to do with their different uses of language?

LOREN EISELEY

The Flow of the River

Even as a child, Loren Eiseley (1907–1977) was of two minds—or rather, he defied the now familiar "two cultures" opposition of the humanities and the natural sciences in order to pursue his own combined fascination with the world itself and the human response to external nature. Born in Lincoln, Nebraska, the son of an itinerant salesman and a hearing-impaired, artistic mother, Eiseley demonstrated an aptitude for reading and writing at an early age. In *All the Strange Hours: The Excavation of a Life* (1975), his autobiography, he recalls reading *Robinson Crusoe* at the age of five. Eiseley entered the University of Nebraska in 1925 and published his first poetry in *The Prairie Schooner*, a literary magazine at the university, two years later. As he recounts in his autobiography, Eiseley spent the next five years struggling to complete his degree at Nebraska, dropping out intermittently to work in a chicken hatchery, to recuperate from tuberculosis by working on a ranch in the Mohave Desert, and to ride the rails with hobos. Eiseley finally graduated from college in 1933 with a double major in English and sociology (anthropology). That same year he enrolled in the graduate program in anthropology at the University of Pennsylvania, where he completed his Ph.D. four years later. Eiseley's teaching career included brief stints at the University of Kansas and Oberlin College before he returned to the University of Pennsylvania in 1947 as department chairman and professor of anthropology; he remained at Penn until his death in 1977. Among his many honors are his selection as the president of the Institute of Human Paleontology in 1949 and his election to the National Institute of Arts and Letters in 1971. Eiseley published fifteen books of poetry, scientific essays, and personal essays before his death, and several more collections have appeared posthumously. As an essayist, Eiseley is widely regarded as one of the principal rescuers of nonfiction as a literary genre after years of overshadowing by poetry and fiction; in her introduction to *The Best American Essays 1988*, Annie Dillard, despite poking fun at the way Eiseley "lays in narrative symbols with a trowel," acknowledges that Eiseley "restored the essay's place in imaginative literature and... extended its symbolic capacity."

The following essay, "The Flow of the River," appeared in Eiseley's first book, *The Immense Journey* (1957). It demonstrates what Eiseley himself described as the "concealed essay" in *All the Strange Hours*, a form "in which personal anecdote was allowed gently to bring under observation thoughts of a more purely scientific nature." In this essay he recalls a time—which may or may not be true in the strictest, most superficial sense—when he allowed himself "to escape the actual confines of the flesh," and join the flow, not just of the Platte River, but of life itself. Eiseley suggests in the essay that the living individual, whether a human being or a catfish, possesses extreme significance, and yet this same individual, consisting mainly of water, is "a minute pulse like the eternal pulse that lifts Himalayas." The self is part and parcel of the larger natural universe, a momentary pause in the ongoing process of evolution.

If there is magic on this planet, it is contained in water. Its least stir even, as now in a rain pond on a flat roof opposite my office, is enough to bring me searching to the window. A wind ripple may be translating itself into life. I have a constant feeling that some time I may witness that momentous miracle on a city roof, see life veritably and suddenly boiling out of a heap of rusted pipes and old television aerials. I marvel at how suddenly a water beetle has come and is submarining there in a spatter of green algae. Thin vapors, rust, wet tar and sun are an alembic remarkably like the mind; they throw off odorous shadows that threaten to take real shape when no one is looking.

Once in a lifetime, perhaps, one escapes the actual confines of the flesh. Once in a lifetime, if one is lucky, one so merges with sunlight and air and running water that whole eons, the eons that mountains and deserts know, might pass in a single afternoon without discomfort. The mind has sunk away into its beginnings among old roots and the obscure tricklings and movings that stir inanimate things. Like the charmed fairy circle into which a man once stepped, and upon emergence learned that a whole century had passed in a single night, one can never quite define this secret; but it has something to do, I am sure, with common water. Its substance reaches everywhere; it touches the past and prepares the future; it moves under the poles and wanders thinly in the heights of air. It can assume forms of exquisite perfection in a snowflake, or strip the living to a single shining bone cast up by the sea.

Many years ago, in the course of some scientific investigations in a remote western county, I experienced, by chance, precisely the sort of curious absorption by water—the extension of shape by osmosis— at which I have been hinting. You have probably never experienced in yourself the meandering roots of a whole watershed or felt your outstretched fingers touching, by some kind of clairvoyant extension, the brooks of snow-line glaciers at the same time that you were flowing toward the Gulf over the eroded debris of worn-down mountains. A poet, MacKnight Black, has spoken of being "limbed... with waters gripping pole and pole." He had the idea, all right, and it is obvious that these sensations are not unique, but they are hard to come by; and the sort of extension of the senses that people will accept when they put their ear against a sea shell, they will smile at in the confessions of a bookish professor. What makes it worse is the fact that because of a traumatic experience in childhood, I am not a swimmer, and am inclined to be timid before any large body of water. Perhaps it was just this, in a way, that contributed to my experience.

As it leaves the Rockies and moves downward over the high plains towards the Missouri, the Platte River is a curious stream. In the spring floods, on occasion, it can be a mile-wide roaring torrent of destruction, gulping farms and bridges. Normally, however, it is a rambling, dispersed series of streamlets flowing erratically over great sand and gravel fans that are, in part, the remnants of a mightier Ice Age stream bed. Quicksand and shifting islands haunt its waters. Over it the prairie suns beat mercilessly throughout the summer. The Platte, "a mile wide and an inch deep," is a refuge for any heat-weary pilgrim along its shores.

This is particularly true on the high plains before its long march by the cities begins.

The reason that I came upon it when I did, breaking through a willow thicket and stumbling out through ankle-deep water to a dune in the shade, is of no concern to this narrative. On various purposes of science I have ranged over a good bit of that country on foot, and I know the kinds of bones that come gurgling up through the gravel pumps, and the arrowheads of shining chalcedony that occasionally spill out of water-loosened sand. On that day, however, the sight of sky and willows and the weaving net of water murmuring a little in the shallows on its way to the Gulf stirred me, parched as I was with miles of walking, with a new idea: I was going to float. I was going to undergo a tremendous adventure.

The notion came to me, I suppose, by degrees. I had shed my clothes and was floundering pleasantly in a hole among some reeds when a great desire to stretch out and go with this gently insistent water began to pluck at me. Now to this bronzed, bold, modern generation, the struggle I waged with timidity while standing there in knee-deep water can only seem farcical; yet actually for me it was not so. A near-drowning accident in childhood had scarred my reactions; in addition to the fact that I was a nonswimmer, this "inch-deep river" was treacherous with holes and quicksands. Death was not precisely infrequent along its wandering and illusory channels. Like all broad wastes of this kind, where neither water nor land quite prevails, its thickets were lonely and untraversed. A man in trouble would cry out in vain.

I thought of all this, standing quietly in the water, feeling the sand shifting away under my toes. Then I lay back in the floating position that left my face to the sky, and shoved off. The sky wheeled over me. For an instant, as I bobbed into the main channel, I had the sensation of sliding down the vast tilted face of the continent. It was then that I felt the cold needles of the alpine springs at my fingertips, and the warmth of the Gulf pulling me southward. Moving with me, leaving its taste upon my mouth and spouting under me in dancing springs of sand, was the immense body of the continent itself, flowing like the river was flowing, grain by grain, mountain by mountain, down to the sea. I was streaming over ancient sea beds thrust aloft where giant reptiles had once sported; I was wearing down the face of time and trundling cloud-wreathed ranges into oblivion. I touched my margins with the delicacy of a crayfish's antennae, and felt great fishes glide about their work.

I drifted by stranded timber cut by beaver in mountain fastnesses; I slid over shallows that had buried the broken axles of prairie schooners and the mired bones of mammoth. I was streaming alive through the hot and working ferment of the sun, or oozing secretively through shady thickets. I *was* water and the unspeakable alchemies that gestate and take shape in water, the slimy jellies that under the enormous magnification of the sun writhe and whip upward as great barbeled fish mouths, or sink indistinctly back into the murk out of which they arose. Turtle and fish and the pinpoint chirpings of individual frogs are all watery projections, concentrations—as man himself is a concentration—of that indescribable and liquid brew which is compounded in varying proportions of salt and sun and time. It has appearances, but at its heart lies water, and as I was finally edged gently against a sand bar and dropped like any log, I tottered as I rose. I knew once more the body's revolt against emergence into the harsh and unsupporting air, its reluctance to break contact with that mother element which still, at this late point in time, shelters and brings into being nine tenths of everything alive.

As for men, those myriad little detached ponds with their own swarming corpuscular life, what were they but a way that water has of going about beyond the reach of rivers? I, too, was a microcosm of pouring rivulets and floating driftwood gnawed by the mysterious animalcules of my own creation. I was three fourths water, rising and subsiding according to the hollow knocking in my veins: a minute pulse like the eternal pulse that lifts Himalayas and which, in the following systole, will carry them away.

Thoreau, peering at the emerald pickerel in Walden Pond, called them "animalized water" in one of his moments of strange insight. If he had been possessed of the geological knowledge so laboriously accumulated since his time, he might have gone further and amusedly detected in the planetary rumblings and eructations which so delighted him in the gross habits of certain frogs, signs of that dark interior stress which has reared sea bottoms up to mountainous heights. He might have developed an acute inner ear for the sound of the surf on Cretaceous beaches where now the wheat of Kansas rolls. In any case, he would have seen, as the long trail of life was unfolded by the fossil hunters, that his animalized water had changed its shapes eon by eon to the beating of the earth's dark millennial heart. In the swamps of the low continents, the amphibians had flourished and had their day; and as the long skyward swing—the isostatic response of the crust—had come about, the era of the cooling grasslands and mammalian life had come into being.

A few winters ago, clothed heavily against the weather, I wandered several miles along one of the tributaries of that same Platte I had floated down years before. The land was stark and ice-locked. The rivulets were frozen, and over the marshlands the willow thickets made such an array of vertical lines against the snow that tramping through them produced strange optical illusions and dizziness. On the edge of a frozen backwater, I stopped and rubbed my eyes. At my feet a raw prairie wind had swept the ice clean of snow. A peculiar green object caught my eye; there was no mistaking it.

Staring up at me with all his barbels spread pathetically, frozen solidly in the wind-ruffled ice, was a huge familiar face. It was one of those catfish of the twisting channels, those dwellers in the yellow murk, who had been about me and beneath me on the day of my great voyage. Whatever sunny dream had kept him paddling there while the mercury plummeted downward and that Cheshire smile froze slowly, it would be hard to say. Or perhaps he was trapped in a blocked channel and had simply kept swimming until the ice contracted around him. At any rate, there he would lie till the spring thaw.

At that moment I started to turn away, but something in the bleak, whiskered face reproached me, or perhaps it was the river calling to her children. I termed it science, however—a convenient rational phrase I reserve for such occasions—and decided that I would cut the fish out of the ice and take him home. I had no intention of eating him. I was merely struck by a sudden impulse to test the survival qualities of high-plains fishes, particularly fishes of this type who get themselves immured in oxygenless ponds or in cut-off oxbows buried in winter drifts. I blocked him out as gently as possible and dropped him, ice and all, into a collecting can in the car. Then we set out for home.

Unfortunately, the first stages of what was to prove a remarkable resurrection escaped me. Cold and tired after a long drive, I deposited the can with its melting water and ice in the basement. The accompanying corpse I anticipated I would either dispose of or dissect on the following day. A hurried glance had revealed no signs of life.

To my astonishment, however, upon descending into the basement several hours later, I heard stirrings in the receptacle and peered in. The ice had melted. A vast pouting mouth ringed with sensitive feelers confronted me, and the creature's gills labored slowly. A thin stream of silver bubbles rose to the surface and popped. A fishy eye gazed up at me protestingly.

"A tank," it said. This was no Walden pickerel. This was a yellow-green, mud-grubbing, evil-tempered inhabitant of floods and droughts and cyclones. It was the selective product of the high continent and the waters that pour across it. It had outlasted prairie blizzards that left cattle standing frozen upright in the drifts.

"I'll get the tank," I said respectfully.

He lived with me all that winter, and his departure was totally in keeping with his sturdy, independent character. In the spring a migratory impulse or perhaps sheer boredom struck him. Maybe, in some little lost corner of his brain, he felt, far off, the pouring of the mountain waters through the sandy coverts of the Platte. Anyhow, something called to him, and he went. One night when no one was about, he simply jumped out of his tank. I found him dead on the floor next morning. He had made his gamble like a man—or, I should say, a fish. In the proper place it would not have been a fool's gamble. Fishes in the drying shallows of intermittent prairie streams who feel their confinement and have the impulse to leap while there is yet time may regain the main channel and survive. A million ancestral years had gone into that jump, I thought as I looked at him, a million years of climbing through prairie sunflowers and twining in and out through the pillared legs of drinking mammoth.

"Some of your close relatives have been experimenting with air breathing," I remarked, apropos of nothing, as I gathered him up. "Suppose we meet again up there in the cottonwoods in a million years or so."

I missed him a little as I said it. He had for me the kind of lost archaic glory that comes from the water brotherhood. We were both projections out of that timeless ferment and locked as well in some greater unity that lay incalculably beyond us. In many a fin and reptile foot I have seen myself passing by—some part of myself, that is, some part that lies unrealized in the momentary shape I inhabit. People have occasionally written me harsh letters and castigated me for a lack of faith in man when I have ventured to speak of this matter in print. They distrust, it would seem, all shapes and thoughts but their own. They would bring God into the compass of a shopkeeper's understanding and confine Him to those limits, lest He proceed to some unimaginable and shocking act—create perhaps, as a casual afterthought, a being more beautiful than man. As for me, I believe nature capable of this, and having been part of the flow of the river, I feel no envy—any more than the frog envies the reptile or an ancestral ape should envy man.

Every spring in the wet meadows and ditches I hear a little shrilling chorus which sounds for all the world like an endlessly reiterated "We're here, we're here, we're here." And so they are, as frogs, of course. Confident little fellows. I suspect that to some greater ear than ours, man's optimistic pronouncements about his role and destiny may make a similar little ringing sound that travels a small way out into the night. It is only its nearness that is offensive. From the heights of a mountain, or a marsh at evening, it blends, not too badly, with all the other sleepy voices that, in croaks or chirrups, are saying the same thing.

After a while the skilled listener can distinguish man's noise from the katydid's rhythmic assertion, allow for the offbeat of a rabbit's thumping, pick up the autumnal monotone of crickets, and find in all of them a grave pleasure without admitting any to a place of preëminence in his thoughts. It is when all these voices cease and the waters are still, when along the frozen river nothing cries, screams or howls, that the enormous mindlessness of space settles down upon the soul. Somewhere out in that waste of crushed ice and reflected stars, the black waters may be running, but they appear to be running without life toward a destiny in which the whole of space may be locked in some silvery winter of dispersed radiation.

It is then, when the wind comes straitly across the barren marshes and the snow rises and beats in endless waves against the traveler, that

I remember best, by some trick of the imagination, my summer voyage on the river. I remember my green extensions, my catfish nuzzlings and minnow wrigglings, my gelatinous materializations out of the mother ooze. And as I walk on through the white smother, it is the magic of water that leaves me a final sign.

Men talk much of matter and energy, of the struggle for existence that molds the shape of life. These things exist, it is true; but more delicate, elusive, quicker than the fins in water, is that mysterious principle known as "organization," which leaves all other mysteries concerned with life stale and insignificant by comparison. For that without organization life does not persist is obvious. Yet this organization itself is not strictly the product of life, nor of selection. Like some dark and passing shadow within matter, it cups out the eyes' small windows or spaces the notes of a meadow lark's song in the interior of a mottled egg. That principle—I am beginning to suspect—was there before the living in the deeps of water.

The temperature has risen. The little stinging needles have given way to huge flakes floating in like white leaves blown from some great tree in open space. In the car, switching on the lights, I examine one intricate crystal on my sleeve before it melts. No utilitarian philosophy explains a snow crystal, no doctrine of use or disuse. Water has merely leapt out of vapor and thin nothingness in the night sky to array itself in form. There is no logical reason for the existence of a snowflake any more than there is for evolution. It is an apparition from that mysterious shadow world beyond nature, that final world which contains—if anything contains—the explanation of men and catfish and green leaves.

Analyzing and Discussing the Text

1. What is so special about water? Does Eiseley's opening celebration of water seem exaggerated? What mood does he create?
2. When Eiseley refers to his mystical experience with the words "the extension of shape by osmosis," what kind of language is he using? What does such a phrase imply about the experience?
3. Does it affect your response to Eiseley's narrative when you learn that he is "a bookish professor"? What other personal details does the author reveal about himself?
4. What do we learn about the setting of Eiseley's adventure? Why is setting significant?
5. How does the essay reflect the author's abiding interest in the process of evolution?

6. Why does Eiseley include the story about the catfish?
7. What consolation does Eiseley derive from the memory of his "summer voyage on the river"?

Experiencing and Writing About the World

1. Write a letter to Loren Eiseley in which you respond to the attitudes he reveals in this essay toward humans and the rest of the sentient world. Is your own perspective on the world so different from Eiseley's that you would hardly know how to begin a "dialogue"? Use this "letter" (remember, Eiseley is no longer alive) as an informal medium for the exploration of Eiseley's writing techniques and ideas about the world—ask questions about specific passages in the text and propose your own interpretations. You may find that in the process of explaining your own questions you'll come up with useful answers.
2. Tell the story of a time in your own life when you achieved some kind of magical convergence with your natural surroundings, in water or on land. If you've never had such an experience, imagine one.
3. Analyze Eiseley's description of his mystical experience on the Platte River and compare his description with one or more of the other mystical narratives in this anthology: for instance, Peter Matthiessen's *The Snow Leopard*, Linda Hogan's "Walking," or Rudolfo Anaya's "The Golden Carp."

RUDOLFO ANAYA

From **Bless Me, Ultima**

Born in Pastura, New Mexico, Rudolfo Anaya (1937–   ) has lived most of his life in his native state. He graduated from high school in Albuquerque, attended the Browning Business School for two years, and eventually earned three degrees from the University of New Mexico (including two M.A. degrees, one in guidance and counseling, the other in literature), where he has taught since 1974. Anaya is the author and editor of many books, including such novels as *Bless Me, Ultima* (1972), *Heart of Aztlán* (1976), *The Legend of La Llorona* (1985), and *Lord of the Dawn, the Legend of Quetzalcoatl* (1987). Most recently he has published *Aztlán, Essays on the Chicano Homeland* (1989), *Tierra, Contemporary Short Fiction of New Mexico* (1989), and the novel *Alburquerque* (1992). Many of Anaya's short stories have appeared in national magazines and journals. His honors and awards include a Rockefeller Foundation residency in Bellagio, Italy, in 1991; a three-year W. W. Kellogg Foundation Fellowship (1983–1985); and several honorary doctorates. *Bless Me, Ultima,* from which the following selection has been taken, received the Premio Quinto Sol Award in 1971. Anaya has commented that "writing is not easy. It is a lonely, and oftentimes unappreciated endeavor. But I had to keep creating, I had to keep trying to organize all the beautiful, chaotic things into some pattern. Writing is never quite learned. I have to rewrite and rewrite each manuscript before I am satisfied."

In the novel *Bless Me, Ultima,* the narrator, Tony Márez, recalls being torn as a child between the predominantly Catholic beliefs of his community (a small town in New Mexico) and the natural mysticism of an old woman named Ultima, who comes to live with Tony's family. As Tony begins to appreciate the wisdom of Ultima, a renowned "curandera," he also learns from his friend Cico to discern the magical presence of the natural world. The beauty of the golden carp, glimpsed in the river near his town, fills Tony with a sense of responsibility; the carp, the "Lord of the waters," suggests to Tony the need for humans to halt their cruel and vicious ways or suffer a flood of biblical proportions. This narration of mystical revelation, which concludes with a nighttime dream of salvation, depicts an important stage in the narrator's development from child to adult, a change triggered by his response to the natural world.

[The Golden Carp]

"Hey Toni-eeeeee. Hulooooooo Antonioforous!"

A voice called.

At first I thought I was dreaming. I was fishing, and sitting on a rock; the sun beating on my back had made me sleepy. I had been thinking how Ultima's medicine had cured my uncle and how he was well and could work again. I had been thinking how the medicine of the doctors and of the priest had failed. In my mind I could not understand how the power of God could fail. But it had.

"Toni-eeeeee!" the voice called again.

I opened my eyes and peered into the green brush of the river. Silently, like a deer, the figure of Cico emerged. He was barefoot, he made no noise. He moved to the rock and squatted in front of me. I guess it was then that he decided to trust me with the secret of the golden carp.

"Cico?" I said. He nodded his dark, freckled face.

"Samuel told you about the golden carp," he said.

"Yes," I replied.

"Have you ever fished for carp?" he asked. "Here in the river, or anywhere?"

"No," I shook my head. I felt as if I was making a solemn oath.

"Do you want to see the golden carp?" he whispered.

"I have hoped to see him all summer," I said breathlessly.

"Do you believe the golden carp is a god?" he asked.

The commandment of the Lord said, Thou shalt have no other gods before me. . . .

I could not lie. I knew he would find the lie in my eyes if I did. But maybe there were other gods? Why had the power of God failed to cure my uncle?

"I am a Catholic," I stuttered, "I can believe only in the God of the church—" I looked down. I was sorry because now he would not take me to see the golden carp. For a long time Cico did not speak.

"At least you are truthful, Tony," he said. He stood up. The quiet waters of the river washed gently southward. "We have never taken a non-believer to see him," he said solemnly.

"But I want to believe," I looked up and pleaded, "it's just that I have to believe in Him?" I pointed across the river to where the cross of the church showed above the tree tops.

"Perhaps—" he mused for a long time. "Will you make an oath?" he asked.

"Yes," I answered. But the commandment said, Thou shalt not take the Lord's name in vain.

"Swear by the cross of the church that you will never hunt or kill a carp." He pointed to the cross. I had never sworn on the cross before. I knew that if you broke your oath it was the biggest sin a man could commit, because God was witness to the swearing on his name. But I would keep my promise! I would never break my oath!

"I swear," I said.

"Come!" Cico was off, wading across the river. I followed. I had waded across that river many times, but I never felt an urgency like today. I was excited about seeing the magical golden carp.

"The golden carp will be swimming down the creek today," Cico whispered. We scrambled up the bank and through the thick brush. We climbed the steep hill to the town and headed towards the school. I never came up this street to go to school and so the houses were not familiar to me. We paused at one place.

"Do you know who lives there?" Cico pointed at a green arbor. There was a fence with green vines on it, and many trees. Every house in town had trees but I had never seen a place so green. It was thick like some of the jungles I saw in the movies in town.

"No," I said. We drew closer and peered through the dense curtain of green that surrounded a small adobe hut.

"Narciso," Cico whispered.

Narciso had been on the bridge the night Lupito was murdered. He had tried to reason with the men, he had tried to save Lupito's life. He had been called a drunk.

"My father and my mother know him," I said. I could not take my eyes from the garden that surrounded the small house. Every kind of fruit and vegetable I knew seemed to grow in the garden, and there was even more abundance here than on my uncles' farms.

"I know," Cico said, "they are from the llano—"

"I have never seen such a place," I whispered. Even the air of the garden was sweet to smell.

"The garden of Narciso," Cico said with reverence, "is envied by all— Would you like to taste its fruits?"

"We can't," I said. It was a sin to take anything without permission.

"Narciso is my friend," Cico said. He reached through the green wall and a secret latch opened an ivy-laden door. We walked into the garden. Cico closed the door behind him and said, "Narciso is in jail. The sheriff found him drunk."

I was fascinated by the garden. I forgot about seeing the golden carp. The air was cool and clear, not dusty and hot like the street. Somewhere I heard the sound of gurgling water.

"Somewhere here there is a spring," Cico said. "I don't know where. That is what makes the garden so green. That and the magic of Narciso—"

I was bewildered by the garden. Everywhere I looked there were fruit-laden trees and rows and rows of vegetables. I knew the earth was fruitful because I had seen my uncles make it bear in abundance; but I never realized it could be like this! The ground was soft to walk on. The fragrance of sun-dazzling flowers was deep, and soft, and beautiful.

"The garden of Narciso," I whispered.

"Narciso is my friend," Cico intoned. He pulled some carrots from the soft, dark earth and we sat down to eat.

"I cannot," I said. It was silent and peaceful in the garden. I felt that someone was watching us.

"It is all right," Cico said.

And although I did not feel good about it, I ate the golden carrot. I had never eaten anything sweeter or juicier in my life.

"Why does Narciso drink?" I asked.

"To forget," Cico answered.

"Does he know about the golden carp?" I asked.

"The magic people all know about the coming day of the golden carp," Cico answered. His bright eyes twinkled. "Do you know how Narciso plants?" he asked.

"No," I answered. I had always thought farmers were sober men. I could not imagine a drunk man planting and reaping such fruits!

"By the light of the moon," Cico whispered.

"Like my uncles, the Lunas—"

"In the spring Narciso gets drunk," Cico continued. "He stays drunk until the bad blood of spring is washed away. Then the moon of planting comes over the elm trees and shines on the horde of last year's seeds— It is then that he gathers the seeds and plants. He dances as he plants, and he sings. He scatters the seeds by moonlight, and they fall and grow— The garden is like Narciso, it is drunk."

"My father knows Narciso," I said. The story Cico had told me was fascinating. It seemed that the more I knew about people the more I knew about the strange magic hidden in their hearts.

"In this town, everybody knows everybody," Cico said.

"Do you know everyone?" I asked.

"Uh-huh," he nodded.

"You know Jasón's Indian?"

"Yes."

"Do you know Ultima?" I asked.

"I know about her cure," he said. "It was good. Come on now, let's be on our way. The golden carp will be swimming soon—"

We slipped out of the coolness of the garden into the hot, dusty street. On the east side of the school building was a barren playground with a basketball goal. The gang was playing basketball in the hot sun.

"Does the gang know about the golden carp?" I asked as we approached the group.

"Only Samuel," Cico said, "only Samuel can be trusted."

"Why do you trust me?" I asked. He paused and looked at me.

"Because you are a fisherman," he said. "There are no rules on who we trust, Tony, there is just a feeling. The Indian told Samuel the story; Narciso told me; now we tell you. I have a feeling someone, maybe Ultima, would have told you. We all share—"

"Hey!" Ernie called, "you guys want to play!" They ran towards us.

"Nah," Cico said. He turned away. He did not face them.

"Hi, Tony," they greeted me.

"Hey, you guys headed for Blue Lake? Let's go swimming," Florence suggested.

"It's too hot to play," Horse griped. He was dripping with sweat.

"Hey, Tony, is it true what they say? Is there a bruja at your house?" Ernie asked.

"¡A bruja!" "¡Chingada!" "¡A la veca!"

"No," I said simply.

"My father said she cursed someone and three days later that person changed into a frog—"

"Hey! Is that the old lady that goes to church with your family!" Bones shrieked.

"Let's go," Cico said.

"Knock it off, you guys, are we going to play or not!" Red pleaded. Ernie spun the basketball on his finger. He was standing close to me and grinning as the ball spun.

"Hey, Tony, can you make the ball disappear?" He laughed. The others laughed too.

"Hey, Tony, do some magic!" Horse threw a hold around my neck and locked me into his half-nelson.

"Yeah!" Ernie shouted in my face. I did not know why he hated me.

"Leave him alone, Horse," Red said.

"Stay out of it, Red," Ernie shouted, "you're a Protestant. You don't know about the brujas!"

"They turn to owls and fly at night," Abel shouted.

"You have to kill them with a bullet marked with a cross," Lloyd added. "It's the law."

"Do magic," Horse grunted in my ear. His half-nelson was tight now. My stomach felt sick.

"Voodoo!" Ernie spun the ball in my face.

"Okay!" I cried. It must have scared Horse because he let loose and jumped back. They were all still, watching me.

The heat and what I had heard made me sick. I bent over, retched and vomited. The yellow froth and juice of the carrots splattered at their feet.

"Jesuschriss!" "¡Chingada!" "¡Puta!" "¡A la madre!"

"Come on," Cico said. We took advantage of their surprise and ran. We were over the hill, past the last few houses, and at Blue Lake before they recovered from the astonishment I saw in their faces. We stopped to rest and laugh.

"That was great, Tony," Cico gasped, "that really put Ernie in his place—"

"Yeah," I nodded. I felt better after vomiting and running. I felt better about taking the carrots, but I did not feel good about what they had said about Ultima.

"Why are they like that?" I asked Cico. We skirted Blue Lake and worked our way through the tall, golden grass to the creek.

"I don't know," Cico answered, "except that people, grownups and kids, seem to want to hurt each other—and it's worse when they're in a group."

We walked on in silence. I had never been this far before so the land interested me. I knew that the waters of el Rito flowed from springs in the dark hills. I knew that those hills cradled the mysterious Hidden Lakes, but I had never been there. The creek flowed around the town, crossed beneath the bridge to El Puerto, then turned towards the river. There was a small reservoir there, and where the water emptied into the river the watercress grew thick and green. Ultima and I had visited the place in search of roots and herbs.

The water of el Rito was clear and clean. It was not muddy like the water of the river. We followed the footpath along the creek until we came to a thicket of brush and trees. The trail skirted around the bosque.

Cico paused and looked around. He pretended to be removing a splinter from his foot, but he was cautiously scanning the trail and the grass around us. I was sure we were alone; the last people we had seen were the swimmers at the Blue Lake a few miles back. Cico pointed to the path.

"The fishermen follow the trail around the brush," he whispered, "they hit the creek again just below the pond that's hidden in here." He squirmed into the thicket on hands and knees, and I followed. After a while we could stand up again and follow the creek to a place where an old beaver dam made a large pond.

It was a beautiful spot. The pond was dark and clear, and the water trickled and gurgled over the top of the dam. There was plenty of grass along the bank, and on all sides the tall brush and trees rose to shut off the world.

Cico pointed. "The golden carp will come through there." The cool waters of the creek came out of a dark, shadowy grotto of overhanging thicket, then flowed about thirty feet before they entered the large pond. Cico reached into a clump of grass and brought out a long, thin salt cedar branch with a spear at the end. The razor-sharp steel glistened in the sun. The other end of the spear had a nylon cord attached to it for retrieving.

"I fish for the black bass of the pond," Cico said. He took a position on a high clump of grass at the edge of the bank and motioned for me to sit by the bank, but away from him.

"How can you see him?" I asked. The waters of the pool were clear and pure, but dark from their depth and shadows of the surrounding brush. The sun was crystalline white in the clear, blue sky, but still there was the darkness of shadows in this sacred spot.

"The golden carp will scare him up," Cico whispered. "The black bass thinks he can be king of the fish, but all he wants is to eat them. The black bass is a killer. But the real king is the golden carp, Tony. He does not eat his own kind—"

Cico's eyes remained glued on the dark waters. His body was motionless, like a spring awaiting release. We had been whispering since we arrived at the pond, why I didn't know, except that it was just one of those places where one can communicate only in whispers, like church.

We sat for a long time, waiting for the golden carp. It was very pleasant to sit in the warm sunshine and watch the pure waters drift by. The drone of the summer insects and grasshoppers made me sleepy. The lush green of the grass was cool, and beneath the grass was the dark earth, patient, waiting. . . .

To the northeast two hawks circled endlessly in the clear sky. There must be something dead on the road to Tucumcari, I thought.

Then the golden carp came. Cico pointed and I turned to where the stream came out of the dark grotto of overhanging tree branches. At first I thought I must be dreaming. I had expected to see a carp the size of a river carp, perhaps a little bigger and slightly orange instead of brown. I rubbed my eyes and watched in astonishment.

"Behold the golden carp, Lord of the waters—" I turned and saw Cico standing, his spear held across his chest as if in acknowledgement of the presence of a ruler.

The huge, beautiful form glided through the blue waters. I could not believe its size. It was bigger than me! And bright orange! The sunlight glistened off his golden scales. He glided down the creek with a couple of smaller carp following, but they were like minnows compared to him.

"The golden carp," I whispered in awe. I could not have been more entranced if I had seen the Virgin, or God Himself. The golden carp had seen me. It made a wide sweep, its back making ripples in the dark water. I could have reached out into the water and touched the holy fish!

"He knows you are a friend," Cico whispered.

Then the golden carp swam by Cico and disappeared into the darkness of the pond. I felt my body trembling as I saw the bright golden form disappear. I knew I had witnessed a miraculous thing, the appearance of a pagan god, a thing as miraculous as the curing of my uncle Lucas. And I thought, the power of God failed where Ultima's worked; and then a sudden illumination of beauty and understanding flashed through my mind. This is what I had expected God to do at my first holy communion! If God was witness to my beholding of the golden carp then I had sinned! I clasped my hands and was about to pray to the heavens when the waters of the pond exploded.

I turned in time to see Cico hurl his spear at the monstrous black bass that had broken the surface of the waters. The evil mouth of the black bass was open and red. Its eyes were glazed with hate as it hung in the air surrounded by churning water and a million diamond droplets of water. The spear whistled through the air, but the aim was low. The huge tail swished and contemptuously flipped it aside. Then the black form dropped into the foaming waters.

"Missed," Cico groaned. He retrieved his line slowly.

I nodded my head. "I can't believe what I have seen," I heard myself say, "are all the fish that big here—"

"No," Cico smiled, "they catch two and three pounders below the beaver dam, the black bass must weigh close to twenty—" He threw his spear and line behind the clump of grass and came to sit by me. "Come on, let's put our feet in the water. The golden carp will be returning—"

"Are you sorry you missed?" I asked as we slid our feet into the cool water.

"No," Cico said, "it's just a game."

The orange of the golden carp appeared at the edge of the pond. As he came out of the darkness of the pond the sun caught his shiny scales and the light reflected orange and yellow and red. He swam very close to our feet. His body was round and smooth in the clear water. We watched in silence at the beauty and grandeur of the great fish. Out of the corners of my eyes I saw Cico hold his hand to his breast as the golden carp glided by. Then with a switch of his powerful tail the golden carp disappeared into the shadowy water under the thicket.

I shook my head. "What will happen to the golden carp?"

"What do you mean?" Cico asked.

"There are many men who fish here—"

Cico smiled. "They can't see him, Tony, they can't see him. I know every man from Guadalupe who fishes, and there ain't a one who has ever mentioned seeing the golden carp. So I guess the grown-ups can't see him—"

"The Indian, Narciso, Ultima—"

"They're different, Tony. Like Samuel, and me, and you—"

"I see," I said. I did not know what that difference was, but I did feel a strange brotherhood with Cico. We shared a secret that would always bind us.

"Where does the golden carp go?" I asked and nodded upstream.

"He swims upstream to the lakes of the mermaid, the Hidden Lakes—"

"The mermaid?" I questioned him.

"There are two deep, hidden lakes up in the hills," he continued, "they feed the creek. Some people say those lakes have no bottom. There's good fishing, but very few people go there. There's something strange about those lakes, like they are haunted. There's a strange power, it seems to watch you—"

"Like the *presence* of the river?" I asked softly. Cico looked at me and nodded.

"You've felt it," he said.

"Yes."

"Then you understand. But this thing at the lakes is stronger, or maybe not stronger, it just seems to want you more. The time I was there—I climbed to one of the overhanging cliffs, and I just sat there, watching the fish in the clear water—I didn't know about the power then, I was just thinking how good the fishing would be, when I began to hear strange music. It came from far away. It was a low, lonely murmuring, maybe like something a sad girl would sing. I looked around, but I was alone. I looked over the ledge of the cliff and the singing seemed to be coming from the water, and it seemed to be calling me—"

I was spellbound with Cico's whispered story. If I had not seen the golden carp perhaps I would not have believed him. But I had seen too much today to doubt him.

"I swear, Tony, the music was pulling me into the dark waters below! The only thing that saved me from plunging into the lake was the golden carp. He appeared and the music stopped. Only then could I tear myself away from that place. Man, I ran! Oh how I ran! I had never been afraid before, but I was afraid then. And it wasn't that the singing was evil, it was just that it called for me to join it. One more step and I'da stepped over the ledge and drowned in the waters of the lake—"

I waited a long time before I asked the next question. I waited for him to finish reliving his experience. "Did you see the mermaid?"

"No," he answered.

"Who is she?" I whispered.

"No one knows. A deserted woman—or just the wind singing around the edges of those cliffs. No one really knows. It just calls people to it—"

"Who?"

He looked at me carefully. His eyes were clear and bright, like Ultima's, and there were lines of age already showing.

"Last summer the mermaid took a shepherd. He was a man from Méjico, new here and working for a ranch beyond the hills. He had not heard the story about the lakes. He brought his sheep to water there, and he heard the singing. He made it back to town and even swore that he had seen the mermaid. He said it was a woman, resting on the water and singing a lonely song. She was half woman and half fish— He said the song made him want to wade out to the middle of the lake to help her, but his fear had made him run. He told everyone the story, but no one believed him. He ended up getting drunk in town and swearing he would prove his story by going back to the lakes and bringing back the mer-woman. He never returned. A week later the flock was found near the lakes. He had vanished—"

"Do you think the mermaid took him?" I asked.

"I don't know, Tony," Cico said and knit his brow, "there's a lot of things I don't know. But never go to the Hidden Lakes alone, Tony, never. It's not safe."

I nodded that I would honor his warning. "It is so strange," I said, "the things that happen. The things that I have seen, or heard about."

"Yes," he agreed.

"These things of the water, the mermaid, the golden carp. They are strange. There is so much water around the town, the river, the creek, the lakes—"

Cico leaned back and stared into the bright sky. "This whole land was once covered by a sea, a long time ago—"

"My name means sea," I pondered aloud.

"Hey, that's right," he said, "Márez means sea, it means you come from the ocean, Tony Márez arisen from the sea—"

"My father says our blood is restless, like the sea—"

"That is beautiful," he said. He laughed. "You know, this land belonged to the fish before it belonged to us. I have no doubt about the prophecy of the golden carp. He will come to rule again!"

"What do you mean?" I asked.

"What do I mean?" Cico asked quizzically, "I mean that the golden carp will come to rule again. Didn't Samuel tell you?"

"No," I shook my head.

"Well he told you about the people who killed the carp of the river and were punished by being turned into fish themselves. After that happened, many years later, a new people came to live in this valley. And they were no better than the first inhabitants, in fact they were worse. They sinned a lot, they sinned against each other, and they sinned against the legends they knew. And so the golden carp sent them a prophecy. He said that the sins of the people would weigh so heavy upon the land that in the end the whole town would collapse and be swallowed by water—"

I must have whistled in exclamation and sighed.

"Tony," Cico said, "this whole town is sitting over a deep, underground lake! Everybody knows that. Look." He drew on the sand with a stick. "Here's the river. The creek flows up here and curves into the river. The Hidden Lakes complete the other border. See?"

I nodded. The town was surrounded by water. It was frightening to know that! "The whole town!" I whispered in amazement.

"Yup," Cico said, "the whole town. The golden carp has warned us that the land cannot take the weight of the sins—the land will finally sink!"

"But you live in town!" I exclaimed.

He smiled and stood up. "The golden carp is my god, Tony. He will rule the new waters. I will be happy to be with my god—"

It was unbelievable, and yet it made a wild kind of sense! All the pieces fitted!

"Do the people of the town know?" I asked anxiously.

"They know," he nodded, "and they keep on sinning."

"But it's not fair to those who don't sin!" I countered.

"Tony," Cico said softly, "all men sin."

I had no answer to that. My own mother had said that losing your innocence and becoming a man was learning to sin. I felt weak and powerless in the knowledge of the impending doom.

"When will it happen?" I asked.

"No one knows," Cico answered. "It could be today, tomorrow, a week, a hundred years—but it will happen."

"What can we do?" I asked. I heard my voice tremble.

"Sin against no one," Cico answered.

I walked away from that haven which held the pond and the swimming waters of the golden carp feeling a great weight in my heart. I was saddened by what I had learned. I had seen beauty, but the beauty had burdened me with responsibility. Cico wanted to fish at the dam, but I was not in the mood for it. I thanked him for letting me see the golden carp, crossed the river, and trudged up the hill homeward.

I thought about telling everyone in town to stop their sinning, or drown and die. But they would not believe me. How could I preach to the whole town, I was only a boy. They would not listen. They would say I was crazy, or bewitched by Ultima's magic.

I went home and thought about what I had seen and the story Cico told. I went to Ultima and told her the story. She said nothing. She only smiled. It was as if she knew the story and found nothing fantastic or impending in it. "I would have told you the story myself," she nodded wisely, "but it is better that you hear the legend from someone your own age. . . ."

"Am I to believe the story?" I asked. I was worried.

"Antonio," she said calmly and placed her hand on my shoulder, "I cannot tell you what to believe. Your father and your mother can tell you, because you are their blood, but I cannot. As you grow into manhood you must find your own truths—"

That night in my dreams I walked by the shore of a great lake. A bewitching melody filled the air. It was the song of the mer-woman! I looked into the dark depths of the lake and saw the golden carp, and all around him were the people he had saved. On the bleached shores of the lake the carcasses of sinners rotted.

Then a huge golden moon came down from the heavens and settled on the surface of the calm waters. I looked towards the enchanting light, expecting to see the Virgin of Guadalupe, but in her place I saw my mother!

Mother, I cried, you are saved! We are all saved!

Yes, my Antonio, she smiled, we who were baptized in the water of the moon which was made holy by our Holy Mother the Church are saved.

Lies! my father shouted, Antonio was not baptized in the holy water of the moon, but in the salt water of the sea!

I turned and saw him standing on the corpse-strewn shore. I felt a searing pain spread through my body.

Oh please tell me which is the water that runs through my veins, I moaned;
oh please tell me which is the water that washes my burning eyes!

It is the sweet water of the moon, my mother crooned softly, it is the water
the Church chooses to make holy and place in its font. It is the water of your
baptism.

Lies, lies, my father laughed, through your body runs the salt water of the
oceans. It is that water which makes you Márez and not Luna. It is the water
that binds you to the pagan god of the Cico, the golden carp!

Oh, I cried, please tell me. The agony of pain was more than I could bear.
The excruciating pain broke and I sweated blood.

There was a howling wind as the moon rose and its powers pulled at the
still waters of the lake. Thunder split the air and the lightning bursts illuminated
the churning, frothy tempest. The ghosts stood and walked upon the shore.

The lake seemed to respond with rage and fury. It cracked with the laughter
of madness as it inflicted death upon the people. I thought the end had come to
everything. The cosmic struggle of the two forces would destroy everything!

The doom which Cico had predicted was upon us! I clasped my hands and
knelt to pray. The terrifying end was near. Then I heard a voice speak above the
sound of the storm. I looked up and saw Ultima.

Cease! she cried to the raging powers, and the power from the heavens and
the power from the earth obeyed her. The storm abated.

Stand, Antonio, she commanded, and I stood. You both know, she spoke to
my father and my mother, that the sweet water of the moon which falls as rain
is the same water that gathers into rivers and flows to fill the seas. Without
the waters of the moon to replenish the oceans there would be no oceans. And
the same salt waters of the oceans are drawn by the sun to the heavens, and in
turn become again the waters of the moon. Without the sun there would be no
waters formed to slake the dark earth's thirst.

The waters are one, Antonio. I looked into her bright, clear eyes and un-
derstood her truth.

You have been seeing only parts, she finished, and not looking beyond into
the great cycle that binds us all.

Then there was peace in my dreams and I could rest.

Analyzing and Discussing the Text

1. What does Tony realize about the natural world during the course
   of this narrative? How does *he* change because of these experiences?
   How does his relationship with Cico change?
2. Why does Anaya emphasize the "golden" color of the carrot in Narciso's garden? Where else does this motif appear?

3. Does this seem like a realistic portrayal of children? How does Anaya attempt to make it so?
4. What is the effect of Cico's caution and secrecy on the narrative?
5. How does Tony realize he has "witnessed a miraculous thing"?
6. Explain the significance of the narrator's name, "Tony Márez."
7. Is there an ecological message in this story, a moral about the relationship between humans and the natural world? Ultima, the old curandera, the healer, tells Tony, "As you grow into manhood you must find your own truths." Does Anaya leave room for his readers to find their own truths? Examine the didactic element in this story.

Experiencing and Writing About the World

1. Write a brief analysis of the fictional narrative as a mode of environmental discourse. How is Anaya's fiction especially effective in communicating ideas about the natural world? What are the didactic limitations that result from the obliqueness and symbolic complexity of fiction? Point to specific passages in this section of the novel that seem likely to compel readers to experience the world in a new way.
2. Create a short story of your own about children making discoveries in the world. Use characters and a setting that come out of your own childhood, incorporating details of speech and behavior from memory. Perhaps, like Anaya, you could establish one character as a guide or teacher and the others as people struggling to decide what is "true" or determined to resist new knowledge at all costs. Use a combination of dialogue, description, and internal meditation. You might even include a visionary, dreamlike passage in the midst of your narrative, as Anaya does at the end of this selection.
3. Have you ever felt a tension between formal religious beliefs and a spirituality rooted in natural experiences? Contemplate this tension by depicting several specific scenes—can you resolve your own conflict as neatly as Tony Márez seems to resolve his? Rather than using only narrative to consider your experiences, attempt to analyze more abstractly the differences between formal religion and natural mysticism or private belief. You might also contemplate the processes and implications of changing beliefs.

JEANNE WAKATSUKI HOUSTON
AND JAMES D. HOUSTON

Manzanar, U.S.A.

Jeanne Wakatsuki Houston (1934–   ) was born in Inglewood, California. During World War II, she and her family, like many other Japanese-Americans, were forced to live in an internment camp called Manzanar, a community assembled hastily in the high desert country on the eastern side of the Sierra Nevada mountains. Jeanne Wakatsuki was seven years old when her family arrived at Manzanar. After the war she studied journalism and sociology at San Jose State College, earning her bachelor's degree in 1956. A year later she married James D. Houston (1933–   ), whom she had met at San Jose State. They worked together on *Farewell to Manzanar: A True Story of Japanese American Experience During and After the World War II Internment* (1973). The book and the subsequent screenplay have received the Humanities Prize, the Christopher Award, and the award of the National Women's Political Caucus. James D. Houston's other books include, most recently, *Californians* (1985) and *Gig* (1988). The two authors have also written *One Can Think About Life After the Fish Is in the Canoe: Beyond Manzanar* (1988).

The following chapter from *Farewell to Manzanar* demonstrates various kinds of aesthetic responses to the natural world. The narrator, recalling her experiences in the camp nearly thirty years after they occurred, uses the vision of an abandoned pear orchard near "Block 28" to symbolize an important change in her family's situation "from the outrageous to the tolerable." Part of what made life in the camp "tolerable" was the view of the Sierras beyond the gates. The internees, such as the narrator's father, made the most of their predicament and perhaps even overcame it by appreciating the beauty of their surroundings, indeed by contributing to this beauty through the creation of "rock gardens, vegetable gardens and flower gardens." The dazzling mountains, viewed from the camp, provided both "spiritual sustenance" and reminders that there are forces in nature "that sometimes [human beings] must simply endure."

In Spanish, Manzanar means "apple orchard." Great stretches of Owens Valley were once green with orchards and alfalfa fields. It has been a desert ever since its water started flowing south into Los

Angeles, sometime during the twenties. But a few rows of untended pear and apple trees were still growing there when the camp opened, where a shallow water table had kept them alive. In the spring of 1943 we moved to Block 28, right up next to one of the old pear orchards. That's where we stayed until the end of the war, and those trees stand in my memory for the turning of our life in camp, from the outrageous to the tolerable.

Papa pruned and cared for the nearest trees. Late that summer we picked the fruit green and stored it in a root cellar he had dug under our new barracks. At night the wind through the leaves would sound like the surf had sounded in Ocean Park, and while drifting off to sleep I could almost imagine we were still living by the beach.

Mama had set up this move. Block 28 was also close to the camp hospital. For the most part, people lived there who had to have easy access to it. Mama's connection was her job as dietician. A whole half of one barracks had fallen empty when another family relocated. Mama hustled us in there almost before they'd snapped their suitcases shut.

For all the pain it caused, the loyalty oath finally did speed up the relocation program. One result was a gradual easing of the congestion in the barracks. A shrewd househunter like Mama could set things up fairly comfortably—by Manzanar standards—if she kept her eyes open. But you had to move fast. As soon as the word got around that so-and-so had been cleared to leave, there would be a kind of tribal restlessness, a nervous rise in the level of neighborhood gossip as wives jockeyed for position to see who would get the empty cubicles.

In Block 28 we doubled our living space—four rooms for the twelve of us. Ray and Woody walled them with sheetrock. We had ceilings this time, and linoleum floors of solid maroon. You had three colors to choose from—maroon, black, and forest green—and there was plenty of it around by this time. Some families would vie with one another for the most elegant floor designs, obtaining a roll of each color from the supply shed, cutting it into diamonds, squares, or triangles, shining it with heating oil, then leaving their doors open so that passers-by could admire the handiwork.

Papa brought his still with him when we moved. He set it up behind the door, where he continued to brew his own sake and brandy. He wasn't drinking as much now, though. He spent a lot of time outdoors. Like many of the older Issei men, he didn't take a regular job in camp. He puttered. He had been working hard for thirty years and, bad as it was for him in some ways, camp did allow him time to dabble with hobbies he would never have found time for otherwise.

Once the first year's turmoil cooled down, the authorities started letting us outside the wire for recreation. Papa used to hike along the creeks that channeled down from the base of the Sierras. He brought back chunks of driftwood, and he would pass long hours sitting on the steps carving myrtle limbs into benches, table legs, and lamps, filling our rooms with bits of gnarled, polished furniture.

He hauled stones in off the desert and built a small rock garden outside our doorway, with succulents and a patch of moss. Near it he laid flat steppingstones leading to the stairs.

He also painted watercolors. Until this time I had not known he could paint. He loved to sketch the mountains. If anything made that country habitable it was the mountains themselves, purple when the sun dropped and so sharply etched in the morning light the granite dazzled almost more than the bright snow lacing it. The nearest peaks rose ten thousand feet higher than the valley floor, with Whitney, the highest, just off to the south. They were important for all of us, but especially for the Issei. Whitney reminded Papa of Fujiyama, that is, it gave him the same kind of spiritual sustenance. The tremendous beauty of those peaks was inspirational, as so many natural forms are to the Japanese (the rocks outside our doorway could be those mountains in miniature). They also represented those forces in nature, those powerful and inevitable forces that cannot be resisted, reminding a man that sometimes he must simply endure that which cannot be changed.

Subdued, resigned, Papa's life—all our lives—took on a pattern that would hold for the duration of the war. Public shows of resentment pretty much spent themselves over the loyalty oath crises. *Shikata ga nai* again became the motto, but under altered circumstances. What had to be endured was the climate, the confinement, the steady crumbling away of family life. But the camp itself had been made livable. The government provided for our physical needs. My parents and older brothers and sisters, like most of the internees, accepted their lot and did what they could to make the best of a bad situation. "We're here," Woody would say. "We're here, and there's no use moaning about it forever."

Gardens had sprung up everywhere, in the firebreaks, between the rows of barracks—rock gardens, vegetable gardens, cactus and flower gardens. People who lived in Owens Valley during the war still remember the flowers and lush greenery they could see from the highway as they drove past the main gate. The soil around Manzanar is alluvial and very rich. With water siphoned off from the Los Angeles-bound aqueduct, a large farm was under cultivation just outside the camp, providing the mess halls with lettuce, corn, tomatoes, eggplant, string beans, horseradish, and cucumbers. Near Block 28 some of the men who had been professional gardeners built a small park, with mossy nooks, ponds, waterfalls, and curved wooden bridges. Sometimes in the evenings we could walk down the raked gravel paths. You could face away from the barracks, look past a tiny rapids toward the darkening mountains, and for a while not be a prisoner at all. You could hang suspended in some odd, almost lovely land you could not escape from yet almost didn't want to leave.

As the months at Manzanar turned to years, it became a world unto itself, with its own logic and familiar ways. In time, staying there seemed far simpler than moving once again to another, unknown place. It was as if the war were forgotten, our reason for being there forgotten. The present, the little bit of busywork you had right in front of you, became the most urgent thing. In such a narrowed world, in order to survive, you learn to contain your rage and your despair, and you try to re-create, as well as you can, your normality, some sense of things continuing. The fact that America had accused us, or excluded us, or imprisoned us, or whatever it might be called, did not change the kind of world we wanted. Most of us were born in this country; we had no other models. Those parks and gardens lent it an oriental character, but in most ways it was a totally equipped American small town, complete with schools, churches, Boy Scouts, beauty parlors, neighborhood gossip, fire and police departments, glee clubs, softball leagues, Abbott and Costello movies, tennis courts, and traveling shows. (I still remember an Indian who turned up one Saturday billing himself as a Sioux chief, wearing bear claws and head feathers. In the firebreak he sang songs and danced his tribal dances while hundreds of us watched.)

In our family, while Papa puttered, Mama made her daily rounds to the mess halls, helping young mothers with their feeding, planning diets for the various ailments people suffered from. She wore a bright yellow, long-billed sun hat she had made herself and always kept stiffly starched. Afternoons I would see her coming from blocks away, heading home, her tiny figure warped by heat waves and that bonnet a yellow flower wavering in the glare.

In their disagreement over serving the country, Woody and Papa had struck a kind of compromise. Papa talked him out of volunteering; Woody waited for the army to induct him. Meanwhile he clerked in the co-op general store. Kiyo, nearly thirteen by this time, looked forward to the heavy winds. They moved the sand around and uncovered obsidian arrowheads he could sell to old men in camp for fifty cents apiece. Ray, a few years older, played in the six-man touch football league, sometimes against Caucasian teams who would come in from Lone Pine or Independence. My sister Lillian was in high school and singing with a hillbilly band called The Sierra Stars—jeans, cowboy hats, two guitars, and a tub bass. And my oldest brother, Bill, led a dance band called The Jive Bombers—brass and rhythm, with cardboard fold-out music stands lettered J. B. Dances were held every weekend in one of the recreation halls. Bill played trumpet and took vocals on Glenn Miller arrangements of such tunes as *In the Mood, String of Pearls,* and *Don't Fence Me In.* He didn't sing *Don't Fence Me In* out of protest, as if trying quietly to mock the authorities. It just happened to be a hit song one year, and they all wanted to be an up-to-date American swing band. They would blast it out into recreation barracks full of bobby-soxed, jitterbugging couples:

Oh, give me land, lots of land
Under starry skies above,
Don't fence me in.
Let me ride through the wide
Open country that I love . . .

Pictures of the band, in their bow ties and jackets, appeared in the high school yearbook for 1943–1944, along with pictures of just about everything else in camp that year. It was called *Our World.* In its pages you see school kids with armloads of books, wearing cardigan sweaters and walking past rows of tarpapered shacks. You see chubby girl yell leaders, pompons flying as they leap with glee. You read about the school play, called *Growing Pains* " . . . the story of a typical American home, in this case that of the McIntyres. They see their boy and girl tossed into the normal awkward growing up stage, but can offer little assistance or direction in their turbulent course . . . " with Shoji Katayama as George McIntyre, Takudo Ando as Terry McIntyre, and Mrs. McIntyre played by Kazuko Nagai.

All the class pictures are in there, from the seventh grade through twelfth, with individual head shots of seniors, their names followed by the names of the high schools they would have graduated from on the outside: Theodore Roosevelt, Thomas Jefferson, Herbert Hoover, Sacred Heart. You see pretty girls on bicycles, chicken yards full of fat pullets, patients back-tilted in dental chairs, lines of laundry, and finally, two large blowups, the first of a high tower with a searchlight, against a Sierra backdrop, the next a two-page endsheet showing a wide path that curves among rows of elm trees. White stones border the path. Two dogs are following an old woman in gardening clothes as she strolls along. She is in the middle distance, small beneath the trees, beneath the snowy peaks. It is winter. All the elms are bare. The scene is both stark and comforting. This path leads toward one edge of camp, but the wire is out of sight, or out of focus. The tiny woman seems very much at ease. She and her tiny dogs seem almost swallowed by the landscape, or floating in it.

Analyzing and Discussing the Text

1. "Manzanar, U.S.A." shows both the beauty and the ugliness of life in an internment camp. Point out examples of each extreme and explain why the authors juxtapose the two.
2. Why do the authors use the trees as a symbol of tolerability? What seems to have been the psychological value of the trees and their

leaves for the young Jeanne Wakatsuki? How do these natural objects go beyond being ordinary elements of the setting to serve as symbols?
3. What seems to be the primary purpose of this essay? Telling a story, describing a setting, or analyzing a phenomenon? Determine whether the dominant expressive mode is narration, description, exposition, or argumentation.
4. What does this chapter teach us about ways of tolerating hardship? Explain the role(s) of nature in this process.
5. The human figures in this chapter are often characterized as tiny, feeble, distorted, aimless. What effect does this create and how does it seem to suit the authors' purpose?

Experiencing and Writing About the World

1. Describe the view from the window of one of your university classrooms. Devote two or three substantial paragraphs to this physical description, perhaps contrasting the world beyond the window with the appearance of the window itself and the rest of the classroom. You might supplement this prose description with a drawing.
2. The repeated use of an image or a phrase often gives it a symbolic resonance. Take a description from your response to the preceding writing suggestion and rewrite it in an attempt to transform one or two items from the initial description into evocative (not necessarily explicit) symbols of what you feel as you look out from the classroom window.
3. Write an essay on the idea of aesthetic appreciation of the natural world as a means of coping with any kind of restriction or imprisonment. You could begin with an analysis of this concept as revealed in "Manzanar, U.S.A." and other works, such as Edward Abbey's *Desert Solitaire* (1968) or Christopher Nolan's *Under the Eye of the Clock* (1987), in which automobiles or physical handicaps, respectively, present obstacles to engagement with the nonhuman world. Attempt to explain the psychology of aesthetic experience (the perception of "the beautiful") and its use as a means of escape or intensification.

LARRY LITTLEBIRD

The Hunter

Larry Littlebird (1941–   ) was born on the Laguna Pueblo Reservation in northern New Mexico, where he grew up in the village of Paguate. He briefly attended Oakland City College (in California) before moving to Santa Fe, New Mexico, in the early 1960s to study at the Institute of American Indian Art and the Anthropology Film Center. He now lives outside Santa Fe in the town of Tesuque. Littlebird has published essays in several periodicals and anthologies, but for the past two decades he has focused his attention on documentary filmmaking and oral storytelling performances; he serves as the director of the Circle Film Production Company and Coyote Gathers His Children (a tribal American performance troupe), both located in Santa Fe. In March of 1992 Littlebird helped to organize the first annual Hama-Ha Conference, devoted to tribal American oral storytelling, which he hopes will provide a "new paradigm for education" in this country. Our society is constantly acquiring and distributing "information," asserts Littlebird, but there is very little "wisdom" in this information. Tribal Americans (Native Americans still associated with a "living tribal community") such as Littlebird hope to teach people outside of their community "how to listen." *Hama-Ha*, a Pueblo phrase, means "time for storytelling."

The following essay (Littlebird refers to it as a "story") was written in 1980 at the request of Simon Ortiz, who was in the process of assembling a collection of writings published in 1983 as *Earth Power Coming*. Littlebird later recorded this and other stories about hunting on his tape "Hunter's Heart" (Lotus Press), which explains the development from learning the Pueblo hunting ritual described in "The Hunter" to becoming a "keeper of ritual"; he is currently preparing an essay collection on this same theme. When asked if it seems phony or crudely imitative for nontribal Americans to aspire to a tribal outlook on the natural world, Littlebird stated that "every individual has a perspective and is entitled to express that perspective." The following essay shows how a young child learns that a deer "cannot simply be slaughtered and used" but must be approached with "supplication, understanding, and reverence," with an attitude that Littlebird would call "tribal wisdom."

Maybe it was because I was a child and saw it that way, or maybe it really is the way I remember it, growing up in my mother's village.

It is fall. There is a special clarity in the way light appears at this time of year. And it gives my memory a sense of another time, a time when my young eyes can see beyond the haze and the world stands out, still, brilliant, and defined. In the fall, all talk and thoughts turn to hunting. As the stories of the deer and the hunter unfold detail by detail, in my child's mind, images of the deer appear and take shape.

They say the deer is a spirit. A creature of God's creation, it needs supplication, understanding, and reverence. It is a blessing, a gift bestowed upon humankind as a remembrance of our own life's interconnected course, an interwoven thread from the beginning of all living time. It is meat for the body and soul.

Endowed with a keen sense of sight, smell, and hearing plus additional uncanny abilities beyond human dimension, this creature cannot be simply slaughtered and used. The deer's realm is the pristine spaces of mountain and plain, its very domain is a sanctuary. Its essence is life; to kill it is to waste it.

This new and wondrous creature begins to occupy me, looming magnificently magnified and imagined in my thoughts as I roam mesas and arroyos playing, as I eat and sleep.

I want to be a hunter, one of the men afield in the fall, gun in hand, bandolier of shiny bullets around my waist, a bright red kerchief about my head. Can I be a man who will endure the rigors of the hunt? The all-night prayer and singing? A man who from daylight till sunset, without food, without drink, will evidence the stamina of a strong people? I wonder.

With a child's anticipation and delight, the fall evenings are spent around the little outdoor fires on the village edge waiting into the night for the signal that will tell everyone a hunter returns. For seeming nights on end, we wait until at last the bright orange spark that lights the shadow of the far southern hill sends me scurrying with the other boys and girls toward the only road by which the hunters will enter. Gathering excitedly at the road's edge, laughing and whispering, speculating about which party of men are returning, our noisy exuberance is suddenly cut silent. A low murmuring sounds from the far deep night. The joyous rise of men's voices singing their songs of the deer coming home to our village reaches us through the darkness.

Someday I will arrive home like these men, my face painted to signify my sacred purpose, greeted reverently by the people, blessed and made welcome. I dream of that day, but how?

One day my grandmother simply tells me, "Day by day, little by little, you will learn. Keep your eyes open, your mouth shut and become obedient to those in authority around you. Life is sacred to us, and you are sacred. You carry it in your heart the best you can. Treat all things as you want to be treated, then some day you will be ready." It is simple and I believe her. But I still want to kill a deer.

With a little boy's forgetfulness, these questions I ponder so seriously easily give way to other equally important concerns as the season
passes. Will there be enough snow this year for my homemade sled
I've worked so hard to find enough scrap boards to make? Will I ever
learn to spin my brightly painted wooden top, whipping it off the tight
string as accurately as my older cousin? Will my small frail hand ever
grasp the correct grip on the beautiful glass marble that would allow
me to win a few? The seasons come and go, invisibly blending one into
another, and even though I still leave more marbles in the ring than fill
my pockets, visions of the deer never quite leave me.

During this time I learn to use a home-made inner tube band
slingshot until cans, bottles, even objects tossed into the air are accurately and consistently knocked down. After that, proficiency with a
rifle comes easily. Even then, something tells me hunting is more than
expertise with a weapon. Gradually, I am obsessed by one recurrent
thought, "to kill a deer without wasting it."

The year of my first deer hunt, my uncles carefully instruct me on
what a man does when he wants to hunt. I do as I am taught; I do it
all correctly but I don't kill a deer.

"Killing a deer isn't everything to hunting," my uncles say. "Fast-
ing and praying, a man works hard giving his self to the spirit the deer
belongs to. We are only human, we cannot say what our giving should
bring. Yes, we want badly to bring home that big buck; we can only
work truthfully at doing that. The Creator will see our honesty; we
must believe our reward will come about. There should be no disappointment."

Trying not to feel disappointed, I think all this over. I prepared so
carefully—my rifle, my bullets, my actions, my thoughts, my prayers.
Where am I at fault? Then I remember.

I remember that little boy sitting by the outdoor fires watching for
the returning hunters. I remember what he felt in his heart when he
saw the stripe-painted faces of the men arriving home from the deer's
mountain sanctuary, their beings permeated with invisible blessings,
strength, well-being.

I remember water that is made holy as the paint is washed from
their faces by the women. I remember the little boy who is told to
drink that sacred water. I remember eagerly drinking that murky brown
liquid, the taste of sweet sediment in my mouth. The grownups laugh
and make joking remarks but I drink it anyway because I believe them
when they tell me it will make me a strong hunter. I feel my body
shudder as the essence touches my young heart that wants only to be
a hunter.

It is the desire to be a hunter who will not waste a deer's life that I
remember. My feet have touched the mountains where deer live; I have
breathed in the same air and drunk of their water. I've gotten close, yet

no deer has come to my hungry gun. There is no fault. Had I killed a deer that first year, would I have recalled the little boy who wanted to be a hunter? Or remembered the child who believed the stories old men and old women tell in that other long ago time?

Surely, the deer is a spirit, and I must die if I am to be one. Day by day, little by little, as I embrace and struggle with this gift, my worldly desires must die, my physical needs must die. I must die to the selfish lusts that would entice my body and entrap my soul, until at last, unthinking and clear-eyes, innocent like a child, I am free to believe and know the secret pulsing in the hot flowing blood the hunter hunts. And, somewhere, the red living waters of the pure-eyed deer wait for me.

Analyzing and Discussing the Text

1. For Littlebird, the process of learning is principally a process of listening. How does he show the importance of listening in this essay?
2. Analyze the relationships within the human community described in this essay and between humans and the rest of nature. How are these relationships defined by a belief that "life is sacred"?
3. "Killing a deer isn't everything to hunting," says one of Littlebird's uncles. What does this mean? How does this idea compare to your own notion of what hunting is?
4. Is this a hunting story or a learning story? Explain your response.

Experiencing and Writing About the World

1. Have you ever viewed some natural object or outdoor activity as mundane and merely pragmatic and then come to recognize its deeper spiritual or psychological value? If you have ever experienced such a shift in perspective, devote three or four pages to telling the story of this change. Attempt to describe your attitudes before and after the change and to narrate the specific events (excursions, conversations, reading) that resulted in new understanding. If you have never experienced such a transformation, imagine one—produce a hypothetical narrative of spiritual discovery.
2. Write an essay of your own called "The Hunter." Attempt to define the essential purposes and processes of hunting. Although you may

wish to use personal experience as evidence for your claims, aim to make your definition universal, not merely personal.

3. Write a critique of your own learning process (or your relationship to teachers, parents, coaches, bosses, and other authority figures) in any context, not strictly an environmental one. Depict, explain, and assess your approach to learning how to play basketball, paint, write, or do anything else that requires considerable effort, time, and interaction with a "teacher." Use both narrative and expository analysis in this discussion of yourself as a learner.

SUSAN MITCHELL

Dreaming in Public:
A Provincetown Memoir

Born and raised in New York City, Susan Mitchell (1944–   ) began writing poetry at the age of seven, although she did not begin submitting her work for publication until the 1970s, following college at Wellesley and graduate school at Georgetown, where she earned an M.A. in English with a focus on medieval literature. Mitchell also attended the Bread Loaf Writers' Conference in Vermont and several poetry workshops at the Columbia School of the Arts in New York before becoming a fellow at the Fine Arts Work Center in Provincetown, Massachusetts, at the outermost tip of Cape Cod, in 1977. After living in Provincetown for three years, Mitchell taught at Northeastern Illinois University in Chicago and at Middlebury College, then moved to Boca Raton in 1987 to become the Mary Blossom Lee Professor in Poetry at Florida Atlantic University. Her first book of poetry, *The Water Inside the Water*, appeared in 1983. *Rapture*, a second collection of poetry, was published in 1992. Mitchell is currently working on a collection of essays, some of which have been published in *Provincetown Arts*, *Parnassus*, and *Marlow RFD*.

The poet's sensitivity to both language and the visual power of the natural world is noticeable even in her nonfiction. "Dreaming in Public," a memoir of Mitchell's experiences in Provincetown, was published in 1987 in *Provincetown Arts* and then selected by Annie Dillard for inclusion in the 1988 edition of *The Best American Essays*. In her introduction to the anthology, Dillard expresses her interest in the way several of the "narrative essays," including Mitchell's, manage to mix "plain facts and symbolic facts," sometimes even transforming the "plain facts" into symbols. Mitchell herself tends to distinguish between the worldly "speaker" in her essays and the speaker in her poetry, who "does not say things one would say in ordinary conversation." But in all of her writing, Mitchell seeks to push language to the limits of everyday speech. Metaphor, she says, may represent the mind's original response to the world, the way "the brain goes through wrong ideas while trying to figure out what something is." When she toured the cypress swamps of south Florida in the process of writing "Gates of Grass: The Road to Loxahatchee" (*Marlow RFD*, 1991), Mitchell says she saw the baton rouge fungus on trees and thought immediately of "splashed blood." Similarly, when she viewed the sky in Provincetown, she thought of "foliage," "vast calligraphy," and "thick squid ink." Throughout her work we encounter the intense aesthetic responses to nature that most people repress or leave unexpressed.

The winter of 1979, I lived in a condominium down by the tennis courts at the east end of Provincetown. The apartment was large enough to span the land world and the sea world, each with its own flora and fauna, sounds and smells. When I stood under the skylight on the land side and looked out on Commercial Street, men slim as their ten-speed bicycles shadowed past, and pink-jeaned girls with enormous eyes whizzed by on roller skates faster than my IBM Selectric could type "anorexia" or "cocaine." Under the skylight was a waterbed, and drifting out on it, I stared up into the sky. "I have done a good deal of skying," Constable wrote in 1822, the year he painted most of his cloud studies. I did a good deal of skying, too—into the green and black foliage of cumulonimbus, into that gaseous, chloroformed light that precedes sudden and violent storms. Sometimes a strong wind tossed and lowered a tree branch against the skylight. In fine weather, that tree pulsed with small golden birds, finches that must have eaten food touched by Midas—even their excrement was liquid gold. I loved skying into weather just developing: clouds rapidly changing to mist, swirling apart until suddenly the skylight framed shades of blue; blurs and blots of clouds, a vast calligraphy that kept erasing, then rewriting itself in an excess, an exuberance of alphabets, or into a patois of bruises, a jargon of violet streakings, thick squid ink that seemed the very opacity of language and desire.

The bedroom, with its white chest of drawers, white chair, blue rug, and white curtains was on the bay side. The low bed seemed a part of that bay: propped on one elbow, I could look out at 4 A.M.—the fishing boats returning to Provincetown harbor, all thirteen of them, their lights a rope pulling toward shore. Their return was a clock chiming, a parent's key turning in the lock of childhood. At high tide, waves would break against the foundation of the building, so that even in the dark, even with eyes closed, I knew, as if something had shifted in my own blood and marrow, the bay was at flood. During hurricanes and gales, the Atlantic was shaken into me, a vibration so deep—that boom, boom of fist against body bag when Marvin Hagler worked out at the Provincetown Inn the following fall—its percussions became part of my sleep, a disturbance of the flesh. Even after I left that apartment and Provincetown, even in Charlottesville and in those breathtaking absences of the Midwest, I could have sworn I felt it—the tide changing, the Atlantic heaving itself on Truro, Wellfleet, Race Point, the waist-high grass of Indiana prairie bending westward.

I grew up in N.Y.C., where I learned to drift with crowds, to be one shining particle in those streaming currents of phosphorescense that merge and intersect around Fifth and Fifty-seventh, especially on late winter afternoons. As one sparkling corpuscle, I delighted in the speed, the thrust, even the bumps and jolts of all those other glittering corpuscles. Black, white, Hispanic, Asian, Native American, we made up one Amazonian bloodstream. In those crowds, I savored my anonymity, that deliciously sensuous private space where I could dream in public, sensing the outermost edges of other people's dreams: that woman striding past me in a green suede coat, lighting up a Mary J—the burned eggplant smell drifted back to me, spreading, smudging the purely olfactory calligraphy of her dream. Long after she disappeared into the crowded distance, her dream flowed from her nostrils, enigmatic, persistent.

In Provincetown, everyone seems to dream in public. The summer I lived in a studio at the west end, Georgie would stand in front of me as I sunbathed in the garden and dream out loud. We had moved into the cottage on the same day, Georgie in the studio below mine. "Hi," he said, "I'm Georgie the Whore," the only name I ever knew him by. Midmorning, as I stirred silty coffee with a twig and watched black islands break loose from the sun, Georgie would read to me from the dream diaries clients had left with him, clients he usually met at Tuesday afternoon tea dances at one of the restaurants on Commercial Street. Georgie was a perfectionist who found ways to concretize down to the last detail his clients' amorphous yearnings for mingled pain and pleasure. But what Georgie loved to dream most was the male body. If he could have found a way, he would have entered through the anus and exited from the mouth, having traveled every tortuous channel of mazy entrails, as if lovemaking, to be any good, had to re-enact our births, the cry of orgasm recalling the glistening moment when we scream out our arrival on earth. How many times that summer I heard his clients arrive, four maybe five arrivals each night, the cars racing up, then falling back down the gravel driveway, as the men replaced one another, their cries always sounding somehow the same. As Georgie talked, the male body turned inside out or rolled into a gleaming ball, arms grasping ankles, or became a wheel, legs reaching back toward the head—all those intricate combinations of cat's cradle I played as a child, Georgie never tiring of the game, the knots never slipping through his fingers, but only through his heart: they were all "teddy bears" whose small bodies nestled against his chest. Georgie's lovers were contortionists, sexual acrobats, so that finally, for me, the image that represented them all was Picasso's *Femme Couche*, with its simultaneous, all-embracing view of breasts, buttocks, and vaginal face. What Georgie dreamed out loud each morning was sex as collage: every possible way of taking a man, fantasy superimposed on fantasy, maps and ground plans for fantastic cities of desire, the cities lapping and overlapping one another, each city with its own lymphatic network pumping, pulsating, spilling from fountain to baroque fountain.

Sometimes when a morning listening to Georgie made me feel too lethargic to write, I'd devote the afternoon to a small shop on Commercial Street that sold magic tricks and costumes. The magic tricks—hats that promised disappearance, rubber spiders quivering on black legs, glasses with false bottoms—were not what interested me: it was the masks, those rubber faces that fit over my own like a second, or a first, skin. There were animal masks—cat, gorilla, bear, and an odd one-of-a-kind fanged face that reminded me of Cocteau's dream animal for *Beauty and the Beast*. The fanged face even came with a costume that swathed and engulfed the body in velvet. Masks are not to be put on frivolously. All through the filming of *Beauty and the Beast* Cocteau was so disfigured by eczema that he wore "a veil made of black paper, fastened to the brim of his hat with clothespins, with holes for his eyes and mouth." What I never tired of were masks that opened to reveal still another mask: a dream inside a dream—or a dream with its own false bottom, the shock of mistaken identity. There was, for example, the Beautiful Lady mask from Italy, with her straight nose, thick mascaraed lashes, porcelain skin blushing at the cheeks—and a black chiffon scarf draped across the mouth. Unfasten the scarf: the mouth bloomed up a crimson gash, a gaping blood-smeared wound. The Beautiful Lady was so versatile, an alluring woman who, at the drop of a veil, could transform herself into something hideous—or, depending on the viewer's taste, perhaps something more alluring. Beautiful Lady reminded me of the mask worn by the Echo Dancer in Kwakiutl winter ceremonies. When the Echo Dancer appears, he wears a mask bearing humanlike features. Moving around the fire, he covers his face with the corner of his blanket, then suddenly lets the covering drop to reveal a different mouthpiece on the mask. As the dance progresses, the performer displays a series of mouthpieces—animal, bird, sea creature. But the Beautiful Lady also brought to mind those Ovidian myths where the hunter is transformed into the victim—Actaeon changed into a stag, then torn to pieces by his own dogs, which mistake him for the animal he was pursuing. But unlike Actaeon, the Beautiful Lady had the ability to heal herself: only cover her mouth, and what was bloody and torn is made whole; cover her mouth, and whatever story she inspires can start over from its innocent beginning.

I approached the Beautiful Lady mask gingerly, with respect, but never tried it on. It was the King Kong hands that I loved to slip over my own like burglar's gloves, that leathery black skin exchanging cells with mine: the gorilla hands were somewhat humanized by my gestures while some animal trace revived my body, electrifying each hair on my head. I have seen every one of the King Kong films, each refilming a reflection of some subtle change in our idea of the erotic. In the version that stars Jessica Lange, the essence of the heroine's sexuality is amnesia, her ability to forget each narrow escape as soon as it's over. As a result, she starts each adventure anew, fearless. When the geological team arrives on Kong's island, Jessica rushes ahead on the stony beach, despite the foreboding chill created by the ominously swirling mists. It's not a beach I would care to walk alone. But Jessica, ignorant of the cues that immediately alert the aficionado of the fantasy genre, senses no danger. Like the Beautiful Lady, she is self-healing, a perpetual virgin in the garden of fantasy sex.

During the winter of 1979, as I read in front of a window overlooking Provincetown Bay, I often thought of Keats the reader: "I should like the window to open onto the Lake of Geneva," he wrote Fanny, "and there I'd sit and read all day, like the picture of somebody reading." Perhaps like those women looking out of windows in paintings by Caspar David Friedrich and M. V. Schwind that had such a vogue in the early and mid 1800s. Backs turned on the dark interiors that make up most of the pictorial space, these women seem to drift out of the paintings— not toward, but away from us, out over the horizon where our own thoughts are traveling. Painters of this period frequently portrayed themselves before windows, and there is even a painting, attributed to M. Drolling the elder, of a Paris interior (Wadsworth Atheneum, Hartford) where the view through the open window is depicted on a canvas on the easel. Like these artists, like Keats looking out on Lake Geneva, I was simultaneously inside and outside, snug and far away, contained and dispersed as I sat by my window. The natural world with its gulls, sandpipers, boats, and winding windrows of kelp and seagrape intermingled with the poems and novels I read, such as in Spenser's Bower of Bliss living vines and tendrils entwine themselves around artificial plants. That strange long-drawn cry that Emma Bovary hears after making love with Rudolphe, the cry that hangs on the air of Steegmuller's superb translation before it mingles with Emma's own jangled nerves seemed to come from out over the bay, the cry of a gull suddenly rising from the silence. The natural world flowed into, washed over, and nurtured whatever I read, dreamed, and wrote. I was a creature in a tidal pool, sometimes drinking the incoming waves at flood, other times breathing air and that extraordinary Provincetown light that always comes from several directions at once—bouncing off the bay, raining down through the skylight, crackling out of the wood stove. I was a straddler, inhabiting a world of art prolonged by dream and a natural world guided by some deeper dream. On sunny, surprisingly warm December afternoons, I sipped margaritas at the Red Inn, and as the sun set, licked salt from the rim of the ocean. This was my third year in Provincetown. No longer a fellow at the Fine Arts Work Center, I stayed on with a grant from the Artists Foundation, sometimes sharing the sunset with two other former fellows, a sculptor and a painter. What I remember now were our long, impassioned talks about Nancy Holt, whose *Sun Tunnels,* constructed during the seventies in Utah's Great Basin Desert, invited us to meditate on inside and outside, sensations from within the body and perceptions sucked in through openings in the tunnels and pipes. Late at night, when the moon loomed, an enormous floating city that illuminated whatever I was reading, I thought of the moon penetrating Holt's tunnels, the different shapes that light takes as it encroaches on darkness. Even when I read in the bath, glass of scotch beside the soap, I could sense the lunar tug, the pull the moon exerted on the bay, on the syrupy undulations of the waterbed, on the water I bathed in. On the stereo, John Anderson slurred "Going Down Hill," the moon dragging at his vocal cords, thickening the sound.

Late at night, I drifted through all the apartments I had ever lived in: the little apartment on the rue du Cherche Midi that looked down on a cobblestone courtyard that gleamed on chill, wet October nights; the hotel room in Paris, its windows opening onto a garden of blossoming pear trees—my home for a year, it also looked into another room where each night a man and woman made love without bothering to draw the curtains; the pink stucco apartment that looked out on Porto Cervo where a harbor vendor sold bright orange roe of sea urchins, the sticky tickertape of history I gulped down with lemon and the rough burn of Sardinian Vernaccia, future urchin beds swallowed whole; the balcony in N.Y.C. that looked down on swaying barges of light, hanging bridges, neon gardens floating miraculously thirty stories above the street; the dark blue tiles of the apartment overlooking Positano, cool under bare feet, the *persiani* half closed on hot afternoons, the ocean boiling at the cliff bottom, sizzling, breeze of garlic and onion. Through the window at Provincetown I looked out through all those other windows, the window in Paris opening to reveal the window in Porto Cervo, which opened wide to reveal the balcony in N.Y.C.—as if I were pulling a spy glass to its furthest extension. Or as if the windows opened onto each other like those stories in the *Arabian Nights* that do not really end but, instead, spill into one another, story overflowing into story, until I am standing in the garden at Positano where Danish's cat has just given birth to the rhythm of "Sergeant Pepper's Lonely Hearts Club Band." The rooster crows and dawn arrives with the smell of lemon and mimosa. The rooster knows the exact moment. All roosters everywhere know the moment. In Provincetown, it's conch pink, slippery, the thin line that separates night from day, the exact moment when morning appears like a sail on the horizon. Such thresholds have always seemed magical to me, those fine threads of the world that have the power to renew us if we can only grab hold of them: the flicker of light that appears between bands of color in Rothko's paintings, that marginal world, the dividing line, the moment of change when everything still seems possible. Once, walking near Pilgrim Heights, I tried to follow the shrill of peepers to its source, that spring where the sound wells up and spills into rivulets of water. Louder and louder the shrilling grew—and then, just when I had almost found its source, the shrilling stopped, all the peepers holding their breath at once. So the source is secret, magical, withholding itself, retreating into what Mallarmé called the "last spiritual casket."

It was at Pilgrim Heights that William Bradford and an exploring party from the *Mayflower* had their first drink of American water. Before going on to Plymouth and founding our nation on rock, the Pilgrims first tried to found it on water in Provincetown Harbor. It was in Provincetown Bay that the women of the *Mayflower* washed their clothes after the long crossing. And it was in Provincetown Bay that Bradford's wife, Anne, in a state of despair, drowned herself. You will not find her mentioned in the *Encyclopaedia Britannica*, though William's career is summarized there. You will not find her suicide mentioned in Bradford's chronicle, *The History of Plimoth Plantation:* not a ripple of her passing disturbs his account of the Pilgrim venture. Within the fullness of the first Thanksgiving there is this absence, Anne's: within the desire to build, to construct, to found, to create something new, this tug in the opposite direction, this desire not to begin, not to, not to—the secret absence out of which all great things start up.

I have visited the spring where supposedly Bradford and his exploring expedition had their first taste of "sweet water." The first time alone, the second time with Otukwei Okai, a poet from Ghana in residence at the Fine Arts Work Center. This was my second year as a fellow, the spring of 1979. The car I had bought the previous year still smelled new, and its shiny black exterior had not yet lost its sex appeal. Every afternoon, Otukwei passed the car, patted the hood, and said something complimentary, until finally it dawned on me: he wanted us to go for a drive and fulfill his version of the American dream—fast car, loud rock, hamburgers, shakes and fries, and all the windows open. It seemed so clichéd to me, this dream, but well, why not do it?—especially since my own myth of Africa was probably just as hackneyed: tawny lions, as marvelously unreal as Rousseau's, creeping up on villagers. My pleas for lion stories invariably reduced Otukwei to frowning silence. The day I satisfied his dream down to the last greasy fried potato, Otukwei, his wife Beatrice, and their infant daughter, swaddled in pink, drove with me to Pilgrim Heights for our own taste of the famous spring. Along the way, Otukwei and I spilled out ideas for poems, our creative juices keeping pace with the rock music, the membranes of our fetal poems so thin that images swam back and forth between us. It was one enormous poem we were writing as we got out of the car and walked the spongy forest trail covered with amber needles to a high place that looks down on the water, which barely seems to move between banks of yellow-brown reeds. An egret shuddered up, its flight hardly faster than the river's. The air shuddered up, its flight hardly faster than the river's. The air was redolent of pine. It was here, supposedly, that the Pilgrims saw footprints made by local Native Americans. I spared Otukwei my skepticism about the role of this particular spring in American history and simply knelt with him: it tasted as before—warm, sandy. On the drive back to Provincetown, suddenly out of the flow of conversation, it erupted—Otukwei's lion story. A very large lion. The men carrying it on a pole back to the village, its tail so long it dragged in the dust.

Recently, on a flight to West Palm Beach, as a south wind carried wave after wave of rain against the windows, I felt it again, the deep boom of Provincetown Bay slapping at foundations, sucking its breath in, holding it, holding it, then heaving it out. We were threading our way between storm systems in an eerie yellow-green light, the wake of a passing tornado. Bouldery clouds, stacked precariously on one another, trembled, stretching, towering higher and higher above the plane, then suddenly toppled, the plane falling with them as if through a trap door. I had entered the realm of process, where skying was all that mattered. To the left, racing us, was a thick black cloud, flat as a mattress, a flying carpet with three dark threads tentacling down. As we banked, cloud after cloud tumbled toward us, breakers, whitecapped, foaming, spewing spray—and then it was the ocean, all its teeth bared.

Sometimes the ocean returns to me in surprising ways—as this past Christmas in the powder room of a N.Y.C. department store. It was my favorite hour. Outside, the lights had just come on, snow was beginning to fall, each flake a momentary jewel in the hair of passersby. As I yawned into the mirror, a stall door opened behind me: the woman enthroned on the toilet puckered her glossy red lips, sweeping her hands up her shiny black hair caught in a chignon. Still sitting, she wiggled out of black lace pantyhose and into crotchless panties. The woman who had just left her stall resembled the woman I had chatted with the night before at a dinner party: same blond bangs, same thick hair squared at the jaw, same sad eyes and drained face. Now I watched them both in the mirror. The prostitute was radiant, glowing, as she removed the crotchless panties, lowering them slowly to the floor, a gesture that suddenly seemed the essence of her appeal. Nothing can dirty me, that gesture said. Not the dirt on the floor. Not the water oozing out of the toilets. Not the urine spotting the toilet seats. Not the faded blonde whose sadness leaves a sour taste only in her own mouth. The prostitute waved a leg in my direction and smiled: "Boy, oh boy, oh boy," she said, her voice entirely different from what I had expected; it seemed to come from another body, from a delivery boy's or a cab driver's. Still looking in the mirror, I smiled back, thinking of the ocean licking itself clean all those nights in Provincetown as I listened in the dark. The ocean that heals instantly around whatever penetrates it. The ocean lubed to a shine. In a mirror, the ocean looks at itself and sees that it is wearing a rose. And sees that it has no hats. This ocean that goes on talking in my sleep, that keeps kneading itself like dough, like prayer.

Analyzing and Discussing the Text

1. Examine Mitchell's depictions of the Provincetown sky, its light. Compare these descriptions with Georgia O'Keeffe's comments about the plains sky in Texas. How do Mitchell's words also compare with Joel Meyerowitz's photograph of the sea and sky near Provincetown?
2. Mitchell calls her piece "Dreaming in Public." Does her language somehow suggest *dreaminess*? Respond with specific examples. Exactly what does the title mean?
3. Mitchell compares the natural place to art, calling the clouds "a vast calligraphy that kept erasing, then rewriting itself in an excess, an exuberance of alphabets." What does this suggest about her attitude toward nature?
4. What is the connection between Georgie's public dreaming and the author's? Explain the analogy between Georgie's "sexual acrobatics" and Picasso's painting.

5. Writers like Barry Lopez, Loren Eiseley, and Richard Nelson strain to make contact with the solidity, the permanence, of the external world. What is Mitchell's attitude toward this world? In what way does *she* make contact?
6. What does Mitchell mean when she writes "I was a straddler, inhabiting a world of art prolonged by dream and a natural world guided by some deeper dream"?
7. Look at the dreams Mitchell and the Ghanaian poet Otukwei Okai share with each other. Does Mitchell trivialize these stereotypes or ultimately restore their importance?
8. Explain the connection between the prostitute and the ocean in the final scene.

Experiencing and Writing About the World

1. Early in her essay, Mitchell quotes the British painter John Constable as having written "I have done a good deal of skying." Do some skying of your own. Write a series of five separate, paragraph-long skyscapes, depicting the sky in your own part of the world.
2. "The natural world . . . intermingled with the poems and novels I read," writes Mitchell. Read some nature poetry and allow it to influence *your* perceptions of the world around you. Write a brief description of your immediate environment in which you mingle your own words with those of the poets and perhaps with those of the essayists from this anthology.
3. Attempt to write an account of a personal experience in which you make absolutely no reference to anything natural. Then rewrite the account, allowing nature to seep into the narrative. How does this change the writing?

Suggestions for Further Reading

Beston, Henry. *The Outermost House.* 1928. New York: Penguin, 1976.
Chatwin, Bruce. *The Songlines.* New York: Viking-Penguin, 1987.
Dillard, Annie. *Holy the Firm.* New York: Harper, 1977.
Edwards, Jonathan. "Personal Narrative." *Jonathan Edwards: Basic Writings.* 1765. New York: NAL, 1966.
Kinseth, Lance. *River Eternal.* New York: Viking, 1989.

Lopez, Barry. "Ice and Light." *Arctic Dreams: Imagination and Desire in a Northern Landscape*. New York: Bantam, 1986.

_____.*River Notes: The Dance of Herons*. New York: Avon, 1979.

Mather, Cotton. "A Voice from Heaven." 1719. *Days of Humiliation: Times of Affliction and Disaster (Nine Sermons for Restoring Favor with an Angry God)*. Ed. George Harrison Orians. Gainesville, FL: Scholars' Facsimiles, 1970.

Schultheis, Rob. *The Hidden West: Journeys in the American Outback*. San Francisco: North Point, 1983.

Van Dyke, John C. *The Mountain: Renewed Studies in Impressions and Appearances*. 1916. Foreword Peter Wild. Salt Lake City: U of Utah P, 1992.

PART FOUR

Abstractions: Thinking About the Environment

Dennis Stock/©1970 Magnum Photos

CHAPTER ONE

Nature and the Mind

Human beings are essentially intellectual creatures. Many of our most powerful and meaningful experiences occur within our own minds, removed from physical contact with the external world. Sometimes, however, our interaction with other people, and even with the nonhuman universe, produces a mirror in which we can see how our minds work and thus sharpen our self-understanding. It is not surprising that writers are often fascinated with their own mental processes, even if their explicit subject matter seems impersonal and nonpsychological. The critic Sharon Cameron has written in her 1985 book, *Writing Nature: Henry Thoreau's Journal,* that "to write about nature is to write about how the mind sees nature, and sometimes about how the mind sees itself." Both nature and writing (the former being an external presence, the latter a process of putting experience into words) demand and contribute to an author's awareness of self and nonself. By confronting the separate realm of nature, by becoming aware of its otherness, the writer implicitly becomes more deeply aware of his or her own dimensions, limitations of form and understanding, and processes of grappling with the unknown. Late in his life John Muir wrote in his journal, "I only went out for a walk, and finally concluded to stay out till sundown, for going out, I found, was really going in." This comment suggests not only the ease and comfort Muir felt in the wilderness, but also, symbolically, the interiority of outdoor experience.

The authors of the following selections demonstrate a wide variety of psychological responses to the natural world. Loren Eiseley contemplates the deep, eternal "fear" of a renewed "ice age" that preoccupies the human subconscious; the very "latent and shadowy powers" of nature become, for thinkers like Eiseley, imprinted on the mind itself. Barry Lopez examines the remarkable ability of children to notice patterns and relationships in nature, and he seeks to explain the role of adults in helping children to fathom their own place in the world. The connections between landscape (physical place and all life within it), history (the passage of time and the recording of events in stories), and imagination (the human intellectual response to the world) are precisely the topic of the excerpts from Leslie Marmon Silko's study of the traditional Pueblo people's nondualistic way of understanding the relationship between the mind and the world. Gary Soto, using childhood memories as the basis for his discussion, focuses on one particular aspect of nature—blue sky—and its wholesome effect on the human mind. In the excerpt from Randall Kenan's novel, we see the young character imagining himself transforming into a bird as a way of surmounting his human limitations. John Daniel, in the final essay of this chapter, makes an important distinction between "sightseeing" (detached, aesthetic perception of nature) and direct, participatory experience of the world, considering the psychological dangers and values of the two approaches.

LOREN EISELEY

The Winter of Man

For biographical information, see the headnote for "The Flow of the River" in Part Three, Chapter Three.

"The Flow of the River" is an example of Eiseley's personal or "concealed" essay. In "The Winter of Man," however, Eiseley speaks in a less private way about people's attitudes toward the place of humanity within the natural world, beginning in the third person ("he") and gradually adopting in his own discussion the explorer Knud Rasmussen's embracing pronoun "we" as a way of suggesting that even modern readers harbor a fear of the universe. Whereas the other writers in this chapter of the anthology emphasize the various ways in which individuals or communities experience the world on a daily basis, Eiseley contemplates the more fundamental, more enduring implications of human attitudes and behavior. He discusses the apparent domination of nature by mankind, only to introduce the idea of *hubris,* "the term for overweening pride." Writing for the *New York Times* in 1972, at a time when "nuclear winter" seemed more threatening than the global warming now known as the greenhouse effect, Eiseley points out that "no living scientist can say with surety the ice will not return. If it does the swarming millions who now populate the planet may mostly perish in misery and darkness, inexorably pushed from their own lands to be rejected in desperation by their neighbors." The external world—including its phases of warmth and cold—becomes for Eiseley a mirror of the human mind: "Today we are aware of the latent and shadowy powers contained in the subconscious: the alternating winter and sunlight of the human soul." Although we may feel ourselves in control, the author suggests in conclusion that "we are in the winter. We have never left its breath." Is this a warning to avoid nuclear catastrophe? A resigned acceptance of the bleakness of all mortal existence? Eiseley, typically, leaves this point ambiguous. We must take his suggestions and weigh them against our own experience.

"We fear," remarked an Eskimo shaman responding to a religious question from the explorer Knud Rasmussen some fifty years ago. "We fear the cold and the things we do not understand. But most of all we fear the doings of the heedless ones among ourselves."

Students of the earth's climate have observed that man, in spite of the disappearance of the great continental ice fields, still lives on the steep edge of winter or early spring. The pulsations of these great ice deserts, thousands of feet thick and capable of overflowing mountains and valleys, have characterized the nature of the world since man, in his thinking and speaking phase, arose. The ice which has left the marks of its passing upon the landscape of the Northern Hemisphere has also accounted, in its long, slow advances and retreats, for movements, migrations and extinctions throughout the plant and animal kingdoms.

Though man is originally tropical in his origins, the ice has played a great role in his unwritten history. At times it has constricted his movements, affecting the genetic selection that has created him. Again, ice has established conditions in which man has had to exert all his ingenuity in order to survive. By contrast, there have been other times when the ice has withdrawn farther than today and then, like a kind of sleepy dragon, has crept forth to harry man once more. For something like a million years this strange and alternating context has continued between man and the ice.

When the dragon withdrew again some fifteen or twenty thousand years ago, man was on the verge of literacy. He already possessed great art, as the paintings in the Lascaux cavern reveal. It was an art devoted to the unseen, to the powers that control the movement of game and the magic that drives the hunter's shaft to its target. Without such magic man felt weak and helpless against the vagaries of nature. It was his first attempt at technology, at control of nature by dominating the luck element, the principle of uncertainty in the universe.

A few millennia further on in time man had forgotten the doorway of snow through which he had emerged. He would only rediscover the traces of the ice age in the nineteenth century by means of the new science of geology. At first he would not believe his own history or the reality of the hidden ice dragon, even though Greenland and the polar world today lie shrouded beneath that same ice. He would not see that what the Eskimo said to Rasmussen was a belated modern enactment of an age-old drama in which we, too, had once participated. "We fear," the Eskimo sage had said in essence, "we fear the ice and cold. We fear nature which we do not understand and which provides us with food or brings famine."

Man, achieving literacy on the far Mediterranean shores in an instant of golden sunlight would take the world as it was, to be forever. He would explore the intricacies of thought and wisdom in Athens. He would dream the first dreams of science and record them upon scrolls of parchment. Twenty-five centuries later those dreams would culminate in vast agricultural projects, green revolutions, power pouring through great pipelines, or electric energy surging across continents. Voices would speak into the distances of space. Huge jet transports would hurtle through the skies. Radio telescopes would listen to cosmic whispers from beyond our galaxy. Enormous concentrations of people would gather and be fed in towering metropolises. Few would remember the Greek word *hubris*, the term for overweening pride, that pride which eventually causes some unseen balance to swing in the opposite direction.

Today the ice at the poles lies quiet. There have been times in the past when it has maintained that passivity scores of thousands of years—times longer, in fact, than the endurance of the whole of urban civilization since its first incipient beginnings no more than seven thousand years ago. The temperature gradient from the poles to the equator is still steeper than throughout much of the unglaciated periods of the past. The doorway through which man has come is just tentatively closing behind him.

So complex is the problem of the glacial rhythms that no living scientist can say with surety the ice will not return. If it does the swarming millions who now populate the planet may mostly perish in misery and darkness, inexorably pushed from their own lands to be rejected in desperation by their neighbors. Like the devouring locust swarms that gather in favorable summers, man may have some of that same light-winged ephemeral quality about him. One senses it occasionally in those places where the dropped, transported boulders of the ice fields still hint of formidable powers lurking somewhere behind the face of present nature.

These fractured mementoes of devastating cold need to be contemplated for another reason than themselves. They constitute exteriorly what may be contemplated interiorly. They contain a veiled warning, perhaps the greatest symbolic warning man has ever received from nature. The giant fragments whisper, in the words of Einstein, that "nature does not always play the same game." Nature is devious in spite of what we have learned of her. The greatest scholars have always sensed this. "She will tell you a direct lie if she can," Charles Darwin once warned a sympathetic listener. Even Darwin, however, alert as he was to vestigial traces of former evolutionary structures in our bodies, was not in a position to foresee the kind of strange mental archaeology by which Sigmund Freud would probe the depths of the human mind. Today we are aware of the latent and shadowy powers contained in the subconscious: the alternating winter and sunlight of the human soul.

Has the earth's glacial winter, for all our mastery of science, surely subsided? No, the geologist would answer. We merely stand in a transitory spot of sunshine that takes on the illusion of permanence only because the human generations are short.

Has the wintry bleakness in the troubled heart of humanity at least equally retreated?—that aspect of man referred to when the Eskimo, adorned with amulets to ward off evil, reiterated: "Most of all we fear the secret misdoings of the heedless ones among ourselves."

No, the social scientist would have to answer, the winter of man has not departed. The Eskimo standing in the snow, when questioned about his beliefs, said: "We do not believe. We only fear. We fear those things which are about us and of which we have no sure knowledge...."

But surely we can counter that this old man was an ignorant remnant of the Ice Age, fearful of a nature he did not understand. Today we have science; we do not fear the Eskimo's malevolent ghosts. We do not wear amulets to ward off evil spirits. We have pierced to the far rim of the universe. We roam mentally through light-years of time.

Yes, this could be admitted, but we also fear. We fear more deeply than the old man in the snow. It comes to us, if we are honest, that perhaps nothing has changed the grip of winter in our hearts, that winter before which we cringed amidst the ice long ages ago.

For what is it that we do? We fear. We do not fear ghosts but we fear the ghost of ourselves. We have come now, in this time, to fear the water we drink, the air we breathe, the insecticides that are dusted over our giant fruits. Because of the substances we have poured into our contaminated rivers, we fear the food that comes to us from the sea. There are also those who tell us that by our own heedless acts the sea is dying.

We fear the awesome powers we have lifted out of nature and cannot return to her. We fear the weapons we have made, the hatreds we have engendered. We fear the crush of fanatic people to whom we readily sell these weapons. We fear for the value of the money in our pockets that stands symbolically for food and shelter. We fear the growing power of the state to take all these things from us. We fear to walk in our streets at evening. We have come to fear even our scientists and their gifts.

We fear, in short, as that self-sufficient Eskimo of the long night had never feared. Our minds, if not our clothes, are hung with invisible amulets: nostrums changed each year for our bodies whether it be chlorophyl toothpaste, the signs of astrology, or cold cures that do not cure: witchcraft nostrums for our society as it fractures into contending multitudes all crying for liberation without responsibility.

We fear, and never in this century will we cease to fear. We fear the end of man as that old shaman in the snow had never had cause to fear it. There is a winter still about us—the winter of man that has followed him relentlessly from the caverns and the ice. The old Eskimo spoke well. It is the winter of the heedless ones. We are in the winter. We have never left its breath.

Analyzing and Discussing the Text

1. Explain the role of "ice" in the "unwritten history" of the human species.
2. What, according to Eiseley, is the typical human response to "the principle of uncertainty in the universe"? What is the uncertainty principle? Do you agree with Eiseley's ideas?
3. How do *fear* and *hubris* define the extreme ways that people have thought about nature?
4. Regarding large boulders transported by ancient glaciers, Eiseley explains, "These fractured mementoes of devastating cold need to be contemplated for another reason than themselves. They constitute exteriorly what may be contemplated interiorly." Explain this idea. Do you sympathize with Eiseley's response or disagree?
5. Most people nowadays are more concerned with the greenhouse effect than with the possibility of a renewed ice age. What is the greenhouse effect? Should we feel toward the disintegration of the earth's ozone layer just as Eiseley's Eskimo feels about the return of "the ice"?

Experiencing and Writing About the World

1. Do you feel wholly in control of your life or of your immediate surroundings? Write a short essay in which you contemplate the vast mystery and power of the universe and the puniness of human existence. Open yourself to the feelings such a concept produces. Do you feel fear, a sense of absurdity, wonder? Explain the relationship between your normal worldview and the worldview depicted in Eiseley's essay.
2. Have you ever had a particular outdoor experience in which you felt intense fear? Write a narrative of this fearful experience in which you also consider the implications of living on a planet where all is not safe and benign. What happened to your "innocence" as a result of this experience?
3. Write an analytical essay in which you compare the various styles of persuasive warning in Stephen Jay Gould's "Sex, Drugs, Disasters, and the Extinction of Dinosaurs" (conclusion), Eiseley's "The Winter of Man," and the excerpt from Jonathan Weiner's "The New Question" (in the final chapter of this text).
4. Do research on the greenhouse effect and/or the idea of a nuclear winter, then write an essay in which you consider the broad implications of these processes. Is the fear expressed in Eiseley's essay

now completely obsolete? Has it been securely replaced by a new fear? Can you imagine a time when thoughtful human beings will ever live without some kind of deep uneasiness about the fate of the species, perhaps of the planet as a whole?

BARRY LOPEZ

Children in the Woods

For biographical information, see the headnote for "The Image of the Unicorn" in Part Two, Chapter One.

"A child's world is fresh and new and beautiful, full of wonder and excitement," writes Rachel Carson in her short picture book, *A Sense of Wonder* (1956). "It is our misfortune," she continues, "that for most of us that clear-eyed vision, that true instinct for what is beautiful and awe-inspiring is dimmed and lost before we reach adulthood." In the following selection from the book *Crossing Open Ground* (1988), Barry Lopez presents his own version of Carson's celebration of children's unique ability to pay attention to the natural world, but Lopez's concern is for the role of the adult (himself) in guiding children to a deeper understanding of what they notice. "If [a child] senses something ineffable in the landscape," he wonders, "will I know enough to encourage it?" After explaining the process of learning and teaching about the natural world, Lopez finally considers the psychological value of such knowledge for the human individual—his ideas differ drastically from the ominous suggestions in Eiseley's "The Winter of Man."

When I was a child growing up in the San Fernando Valley in California, a trip into Los Angeles was special. The sensation of movement from a rural area into an urban one was sharp. On one of these charged occasions, walking down a sidewalk with my mother, I stopped suddenly, caught by a pattern of sunlight trapped in a spiraling imperfection in a windowpane. A stranger, an elderly woman in a cloth coat and a dark hat, spoke out spontaneously, saying how remarkable it is that children notice these things.

I have never forgotten the texture of this incident. Whenever I recall it I am moved not so much by any sense of my young self but by a sense of responsibility toward children, knowing how acutely I was affected in that moment by that woman's words. The effect, for all I know, has lasted a lifetime.

Now, years later, I live in a rain forest in western Oregon, on the banks of a mountain river in relatively undisturbed country, surrounded by 150-foot-tall Douglas firs, delicate deer-head orchids, and clearings where wild berries grow. White-footed mice and mule deer, mink and coyote move through here. My wife and I do not have children, but children we know, or children whose parents we are close to, are often here. They always want to go into the woods. And I wonder what to tell them.

In the beginning, years ago, I think I said too much. I spoke with an encyclopedic knowledge of the names of plants or the names of birds passing through in season. Gradually I came to say less. After a while the only words I spoke, beyond answering a question or calling attention quickly to the slight difference between a sprig of red cedar and a sprig of incense cedar, were to elucidate single objects.

I remember once finding a fragment of a raccoon's jaw in an alder thicket. I sat down alongside the two children with me and encouraged them to find out who this was—with only the three teeth still intact in a piece of the animal's maxilla to guide them. The teeth told by their shape and placement what this animal ate. By a kind of visual extrapolation its size became clear. There were other clues, immediately present, which told, with what I could add of climate and terrain, how this animal lived, how its broken jaw came to be lying here. Raccoon, they surmised. And tiny tooth marks along the bone's broken edge told of a mouse's hunger for calcium.

We set the jaw back and went on.

If I had known more about raccoons, finer points of osteology, we might have guessed more: say, whether it was male or female. But what we deduced was all we needed. Hours later, the maxilla, lost behind us in the detritus of the forest floor, continued to effervesce. It was tied faintly to all else we spoke of that afternoon.

In speaking with children who might one day take a permanent interest in natural history—as writers, as scientists, as filmmakers, as anthropologists—I have sensed that an extrapolation from a single fragment of the whole is the most invigorating experience I can share with them. I think children know that nearly anyone can learn the names of things; the impression made on them at this level is fleeting. What takes a lifetime to learn, they comprehend, is the existence and substance of myriad relationships: it is these relationships, not the things themselves, that ultimately hold the human imagination.

The brightest children, it has often struck me, are fascinated by metaphor—with what is shown in the set of relationships bearing on the raccoon, for example, to lie quiet beyond the raccoon. In the end, you are trying to make clear to them that everything found at the edge of one's senses—the high note of the winter wren, the thick perfume of propolis that drifts downwind from spring willows, the brightness of wood chips scattered by beaver—that all this fits together. The indestructibility of these associations conveys a sense of permanence that nurtures the heart, that cripples one of the most insidious of human anxieties, the one that says, you do not belong here, you are unnecessary.

Whenever I walk with a child, I think how much I have seen disappear in my own life. What will there be for this person when he is my age? If he senses something ineffable in the landscape, will I know enough to encourage it?—to somehow show him that, yes, when people talk about violent death, spiritual exhilaration, compassion, futility, final causes, they are drawing on forty thousand years of human meditation on *this*—as we embrace Douglas firs, or stand by a river across whose undulating back we skip stones, or dig out a camas bulb, biting down into a taste so much wilder than last night's potatoes.

The most moving look I ever saw from a child in the woods was on a mud bar by the footprints of a heron. We were on our knees, making handprints beside the footprints. You could feel the creek vibrating in the silt and sand. The sun beat down heavily on our hair. Our shoes were soaking wet. The look said: I did not know until now that I needed someone much older to confirm this, the feeling I have of life here. I can now grow older, knowing it need never be lost.

The quickest door to open in the woods for a child is the one that leads to the smallest room, by knowing the name each thing is called. The door that leads to the cathedral is marked by a hesitancy to speak at all, rather to encourage by example a sharpness of the senses. If one speaks it should only be to say, as well as one can, how wonderfully all this fits together, to indicate what a long, fierce peace can derive from this knowledge.

Analyzing and Discussing the Text

1. How does the child's mind respond to the world?
2. According to Lopez, what is the best way for an adult to participate in a child's discovery of nature? Why?
3. What is it about the natural world that "ultimately hold[s] the human imagination"? Which aspects of the world are the most meaningful?
4. "[A] long, fierce peace can derive from this knowledge," writes Lopez. What knowledge? What kind of "peace" does he mean?

Experiencing and Writing About the World

1. Can you recall a time from your own childhood when you happened to pay especially close attention to some detail in the natural world? What was it about this detail that so captivated you? Explain your behavior on this occasion, either agreeing with Lopez's notion of the human imagination or proposing your own "psychology."

2. Have you recently accompanied children on an excursion in nature? If so, try to recollect and describe in detail their behavior. Explain your own thoughts and behavior as well. If you haven't ever taken children on a walk outside, try to find an opportunity to do so—offer to babysit, visit friends or relatives who have kids (or take your *own* kids out), or go observe at a school when the children are outdoors. Write about your observations.

3. Are children the only people who know how to pay close attention to the world? Find someone else, perhaps a scientist or an artist, who will allow you to tag along and watch during an outing. Write about the way this person responds to the world. You might supplement this experiential research by reading books on the theory of science or art, or perhaps on the psychology of perception and attention.

LESLIE MARMON SILKO

From Landscape, History, and the Pueblo Imagination

Leslie Marmon Silko (1948–   ) was born in Albuquerque, New Mexico, but grew up on the Laguna Pueblo Reservation. After the fourth grade, she was educated at Catholic schools in Albuquerque. In 1969 Silko graduated summa cum laude from the University of New Mexico with a B.A. in English, and that same year she published her first short story, called "The Man to Send Rain Clouds." After attending law school briefly, Silko left to devote her attention to writing. She spent two years teaching at Navajo Community College in Many Farms, Arizona, and then lived in Ketchikan, Alaska, while writing her first novel, *Ceremony*, which was published in 1977. Since then she has taught at the University of New Mexico and the University of Arizona. In 1983 Silko was awarded the prestigious and lucrative ($176,000) five-year MacArthur Fellowship, which enabled her to take an extended leave from her teaching position at the University of Arizona. Her other books include *Laguna Woman: Poems* (1974), *Storyteller* (1981), and most recently, *The Almanac of the Dead* (1991). In 1985 the volume *With the Delicacy and Strength of Lace: Letters Between Leslie Marmon Silko and James Wright* was published, revealing Silko's friendship with the poet, who died in 1980.

The following excerpts from the essay "Landscape, History, and the Pueblo Imagination" (1986) explain the traditional Pueblo way of viewing the natural world, not as outsiders but as part of the place: "So long as the human consciousness remains *within* the hills, canyons, cliffs, and the plants, clouds, and sky, the term *landscape,* as it entered the English language, is misleading. . . . Viewers are as much a part of the landscape as the boulders they stand on." Thus the Pueblo worldview differs radically from the western or European outlook, which emphasizes the division between the viewing self and the subject under scrutiny—Silko refers to this as "Cartesian dualism," alluding to the ideas of the seventeenth-century French philosopher René Descartes. The value of avoiding this dualistic perspective was, for the traditional Pueblo, not only spiritual, but practical. "Interrelationships in the Pueblo landscape are complex and fragile," writes Silko. "The unpredictability of the weather, the aridity and harshness of much of the terrain in the high plateau country explain in large part the relentless attention the ancient Pueblo people gave the sky and the earth around them. Survival depended upon harmony and cooperation not only among human beings, but among all things." The Pueblo people transmit their culture and their understanding of the land through stories—oral narratives—which function as survival strategies. In the following sections from "Landscape, History, and the Pueblo Imagination," Silko both discusses and demonstrates the inclusive Pueblo view of "landscape" and the use of stories as a means of integrating the human and the nonhuman.

Through the Stories We Hear Who We Are

All summer the people watch the west horizon, scanning the sky from south to north for rain clouds. Corn must have moisture at the time the tassels form. Otherwise pollination will be incomplete, and the ears will be stunted and shriveled. An inadequate harvest may bring disaster. Stories told at Hopi, Zuni, and at Acoma and Laguna describe drought and starvation as recently as 1900. Precipitation in west-central New Mexico averages fourteen inches annually. The western pueblos are located at altitudes over 5,600 feet above sea level, where winter

temperatures at night fall below freezing. Yet evidence of their presence in the high desert plateau country goes back ten thousand years.
The ancient Pueblo people not only survived in this environment, but
many years they thrived. In A.D. 1100 the people at Chaco Canyon had
built cities with apartment buildings of stone five stories high. Their
sophistication as sky-watchers was surpassed only by Mayan and Inca
astronomers. Yet this vast complex of knowledge and belief, amassed
for thousands of years, was never recorded in writing.

Instead, the ancient Pueblo people depended upon collective memory through successive generations to maintain and transmit an entire
culture, a world view complete with proven strategies for survival. The
oral narrative, or "story," became the medium in which the complex
of Pueblo knowledge and belief was maintained. Whatever the event
or the subject, the ancient people perceived the world and themselves
within that world as part of an ancient continuous story composed of
innumerable bundles of other stories.

The ancient Pueblo vision of the world was inclusive. The impulse
was to leave nothing out. Pueblo oral tradition necessarily embraced all
levels of human experience. Otherwise, the collective knowledge and
beliefs comprising ancient Pueblo culture would have been incomplete.
Thus stories about the Creation and Emergence of human beings and
animals into this World continue to be retold each year for four days and
four nights during the winter solstice. The "humma-hah" stories related
events from the time long ago when human beings were still able to
communicate with animals and other living things. But, beyond these
two preceding categories, the Pueblo oral tradition knew no boundaries.
Accounts of the appearance of the first Europeans in Pueblo country or
of the tragic encounters between Pueblo people and Apache raiders
were no more and no less important than stories about the biggest
mule deer ever taken or adulterous couples surprised in cornfields and
chicken coops. Whatever happened, the ancient people instinctively
sorted events and details into a loose narrative structure. Everything
became a story.

Traditionally everyone, from the youngest child to the oldest person, was expected to listen and to be able to recall or tell a portion, if
only a small detail, from a narrative account or story. Thus the remembering and retelling were a communal process. Even if a key figure, an
elder who knew much more than others, were to die unexpectedly, the
system would remain intact. Through the efforts of a great many people, the community was able to piece together valuable accounts and
crucial information that might otherwise have died with an individual.

Communal storytelling was a self-correcting process in which listeners were encouraged to speak up if they noted an important fact or
detail omitted. The people were happy to listen to two or three different
versions of the same event or the same humma-hah story. Even conflict-

ing versions of an incident were welcomed for the entertainment they provided. Defenders of each version might joke and tease one another, but seldom were there any direct confrontations. Implicit in the Pueblo oral tradition was the awareness that loyalties, grudges, and kinship must always influence the narrator's choices as she emphasizes to listeners this is the way *she* has always heard the story told. The ancient Pueblo people sought a communal truth, not an absolute. For them this truth lived somewhere within the web of differing versions, disputes over minor points, outright contradictions tangling with old feuds and village rivalries.

A dinner-table conversation, recalling a deer hunt forty years ago when the largest mule deer ever was taken, inevitably stimulates similar memories in listeners. But hunting stories were not merely after-dinner entertainment. These accounts contained information of critical importance about behavior and migration patterns of mule deer. Hunting stories carefully described key landmarks and locations of fresh water. Thus a deer-hunt story might also serve as a "map." Lost travelers, and lost piñon-nut gatherers, have been saved by sighting a rock formation they recognize only because they once heard a hunting story describing this rock formation.

The importance of cliff formations and water holes does not end with hunting stories. As offspring of the Mother Earth, the ancient Pueblo people could not conceive of themselves within a specific landscape. Location, or "place," nearly always plays a central role in the Pueblo oral narratives. Indeed, stories are most frequently recalled as people are passing by a specific geographical feature or the exact place where a story takes place. The precise date of the incident often is less important than the place or location of the happening. "Long, long ago," "a long time ago," "not too long ago," and "recently" are usually how stories are classified in terms of time. But the places where the stories occur are precisely located, and prominent geographical details recalled, even if the landscape is well-known to listeners. Often because the turning point in the narrative involved a peculiarity or special quality of a rock or tree or plant found only at that place. Thus, in the case of many of the Pueblo narratives, it is impossible to determine which came first: the incident or the geographical feature which begs to be brought alive in a story that features some unusual aspect of this location.

There is a giant sandstone boulder about a mile north of Old Laguna, on the road to Paguate. It is ten feet tall and twenty feet in circumference. When I was a child, and we would pass this boulder driving to Paguate village, someone usually made reference to the story about Kochininako, Yellow Woman, and the Estrucuyo, a monstrous giant who nearly ate her. The Twin Hero Brothers saved Kochininako, who had been out hunting rabbits to take home to feed her mother and sisters. The Hero Brothers had heard her cries just in time. The Estrucuyo had cornered her in a cave too small to fit its monstrous head. Kochininako had already thrown to the Estrucuyo all her rabbits, as well as her moccasins and most of her clothing. Still the creature had not been satisfied. After killing the Estrucuyo with their bows and arrows, the Twin Hero Brothers slit open the Estrucuyo and cut out its heart. They threw the heart as far as they could. The monster's heart landed there, beside the old trail to Paguate village, where the sandstone boulder rests now.

It may be argued that the existence of the boulder precipitated the creation of a story to explain it. But sandstone boulders and sandstone formations of strange shapes abound in the Laguna Pueblo area. Yet most of them do not have stories. Often the crucial element in a narrative is the terrain—some specific detail of the setting.

A high dark mesa rises dramatically from a grassy plain fifteen miles southeast of Laguna, in an area known as Swanee. On the grassy plain one hundred and forty years ago, my great-grandmother's uncle and his brother-in-law were grazing their herd of sheep. Because visibility on the plain extends for over twenty miles, it wasn't until the two sheep-herders came near the high dark mesa that the Apaches were able to stalk them. Using the mesa to obscure their approach, the raiders swept around from both ends of the mesa. My great-grandmother's relatives were killed, and the herd lost. The high dark mesa played a critical role: the mesa had compromised the safety which the openness of the plains had seemed to assure. Pueblo and Apache alike relied upon the terrain, the very earth herself, to give them protection and aid. Human activities or needs were maneuvered to fit the existing surroundings and conditions. I imagine the last afternoon of my distant ancestors as warm and sunny for late September. They might have been traveling slowly, bringing the sheep closer to Laguna in preparation for the approach of colder weather. The grass was tall and only beginning to change from green to a yellow which matched the late-afternoon sun shining off it. There might have been comfort in the warmth and the sight of the sheep fattening on good pasture which lulled my ancestors into their fatal inattention. They might have had a rifle whereas the Apaches had only bows and arrows. But there would have been four or five Apache riders, and the surprise attack would have canceled any advantage the rifles gave them.

Survival in any landscape comes down to making the best use of all available resources. On that particular September afternoon, the raiders made better use of the Swanee terrain than my poor ancestors did. Thus the high dark mesa and the story of the two lost Laguna herders became inextricably linked. The memory of them and their story resides in part with the high black mesa. For as long as the mesa stands, people within the family and clan will be reminded of the story of that afternoon long ago. Thus the continuity and accuracy of the oral narratives are reinforced by the landscape—and the Pueblo interpretation of that landscape is *maintained.*

The Migration Story: An Interior Journey

The Laguna Pueblo migration stories refer to specific places—mesas, springs, or cottonwood trees—not only locations which can be visited still, but also locations which lie directly on the state highway route linking Paguate village with Laguna village. In traveling this road as a child with older Laguna people I first heard a few of the stories from that much larger body of stories linked with the Emergence and Migration.[1] It may be coincidental that Laguna people continue to follow the same route which, according to the Migration story, the ancestors followed south from the Emergence Place. It may be that the route is merely the shortest and best route for car, horse, or foot traffic between Laguna and Paguate villages. But if the stories about boulders, springs, and hills are actually remnants from a ritual that retraces the creation and emergence of the Laguna Pueblo people as a culture, as the people they became, then continued use of that route creates a unique relationship between the ritual-mythic world and the actual, everyday world. A journey from Paguate to Laguna down the long incline of Paguate Hill retraces the original journey from the Emergence Place, which is located slightly north of the Paguate village. Thus the landscape between Paguate and Laguna takes on a deeper significance: the landscape resonates the spiritual or mythic dimension of the Pueblo world even today.

Although each Pueblo culture designates a specific Emergence Place—usually a small natural spring edged with mossy sandstone and full of cattails and wild watercress—it is clear that they do not agree on any single location or natural spring as the one and only true Emergence Place. Each Pueblo group recounts its own stories about Creation, Emergence, and Migration, although they all believe that all human beings, with all the animals and plants, emerged at the same place and at the same time.[2]

Natural springs are crucial sources of water for all life in the high desert plateau country. So the small spring near Paguate village is literally the source and continuance of life for the people in the area. The spring also functions on a spiritual level, recalling the original Emergence Place and linking the people and the spring water to all other people and to that moment when the Pueblo people became aware

[1]The Emergence—All the human beings, animals, and life which had been created emerged from the four worlds below when the earth became habitable.
The Migration—The Pueblo people emerged into the Fifth World, but they had already been warned they would have to travel and search before they found the place they were meant to live.—Author's note.
[2]Creation—Tse'itsi'nako, Thought Woman, the Spider, thought about it, and everything she thought came into being. First she thought of three sisters for herself, and they helped her think of the rest of the Universe, including the Fifth World and the four worlds below. The Fifth World is the world we are living in today. There are four previous worlds below this world.—Author's note.

of themselves as they are even now. The Emergence was an emergence into a precise cultural identity. Thus the Pueblo stories about the Emergence and Migration are not to be taken as literally as the anthropologists might wish. Prominent geographical features and landmarks which are mentioned in the narratives exist for ritual purposes, not because the Laguna people actually journeyed south for hundreds of years from Chaco Canyon or Mesa Verde, as the archaeologists say, or eight miles from the site of the natural springs at Paguate to the sandstone hilltop at Laguna.

The eight miles, marked with boulders, mesas, springs, and river crossings, are actually a ritual circuit or path which marks the interior journey the Laguna people made: a journey of awareness and imagination in which they emerged from being within the earth and from everything included in earth to the culture and people they became, differentiating themselves for the first time from all that had surrounded them, always aware that interior distances cannot be reckoned in physical miles or in calendar years.

The narratives linked with prominent features of the landscape between Paguate and Laguna delineate the complexities of the relationship which human beings must maintain with the surrounding natural world if they hope to survive in this place. Thus the journey was an interior process of the imagination, a growing awareness that being human is somehow different from all other life—animal, plant, and inanimate. Yet we are all from the same source: the awareness never deteriorated into Cartesian duality, cutting off the human from the natural world.

The people found the opening into the Fifth World too small to allow them or any of the animals to escape. They had sent a fly out through the small hole to tell them if it was the world which the Mother Creator had promised. It was, but there was the problem of getting out. The antelope tried to butt the opening to enlarge it, but the antelope enlarged it only a little. It was necessary for the badger with her long claws to assist the antelope, and at last the opening was enlarged enough so that all the people and animals were able to emerge up into the Fifth World. The human beings could not have emerged without the aid of antelope and badger. The human beings depended upon the aid and charity of the animals. Only through interdependence could the human beings survive. Families belonged to clans, and it was by clan that the human being joined with the animal and plant world. Life on the high arid plateau became viable when the human beings were able to imagine themselves as sisters and brothers to the badger, antelope, clay, yucca, and sun. Not until they could find a viable relationship to the terrain, the landscape they found themselves in, could they *emerge*. Only at the moment the requisite balance between human and *other* was realized could the Pueblo people become a culture, a distinct group whose population and survival remained stable despite the vicissitudes of climate and terrain.

Landscape thus has similarities with dreams. Both have the power to seize terrifying feelings and deep instincts and translate them into images—visual, aural, tactile—into the concrete where human beings may more readily confront and channel the terrifying instincts or powerful emotions into rituals and narratives which reassure the individual while reaffirming cherished values of the group. The identity of the individual as a part of the group and the greater Whole is strengthened, and the terror of facing the world alone is extinguished.

Even now, the people at Laguna Pueblo spend the greater portion of social occasions recounting recent incidents or events which have occurred in the Laguna area. Nearly always, the discussion will precipitate the retelling of older stories about similar incidents or other stories connected with a specific place. The stories often contain disturbing or provocative material, but are nonetheless told in the presence of children and women. The effect of these inter-family or inter-clan exchanges is the reassurance for each person that she or he will never be separated or apart from the clan, no matter what might happen. Neither the worst blunders or disasters nor the greatest financial prosperity and joy will ever be permitted to isolate anyone from the rest of the group. In the ancient times, cohesiveness was all that stood between extinction and survival, and, while the individual certainly was recognized, it was always as an individual simultaneously bonded to family and clan by a complex bundle of custom and ritual. You are never the first to suffer a grave loss or profound humiliation. You are never the first, and you understand that you will probably not be the last to commit or be victimized by a repugnant act. Your family and clan are able to go on at length about others now passed on, others older or more experienced than you who suffered similar losses.

The wide deep arroyo near the Kings Bar (located across the reservation borderline) has over the years claimed many vehicles. A few years ago, when a Viet Nam veteran's new red Volkswagen rolled backwards into the arroyo while he was inside buying a six-pack of beer, the story of his loss joined the lively and large collection of stories already connected with that big arroyo. I do not know whether the Viet Nam veteran was consoled when he was told the stories about the other cars claimed by the ravenous arroyo. All his savings of combat pay had gone for the red Volkswagen. But this man could not have felt any worse than the man who, some years before, had left his children and mother-in-law in his station wagon with the engine running. When he came out of the liquor store his station wagon was gone. He found it and its passengers upside down in the big arroyo. Broken bones, cuts and bruises, and a total wreck of the car. The big arroyo has a wide mouth. Its existence needs no explanation. People in the area regard the arroyo much as they might regard a living being, which has a certain character and personality. I seldom drive past that wide deep arroyo without feeling a familiarity with and even a strange affection for this arroyo. Because as treacherous as it may be, the arroyo maintains a strong connection between human beings and the earth. The arroyo demands from us the caution and attention that constitute respect. It is this sort of respect the old believers have in mind when they tell us we must respect and love the earth.

Hopi Pueblo elders have said that the austere and, to some eyes, barren plains and hills surrounding their mesa-top villages actually help to nurture the spirituality of the Hopi *way*. The Hopi elders say the Hopi people might have settled in locations far more lush where daily life would not have been so grueling. But there on the high silent sandstone mesas that overlook the sandy arid expanses stretching to all horizons, the Hopi elders say the Hopi people must "live by their prayers" if they are to survive. The Hopi way cherishes the intangible: the riches realized from interaction and interrelationships with all beings above all else. Great abundances of material things, even food, the Hopi elders believe, tend to lure human attention away from what is most valuable and important. The views of the Hopi elders are not much different from those elders in all the Pueblos.

The bare vastness of the Hopi landscape emphasizes the visual impact of every plant, every rock, every arroyo. Nothing is over-looked or taken for granted. Each ant, each lizard, each lark is imbued with great value simply because the creature is there, simply because the creature is alive in a place where any life at all is precious. Stand on the mesa edge at Walpai and look west over the bare distances toward the pale blue outlines of the San Francisco peaks where the ka'tsina spirits reside. So little lies between you and the sky. So little lies between you and the earth. One look and you know that simply to survive is a great triumph, that every possible resource is needed, every possible ally—even the most humble insect or reptile. You realize you will be speaking with all of them if you intend to last out the year. Thus it is that the Hopi elders are grateful to the landscape for aiding them in their quest as spiritual people.

Analyzing and Discussing the Text

1. What, for the traditional Pueblo people, is the connection between history (stories) and the landscape? How do these stories help the people survive?
2. Why did the communal storytellers tolerate multiple versions of the same stories? What is the difference between a "communal truth" and an "absolute truth"?

3. What kinds of details does Silko include in her narrative of the Apache raid on Pueblo sheepherders? Be specific. How does such information demonstrate the value of knowing one's local landscape?

4. Even if the Pueblo people are aware of the difference between human and other life, Silko argues, "the awareness never deteriorate[s] into Cartesian duality, cutting off the human from the natural world." Explain what this means and why, for the Pueblo, it is important. Is such a mental state irrelevant to modern, urban existence?

5. Explain Silko's point that "Landscape . . . has similarities with dreams." How does this statement support the idea that the human consciousness is part of the landscape?

Experiencing and Writing About the World

1. Because the route between Paguate and Laguna villages "retraces the original journey from the Emergence Place," says Silko, "the landscape resonates the spiritual or mythic dimension of the Pueblo world even today." How does it feel to be in a landscape that has a powerful "spiritual or mythic" dimension? Religious Jews and Christians often feel this way then they visit Israel, where many features of the landscape are associated with specific biblical stories. If you have ever spent time in a place that had profound spiritual meaning for you, write a paper about this experience and attempt, like Silko, to analyze and generalize about the state of mind it produced in you.

2. Tell a story about your own typical environment, urban or not, in which you attempt to create a "map" for your readers. Reread Silko's discussion of Pueblo hunting stories; give your own story a similar practical value (survival information!) by using specific details from your surroundings.

3. Write an analytical essay in which you compare the worldview (the relationship between the human mind and the natural world) described in Silko's essay to the perspectives demonstrated in such essays as David Black's "Walking the Cape" and John Daniel's "The Impoverishment of Sightseeing." Use the notion of "Cartesian dualism" (the split between the mind and the world) as a way of distinguishing between the authors' views. Attempt to analyze the literary devices the authors use in depicting the particular habits of their own minds. Can you find other essays in this anthology that present interesting versions of dualism or its opposite, "monism"?

GARY SOTO

Blue

Gary Soto (1952–   ), who teaches Chicano studies and English at the University of California at Berkeley, was born and raised in Fresno, in the inland agricultural part of California. Soto studied poetry with Philip Levine at Cal State–Fresno, where he earned his B.A. in 1974; two years later he completed his M.F.A. at the University of California–Irvine. He began college intending to major in geography, but found himself pulled toward literature after discovering Donald Allen's anthology, called *The New American Poetry,* in the library; "This is terrific," he recalls saying to himself, "I'd like to do something like this." Since graduate school Soto has published six poetry collections, including *The Elements of San Joaquin* (1977), *The Tale of Sunlight* (1978), and *Who Will Know Us, New Poems* (1990). *Living up the Street,* a volume of prose recollections about his childhood in Fresno, received the American Book Award in 1985. Soto's third and most recent collection of essays, *Lesser Evils: Ten Quartets,* appeared in 1988. In 1990 he published his first volume of fiction, entitled *Baseball in April and Other Stories.*

In both his poetry and his prose, Soto demonstrates an important shift in Chicano literature "toward a more personal, less politically motivated" perspective, as the critic Juan Bruce-Novoa put it. Another scholar, Raymund Paredes, has observed with regard to the early essay collections that "it is a measure of Soto's skill that he so effectively invigorates and sharpens our understanding of the commonplace"; this is an achievement Soto has in common with many of the other writers in this anthology, beginning with Thoreau. A year after *Living up the Street* came out, Soto published *Small Faces,* more essays about, for the most part, his own childhood. In the final essay of *Small Faces,* a piece called "Saying Things," Soto reflects on what he contributes to the world, the world of environmental crises and human cruelty, through his work as a writer. "This hand that speaks to a pencil, then a typewriter, can go on and on," he writes. "I can say things that may solve a fingernail of pain—and isn't that a start?" The following essay, also from this 1986 collection, considers the "fingernail of pain" that may result when people lose contact with something as simple as the blueness of the sky. Soto seeks in this narrative both an understanding of the problem and the solace of reconstructed memories—and he does this by "saying things."

How much sky do we need? If we're going to remain whole, healthy in mind, we need to walk, dream, lie inquisitively under the sky each day, or so writes a researcher who thinks neurosis arises from our disconnection from the sky. Look at the major cities—say New York or San Francisco—where the sky is often eclipsed by buildings, crossed up with wires, slivered and cut into pieces by bridges and towers, so that we can never look up to an unbroken sky. We get portions, flimsy postcards of blue, from where we sit at work or slouch at home. In such cities neurosis is prevalent, more visible daily than in places where the sky is not blocked out but fills the day and rains its complete, unfractured blue. Arizona. Montana. Canada. Those are the places. Australia. Africa. I only half-remember the places and don't recall how the researcher came to study this phenomenon, but I believed him.

When I was a kid of ten or so, a time when I could wander as I pleased, the sky seemed to show up more often, especially when my friend Jackie and I sat in fruit trees: orange, apricot, plum, and peach. We walked up alleys until we found one heavy with fruit half-guarded behind a wire fence and leaped so carelessly that sometimes we fell and got up with dust powdered on our eyelashes. We climbed trees and ate like birds, pecking holes in fruit that we dropped unfinished to the ground. We liked plums the best—the juice splashed against the insides of our cheeks and the roofs of our mouths. It excited us. When we smiled, our teeth were red and dripping.

After eating our fill we stayed in the trees to talk. And about what? Girls we were in love with, God, family, mean brothers on bicycles, school fights that did no one any good. As we spoke we seldom looked at one another. Instead, we looked skyward where, if it were spring, an occasional cloud chugged by, sloshing a belly full of rain, and if it were summer, the blue was the color of a crayon. I remember that well. I also remember Jackie and the beatings his father gave him, his body balled up under a bed and screaming *Daddy No!* I said these things too, and almost cried. Because we confided in one another with our eyes on the sky, we felt less troubled when we finally did drop to the ground and went back to our homes where, however slowly, it would begin again.

I remember the Fresno sky after a rain and how puddles flashed like knives when I walked past on my way to nowhere in particular, just looking about as I walked from my street into an alley, happy that I was outside and things were as clear as they were going to get in my young life. I walked toward Jackie's house, but instead of calling him I sneaked into his backyard, tore a couple of pomegranates from his tree, and raced down the alley to another friend's house. When I called and no one came out, I climbed onto his pigeon coop and up onto the roof of his garage. There I tore open a pomegranate whose juice ran like fingers of blood down my sleeve to my elbows. While I ate I looked around until the sky seemed more beautiful than I remembered: the clouds were piled up, like fat Chinese faces and, from where I sat, the Sierras in the east were tipped white with snow and jagged like a child's scribbling. It was the first time I had seen them, snow or no snow, with so much blue behind them.

That was when I was ten. Now that I am so much older, the possibility of climbing a tree to eat fruit with a friend is almost nonexistent. How would I explain myself if someone, neighbor or wife, looked up among the ladders of leafy branches and saw a pant leg, a shirt, and finally a face, which would be mine? And what friends would climb for fruit they could enjoy on the ground?

But it's not a tree you need or a friend. It's the sky and the feeling that you're connected, that things are circular, beginning with the sky and all it holds: sun, moon, stars, wind, birds that come and go with the seasons.

I believe this more and more. Lying on a blanket at Tilden Park, I have listened to the wind in the trees recalling a childhood day, a friend, my wife, my daughter with clever tricks up her sleeve. I've laid half in shade, half in sun, and recalled all that I've enjoyed and, on occasion, have tried to clear my mind so that the sky is my only thought, its brightness like no other. When I close my eyes, the blue stays. When I listen to the wind, the blue stays. And a little green that makes me think of the sea.

Analyzing and Discussing the Text

1. Soto refers to a researcher who thinks that urban neurosis results "from our disconnection from the sky." Do you believe this research? If you happen to come from a place where it's cloudy much of the time, like the Pacific Northwest, do you still agree with this research? Does gray sky have the same healthy effect as blue sky?
2. Does Soto portray the ten-year-olds believably? What is most effective about his characterizations?
3. Try to explain why Soto, as a child, once stole pomegranates from the tree in Jackie's yard. Why did the sky seem even more beautiful as he ate the illicit fruit?
4. Does Soto suggest at the end of his essay that the sky helps adults, too? Is his own essay "scientific"? What kinds of "data" and language does he rely on to make his point?

Experiencing and Writing About the World

1. Is the sky the only feature of the natural world that people need, that *you* need, in order to feel healthy or at peace? Select a natural phenomenon—trees, wind, the moon, for instance—and write your own essay asserting the importance of this particular phenomenon to the human mind. Make this an argumentative paper. If you can find any formal research to back up your ideas (check recent studies in environmental psychology), so much the better. Otherwise, rely on experiential evidence, logical explanations, and vivid imagery to make your point.

2. Try to recall your own feelings about the natural world at the age of ten. Do any particular images or incidents come to mind? Adventures with friends? Encounters with siblings or parents? Begin with these memories, then proceed to develop a more general thesis about the influence of nature on the human mind. You don't have to say that nature is always wholesome and benign. If your early experiences were bad ones (a tornado, a boating accident, an earthquake), feel free to develop those feelings.

3. Select several readings from this anthology and write a comparative essay that analyzes the various ways in which the authors think and write about the sky. In addition to Soto's essay, consider such pieces as John Hay's "A Season for Swallows," Chet Raymo's "The Blandishments of Color," Scott Russell Sanders's "Cloud Crossing," Ursula Le Guin's "Riding Shotgun," William Least Heat-Moon's "Atop the Mound," Georgia O'Keeffe's "Letter to Anita Pollitzer," and Susan Mitchell's "Dreaming in Public: A Provincetown Memoir" (choose two or three from among these). Do all of these writers respond to the sky in wholly aesthetic ways? What other kinds of intellectual responses (besides the appreciation of beauty) do you notice in these essays? How do their descriptive techniques achieve different effects on you? Does the concentrated reading of so much "sky writing" change the way *you* look at an ordinary sky?

RANDALL KENAN

From **A Visitation of Spirits**

Although born in New York City, Randall Kenan (1963–   ) moved
to North Carolina before he was a month old. Kenan grew up in Chin-
quapin, a town of "five hundred souls" about forty-five miles from
Wilmington, and went to school in Duplin County before attending the
University of North Carolina at Chapel Hill, where he majored in English (earning honors in creative writing) and physics. Immediately after
college, Kenan returned to New York to seek a career in the publishing
business; he began as an "office boy in waiting" at Random House,
later became a receptionist, and after five years was an assistant editor
at Alfred A. Knopf. In the fall of 1989, the year his novel A *Visitation of
Spirits* was published, Kenan left Knopf to begin teaching fiction writing
at Sarah Lawrence College in Bronxville, New York. Since then, in addition to teaching at Sarah Lawrence, he has taught writing at Columbia
University and a course called "The City in Literature" at Vassar College. His second book, a collection of short fiction called *Let the Dead
Bury Their Dead*, appeared in 1992. He is currently completing a book
of interviews with black people from all around North America (some
thirty states and four Canadian provinces), trying to discover what it
means to be black in present-day America.

Kenan lists an eclectic group of writers as influences on his own
work, including Zora Neale Hurston, Cormac McCarthy, Edward Hoagland, and Barry Lopez. "The South is a place of myth and mystery," says
Kenan, and in his own writing, such as the following excerpt from the
beginning of A *Visitation of Spirits,* he attempts to represent the "amorphous" southern way of seeing nature, allowing "the preternatural, the
supernatural, and the natural" to coexist. In this piece of fiction, we can
see Kenan's inclination toward "magical realism" as his character imagines himself transforming from human to bird. The character Horace also
demonstrates Kenan's belief that people in the South, no matter how urban their surroundings may seem, "aren't far from the land," from the
mysterious forces of the fields and gardens and woods.

April 29, 1984
11:30 A.M.

. . . What to become?

At first Horace was sure he would turn himself into a rabbit. But
then, no. Though they were swift as pebbles skipping across a pond,

they were vulnerable, liable to be snatched up in a fox's jaws or a hawk's talons. Squirrels fell too easily into traps. And though mice and wood rats had a magical smallness, in the end they were much smaller than he wished to be. Snakes' heads were too easily crushed, and he didn't like the idea of his entire body slithering across all those twigs and feces and spit. Dogs lacked the physical grace he needed. More than anything else, he wanted to have grace. If he was going to the trouble of transforming himself, he might as well get exactly that. Butterflies were too frail, victims to wind. Cats had a physical freedom he loved to watch, the svelte, smooth, sliding motion of the great cats of Africa, but he could not see transforming himself into anything that would not fit the swampy woodlands of southeastern North Carolina. He had to stay here.

No, truth to tell, what he wanted more than anything else, he now realized, was to fly. A bird. He had known before, but he felt the need to sit down and ponder the possibilities. A ritual of choice, to make it real. A bird.

With that thought he rose, his stomach churning with excitement. A bird. Now to select the type. The species. The genus. He knew the very book to use in the school library; he knew the shelf, and could see the book there in its exact placement, now, slightly askew between a volume on birdfeeders no one ever moved and a treatise on egg collecting; he could see the exact angle at which it would be resting. Hadn't the librarian, Mrs. Stokes, always teased him that he knew the library better than she ever would? And wasn't she right?

He was sitting on the wall at the far end of the school campus, on the other side of the football field, beyond the gymnasium, beyond the main school building. He had wanted to be alone, to think undistracted. But now he was buoyed by the realization that he knew how he would spend the rest of his appointed time on this earth. Not as a tortured human, but as a bird free to swoop and dive, to dip and swerve over the cornfields and tobacco patches he had slaved in for what already seemed decades to his sixteen years. No longer would he be bound by human laws and human rules that he had constantly tripped over and frowned at. Now was his chance, for he had stumbled upon a passage by an ancient mystic, a monk, a man of God, and had found his salvation. It was so simple he wondered why no one had discovered it before. Yet how would anyone know? Suddenly poor old Jeremiah or poor old Julia disappears. Everybody's distraught; everybody worries. They search. They wait. Finally the missing person is declared dead. And the silly folk go on about their business and don't realize that old Julia turned herself into an eel and went to the bottom of the deep blue sea to see what she could see. There are no moral laws that say: You must remain human. And he would not.

His morning break was over. The other students were hustling back to third period. But he decided to skip. What did it matter? In a few days he would be transformed into a creature of the air. He could soar by his physics class and listen to Mrs. Hedgeson deliver her monotone lecture about electrons; he could perch on the ledge and watch the biology students dissect pickled frogs; hear the Spanish class tripping over their tongues; glide over the school band as they practiced their awkward maneuvers on the football field, squawking their gleaming instruments. All unfettered, unbound, and free.

As he walked down the hall, he suddenly realized he had no hall pass and that the vice-principal might walk by and demand it. But no. He was Horace Thomas Cross, the Great Black Hope, as his friend John Anthony had called him. The Straight-A Kid. Or once, at least. Where most students would be pulled aside and severely reprimanded, he could walk unquestioned. In his mind he could see his Cousin Ann smiling her cinnamon smile and hear her say in her small, raspy voice: But don't you know it yet, Horace? You the Chosen Nigger.

The library was empty except for old Mrs. Stokes, who stood by the card catalogue and smiled at him, nodding knowingly. If she only realized—her gray hair would turn white. He walked straight to the exact aisle, the exact shelf, selected the exact book, and took it to a table in the back of the library, even though he was the only other person in that large room. He sat by a window overlooking the long, sloping lawn, spring green, that dipped into the pine-filled woods.

It was a huge book. White cloth with elegant gold lettering: *Encyclopedia of North American Birds,* a book he had known since elementary school, with its crisp photographs and neat diagrams and its definitions upon definitions upon definitions. Because it was a reference book he couldn't check it out, so for long hours he would sit and read about migratory paths, the use of tail feathers, the gestation periods of eggs. . . .

As he opened the book he felt the blood rush to his head, and the first color plates cranked up his imagination like a locomotive: gulls, cranes, owls, storks, turkeys, eagles. He flipped through the book, faster and faster. Which bird? Sparrow, wren, jay. No, *larger.* Mallard, grouse, pheasant. *Larger.* Goose, swan, cormorant. *Larger.* Egret, heron, condor. Pages flipped; his heart beat faster; his mind grew fuzzy with possibilities. Raven, rook, blackbird. Crow . . .

He slammed the book shut, realizing that he had been riffling through the pages like a madman. Mrs. Stokes looked up quickly, startled, then gave him that brief, knowing smile.

He closed his eyes and thought of the only way he could make his decision. He thought about the land: the soybean fields surrounding his grandfather's house, the woods that surrounded the fields, the tall, massive long-leaf pines. He thought of the miles and miles of highways, asphalt poured over mule trails that etched themselves into the North Carolina landscape, onto the beach, sandy white, the sea, a murky churning, the foam, spray, white, the smell of fish and rotting wood.

He thought of winters, the floor of the woods a carpet of dry leaves, brown-and-black patchwork carpet. He thought of the sky, not a blue picture-book sky with a few thin clouds, but a storm sky, black and mean, full of wind and hate, God's wrath, thunder, pelting rain. He thought of houses, new and old, brick and wood, high and low, roofs mildewed and black, chimneys, lightning rods, TV antennas. He was trying to think like a bird, *the* bird, the only bird he could become. And when he saw a rabbit, dashing, darting through a field of brown rye grass, and when he saw talons sink into the soft brown fur, he knew.

But he had known before, had realized when he stumbled across the pact the old monk had made with the demon in the book, that if he were to transform himself, irrevocably, unconditionally, he would choose a red-tailed hawk. He opened the book to the hawk family—pausing at the eagle, but knowing that was too corny, too noticeable, not indigenous to North Carolina—and flipped to the picture of his future self. He could not help but smile. The creature sat perched on a fence post, its wings brought up about its neck, its eyes murderous. Many times he had admired the strong flight of the bird, the way it would circle the field like a buzzard, but not like a buzzard, since the rat or the rabbit or the coon it was after was not dead—yet. Talons would clutch the thrashing critter tighter than a vise, its little heart would beat in sixteenth notes, excited even more by the flapping wings that beat the air like hammers and blocked the sun like Armageddon. Then the piercing of the neck, the rush of hot, sticky blood. The taste of red flesh. He felt a touch of empathy for the small mammal, its tail caught in the violent twitching of death thralls, but he was still thrilled.

He turned and looked to the woods and sighed, the sigh of an old man, of resigned resolve and inevitable conclusion. A sigh too old for a sixteen-year-old boy. He rose and replaced the book. The bell rang, signaling the end of third period. He thought of never walking down this aisle and past that shelf again; he would read none of these volumes again. He allowed himself to swell up. Not with sadness, but with pride. He had found the escape route, of which they were all ignorant. Mrs. Stokes once again gave her knowing nod. He winked at her and did not look back.

Analyzing and Discussing the Text

1. This passage of Kenan's novel begins *in medias res*—"in the middle of things." How does this affect your response to Horace's way of thinking? Do you understand what's going on in his mind or do you need more explicit explanation in the text?

2. What seems to be Horace's attitude toward the natural world? Find specific passages in the text that display his attitudes.
3. Why does Horace need "an escape route"? How does his imagined transformation constitute a legitimate escape?
4. How does Kenan's prose style depict the character's inner thoughts? Look for passages that seem particularly internalized and discuss precise aspects of the narrative language (such as sentence structure, sensory images, complexity or simplicity of diction).

Experiencing and Writing About the World

1. Write your own narrative (fictional or nonfictional) on the subject of transmutation from the human to the nonhuman. Try to justify this change without allowing your prose to become ploddingly abstract. Attempt to show in this narrative what it would be like to exist as something nonhuman—a bird, a tree, a rock, a raccoon. Choose an animal or another natural object that especially appeals to you.
2. Compare Horace's imagined transformation into a red-tailed hawk with Sue Hubbell's idea of transformation in "Becoming Feral." Write a short analytical essay in which you consider how the two authors, Kenan and Hubbell, present the relationship between the human and the nonhuman.
3. Write an argumentative essay in which you analyze the virtues and deficiencies of nature as a realm of physical and/or psychological escape. Consider Edward Abbey's notion that someone "could be a lover and a defender of wilderness without ever leaving the boundaries of asphalt, powerlines, and right-angled surfaces" (*Desert Solitaire*). You might search for additional environmental literature and studies in environmental psychology to back up your own theories about the escape value of nature. How does Kenan's story contribute to your understanding of this issue?

JOHN DANIEL

The Impoverishment of Sightseeing

For biographical information, see the headnote for "Some Mortal Speculations" in Part One, Chapter Two.

In his 1991 article "Nature as Picture/Nature as Milieu," Paul T. Bryant traces the historical roots of the picturesque in American literature and argues that "by rendering a scene static and stepping back to see it objectively, we have become separated from it"; however, Bryant observes that in "the most informed nature writing" the authors "put themselves into the picture and the picture becomes a scene, with action and change and interplay of humans with nature." Along these same lines, John Daniel criticizes both the "cult of utility" and the "cult of beauty," asserting in the following essay that "neither [view] recognizes nature as a living system of which our human lives are part, on which our lives and all lives depend, and which places strict limits upon us even as it sustains us." Rather than allowing ourselves to pull back even further from the natural world, Daniel urges us to submit ourselves to the "ancient influences" of nature, to regain the "primordial alertness" that comes from direct exposure to wild places and wildlife, so as to overcome "the impoverishment of sightseeing" and become active participants in the world. Daniel's argument certainly has ecological implications, for how can we casually neglect a biotic system to which we understand ourselves to be integrally connected? And yet Daniel's principal goal in this essay seems to be the enrichment of the individual person's experience.

When I was a boy my family had a weekend cabin on the Blue Ridge of northern Virginia, and it was on one of my hikes in the woods nearby that I experienced a new standard of fear. I was walking alone on a sunny day when I came to a slope of small gray boulders, bare of vegetation. I had skirted this boulder patch on previous rambles, and wondered about it, and now I decided to cross it. As I hopped from rock to rock, a quick buzz from below froze me. *Cicada,* I thought hopefully, but I knew what it was. I jumped to another rock and another buzz sounded, then another. The whole bright strew of boulders seemed to be buzzing around me, beneath me, and one more step, I was sure, would bring lightning fangs. I tried to quiet my tremoring legs, to stand as still and light and thin as it was possible to stand. I'm sure I prayed—prayer was my habit in those days when things weren't going well. I stood for probably half an hour, long after the buzzes had stopped. Finally I boosted my courage, stepped to the very crown of the next rock, and accompanied by sporadic buzzes, danced out of the boulder field with the nimbleness of dread.

I thought of that childhood ordeal when I visited Yosemite Valley recently for the first time in over a decade. In my mid-twenties I knew the Valley as a rock climber of high enthusiasm and modest ability. Now, at thirty-seven, I was returning with my wife and mother, neither of whom had seen Yosemite before. I wanted to show them the exhilarating playground I had known. Because my mother wasn't a strong walker, we decided to take our first long look from one of those buses that loop around the Valley floor. With its solid bank of windows curving up over our heads, we thought the bus would give us many good views, and it did. But how disappointing those views were, how unaccountably dull. The familiar rock faces all were there, as sheer and massive as ever, but *merely* there. As the bus trundled along they paraded through the frame of my window, one after another, as I tried hard to feel excited.

What I saw was dull, I realized after a while, because I was walking the boulder field without the snakes. The places that had once been alive to me, imbued with my zeal and fears, now were reduced to plain visual images, seen for the sake of seeing, *scenes* in the bus window. My wife and mother, viewing Glacier Point and Half Dome for the first time, were more satisfied with what they saw. But I sensed no real enthusiasm from them as the sunny granite shifted in our window view, nor from the other passengers, most of whom were clearly new to the Valley. "Look at that," the man in front of us kept murmuring, but listlessly, like a recorded message. "Isn't that a sight. Isn't that a sight."

When I climbed those rocks—only a few hundred feet up, most of them—they were not sights but presences. As I focused on cracks and tiny nubbins in front of my face, bright granite expanse was always flaring in the periphery of my vision—all the more vivid, all the more present, for being only obliquely seen. And just as vivid and present was what I couldn't yet see, the challenges that lay hidden where the route disappeared above an overhang or around a corner. It was that perpetual unknown that buzzed me with scary excitement, like rattlesnakes hidden beneath boulders—that was what I climbed after, more beautiful than anything I saw with my eyes.

As I looked out from a belay ledge after a hard pitch, the far Valley wall wavered and swam with squiggly spots, nothing solid about it, then settled in my vision not merely to stone but to an embodiment of spirit. Having made a pitch I wasn't sure I could make, I was suffused with a sense of body and mind doing exactly what they were meant to do, blended perfectly in their most rightful act. And what was that arched and pinnacled rising of granite I gazed at, shining through a gulf of air, but the world's own most perfect and rightful act?

One July weekend my partner and I tried the Chouinard-Herbert route on Sentinel Rock, a 1,700-foot face normally done in two days. Mid-morning on the second day, after a bivouac on a ledge, we killed our last bottle of water—we had badly miscalculated our need—and climbed ahead into the ninety-degree afternoon. We became so weak we couldn't finish the climb by dark, though we had reached the easy ledges near the top. We spent another night, sleeping like stones as the brightest colors I have ever seen flamed through my dreams. In the morning we made our way to the top, there to find an enormous orange-barked ponderosa pine, standing alone. It seemed to glow from within, a tree, but more than a tree, an emblem of being itself. And the stream we finally came to, after what seemed hours of stumbling descent down the dry gully behind Sentinel, was no ordinary stream with a fringe of plants—how *green* those plants were—but the very Garden itself. We knelt there, feeling the icy glow of water inside us with our booming and skittering hearts.

Rock climbing and mountaineering are unnecessary, artificial activities, invented by a privileged leisure class. Yet the act of climbing can yield an engagement with the natural world that is anything but artificial. That, I believe, is the reason it arose among the European well-to-do of the eighteenth century—it answered a need for reconnection to the wild nature from which they had so successfully separated themselves. Other kinds of outdoor activities answer the same need for many who pursue them—backpacking, birding, hunting, fishing, white-water rafting. They offer in common the opportunity to be actively involved with nature instead of passively receiving it. Climbers and fishermen may not be at one with nature, but they are immersed in it, interact with it, and in that sense they are part of their surroundings. They experience a sense of place in nature, or at least the experience is potentially available to them. Those who come to sightsee, on the other hand, are not part of the place they look at. They are observers, subjects seeking an object, passing through.

I don't mean that the population can be divided into two groups, the doers and the lookers. I am both, at different times. All of us at various moments are the man on the bus gazing out and murmuring, "Isn't that a sight." Nor do I believe that that man was completely disconnected from what he saw; he was impressed, perhaps even moved, by the spectacle of Yosemite's walls. But he wasn't moved in any way that energized him much, that evoked any sign of elation or fear or awe. Like me at the time, he wasn't in the *presence* of those soaring faces. And as I watched him and others clicking photographs later, I couldn't help thinking that by recording what they saw they were trying to verify that it was real, and that they were actually there.

I've experienced that odd feeling myself. The first time I saw the Tetons I was a teenager sightseeing with my family. We sat at an outdoor chuckwagon breakfast place, eating pancakes and staring at the most dramatic mountains I had ever seen, so dramatic my eyes didn't quite believe them. They seemed to have no depth, hardly any substance—I kept thinking they looked like cut-outs someone had propped up on the other side of the lake. Part of my trouble, I'm sure, was due to the fact that an eastern kid was seeing his first western mountains. But I think there was more. I was expecting to experience those mountains, to perceive their full reality, simply by looking at them from a distance. They seemed to lack substance because I was reducing them to an image on the screen of my vision.

I suspect that television—I used to watch a lot of it—had much to do with my perception of the Tetons, as I suspect it has much to do with the way many of us experience the natural world. Television viewers give up the active movements of awareness—glancing around, comparing, looking long or only briefly—to the autocratic screen, reducing themselves to mere absorbers of the presented image. All of us who spend much time in such a mode of consciousness will necessarily transfer it to other areas of experience. When we go into nature, we will expect the things we see to reveal themselves, to tender their full value merely by lying in our field of vision. And to the extent that nature seems static and dramatically blank compared to TV entertainment, it is likely to seem disappointing, lifeless, and unreal.

Even nature documentaries, despite their educational value, may tend ultimately to diminish the viewer's engagement with nature rather than enhance it. Those who are used to such programs are likely to find real nature—subliminally, at least—disorderly and dull, because its images aren't preselected for visual impact and framed within a screen. Shows about nature may come to seem more real than nature itself. For millions of Americans, it may be that the viewing of such programs, and of television in general, is substantially replacing direct experience of the wild natural world. When an old-growth forest is delivered to the living room, some viewers will want to go there. But far more, I think, will feel they have already been.

What that majority will miss, of course, is the unframed sensory texture of the thing itself—the scale of the trees, the pervasive stillness and the filtered ambient light, the dark smells of the forest floor, the feel of moss under their feet. They will miss the varying rhythms of their walking and the unconstrained movements of awareness in such a place. They will miss the primordial alertness that comes in the presence of trees, shadows, and small forest sounds, of wildlife seen and unseen. Consuming the image rather than the thing, they will have walked the boulder field not only without the snakes but without the boulders, and without themselves.

But more is at stake than the quality of our perception. Reducing nature to a collection of visual objects seen on television, or even first-hand, is not only impoverishing to us, but dangerous to the land as well. Nature-as-sight affords a purely aesthetic appeal to the seer, a pleasing pattern of form and color—what we call generically "natural beauty." There is nothing wrong with aesthetic appreciation, and it can lead to other ways of valuing nature, but it seems to me a very fragile basis for preserving what relatively wild, undisturbed lands we have left. When push comes to shove, as the settlement of North America has made clear, aesthetic values have a way of toppling in the practical path of progress. Tall-grass prairie was beautiful to the Ohio Valley settlers, but they plowed it under. The passenger pigeon was beautiful to the hunters who shot it down. Even timber executives see beauty in old-growth Douglas fir, but its beauty doesn't stop them from reducing it to clear-cuts.

Appreciation of nature in our society takes two forms above all others. The prevailing form, the cult of utility, shapes and perpetuates our sense of land as something from which to extract uses and materials. The other, the cult of beauty, values land for its own sake, but chiefly for its visual appearance. The cult of beauty has had important positive consequences—most of our national and state parks were set aside because of their scenic splendor—but it also works hand-in-hand with the cult of utility. Our working assumption as a people has been that except for a scattering of parks and designated wilderness areas, many of them in alpine regions difficult of commercial access anyway, all other land is subject to utility first and other considerations second. On public lands, the much-voiced concept of multiple-use says that scenery and recreation are equal in importance to the land's utilitarian value; but in practice, multiple-use in our national forests means logging first and other uses where logging permits. And in the desert West, which even in the eyes of many nature lovers still lies outside the category of the beautiful, mining, oil and gas drilling, and the wholesale stripping of forest to create range for cows all proceed with practically no restraint.

When those who oppose such "improvements" invoke in its defense only (or mainly) the land's beauty, they are dismissed as sentimental and unrealistic. And there is a certain justice in the dismissal, because at bottom the cult of beauty shares with the cult of utility the same flaw: it views nature as an object separate from the human subject. The timber or mineral executive reduces nature to a commodity, something to be taken out. The tourist seeking scenic beauty reduces nature to pleasing images, enjoyed and taken home on film. Neither recognizes nature as a living system of which our human lives are part, on which our lives and all lives depend, one which places strict limits upon us even as it sustains us.

That is an ecological view, and though most of us have some familiarity with the ideas of ecology, ecology remains *only* ideas, abstract and forceless in our lives, so long as we perceive nature merely as a collection of objects, however lovely. It takes not just looking at nature but getting into it—into some of its unloveliness as well as its splendor—for ideas to begin to bear the fruit of understanding. The rattlesnakes beneath the boulders instructed me, in a way no book could have, that the natural world did not exist entirely for my comfort and pleasure; indeed, that it did not particularly care whether my small human life continued to exist at all. Being terribly thirsty on Sentinel Rock helped me understand in my body what my mind already knew, or thought it knew—how moisture both makes life possible and sets unequivocal limits on where it can exist. And once I had spent some time in old-growth forests, the profusion of dead trees that had daunted me at first began to elicit an appreciation of how death and life dance to a single music, how a healthy natural community carefully conserves and recycles its living wealth, and so sustains itself through time.

Such perceptions, in their rudimentary way, point toward an ecological understanding of the natural world. Clearly, to fully realize this understanding, we as a people need to follow the lead of the ecological sciences and learn to live by their principles. We need to heal the injuries we have caused in the biosphere. But even as we scientifically study the inner workings of nature and the ways we have disrupted it, we must learn how to experience it again, how to apprehend it in its fullness. As Edward Abbey told us many times, we can't experience the outdoors through a car window. We must take the time to enter the natural world, to engage it, not just to run our eyes along its surfaces but to place ourselves among its things and weathers—to let it exert, at least for intervals in our lives, the ancient influences that once surrounded and formed us.

Enough time under those influences can teach us to use our eyes actively again, as something more than receptacles. They seek a route through trees, across a creek, over a ridge, working in concert with body and mind. They follow the darts and veers of a hummingbird, a lizard skimming across stones, the quick glint of a trout. Things much smaller than El Capitan or the Tetons, things easy to miss, begin to reveal themselves—tiny white flowers of saxifrage, the quarter-sized, web-lined shaft of a tarantula's den, a six-inch screech owl flicking limb to limb in the dusk.

And when later in the evening the owl sounds its soft, tremulous call, and small snaps and rustlings reveal the presence of other lives, the eyes have reached their proper limit. The sense we rely on above all others can never completely know the natural world, for nature's being is only partly what it shows. Its greater part, and greater beauty, is always past what human eyes can understand. When I started hiking desert canyons a few years ago, I kept hearing the song of a bird I couldn't see, a long descending series of sharply whistled notes. It was a canyon wren, I learned from the books, but what I learned from the bird was more important. It sang as I woke up, a brilliant sun spread down the great red walls, and it sang as I started farther up the twisting canyon, sloshing through pools and scrambling up dry water chutes, higher and deeper into the carving of time. And what I remember most vividly from those early hikes is no particular thing I saw, no one fern grotto or sandstone spire, no cottonwood or cactus garden. I remember a bird I couldn't see that called from around the next bend, from over the brink of a dry waterfall where the upper walls held the blaze of sky, where even as it steadily opened itself to sight, the canyon receded further and further into the depth of its mystery.

Analyzing and Discussing the Text

1. What's wrong with the "sightseeing" mentality that Daniel describes in this essay? In what sense is it an "impoverishment"?
2. Does Daniel envision a renewal of the traditional nondualistic way of perceiving the natural world described in Leslie Marmon Silko's essay? Is such a return to the direct experience of nature's "ancient influences" really necessary?
3. Try to image how Daniel would regard John Muir's aggressive participation in the same Yosemite scene viewed so safely and antiseptically by the sightseers described in his own essay (see Muir's "An Unexpected Adventure" in Part Two, Chapter Four).
4. Notice the difference between Daniel's combination of first-person narrative and abstract analysis and the more uniformly abstract and impersonal prose style of Silko. What would be the effect if Daniel removed all of the narrative passages from his essay and left only the abstract passages (such as paragraphs 10 to 16)?
5. Observe how Daniel strategically uses his narrative material (not a single narrative, but several brief stories) at the beginning and the conclusion of his essay. Why not begin and end with the abstract? Does the style of this essay itself, in its prominent reliance on vivid personal anecdote, seem to underscore Daniel's message about how to overcome the "sightseeing" mentality?

Experiencing and Writing About the World

1. Write a picturesque description of a nearby natural scene. Try to view the landscape from a wholly aesthetic point of view, making it seem static and perfect and somehow separate from you, the viewer. You might even frame the scene with the edges of a dorm room window or that of a tour bus.
2. Write a narrative of the last time you submitted yourself to the "ancient influences" of the natural world. When did you last hike up a steep hill, encounter a truly wild animal, or find yourself caught in a freak storm? Tell the story of this experience and emphasize the way you responded psychologically to this exposure to nature. If you were not particularly conscious of nature even in the midst of this experience, consider the implications of this unawareness.
3. Is Daniel's essay an implicit critique of the aesthetic perspectives adopted in the pieces by Georgia O'Keeffe and Susan Mitchell in the preceding chapter? Write an analytical essay in which you compare and contrast Daniel's ideas and approach to writing with the aestheticism of the other writers.
4. Take a stand on the issue of detached observation versus participatory experience, and devote several paragraphs to explaining this idea logically. Then, in imitation of Daniel, write a brief but detailed narrative of a personal experience that reinforces this argument. Now join this narrative to your meditation/argument about the "proper" relationship between nature and the mind, either by breaking up the narrative and using portions of it throughout your meditation or by placing the entire narrative in one key section of the combined essay.

Suggestions for Further Reading

Atwood, Margaret. *Surfacing*. Greenwich, CT: Fawcett, 1972.

Bass, Rick. *Wild to the Heart*. New York: Norton, 1987.

Berger, Bruce. *The Telling Distance: Conversations with the American Desert*. 1990. New York: Doubleday, 1991.

Finch, Robert. "Being at Two with Nature." *Georgia Review* (Spring 1991): 97–104.

Hawthorne, Nathaniel. "Roger Malvin's Burial." 1832. *The Celestial Railroad and Other Stories*. New York: New American Library, 1963.

Johnson, Cathy. *On Becoming Lost: A Naturalist's Search for Meaning*. Salt Lake City: Gibbs M. Smith, 1990.

Kaplan, Stephen, and Rachel Kaplan. *The Experience of Nature: A Psychological Perspective*. New York: Cambridge UP, 1989.

Lopez, Barry. "Landscape and Narrative." *Crossing Open Ground*. New York: Scribner's, 1988.

McCullers, Carson. "A Tree, a Rock, a Cloud." *The Ballad of the Sad Cafe and Other Stories*. New York: Bantam, 1977.

Nelson, Kent. *All Around Me Peaceful*. New York: Dell, 1989.

Poe, Edgar Allan. "A Descent into the Maelström" (1841) and "A Tale of the Ragged Mountains" (1844). *Great Short Works of Edgar Allan Poe*. Ed. G. R. Thompson. New York: Harper, 1970.

Sanders, Scott Russell. "Landscape and Imagination." *North American Review* 274.3 (September 1989): 63–66.

Shoumatoff, Alex. *African Madness*. New York: Vintage, 1990.

©Robert Fox, 1990/Impact Visuals

CHAPTER TWO

Public Statements: Polemics, Conjectures, Records of Conflict

"In this era of prepackaged thought," writes Scott Russell Sanders in "The Singular First Person," "the essay is the closest thing we have, on paper, to a record of the individual mind at work and play." The language in the essays collected in this chapter may at times seem playful, but these pieces attempt even more explicitly than the essays elsewhere in this anthology to describe and explore basic "environmental issues" and to argue in favor of particular stances on these issues. Like the soapbox orator Sanders mentions at the beginning of his essay, these writers stand up and state their opinions on subjects ranging from land use to nuclear power "with all the eloquence [they] can muster," although no one may have asked for their particular opinions. What most of the diverse voices now speaking for nature have in common is their opposition to the view that humans stand outside of nature and are destined to dominate it. From this central starting point, however, the discussions go in many different directions.

For N. Scott Momaday, the appropriate and necessary new land ethic is really an older one, rooted in the tradition of the Kiowa Indians, which honors the land and those people who live their lives in close relationship to it. William Kittredge's remembrance and confession take the form of personal history as he recounts his own attempts to live in accordance with the land ethic he learned as a boy that encouraged the conquering and remaking of the land of the American West. Joseph Meeker's highly compressed essay works from a larger, more inclusive cultural perspective than either of the first two essays; he reminds us of the fears that all cultures have in common and ties them to our current attempts to use nuclear energy. Scott Russell Sanders, Joy Williams, and David Quammen all concern themselves with questions of language and voice: how, they ask in various ways, does the essayist best express his or her sense of what is wrong with our treatment of the earth, and how can we convince others to work with us for change? For Sanders, whose subject is the personal essay itself, this is done through the individual human voice, grounded in awareness of the earth and attuned to truths discovered through personal experience. Williams wants to make her point more dramatically; she uses some of the tools of the fiction writer, such as extensive dialogue and the dramatic monologue form, to catch and hold her reader's attention on the topic of environmental abuses. By playing with the "you" and "me" of the dialogue form, she involves her readers in the idea that we must all finally bear the responsibility for the condition of the environment. Quammen's essay uses the more traditional tools of the formal essayist—an understanding of the historical use of such words as "environment" and "conservation" and the ironic vision of a clean, but dull, environmental dystopia, which he calls the "Planet of Weeds"—to emphasize how clear, honest language is essential to the conservation movement's efforts to see beyond narrow, human interests.

N. SCOTT MOMADAY

An American Land Ethic

N. Scott Momaday (1934–   ), a painter, writer, and teacher, was born in Lawton, Oklahoma. His father was a Kiowa artist and art teacher; his mother, Mayme Natachee Scott, was a teacher and writer who descended from early American pioneers, but took her middle name from her Cherokee great-grandmother. Momaday earned his B.A. (1958) from the University of New Mexico and his M.A. (1960) and Ph.D. (1963) from Stanford University. He has taught at Stanford and the University of California at Berkeley and is now Regents Professor of English at the University of Arizona. His many honors include a Guggenheim Fellowship and a grant from the National Institute of Arts and Letters. *House Made of Dawn* (1969), his first novel, won the Pulitzer Prize for fiction. He has also published a book of poetry called *The Gourd Dancer* (1976) and an autobiography and family history called *The Names: A Memoir* (1977). An essay collection, *The Way to Rainy Mountain*, appeared in 1969, and another novel, *The Ancient Child*, was published in 1989. However, in all of his creative work, the ordinary generic categories have little meaning. Momaday's distinctive style brings together myth, family tales, tribal history, and personal recollection within a fluid, original structure that is not neatly captured by our usual categories.

This highly personal adaptation of form also characterizes the following statement (published in 1970) on the American relationship to the land. Momaday's title, which sounds as if it might be announcing an abstract and argumentative thesis, gives way immediately to his account of a "strange thing" that happened one night when he was writing the epilogue of *The Way to Rainy Mountain*: as he wrote about Ko-sahn, a wise old Kiowa woman, she actually seemed to step out of the page and into Momaday's room, where she sang and spoke to the author. This "ancient, one-eyed woman," who embodied so much of his tribal history, evoked both Momaday's ethical creed—"Once in his life a man ought to concentrate his mind upon the remembered earth"—and his beautiful description of the Kiowa homeland in the Wichita Mountains of Oklahoma. This "American Land Ethic" not only explains and prescribes an ethical regard for the land, but also, through the rendering of personal and tribal landscapes, engenders such an ethic in us.

[I]

One night a strange thing happened. I had written the greater part of *The Way to Rainy Mountain*—all of it, in fact, except the epilogue. I had set down the last of the old Kiowa tales, and I had composed both the historical and the autobiographical commentaries for it. I had the sense of being out of breath, of having said what it was in me to say on that subject. The manuscript lay before me in the bright light, small, to be sure, but complete; or nearly so. I had written the second of the two poems in which that book is framed. I had uttered the last word, as it were. And yet a whole, penultimate piece was missing. I began once again to write:

> *During the first hours after midnight on the morning of November 13, 1833, it seemed that the world was coming to an end. Suddenly the stillness of the night was broken; there were brilliant flashes of light in the sky, light of such intensity that people were awakened by it. With the speed and density of a driving rain, stars were falling in the universe. Some were brighter than Venus; one was said to be as large as the moon.*

I went on to say that that event, the falling of the stars on North America, that explosion of Leonid meteors which occurred 137 years ago, is among the earliest entries in the Kiowa calendars. So deeply impressed upon the imagination of the Kiowas is that old phenomenon that it is remembered still; it has become a part of the racial memory.

"The living memory," I wrote, "and the verbal tradition which transcends it, were brought together for me once and for all in the person of Ko-sahn." It seemed eminently right for me to deal, after all, with that old woman. Ko-sahn is among the most venerable people I have ever known. She spoke and sang to me one summer afternoon in Oklahoma. It was like a dream. When I was born she was already old; she was a grown woman when my grandparents came into the world. She sat perfectly still, folded over on herself. It did not seem possible that so many years—a century of years—could be so compacted and distilled. Her voice shuddered, but it did not fail. Her songs were sad. An old whimsy, a delight in language and in remembrance, shone in her one good eye. She conjured up the past, imagining perfectly the long continuity of her being. She imagined the lovely young girl, wild and vital, she had been. She imagined the Sun Dance:

> *There was an old, old woman. She had something on her back. The boys went out to see. The old woman had a bag full of earth on her back. It was a certain kind of sandy earth. That is what they must have in the lodge. The dancers must dance upon the sandy earth. The old woman held a digging tool in her hand.*

She turned towards the south and pointed with her lips. It was like a kiss, and she began to sing:

> *We have brought the earth.*
> *Now it is time to play;*
> *As old as I am, I still have the feeling of play.*

That was the beginning of the Sun Dance.

By this time I was back into the book, caught up completely in the act of writing. I had projected myself—imagined myself—out of the room and out of time. I was there with Ko-sahn in the Oklahoma July. We laughed easily together; I felt that I had known her all of my life—all of hers. I did not want to let her go. But I had come to the end. I set down, almost grudgingly, the last sentences:

> *It was—all of this and more—a quest, a going forth upon the way to Rainy Mountain. Probably Ko-sahn too is dead now. At times, in the quiet of evening, I think she must have wondered, dreaming, who she was. Was she become in her sleep that old purveyor of the sacred earth, perhaps, that ancient one who, old as she was, still had the feeling of play? And in her mind, at times, did she see the falling stars?*

For some time I sat looking down at these words on the page, trying to deal with the emptiness that had come about inside of me. The words did not seem real. The longer I looked at them, the more unfamiliar they became. At last I could scarcely believe that they made sense, that they had anything whatsoever to do with meaning. In desperation almost, I went back over the final paragraphs, backwards and forwards, hurriedly. My eyes fell upon the name Ko-sahn. And all at once everything seemed suddenly to refer to that name. The name seemed to humanize the whole complexity of language. All at once, absolutely, I had the sense of the magic of words and of names. Ko-sahn, I said. And I said again KO-SAHN.

Then it was that that ancient, one-eyed woman Ko-sahn stepped out of the language and stood before me on the page. I was amazed, of course, and yet it seemed to me entirely appropriate that this should happen.

"Yes, grandson," she said. "What is it? What do you want?"

"I was just now writing about you," I replied, stammering. "I thought—forgive me—I thought that perhaps you were . . . that you had . . ."

"No," she said. And she cackled, I thought. And she went on. "You have imagined me well, and so I am. You have imagined that I dream, and so I do. I have seen the falling stars."

"But all of this, this *imagining*," I protested, "this has taken place—is taking place in my mind. You are not actually here, not here in this room." It occurred to me that I was being extremely rude, but I could not help myself. She seemed to understand.

"Be careful of your pronouncements, grandson," she answered. "You imagine that I am here in this room, do you not? That is worth something. You see, I have existence, whole being, in your imagination. It is but one kind of being, to be sure, but it is perhaps the best of all kinds. If I am not here in this room, grandson, then surely neither are you."

"I think I see what you mean," I said. I felt justly rebuked. "Tell me, grandmother, how old are you?"

"I do not know," she replied. "There are times when I think that I am the oldest woman on earth. You know, the Kiowas came into the world through a hollow log. In my mind's eye I have seen them emerge, one by one, from the mouth of the log. I have seen them so clearly, how they were dressed, how delighted they were to see the world around them. I *must* have been there. And I must have taken part in that old migration of the Kiowas from the Yellowstone to the Southern Plains, for I have seen antelope bounding in the tall grass near the Big Horn River, and I have seen the ghost forests in the Black Hills. Once I saw the red cliffs of Palo Duro Canyon. I was with those who were camped in the Wichita Mountains when the stars fell."

"You are indeed very old," I said, "and you have seen many things."

"Yes, I imagine that I have," she replied. Then she turned slowly around, nodding once, and receded into the language I had made. And then I imagined I was alone in the room.

[II]

Once in his life a man ought to concentrate his mind upon the remembered earth, I believe. He ought to give himself up to a particular landscape in his experience, to look at it from as many angles as he can, to wonder about it, to dwell upon it. He ought to imagine that he touches it with his hands at every season and listens to the sounds that are made upon it. He ought to imagine the creatures there and all the faintest motions of the wind. He ought to recollect the glare of noon and all the colors of the dawn and dusk.

The Wichita Mountains rise out of the Southern Plains in a long crooked line that runs from east to west. The mountains are made of red earth, and of rock that is neither red nor blue but some very rare admixture of the two, like the feathers of certain birds. They are not so high and mighty as the mountains of the Far West, and they bear a different relationship to the land around them. One does not imagine that they are distinctive in themselves, or indeed that they exist apart from the plain in any sense. If you try to think of them in the abstract, they lose the look of mountains. They are preeminently an expression of the larger landscape, more perfectly organic than one can easily imagine. To behold these mountains from the plain is one thing; to see the plain from the mountains is something else. I have stood on the top of Mt. Scott and seen the earth below, bending out into the whole circle of the sky. The wind runs always close upon the slopes, and there are times when you can hear the rush of it like water in the ravines.

Here is the hub of an old commerce. A hundred years ago the Kiowas and Comanches journeyed outward from the Wichitas in every direction, seeking after mischief and medicine, horses and hostages. Sometimes they went away for years, but they always returned, for the land had got hold of them. It is a consecrated place, and even now there is something of the wilderness about it. There is a game preserve in the hills. Animals graze away in the open meadows or, closer by, keep to the shadows of the groves: antelope and deer, longhorns and buffalo. It was here, the Kiowas say, that the first buffalo came into the world.

The yellow, grassy knoll that is called Rainy Mountain lies a short distance to the north and west. There, on the west side, is the ruin of an old school where my grandmother went as a wild young girl in blanket and braids to learn of numbers and of names in English. And there she is buried.

> Most is your name the name of this dark stone.
> Deranged in death, the mind to be inheres
> Forever in the nominal unknown,
> The wake of nothing audible he hears
> Who listens here and now to hear your name.
>
> The early sun, red as a hunter's moon,
> Runs in the plain. The mountain burns and shines;
> And silence is the long approach of noon
> Upon the shadow that your name defines—
> And death this cold, black density of stone.

[III]

I am interested in the way that a man looks at a given landscape and takes possession of it in his blood and brain. For this happens, I am certain, in the ordinary motion of life. None of us lives apart from the land entirely; such an isolation is unimaginable. We have sooner or later to come to terms with the world around us—and I mean especially the physical world, not only as it is revealed to us immediately through our senses, but also as it is perceived more truly in the long turn of

segments and of years. And we must come to moral terms. There is no
alternative, I believe, if we are to realize and maintain our humanity, for
our humanity must consist in part in the ethical as well as the practical
ideal of preservation. And particularly here and now is that true. We
Americans need now more than ever before—and indeed more than
we know—to imagine who and what we are with respect to the earth
and sky. I am talking about an act of the imagination essentially, and
the concept of an American land ethic.

It is no doubt more difficult to imagine in 1970 the landscape of
America than it was in, say, 1900. Our whole experience as a nation in
this century has been a repudiation of the pastoral ideal which informs
so much of the art and literature of the nineteenth century. One effect
of the Technological Revolution has been to uproot us from the soil. We
have become disoriented, I believe; we have suffered a kind of psychic
dislocation of ourselves in time and space. We may be perfectly sure of
where we are in relation to the supermarket and the next coffee break,
but I doubt that any of us knows where he is in relation to the stars
and to the solstices. Our sense of the natural order has become dull
and unreliable. Like the wilderness itself, our sphere of instinct has
diminished in proportion as we have failed to imagine truly what it
is. And yet I believe that it is possible to formulate an ethical idea of
the land—a notion of what it is and must be in our daily lives—and I
believe moreover that it is absolutely necessary to do so.

It would seem on the surface of things that a land ethic is something
that is alien to, or at least dormant in, most Americans. Most of us in
general have developed an attitude of indifference toward the land. In
terms of my own experience, it is difficult to see how such an attitude
could ever have come about.

[IV]

Ko-sahn could remember where my grandmother was born. "It
was just there," she said, pointing to a tree, and the tree was like a
hundred others that grew up in the broad depression of the Washita
River. I could see nothing to indicate that anyone had ever been there,
spoken so much as a word, or touched the tips of his fingers to the
tree. But in her memory Ko-sahn could see the child. I think she must
have remembered my grandmother's voice, for she seemed for a long
moment to listen and to hear. There was a still, heavy heat upon that
place; I had the sense that ghosts were gathering there.

And in the racial memory, Ko-sahn had seen the falling stars. For
her there was no distinction between the individual and the racial experience, even as there was none between the mythical and the historical.
Both were realized for her in the one memory, and that was of the

land. This landscape, in which she had lived for a hundred years, was the common denominator of everything that she knew and would ever know—and her knowledge was profound. Her roots ran deep into the earth, and from those depths she drew strength enough to hold still against all the forces of chance and disorder. And she drew therefrom the sustenance of meaning and of mystery as well. The falling stars were not for Ko-sahn an isolated or accidental phenomenon. She had a great personal investment in that awful commotion of light in the night sky. For it remained to be imagined. She must at last deal with it in words; she must appropriate it to her understanding of the whole universe. And, again, when she spoke of the Sun Dance, it was an essential expression of her relationship to the life of the earth and to the sun and moon.

In Ko-sahn and in her people we have always had the example of a deep, ethical regard for the land. We had better learn from it. Surely that ethic is merely latent in ourselves. It must now be activated, I believe. We Americans must come again to a moral comprehension of the earth and air. We must live according to the principle of a land ethic. The alternative is that we shall not live at all.

Analyzing and Discussing the Text

1. Why does Momaday emphasize the role of the imagination in the interaction between himself and Ko-sahn? In what ways do the appearance and conversation prepare us for the second section of the essay, with its more direct focus on the landscape?
2. The injunction to concentrate more on "the remembered earth," to give oneself up "to a particular landscape," becomes the impetus for Momaday's three-paragraph description of the Wichita Mountains. Analyze the specific descriptive techniques Momaday uses to convey the beauty and importance of the mountains.
3. What changes in tone and focus occur in the third section of this essay? How does this section tie in with the preceding ones? Do you agree that our "sense of the natural order has become dull and unreliable"? Do you see evidence of what Momaday later describes as a latent "land ethic"?
4. How does the essay's fourth section bring together all of the other strands in the piece? Is it an effective, persuasive blend of rhetorical modes and strategies? Explain.

Experiencing and Writing About the World

1. Create an imaginary dialogue with one of your own ancestors about a landscape that is central to your family's history and sense of themselves. Does your heritage parallel Momaday's attitudes or embody other relationships to the land? Include in this paper some expression of your sense of what is important about "place." Is it beauty, private memory, community history, or some blend of these aspects?

2. Write an argumentative essay that starts with Momaday's statement that we "must come again to a moral comprehension of the earth and air" and proceeds to explain exactly what should be included in this "moral comprehension" and how this viewpoint can be gained.

3. Like Momaday, William Kittredge espouses a "land ethic" in the excerpt from his essay "Owning It All," but Kittredge's essay emphasizes the criticism of unsatisfactory land use rather than the celebration of a wholesome, traditional relationship between people and place. Write a detailed comparison of the persuasive strategies in each of these essays and evaluate the effectiveness of each approach in stirring you to think about natural places in new ways. In a 1925 essay called "Negation," the psychologist Sigmund Freud argued that the "negative formulation" of an idea (the critique) captures our attention more forcefully than the positive statement of the same idea (the celebration). Do you agree with this theory? Use specific references to these two essays in evaluating the usefulness of critique and celebration as styles of argumentation.

WILLIAM KITTREDGE

From **Owning It All**

William Kittredge (1932–   ) was born on his family's cattle ranch in southeastern Oregon at the end of a time "in which people lived in everyday proximity to animals on territory they knew more precisely than the patterns in the palms of their hands." He received a B.S. in agriculture from Oregon State University (where he also took classes from the novelist Bernard Malamud) in 1953 and went straight from there to Guam, where he did photo intelligence work for the U.S. Air Force. Kittredge returned to the MC Ranch in the Warner Valley in 1958 and, in a process that he discusses in the following essay, began to turn "the fertile homeplace of [his] childhood into a machine for agriculture." After the farming and ranching agribusiness lost its appeal and the ranch was sold, Kittredge went to the University of Oregon for a year and then attended the University of Iowa, where he earned his M.F.A. in creative writing in 1969. Since then, apart from spending a year (1973–1974) as a Stegner Fellow at Stanford University, he has lived in Montana and taught creative writing at the University of Montana in Missoula. The recipient of two grants from the National Endowment for the Arts (1974 and 1981), Kittredge is the author of two short story collections, *The Van Gogh Field and Other Stories* (1979) and *We Are Not in This Together* (1984), and he is the co-editor of *The Last Best Place: A Montana Anthology* (1988). Under the joint pseudonym of "Owen Rountree," Kittredge and S. M. Krauzer published a series of "action stories"—including *Lord* and *Lord: The Nevada War*—in the early 1980s. The following essay is excerpted from the title piece in his 1987 book of autobiographical essays, *Owning It All*. In 1992 Kittredge published a memoir called *Hole in the Sky*.

The following essay, like the volume in which it was published, demonstrates both senses of "owning": possession and "owning up." Confession, in Kittredge's case, means to acknowledge the changes wrought by his false dreams of ownership and control, rather than stewardship, of the land. Here he looks back on his life as an agricultural manager—a time when he had laid out patterns for irrigation, manipulated more than five thousand water control devices, and constructed "a perfect agricultural palace"—to ask where he, and the whole mythology of American culture, went wrong.

Agriculture is often envisioned as an art, and it can be. Of course there is always survival, and bank notes, and all that. But your basic bottom line on the farm is again and again some notion of how life should be lived. The majority of agricultural people, if you press them hard enough, even though most of them despise sentimental abstractions, will admit they are trying to create a good place, and to live as part of that goodness, in the kind of connection which with fine reason we call *rootedness*. It's just that there is good art and bad art.

These are thoughts which come back when I visit eastern Oregon. I park and stand looking down into the lava-rock and juniper-tree canyon where Deep Creek cuts its way out of the Warner Mountains, and the great turkey buzzard soars high in the yellow-orange light above the evening. The fishing water is low, as it always is in late August, unfurling itself around dark and broken boulders. The trout, I know, are hanging where the currents swirl across themselves, waiting for the one entirely precise and lucky cast, the Renegade fly bobbing toward them.

Even now I can see it, each turn of water along miles of that creek. Walk some stretch enough times with a fly rod and its configurations will imprint themselves on your being with Newtonian exactitude. Which is beyond doubt one of the attractions of such fishing—the hours of learning, and then the intimacy with a living system that carries you beyond the sadness of mere gaming for sport.

What I liked to do, back in the old days, was pack in some spuds and an onion and corn flour and spices mixed up in a plastic bag, a small cast-iron frying pan in my wicker creel and, in the last twilight on a gravel bar by the water, cook up a couple of rainbows over a fire of snapping dead willow and sage, eating alone while the birds flitted through the last hatch, wiping my greasy fingers on my pants while the heavy trout began rolling at the lower ends of the pools.

The canyon would be shadowed under the moon when I walked out to show up home empty-handed, to sit with my wife over a drink of whiskey at the kitchen table. Those nights I would go to bed and sleep without dreams, a grown-up man secure in the house and the western valley where he had been a child, enclosed in a topography of spirit he assumed he knew more closely than his own features in the shaving mirror.

So, I ask myself, if it was such a pretty life, why didn't I stay? The peat soil in Warner Valley was deep and rich, we ran good cattle, and my most sacred memories are centered there. What could run me off?

Well, for openers, it got harder and harder to get out of bed in the mornings and face the days, for reasons I didn't understand. More and more I sought the comfort of fishing that knowable creek. Or in winter the blindness of television.

My father grew up on a homestead place on the sagebrush flats outside Silver Lake, Oregon. He tells of hiding under the bed with his sisters when strangers came to the gate. He grew up, as we all did in that country and era, believing that the one sure defense against the world was property. I was born in 1932, and recall a life before the end of World War II in which it was possible for a child to imagine that his family owned the world.

Warner Valley was largely swampland when my grandfather bought the M C Ranch with no downpayment in 1936, right at the heart of the Great Depression. The outside work was done mostly by men and horses and mules, and our ranch valley was filled with life. In 1937 my father bought his first track-layer, a secondhand RD6 Caterpillar he used to build a 17-mile diversion canal to carry the spring floodwater around the east side of the valley, and we were on our way to draining all swamps. The next year he bought an RD7 and a John Deere 36 combine which cut an 18-foot swath, and we were deeper into the dream of power over nature and men, which I had begun to inhabit while playing those long-ago games of war.

The peat ground left by the decaying remnants of ancient tule beds was diked into huge undulating grainfields—Houston Swamp with 750 irrigated acres, Dodson Lake with 800—a final total of almost 8,000 acres under cultivation, and for reasons of what seemed like common sense and efficiency, the work became industrialized. Our artistry worked toward a model whose central image was the machine.

The natural patterns of drainage were squared into dragline ditches, the tules and the aftermath of the oat and barley crops were burned— along with a little more of the combustible peat soil every year. We flood-irrigated when the water came in spring, drained in late March, and planted in a 24-hour-a-day frenzy which began around April 25 and ended—with luck—by the 10th of May, just as leaves on the Lombardy poplar were breaking from their buds. We summered our cattle on more than a million acres of Taylor Grazing Land across the high lava rock and sagebrush desert out east of the valley, miles of territory where we owned most of what water there was, and it was ours. We owned it all, or so we felt. The government was as distant as news on the radio.

The most intricate part of my job was called "balancing water," a night and day process of opening and closing pipes and redwood headgates and running the 18-inch drainage pumps. That system was the finest plaything I ever had.

And despite the mud and endless hours, the work remained play for a long time, the making of a thing both functional and elegant. We were doing God's labor and creating a good place on earth, living the pastoral yeoman dream—that's how our mythology defined it, although nobody would ever have thought to talk about work in that way.

And then it all went dead, over years, but swiftly.

You can imagine our surprise and despair, our sense of having been profoundly cheated. It took us a long while to realize some unnamable thing was wrong, and then we blamed it on ourselves, our inability to manage enough. But the fault wasn't ours, beyond the fact that we had all been educated to believe in a grand bad factory-land notion as our prime model of excellence.

We felt enormously betrayed. For so many years, through endless efforts, we had proceeded in good faith, and it turned out we had wrecked all we had not left untouched. The beloved migratory rafts of waterbirds, the green-headed mallards and the redheads and canvasbacks, the cinnamon teal and the great Canadian honkers, were mostly gone along with their swampland habitat. The hunting, in so many ways, was no longer what it had been.

We wanted to build a reservoir, and litigation started. Our laws were being used against us, by people who wanted a share of what we thought of as our water. We could not endure the boredom of our mechanical work, and couldn't hire anyone who cared enough to do it right. We baited the coyotes with 1080, and rodents destroyed our alfalfa; we sprayed weeds and insects with 2-4-D Ethyl and Malathion, and Parathion for clover mite, and we shortened our own lives.

In quite an actual way we had come to victory in the artistry of our playground warfare against all that was naturally alive in our native home. We had reinvented our valley according to the most persuasive ideal given us by our culture, and we ended with a landscape organized like a machine for growing crops and fattening cattle, a machine that creaked a little louder each year, a dreamland gone wrong.

One of my strongest memories comes from a morning when I was maybe 10 years old, out on the lawn before our country home in spring, beneath a bluebird sky. I was watching the waterbirds coming off the valley swamps and grainfields where they had been feeding overnight. They were going north to nesting grounds on the Canadian tundra, and that piece of morning, inhabited by the sounds of their wings and their calling in the clean air, was wonder-filled and magical. I was enclosed in a living place.

No doubt that memory has persisted because it was a sight of possibility which I will always cherish—an image of the great good place rubbed smooth over the years like a river stone, which I touch again as I consider why life in Warner Valley went so seriously haywire. But never again in my lifetime will it be possible for a child to stand out on a bright spring morning in Warner Valley and watch the waterbirds come through in enormous, rafting vee-shaped flocks of thousands—and I grieve.

My father is a very old man. A while back we were driving up the Bitterroot Valley of Montana, and he was gazing away to the mountains. "They'll never see it the way we did," he said, and I wonder what he saw.

We shaped our piece of the West according to the model provided by our mythology, and instead of a great good place such order had given us enormous power over nature, and a blank perfection of fields.

A mythology can be understood as a story that contains a set of implicit instructions from a society to its members, telling them what is valuable and how to conduct themselves if they are to preserve the things they value.

The teaching mythology we grew up with in the American West is a pastoral story of agricultural ownership. The story begins with a vast innocent continent, natural and almost magically alive, capable of inspiring us to reverence and awe, and yet savage, a wilderness. A good rural people come from the East, and they take the land from its native inhabitants, and tame it for agricultural purposes, bringing civilization: a notion of how to live embodied in law. The story is as old as invading armies, and at heart it is a racist, sexist, imperialist mythology of conquest; a rationale for violence—against other people and against nature.

At the same time, that mythology is a lens through which we continue to see ourselves. Many of us like to imagine ourselves as honest yeomen who sweat and work in the woods or the mines or the fields for a living. And many of us are. We live in a real family, a work-centered society, and we like to see ourselves as people with the good luck and sense to live in a place where some vestige of the natural world still exists in working order. Many of us hold that natural world as sacred to some degree, just as it is in our myth. Lately, more and more of us are coming to understand our society in the American West as an exploited colony, threatened by greedy outsiders who want to take our sacred place away from us, or at least to strip and degrade it.

In short, we see ourselves as a society of mostly decent people who live with some connection to a holy wilderness, threatened by those who lust for power and property. We look for Shane to come riding out of the Tetons, and instead we see Exxon and the Sierra Club. One looks virtually as alien as the other.

And our mythology tells us we own the West, absolutely and morally—we own it because of our history. Our people brought law to this difficult place, they suffered and they shed blood and they survived, and they earned this land for us. Our efforts have surely earned us the right to absolute control over the thing we created. The myth tells us this place is ours, and will always be ours, to do with as we see fit.

That's a most troubling and enduring message, because we want to believe it, and we do believe it, so many of us, despite its implicit ironies and wrongheadedness, despite the fact that we took the land from someone else. We try to ignore a genocidal history of violence against the Native Americans.

In the American West we are struggling to revise our dominant mythology, and to find a new story to inhabit. Laws control our lives, and they are designed to preserve a model of society based on values learned from mythology. Only after re-imagining our myths can we coherently remodel our laws, and hope to keep our society in a realistic relationship to what is actual.

In Warner Valley we thought we were living the right lives, creating a great precise perfection of fields, and we found the mythology had been telling us an enormous lie. The world had proven too complex, or the myth too simpleminded. And we were mortally angered.

The truth is, we never owned all the land and water. We don't even own very much of them, privately. And we don't own anything absolutely or forever. As our society grows more and more complex and interwoven, our entitlement becomes less and less absolute, more and more likely to be legally diminished. Our rights to property will never take precedence over the needs of society. Nor should they, we all must agree in our grudging hearts. Ownership of property has always been a privilege granted by society, and revokable.

Analyzing and Discussing the Text

1. What does Kittredge include in his definition of "rootedness"? How is that definition central to this essay?
2. The first segment of this excerpted essay (paragraph 5) seems to end with the author securely "enclosed in a topography of spirit." Explain precisely what he means with this phrase.
3. Why does Kittredge describe the irrigation system on his farm as "the finest plaything that I ever had"? What do the connotations of "plaything" suggest about his attitude toward irrigating the land?
4. Late in the essay (paragraphs 15 through 18) Kittredge describes the dream gone bad. What precisely causes this shift in viewpoint? How does the bad dream differ from the labor to control the land—to gain power over nature—that preceded it? How is the dream like what has gone before it?
5. What does Kittredge mean by the phrase "blank perfection of fields"?

Experiencing and Writing About the World

1. Construct a definition of *rootedness*. Illustrate your definition with examples from your own observations and personal experiences.
2. Consider some aspect of your life that once seemed essential to your attitude toward the world, but that you have come to reject and perhaps even regret. Write an argument in favor of your new understanding of the "right way to live"—for instance, working hard in school, paying attention to "safe sex" procedures, avoiding drug or alcohol abuse, learning to "live deep and suck out all the marrow of life," or simply trying not to throw litter on the ground—but present your "case" by way of a critique of your previous habits. Make the

alternatives clear to your reader by moving beyond critique in your essay and pointing out more constructive, more wholesome, ways of behaving.

3. Write an essay in which you argue that the cultural mythology described in Kittredge's chapter is being challenged by other land values. Describe, define, and give examples of the values that are replacing the old and destructive mythology.

JOSEPH MEEKER

Nuclear Time

Joseph Meeker (1932–   ) was born in Iowa. He earned his B.A. (1954), M.A. (1962), and Ph.D. (1963) from Occidental College in southern California, having taken courses at the University of California at Berkeley and the University of Oregon before returning to Occidental for graduate school. Meeker has worked as a seasonal park ranger, a professor of languages and literature, the chair of an English Department, a professor of environmental studies, a radio announcer, a visiting professor of ethics, a technical writer and editor, and the host of a weekly radio series called "Minding the Earth." He has also written widely on the environment, including such books as *The Comedy of Survival: Studies in Literary Ecology* (1973); *The Spheres of Life: An Introduction to World Ecology* (1974); and the collection of essays from which "Nuclear Time" is taken, *Minding the Earth: Thinly Disguised Essays on Human Ecology* (1988). The theme that runs throughout Meeker's writing is the "attempt to change people's perceptions about the natural environment. I think that the quickest way to change things is to find a new way of seeing and feeling our relationships to one another and to all other creatures." One instance of this effort to change how people think about nonhumans—and about ourselves—occurs at the outset of *The Comedy of Survival*, when Meeker notes that "it is generally assumed that [our] unique literary talent bestows upon mankind a special dignity not enjoyed by other animals. Whooping cranes, were they blessed with self-consciousness, might feel the same about their sophisticated mating rituals. Like us, they might translate their specific peculiarities into status symbols affirming their worth in the world. We would laugh at them, for in honest moments we know well enough that uniqueness does not in itself confer superiority." In his work, Meeker repeatedly voices the ideas that come during his own "honest moments," moments of humility and concern for the world beyond the self.

The brief, meditative essays in *Minding the Earth* carefully play off the multiple meanings contained in the term *minding;* they urge us to be thinking, remembering, and caring, not mindlessly destructive, in our relationships with the planet and its various life forms. The essay "Nuclear Time" is a strikingly original analysis and discussion of "modern feelings about nuclear energy," as remarkable for how it frames its discussion without reference to the usual arguments about technological safety as for its brevity and force.

Spiritual traditions worldwide agree upon a couple of principles: the origins of things are sacred, and what is sacred is always dangerous. Creation stories and accounts of frightening encounters with deities affirm these principles from widely divergent cultures and periods of time, suggesting that they represent fundamental human attitudes toward the cosmos we live in. The powers and dangers of origins are present in modern feelings about nuclear energy.

How far back in time do we need to go to find energy sources? The wood I burn to heat my home has mostly grown during my lifetime, as the trees around me have stored some of the same solar energy that also shines on me. When I burn coal, oil products, or natural gas, I am drawing upon their cambrian origins some 600 million years ago. If I choose to add nuclear energy to my repertoire, I am dipping deeply into the time before the origin of the solar system when energy was stored in atomic nuclei. The farther back in time I go for my energy, the scarier it gets.

Much effort has gone into making the development of nuclear energy seem a thoroughly profane affair, useful to make weapons and to power machines, but without spiritual content. Sanitary-looking facilities are built to confine bizarre forces at work within them, and it all looks like a tidy technology under human control. Now and then, however, the meaning of nuclear energy peeks out from a Three Mile Island or a Chernobyl to confront us with the origins of the universe and the terrors of ultimate forces. Our spirits are moved, not just our minds, when we are reminded that containment buildings are not enough to restrain the original powers of creation and death.

The tree dies, too, before I burn it to release its energy, and that process also has spiritual content. But the tree and I are contemporaries who understand one another, and each of us can be nourished by the death of the other. When energy comes from sources billions of years distant in time, then I enter a cosmic context where life and its needs are insignificant, and the trees and I don't count. That godlike perspective is beyond me, and I fear its dangers. Let me burn the friendly wood, and live within my own time.

Analyzing and Discussing the Text

1. How does Meeker link our distrust of nuclear energy to spiritual traditions? Why is this an important link to establish?
2. In the second paragraph of the essay, Meeker mentions older energy sources. What are the implications in this paragraph for our reliance on these non-nuclear sources of energy?
3. Explain what Meeker means when he states that "the tree and I are contemporaries who understand one another, and each of us can be nourished by the death of the other." Does our society tend to share the view implied here? What changes in our attitudes toward energy use would emerge if this attitude toward nonhuman life were a basis for policy?

Experiencing and Writing About the World

1. Write an essay that identifies and discusses other contemporary environmental issues from which a disguised, ignored, or hidden "spiritual content" occasionally emerges. What are our society's attitudes toward "the spiritual"? Does it make sense to raise spiritual concerns in discussing land use, logging, energy sources, commercial fishing techniques, wilderness preservation, and other environmental issues, or do these concerns merely cloud the technical discussion and make environmentalists seem "flaky"? Explain the appropriate and inappropriate uses of environmental spirituality in this essay.
2. Using Meeker's essay as a starting point for your own thoughts, write an essay in which you expand the discussion by analyzing other aspects of our country's energy policy. Are there practical as well as spiritual arguments that need to be addressed? How do such considerations guide our understanding of energy production and use? Rather than merely spouting opinions off the top of your head, go to the library and, using current periodicals, do research on energy in general or a specific form of energy.

3. Write an analytical essay in which you contrast Meeker's style of environmental discussion with the more explicitly down-to-earth, "hardheaded" approach in such essays as William Kittredge's "Owning It All" and David Quammen's "Dirty Word, Clean Place" (later in this chapter). Using specific passages from the texts to support your claims, try to explain who the expected audiences of the various essays seem to be. What types of readers seem likely to respond favorably to the essays you're discussing, and which readers might be unaffected or turned off?

SCOTT RUSSELL SANDERS

The Singular First Person

For biographical information, see the headnote for "Listening to Owls" in Part One, Chapter Three.

If, as Scott Russell Sanders suggests, the essayist differs from the novelist and the short story writer in that he or she has "nowhere to hide," then the essayist who dares to write *about* the personal essay (his or her very medium of expression) is doubly exposed. In the following piece, Sanders deliberately places himself in a position to give away his own, and his fellow essayists', trade secrets, prejudices, and tricks of the craft. Both essay readers and fellow essayists (including student writers) have something to gain from considering this accomplished and unusually candid writer's explanation of the essay as a mode of expression. Sanders's singular essay on "The Singular First Person" (a play on the phrase "first-person singular," which describes the point of view of the personal essayist) gives us mainly one practitioner's entertaining ideas about why the essay form attracts him, why the essay attracts both . excellent writers and an abundance of readers, and how the singularity (the uniqueness) of individual essayists emerges in this genre. This essay also helps us, as readers and writers, by providing ways of talking about essays, about how and why they succeed or fail.

The first soapbox orator I ever saw was haranguing a crowd beside the Greyhound Station in Providence about the evils of fluoridated water. What the man stood on was actually an upturned milk crate, all the genuine soapboxes presumably having been snapped up by antique dealers. He wore an orange plaid sportscoat and matching bow tie and held aloft a bottle filled with mossy green liquid. I don't remember the details of his spiel, except his warning that fluoride was an invention of the communists designed to weaken our bones and thereby make us pushovers for a Red invasion. What amazed me, as a tongue-tied kid of seventeen newly arrived in the city from the boondocks, was not his message but his courage in delivering it to a mob of strangers. I figured it would have been easier for me to jump straight over the Greyhound Station than to stand there on that milk crate and utter my thoughts.

To this day, when I read or when I compose one of those curious monologues we call the personal essay, I often think of that soapbox orator. Nobody had asked him for his two cents' worth, but there he was declaring it with all the eloquence he could muster. The essay, although enacted in private, is no less arrogant a performance. Unlike novelists and playwrights, who lurk behind the scenes while distracting our attention with the puppet show of imaginary characters, unlike scholars and journalists, who quote the opinions of others and shelter behind the hedges of neutrality, the essayist has nowhere to hide. While the poet can lean back on a several-thousand-year-old legacy of ecstatic speech, the essayist inherits a much briefer and skimpier tradition. The poet is allowed to quit in less than a page, but the essayist must generally hold forth over several thousand words. It is an arrogant and foolhardy form, this one-man or one-woman circus, which relies on the tricks of anecdote, memory, conjecture, and wit to hold our attention.

Addressing a monologue to the world seems all the more brazen or preposterous an act when you consider what a tiny fraction of the human chorus any single voice is. At the Boston Museum of Science an electronic meter records with flashing lights the population of the United States. Figuring in the rate of births, deaths, emigrants leaving the country and immigrants arriving, the meter calculates that we add one fellow citizen every twenty-one seconds. When I looked at it recently, the count stood at 242,958,483. As I wrote that figure in my notebook, the final number jumped from three to four. Another mouth, another set of ears and eyes, another brain. A counter for the earth's population would stand somewhere past five billion at the moment, and would be rising in a blur of digits. Amid this avalanche of selves it is a wonder that anyone finds the gumption to sit down and write one of those naked, lonely, quixotic letters-to-the-world.

A surprising number do find the gumption. In fact I have the impression there are more essayists at work in America today, and more gifted ones, than at any time in recent decades. Whom do I have in mind? Here is a sampler: Edward Abbey, James Baldwin, Wendell Berry, Carol Bly, Joan Didion, Annie Dillard, Stephen Jay Gould, Elizabeth Hardwick, Edward Hoagland, Barry Lopez, Peter Matthiessen, John McPhee, Cynthia Ozick, Paul Theroux, Lewis Thomas, Tom Wolfe. No doubt you could make up a wiser list of your own—with a greater ethnic range, say, or fewer nature enthusiasts—a list that would provide even more convincing support for my view that we are blessed right now with an abundance of essayists. We do not have anyone to rival Emerson or Thoreau, but in sheer quantity of first-rate work our time stands comparison with any period since the heyday of the form in the mid-nineteenth century.

In the manner of a soapbox orator I now turn my hunch into a fact and state boldly that in America these days the personal essay is flourishing. Why are so many writers taking up this risky form, and why are so many readers—to judge by the statistics of book and magazine publication—seeking it out?

In this era of prepackaged thought the essay is the closest thing we have, on paper, to a record of the individual mind at work and play. It is an amateur's raid in a world of specialists. Feeling overwhelmed by data, random information, the flotsam and jetsam of mass culture, we relish the spectacle of a single consciousness making sense of a part of the chaos. We are grateful to Lewis Thomas for shining his light into the dark corners of biology, to John McPhee for laying bare the geology beneath our landscape, to Annie Dillard for showing us the universal fire blazing in the branches of a cedar, to Peter Matthiessen for chasing after snow leopards and mystical insights in the Himalayas. No matter if they are sketchy—these maps of meaning are still welcome. As Joan Didion observes in *The White Album*, "We live entirely, especially if we are writers, by the imposition of a narrative line upon disparate images, by the 'ideas' with which we have learned to freeze the shifting phantasmagoria which is our actual experience." Dizzy from a dance that seems to accelerate hour by hour, we cling to the narrative line, even though it may be as pure an invention as the shapes drawn by Greeks to identify the constellations.

The essay is a haven for the private idiosyncratic voice in an era of anonymous babble. Like the blandburgers served in their millions along our highways, most language served up in public these days is textureless tasteless mush. On television, over the phone, in the newspaper, wherever human beings bandy words, we encounter more and more abstractions, more empty formulas. Think of the pablum ladled out by politicians. Think of the fluffy white bread of advertising. Think, lord help us, of committee reports. By contrast the essay remains stubbornly concrete and particular: it confronts you with an oil-smeared toilet at the Sunoco station, a red vinyl purse shaped like a valentine heart, a bowlegged dentist hunting deer with an elephant gun. As Orwell forcefully argued, and as dictators seem to agree, such a bypassing of abstractions, such an insistence on the concrete, is a politically subversive act. Clinging to this door, that child, this grief, following the zigzag motions of an inquisitive mind, the essay renews language and clears trash from the springs of thought. A century and a half ago Emerson called on a new generation of writers to cast off the hand-me-down rhetoric of the day, to "pierce this rotten diction and fasten words again to visible things." The essayist aspires to do just that.

As if all these virtues were not enough to account for a renaissance of this protean genre, the essay has also taken over some of the territory abdicated by contemporary fiction. Pared down to the brittle bones of plot, camouflaged with irony, muttering in brief sentences and grade-school vocabulary, today's fashionable fiction avoids disclosing where the author stands on anything. Most of the trends in the novel and short story over the past twenty years have led away from candor—toward satire, artsy jokes, close-lipped coyness, metafictional hocus-pocus, anything but a direct statement of what the author thinks and feels. If you hide behind enough screens, no one will ever hold you to an opinion or demand from you a coherent vision or take you for a charlatan.

The essay is not fenced round by these literary inhibitions. You may speak without disguise of what moves and worries and excites you. In fact you had better speak from a region pretty close to the heart or the reader will detect the wind of phoniness whistling through your hollow phrases. In the essay you may be caught with your pants down, your ignorance and sentimentality showing, while you trot recklessly about on one of our hobbyhorses. You cannot stand back from the action, as Joyce instructed us to do, and pare your fingernails. You cannot palm off your cockamamy notions on some hapless character. If the words you put down are foolish, everyone knows precisely who the fool is.

To our list of the essay's contemporary attractions we should add the perennial ones of verbal play, mental adventure, and sheer anarchic high spirits. The writing of an essay is like finding one's way through a forest without being quite sure what game you are chasing, what landmark you are seeking. You sniff down one path until some heady smell tugs you in a new direction, and then off you go, dodging and circling, lured on by the songs of unfamiliar birds, puzzled by the tracks of strange beasts, leaping from stone to stone across rivers, barking up one tree after another. Much of the pleasure in writing an essay—and, when the writing is any good, the pleasure in reading it—comes from this dodging and leaping, this movement of the mind. It must not be idle movement, however, if the essay is to hold up; it must be driven by deep concerns. The surface of a river is alive with lights and reflections, the breaking of foam over rocks, but underneath that dazzle it is going somewhere. We should expect as much from an essay: the shimmer and play of mind on the surface and in the depths a strong current.

To see how the capricious mind can be led astray, consider my last paragraph, in which the making of essays is likened first to the romping of a dog and then to the surge of a river. That is bad enough, but it could have been worse. For example I began to draft a sentence in that paragraph with the following words: "More than once, in sitting down to beaver away at a narrative, felling trees of memory and dragging brush to build a dam that might slow down the waters of time. . . . " I had set out to make some innocent remark, and here I was gnawing down trees and building dams, all because I had let that *beaver* slip in. On this occasion I had the good sense to throw out the unruly word. I don't always, as no doubt you will have noticed. I might as well drag in another metaphor—and another unoffending animal—by saying that each doggy sentence, as it noses forward into the underbrush of thought, scatters a bunch of rabbits that go rushing off in all directions. The essayist can afford to chase more of those rabbits than the fiction writer can, but fewer than the poet. If you refuse to chase any of them, and keep plodding along in a straight line, you and your reader will have a dull outing. If you chase too many, you will soon wind up lost in a thicket of confusion with your tongue hanging out.

The pursuit of mental rabbits was strictly forbidden by the teachers who instructed me in English composition. For that matter nearly all the qualities of the personal essay, as I have been sketching them, violate the rules that many of us were taught in school. You recall we were supposed to begin with an outline and stick by it faithfully, like a train riding its rails, avoiding sidetracks. Each paragraph was to have a topic sentence pasted near the front, and these orderly paragraphs were to be coupled end-to-end like so many boxcars. Every item in those boxcars was to bear the stamp of some external authority, preferably a footnote referring to a thick book, although appeals to magazines and news-papers would do in a pinch. Our diction was to be formal, dignified, shunning the vernacular. Polysyllabic words derived from Latin were preferable to the blunt lingo of the streets. Metaphors were to be used only in emergencies, and no two of them were to be mixed. And even in emergencies we could not speak in the first-person singular.

Already, as a schoolboy, I chafed against those rules. Now I break them shamelessly—in particular the taboo against using the lonely cap-ital *I*. Just look at what I'm doing right now. My speculations about the state of the essay arise, needless to say, from my own practice as reader and writer, and they reflect my own tastes, no matter how I may pretend to gaze dispassionately down on the question from a hot-air balloon. As Thoreau declares in his brash manner on the opening page of *Walden:* "In most books the *I*, or first person, is omitted; in this it will be retained; that, in respect to egotism, is the main difference. We commonly do not remember that it is, after all, always the first person that is speaking. I should not talk so much about myself if there were anybody else whom I knew as well." True for the personal essay, it is doubly true for an essay about the essay: one speaks always and inescapably in the first-person singular.

We could sort out essays along a spectrum according to the degree to which the writer's ego is on display—with John McPhee, perhaps, at the extreme of self-effacement, and Norman Mailer at the opposite extreme of self-dramatization. Brassy or shy, stage-center or hanging back in the wings, the author's persona commands our attention. For the length of an essay, or a book of essays, we respond to that persona as we would to a friend caught up in a rapturous monologue. When the monologue is finished, we may not be able to say precisely what it was about, any more than we can draw conclusions from a piece of music. "Essays don't usually boil down to a summary, as articles do," notes Edward Hoagland, one of the least summarizable of companions, "and the style of the writer has a 'nap' to it, a combination of personality and originality and energetic loose ends that stand up like the nap of a piece of wool and can't be brushed flat." We make assumptions about that speaking voice, assumptions we cannot validly make about the narrators in fiction. Only a sophomore is permitted to ask how many children had Huckleberry Finn. But even literary sophisticates wonder in print about Thoreau's love life, Montaigne's domestic arrangements, De Quincey's opium habit, Virginia Woolf's depression.

Montaigne, who not only invented the form but perfected it as well, announced from the start that his true subject was himself. In his note "To the Reader," he slyly proclaimed:

> I want to be seen here in my simple, natural, ordinary fashion, without straining or artifice; for it is myself that I portray. My defects will here be read to the life, and also my natural form, as far as respect for the public has allowed. Had I been placed among those nations which are said to live still in the sweet freedom of nature's first laws, I assure you I should very gladly have portrayed myself here entire and wholly naked.

A few pages after this disarming introduction we are told of the Emperor Maximilian, who was so prudish about displaying his private parts that he would not let a servant dress him or see him in the bath. The emperor went so far as to give orders that he be buried in his under-drawers. Having let us in on this intimacy about Maximilian, Montaigne then confessed that he himself, although "bold-mouthed," was equally prudish, and that "except under great stress of necessity or voluptuous-ness," he never allowed anyone to see him naked. Such modesty, he feared, was unbecoming in a soldier. But such honesty is quite becom-ing in an essayist. The very confession of his prudery is a far more revealing gesture than any doffing of clothes.

Every English major knows that the word *essay,* as adapted by Montaigne, means a trial or attempt. The Latin root carries the more vivid sense of a weighing out. In the days when that root was alive and green, merchants discovered the value of goods and alchemists discovered the composition of unknown metals by the use of scales. Just so the essay, as Montaigne was the first to show, is a weighing out, an inquiry into the value, meaning, and true nature of experience; it is a private experiment carried out in public. In each of three successive editions Montaigne inserted new material into his essays without revising the old material. Often the new statements contradicted the original ones, but Montaigne let them stand, since he believed that the only consistent fact about human beings is their inconsistency. Lewis Thomas has remarked of him that he was "fond of his mind, and affectionately entertained by everything in his head." Whatever Montaigne wrote about (and he wrote about everything under the sun—fears, smells, growing old, the pleasures of scratching) he weighed on the scales of his own character.

It is the *singularity* of the first person—its warts and crotchets and turn of voice—that lures many of us into reading essays, and that lingers with us after we finish. Consider the lonely melancholy persona of Loren Eiseley, forever wandering, forever brooding on our dim and bestial past, his lips frosty with the chill of the Ice Age. Consider the volatile dionysian persona of D. H. Lawrence, with his incandescent gaze, his habit of turning peasants into gods and trees into flames, his quick hatred and quicker love. Consider that philosophical farmer Wendell Berry, who speaks with a countryman's knowledge and a deacon's severity. Consider E. B. White, with his cheery affection for brown eggs and dachshunds, his unflappable way of herding geese while the radio warns of an approaching hurricane.

White, that engaging master of the genre, a champion of idiosyncrasy, introduced one of his own collections by admitting the danger of narcissism:

> I think some people find the essay the last resort of the egoist, a much too self-conscious and self-serving form for their taste; they feel that it is presumptuous of a writer to assume that his little excursions or his small observations will interest the reader. There is some justice in their complaint. I have always been aware that I am by nature self-absorbed and egoistical; to write of myself to the extent I have done indicates a too great attention to my own life, not enough to the lives of others.

Yet the self-absorbed Mr. White was in fact a delighted observer of the world, and shared that delight with us. Thus, after describing memorably how a circus girl practiced her bareback riding in the leisure moments between shows ("The Ring of Time"), he confessed: "As a writing man, or secretary, I have always felt charged with the safekeeping of all unexpected items of worldly or unworldly enchantment, as though I might be held personally responsible if even a small one were to be lost." That may still be presumptuous, but it is presumption turned outward on the world.

This looking outward on the world helps distinguish the essay from pure autobiography, which dwells more complacently on the self. Mass murderers, movie stars, sports heroes, Wall Street crooks, and defrocked politicians may blather on about whatever high jinks or low jinks made them temporarily famous, may chronicle their exploits, their diets, their hobbies, in perfect confidence that the public is eager to gobble up every last gossipy scrap. And the public, according to sales figures, generally is. On the other hand I assume the public does not give a hoot about my private life (an assumption also borne out by sales figures). If I write of hiking up a mountain with my one-year-old boy riding like a papoose on my back, and of what he babbled to me while we gazed down from the summit onto the scudding clouds, it is not because I am deluded into believing that my baby, like the offspring of Prince Charles, matters to the great world. It is because I know the great world produces babies of its own and watches them change cloud-fast before its doting eyes. To make that climb up the mountain vividly present for readers is harder work than the climb itself. I choose to write about my experience not because it is mine, but because it seems to me a door through which others might pass.

On that cocky first page of *Walden* Thoreau justified his own seeming self-absorption by saying that he wrote the book for the sake of his fellow citizens, who kept asking him to account for his peculiar experiment by the pond. There is at least a sliver of truth to this, since Thoreau, a town character, had been invited more than once to speak his mind at the public lectern. Most of us, however, cannot honestly say the townspeople have been clamoring for our words. I suspect that all writers of the essay, even Norman Mailer and Gore Vidal, must occasionally wonder if they are egomaniacs. For the essayist, in other words, the problem of authority is inescapable. By what right does one speak? Why should anyone listen? The traditional sources of authority no longer serve. You cannot justify your words by appealing to the Bible or some other holy text, you cannot merely stitch together a patchwork of quotations from classical authors, you cannot lean on a podium at the Atheneum and deliver your wisdom to a rapt audience.

In searching for your own soapbox, a sturdy platform from which to deliver your opinionated monologues, it helps if you have already distinguished yourself at making some other, less fishy form. When Yeats describes his longing for Maud Gonne or muses on Ireland's misty lore, everything he says is charged with the prior strength of his poetry. When Virginia Woolf, in *A Room of One's Own*, reflects on the status of women and the conditions necessary for making art, she speaks as the author of *Mrs. Dalloway* and *To the Lighthouse*. The essayist may also claim our attention by having lived through events or traveled through terrains that already bear a richness of meaning. When James Baldwin writes his *Notes of a Native Son*, he does not have to convince us that racism is a troubling reality. When Barry Lopez takes us on a meditative tour of the far north in *Arctic Dreams*, he can rely on our curiosity about that fabled and forbidding place. When Paul Theroux climbs aboard a train and invites us on a journey to some exotic destination, he can count on the romance of railroads and the allure of remote cities to bear us along.

Most essayists, however, cannot draw on any source of authority from beyond the page to lend force to the page itself. They can only use language to put themselves on display and to gesture at the world. When Annie Dillard tells us in the opening lines of *Pilgrim at Tinker Creek* about the tomcat with bloody paws who jumps through the window onto her chest, why should we listen? Well, because of the voice that goes on to say: "And some mornings I'd wake in daylight to find my body covered with paw prints in blood; I looked as though I'd been painted with roses." Listen to her explaining a few pages later what she is up to in this book, this broody zestful record of her stay in the Roanoke Valley: "I propose to keep here what Thoreau called 'a meteorological journal of the mind,' telling some tales and describing some of the sights of this rather tamed valley, and exploring, in fear and trembling, some of the unmapped dim reaches and unholy fastnesses to which those tales and sights so dizzyingly lead." The sentence not only describes the method of her literary search, but also displays the breathless, often giddy, always eloquent and spiritually hungry soul who will do the searching. If you enjoy her company, you will relish Annie Dillard's essays; if you don't, you won't.

Listen to another voice which readers tend to find either captivating or insufferable:

> That summer I began to see, however dimly, that one of my ambitions, perhaps my governing ambition, was to belong fully to this place, to belong as the thrushes and the herons and the muskrats belonged, to be altogether at home here. That is still my ambition. But now I have come to see that it proposes an enormous labor. It is a spiritual ambition, like goodness. The wild creatures belong to the place by nature, but as a man I can belong to it only by understanding and by virtue. It is an ambition I cannot hope to succeed in wholly, but I have come to believe that it is the most worthy of all.

That is Wendell Berry writing about his patch of Kentucky. Once you have heard that stately, moralizing, cherishing voice, laced through with references to the land, you will not mistake it for anyone else's. Berry's themes are profound and arresting ones. But it is his voice, more than anything he speaks about, that either seizes us or drives us away.

Even so distinct a persona as Wendell Berry's or Annie Dillard's is still only a literary fabrication, of course. The first-person singular is too narrow a gate for the whole writer to pass through. What we meet on the page is not the flesh-and-blood author, but a simulacrum, a character who wears the label *I*. Introducing the lectures that became *A Room of One's Own*, Virginia Woolf reminded her listeners that " 'I' is only a convenient term for somebody who has no real being. Lies will flow from my lips, but there may perhaps be some truth mixed up with them; it is for you to seek out this truth and to decide whether any part of it is worth keeping." Here is a part I consider worth keeping: "Women have served all these centuries as looking-glasses possessing the magic and delicious power of reflecting the figure of man at twice its natural size." From such elegant revelatory sentences we build up our notion of the "I" who speaks to us under the name of Virginia Woolf.

What the essay tells us may not be true in any sense that would satisfy a court of law. As an example think of Orwell's brief narrative "A Hanging," which describes an execution in Burma. Anyone who has read it remembers how the condemned man as he walked to the gallows stepped aside to avoid a puddle. That is the sort of haunting detail only an eyewitness should be able to report. Alas, biographers, those zealous debunkers, have recently claimed that Orwell never saw such a hanging; that he reconstructed it from hearsay. What then do we make of his essay? Or has it become the sort of barefaced lie we prefer to call a story?

I don't much care what label we put on "A Hanging"—fiction or nonfiction: it is a powerful statement either way; but Orwell might have cared a great deal. I say this because not long ago I found one of my own essays treated in a scholarly article as a work of fiction, and when I got over the shock of finding any reference to my work at all, I was outraged. Here was my earnest report about growing up on a military base, my heartfelt rendering of indelible memories, being confused with the airy figments of novelists! To be sure, in writing the piece I had used dialogue, scenes, settings, character descriptions, the whole fictional bag of tricks; sure, I picked and chose among a thousand beckoning details; sure, I down-played some facts and highlighted others; but I was writing about the actual, not the invented. I shaped the matter, but I did not make it up.

To explain my outrage I must break another taboo, which is to speak of the author's intention. My teachers warned me strenuously to avoid the intentional fallacy. They told me to regard poems and plays and stories as objects washed up on the page from some unknown and unknowable shores. Now that I am on the other side of the page, so to speak, I think quite recklessly of intention all the time. I believe that if we allow the question of intent in the case of murder, we should allow it in literature. The essay is distinguished from the short story not by the presence or absence of literary devices, not by tone or theme or subject, but by the writer's stance toward the material. In composing an essay about what it was like to grow up on that military base, I *meant* something quite different from what I mean when concocting a story. I meant to preserve and record and help give voice to a reality that existed independently of me. I meant to pay my respects to a minor passage of history in an out-of-the-way place. I felt responsible to the truth as known by other people. I wanted to speak directly out of my own life into the lives of others.

You can see I am teetering on the brink of metaphysics. One step farther and I will plunge into the void, wondering as I fall how to prove there is any external truth for the essayist to pay homage to. I draw back from the brink and simply declare that I believe one writes, in essays, with a regard for the actual world, with a respect for the shared substance of history, the autonomy of other lives, the being of nature, the mystery and majesty of a creation we have not made.

When it comes to speculating about the creation, I feel more at ease with physics than with metaphysics. According to certain bold and lyrical cosmologists, there is at the center of black holes a geometrical point, the tiniest conceivable speck, where all the matter of a collapsed star has been concentrated, and where everyday notions of time, space, and force break down. That point is called a singularity. The boldest and most poetic theories suggest that anything sucked into a singularity might be flung back out again, utterly changed, somewhere else in the universe. The lonely first person, the essayist's microcosmic "I," may be thought of as a verbal singularity at the center of the mind's black hole. The raw matter of experience, torn away from the axes of time and space, falls in constantly from all sides, undergoes the mind's inscrutable alchemy, and reemerges in the quirky unprecedented shape of an essay.

Now it is time for me to step down, before another metaphor seizes hold of me, before you notice that I am standing, not on a soapbox, but on the purest air.

Analyzing and Discussing the Text

1. Why does Sanders select the soapbox orator as his model for the first-person essayist? Does the metaphor have implications that he doesn't explore?
2. Explain why Sanders sees the essay growing in popularity in our era.
3. How does Sanders characterize himself in this essay? Who is the "character who wears the label *I*"? Does the author's persona in this

context differ from the personae he creates in such essays as "Listening to Owls" (Part One, Chapter Three) and "Cloud Crossing" (Part Two, Chapter Three)? Explain the similarities and differences.

4. Does this essay reveal Sanders's own preferences as a reader of essays, or is he totally objective in his discussion of other writers? Explain why he responds in this way.

5. Does the author's credo in the next-to-last paragraph seem to have applications beyond his own work? Does it apply to any of the other nature essayists collected in this book? What, if anything, needs to be added or subtracted or emphasized more fully in order to make it applicable?

6. In what ways does the metaphor for literary creation that appears at the end of the essay seem to be a product of the author's own unique training and experience?

Experiencing and Writing About the World

1. Write a brief essay explaining your choice of rhetorical strategies (including your use or nonuse of the pronoun *I*) in at least two of the papers you have written in your current writing class.

2. Does Sanders's essay suggest a set of criteria that we can apply to other first-person essayists? Can we, for example, use the suggestion that we "sort out essays along a spectrum according to the degree to which the writer's ego is on display" as a way to discuss other essayists in this anthology? Do you agree with Sanders's sense that "the shimmer and play of mind" and a deep "strong current" are necessary ingredients in good essay writing? Prepare an analytical/philosophical essay in which you use these and/or other aspects of Sanders's implied or stated criteria as the basis for making literary judgments about other essayists. Analyze a few specific examples from the anthology according to the criteria you select; you might even subject a few of your own earlier essays to examination with these criteria in mind.

3. Sanders's discussion of the first-person essay does not mention other modes and traditions within the broad genre of literary nonfiction about the relationship between humans and nonhuman nature ("nature writing"). Using specific examples from this anthology—or from other books or periodicals that you've come across—write an essay discussing the significance of subordinating the singular first-person viewpoint to other literary strategies and intellectual concerns. What essential differences are there between personal and "impersonal" essays beyond the mere switch in pronouns? Why do some essayists opt to avoid the pronoun *I,* to leave themselves out of the discussion as much as possible? Do you, as both a reader and a writer, have a personal preference for personal or impersonal essays? When does each style seem most appropriate?

JOY WILLIAMS

Save the Whales, Screw the Shrimp

Joy Williams (1944–   ) was born in Chelmsford, Massachusetts, and now lives in Florida. She received her M.A. from Marietta College in Ohio (1963) and her M.F.A. from the University of Iowa (1965), and she has taught creative writing at a number of universities, including Houston, Florida, California (Irvine), Iowa, and Arizona. Williams, who is married to the writer and editor Rust Hills, is best known for her work as a fiction writer; her books include the story collections *Taking Care* (1982) and *Escapes* (1991) and the novels *State of Grace* (1973), *The Changeling* (1978), and *Breaking and Entering* (1989). Her fiction, which provides a surrealistic and despairing picture of contemporary lives, has been recognized with a National Endowment for the Arts Award (1973) and a Guggenheim Fellowship (1974). Williams spent 1974–1975 as a Wallace Stegner Fellow at Stanford University.

Recently, Williams has begun to write literary essays on environmental topics. While these essays do create some of the same despair that emerges in her fiction, they also give Williams the opportunity to bring to the essay form some stylistic devices that differ from those we normally associate with the genre and to express her deeply felt concerns on environmental topics. All of these qualities are evident in the essay "Save the Whales, Screw the Shrimp," which first appeared in *Esquire* and was reprinted in *The Best American Essays 1990*. In this piece, Williams's use of both dialogue and the dramatic monologue enable her to harness effectively the anger she feels in response to humanity's casual misuse of the planet, our easy pretending that such behavior is just one of many inconsequential trends in modern society.

I don't want to talk about *me*, of course, but it seems as though far too much attention has been lavished on *you* lately—that your greed and vanities and quest for self-fulfillment have been catered to far too much. You just want and want and want. You haven't had a mandala dream since the eighties began. To have a mandala dream you'd have to instinctively know that it was an attempt at self-healing on the part of Nature, and you don't believe in Nature anymore. It's too isolated from you. You've abstracted it. It's so messy and damaged and sad. Your eyes glaze as you travel life's highway past all the crushed animals and the Big Gulp cups. You don't even take pleasure in looking at nature photographs these days. Oh, they can be just as pretty, as always, but don't they make you feel increasingly . . . anxious? Filled with more trepidation than peace? So what's the point? You see the picture of the baby condor or the panda munching on a bamboo shoot, and your heart just sinks, doesn't it? A picture of a poor old sea turtle with barnacles on her back, all ancient and exhausted, depositing her five gallons of doomed eggs in the sand hardly fills you with joy, because you realize, quite rightly, that just outside the frame falls the shadow of the condo. What's cropped from the shot of ocean waves crashing on a pristine shore is the plastics plant, and just beyond the dunes lies a parking lot. Hidden from immediate view in the butterfly-bright meadow, in the dusky thicket, in the oak and holly wood, are the surveyors' stakes, for someone wants to build a mall exactly there—some gas stations and supermarkets, some pizza and video shops, a health club, maybe a bulimia treatment center. Those lovely pictures of leopards and herons and wild rivers, well, you just know they're going to be accompanied by a text that will serve only to bring you down. You don't want to think about it! It's all so uncool. And you don't want to feel guilty either. Guilt is uncool. Regret maybe you'll consider. *Maybe.* Regret is a possibility, but don't push me, you say. Nature photographs have become something of a problem, along with almost everything else. Even though they leave the bad stuff out—maybe because you *know* they're leaving all the bad stuff out—such pictures are making you increasingly aware that you're a little too late for Nature. Do you feel that? Twenty years too late, maybe only ten? Not *way* too late, just a little too late? Well, it appears that you are. And since you are, you've decided you're just not going to attend this particular party.

Pascal said that it is easier to endure death without thinking about it than to endure the thought of death without dying. This is how you manage to dance the strange dance with that grim partner, nuclear annihilation. When the U.S. Army notified Winston Churchill that the first atom bomb had been detonated in New Mexico, it chose the code phrase BABIES SATISFACTORILY BORN. So you entered the age of irony, and the strange double life you've been leading with the world ever since. Joyce Carol Oates suggests that the reason writers—*real* writers, one assumes—don't write about Nature is that it lacks a sense of humor and registers no irony. It just doesn't seem to be of the times—these slick, sleek, knowing, objective, indulgent times. And the word *Environment.* Such a bloodless word. A flat-footed word with a shrunken heart. A word increasingly disengaged from its association with the natural world. Urban planners, industrialists, economists, and developers use it. It's a lost word, really. A cold word, mechanistic, suited strangely to the coldness generally felt toward Nature. It's their word now. You don't mind giving it up. As for *Environmentalist*, that's one that can really bring on the yawns, for you've tamed and tidied it, neutered it quite nicely. An environmentalist must be calm, rational, reasonable, and willing to compromise, otherwise you won't listen to him. Still, his beliefs are *opinions* only, for this is the age of radical subjectivism. Not long ago, Barry Commoner spoke to the Environmental Protection Agency. He scolded them. They loved it. The way they protect the environment these days is apparently to find an "acceptable level of harm from a pollutant and then issue rules allowing industry to pollute to that level." Commoner suggested that this was inappropriate. An EPA employee suggested that any other approach would place limits on economic growth and implied that Commoner was advocating this. Limits on economic growth! Commoner vigorously denied this. Oh, it was a healthy exchange of ideas, healthier certainly than our air and water. We needed that little spanking, the EPA felt. It was refreshing. The agency has recently lumbered into action in its campaign to ban dinoseb. You seem to have liked your dinoseb. It's been a popular weed killer, even though it has been directly linked with birth defects. You must hate weeds a lot. Although the EPA appears successful in banning the poison, it will still have to pay the disposal costs and compensate the manufacturers for the market value of the chemicals they still have in stock.

That's ironic, you say, but farmers will suffer losses, too, oh dreadful financial losses, if herbicide and pesticide use is restricted.

Farmers grow way too much stuff anyway. They grow surplus crops with subsidized water created by turning rivers great and small into a plumbing system of dams and canals. Rivers have become *systems*. Wetlands are increasingly being referred to as *filtering systems*—things deigned *useful* because of their ability to absorb urban run-off, oil from roads, et cetera.

We know that. We've known that for years about farmers. We know a lot these days. We're very well informed. If farmers aren't allowed to make a profit by growing surplus crops, they'll have to sell their land to developers, who'll turn all that *arable land* into office parks. Arable land isn't Nature anyway, and besides, we like those office parks and shopping plazas, with their monster supermarkets open twenty-four hours a day with aisle after aisle after aisle of *products*. It's fun. Products are fun.

Farmers like their poisons, but ranchers like them even more. There are well-funded predominantly federal and cooperative programs like the Agriculture Department's Animal Damage Control Unit that poison, shoot, and trap several thousand animals each year. This unit loves to kill things. It was created to kill things—bobcats, foxes, black bears, mountain lions, rabbits, badgers, countless birds—all to make this great land safe for the string bean and the corn, the sheep and the cow, even though you're not consuming as much cow these days. A burger now and then, but burgers are hardly cows at all, you feel. They're not all *our* cows in any case, for some burger matter is imported. There's a bit of Central American burger matter in your bun. Which is contributing to the conversion of tropical rain forest into cow pasture. Even so, you're getting away from meat these days. You're eschewing cow. It's seafood you love, shrimp most of all. And when you love something, it had better watch out, because you have a tendency to love it to death. Shrimp, shrimp, shrimp. It's more common on menus than chicken. In the wilds of Ohio, far, far from watery shores, four out of the six entrées on a menu will be shrimp, for some modest sum. Everywhere, it's all the shrimp you can eat or all you *care* to eat, for sometimes you just don't feel like eating all you *can*. You are intensively *harvesting* shrimp. Soon there won't be any left and then you can stop. It takes that, often, to make you stop. Shrimpers shrimp, of course. That's their *business*. They put out these big nets and in these nets, for each pound of shrimp, they catch more than ten times that amount of fish, turtles, and dolphins. These, quite the worse for wear, they dump back in. There is an object called TED (Turtle Excluder Device), which would save thousands of turtles and some dolphins from dying in the nets, but the shrimpers are loath to use TEDs, as they say it would cut the size of their shrimp catch.

We've heard about TED, you say.

They want you, all of you, to have all the shrimp you can eat and more. At Kiawah Island, off the coast of South Carolina, visitors go out on Jeep "safaris" through the part of the island that hasn't been developed yet. ("Wherever you see trees," the guide says, "really, that's a lot.") The safari comprises six Jeeps, and these days they go out at least four times a day, with more trips promised soon. The tourists drive their own Jeeps and the guide talks to them by radio. Kiawah has nice beaches, and the guide talks about turtles. When he mentions the shrimpers' role in the decline of the turtle, the shrimpers, who share the same frequency, scream at him. Shrimpers and most commercial fishermen (many of them working with drift and gill nets anywhere from six to thirty miles long) think of themselves as an *endangered species*. A recent newspaper headline said, "Shrimpers Spared Anti-Turtle Devices." Even so, with the continuing wanton depletion of shrimp beds, they will undoubtedly have to find some other means of employment soon. They might, for instance, become part of that vast throng laboring in the *tourist industry*.

Tourism has become an industry as destructive as any other. You are no longer benign in your traveling somewhere to look at the scenery. You never thought there was much gain in just looking anyway, you've always preferred to *use* the scenery in some manner. In your desire to get away from what you've got, you've caused there to be no place to get away *to*. You're just all bumpered up out there. Sewage and dumps have become prime indicators of America's lifestyle. In resort towns in

New England and the Adirondacks, measuring the flow into the sewage plant serves as a business barometer. Tourism is a growth industry. You believe in growth. *Controlled* growth, of course. Controlled exponential growth is what you'd really like to see. You certainly don't want to put a moratorium or a cap on anything. That's illegal, isn't it? Retro you're not. You don't want to go back or anything. Forward. Maybe ask directions later. Growth is *desirable* as well as being *inevitable*. Growth is the one thing you seem to be powerless before, so you try to be realistic about it. Growth is—it's weird—it's like cancer or something.

Recently you, as tourist, have discovered your national parks and are quickly *overburdening* them. Spare land and it belongs to you! It's exotic land too, not looking like all the stuff around it that looks like everything else. You want to take advantage of this land, of course, and use it in every way you can. Thus the managers—or *stewards,* as they like to be called—have developed *wise* and *multiple-use* plans, keeping in mind exploiters' interests (for they have their needs, too) as well as the desires of the backpackers. Thus mining, timbering, and ranching activities take place in the national forests, where the Forest Service maintains a system of logging roads eight times larger than the interstate highway system. The national parks are more of a public playground and are becoming increasingly Europeanized in their look and management. Lots of concessions and motels. You deserve a clean bed and a hot meal when you go into the wilderness. At least your stewards think that you do. You keep your stewards busy. Not only must they cater to your multiple and conflicting desires, they have to manage your wildlife *resources.* They have managed wildfowl to such an extent that the reasoning has become, If it weren't for hunters, ducks would disappear. Duck stamps and licensing fees support the whole rickety duck-management system. Yes! If it weren't for the people who killed them, wild ducks wouldn't exist! Managers are managing all wild creatures, not just those that fly. They track and tape and tag and band. They relocate, restock, and reintroduce. They cull and control. It's hard to keep it all straight. Protect or poison? Extirpate or just mostly eliminate? Sometimes even the stewards get mixed up.

This is the time of machines and models, hands-on management and master plans. Don't you ever wonder as you pass that billboard advertising another MASTER-PLANNED COMMUNITY just what master they are actually talking about? Not the Big Master, certainly. Something brought to you by one of the tiny masters, of which there are many. But you like these tiny masters and have even come to expect and require them. In Florida they've just started a ten-thousand-acre city in the Everglades. It's a *megaproject,* one of the largest ever in the state. Yes, they must have thought you wanted it. No, what you thought of as the Everglades, the Park, is only a little bitty part of the Everglades. Developers have been gnawing at this irreplaceable, strange land for years. It's like they just *hate* this ancient sea of grass. Maybe you could ask them about this sometime. Roy Rogers is the senior vice president of strategic planning, and the old cowboy says that every tree and bush and inch of sidewalk in the project has been planned. Nevertheless, because the whole thing will take twenty-five years to complete, the plan is going to be constantly changed. You can understand this. The important thing is that there be a blueprint. You trust a blueprint. The tiny masters know what you like. You like *a secure landscape* and *access to services*. You like grass—that is, lawns. The ultimate lawn is the golf course, which you've been told has "some ecological value." You believe this! Not that it really matters, you just like to play golf. These golf courses require a lot of watering. So much that the more inspired of the masters have taken to watering them with effluent, *treated* effluent, but yours, from all the condos and villas built around the stocked artificial lakes you fancy.

I really don't want to think about sewage, you say, but it sounds like progress.

It is true that the masters are struggling with the problems of your incessant flushing. Cuisine is also one of their concerns. Advances in sorbets—sorbet intermezzos—in their clubs and fine restaurants. They know what you want. You want A HAVEN FROM THE ORDINARY WORLD. If you're A NATURE LOVER in the West you want to live in a $200,000 home in A WILD ANIMAL HABITAT. If you're eastern and consider yourself more hip, you want to live in new towns—brand-new reconstructed-from-scratch towns—in a house of NINETEENTH-CENTURY DESIGN. But in these new towns the masters are building, getting around can be confusing. There is an abundance of curves and an infrequency of through streets. It's the new wilderness without any trees. You can get lost, even with all the "mental bread crumbs" the masters scatter about as visual landmarks—the windmill, the water views, the various groupings of landscape "material." You *are* lost, you know. But you trust a Realtor will show you the way. There are many more Realtors than tiny masters, and many of them have to make do with less than a loaf—that is, trying to sell stuff that's already been built in an environment already "enhanced" rather than something being planned—but they're everywhere, willing to show you the path. If Dante returned to Hell today, he'd probably be escorted down by a Realtor, talking all the while about how it was just another level of Paradise.

When have you last watched a sunset? Do you remember where you were? With whom? At Loews Ventana Canyon Resort, the Grand Foyer will provide you with that opportunity through lighting which is computerized to diminish with the approaching sunset!

The tiny masters are willing to arrange Nature for you. They will compose it into a picture that you can look at at your leisure, when you're not doing work or something like that. Nature becomes scenery, a prop. At some golf courses in the Southwest, the saguaro cacti are reported to be repaired with green paste when balls blast into their skin. The saguaro can attempt to heal themselves by growing over the balls, but this takes time, and the effect can be somewhat...baroque. It's better to get out the pastepot. Nature has become simply a visual form of entertainment, and it had better look snappy.

Listen, you say, we've been at Ventana Canyon. It's in the desert, right? It's very, very nice, a world-class resort. A totally self-contained environment with everything that a person could possibly want, on more than a thousand acres in the middle of zip. It sprawls but nestles, like. And they've maintained the integrity of as much of the desert ecosystem as possible. Give them credit for that. *Great* restaurant, too. We had baby bay scallops there. Coming into the lobby there are these two big hand-carved coyotes, mutely howling. And that's the way we like them, *mute*. God, why do those things howl like that?

Wildlife is a personal matter, you think. The attitude is up to you. You can prefer to see it dead or not dead. You might want to let it mosey about its business or blow it away. Wild things exist only if you have the graciousness to allow them to. Just outside Tucson, Arizona, there is a brand-new structure modeled after a French foreign legion outpost. It's the *International Wildlife Museum,* and it's full of dead animals. Three hundred species are there, at least a third of them—the rarest ones—killed and collected by one C. J. McElroy, who enjoyed doing it and now shares what's left with you. The museum claims to be educational because you can watch a taxidermist at work or touch a lion's tooth. You can get real close to these dead animals, closer than you can in a zoo. Some of you prefer zoos, however, which are becoming bigger, better, and bioclimatic. New-age zoo designers want the animals to *flow right out into your space.* In Dallas there will soon be a Wilds of Africa exhibit; in San Diego there's a simulated rain forest, where you can thread your way "down the side of a lush canyon, the air filled with a fine mist from 300 high-pressure nozzles"; in New Orleans you've constructed a swamp, the real swamp not far away on the verge of disappearing. Animals in these places are abstractions—wandering relics of their true selves, but that doesn't matter. Animal behavior in a zoo is nothing like natural behavior, but that doesn't really matter, either. Zoos are pretty, contained, and accessible. These new habitats can contain one hundred different species—not more than one or two of each thing, of course—on seven acres, three, one. You don't want to see *too much* of anything, certainly. An *example* will suffice. Sort of like a biological Crabtree & Evelyn basket selected with *you* in mind. You like things reduced, simplified. It's easier to take it all in, park it in your mind. You like things inside better than outside anyway. You are increasingly looking at and living in proxy environments created by substitution and simulation. *Resource economists* are a wee branch in the tree of tiny masters, and one, Martin Krieger, wrote, "Artificial prairies and wildernesses have been created, and there is no reason to believe that these artificial environments need be unsatisfactory for those who experience them. . . . We will have to realize that the way in which we experience nature is conditioned by our society—which more and more is seen to be receptive to responsible intervention."

Nature has become a world of appearances, a mere source of materials. You've been editing it for quite some time; now you're in the process of deleting it. Earth is beginning to look like not much more than a launching pad. Back near Tucson, on the opposite side of the mountain from the dead-animal habitat, you're building Biosphere II (as compared with or opposed to Biosphere I, more commonly known as Earth)—a $2\frac{1}{2}$-acre terrarium, an artificial ecosystem that will include a rain forest, a desert, a thirty-five-foot ocean, and several thousand species of life (lots of microbes), including eight human beings, who will cultivate a bit of farmland. You think it would be nice to colonize other worlds after you've made it necessary to leave this one.

Hey, that's pretty good, you say, all that stuff packed into just $2\frac{1}{2}$ acres. That's only about three times bigger than my entire *house*.

It's small all right, but still not small enough to be, apparently, useful. For the purposes of NASA, say, it would have to be smaller, oh much smaller, and energy-efficient too. Fiddle, fiddle, fiddle. You support fiddling, as well as meddling. This is how you learn. Though it's quite apparent the environment has been grossly polluted and the natural world abused and defiled, you seem to prefer to continue pondering effects rather than preventing causes. You want proof, you insist on proof. A Dr. Lave from Carnegie-Mellon—and he's an expert, an economist, and an environmental *expert*—says that scientists will have to prove to you that you will suffer if you don't become less of a "throwaway society." *If you really want me to give up my car or my air conditioner, you'd better prove to me first that the earth would otherwise be uninhabitable,* Dr. Lave says. *Me* is *you*, I presume, whereas *you* refers to them. You as in me—that is, *me, me, me*—certainly strike a hard bargain. Uninhabitable the world has to get before you rein in your requirements. You're a consumer after all, *the* consumer upon whom so much attention is lavished, the ultimate user of a commodity that has become, these days, everything. To try to appease your appetite for proof, for example, scientists have been leasing for experimentation forty-six pristine lakes in Canada.

They don't want to *keep* them, they just want to *borrow* them.

They've been intentionally contaminating many of the lakes with a variety of pollutants dribbled into the propeller wash of research boats. *It's one of the boldest experiments in lake ecology ever conducted.* They've turned these remote lakes into huge *real-world test tubes*. They've been doing this since 1976! And what they've found so far in these *preliminary* studies is that pollutants are really destructive. The lakes get gross. Life in them ceases. It took about eight years to make this happen in one of them, everything carefully measured and controlled all the while. Now the scientists are slowly reversing the process. But it will take hundreds of years for the lakes to recover. They think.

Remember when you used to like rain, the sound of it, the feel of it, the way it made the plants and trees all glisten. We needed that rain, you would say. It looked pretty too, you thought, particularly in the movies. Now it rains and you go, Oh-oh. A nice walloping rain these days means *overtaxing our sewage treatment plants*. It means *untreated waste discharged directly into our waterways*. It means . . .
Okay. Okay.
Acid rain! And we all know what this is. Or most of us do. People of power in government and industry still don't seem to know what it is. Whatever it is, they say, they don't want to curb it, but they're willing to study it some more. Economists call air and water pollution "externalities" anyway. Oh, acid rain. You do get so sick of hearing about it. The words have already become a white-noise kind of thing. But you think in terms of *mitigating* it maybe. As for *the greenhouse effect,* you think in terms of *countering* that. One way that's been discussed recently is the planting of new forests, not for the sake of the forests alone, oh my heavens, no. Not for the sake of majesty and mystery or of Thumper and Bambi, are you kidding me, but because, as every schoolchild knows, trees absorb carbon dioxide. They just soak it up and store it. They just love it. So this is the plan: you plant millions of acres of trees, and you can go on doing pretty much whatever you're doing—driving around, using staggering amounts of energy, keeping those power plants fired to the max. Isn't Nature remarkable? So willing to serve? You wouldn't think it had anything more to offer, but it seems it does. Of course these "forests" wouldn't exactly be forests. They would be more like trees. *Managed* trees. The Forest Service, which now manages our forests by cutting them down, might be called upon to evolve in their thinking and allow these trees to grow. They would probably be patented trees after a time. Fast-growing, uniform, genetically-created-to-be-toxin-eating *machines*. They would be *new-age* trees, because the problem with planting the old-fashioned variety to *combat* the greenhouse effect, which is caused by pollution, is that they're already dying from it. All along the crest of the Appalachians from Maine to Georgia, forests struggle to survive in a toxic soup of poisons. They can't *help* us if we've killed them, now can they?

All right, you say, wow, lighten up will you? Relax. Tell about yourself.
Well, I say, I live in Florida . . .

Oh my God, you say. Florida! Florida is a joke! How do you expect us to take you seriously if you still live there! Florida is crazy, it's pink concrete. It's paved, it's over. And a little girl just got eaten by an alligator down there. It came out of some swamp next to a subdivision and just carried her off. That set your Endangered Species Act back fifty years, you can bet.

I . . .

Listen, we don't want to hear any more about Florida. We don't want to hear about Phoenix or Hilton Head or California's Central Valley. If our wetlands—our *vanishing* wetlands—are mentioned one more time, we'll scream. And the talk about condors and grizzlies and wolves is becoming too de trop. We had just managed to get whales out of our minds when those three showed up under the ice in Alaska. They even had *names*. Bone is the dead one, right? It's almost the twenty-first century! Those last condors are *pathetic*. Can't we just get this over with?

Aristotle said that all living things are ensouled and striving to participate in eternity.

Oh, I just bet he said that, you say. That doesn't sound like Aristotle. He was a humanist. We're all humanists here. This is the age of humanism. And it has been for a long time.

You are driving with a stranger in the car, and it is the stranger behind the wheel. In the back seat are your pals for many years now—DO WHAT YOU LIKE and his swilling sidekick, WHY NOT. A deer, or some emblematic animal, something from that myriad natural world you've come from that you now treat with such indifference and scorn—steps from the dimming woods and tentatively upon the highway. The stranger does not decelerate or brake, not yet, maybe not at all. The feeling is that whatever it is *will get out of the way*. Oh, it's a fine car you've got, a fine machine, and oddly you don't mind the stranger driving it, because in a way, everything has gotten too complicated, way, way out of your control. You've given the wheel to the masters, the managers, the comptrollers. Something is wrong, *maybe*, you feel a little sick, *actually*, but the car is luxurious and fast and you're *moving*, which is the most important thing by far.

Why make a fuss when you're so comfortable? Don't make a fuss, make a baby. Go out and get something to eat, build something. Make *another* baby. Babies are cute. Babies show you have faith in the future. Although faith is perhaps too strong a word. They're everywhere these days, in all the crowds and traffic jams, there are the babies too. You don't seem to associate them with the problems of population increase. They're just babies! And you've come to believe in them again. They're a lot more tangible than the afterlife, which, of course, you haven't believed in in ages. At least not for yourself. The afterlife now belongs to plastics and poisons. Yes, plastics and poisons will have a far more extensive afterlife than you, that's known. A disposable diaper, for example, which is all plastic and wood pulp—you like them for all those babies, so easy to use and toss—will take around four centuries to degrade. Almost all plastics do, centuries and centuries. In the sea, many marine animals die from ingesting or being entangled in discarded plastic. In the dumps, plastic squats on more than 25 percent of dump space. But your heart is disposed toward plastic. Someone, no doubt the plastics industry, told you it was convenient. This same industry is now looking into recycling in an attempt to get the critics of their nefarious, multifarious products off their backs. That should make you feel better, because *recycling* has become an honorable word, no longer merely the hobby of Volvo owners. The fact is that people in plastics are born obscurants. Recycling (practically impossible) won't solve the plastic glut, only reduction of production will, and the plastics industry isn't looking into that, you can be sure. Waste is not just the stuff you throw away, of course, it's the stuff you use to excess. With the exception of *hazardous waste*, which you do worry about from time to time, it's even thought you have a declining sense of emergency about the problem. Builders are building bigger houses because you want bigger. You're trading up. Utility companies are beginning to worry about your constantly rising consumption. Utility companies! You haven't entered a new age at all but one of upscale nihilism, deluxe nihilism.

In the summer, particularly in *the industrial Northeast,* you did get a little excited. The filth cut into your fun time. Dead stuff floating around. Sludge and bloody vials. Hygienic devices—appearing not quite so hygienic out of context—all coming in on the tide. The air smelled funny, too. You tolerate a great deal, but the summer of '88 was truly creepy. It was even thought for a moment that the environment would become a political issue. But it didn't. You didn't want it to be, preferring instead to continue in your politics of subsidizing and advancing avarice. The issues were the same as always—jobs, defense, the economy, maintaining and improving the standard of living in this greedy, selfish, expansionistic, industrialized society.

You're getting a little shrill here, you say.

You're pretty well off. You expect to be better off soon. You do. What does this mean? More software, more scampi, more square footage? You have created an ecological crisis. The earth is infinitely variable and alive, and you are killing it. It seems safer this way. But you are not safe. You want to find wholeness and happiness in a land increasingly damaged and betrayed, and you never will. More than material matters. You must change your ways.

What is this? *Sinners in the Hands of an Angry God?*

The ecological crisis cannot be resolved by politics. It cannot be solved by science or technology. It is a crisis caused by culture and character, and a deep change in personal consciousness is needed. Your fundamental attitudes toward the earth have become twisted. You have made only brutal contact with Nature, you cannot comprehend its grace. You must change. Have few desires and simple pleasures. Honor non-human life. Control yourself, become more authentic. Live lightly upon the earth and treat it with respect. Redefine the word *progress* and dismiss the managers and masters. Grow inwardly and with knowledge become truly wiser. Make connections. Think differently, behave differently. For this is essentially a moral issue we face and moral decisions must be made.

A *moral issue!* Okay, this discussion is now toast. A *moral* issue . . . And who's this *we* now? Who are *you* is what I'd like to know. You're not me, anyway. I admit, someone's to blame and something should be done. But I've got to go. It's getting late. That's dusk out there. That is dusk, isn't it? It certainly doesn't look like any dawn I've ever seen. Well, take care.

Analyzing and Discussing the Text

1. Throughout this essay we hear the voice of a character Williams has created and launched on a long (and somewhat one-sided and scolding) environmental discussion. What do the word choice and tone suggest about the character's class, life-style, environmental awareness, and level of commitment to the environment? How does the speaker seem to view the listener, the "you" of the essay?

2. Describe the speaker's tone when suggesting that nature photographs "are making you increasingly aware that you're a little too late for Nature" and accusing the listener of deciding that "you're just not going to attend this particular party." What is Williams's point in these passages?

3. Why does Williams call *environment* a "lost word really" early in this essay? How does her discussion compare, in attitude and style, with David Quammen's essays "The White Tigers of Cincinnati" and "Dirty Word, Clean Place"? How does Williams's discussion of zoos relate to Quammen's essay on zoos?

4. How does Williams characterize American society in paragraph 5? Does this characterization change at all in paragraphs 9 and 10?

5. Who are the "tiny masters" mentioned in this essay?

6. Is the image of the car in paragraph 31 an effective metaphor for contemporary American culture and its environmental attitudes?
7. How and why does the tone of the essay shift in paragraphs 35 to 38?

Experiencing and Writing About the World

1. Write a short essay in which you create a dramatic monologue about one aspect of the environment. Try to give your speaker a different personality and set of attitudes than Williams's speaker, but make your character just as distinctive and opinionated.
2. Choose one of the topics addressed in Williams's essay—overdevelopment, overpopulation, pesticides, and so forth—as the subject of a more straightforward expository essay. As you write, notice how the different approach determines the amount and type of information you need in order to make your points persuasively. Go to the library and gather information on your specific topic from current periodicals before writing this essay, rather than merely spouting ideas off the top of your head.
3. Do you find Williams's essay engagingly humorous or offensively strident? Write an analytical essay in which you compare Williams's effort to present environmental attitudes humorously with other examples of humorous writing about the environment from this anthology. How, for instance, does Williams's style of humor compare with Edward Abbey's? David Quammen's?

DAVID QUAMMEN

Dirty Word, Clean Place

For biographical information, see the headnote for "The Face of a Spider" in Part One, Chapter One.

Because most people today typically view "environmentalism" as preferable to the ills (increased toxic waste, overdevelopment, destruction of the ozone layer, acid rain, and so forth) that threaten us and the planet, Quammen's argument in this essay may startle us at first. The "e-word" is so strongly interwoven with our day-to-day discussions about how to protect the planet that we may find it difficult to believe that Quammen really means to suggest that environmentalism is a dangerous instance of "semantic perversion." We assume, perhaps, that this assertion is designed simply to be provocative, to grab our attention before the author moves on to state his real, and presumably "environmental," agenda. As we read through Quammen's "Dirty Word, Clean Place," however, it becomes clear that what he seeks is to persuade us to think, talk, and write with more clarity and precision as we determine what we want for ourselves and our planet. Thus Quammen attempts to move beyond the limited thinking that he now sees embodied in the term *environmentalism*. In this essay published originally in *Outside* (August 1991), Quammen uses his formidable range of knowledge and his precise verbal logic to sort out just why the term *environmentalism* has become, for him, a "dirty word," a word that implies that "humanity is the star of a one-character drama," with the rest of nature serving merely as stage and scenery. Thus, according to the essayist, the "e-word" advocates a selfish and, ultimately, sterile cleanliness.

At some point during the past 25 years we have perverted a word, and that semantic perversion has brought upon us a perverted idea. The perverted idea is well intentioned, innocent-seeming, currently rather fashionable, and dangerous. The perverted word is "environmentalism." A sawmill foreman in Oregon, a liability lawyer for Exxon, an Assistant Secretary of Agriculture in the Bush administration might not agree with much of what I'm about to say, but I suspect that they each would agree (for their own reasons, antithetical to mine) with this point at least: Environmentalism, word and idea, is inimical to all that's precious.

Bear with me a moment. The fact that a lawyer for Exxon might agree with some notion doesn't necessarily make that notion false. The next stage of the argument is: dangerous and perverted compared to what? I'm not talking about environmentalism versus development, or environmentalism versus business, or (the phoniest, most duplicitous dichotomy of them all) environmentalism versus jobs. I'm talking about environmentalism versus conservation. My complaint is that people keep fussing about "the environment" when they should be concerned with something more intricate, less flat, less peripheral, more important. What's more intricate and more important than the environment? This is: the collective assemblage of beings and relationships and processes and physical objects that we might choose to call by the term "nature."

An alternative term is "the biosphere." Another alternative, less precise but just as accurate, is "the world." We live in the world, we're destroying the world. The world is more dimensional, less subordinate, than the environment. The world consists of granite and rivers and wind and limestone, of beetles and falcons and rhinos, of rainforest and chaparral, of predation and competition and pollination and mutualism, as well as a bit of concrete, a bit of steel, and five billion *Homo sapiens*. The world is foreground whereas the environment is background. This is not just a matter of words. This involves the concepts and attitudes to which words give shape and power. The term "environment" implies a set of surroundings for some central, preeminent subject. That central subject, under our prevailing assumptions, is human life. Therefore the very word "environment" entails a presumption that humanity is the star of a one-character drama around which everything else is just scenery and proscenium. Still, "environmentalism" is an apt bit of terminology for use by whoever might want to declare themselves utterly, unapologetically anthropocentric. "Nature," on the other hand, implies something deeper and more meaningful than a set of surroundings, and "conservation of nature" is an enterprise of far wider ambition than getting asbestos off the market or keeping tap water fit to drink. Conservation admits to the premise that nonhuman species and natural systems are intrinsically valuable; environmentalism is utilitarian. That distinction is a huge one. For a conservationist to talk about "the environment," as though it were synonymous with "nature," seems as jarringly wrongheaded as for a white liberal to talk about "darkies" and "gooks."

Of course I've done it myself. You've done it. We all speak the words that are familiar and handy and streamlined. But then sometimes there comes a point where we rebel. We become sensitive to subtext and context, as well as text. We begin to choose better, less damaging language.

There's a place for the word "environmentalism." It's an appropriate label for a certain, limited set of concerns: nontoxic water, nontoxic air, nontoxic tomatoes, no used hypodermics littering the beaches of Long Island or Massachusetts or California, and the freedom for humans to go on expropriating every inch of the planet without fear that someone might get poisoned. The last of those items—freedom from toxic feedback while we overrun the planet—is not an explicit part of the environmentalist program, but it does lurk in shadows among the language and the priorities. Granted, no popular movement should be held culpable for everything it omits, and I want to be fair as well as harsh. So I'll state the obvious: The fight to reverse our species' inclination toward industrial-strength biochemical suicide has a noble history, dating back at least to Rachel Carson, and that fight is rightly called "environmentalism." But we ought to be clear about what it denotes, what it connotes, and what it ignores. I started this argument with wild talk of perversion. Environmentalism is not in its essence perverted. It's just an understandable campaign of self-interest, by our species, with potentially dire implications for the world at large. What does seem perverted is confusing environmentalism with conservation.

Several months ago Michael Oppenheimer, a senior scientist at the Environmental Defense Fund, noted passingly in a book review: "Environmentalism is no longer about wilderness protection; it's about saving the collective neck of humanity." Unfortunately, he's right.

But what Oppenheimer suggests, with this statement, is that environmentalism in the course of its maturation has gotten bigger. I think it's gotten smaller.

"Conservation" is a respectable old word. When did "conservation" become "environmentalism"? I consulted the *Oxford English Dictionary*, which tells us about the history of our language as well as its present condition.

The adjective "environmental" has been around for at least a century, though its meaning has changed. The noun forms seem to be slightly newer. Back in 1923, in a book titled *Early Civilization*, A. A. Goldenweiser used "environmentalism" to label a school of thought that interpreted forms of civilization in light of environmental conditions. About the same time, that usage was echoed by a certain F. Thomas, in a volume called *The Environmental Basis of Society*. According to Thomas: "The environmentalist holds, for example, that the snow house of the Eskimo is determined by the surrounding Arctic environment." In 1931, the *Encyclopedia of Social Sciences* declared that "environmentalism is the tendency to stress the importance of physical, biological, psychological or cultural environment as a factor influencing the structure or behavior of animals, including man." In 1940, R. S. Woodworth wrote of the "age-long dispute between the hereditarians and the environmentalists," and as late as 1959, in *Architectural Review*, "Environmentalists" with a capital E was applied to architectural thinkers holding particular views of the relationships between buildings and spaces. But by the time of the first Earth Day, in 1970, a completely new meaning was in place.

That year, in *The New Yorker*, it was reported that "Dr. Robert N. Rickles, a thirty-four-year-old chemist and an environmentalist," had become head of New York's Department of Air Resources. Dr. Rickles seems nicely appropriate as the earliest environmentalist (in the modern sense of the word) to be recognized by the *Oxford English Dictionary*, in that he was professionally responsible for air quality in the city of New York. No one should confuse that job with the conservation of nature.

What was it that occurred between 1959 and 1970 to give a new definition to this protean word? Well, that was a hectic time, as you might recall. We were thumping around like beached belugas, trying to redefine ourselves as a civilized culture. Plenty happened. One of the more consequential events, I suspect, was the publication in 1962 of Rachel Carson's most famous book, *Silent Spring*.

Carson was trained as an aquatic biologist. She worked for the U.S. Bureau of Fisheries, then for the Fish and Wildlife Service. Her earlier books, more descriptive than polemic, were about the sea. *Silent Spring* was her last, and it was part of a different era; in fact, it was the heraldic horn-blast to that era. Before her, we had been blessed with some pioneer conservationists such as John Muir, Gifford Pinchot, Aldo Leopold, Charles Elton, whose hearts were in the woodland and whose expertise (except for Muir, no expert but profoundly an amateur) was in forestry or ecology. Rachel Carson brought biochemistry into the picture. She didn't use the word "environmentalism" (unless I've missed it, in looking back at her book), but I suspect that she more than anyone else caused it to come into being. She did declare, before such statements were fashionable, that the "most alarming of all man's assaults upon the environment is the contamination of air, earth, rivers, and sea with dangerous and even lethal materials." And she did write: "The problem of water pollution by pesticides can be understood only in context, as part of the whole to which it belongs—the pollution of the total environment of mankind." Although Carson seems to have cared deeply about the integrity of ecosystems and the survival of other species, her central and stated concern in this book was the poisoning of the "environment of mankind," and to that concern she did eloquent service.

Without the work of Rachel Carson, Dr. Robert N. Rickles might not have been labeled, in 1970, an environmentalist. Maybe he would have fought the same skirmishes under some other flag. Or maybe, in the absence of Carson, there might have been no New York Department of Air Resources for him to command.

The only bad aspect of Carson's legacy is that her influence, so timely and potent, may have led the rest of us to commit that act of perverting synecdoche. We have mistaken the part for the whole. We have confused environmentalism with conservation.

I want to pose you a dire hypothesis. Let's imagine that the world had nothing to protect it but environmentalism.

We would all enjoy clean water. The soil would be certifiably free of plutonium and arsenic. The air would be filtered, scrubbed, ceaselessly monitored, invisible, and pure. Our electric buses and cars would emit no hydrocarbons, the ozone would be intact, and the problem of global warming would be solved, don't ask me how. We're on board the flying carpet of fantasy, remember, sailing into a future where all this is plausible. Our tomatoes and our cotton are grown without pesticides.

We carry our groceries in cloth bags. Malaria is prevented by window screens. Love Canal is a showcase community full of vigorous children and organic asparagus, the most improbable rehabilitation since Richard Nixon's. We have invented ways to detoxify our environment and keep it detoxified. We are all healthy, and the Earth is a miserable, desolate, lonely place.

It's clean. But ecologically, it's empty. Simplified. Depleted of biotic diversity. We share the planet with just a small number of other species, and they all tend to resemble us in ecological character, if not in physical shape: rats, gray squirrels, raccoons, crab-eating macaques, mongooses, feral pigeons, crows, coyotes, white-tailed deer, cockroaches, *Ailanthus* trees, *Cecropia* trees, sea lampreys, Nile perch, European starlings, burrowing owls, *Spartina* grass, geckos, muskrats, rabbits, and possibly black bears, though certainly no polar bears and no grizzlies. The list isn't random. They are all stubborn, forgiving survivors. What we ourselves have in common with this relative handful of virtually ineradicable species is the ability to thrive on a disrupted landscape, to tolerate a wide range of conditions, to subsist on a wide range of foods, to colonize new places, and to reproduce quickly. In other words, we are all weeds.

That's why I call this gloomy vision the Planet of Weeds scenario.

We have abolished rainforest without depriving ourselves of oxygen. (Sadly, that may be possible.) We have also clear-cut and pulped the last of the temperate forests, elbowed the spotted owl into oblivion, and planted eucalyptus and gmelina in neat rows. Our economy is sound. Our land is productive. The most plentiful large animal on the face of creation, next to us, is the Hereford. Forty-five zillion acres are devoted to high-yield strains of wheat and rice. Nothing is wasted, nothing exists only for its own narrow sake, except us. Nothing is intrinsically valued. The inconvenient animals are gone—the tiger, the bison, the wolf, the wolverine, the cougar, the mountain gorilla. The innocuous but useless animals, the specialists adapted to mature habitats, the occupiers of slim niches, the slow reproducers, are gone too—beginning with all the world's tortoises. We have pared down the number of beetle species on Earth from ten million to roughly three dozen, but we've saved the ladybug for recreational gardening. Chickens and dogs are now thought of as wildlife. African lions still exist in zoos, for reasons of entertainment and nostalgia, and high-quality ivory is synthesized in labs. Butterflies are bred in greenhouses and processed into decorative works of craft, but the inventory of species is tiny; they are offered in metallic blue, in yellow, and in orange-and-black. The cabbage butterfly lives wild, another weed. An agricultural landscape in New Zealand is indistinguishable biologically from an agricultural landscape in Wisconsin.

There's been a pleasant surprise: The life-support capacity of the continents and the oceans and the atmosphere has not collapsed in ruins, as some people predicted it would. We have not, as it turns out, destroyed ourselves by destroying most of the other species on Earth. In the process of transforming wild habitat into cities and suburbs and fields of soybeans and corn, we have reduced global biodiversity by 99.9 percent, yes, but so what? The world continues to function. It simply has fewer moving parts. It seems to be reasonably stable, and when it waggles askew from the equilibrium state we can nudge it back with ingenious technological fixes. We and our handful of fellow weed-species seem to be doing just fine. The predictions of doom—the doom that was promised to follow our elimination of all those rich ecosystems, all those other species—haven't come true. We can laugh with relief. The planet is clean, it's healthy, and it belongs completely to us.

Human population has leveled off at a comfortable ten billion, and yet for some reason everybody feels lonely. Environmentalism is the leading global religion.

In the United States, that religion is professed unanimously; it's as American as apple pie. Apple pies are made only with the single surviving brand, Red Delicious. The apple pests have all gone extinct, but spots and blemishes are painted on cosmetically.

I'm not the only person unhappy with "environmentalism" and the set of priorities that term implies. An admirably cranky fellow named Colin Tudge had his own say on the subject some months ago in the magazine *Wildlife Conservation,* and I saved his piece in my environmentalism-be-damned file. Tudge agrees that the E word is either a bad label for a good idea or a good label for a bad one. He reminds us that "it is not enough to keep the beaches clean and the air fit to breathe, or even to keep parrots in the trees. We could make a world that was wonderful for humans—vast numbers of humans—and yet perpetrate a mass extinction." Another man who seems uneasy about sheer anthropocentric environmentalism is in far better position than either Colin Tudge or myself to do something about it: William K. Reilly.

As you know, Mr. Reilly is head of the Environmental Protection Agency. He is America's official scourge of toxicity. As you may or may not also remember, he was formerly president of the U.S. branch of the World Wildlife Fund, a private conservation group dedicated precisely to forestalling the Planet of Weeds scenario. I can recall thinking, when the incoming Bush administration announced his appointment, that if Reilly was acceptable in such august Republican circles, it was a shame to see him wasted on the EPA. Let him be Secretary of the Interior, I thought, and maybe he could save a few old-growth forests or rescue a few threatened species. But George Bush seldom seeks my advice on these matters and he probably saw clearly that as Secretary of the

Interior a real conservationist could cause real trouble. Anyway, Mr. Reilly is now generating some interesting ripples where he is. In January he appeared at a Senate hearing to explain his view that the priorities of the EPA need a fundamental reassessment.

Reilly, with help from his Science Advisory Board, has bravely concluded that the most truly serious "environmental" concerns are not the same ones that loom biggest in the minds of the American public. What worries the public? Oil spills rank high, probably because oil spills are easily comprehensible, make for dramatic TV, and can be blamed on somebody else. Hazardous wastes, industrial accidents like the one at Bhopal, and radioactive leakage are also devoutly abhorred. And who could deny the nastiness of such things? But the actual significance of those problems, in the judgment of Reilly's advisory scientists, is minor compared to such slightly more abstract concerns as habitat destruction, species extinction, overall loss of biodiversity, and global warming. Environmental cleanliness, say the EPA experts themselves, isn't enough.

William Reilly's task—selling this reordered set of priorities to the American people and to his own boss—won't be easy. Language is part of it, and the language is stacked against him. Possibly he should start by asking Congress and the public to let his agency take a new name.

While we're at it, Congress and you and me, we could reshape a few bureaucratic jurisdictions. Get the national forests out of the Department of Agriculture, for God's sake, and put them within this newer, less utilitarian entity; incorporate also the entire Department of the Interior, with the exception of Manuel Lujan; add a directorate for monitoring biodiversity in America, a directorate for promoting ecological research with the same zeal as the National Science Foundation promotes physics, and a soft-handed directorate for helping the rest of the world find ways to conserve their own wild landscapes while nevertheless feeding their own people. We're a big country so why think small? Give the new entity cabinet-level status, of course, and let the presentable Mr. Reilly be in charge. Create an official seal depicting the snail darter. We could do worse than call it the Department of Nature.

Analyzing and Discussing the Text

1. Much of the first part of "Dirty Word, Clean Place" seeks to redefine the word *environmentalism*. How, precisely, does Quammen attempt this? Analyze his specific approach to definition. Does he rely on etymology (as Thoreau does in "Walking")?

2. The second section of this argument traces the history of how "conservation" came to mean "environmentalism." What role does Rachel Carson's writing play in this history? Does Quammen criticize her part in this or see her work as useful?
3. Is Quammen's environmental "dystopia" (a miserable imaginary place) convincing? How does he try to persuade us that this clean, dull "Planet of Weeds" could really exist?
4. Where does the final segment of the essay go with the process of redefinition? Is the political focus appropriate here? Why or why not?

Experiencing and Writing About the World

1. In opposition to Quammen's dystopia, describe what you imagine to be a truly viable environmental *utopia*.
2. Analyze one or more other examples of "semantic perversion" in our national political debates about protecting/using the planet. What happens, for example, when we talk about drilling for oil in "A.N.W.R." (often pronounced "an-wahr") rather than in "the Arctic National Wildlife Refuge? If we refer to a region as a swamp or a desert or a jungle, is it easier to contemplate its destruction than if we refer to it as a wetland wildlife habitat or a rainforest? Are there other examples particular to your region? How and why do such "perversions" arise? Write an argument against (or for) such uses of language, explaining the special dangers or values of the verbal practices you've observed.
3. Write an extended analysis of a word like *nature, wilderness, city, park, automobile, fence, agriculture,* or *animal*—a word that we all use routinely and almost unthinkingly. Attempt to explain the complexity, ambiguity, and importance of this word, using your linguistic analysis as a way of advancing a theory about the relationship between human beings and the rest of the world. Try to structure your essay (using distinct sections) in a way that resembles Quammen's structure in "Dirty Word, Clean Place," although your essay may not be quite as long. You might begin by explaining the current usage of the word you are discussing, then tell the history of the word and/or the thing it represents, imagine how the planet's future may be determined by ideas related to the word, and conclude by suggesting ways of refining or altering our language and behavior.

Suggestions for Further Reading

Bailey, Liberty. *The Holy Earth.* New York: Macmillan, 1915.

Berry, Wendell. "Mayhem in the Industrial Paradise." *A Continuous Harmony: Essays Cultural and Agricultural.* New York: Harcourt, 1972.

Bookchin, Murray. *Toward an Ecological Society.* Montreal: Black Rose Books, 1980.

Brower, David. *For Earth's Sake: The Life & Times of David Brower.* Salt Lake City: Gibbs Smith, 1990.

Carson, Rachel. *Silent Spring.* Boston: Houghton, 1962.

Codrescu, Andrei. *The Disappearance of the Outside: A Manifesto for Escape.* Reading, MA: Addison, 1990.

Collard, Andrée, with Joyce Contrucci. *The Rape of the Wild: Man's Violence Against Animals and the Earth.* Bloomington: Indiana UP, 1989.

Commoner, Barry. *The Closing Circle: Nature, Man & Technology.* New York: Knopf, 1971.

Disch, Robert, ed. *The Ecological Consciousness: Values for Survival.* Englewood Cliffs, NJ: Prentice, 1970.

Dobson, Andrew, ed. *The Green Reader: Essays Toward a Sustainable Society.* San Francisco: Mercury, 1991.

Ehrenfeld, David. *The Arrogance of Humanism.* New York: Oxford UP, 1978.

Ehrlich, Paul. *The Population Bomb.* 1968. New York: Ballantine, 1986.

Foreman, Dave, and T. O. Hellenback. *Ecodefense: A Field Guide to Monkeywrenching.* Tucson: Ned Ludd, 1989.

Leopold, Aldo. "The Land Ethic." *A Sand County Almanac.* New York: Oxford UP, 1949.

Levine, Michael. *The Environmental Address Book: How to Reach the Environment's Greatest Champions and Worst Offenders.* New York: Perigree, 1991.

Lopez, Barry. *The Rediscovery of North America.* Lexington: UP of Kentucky, 1991.

Lovins, Amory. *Soft Energy Paths: Towards a Durable Peace.* London: Penguin, 1977.

McKibben, Bill. *The End of Nature.* New York: Doubleday, 1989.

Manes, Christopher. *Green Rage: Radical Environmentalism and the Unmaking of Civilization.* Boston: Little, 1990.

Manning, Richard. *Last Stand: Logging, Journalism, and the Case for Humility.* Salt Lake City: Gibbs Smith, 1991.

Mitchell, Don. "Dancing with Nature." *The Bread Loaf Anthology.* Hanover, NH: UP of New England, 1989.

Nichols, John. *The Sky's the Limit: A Defense of the Earth.* New York: Norton, 1990.

Olson, Sigurd. "Silence." *The Singing Wilderness.* New York: Knopf, 1956.

Reisner, Marc. *Cadillac Desert: The American West and Its Disappearing Water.* New York: Viking-Penguin, 1986.

——.*Game Wars: The Undercover Pursuit of Wildlife Poachers.* New York: Viking-Penguin, 1991.

Rienow, Robert, and Leona Train Rienow. *Moment in the Sun: A Report on the Deteriorating Quality of the American Environment.* New York: Ballantine, 1967.

Sanders, Scott Russell. "Speaking a Word for Nature." *Michigan Quarterly Review* (1987): 648–62.

Schell, Jonathan. *The Fate of the Earth.* New York: Avon, 1982.

Snyder, Gary. *The Practice of the Wild.* San Francisco: North Point, 1990.

Stegner, Wallace. "The Wilderness Idea." *Wilderness: America's Living Heritage.* Ed. David Brower. San Francisco: Sierra Club, 1961.

Wolfe, Tom. "The New Journalism." *The New Journalism.* Ed. Tom Wolfe and E. W. Johnson. New York: Harper, 1973.

Suzanne Kreiter/Globe Staff

CHAPTER THREE

Global Thoughts, Local Actions

In the summer of 1869, after a joyful day of hiking in the high Sierras, John Muir, feeling deeply united with his surroundings, made a now famous entry in his journal. "When we try to pick out anything by itself," he wrote, "we find it hitched to everything else in the universe." In our own time, however, Muir's words have taken on a more ominous meaning, suggesting that environmental problems cannot be regarded solely on an immediate, local level. When industrialized countries send ozone-depleting pollution into the earth's atmosphere, the entire planet must face the dangers of the greenhouse effect—the potential melting of the polar icecaps and the flooding of low-lying land masses throughout the world. When dangerous pesticides are used, radiation leaks from nuclear power plants, and chemicals escape from supposedly secure storage tanks, these pollutants leach into nearby soil and water, then enter the food chain, potentially affecting plant and animal life (including humans) even in distant regions of the world. It is necessary, therefore, for us to think *globally* as we consider the environmental dangers we face in the final decade of the twentieth century. How will our own behavior and the events in our particular part of the world have an impact on the planet as a whole? When people have achieved a certain level of awareness, they often feel compelled to *act,* but seldom can individuals directly affect the distant reaches of the world. For this reason we must understand that our *local* actions—good and bad—may have widespread consequences and that the consequences will be cumulative if people in other places think and behave as we do.

The following essays take a wide range of approaches to the idea of global thoughts and local actions. Jonathan Weiner, in the warning tradition of Rachel Carson's *Silent Spring* (1962), seeks to direct readers' attention to a new source of possible environmental catastrophe—global warming—which is more difficult to recognize, although no less dangerous, than the threat of nuclear war, which has preoccupied much of the world since 1945. Richard Nelson, in his response to the 1989 *Exxon Valdez* oil spill off the coast of Alaska, asks us to consider our own responsibility for the devastating accident—how can we, as active participants in an oil-consuming society, facilely accuse the oil providers of being the sole culprits? John Nichols, as if in reaction to Nelson's prodding, explains how a new global- and self-consciousness have led him to change his life-style, so as to "keep it simple." Baruch Fischhoff and Wangari Maathai serve as distributors of information, reporting to the American public about environmental problems and efforts to solve them elsewhere in the world. Fischhoff's article is one of many to emerge from visits by Americans to newly open Eastern Europe in recent years. Maathai writes about a grassroots tree-planting operation in her native Kenya. In the final essay of the chapter, Paula DiPerna considers how difficult it can be to determine the true nature and scale of environmental problems. And distinguishing "truth" from "facts," as she points out, is fundamental to the writer's ability to catalyze his or her audience.

JONATHAN WEINER

From **The New Question**

Jonathan Weiner (1953–   ) was born in New York City but grew up mostly in New Jersey and Rhode Island, with one year in Italy and another in Israel. His father is a professor of engineering at Brown University, but Weiner attended Harvard, graduating with honors in English and American literatures in 1977. At Harvard, Weiner edited two literary magazines, the *Harvard Advocate* and *Aspect,* and wrote for the *Harvard Independent.* After college he taught for a year at The Mountain School in Vershire, Vermont, and then became a freelance writer, preparing articles on science and the arts for various publications. Weiner worked for six months as an assistant editor at *Moment,* a popular Jewish intellectual magazine, before becoming an associate editor at *The Sciences,* the bimonthly magazine of the New York Academy of Sciences, where he contributed dozens of short feature articles and began writing a column called "Field Notes," which consists of personal essays on such topics as waterfalls, butterflies, pebbles, and planets. Weiner became senior editor at *The Sciences* in 1981, and he stayed with the magazine until 1986, when his successful first book, *Planet Earth,* was published. He spent the next three years researching and writing *The Next One Hundred Years: Shaping the Fate of Our Living Earth* (1990), from which the following selection is taken. Weiner now lives with his wife and two sons in Bucks County, Pennsylvania, and is currently writing a book on evolution.

The final chapter of *The Next One Hundred Years* raises a "new question" about the fate of the earth that supersedes the predominant question of the latter half of the twentieth century, the threat of nuclear holocaust, which is mentioned elsewhere in this anthology in such essays as Stephen Jay Gould's "Sex, Drugs, Disasters, and the Extinction of Dinosaurs" and Loren Eiseley's "The Winter of Man." Although Weiner's entire book is a study of the greenhouse effect, his message of warning comes across with particular resonance in the concluding extended analogy between the early nuclear weapons experiments at Alamagordo, New Mexico, and the "experiment" the world is now conducting with its threatened ozone layer. However, Weiner points out that this new experiment is much slower and subtler than the last one, and

661

its results potentially even more devastating. "This time there is no place to call Ground Zero," he writes. "Every continent is Ground Zero; Earth is Ground Zero."

> All changed, changed utterly:
> A terrible beauty is born.
>   William Butler Yeats
>   "Easter, 1916"

We are conducting an experiment as fateful as the one that took place half a century ago near Alamagordo, New Mexico.

That experiment was called Trinity. Its focal point was a steel sphere called Fat Man. The sphere reposed on top of a steel tower at a point called Ground Zero, in a part of the desert known since the time of the Spanish conquistadores as *Jornada del Muerto,* Dead Man's Trail, the Journey of Death.

Even the physicists who built the sphere did not know what it would do. In a betting pool before the test, Robert Oppenheimer had put a dollar on an explosion equivalent to 300 tons of TNT—a modest guess, befitting the scientific director of the experiment. George Kistiakowsky bet 1,400 tons; Hans Bethe, 8,000 tons; I. I. Rabi, 18,000 tons; Edward Teller, 45,000 tons.

Enrico Fermi offered to take wagers that the explosion would ignite the atmosphere. This was a possibility no one could quite rule out. "In this event," one physicist had written lyrically, some years before, "the whole of the hydrogen on the Earth might be transformed at once and the success of the experiment published at large to the universe as a new star."

There was only one way to narrow the range of uncertainties. In the *Jornada del Muerto* on July 16, 1945, Teller, Bethe, and others listened to the countdown by shortwave radio. They were stationed on a hill twenty miles from Ground Zero. It was 5:00 A.M. and pitch dark. They had been advised to lie down and bury their faces in the sand. But Teller was determined (he said years afterward) "to look the beast in the eye." In the darkness, he put on suntan lotion, then passed the lotion around.

Five miles from Ground Zero, Fermi, Rabi, and hundreds of other scientists, technicians, and soldiers lay down with their backsides up and their feet pointing toward the bomb. At 5:29:35, a loudspeaker began tolling the last ten seconds. "There were just a few streaks of gold in the east," Rabi recalled in Richard Rhodes's history, *The Making of the Atomic Bomb;* "you could see your neighbor very dimly. Those ten seconds were the longest ten seconds I have ever experienced."

Less than two miles from Zero, in an earth-shielded bunker, Oppenheimer said, "Lord, these affairs are hard on the heart." He was hardly breathing. He held on to a post to steady himself.

The flash that illuminated the *Jornada del Muerto* was the biggest explosion in history, equivalent to 18,600 tons of TNT. The test was a success. Hiroshima and Nagasaki followed within three weeks.

Scientists who study the changes that are now in progress in the atmosphere and the biosphere must strive for a calm and disembodied objectivity. They need to work as if from a cosmic distance if they are to put into society's possession facts that do not lie. They prefer the studied neutrality of the term "global change" to the term they might use for events this big in the geological record: "global catastrophe."

They are also aware that there may be a mistake somewhere in their calculations (which was a possibility at Trinity, too, even at T-1 seconds). For decades they have been afraid of sounding an alarm too soon. They themselves would never compare their watch to the physicists' in the desert.

Nevertheless as this troubled century closes, we find ourselves in the middle of another countdown. Again scientists from around the world have converged upon it. Again their calculations have been extensive. Again they do not agree on the outcome: whether the planet Earth will soon grow hotter than it has been in thousands, tens of thousands, hundreds of thousands, millions, or tens of millions of years.

This time there is no place to call Ground Zero. Every continent is Ground Zero; Earth is Ground Zero. There is no one moment when the firing circuit will close. It began closing long ago, although we did not know it then. And there will be no single moment when we learn the extent of the reaction. The reaction may build for the next one thousand years.

To compare these countdowns is not hyperbolic. Indeed it would be hard to say which test is beggared in the comparison. John Maddox, the editor of *Nature,* has observed that "avoiding nuclear war by means of arms control would be a hollow boast if the vestigial ice caps were then allowed to melt." By the most modest estimate in the betting pool, we are in for climate changes as great as any since the dawn of civilization. By the most extreme estimate, Earth is on the brink of climatic upheavals and mass extinctions as great as any since the end of the age of the dinosaurs.

If we do not destroy ourselves with the A-bomb and the H-bomb, then we may destroy ourselves with the C-bomb, the Change Bomb. And in a world as interlinked as ours, one explosion may lead to the other. Already in the Middle East, from North Africa to the Persian Gulf and from the Nile to the Euphrates, tensions over dwindling water supplies and rising populations are reaching what many experts describe as a flashpoint. A climate shift in that single battle-scarred nexus might trigger international tensions that will unleash some of the 60,000 nuclear warheads the world has stockpiled since Trinity.

No one says that the worst will happen, only that it could happen. It need not happen, but we are priming the planet for it every year, with loads of carbon measured in gigatons. The codename "Trinity" was inspired by a poem by John Donne ("Batter my heart, three-person'd God;—"). We have no adequate name for an experiment in which one planetary sphere tests the stability of seven. I have compared this geological upheaval to a volcano, and also to Atropos, the Greek Fate who cut the thread of life. But the more one sees of this experiment's scale and suspense, the more it is reminiscent of Alamagordo.

In a sense the experiment began in the mid-1700s with Black, Watt, and the Industrial Revolution. For a few Earth scientists, the countdown began in March of 1958, when Keeling began measuring carbon dioxide from the volcano Mauna Loa. For most of the world the countdown began precisely thirty years later to the month, in the first heat of 1988. In that year, as Thoreau once wrote in a very different mood and in very different weather, "I awoke to an answered question."

We understand now that the uncertainties will remain wide. There is only one way to eliminate them, and that is the method of the physicists in the desert. The physicists had their results in seconds, but ours will unfold for millennia, and as in the *Jornada del Muerto,* if we do not like what we see there will be no turning back.

For many people around the world this method of eliminating uncertainties now seems unacceptable. This is the most frightening countdown since Oppenheimer held his breath at Alamagordo. After the Summer of '88 the only important question became what we can do to stop the experiment. Not—is this something to worry about? Not—how bad will it be? But—what must we do?

That summer the world started trying to answer this new question. One week after James Hansen's dramatic testimony in Washington in 1988, delegates from almost fifty countries met in Toronto, Canada. Prominent climate experts convened with national leaders, including Prime Ministers Brian Mulroney, of Canada, and Gro Harlem Brundtland, of Norway, to discuss the task of bringing Earth's temperature back under control. It was the first International Conference on the Changing Atmosphere.

That fall in Geneva, Switzerland, delegates met again and formed an Intergovernmental Panel on Climate Change. Some of the panelists represented countries that contribute the lion's share of greenhouse gases—including the U.S., the U.S.S.R., China, and Brazil. Others came from countries that contribute almost nothing to the problem but have a lot to lose, including the Maldives and Malta. Together they began hammering out a global action plan, country by country.

Given the enormous political obstacles to such a plan, some of these countries may have been trying to "panel over" the problem until the world's attention turned away again. Calling for action is easier than taking action. The only certain outcome of talk is carbon dioxide. Nevertheless, with that rapid-fire series of meetings the nations of the world did acknowledge the magnitude of the threat. As the Chinese say, a journey of a thousand miles must begin with a single step. The first step had been taken.

And the step had momentum. By the fall of '88, at least fifteen high-level international meetings on the greenhouse effect had been scheduled for the following year. Arms control talks were making remarkable progress in '88; and suddenly it seemed possible that carbon control talks would join or even replace arms control in the main ring of diplomacy's travelling circus. (Either way we are talking about global survival.) One veteran environmentalist, Michael Oppenheimer, a senior scientist with the Environmental Defense Fund, wrote, "It is no exaggeration to say that global environment may become the overarching issue for the next forty years in the way the cold war defined our world view during the last forty years."

The planetary prospect looks something like this. In the next one hundred years, Earth's fever may rise on one of three paths:

The steepest curve shows what could happen if human beings devour resources at faster and faster rates. Suppose next year we put a greater quantity of carbon into the air than we did this year. Suppose we do the same thing the year after next and the year after that: an ever-larger tonnage of greenhouse gases. And suppose the climate of the planet turns out to be extremely sensitive. Then, according to one state-of-the-art estimate, Earth's temperature could rise as much as 16° C. (30° F.) in the next century. This way to the Inferno.

Suppose instead that human beings inject the *same* amount of carbon into the air next year as we did this year, and so on for the next hundred years. That is the scenario of the middle curve: business as usual.[1] Suppose we follow this path, and suppose our climate turns out to be only moderately sensitive. Then the planet's temperature may rise between 3 and 8° C. (5 and 15° F.). No one knows if the human sphere could survive the stress of a rise of 5° F. But 15° would probably be just as devastating as 30. This may be another road to the Inferno.

[1]Business as usual implies that carbon dioxide will rise at the rate it is rising right now. However, there are greenhouse gases, including methane and nitrous oxide, that are rising at faster and faster rates today. Business as usual implies that they will continue rising faster and faster. — Author's note.

The lowest curve shows what might happen if we cut back. Suppose our species puts less and less carbon into the air each year, cutting down to 2.5 gigatons of carbon per year, which is about half of what we are doing right now. And suppose we are also very lucky, and the global climate turns out to be relatively stable and insensitive to this insult. The result might be a rise of 1.5 to 4.5° C. (3 to 8° F.) in the next one hundred years.

Of course, a rise of even 3° F. is nothing to look forward to. It is three times greater than the rise in global temperatures that accompanied the heat waves and droughts of the 1980s. Its blessings are strictly comparative. The difference between the best case and the worst case is about 25° F. For our species and for millions of others, that is the difference between survival and extinction.

To get on the safest of these paths, the world must cut back on its production of carbon. Each year we must put a little less carbon into the air than the year before.

The human sphere did accomplish something like that within recent memory. When the OPEC cartel created an international energy crisis, beginning with the Arab oil embargo of 1973, the price of oil began to jump. In ten years it rose from a little more than ten dollars a barrel to almost forty dollars a barrel. The consequences did not show up right away, because our world of getting and spending has so much momentum. Eventually, however, the actions of that single cartel affected our behavior as a geological force. We burned so much less oil that we began to reduce the total amount of carbon we put into the air each year. In 1973, the year of the embargo, the amount of carbon we burned was still higher than the year before. This is the world's year-by-year carbon scorecard for the decade that followed:

in 1974, higher
1975, lower (for the first time since World War II)
1976, higher
1977, higher
1978, higher
1979, higher
1980, a little lower
1981, lower
1982, lower
1983, lower

It may not look like much, but the cartel accomplished something that one world depression and two world wars had failed to do. Four years in a row, the world burned less carbon than it had the year before. The high price of oil forced people around the world to look for ways to do more work while burning less fuel. Industries eked out more heat, light, and mileage from each drop of oil. People did the same thing in their homes.

Unlike the depression and the world wars, the period was not generally unpleasant. So many enterprises grew so much more efficient that national economies expanded even while the burning of carbon dropped. The U.S. economy grew by almost 40 percent, producing more and more goods and services with less and less oil. In fact, thanks to the energy-efficiency measures the country adopted, the U.S. is now saving an estimated $160 billion a year on an annual energy bill of $430 billion.

Japan adopted more efficiency measures than the U.S. or Western Europe. That gave it a secret weapon in world markets. It costs less to make things in Japan, partly because the Japanese burn less oil and coal to make them. According to one American analyst, this single factor gives Japan "about a 5 percent economic edge on everything they sell."

The price of oil started falling again in the early 1980s, and by the end of the decade we were once again burning more carbon each year than the year before. ("We've recovered," says one greenhouse expert, with a dark laugh.) But that run of four years is a very encouraging sign. If the world responds to the global warming the way it responded to OPEC, we may yet avert the worst.

As experts point out, another drive toward efficiency would pay off even without the threat of a warming. Analysts at the Worldwatch Institute and other environmental groups argue that Americans could cut energy consumption another 50 percent, reduce carbon dioxide emissions by 50 percent, *and* save another $200 billion a year, all without much sacrifice.

American cars, for example, are putting gigatons of carbon into the atmosphere. Yet the gas tax in the U.S. is scandalously low, compared to that of other industrial powers. For the U.S. to keep the tax so low is to encourage waste and to fuel the greenhouse effect.

U.S. mileage standards are another scandal. In 1975, during the oil crisis, the U.S. government gave American automakers ten years to improve their cars' mileage rate from 14 miles per gallon to 27.5 miles per gallon. When oil prices came back down in the 1980s, the government relaxed the standard again. Transportation experts at the E.P.A. argue that the mileage requirement might reasonably be raised to 40 miles per gallon. Meanwhile, every time we turn the key in a car's ignition we turn up the planet's thermostat.

There is also room for improvement indoors. During the energy crisis, President Jimmy Carter declared "the moral equivalent of war" on the waste of energy. Part of the war included a strong tax incentive program to improve home insulation. The program worked: it benefited homeowners, the atmosphere, the climate, and the national budget. A recent E.P.A. report recommends that the U.S. now revive the program, cutting the fuel used to heat its homes by half the amount used in the year 1980.

The refrigerator is the biggest single user of electricity in the average American home, and it could be made much more efficient. The typical Japanese refrigerator is so much better made that it uses half as much electricity. (It is also somewhat smaller. The typical American refrigerator could serve a small restaurant.)

Replacing every old fluorescent light fixture in the U.S. with a cooler and more efficient type (already commercially available) could save the nation one very large oil field every twenty years. Changing light bulbs is simpler and safer than pumping oil in Alaska.

There are new windows that steal a trick from the greenhouse effect. Scientists at the National Lighting Laboratory, in Berkeley, California, are coating one surface of double- and triple-glazed windowpanes with tin oxide. This coating lets visible light through but bounces infrared light back into the room. Touch the glass and it feels as warm as the wall.

The same lessons apply around the world. Brazil, for example, is planning the construction of about one hundred new hydroelectric dams, mostly to supply electricity to sprawling cities like São Paolo and Rio de Janeiro. As many as seventy of the new dam sites are in the Amazon Basin. There, because the terrain is flat and the flow of water is sluggish, vast tracts have been flooded in the past to provide small amounts of electricity. The Balbina dam drowned 900 square miles of rain forest to supply about half the electricity needs of the city of Manaus.

Sometimes, observes Jessica Tuchman Matthews, of the World Resources Institute, "poverty is as great a cause of wasteful energy use as great wealth." If Brazil were to invest $4 billion in new and more efficient refrigerators, lights, and motors, the country would save enough energy to supplant twenty-one large new power plants. The country would also save $19 billion between now and the year 2000.

However, Brazil is expected to grow by some 60 million people in the next two decades, to more than 200 million. The prospect is putting enormous pressure on government planners, and they want the dams.

This pressure of human numbers makes the task of cutting back more complicated and more painful. The heart blanches at the moral, political, and religious dilemmas that face us. Each year there are another 80 million people on the planet, each decade another India. Demography is among the most reliable sciences of the future, and demographers expect the human sphere to double in size in the next one hundred years. Barring a global catastrophe (a possibility that lies outside the scope of demography) Planet Earth will be carrying more than ten billion human beings around the sun within the next century—say, by the year 2050.

According to the demographers, at least eight billion of us will then be living in places that have trouble sustaining their present populations. Indeed the very poorest countries of the world—the most malnourished, ill-housed, unstable—will double in population within about *thirty-five* years. In Asia, this list includes Bangladesh, Pakistan, the Philippines, Vietnam. In the Middle East: Egypt, Jordan, Syria. In Latin America: Nicaragua, Guatemala, El Salvador, Honduras. In South America: Ecuador, Paraguay. In the Caribbean: Haiti.

In Africa, nearly half the population is under the age of fifteen. With so many Africans just beginning their child-bearing years, the population of the whole continent—the poorest continent in the world—will more than double by the year 2020.

Again, demographers' predictions do not take into account war, famine, plague, or global chaos. Given the sensitivity of the spheres, it seems best to speak of ten billion people in the conditional tense. For long before there were ten billion people on this Earth almost everyone would be living on the edge. With the planet so crowded even the danger of earthquakes would become spectacular. More people will not make more earthquakes, of course. The lithosphere is still beyond our influence. But the population explosion will have a surprising effect on the number of people at risk. Roger Bilham, a geologist at the University of Colorado, has noted that by the year 2000, one hundred cities will have populations exceeding two million, and by pure chance, almost half these cities are located in places where the shifting plates of the lithosphere create earthquake hazard zones. "It appears," Bilham warned in 1988, "that within twelve years 290 million 'supercity' dwellers, 80 percent of them living in developing nations, will live in a region of seismic risk." In fact, so many of us are clustering along the planet's fault lines that the number of people in danger of dying in an earthquake will have doubled by the year 2035. (It is a dark coincidence that in the human sphere and the lithosphere, tension and friction should be building at so many of the same foci.)

Greater dangers will come from shifts in the air. The more we grow the more we change the atmosphere. This lesson is inscribed in the very icecaps. Compare the rise of our population, as recorded by the demographers, and the rise of methane gas, as recorded by the polar ice sheets. The two curves have been rising in unison for six hundred years, since the first years of the Renaissance. The solid line represents people and the dots represent methane:

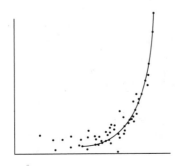

Why should the number of people on the ground and the number of methane molecules in the air have exploded in parallel? Because people generate methane by so many different kinds of disturbances in the biosphere. Each new rice paddy in China, chopped tree in England, ruminating cow and goat in India, garbage dump in Mexico, and leaking natural-gas pipe in Texas, makes methane. Methane is almost as universal a product of progress as carbon dioxide. People have a methane effect and methane has a greenhouse effect. So people have a greenhouse effect.

If our numbers continue to spiral upward, so will greenhouse gases, and so will the temperature of the planet. To say nothing of the number of tons of topsoil lost to the sea, the number of acres lost to deserts, and the number of species lost forever. If we cannot manage our impact on the planet now, how would we do so if there were many more of us? Can we defuse the Change Bomb while human numbers explode? Can we cut our carbon production in half while doubling the size of the human sphere?

Think of the U.S., which has already seen the most fantastic population explosion in human history, from 18 million in 1750 to 250 million today, an increase of 3,500 percent. The U.S. population will reach almost 300 million in the next one hundred years. And at present rates, of course, each citizen is shoveling about five tons of carbon into the air. Some American economists see U.S. population growth as discomfortingly sluggish. Yet 300 million people consuming resources as fast as Americans do today would produce about 1.5 billion tons of carbon per annum. That is to say, in one hundred years, the United States alone would be producing more than half of the whole world's annual quota of greenhouse gas. Something has to give; the planet cannot afford that many American consumers.

This subject is not only difficult, in many countries it is politically untouchable. But if we do not confront it we cannot stop the explosion in the air over our heads. People say family planning is unnatural. Surely the factors that fuel the population explosion are unnatural, too, as Harrison Brown pointed out in The Challenge of Man's Future back in 1954 (population: 2.6 billion). "Those who maintain that conception control should not be used because it is unnatural would be far more convincing," Brown wrote, "if they urged simultaneously abolishment of all clothing, antiseptics, antibiotics, vaccinations, and hospitals, together with all artificial practices which enable man to extract food from the soil."

Either we will slow our growth by managing birth rates, or the other spheres of the Earth will control ours by managing our death rates. Think of the populations of Bangladesh and the Maldives. Each will double within about 30 years. Then, if sea levels rise as some models predict, each country may start losing land. Before the end of the next century tens of millions of people may have been drowned or forced out of Bangladesh, and the 2,000 tiny atolls of the Maldives may have been erased from the map. (The leader of the Maldives calls his atolls "an endangered nation.")

Where there is a will there is a way. It is amazing what a country can do. Japan halved its population growth rate in the space of about five years—the first half of the 1950s. China did the same thing in the first half of the 1970s. The two nations are very different and they used very different tactics, but both of them are heavily populous and both pulled it off. If the human sphere is to reduce its production of carbon, it will have to do what China and Japan did, country by country, in each place with the appropriate tactics.

No one knows if we will do it, but we really have no decent alternative. Writes Lester Brown, director of the Worldwatch Institute, "It is hard to imagine anything more difficult... except suffering the consequences of failing to do so."

There is a standard illustration in stories about the greenhouse effect: the Statue of Liberty submerged in a rising sea, holding her torch up above the water. This symbol of the global forecast is an artistic exaggeration. The sea would have to rise 300 feet to douse Miss Liberty's torch. Yet the image may be more appropriate than we imagine. The sea would have to rise only a foot to displace a global flood of refugees. Long before the tides had reached the statue's ankles they would have drowned her traditional welcome to the tired and the poor. If the ocean drowns Bangladesh and invades the Nile, where will all the refugees go? Who will take them in? In the 1980s the number of refugees in the world rose from less than 5 million to more than 14 million. Doors were closing in the more fortunate nations in the world, including the United States, where officials were speaking of "compassion fatigue." A warmer planet may not be a warmer world....

Trinity was a secret test in the desert. This is the most public experiment in history. It is a slow-motion explosion manufactured by every last man, woman, and child on the planet.

If we threw 5 gigatons of carbon into the air all in one place, all at one time, in a single great eruption, it would make a spectacle on the scale of the fireball that rose from the desert at Alamagordo. Dust and smoke would be entrained in it. Lightning would flicker through the dust. A pillar of fire would seem to extend higher into the sky and farther into the future than the eye can see.

At Trinity in the command bunker Oppenheimer remembered a line from the *Bhagavad-Gita:* "Now I am become Death, the destroyer of worlds." Oppenheimer's right-hand man Kenneth Bainbridge exclaimed, "Now we are all sons of bitches."

We do not respond to emergencies that unfold in slow motion. We do not respond adequately to the invisible. But we understand explosions. Five gigatons of carbon are the work of one year for the human sphere; or the work of one hundred Tamboras for the lithosphere. It would be a strange experience, watching five gigatons of carbon go up into the air. People meeting us afterward would see it in our faces. A physicist at Los Alamos watched the busloads of experimenters returning from Alamagordo: "I saw that something very grave and strong had happened to their whole outlook on the future."

Long after the winds had dispersed the cloud, it would linger in our minds. We would carry the sight with us like the witnesses in the desert. We would understand that the world will never be the same.

Analyzing and Discussing the Text

1. Explain the phrase "The New Question." Why does Weiner apply it to the phenomenon of the greenhouse effect?
2. Weiner claims that his analogy between the Trinity experiment and the current questions about the greenhouse effect is not "hyperbolic." What does this mean? Is hyperbole perhaps warranted because of the potential magnitude of this problem?
3. Look at the passages in the essay in which Weiner attempts to "translate" technical information into terms accessible (and impressive) to the average, intelligent nonscientist. How does he seem to go about this translation? Does some of his writing still seem too technical for the lay reader?
4. How convincingly does Weiner correlate the apparent causes of the greenhouse effect with the symptoms of this problem? What are these causes? What is the evidence that the polar icecaps are in danger of melting? Why would this melting be a serious problem?
5. Does Weiner merely criticize the societies responsible for the greenhouse effect or does he recommend specific ways of changing behavior in order to alleviate (or at least slow down) this problem? Point out specific passages in the text.

Experiencing and Writing About the World

1. Write a descriptive and analytical essay in which you assess your own life-style in light of Weiner's warnings. What aspects of your life seem likely contributors to the global environmental problems explained in this essay? How do you feel after experiencing a harshly critical essay like "The New Question," and what is the likelihood that those feelings will result in changes (even slight ones) in your daily habits? If your current life-style seems to conflict with Weiner's

suggestions and yet you feel no inclination to change, explain your indifferent response.

2. Read the entirety of *The Next One Hundred Years* and do additional research on the greenhouse effect, then prepare a detailed proposal for local, regional, or national governmental officials in which you recommend specific policy changes that would help to reduce the threat of global warming. Alternatively, prepare a persuasive letter for the administration at your college or university, suggesting ways in which the institution (including individual members of its faculty, staff, and student body) could consume less energy and demonstrating the need for such changes. Emphasize causes and effects in this proposal/letter.

3. Analyze Weiner's elaborate use of analogy in "The New Question." Explain not only *what* the analogy attempts to show, but also *how* Weiner structures it and *which* specific aspects of the atomic-bomb testing and the greenhouse effect he is emphasizing. You could also compare Weiner's use of analogy to one or more of the other analogies indicated in this anthology's Rhetorical Table of Contents (see Comparison and Contrast).

RICHARD NELSON

Oil and Ethics: Adrift on Troubled Waters

Richard K. Nelson (1941–   ) was born in Madison, Wisconsin. He earned his B.S. (1964) and M.S. (1968) at the University of Wisconsin in Madison and his Ph.D. (1971) at the University of California–Santa Barbara. Nelson has published eleven books, his work gradually broadening from the early scientific (anthropological) studies of Alaskan Eskimo and Athabaskan Indians to include explorations of his personal relationships with the natural community. The early books include *Hunters of the Northern Ice* (1969) and *Hunters of the Northern Forest* (1973); the first book in which he consciously sought to reach a wider, nonscientific audience was *Shadow of the Hunter: Stories of Eskimo Life* (1980). Nelson's *Make Prayers to the Raven: A Koyukon View of the Northern Forest*

(1983), a study of the Koyukon Athabaskan Indians and their teachings on how to live with respect for the natural world, directly anticipates his extremely successful and important recent book, *The Island Within* (1989), which won the John Burroughs Medal for outstanding natural history writing in 1991. In this latest book, Nelson tells the story of his family's life on an isolated coast of Alaska, showing how he has worked to incorporate Koyukon teachings about living in harmony with nature into his own life there. This fascination with another culture's attitudes toward nature closely resembles Terry Tempest Williams's feelings in *Pieces of White Shell* (1984). In an excerpt from *The Island Within*, first published as an essay called "The Gifts" in the special issue of *Antaeus* devoted to nature writing (Autumn, 1986), Nelson explains what happened to him when he went to live with Alaskan Eskimos at the age of twenty-two:

> The experience of living with Eskimos made very clear the direct, phys-
> ical connectedness between all humans and the environments they draw
> existence from. Some years later, living with Koyukon Indians in Alaska's
> interior, I encountered a rich new dimension of that connectedness, and
> it profoundly changed my view of the world. Traditional Koyukon people
> follow a code of moral and ethical behavior that keeps a hunter in right
> relationship to the animals. They teach that all of nature is spiritual and
> aware, that it must be treated with respect, and that humans should ap-
> proach the living world with restraint and humility. Now I struggle to learn
> if these same principles can apply in my own life and culture. Can we
> borrow from an ancient wisdom to structure a new relationship between
> ourselves and the environment? Or is Western society irreversibly commit-
> ted to the illusion that humanity is separate from and dominant over the
> natural world? (pp. 118–119)

Here Nelson raises precisely the questions that must occur to any "West-ern" observer of native or non-Western cultures that exhibit particularly wholesome attitudes toward nature. Can we, too, embrace these values or are we inescapably bound to the "illusion" of separation? Nelson's own writings, including the following response to the *Exxon Valdez* oil spill, sug-gest a successful transfer of Koyukon values to his own world view.

Nelson describes himself as someone who has gone from being "a person who never intended to write to one who never intends to stop writing." For him, one of the most important features of the writing process is "to remember that I am writing to serve my subject rather than to serve myself," an attitude reminiscent of Barry Lopez's approach to writing and the natural world. Although the essay "Oil and Ethics" is only one of many accounts that have sought to understand the implications of the 1989 oil spill in Prince William Sound, off the coast of Alaska, Nelson's thoughtful attempt to use the terrible event as a way to make fundamental observations about our society, to show us how we can learn from the event, makes this a piece of writing that transcends the particular catastrophe that inspired it.

I live on the Northwest Pacific coast. Although Prince William Sound is hundreds of miles away, its oil-covered waters now seem perilously close. Sister tankers to the *Exxon Valdez* have passed here daily for twelve years, hidden just beyond the horizon. Until last week I rarely gave them a thought.

Now I realize their destructive potential. I fear them. And I wonder who is to blame for this catastrophe? Who will pay the costs? What can be learned from it? The answers are not as simple as they might seem.

The surroundings I live in are much like those near Cordova and the other Prince William Sound communities: forested mountains rising sheer above islands and bays; violent Pacific storms shrouding the coast in clouds and rain; the land and waters filled with a staggering abundance of life.

At this time of year, herring mass to spawn along the shores and fingerling salmon pour out from rivers and hatchery pens. Drawn by the abundant feed are humpback whales, sea lions, harbor seals, killer whales, porpoises, and countless thousands of sea birds—gulls, ducks, cormorants, kittiwakes, auklets, murres, murrelets, grebes, loons and bald eagles. There are few places on Earth where nature remains so pristine and exuberant.

This was true of Prince William Sound until last week. We can only hope it will someday be true again. Like other Americans, my neighbors and I have watched the tragedy unfold on nightly newscasts: the oil slick covering thirty square miles, a hundred, two hundred, five hundred, then a thousand square miles; sludge pluming into the open Pacific, heading toward Kenai Fjords National Park, Kodiak Island, and the rich waters of Cook Inlet.

Most of us who live along this coast are fishermen of one sort or another—commercial, sport, or subsistence. What corn and wheat are to Midwestern farmers, salmon and halibut are to people here. Now, with brutal suddenness, the residents of Prince William Sound face the equivalent of a year in farm country without a drop of rain; and worse, the possibility that many more will follow.

In a state often deeply divided over environmental issues, an uncommon unity of opinion has emerged. Alaskan editorial pages and radio talk shows are filled with grief and indignation. Blame is assigned first to an arrogant and unprepared oil industry, then to an ineffective and unresponsive government, and then to a more tangible scapegoat—the captain who tested legally drunk after his tanker struck Bligh Reef.

Amid the turmoil and chaos, the anger and recriminations, it is easy to forget the raw tragedy behind it all. In 1969, I was living in Santa Barbara, California, when the first great American oil spill came ashore. Like thousands of others, I walked the blackened beaches and clambered across lathered rocks, an act not only of curiosity but also of conscience, as if simply being there and showing concern might help.

And then I found a bird, hiding among kelp and boulders just above the tide. A western grebe, big as a mallard, long-necked, with a slender needle beak, half-submerged in a puddle of mixed oil and water.

I have forgotten how many barrels of oil went into the Santa Barbara Channel, how much it cost to clean up the spill, how those who suffered damages were compensated, how blame was decided, how punishment was administered, how many animals were calculated to have died and how many were saved. But one memory is lodged forever in my mind—that dying bird, her feathers matted and shining with oil, her wings drooped, her body quivering.

She stared up at me, blinking her bright red eyes, the one part of her that still seemed fully alive. Caught in the bird's unwavering gaze, I could not escape my own feelings of guilt.

Now it has happened again, and far worse this time, on a wilderness coast populated with incalculable numbers of fish, sea birds, mammals and a diverse array of other marine life.

Each day I am haunted by images of birds setting their wings to land in the morass of crude. And I think of the sea otters, those clever and energetic creatures who add such brightness to my days, crawling out to drape themselves on oil-soaked rocks and await a slow death. Prince William Sound has become a dying grounds, filled with thousands of animals, each one another story like the doomed grebe I found twenty years ago.

Soon enough, arguments over who is responsible will shift from the courts of public opinion to the courts of law. By assigning blame we may find satisfaction. But will the legal process identify who is truly guilty? I think not.

Responsibility for the Prince William Sound disaster rests not just on the oil companies, not just on the government, not just on the tanker's captain. Ultimately, you and I must accept our share of the blame—as members of a society that understood the risks and judged them acceptable. A society that valued convenience and monetary gain above the security of its own environment. A society that placed nature outside the sphere of ethical concern and moral restraint. Each of us must accept a portion of the guilt, as members of a human community that has profoundly injured its surroundings. We belong to a society much like the tanker in Prince William Sound, laden with an enormous deadly cargo, making its way through treacherous waters with impaired judgment at the helm.

And who will pay for the Prince William Sound disaster? You and I. We will cover the cost to government when we pay taxes. We will cover the cost to the oil industry when we buy fuel or anything made with petroleum products. The notion that someone else will pay is an illusion.

There is yet another cost to us, this one far greater and more consequential. The natural world of Prince William Sound is not just scenery; it is a vital part of our continent's living community, a community that includes all of us, a community that supplies the air we breathe and the food we eat. Any wound to that community diminishes the environment we depend upon for every moment of our lives, takes away from its capacity to sustain us, whether we live near the disaster or far away, in small villages or huge cities. As we learn more about the connections among all things, we realize that damage to one place is damage to the environment everywhere. We are a part of what we have destroyed.

An environmental officer for the Exxon Corporation asserted that the Alaskan oil spill is "the cost of civilization." What we have lost may never be regained. As a society, we must agree that we will no longer accept this cost. In the future, we must be willing to pay every cost and make every sacrifice to assure that such disasters can never happen. Never again.

I choose those words deliberately. The enslavement and extermination of racial and ethnic groups in Europe and America is a deep stain on our collective memory. Behavior our society once condoned has now literally become unthinkable. Abraham Lincoln said, "If slavery is not wrong, then nothing is wrong." His plea for a moral conscience that embraces all peoples eventually became the law and practice of our land. We must now recognize the need for a further growth of moral conscience, to encompass the whole community of life—the environment that nurtures, uplifts our senses and sustains our existence.

Future generations will look back on our behavior toward the environment—the enslavement and extermination of species who share the world with us—and judge it unthinkable. My deepest hope is that the tragedy of Prince William Sound will help us toward a wiser, healthier, morally balanced relationship to our surroundings.

Analyzing and Discussing the Text

1. Discuss the significance of the opening paragraph. Why does Nelson begin the essay with this information? How does it prepare us for the questions in the second paragraph? What function is served by paragraphs 4 through 6, with their descriptions of the abundance of life along the shores of Prince William Sound?
2. Why does Nelson recall, in paragraphs 8 through 11, the Santa Barbara spill of twenty years earlier? How does this tie in with the points that he makes in the essay's final three paragraphs?

3. Why does Nelson emphasize his own feelings of guilt about the dying western grebe in Santa Barbara? How does this prepare us for his discussion of who is to blame for the *Exxon Valdez* spill?

4. The last sentence in paragraph 15 presents the tanker in Prince William Sound in a different light than most other accounts of the disaster. How accurate is it as a metaphor that describes America's relationship to the natural world?

5. Explain what Nelson means when he says that "we are a part of what we have destroyed."

6. Notice how Nelson defines *environment* in the last two paragraphs. How does his equation of the environment with "the whole community of life" differ from David Quammen's definition of the same word in the previous chapter of the anthology?

Experiencing and Writing About the World

1. Look at the evidence of environmental abuse in your own area, describe what has happened, and then explore whether or not the abuse has been recognized as such, resulting in recent attitude or behavioral changes in your community.

2. The underlying theme of Nelson's argument is that we need to do what our culture has not yet done, which is to include nature in "the sphere of ethical concern and moral restraint." Do you see any evidence in your own life, in your own community, that there is growing acceptance of this belief that nature, too, has rights?

3. Think of one or more aspects of your own life-style that are likely to contribute to environmental degradation in your local area. Do you burn trees in a woodstove, leave lights and other appliances on throughout your house or apartment, drive by yourself to work/school, wash your car frequently even during times of drought, or routinely throw away cans and newspapers rather than recycling them? Write a critique of your society's (*our* society's) environmental situation that focuses on a particular concern in your region of the country (for instance, water shortages in the Southwest or air pollution in any urban area) and explores the issue of *shared responsibility* for this problem. Combine your awareness of both your own life-style and the larger environmental issue in a critical essay that goes beyond facile "finger pointing." Perhaps you could publish this piece as an editorial in the student newspaper at your university or in a city paper.

4. The issue of how to assess the worth of natural places is a major concern these days for scholars working in many different disciplines (economics, law, psychology, philosophy, history, and even literature). Much of the recent research in this area was inspired by the

need to determine the "cost" of the *Exxon Valdez* oil spill—the effect of the spill on both the economic value of Prince William Sound and the "existence value" of the pristine wilderness area. Research the issue of "environmental value" from the perspective of one particular discipline and explain the latest developments in this field in an analytical essay.

JOHN NICHOLS

Keep It Simple

John Nichols (1940–   ) seems to have acquired his interest in the natural world genetically: his paternal grandfather (and namesake) was a prominent zoologist, biologist, and ornithologist who founded the journal *Copeia* (the publication of the American Ichthyologists and Herpetologists Society) and who served as the Curator of Fishes for the American Museum of Natural History in New York City. Nichols was born in Berkeley, California, and was only two years old when his mother died from a congenital heart condition while the family was living in Miami, Florida. Nichols's father (who later became a psychology professor at the University of Colorado) joined the Marines and sent John to live with his sister in Smithtown (Long Island), New York, for the remainder of World War II, after which he remarried and moved the family repeatedly, stopping in Vermont, Smithtown, Virginia, Connecticut, D.C., and Berkeley again. While a student at the Loomis School in 1957, John Nichols took his first trip to the Southwest, traveling cross-country by bus to visit the American Museum of Natural History's field station in southern Arizona, then working as a firefighter in New Mexico's Chiricahua Mountains on his way back east. Although he was an inattentive student and even a disciplinary problem at Loomis, Nichols was becoming an excellent hockey player, and his skills on the ice helped him get into Hamilton College in upstate New York. Already in prep school he had begun writing fiction in imitation of Ernest Hemingway, F. Scott Fitzgerald, Carson McCullers, and Damon Runyon, but his writing became more serious during college. While living in Spain the year after graduating from Hamilton, he drafted his first novel, *The Sterile Cuckoo*, which was published in 1965. Nichols's next novel, *The Wizard of Loneliness,* appeared a year later, and Nichols was soon hired by Alan Pakula to write the screenplay for a film version of *The Sterile Cuckoo.* In 1969, feeling oppressed by New York City, Nichols moved with his wife and two children to northern New Mexico, the region that has inspired his best-known work. His "New Mexico Trilogy" includes the novels *The Milagro Beanfield War* (1974), *The Magic Journey* (1978), and *The Nirvana Blues* (1981), the first of which was made into a successful film by Robert Redford. Despite his success as a writer, Nichols emphasizes that it requires hard work, that "behind every book is essentially a seven day week, and a twelve to fourteen hour day, day in and day out for years, sometimes." In a 1991 interview, he compared writing to distance running: "I ran cross country in college. Cross country always seemed to me like a great metaphor for writing, because it's so long and it's so painful, but you just had to keep going and going....I know for me, it is just an extraordinary amount of work. Frustrating work."

In the late 1970s, Nichols began publishing nonfiction collections such as *If Mountains Die* (1979), *The Last Beautiful Days of Autumn* (1982), *On the Mesa* (1986), and most recently *The Sky's the Limit: A Defense of the Earth* (1990), often combining his polemical prose with powerful photographs of the natural landscape near his home in Taos. The following article, written on Nichols's fiftieth birthday, demonstrates his characteristically hyperbolic writing style and his increasingly strident environmental activism. Although Nichols is writing here about his own life in New Mexico, he is clearly conscious of the global implications of excessively consumptive behavior. His decision to simplify his life reflects not only Thoreau's famous exhortation in *Walden*—"Simplify, simplify"—but also an intense awareness of the environmental issues of the 1990s.

Once I led a pretty modern life. I could juggle many different preoccupations at once: family, garden, children, friendships, chores, grandiose ideas, political activism, fishing, hiking, drinking, novel writing, script writing, nature photography and so forth. In a single year I could travel to Europe, San Francisco, Seattle, Los Angeles, Austin, Boston, Chicago and New York without blinking an eye. While talking on the phone I could at the same time cook supper, scan the newspaper, make love and write notes to myself. I had a 20-track mind. I was seething with manic energy.

Then one day I got sick. My heart started fibrillating. I experienced searing pains in my neck and burst out in cold sweats. The pain traveled upwards, popping in both ears. Tachycardia hit, I went dizzy, nearly sank to my knees, almost blacked out. I thought: Dammit, I'm going to die.

Don't ask how, but I made it to a doctor. He put me through a battery of tests: echograms, dopplers, thalium treadmills. He concluded maybe I'd already had a heart attack. It was decided to catheterize my heart, shoot it full of dye, check out the arteries. I entered the hospital, they did their thing, and announced, "Nope, the arteries look great."

Then they put me on digitalis for the rest of my life.

When I asked what's wrong with me, the doctors shrugged and said I was probably so stressed out I couldn't see straight.

Then one of them said "Why don't you kick back and mellow out a little?"

Another advised, "Take the time to stop and smell the flowers."

A third hoped that I would "... learn how to keep it simple."

Fair enough: I set about making my life simple. I quit answering the telephone and, just to make certain, I petitioned for a new unlisted number. When people somehow got through and asked me to do things, I told any old baldface lie to weasle out of the commitment. I taught myself not to feel guilty for doing this. I ceased driving my old Dodge truck and started riding a bicycle. My sense of time slowed down. Things became less urgent. I stopped drinking coffee and eating salt and gobbling cookies.

Nevertheless, I soon realized that even if I quit killing myself, everybody else on earth was still eager to do me in. The air was so full of carcinogens, my asthma was being triggered regularly. Rays of sunshine galloped through vast holes in the ozone, eager to forge melanomas in me. Big time agribusinessmen continued painting my tomatoes with pesticides. Lee Iacocca was still manufacturing millions of automobiles in hopes of slaying me with carbon monoxide. And researchers on all continents were rushing to discover a cure for AIDS so I would become a mortal statistic in one of the many crises caused by overpopulation.

Bottom line, I soon realized, is that if everybody else on earth doesn't learn how to keep it simple, I'm doomed anyway. Unfortunately, my well-being is a collective effort. It does no good for me to mellow out if Lee Iacocca continues on his rampage.

Obviously, I can't just kick back, it doesn't work that way. To save my own life, I gotta save yours too. If you're not willing to take responsibility for your own health (and mine), then I'll probably have to defend myself by making you very uncomfortable about your habits and actions.

According to John Muir, "Whenever we try to pick out anything by itself, we find it connected to everything else in the universe."

To me, understanding that statement seems like Step One on the road to recovery. Everything is interconnected, and the damage to any one small aspect of the overall picture (like me) usually threatens the entire picture. For example, look what happened tonight when I flicked on a light switch in order to write this article. A bulldozer started up in Arizona and stripmined a few tons of soft coal. Water was cut from a river into a slurry line to carry the coal to a generating plant in Page, Arizona. The generating plant fired up, turning the turbines that made electricity for my house. Smoke pollution spewed into the atmosphere, and prevailing winds blew it over my hometown of Taos and into the mountains and rivers near me. The pollution fell to earth as acid rain. Poisonous water came downstream into my irrigation ditch, and thence into my "organic" garden, which is full of beets and carrots. But when I ate a carrot it was contaminated by poisons which originated at Page, Arizona, whose raison d'être, of course, is millions of people like me who use lights at night, or run a refrigerator, or maybe watch a little TV to mellow out after a hard day at the office trying to save the planet.

The message is painfully clear. I love life, so I'm fighting like hell to make mine (and yours) more simple. I recycle everything possible, and try not to consume much to begin with. I buy all my clothes second hand, real cheap. I try to eat only what I need to survive. (How much of the planet do you think was destroyed by Orson Welles before he died?) Mostly, I don't need things so I don't buy them. If somebody turns on an air conditioner in my presence, I threaten to punch them, because they are personally attacking my well-being by adding to the Greenhouse Effect.

I have published four photo/essay books, and I still take pictures. But, frankly, I'm worried about photography. What happens to all those chemicals? How much poison, needed to print every beautiful image that I create, comes back to shorten my life?

And what about the pulp mills creating the paper upon which this chipper little article is printed?

No matter what, we all do damage. Nevertheless, it's real easy to reduce the damage we do.

Yes, I take a lot of time now to smell the flowers. I photograph them also. I'm training my eye to the simplicity in things, in order to move differently through the world. I always hope that by sharing a vision I'll gain other souls as allies. For in the end, only everybody else can save me.

In the meantime, my world has calmed down a lot, and I can tell the end of my life is receding.

Analyzing and Discussing the Text

1. What was it that alerted Nichols to the need to change his life-style? Do you think he is suggesting that the rest of us should wait for a similar signal? Explain your response.
2. List the specific changes Nichols made in order to simplify his life. What did he sacrifice in the process? What did he gain?
3. "Everything is interconnected," writes Nichols. Why is this concept essential to his effort to persuade us, his readers, to live more simply?

4. "I'll probably have to defend myself by making you very uncomfortable about your habits and actions"—does Nichols's essay make you uncomfortable? Does it succeed in making you want to live simply?
5. Much of Nichols's essay is critical and disturbing. Can you detect any passages, however, that compel us to change our habits by showing the *positive* results of such changes?

Experiencing and Writing About the World

1. Make a brutally honest list of every part of your life-style that seems environmentally unsound. Think of every little detail—even using a dryer rather than a clothesline—that Nichols might consider extravagant.
2. Write three letters—one to a friend; one to your parents; and one to a professor, a boss, or a university or government official—explaining the value, even the necessity, of simplicity. Try to present your ideas differently in each letter so as to appeal to the interests and attitudes of your various audiences.
3. "[I]f everybody else on earth doesn't learn how to keep it simple," writes Nichols, "I'm doomed anyway. Unfortunately, my well-being is a collective effort." Write an analytical essay in which you explain how this idea underlies one or more of the other articles in this chapter of the anthology. Try to detect whether these essays—as well as Nichols's—result from an altruistic concern for others or from direct self-interest.

BARUCH FISCHHOFF

Report from Poland: Science and Politics in the Midst of Environmental Disaster

Baruch Fischhoff (1946–   ) was born in Detroit, Michigan. He attended Wayne State University in his hometown, earning a B.S. in mathematics and psychology in 1967. Fischhoff then joined Kibbutz Gal-On and Kibbutz Lahav in Israel before working on his M.A. and Ph.D. in psychology at the Hebrew University in Jerusalem. In 1974 he moved to Eugene, Oregon, where he became a research associate at the Oregon Research Institute. Two years later he helped to found Decision Research in Eugene, remaining there until 1987, when he received a joint appointment as professor of social and decision sciences and professor of engineering and public policy at Carnegie Mellon University in Pittsburgh, Pennsylvania. Fischhoff has written numerous articles on decision making and risk perception. In 1980 he received the American Psychological Association's Distinguished Achievement Award for Early Career Contribution to Psychology, and in 1991 he was the corecipient of the Distinguished Contribution Award from the Society for Risk Analysis for his work on how people perceive risks, especially those associated with technology.

In 1990 Fischhoff accompanied a film crew from Boston on a trip to Poland to prepare a report for the World Wildlife Fund on environmental problems in that country shortly after the opening of Eastern Europe to western journalists. During the "down time" while the film crew was setting up equipment, Fischhoff began typing his notes about his experiences in Poland on a laptop computer. These notes eventually became what Fischhoff calls a "crude handout," circulated to interested readers via electronic mail after the author's return to the United States. Later, working with the editors at *Environment*, Fischhoff took the loose "e-mail" paragraphs, reorganized them, cut the manuscript, and added the internal headings found in the following version of the article. The goal of the piece was not merely to expose Poland's environmental problems, but also to suggest the need for international cooperation, for people in various countries to share information about environmental problems and solutions. As a result of this article, many American scholars sent information on risk and environmental issues to the Polish officials listed at the end of the piece. Even in a dire story like this one, there is an underlying hope that the writer's expression of interest and concern will motivate action on the part of readers. "Things that give you hope are important in stories," says Fischhoff. Sometimes this hope is based on the discovery and communication of disturbing information.

Horror stories of environmental catastrophe have been leaking out of Eastern Europe in recent years. Last spring, I toured southern Poland with a crew of film producers looking for environmental problems that could be examined in a television special on risk (to be aired on 3 April) being produced by WGBH of Boston in association with the World Wildlife Fund. Our three main stops in Poland were Warsaw, where we met several environmental functionaries and activists; Krakow, where we met several scientists and visited Nowa Huta, site of the largest steel mill in Poland; and Upper Silesia, where we visited Solidarity activists living in what is arguably the most polluted place in the world. The following is a report on the environmental conditions that we witnessed and had described to us by Poles, on people's attitudes toward their environment, and on environmental politics in Poland.

Poland's environment is in desperate shape. By U.S. and European standards, the country has virtually no potable water. People pay extraordinary amounts of money (by Polish standards) to buy bottled water. In Warsaw, we visited an enormous slag heap with residue from one of the plants that provides the city with central heating. It looked fairly benign, although it was disturbingly surrounded by truck farms that supply much of Warsaw's produce. According to a local woman working in her potato field, it is intolerable when the wind blows up the dust. Our driver said that the plant creates enormous quantities of smoke in the winter when it is working. According to Elizabeth Pyroch, who accompanied us in Poland as the fixer for the television project, the plant starts up two months after winter has begun and runs until May or so. People can regulate indoor heat only by opening their windows.

The worst conditions, however, are in the south, around Krakow and Katowice. Human life expectancy is falling while the rate of leukemia is rising. Infant mortality is increasing, in part because many babies are born premature. By age 10, most children are under continuing medical treatment for chronic illnesses. It is uncommon to find someone with a red blood cell count above the norm of 5 million per cubic millimeter, despite high levels of carbon monoxide in the air, which typically increase red blood cell counts. Scientists there speculated that the unhealthily high lead levels in people's blood prevent the normal physiological response.

Although the countryside around Krakow is remarkably green and cultivated, locally grown produce is too contaminated with heavy metals to be edible. Yet it is eaten any way because the distribution system is too poor to bring in fruits and vegetables from elsewhere. When we began to ascend to Krakow, the air became quite acrid. By the time we were in the city, it was terrible. Yet our driver described it as the best time of year because home furnaces were no longer in use. He said that people have constant respiratory problems and that he himself had to leave work frequently in midwinter because he could not stop vomiting. In addition, school officials keep children inside during recess.

Krakow was once the capital of Poland, and it has many fine buildings and a university community of 65,000 students. From a distance, the city looks quite appealing, but, as elsewhere in Poland, the buildings and statues are eaten away by acid rain. The most identifiable source of air pollution in Krakow is the Nowa Huta steelworks, which employs 27,000 Poles. People told us that the plant was built about six kilometers from the center of Krakow to dilute the local intelligentsia with proletarians and peasants from other parts of the country. There are, apparently, no relevant natural resources, such as coal or iron ore, in the immediate area. Steel production began in the mid 1950s, and much of its equipment was antiquated even at that time. On a tour, we saw an open hearth furnace, a converter, a rolling mill, and a badly leaking coke battery—all on a very large scale. The only safety equipment that we saw of any kind was a protective coat worn by workers near the open hearth. Most workers were covered with the soot or residue generated by their particular operation. One worker mentioned that men expect to die by their fifties as a matter of course. A plant manager said that 80 percent of the workers retire because of disability.

In a long interview, the plant's technical manager, an engineer named Ryszard Kaczor, said that the overthrow of communism had allowed him to run the plant as he wanted—investing in modern technology and safety equipment, implementing efficiency procedures, finding new markets, etc.—but that to do so he needed $400 million to become competitive in the world market. Most recent reductions in pollution, however, seem to have come from downsizing, which closed the least efficient (and dirtiest) sections first. Kaczor claimed that Nowa Huta was responsible for only three percent of Krakow's pollution but was taking a lot of blame because it was such an identifiable source. He said that he was doing what he could to stop pollution but needed to preserve jobs. He also mentioned a steady stream of vendors wanting to sell new technologies and, among them, some U.S. businessmen trying to sell used, old technologies. In all our hotels, there were sales representatives and personnel recruiters from the West.

In Krakow, we also visited the Wieliczka salt mines, an enormous operation reaching 300 meters underground, which have been worked since the 1300s and possibly earlier. In the 1950s, a local physician decided that one way of treating the endemic respiratory problems was with a 24-day treatment that involved 100 hours underground in the cool, damp air. So workers periodically leave the surface of the planet just to breath clean air. I did breathe easier down in the mines, but we were not able to find out where the air came from (e.g., whether the mine was just ventilated from the surface) nor how effective the treatment had proved to be. The relative ease of breathing might be due simply to the coolness and dampness of the air. Above ground, the smokestack from the coal-fired power plant that ran the mines was a major polluter itself, probably ensuring a steady supply of customers for the therapy.

The morning after our visit to the salt mines, we drove to Katowice, the entry point to a region, Upper Silesia, with a phenomenal concentration of filthy smokestacks. Everywhere we looked there was smoke spewing into the air and onto nearby dwellings. Even after we had spent almost a week in the area, the view was still mind-boggling. Our hotel was across the street from a large coal mine and power plant. Everything was dirty. Soot drifted in the streets. In a heroic gesture, Upper Silesians maintain a tradition of painting their windowsills and porches in bright colors. In many ways, Katowice reminded me of what Pittsburgh, Pennsylvania, used to look like.

Restricted housing and limited job mobility make it impossible for most people to move away from the worst areas. We talked to a pediatrician whose son had a blood lead level of 56 micrograms per deciliter (20 is alarming), yet was unable to move from the shadow of the battery-recycling plant that she held responsible. A peculiar feature of the old social contract in communist Poland was the virtually total neglect of people's welfare on the prevention side but considerable concern and effort on the treatment side. Thus, once workers got sick because of terrible occupational conditions, resources were devoted toward making their lives more tolerable. For example, most industrial plants in Upper Silesia have spas in other parts of Poland with better air, where workers take regular vacations. This arrangement may have bought off the citizens somewhat and given the bosses the feeling that they were not entirely exploitative. However, one by-product of the current economic reforms is that workers receive fewer days off because firms are more cost-conscious. Perhaps by eliminating the temporary respites at the spas, the economic reforms will provide pressure toward environmental reforms.

Still, many of the most threatened areas have a remarkably normal appearance. They look poor and neglected, but, at least in the spring, the trees were covered by green leaves, children were playing, and couples were strolling in the parks. It would not be too hard to convince oneself that, if this is the most polluted place in the world, pollution cannot be all that bad. But, as someone once suggested, environmentally, the world dies with a whimper, but it takes a bang to get political attention. (For more in-depth information on Poland's environment, see "Poland: Facing the Hidden Costs of Development" in the November 1985 issue of *Environment*.)

The Lack of Data

Although Poland's environmental problems are desperate, no one seems to have the hard data needed to establish a correlation between pollution and the incidence of disease. The old regime suppressed, fabricated, or just failed to collect data about both human exposure to pollutants and health effects. Of course, it is often difficult to establish a cause-and-effect relationship even in cases of apparently serious harm. Occasionally, however, unplanned "experiments" have produced fairly clear evidence. For example, when the electrolysis division of a large aluminum plant in Krakow was closed because of public pressure, there was an observable reduction in the local incidence of osteoporosis. The division, we were told later, had been relocated to Bytom, near Katowice.

Some Poles think of themselves as living in an enormous, open-air laboratory where the effects of the total environmental burden on humans are being tested. Some people seem torn between wanting Western scientific attention, which could help them substantiate their suspicions and get action, and not wanting the dehumanization that comes with being a statistic or a subject in an experiment. One group of physicians said quite explicitly, "Come help us to test, and we will give you unlimited access to subjects."

Understanding the magnitude of the risks in Poland was complicated not only by the general lack of data but also by the uncertain standardization of terms. For example, we were told about alarmingly high rates of mental retardation, pregnancy complication, and long-term medical treatment for children. However, without knowing exactly what those terms mean, it is hard to tell what is really happening. A thorough study would also have to examine the procedures and reporting practices associated with even the more conventional health problems, such as infant mortality.

One obvious consequence of the paucity of credible information is the proliferation of rumors. I often wondered whether even widely accepted facts were true, including "facts" about health procedures, such as what to feed children to reduce the effects of heavy metal poisoning, and about political events, such as whether the electrolysis operation had really been moved from Krakow to Bytom.

Environmental Politics

The environmental activists whom we met were remarkably mainstream—doctors, lawyers, and engineers who had realized that they could not do their jobs in good conscience without challenging the regime. The rough treatment that they have received from the old government has left deep scars. Many people mentioned the accident at Chernobyl as a catalyst for their environmental activism. I was somewhat surprised given that Poland has no nuclear power plants (in part because, since the accident, construction has slowed or stopped on the two plants that Poland had in progress). But perhaps Chernobyl was the last straw for these people. After all, they may have felt that they had less to lose by protesting if the regime and the Soviets were killing them anyway. Moreover, because environmental affairs are an expression of the entire social, economic, and political situation, they must wage a broad battle to get anything done. If the changes in Poland were an important first step toward the changes in Eastern Europe altogether, the accident at Chernobyl might ironically represent a case of atoms for peace.

Most Poles belong or adhere to Solidarity. While we were there, Solidarity candidates received almost 80 percent of the vote in regional elections. But there are several parts to Solidarity. In particular, subgroups have organized on both a work-place and a territorial basis. Thus, jobs-versus-health battles are, to some extent, fought between different branches of the same organization. These are still serious conflicts; one territorial Solidarity member said that he would be lynched if he openly proposed what he really thought should be done for the environment. Compared to the United States, however, there may be greater understanding between the jobs and health "lobbies" in Poland because Polish workers' families usually live very close to the plants, making them victims of the pollution. Moreover, their neighbors—with whom they have struggled together in Solidarity—may be less dependent on the economic fortune of the local plant. Perhaps these common interests and mutual understanding will make it easier to reach some acceptable compromises.

In Warsaw, we met Andrzej Kassenberg, the vice president of the Polish Ecology Club. He is an urban planner who said that he became politically active 10 years ago when he realized that his job was a joke as long as there was nothing to be done about the environmental degradation that was ruining the lives of the people for whom he was planning. Like everyone else with whom we spoke, Kassenberg had been hassled for his activities by the previous regime and saw Solidarity as his vehicle for change. In some ways, the Ecology Club was tolerated more than other groups, even during the darkest days of martial law, perhaps because concern for the environment could be seen as an expression of nationalism and, hence, less of a threat to the political legitimacy of the regime.

The same day, we met Maria Guminska, a biochemist, and Andrzej Szczeklyk, an immunologist, who are both active in Solidarity and the Ecology Club. Each described personal struggles to collect and disseminate data related to environmental health. Guminska and her colleagues have compiled a collection of their research on environmental problems in their region. However, they could not get their findings published because the political changes that have given people the freedom to publish whatever they want have also wrought economic changes that have taken away the financial resources required to do so.

In Upper Silesia, we visited Wojciech Beblo, a mechanical engineer for the local mining institute and also a Solidarity environmental activist. Beblo spoke of people being punished for seeking information under the old regime. While we were there, he was elected to a local government council. We also met Katarzyna Klich, who works as a full-time environmental activist for Solidarity. She said that she knew too much to feel comfortable about having children. She optimistically hoped that she might begin a family in two or three years, when the environment would be better.

Looking Forward

What Poland can do to help itself environmentally is greatly limited by its meager economic resources. According to the theory that "richer is safer," the Poles would close the worst plants if only they could afford to do so. That may be true, but there are a few more complex wrinkles. One is the fact that those who profit from an industry will always feel threatened if the industry is threatened, regardless of how much money they are making. Therefore, waiting does not always make it easier to take action, at least not at the local level. If waiting a while made Poland as a whole wealthier and if the country arrived at an appropriate social contract, then the delay might put the government in a better position to cushion the blow for those who suffer for the sake of the environment. A second wrinkle is that exposing Poland's industries to a market economy may further environmental cleanup because many of the dirtiest plants are among the least sound economically and are being kept alive only by artificially guaranteed suppliers and customers.

A market economy would not be a cure-all, however. In Upper Silesia, we heard references to Katanga, Zaire, a mineral-rich region that was mercilessly exploited by a foreign empire. Such exploitation could easily be repeated in Poland as economic domination by the West replaces military domination by the USSR. Many Western carpetbaggers are going to Poland to find places for disposing hazardous wastes or to sell outmoded technologies. Must of the power to decide about technology purchases lies with the same people who worked for the old regime and have a demonstrated lack of concern for their fellow citizens.

Such threats make the need for environmental regulations obvious. We frequently received requests for information about environmental regulation in the United States. But if U.S. procedures are to be used as a prescription for Poland, many precautions must go with their use. How much of the United States' welter of regulations can really be recommended to a country that is starting to regulate environmental protection from scratch? In this respect, the Poles might have an advantage in that they are not buried under the morass of government rules, court rulings, and entrenched political forces that makes environmental regulation so cumbersome in the United States. Poland needs a regulatory system that makes sense in terms of both Western countries' experience and its own conditions. Such a system would have sensible incentives for people in different parts of the economy. Starting from almost nothing gives Poland much freedom to create such a system but also deprives it of the skilled and seasoned specialists needed to implement the system.

One kind of help that might be relatively easy for the West to deliver is basic scientific information. The people we met asked about current research on energy conservation, the effects of lead poisoning on children, the treatment of heavy metals poisoning, the risks of agricultural pesticides, the historical transition of Pittsburgh, and the use of support groups for the mothers of infants with birth defects, among other things. Although there is now a lot of sharing of information among Polish environmental activists at the national level and among physicians at the regional level, much of the information being shared is very old. People showed us tattered, 15-year-old reprints that were the most recent sources for their own work. (The box [at the end of this article] lists the addresses of four Polish environmentalists, activists, and politicians who would like to receive information on environmental risks and issues.)

Western Europeans have every incentive to help Poland and other Eastern European countries because the poverty of Eastern Europe threatens environmental protection in the West. The most obvious way is through transboundary pollution. Perhaps less obvious is the extent to which the availability of disposal sites and cheap, dirty production processes in the East will provide a disincentive to build facilities in the more heavily regulated West. Some of the businesspeople we met in our hotels made loosely veiled threats to take their dirty facilities eastward if permission were not granted to expand hazardous waste disposal facilities in Western Europe.

The Poles have heard a lot of promises since the overthrow of communism. Many people we spoke to remembered exactly what U.S. president George Bush and other officials and visiting scientists from the West have promised in terms of contacts, scientific instruments, visits, resources, and so forth. I wondered whether the Poles realize how short the attention spans of citizens and politicians in the United States can be. The vividness of a visitor's experience fades very quickly, and many things can change to prevent the fulfillment of promises. The U.S. Congress or the Office of Management and Budget may fail to allow the promised expenditures for reasons unrelated to the worthiness of Poland's cause. Nevertheless, we found it hard to leave without some promise of support. Certainly for the Poles, it must be hard to believe that they are largely alone in their predicament.

The following people are interested in receiving scientific information on environmental risks and issues:

Dr. Maria Guminska
Polish Ecology Club
Department of General
    Biochemistry
ul. Ikopernika 7
31-034 Krakow
POLAND

Dr. Guminska is a biochemist active in both Solidarity and the Polish Ecology Club.

Katarzyna Klich
ul. Tysiaclecia 4/22
40-873 Katowice
POLAND

Ms. Klich is a Solidarity activist who runs an information distribution center in Upper Silesia.

Professor Stefan Kozlowski
Panstwowy Instytut
    Geologiczny
ul. Rakowiecka 4
00-975 Warszawa
POLAND

Professor Kozlowski is an environmental specialist and member of the Polish Parliament.

Dr. Zofia Kuratowska
Wicemarszalek Senatu
ul. Wiejska 6
00-902 Warszawa
POLAND

Dr. Kuratowska is a senator who represented Solidarity in Poland's national roundtable discussions that preceded the overthrow of the communist regime.

Analyzing and Discussing the Text

1. What are the gravest environmental problems in present-day Poland? What are the causes of these problems? How "healthy" does the American environment seem by comparison? Is this a dangerous comparison to make?
2. Who were the "environmental activists" Fischhoff spoke to in Poland? What seem to be their average levels of education and

roles in Polish society? How do they compare to the environmental activists in this country?

3. Fischhoff mentions some atrocious health problems resulting from Poland's environmental disaster. Analyze the language of his descriptions: what kind of diction does he use? What is the tone of his descriptive language? Can you gauge from Fischhoff's prose style who his intended audience must have been and what effect he wanted to achieve?

4. Explain the structure of Fischhoff's article. Why does he begin with the catalogue of environmental problems rather than with the discussion of the lack of scientific data and the nature of environmental politics?

5. What incentives do people outside of Eastern Europe have for helping countries like Poland with their environmental problems?

6. Explain the value that "basic scientific information" would have to the Polish officials listed at the end of Fischhoff's article.

Experiencing and Writing About the World

1. Travel to another part of this country or to a distant part of the world, either physically (if possible) or by digging up journalistic accounts in your library and then produce a "Report from _____" for an educated, concerned audience. Your goal should not be to alarm or annoy your readers with hyperbolic prose but rather to inform them of the current environmental situation in the place you're reporting about and the ways they could contribute to a solution.

2. Think of a major environmental issue in your own city (such as endangered species in nearby rivers or forests, acid rain, industrial water pollution, overcrowded landfills, or urban sprawl), then find out the history of this problem, gather data about the current situation, and assess the prognosis for the future. Use the library for background information, and interview three or more "experts." Structure your material like Fischhoff's article, beginning with a description of the problem, explaining its causes, commenting on the major people involved in responding to the problem, explaining its causes, commenting on the major people involved in responding to the problem, and finally indicating necessary actions.

3. Baruch Fischhoff and Paula DiPerna both suggest the need to scrutinize environmental data carefully, even sceptically, Taking their advice, write an analysis of Jonathan Weiner's use of data in "The New Question." If you have time to do a particularly thorough job, find a copy of Weiner's book, check the sources of information he mentions in his bibliography, and then compare the information in these books and articles with Weiner's own essay.

WANGARI MAATHAI

Foresters Without Diplomas

Wangari Maathai (1940–   ), an American-educated biologist and the first woman in east and central Africa to earn a Ph.D., is best known as the founder and current coordinator of Kenya's grassroots tree-planting program called the Green Belt Movement. Maathai, who was born in Nyeri, Kenya, received a B.S. in biology at Mount St. Scholastics College (Atchison, Kansas) and an M.S. in biology from the University of Pittsburgh before returning to Kenya, where she completed her Ph.D. at the University of Nairobi in 1971. While a senior lecturer at the University of Nairobi in 1973, she began serving as chair of the Department of Anatomy (thus becoming the first woman to chair a department), a position she held until 1981; in 1978 she was promoted to associate professor (another first for a woman in east and central Africa). In addition to her scholarly achievements, Maathai has earned many awards in recognition of her environmental and social activism, including the Windstar Award for Environment, the Conde Nast Environmental Award, the Goldman Environmental Foundation Award, the Better World Society Award, the Woman of the World Award, the Green Century Environmental Award for Courage, and the Africa Prize for Leadership. In 1990, she received an honorary doctor of law degree from Williams College (Williamstown, Massachusetts). Maathai serves on the steering committee of the Women's International Policy Action Committee on Environment and Development (IPAC), and in February of 1992 Bella Abzug, IPAC's co-chair, notified IPAC members that Maathai had recently been arrested and charged with violating a law against either "rumor-mongering" or "incitement to riot" simply because she attended a meeting in Nairobi with supporters of expanded democratic rights and a multiparty political system. Maathai's arrest is the latest event in a series of confrontations with the Kenyan government as a result of her political and environmental activism.

In the following article, which first appeared in Ms. (March/April, 1991), Maathai tells the story of the Green Belt Movement, its goals, its troubles, and its successes. Her optimistic conclusion, so powerfully demonstrated by the preceding account of her own experience, is that "one person can make the difference." Whereas people like John Nichols prefer to help the environment by changing (and reporting about) their personal life-styles, others like Maathai work on a larger scale as political organizers and social critics; even articles such as "Foresters Without Diplomas" function as political statements, rallying readers in support of the causes they publicize. Because the Green Belt Movement has attracted such widespread and favorable attention among the Kenyan people and the international environmental community, there is reason to be hopeful that both the movement and Wangari Maathai herself will weather this latest danger successfully.

The Green Belt movement started in my backyard. I was involved in a political campaign with a man I was married to; I was trying to see what I could do for the people who were helping us during our campaign, people who came from the poor communities. I decided to create jobs for them—cleaning their constituency, planting trees and shrubs, cleaning homes of the richer people in the communities, and getting paid for those services. That never worked, because poor people wanted support right away, and I didn't have money to pay them before the people we were working for had paid *me*. So I dropped the project but stayed with the idea. Then, in 1976—two years after the first backyard idea—I was invited to join the National Council of Women of Kenya.

We were into the U.N.'s "women's decade," and I got exposed to many of the problems women were facing—problems of firewood, malnutrition, lack of food and adequate water, unemployment, soil erosion. Quite often what we see in the streets of our cities, in the rural areas, in the slums, are manifestations of mistakes we make as we pretend we are "developing," as we pursue what we are now calling *mal*development.

And so we decided to go to the women. Why? Well, I am a woman. I was in a women's organization. Women are the ones most affected by these problems. Women are concerned about children, about the future.

So we went to the women and talked about planting trees and overcoming, for example, such problems as the lack of firewood and building and fencing materials, stopping soil erosion, protecting water systems. The women agreed, although they didn't know how to do it.

The next few months we spent teaching them how to do it. We first called the foresters to come and show the women how you plant trees. The foresters proved to be very complicated because they have diplomas, they have complicated ways of dealing with a very simple thing like looking for seeds and planting trees. So eventually we taught the women to just do it using common sense. And they did. They were able to look for seeds in the neighborhood, and learn to recognize seedlings as they germinate when seeds fall on the ground. Women do not have to wait for anybody to grow trees. They are really foresters without a diploma.

We started on World Environment Day, June 5, 1977; that's when we planted the first seven trees. Now, only two are still standing. They are beautiful *nandi* flame trees. The rest died. But by 1988, when we counted according to the records women sent back to us, we had *10 million trees surviving.* Many had already matured to be used by the women. But the most important thing is that the women were now independent; had acquired knowledge, techniques; had become empowered. They have been teaching each other. We started with one tree nursery in the backyard of the office of the National Council of Women. Today we have over 1,500 tree nurseries, 99 percent run by women.

The women get a very small payment for every seedling that survives. The few men who come are extremely poor, so poor that they don't mind working with women. Women do a lot of work that requires caring. And I don't believe that it is solely indoctrination. Women started the environmental movement, and now it has become a movement that even financial donors see they should put money in, because the efforts are providing results. But the minute money is in, the men come in. I would not be surprised that eventually the more successful the Green Belt movement becomes, the more infiltrated it will be by men, who will be there more for the economic benefit than the commitment.

Although men are not involved in the planting at the nursery, they are involved in the planting of trees on farms. These are small-scale farmers. In our part of Africa, men own land; in some communities they own separate titles to the land; in others there is still communal ownership, which is the tradition in Africa. We are most successful in communities where women are involved in land farming.

In Kenya, as in so much of the African continent, 80 percent of the farmers—and the fuel gatherers—are women. Women also keep animals. A large population of Kenyans are nomadic communities: the Maasai, the Samburu, the Somalis, most of the northern communities. We have been unsuccessful there. Yet this is where trees are much needed. Areas that are green now will soon be a desert if not cared for.

We have been approached by other countries, and in 1987–88 we launched what we hoped would become an effort to initiate Green Belt-like activities in other African countries. Unfortunately, we have not been able to follow up. We started having our own problems in Kenya because of our having criticized the government for wanting to put up a big building in a Nairobi public park. But we are encouraging an establishment of a Green Belt Center in Nairobi, where people can come and experience development that is community oriented, with community decision-making, and with development appropriate to the region.

Funding is always a problem. We never received any financial support from the Kenyan government. They gave us an office—which they took away as soon as we criticized them. (In a way, it is good they didn't give us money because they would have withdrawn that.) We receive much of our support from abroad, mostly from women all over this world, who send us small checks. And the United Nations Development Fund for Women gave us a big boost, $100,000 in 1981. We also received support from the Danish Voluntary Fund and the Norwegian

Agency for International Development. In the U.S. we are supported by the African Development Foundation, which helped us make a film about the Green Belt movement in 1985. Information on the film can be obtained from the Public Affairs Officer of the African Development Foundation, 1400 I Street, N.W., Washington, D.C. 20005.

In the field, we now have about 750 people who teach new groups and help with the compilation of the reports, which we monitor to have an idea of what is happening in the field. At the headquarters we now have about 40 people. When we were kicked out of our office, the headquarters moved back to my house; a full-circle return to where we started.

But it's 10 million trees later—not quite where we started. For myself, now that my two boys and a girl are big—the last boy is still in high school—when we have trained enough women in leadership and fund-raising, I would love to go back into an academic institution. I do miss it. My field is biology. But I was into microanatomy and developmental anatomy. I would love to be able to read more about community development and motivation and write about the experience that I have had in the field. And perhaps train people on grass-roots projects. But that will have to wait. I earn maybe a tenth of what I could earn on the international market if I sold my expertise and energy, and I'm sure many people would probably consider me a fool. At home the men don't believe that I don't make a fortune out of the Green Belt movement. But all over the world we women do this sort of thing.

My greatest satisfaction is to look back and see how far we have come. Something so simple but meaning so much, something nobody can take away from the people, something that is changing the face of the landscape.

But my greatest disappointment has been since I returned to Kenya in 1966 after my education in the United States. When I was growing up and going through school, I believed that the sky is the limit. I realized when I went home that the sky is not the limit, that human beings can make the limit for you, stop you from pursuing your full potential. I have had to fight to make a contribution. We lose so much from people because we don't allow them to think freely and do what they can. So they lose their interest; their energy; the opportunity to be creative and positive. And developing countries need all the energy they can get.

I tell people that if they know how to read and write it is an advantage. But that all we really need is a desire to work and common sense. These are usually the last two things people are asked for. They are usually asked to use imposed knowledge they do not relate to, so they become followers rather than leaders.

For example, because I criticized the political leadership, I have been portrayed as subversive, so it's very difficult for me to not feel constrained. I have the energy; I want to do exactly what they spend hours in the U.N. talking about. But when you really want to *do* it you are not allowed, because the political system is not tolerant or encouraging enough.

But we must never lose hope. When any of us feels she has an idea or an opportunity, she should go ahead and do it. I never knew when I was working in my backyard that what I was playing around with would one day become a whole movement. One person *can* make the difference.

Analyzing and Discussing the Text

1. Does the article "Foresters Without Diplomas" seem to be a formal report on the Green Belt Movement or an informal one? Explain your response and try to determine why Maathai wrote her article on this level.
2. This article initially appeared in *Ms.* magazine's "ecofeminism" column. Is this a feminist essay? Where do you notice references to gender, and why is gender relevant to the issue of environmental protection/restoration?
3. Why does Maathai offer information about her family and her academic background? Is it related to the fund-raising goal of the essay?
4. "[H]uman beings can make the limit for you," writes Maathai, "stop you from pursuing your full potential." Do we face similar "limits," similar human obstacles, in this country? What would happen if you tried to start a Green Belt Movement in your local area?
5. Why do you think Maathai tells potential Green Belt workers "if they know how to read and write it is an advantage"? Is she talking about basic literacy skills or something more advanced?

Experiencing and Writing About the World

1. If you were bold enough and had enough time or enough money, what kind of political movement—environmental or otherwise—would you like to start? Write a speculative essay in which you describe this "movement," justify its existence, and explain the process of starting it and keeping it going.
2. John Nichols works on a private level, but thinks globally; Wangari Maathai organizes nationally, but thinks internationally. Analyze these two approaches to environmental action, explaining the purposes, advantages, and drawbacks of each.

3. What does your community need? A recycling program, an environmental education resource center, an urban renewal program that turns inner-city lots into community gardens, a Green Belt Movement? Inquire of city and/or university officials and potential funding sources (including private foundations and government agencies) to find out what it would take to establish such a program. Then prepare a formal proposal (a potentially lengthy project), even if you do not intend to submit it for approval and/or funding. Many present-day jobs require grant-writing skills—consider this project a chance to practice such skills.

PAULA DIPERNA

Truth vs. "Facts"

Paula DiPerna (1949–   ), a freelance writer of books, articles, and films, lives in upstate New York. She earned her B.A. in English and her M.A. in English education by taking night courses at New York University, and then became a teacher at an alternative high school in New York City in 1975. DiPerna began writing articles about public education for the *Village Voice* in the mid-1970s but soon found herself working on various subjects for such publications as the *New York Times,* the *Chicago Tribune,* the *Philadelphia Inquirer,* and many magazines. In 1978 she became an associate producer and writer of films for The Cousteau Society, a job that requires her to travel ahead of film crews looking for stories, arrange for filming, and eventually write scripts. Working for The Cousteau Society, DiPerna has traveled up and down the east coast of Canada, spent a year in Brazil near the Amazon, and worked in New Zealand, Australia, Haiti, Cuba, France, and even Antarctica. In 1990 she wrote *Lilliput in Antarctica,* a one-hour Earth Day television special on a journey to Antarctica with six children. That same year she wrote and coproduced "Outrage at Valdez," a television film about the *Exxon Valdez* oil spill. DiPerna has also published five books since 1979, including *The Cousteau Almanac: An Inventory of Life on Our Water Planet* (1981), *Cluster Mystery: Epidemic and the Children of Woburn,*

Mass. (1985), and *With These Hands: Farmworkers in America* (1986). In 1988 DiPerna was the Thurber Writer-in-Residence at Ohio State University's School of Journalism.

DiPerna published the following article, "Truth vs. 'Facts,' " in *Ms.* (September/October, 1991), drawing in part on research done in the course of her other projects. She tried to use "facts" (i.e., statistics) sparingly in the article because, as she puts it, "the piece itself made the distinction between truth and facts and I wanted my thoughts and ideas to carry the article, rather than information." Still, she cautions, "it is important that all writers, especially those working with slippery facts like those relevant to environmental subjects, learn to be scrupulous with facts and quote them accurately." DiPerna says that she wrote her article for a widely mixed audience, not only for people already committed to the environment: "I would hope that political leaders, bankers, and scientists take the piece to heart." This kind of ambition should motivate students, too, she says: "I think students who want to write about the environment should not expect to change the world with a single article, but they should want to. A student should write each piece of work with the same care and attention—anything worth writing is worth writing well." The process of thinking is also essential to good writing. "[T]he best writers are those who think, rethink, feel, think, rethink, feel, ask, etc.," she says. "Young writers who don't think are doomed not to have much new to say."

It was 1984 and large snowflakes fell on Woburn, Massachusetts. Despite the cold, people gathered for the meeting of their group, For a Cleaner Environment, the storefront throwing a glow into the snowy evening. I was there to cover the story of Woburn, site of toxic waste dumping, public wells contaminated with carcinogens, and a mysterious grouping of leukemia cases among children.

It had been a haggle to convince my editor that what I saw as a fascinating medical detective tale—did the contaminated drinking water cause the leukemia cases?—was worthwhile. Now, there I was; the players gathered, ripe for questioning. But the key person was missing: Anne Anderson, the mother of one of the children who had died. After her son was diagnosed with leukemia in 1972, well before Love Canal, and she became aware of other cases in her neighborhood, Anne Anderson began to suspect the only common factor—the foul tapwater about which she and her neighbors had been complaining for years. But the authorities insisted the water was fine; her own husband, trying to dissuade her from keeping a record of each new leukemia case, told her that "if this was unusual, someone would know." But Anne Anderson remained undeterred, and in 1979, Woburn's toxic waste contamination broke into the news.

When we met the next morning, I sat notebook and pen at the ready. But mindful that she had lost a son, I prefaced my questions: "I know this may be painful to discuss, but I'd like to begin by asking you what made you suspect the water?" Anne interrupted, taking control. "You can't just jump into the facts like that. It is a long and complicated story and it took my Jimmy nine years to die."

My eyes burned with tears of embarrassment, and as I fought not to show them, I listened. She explained that she had missed the meeting the night before because it had been the third anniversary of Jimmy's death. She narrated a long history of trying to get her theory taken seriously. I began to realize that Woburn was not just about toxicology, or chemistry, or how many parts per million of carcinogenic substances were found in the water, or the criminal proceedings against the polluters, or any of the obvious reportorial aspects. The Woburn story eclipsed mere information. It was a human tragedy. Real children, real pain, real death.

There and then I altered my view of environmental issues. I saw that they are inseparable from ethics, indivisible from society. Proceeding from biology, agronomy, oceanography, hydrography, and other disciplines—yet more than their sum—environmentalism is a humanity, perhaps sometimes even more than a science.

Women understand this transcendent quality better than men, which is why women are uniquely suited to lead in environmental matters—not just lead the doing, but the thinking. Women process complexities and still focus on the undeniable fact: a healthy planet is not a luxury but a basic human necessity. In a way, environmentalism shouldn't even exist or be a specialty of any kind, but an "ism" without a name, so pervasive as to be virtually invisible. Anne Anderson did not think of herself as an environmentalist when her son fell ill. Yet she took on the most complicated environmental questions, motivated not only by deep love, but also by her commonsense belief that human beings should not be expected to drink contaminated water. Period.

As society hurtles through this decade, passion for environmental causes has never been higher (theoretically, at least). "Think green" evolved into "buy green" and for those affluent enough to exercise the option, "ecologically correct" behavior is in. But has this ground swell actually established a clean environment as a basic human right? Or have we created the *appearance* of protecting the earth?

Women, of course, know the difference, being experts at discerning substance from tokenism, real work from taking credit for it, the good buy from the bad.

Consider the challenges, against which governments have taken virtually no meaningful action.

Depletion of the ozone layer, which protects the earth and us from harmful solar ultraviolet rays, seems under way. An ozone "hole" in-

disputably occurs seasonally over Antarctica, largely due to chlorofluo-
rocarbons (CFCs) rising into the stratosphere, which shatter the ozone
molecules. Lacking this filter, the sun becomes our enemy, the possible cause of increased skin cancers, immune system suppression, and
the burning of the microscopic plants and animals that are the building
blocks of the food chain, including plankton on the ocean surface.

Global climate change also looms, due to the buildup of certain
gases in the atmosphere, especially carbon dioxide. Much accumulation
occurs because of the destruction of forest and grassland for farmland,
causing organic matter to be oxidized. Thus, deforestation means not
only loss of trees, but roughly one to three billion tons of carbon released
per year, in addition to the approximately six billion tons attributable
to the burning of fossil fuels.

Add to this, run-of-the-mill air pollution—sulfur dioxide, nitrogen
oxide, lead, and their numerous by-products—plus what are called
toxic "trace" elements such as benzene and polychlorinated biphenyls
(PCBs).

The water on which we depend for drinking, irrigation, and the like
can be polluted insidiously by chemicals and human waste. And in most
countries, including the U.S., neither groundwater nor municipal water
is routinely tested for chemical contamination (including pesticides). In
the developing world, nearly one billion people have no access to safe
water at all.

And despite the new consciousness, the world continues to lose 42
million acres of tropical rain forest per year, and gain 14 million acres of
desert. Diversity of species, the multitude of creatures and plants that
account for the pyramid of life, is under siege as approximately 20,000
species become extinct each year.

The Persian Gulf War represented a hellish turning point. Roughly
600 oil wells were set ablaze by retreating Iraqi troops, following the deliberate and "incidental" wartime release of one to three million barrels
of oil. The gulf provides food and a living to many in all the bordering
states. Subsistence fishing suffered immediate losses and the shrimp
industry was reportedly entirely eradicated.

I spoke with Munira Fakhro, an expert in women and development
issues, who had been at her Bahrain home in July. She reported, "There
was black rain everywhere, affecting seafood, fish, so many things that
I cannot name them." Fakhro was sure that "right now, the most important issue is damage caused to children. But everyone suffers from
a kind of virus from the chemicals in the air that affects their eyes and
noses." In general, deadly pollutants can take their first toll on the
female reproductive system, and in miscarriages, stillbirths, and congenital deformities. Yet she knew of no short- or long-term studies being
initiated, or even whether the rate of miscarriages had risen. Concern-

ing the impact of the inferno on health in the future, little data is being offered. As Fakhro says, "Maybe someone should be telling us about that."

Eco-warfare should be terrifying in itself, but especially in view of the regular movement of toxic substances that could be the targets of ambush. All of which pales compared to the projected transport of plutonium to enable Japan and such countries as Belgium, France, Switzerland, and Germany to reprocess spent nuclear fuel for use in a new generation of nuclear reactors. Plutonium is the stuff of nuclear bombs, the most toxic substance we know. A single particle of plutonium inhaled can cause lung cancer.

The transition from fossil fuel to plutonium could mean nations would then be dependent on an *inherently lethal substance* for energy — and by the late 1990s, about 400 shipments per year will take place by land, sea, and air, involving the movement of tons of plutonium.

So, despite growing awareness, dangerous trends persist, often the subject of fruitless debate. Since most environmental impacts don't follow the traditional cause and effect pattern, there is room for "on the one hand, on the other" contention: CFCs do destroy the ozone layer, but not everyone will get cancer; it's true some climate models show increase in global temperature over time, but these could be "flukes"; fish stocks seem lower, but these could be "natural crashes" of the populations; since the fires in Kuwait are unprecedented, no one can accurately predict their impact. The flaming match can be shown to burn the finger, but disease — especially cancer — may appear much later than when the cause exerted its power, and often long after the causative agent can be found in the environment. The tobacco industry is the most shameless in exploiting this drawback.

Therefore, because clear-cut links between cause and effect are elusive, remedies are evaded. Not to mention when information is deliberately covered up, of course, as chillingly described by Rosalie Bertell. But women bring to the discussion badly needed qualities — among them, a scalpel to cut away such evasions: women specialize in early warnings.

For example, few people knew that a woman second mate on the ill-fated *Exxon Valdez*, Maureen Jones, was lookout on deck and first to notice that the tanker was traveling the wrong side of the flashing red buoy. Apparently, she twice warned the third mate, then at the helm. He ignored her, though heeding her warning could have prevented the accident entirely.

The causes of the accident were even deeper. Again, it was an all-too-prescient woman — toxicologist and fisherwoman Frederika (Riki) Ott — who enunciated them. In a speech the night before the grounding, she had predicted what would happen, and why: "Given the high frequency of tankers into Port Valdez, the increasing age and size of that tanker fleet, and the inability to quickly contain and clean up an oil spill in the open waters of Alaska, fishermen feel that we are playing a game of Russian roulette. It's a question of when, not if. . . . " Such women can be found around the world, grasping and acting on connections that seem to elude the men in charge.

In Tasmania, the southerly island state of Australia, a novice politician, schoolteacher Christine Milne, won a seat in the state parliament in 1989. She convincingly exposed the environmental shortcomings of a $1 billion (Australian) paper plant. Her campaign proved that a cleaner paper mill could still be cost-effective, halting the construction of an inferior facility in Tasmania, and helping to raise the standard globally.

Milne received a Global 500 citation for achievement from the United Nations Environment Programme. Only 11 other women (750 awards have been made) have been similarly honored, including journalist Barbara d'Achille of Peru, who died for her trouble. She had been a vanguard voice on environmental subjects in the region for about 18 years, until she was stoned to death in 1989 by Shining Path guerrillas in the highlands.

Wangari Maathai, winner this year of a Goldman Environmental Prize among other awards, endured severe government criticism for her opposition to urban sprawl in Nairobi. Yet the Green Belt movement she began in 1977, through which women mobilized in Kenya to combat desertification, catalyzed similar efforts throughout East Africa.

Last year I met Dagmar Werner, otherwise known as "Iguana Mama." Trained in iguana biology, she is also a fervent interdisciplinarian. Observing the decline of rain forests in the tropical Americas—to make way for short-term slash-and-burn agriculture—Werner began to think that iguanas could stem the trend. But the herbivorous iguanas, long a prized food among the campesinos cutting down the trees, need the rain forest habitat, and their number has declined dramatically. Werner reasoned that if there were enough iguanas to eat, campesinos would rather hunt them than clear land to raise a few chickens or cows or low-paying crops. They could also enter the cash economy by selling iguana skins instead of leather. As she explains her mission, "I work with campesinos all the time and I know how few their economic choices are. Why shouldn't they eat the meat that is part of their culture, especially if northern countries are always telling them not to cut down the trees?" She pioneered the study of iguana reproduction in Panama, and when the U.S. invasion plunged that country into turmoil, she packed her breeding population of iguanas into a van and drove to Costa Rica. Her Fundación Pro Iguana Verde is now installed there, underfunded but functional, a practical and innovative approach to a recalcitrant problem.

Sylvia Earle, a marine biologist renowned for her deepwater diving and for having made the first untethered walk on the ocean floor, is now the chief scientist at the U.S. National Oceanic and Atmospheric Administration. She advocates the establishment of large "ocean wilderness" areas stretching from the surface to the depths, including international waters, where human activities would be prohibited or strictly limited. These swaths would protect not only harvestable fish, but the waters themselves for their role in maintaining global climate and cleansing the earth. As Earl puts it, "Imagine if we tried today to set aside the large sanctuaries on land that we now enjoy." She also notes that "the two billion dollars Exxon spent at Prince William Sound did not bring the tides in twice a day."

Pressing exploration into service for the environment, mountaineer Ann Bancroft hopes to lead the first all-women team across Antarctica in 1992, to call attention to the environmental importance of the earth's last virtually pristine continent. (Though an agreement forged in July 1991 declared Antarctica off-limits to mining and minerals exploration for at least 50 years, tourism proceeds and accidents can happen. An Argentine vessel ran aground in 1989; the oil spill killed large numbers of seabirds and jeopardized scientific research into the effects of ozone depletion on marine organisms.)

Such women inspire us, and testify to the basic connections of women to environmental issues.

For one thing, women are in a position to know. Who more than women—who increasingly head families, and who provide and cook the world's food, gather the world's fuel, pump the world's water, nurse the world's sick children and carry them from camp to camp in famine—experience the effects of dwindling resources and declining environmental quality?

Filomina Chioma Steady, a social anthropologist from Sierra Leone who is serving as a special adviser on women to the United Nations Conference on Environment and Development (UNCED) to be held in Brazil in June 1992, observes: "Women are much more attuned to the idea of sustainability, the need for a steady, not short-term, supply of resources." Steady's role, in collaboration with the United Nations Development Fund for Women, is to ensure that gender issues become integral to the UNCED agenda. Former U.S. Congresswoman Bella Abzug, of the Women's Environment & Development Organization (WEDO), charges: "Women have been almost invisible in policy-making on environment and development issues. They're present in large numbers at the grass roots, but at the top of most important nongovernmental organizations we find only male leadership."

For the past year, Abzug has been a senior adviser to Maurice Strong, secretary-general of the UNCED. The WEDO will sponsor a

World Women's Congress for a Healthy Planet in Miami from November 8 to 12, to develop an action agenda to present in Brazil. One goal of Abzug and Steady is to convince each nation to send a delegation to the UNCED of at least 50 percent women.

In fact, little environmental progress can be achieved without women. For example, in Africa, at least 70 percent of agricultural work is performed by women, yet they have no say in what agricultural practices are adopted. And the need for women's involvement is nowhere more evident than in attempting to stem overpopulation. Without control over their reproductive destiny, empowerment, and fair access to education and income, women will continue, willingly and unwillingly, to bring children into the world the environment cannot support, rendering null the concept of sustainable development.

Some hold the view that the environment is a "women's issue" by virtue of women's "holistic" vision and nurturing tendencies—by now a cliché. But although biology and social conditioning cannot be ignored, I think women's affinity for environmental issues has more to do with the concept of *potential:* the environment, though modern living cloaks the relationship, is the giver of all human potential. Without water, air, natural resources, the diversity of nonhuman species, no human endeavor would be possible. Underpinning all human activity and enabling all human success, therefore, the environment is the true source of human possibility. Thus, women struggling to explore, define, reach, and prove potential, relate not just to the life-creating and life-sustaining aspects of nature, but to its life-*enhancing* role. For women, to protect the environment is to secure not only a minimum level of existence, but a fair quality standard of living.

Since such a concept embroils global economics, women are well positioned to be the architects of a new "eco-economics."

Political economist, goat farmer, and former member of parliament in New Zealand, Marilyn Waring pioneered this area in 1988 in her book, *If Women Counted,* demonstrating how the United Nations System of National Accounts and the world's accounting systems ignore the value of "nonproductive" work performed by women and by nature.

In fact, the paradox of our time, which trumpets a "free market," is that natural resources are worth no money in and of themselves. They convert to money, i.e., marketability, only when used—then the cleanup operations and matériel are considered "productive"—but that use then generates environmental degradation and pollution. Furthermore, the notion that raw materials are free demands debunking. That sufficient trees have been available has been a long-term subsidy to all the wood-using industries as, for example, has been the capacity of rivers and oceans to absorb manufacturing and municipal sludge. The environment has actually been the silent unpaid partner of all economic growth.

Traditional economic theory posits environmental protection and economic activity as mutually exclusive—but today the two may be on a collision course. Some problems, such as climate change and ozone depletion, have grown too large to ignore except at global peril. Moreover, as the Cold War ends, such concepts as "economic planning" and "subsidy" have become dirty words. Yet there can *be* no environmental management without planning, and the private sector will not take risks in still-fledgling industries, like household solar power, without subsidy. Therefore, in a global economy governed only by market forces, how can environmental protection find a viable form?

One promising innovation, though it has turned red ink into an asset rather than truly making new cash available to environmental programs, is the "debt-for-nature" swap. Conservation organizations have raised money to buy a portion of a nation's outstanding debt from commercial debt holders who, eager to realize some repayment, sell the debt at discounted rates. But the sale relieves the government of repaying the full principal amount, as long as it is made available in local currency exclusively for environmental projects.

Kathryn S. Fuller, the first woman president of the World Wildlife Fund and a lawyer and biologist by training, has been active in such landmark transactions in Ecuador, the Philippines, and elsewhere. Fuller has hope for such alternatives. "We are still tinkering on the margins of financing conservation," she notes, "and the first efforts were supposed to catalyze numbers of things and get people thinking about creative financing mechanisms. The question now is to shift to larger institutions."

In the end, the revamping of economics with the environment in mind will have to forge new paths between private and public, especially since the so-called planned economies offered little in environmental protection. On the contrary, dead air, water, and land seem of crisis proportion in Eastern Europe—but nowhere more dramatic than at Chernobyl in the USSR. Five years ago, the infamous reactor exploded. Today, 125,000 persons are at risk of dying from radiation-induced illnesses within five years, 1.5 to 2 million are at long-term risk, and even after entombment, the reactor remains unstable.

Women are eloquent witnesses, though few perhaps as unlikely as Olga Korbut, the Soviet gymnast who, at the age of 17, mesmerized the 1972 Olympic games with the sheer perfection of her forms. Having once epitomized good health and the excellence of the human body, Olga Korbut fled her home in Minsk, only 180 miles from Chernobyl, fearing continued exposure.

She describes with lingering incredulity the innocence in which she and other citizens languished while living in the shadow of disaster. "For some time," she recounts, "nobody told us anything, and I went into the street without knowing what had happened." She remembers knowing women who were pregnant at the time, whose children were born with illnesses and birth defects, and adds, "Only now women know they are taking a risk in getting pregnant." Today, her health and that of her family are good, she says, "but in later time, who knows?"

Indeed. Unwilling to turn her back on the people she left behind, Korbut started the Olga Korbut Foundation at the Fred Hutchinson Cancer Research Center in Seattle, Washington, to raise money for Chernobyl victims, and to finance medical care for the hundreds of leukemic children.

Korbut joins the growing ranks of activist women in the Soviet Union, and when I asked her if this was because women were stronger, she simply answered, "I don't know. But what I do know is that for women, there is no exit. Woman is mother, and mother is always mother, and mothers are always stronger."

As the 1990s unfold, this strength, however defined and whatever the source, can be tapped to reexamine even the language that has dominated decisions affecting the environment. Women can remove the dialogue from the cycle of liberal versus conservative. Nowhere are these labels more inappropriately applied than in discussions of the environment, for though polluters may belittle "liberal environmentalists," what could be more liberal than irreverently dumping toxic sludge into streams, spewing acid into the rain, putting flame into forests? And what, after all, is more conservative than wanting to conserve the place where we live?

And if women have a single truly philosophical contribution to make, I believe it is to render the lack of traditional proof an irrelevant argument in environmental matters, as Anne Anderson did at Woburn.

For it may be that we will not have irrefutable evidence of such disturbances as global warming in time to address them. One can speak of a body of data, but each set has its detractor. The public, already skeptical of authority, shrinks from the cacophony into indifference and is inexcusably led to believe it is safe to do nothing "for now."

So the politician's statement that "all the evidence isn't in yet," is a perversion of science. Science is not the demonstration of fixed knowledge; it is only the quest, the ascent toward answers in aid of policy; it is not a justification for lack of action.

Fortunately, women can imagine the consequences of an act without having had to experience it. Physicist, feminist, and ecologist, Vandana Shiva of India contrasts this with what she has called "...a patriarchal reductionism that values only the part of reality that can be exploited. . . . The rest of reality is ignored." Thus, the prospects of environmental consequences are minimized because those consequences may not be tangible or provable in the classic sense. Turning Shiva's "rest of reality" into reality itself is the critical task of what has come to be called "ecofeminism."

Women can play the crucial role in "nurturing" the public away from expecting absolutes and toward redefining proof in Hippocratic terms—*in the absence of full knowledge, do no harm.* Under this banner, coupled with a rededication to the political process and campaigning for office, women could transform environmental policy.

The 1980s subversively denigrated the role of government, stimulating a wave of privatization and deregulation, demeaning the notion of public good in favor of individual good. But true environmentalism requires the sense of public good, advanced by an imaginative, credible, even passionate government, especially given the unprecedented nature of international cooperation required to solve global problems.

It is no longer enough for environmentalists to remain in parallel relationship to power; however large the movement grows, a lobbying body is on the outside. Similarly, it is no longer sufficient for politicians to remain entrenched and distracted insiders.

Women are perhaps the only ones equipped to cross this gulf. Marshaling philosophy, strategy, experience, and a unique cross-cultural point of view, women can bridge local activism and global leadership, instating *potential environmental consequences as the gauge by which all policy is measured.* Ultimately, women cannot remain mere advocates for the environment but must reestablish the environment as the advocate of human survival.

The next goal may well be to make *all* parties green, even in the smallest hamlets today reeling for lack of leadership on such problems as waste disposal, water treatment, and land use. This widespread political ignition could lead eventually to a new roster of women heads of government uniquely capable of setting new environmental priorities— women thinking globally and *acting* globally. Gro Harlem Bruntland, prime minister of Norway, was perhaps the first of this class, but even Margaret Thatcher was the most outspoken among her colleagues on global warming.

And true priority for environmental questions would be completely consistent with redressing poverty and misery, for the poor are the first victims of environmental degradation and the least able to pay for medical care—and most of the poor are women and children.

Women and the environment is really about women and truth, and redefining politics as the use of truth for the public well-being. This means *truth as distinct from final "facts,"* truth being the best you can get when you thoughtfully weigh everything together. The environment is not a special interest, but the single common interest, and as such acquires unique political and moral force. In the hands of women, this force could be the light of the next century.

Analyzing and Discussing the Text

1. When researching a story on contaminated water in Woburn, Massachusetts, DiPerna realized that the story "eclipsed mere information," a realization that immediately changed the author's view of environmental issues. Explain this change and discuss its implications for the way the rest of us think about the environment.
2. The author argues that "women are uniquely suited to lead in environmental matters." Why does she says this? Is her point convincing?
3. What reason does DiPerna have to suspect that we have achieved only "the *appearances* of protecting the earth"?
4. What is the problem with "factual" information? Isn't such information necessary to our understanding of the environment?
5. What seems to be DiPerna's purpose in listing women from around the world who have made important environmental contributions?
6. Explain why DiPerna connects "women's affinity for environmental issues" with "the concept of *potential.*"
7. Why should "*potential environmental consequences* [be instated] *as the gauge by which all policy is measured*"? Does the instatement of such a gauge seem feasible? Is it likely?
8. How does DiPerna define "truth"?

Experiencing and Writing About the World

1. DiPerna has attempted to explain the special contributions that women have made and can continue to make to the environmental movement. Write your own version of this argument in which you explain the special contributions that another traditionally disempowered group—students—can make. Interview your fellow students (on your campus and at other universities) and do research to discover past environmental activism among students (as individuals and as formal organizations). What are the unique characteristics of college students (such as flexible life-styles, brainpower, idealism, and access to vast libraries and expert scholars) that make them (you!) a likely group of environmental leaders?
2. Based on DiPerna's implied distinctions between men and women, analyze several of the other essays in this anthology to see whether these distinctions (in the use of "information" and in attentiveness to the "transcendent qualit[ies]" of environmental issues) emerge in environmental literature.
3. Interview various "players" involved in an environmental incident in your area to get each participant's version of the story. Then write

an analysis of the interviews to see whether you can predict people's attitudes and/or approaches to problems on the basis of gender, age, profession, ethnic background, socioeconomic status, or educational history. What are the implications of your findings?

Suggestions for Further Reading

Cowell, Adrian. *The Decade of Destruction: The Crusade to Save the Amazon Rain Forest.* New York: Henry Holt, 1990.

DeBardeleben, Joan, ed. *To Breathe Free: Eastern Europe's Environmental Crisis.* Baltimore: Johns Hopkins UP, 1991.

Erickson, Jon. *Greenhouse Earth: Tomorrow's Disaster Today.* Blue Ridge Summit, PA: TAB, 1990.

Friday, Laurie, and Ronald Laskey. *The Fragile Environment: New Approaches to Global Problems.* Cambridge, UK: Cambridge UP, 1989.

Knibb, David G. "Trashing the Marshalls." *Buzzworm* (September/October, 1990): 22–23.

Lovelock, James. *Gaia: A New Look at Life on Earth.* Oxford, UK: Oxford UP, 1979.

Norton, Bryan G. *Why Preserve Natural Variety?* Princeton, NJ: Princeton UP, 1987.

Popescu, Petru. *Amazon Beaming.* New York: Viking-Penguin, 1991.

Schell, Jonathan. *The Fate of the Earth.* New York: Avon, 1982.

Wallace, David Rains. "Wilderness Earth." *Life in the Balance.* New York: Harcourt, 1987.

Wilson, Edward O. *Biophilia.* Cambridge, MA: Harvard UP, 1984.

Yamashita, Karen Tei. *Through the Arc of the Rain Forest.* Minneapolis: Coffee House P, 1990.

Young, Allen. *Sarapiqui Chronicle.* Washington, DC: Smithsonian Inst., 1991.

Glossary of Critical Terms

Aesthetics: The branch of philosophy that considers the theory of beauty. An aesthetic approach to any given subject emphasizes its beauty rather than its meaning or its usefulness.

Allusion: A reference to familiar people, places, events, or artistic/literary works.

Analogy: The extended comparison of two seemingly dissimilar things, typically illuminating the unknown or the unfamiliar by associating it with the known/familiar.

Anecdote: A short account of an interesting or important incident.

Anthropomorphism: The attribution of human form, behavior, ideas, or feelings to something nonhuman.

Argumentation: The effort to convince readers to accept the writer's interpretation of or attitude toward a meaningful, controversial issue. Some arguments may rely on rational appeals to the reader's intellect, whereas other persuasive efforts may attempt to prompt certain emotions in the reader.

Arrangement: The structure or organization of a literary text.

Autobiography: Literally, "self-life-writing." An autobiography is normally a book-length study of the author's own life experiences. Shorter texts (and even work in such genres as fiction and poetry) may be autobiographical if they attempt, directly or indirectly, to convey essential features of the author's life.

Character: A participant, human or otherwise, in the action of a literary text.

712

Cinematic: A literary text that employs certain artistic techniques borrowed from film, such as panoramic descriptions of setting and sudden "cuts" from scene to scene.

Collage: A term borrowed from the visual arts to describe a literary text that consists of strikingly arranged images, scenes, or bits of language, things seemingly "pasted side by side" with minimal transition.

Commentary: Explicit analysis, explanation, or emotional response to a given subject, as opposed to the mere presentation of evocative material.

Comparison and contrast: A mode of composition that aims to show the similarities and differences between various things (physical or abstract). Seldom are any two things (including literary texts) absolutely alike or absolutely different, thus most *comparative* analyses entail some discussion of difference as well.

Conclusion: The final part of either an academic essay or a literary text, which can consist of as much as a multiparagraph section or as little as a few sentences. Conclusions normally aim to satisfy the reader's need for psychological or logical closure; they achieve this by restating main ideas, presenting a key point not yet mentioned, offering a memorable example or quotation, or suggesting the broader implications of the subject matter.

Confessional style: A literary mode (in either poetry or prose) in which the author reveals his or her intimate and sometimes painful experiences.

Depersonalized description: The presentation of a scene, object, person, or abstract idea with minimal explicit involvement on the part of the author.

Depiction: The manner or mode of describing characters, objects, or scenes.

Description: A mode of discourse (linguistic expression) designed to recreate sensory experience by evoking how something looks, feels, sounds, smells, or tastes.

Dialogue: A conversation between two or more characters in a literary text.

Diction: Word choice.

Digression: A deviation from the main (or previous) theme or style of a literary text. Some literary texts employ digression as an intentional technique—a way of forcing readers to stay attentive and make imaginative connections between various sections of a text rather than providing easy transitions.

Dramatic monologue: A literary text in which a speaker addresses a listener who remains silent—the listener may simply be the reader.

Episodic structure: Unlike a continuous chronological narrative, this narrative style leaps from scene to scene, skipping intervening events.

Essay: A short written composition (usually nonfiction) offering either reflections on abstract issues or an account and explanation of actual happenings. Essays that emphasize the author's own experiences or intimate feelings about a subject are called "personal essays."

Etymology: The branch of linguistics concerned with the origin and history of specific words. Writers such as Henry David Thoreau commonly explore the meanings of important concepts (for instance, "sauntering") by tracing the original meanings of the words.

Explanation: The process of making a subject plain or intelligible, or the process of interpreting something. An explanation (sometimes called "exposition" or "discursive prose") is a relatively straightforward and explicit way of revealing ideas.

Exposition: The act of exposing or explaining. The main goal of expository or discursive prose is explanation.

Fiction: A literary genre in which specific characters, places, and events are mainly the products of the author's imagination.

Figurative language: A type of descriptive language that employs metaphors and similes as a means of attracting attention and capturing the reader's imagination. Sometimes figures of speech are used to explain the unknown by connecting it with something more familiar and understandable.

Genre: A literary category emphasizing style or subject matter. For example, nonfiction, fiction, poetry, nature writing, and mountaineering narratives.

Image/imagery: An image is a word or a cluster of words designed to recreate sensory experience (usually *visual* experience), and *imagery* means the purposeful use of images.

Introduction: The opening passage (one or more paragraphs) of a written text. Shorter texts normally have proportionately shorter introductions. Effective introductions usually present the author's topic or thesis; engage the reader through an interesting or exciting quotation, narrative, description, or metaphor; provide helpful background information; or cite the views of an authority on the subject matter of the text.

Journal: Typically, a private medium for recording events, observations, and ideas experienced on a particular day. Journals commonly demonstrate the writer's consciousness of the passage of time; are kept routinely for weeks, months, or years at a time; and seem deeply rooted in concrete details of daily life. Nonfiction writers (and sometimes novelists and poets) occasionally adopt a journal-like structure even in works intended for publication.

Juxtaposition: The technique of placing two or more objects, events, characters, or ideas side by side, often creating a jarring contrast.

Memoir: A personal history; a nonfictional autobiography.

Metaphor: A figure of speech that equates two seemingly unrelated things; for instance, when Robert Finch, describing the dead whale in "Very Like a Whale," writes, "The distended, corrugated lower jaw, 'a giant accordian,' was afloat with the gas of putrifaction. . . . "

Mood: The feeling or atmosphere created by the author's use of setting, characterization, imagery, and events.

Narration/narrator: Narration is the process of telling about an occurrence or a series of occurrences, sometimes with the ultimate goal of making a point beyond the story itself. The narrator, who has often participated in the narrated event, is the character who tells the story.

Nature writing: Literature in any stylistic genre (poetry, fiction, nonfiction, and even drama) that focuses on either natural phenomena or the relationship between human beings and the nonhuman natural world. When scholars refer to nature writing, they often are thinking specifically of literary nonfiction.

Nonfiction: Literary texts (essays, autobiographies, and some journalistic and scientific prose) based on factual experience or observations, but colored and controlled by the author's writing style and interpretation of the subject matter.

Omniscience: An "all-knowing" narrative perspective that surpasses a single human narrator's knowledge about the scene being presented.

Oxymoron: A contradictory or paradoxical phrase, such as Matthew Henson's "magnificent desolation."

Paradox: The use of statements that contradict themselves, other passages in a literary text, or common sense. Essayists sometimes use paradox as a way of forcing their own minds and their readers' beyond the limits of strictly rational understanding.

Persuasion: The desired effect of argumentative writing, either evoking strong feelings in the reader or convincing the reader to accept or deny an idea.

Petroglyph: An archeological and art historical term referring to a rock carving or painting, normally a prehistoric one.

Point of view: The perspective from which an idea or a story is presented. If the speaker uses the pronouns *I* or *we,* the perspective is called "first person." Third-person narratives use the pronouns *he, she, it,* and *they.* Occasionally, for dramatic effect, at least part of an essay or a story may be presented from the second-person perspective, addressing the reader directly as "you."

Prose: A form of written or spoken language that normally does not have a metrical structure. Academic writing, journalism, fiction, and nonfiction are typical examples of prose, as compared to poetry.

Reflection: The process of meditating about subtle or complex ideas. Critics sometimes describe literary passages as "reflections," "meditations," or "ruminations," meaning much the same thing in each case.

Rhetoric: The effective use of language to achieve an intended purpose. Common rhetorical modes include description, narration, exposition, and argumentation.

Scene: The description of a real or imagined event. Sometimes this term refers simply to a physical place, as in "scenery."

Section: A semiautonomous grouping of events or ideas within a larger literary text. In an essay, separate sections are often indicated by leaving an extra blank line between paragraphs. Sections can consist of as little as one paragraph or can be many paragraphs long.

Sentence structure: The arrangement of words within a sentence that shows the relationship between the individual words. Also known as "syntax."

Setting: The time and place in which the action of a literary text occurs. Often this is the role of nature in literature, although in nature writing the nonhuman world generally plays a more prominent role.

Short story: A work of fictional prose that is shorter than a novel.

Simile: An explicit comparison that uses the words *like* or *as* to establish the connection. For example, Barry Lopez writes in *Arctic Dreams* that he saw an iceberg "rounded off smoothly, like a human forehead against the sky. . . ."

Speaker: The character telling a story or presenting the ideas in an essay. The speaker may represent the author directly, but this is not always the case.

Structure: The organization or "architecture" of a written text.

Summary: A condensation and restatement of someone else's ideas, or the brief and relatively undetailed account of one's own experiences.

Symbolism: The use of a thing, person, place, idea, or action to represent something other than itself. Usually, there is a more ambiguous and complex relationship between a symbol and its meaning than the relationship between the two items being compared through a metaphor or simile.

Thesis: The main idea or "argument" of an essay. Sometimes the thesis is directly expressed in one or more sentences early in the essay, but other times (usually in literary, not academic, texts) the main idea may be revealed only gradually or indirectly.

Tone: The author's attitude toward him- or herself, toward the reader, and toward the subject matter. The tone of an essay may be humorous, critical, wondering, respectful, celebratory, cynical, and so forth. Discerning subtle or unexpected tones in literary essays is one of the more difficult and important goals of the sophisticated reader.

Understatement: The opposite of hyperbole or exaggeration. Understatement means the intentional down-playing of something, often for humorous or ironic purposes.

Unity: The arrangement of the parts of a written text, literary or non-literary, in order to achieve a unified or consistent aesthetic effect.

Word choice: The process of selecting appropriate words to fit one's subject matter, audience, and purpose in a specific piece of writing. Also known as "diction."

Acknowledgments

Edward Abbey "Floating," from *Down the River* by Edward Abbey. Copyright© 1982 by Edward Abbey. Used by permission of the publisher, Dutton, an imprint of New American Library, a division of Penguin Books USA Inc. "The Great American Desert," from *The Journey Home* by Edward Abbey. Copyright© 1977 by Edward Abbey. Used by permission of the publisher, Dutton, an imprint of New American Library, a division of Penguin Books USA Inc.

Rudolfo Anaya Excerpt from Chapter 11 in *Bless Me, Ultima* by Rudolfo Anaya. Copyright© 1972 by Rudolfo A. Anaya. Tonatiuh-Quinto Sol International Publishers, P.O. Box 9275, Berkeley, CA 94709. Reprinted by permission.

Gloria Anzaldúa "El retorno," from *Borderlands/La Frontera* by Gloria Anzaldúa. Copyright© 1987 by Gloria Anzaldúa. Reprinted by permission of Spinsters Aunt Lute Books.

Rick Bass Excerpt, "The Nantahala," from *Wild to the Heart* by Rick Bass, published by Stackpole Books, Harrisburg, Pennsylvania, 1987. Reprinted by permission.

Wendell Berry "A Country of Edges," from *The Unforeseen Wilderness,* copyright © 1991 by Wendell Berry. Published by North Point Press and reprinted by permission of Farrar, Straus & Giroux, Inc.

David Black "Walking the Cape: A Distance Measured in Time," copyright© 1985 by *Harper's Magazine.* All rights reserved. Reprinted from the June 1985 issue by special permission.

Arlene Blum Excerpt, "Plans and Changes," from *Annapurna: A Woman's Place* by Arlene Blum. Copyright© 1980 by Arlene Blum. Reprinted with permission of Sierra Club Books.

Sally Carrighar Excerpt, "Parent Birds," from *Wild Heritage* by Sally Carrighar. Copyright© 1965 by Sally Carrighar. Reprinted by permission of Houghton Mifflin Company. All rights reserved.

Rachel Carson "The Marginal World," from *The Edge of the Sea* by Rachel Carson. Copyright© 1955 by Rachel L. Carson. Copyright© renewed 1983 by Roger Christie. Reprinted by permission of Houghton Mifflin Company. All rights reserved.

Sandra Cisneros "Four Skinny Trees," from *The House on Mango Street.* Copyright© 1989 by Sandra Cisneros. Published by Random House, reprinted by permission of Susan Bergholz Literary Agency.

John Daniel "Some Mortal Speculations" and "The Impoverishment of Sightseeing," from *The Trail Home* by John Daniel. Copyright© 1982 by John Daniel. Reprinted by permission of Pantheon Books, a division of Random House, Inc.

Joan Didion "Los Angeles Notebook," from *Slouching Towards Bethlehem.* Copyright© 1967, 1968 by Joan Didion. Reprinted by permission of Farrar, Straus & Giroux, Inc.

Annie Dillard Excerpt, "Fecundity," from *Pilgrim at Tinker Creek* by Annie Dillard. Copyright© 1974 by Annie Dillard. Reprinted by permission of Harper-Collins Publishers. "Living Like Weasels," from *Teaching a Stone to Talk* by Annie Dillard. Copyright © 1982 by Annie Dillard. Reprinted by permission of HarperCollins Publishers. Excerpt from *An American Childhood* by Annie Dillard. Copyright© 1987 by Annie Dillard. Reprinted by permission of HarperCollins Publishers.

Paula DiPerna "Truth vs. 'Facts,' " by Paula DiPerna. Copyright 1991 by Paula DiPerna. Originally published in *Ms.* Magazine, September/October 1991. Reprinted by permission of the author.

Gretel Ehrlich "A Storm, the Cornfield, and Elk," from *The Solace of Open Spaces* by Gretel Ehrlich. Copyright © 1985 by Gretel Ehrlich. Used by permission of Viking Penguin, a division of Penguin Books USA Inc. Excerpt, "On the Pond Again," from *Islands, the Universe, Home* by Gretel Ehrlich. Copyright© 1991 by Gretel Ehrlich. Used by permission of Viking Penguin, a division of Penguin Books USA Inc.

Loren Eiseley "The Flow of the River," from *Immense Journey* by Loren Eiseley. Copyright© 1953 by Loren Eiseley. Reprinted by permission of Random House, Inc. "The Winter of Man," in *The New York Times*, January 16, 1972. Copyright© 1972 by The New York Times Company. Reprinted by permission.

John Elder "The Plane on South Mountain," from *The Bread Loaf Anthology* published by University Press of New England, 1989. Copyright 1989 by John Elder. Reprinted by permission of the author.

Robert Finch "Very Like a Whale," from *Common Ground* by Robert Finch. Copyright© 1981 by Robert Finch. Reprinted by permission of David R. Godine, Publisher.

Baruch Fischhoff "Report from Poland: Science and Politics in the Midst of Environmental Disaster," by Baruch Fischhoff, in *Environment*, March 1991. Reprinted with permission of the Helen Dwight Reid Educational Foundation. Published by Heldref Publications, 1319 Eighteenth St., N.W., Washington, D.C. 20036-1802. Copyright© 1991.

Stephen Jay Gould "Sex, Drugs, Disasters, and the Extinction of Dinosaurs" is reprinted from *The Flamingo's Smile, Reflections in Natural History*, by Stephen Jay Gould, by permission of W. W. Norton & Company, Inc. Copyright© 1985 by Stephen Jay Gould.

Stephen Harrigan "The Secret Life of the Beach," from *A Natural State* by Stephen Harrigan. Copyright© 1988 by Gulf Publishing Company, Houston, TX. Used with permission. All rights reserved.

Eddy L. Harris Excerpt from *Mississippi Solo: A River Quest* by Eddy L. Harris. Copyright© 1988 by Eddy L. Harris. Published by Lyons & Burford, Publishers, 31 West 21st Street, New York, NY 10010.

John Hay "A Season for Swallows" is reprinted from *The Undiscovered Country* by John Hay, by permission of W. W. Norton & Company, Inc. Copyright© 1981 by John Hay.

Betsy Hilbert "Disturbing the Universe," first appeared in *Orion Magazine*, Summer 1987, pp. 63–65. Copyright© 1987 The Myrin Institute. Reprinted with permission of the author and *Orion Magazine*.

Edward Hoagland "Dogs, and the Tug of Life," from *Heart's Desire: The Best of Edward Hoagland* by Edward Hoagland. Copyright© 1988 by Edward Hoagland. Reprinted by permission of Simon & Schuster, Inc.

Linda Hogan "Walking," reprinted from *Parabola, The Magazine of Myth and Tradition*, vol. XV, no. 2 (Summer, 1990). Reprinted with permission of *Parabola* and the author.

David Brendan Hopes "Crossings," from *A Sense of Morning*, published by Simon & Schuster, 1988. Copyright© 1988 by David Brendan Hopes. Reprinted by permission of the author.

Jeanne Wakatsuki Houston and James D. Houston "Manzanar, U.S.A." from *Farewell to Manzanar* by James D. and Jeanne Wakatsuki Houston. Copyright© 1973 by James D. Houston. Reprinted with permission of Houghton Mifflin Company. All rights reserved.

Sue Hubbell Excerpt, "Becoming Feral," from *A Country Year: Living the Question* by Sue Hubbell. Copyright© 1983, 1984, 1985, 1986 by Sue Hubbell. Reprinted by permission of Random House, Inc.

John Janovy, Jr. "Tigers and Toads," from *Back in Keith County*, published by St. Martin's Press, 1981. Copyright© 1981 by John Janovy, Jr. Reprinted by permission of St. Martin's Press.

Randall Kenan Excerpt from *A Visitation of Spirits* by Randall Kenan. Copyright© 1989 by Randall Kenan. Used by permission of Grove Press, Inc.

Jack Kerouac Excerpt from *The Dharma Bums* by Jack Kerouac. Copyright© 1958 by Jack Kerouac, © renewed 1986 by Stella Kerouac and Jan Kerouac. Used by permission of Viking Penguin, a division of Penguin Books USA Inc.

William Kittredge Excerpt from *Owning It All*, copyright 1987 by William Kittredge. Reprinted from *Owning It All* with the permission of Graywolf Press, Saint Paul, Minnesota.

Maxine Kumin "Menial Labor and the Muse," published in *Triquarterly*, 75, Spring/Summer 1989. Reprinted by permission of Curtis Brown, Ltd. Copyright© 1989 by Maxine Kumin.

William Least Heat-Moon "Atop the Mound," from *Prairyerth: A Deep Map* by William Least Heat-Moon. Copyright© 1991 by William Least Heat-Moon. Reprinted by permission of Houghton Mifflin Company. All rights reserved.

Ursula K. Le Guin "Riding Shotgun," from *Dancing at the Edge of the World* by Ursula K. Le Guin. Copyright© 1981 by Ursula K. Le Guin. Used by permission of Grove Press, Inc.

Larry Littlebird "The Hunter," copyright© 1983 by Larry Littlebird. Reprinted by permission of the author.

Barry Lopez "Children in the Woods," reprinted with the permission of Charles Scribner's Sons, an imprint of Macmillan Publishing Company, from *Crossing Open Ground* by Barry Lopez. Copyright© 1982, 1988 Barry Holstun Lopez. First appeared in *Pacific Northwest* (April 1982). "The Image of the Unicorn," reprinted with the permission of Charles Scribner's Sons, an imprint of Macmillan Publishing Company, from *Arctic Dreams* by Barry Lopez. Copyright© 1986 by Barry Holstun Lopez.

Wangari Maathai "Foresters Without Diplomas," in *Ms.* Magazine, March/April 1991. Copyright© 1991 by Wangari Maathai. Reprinted by permission.

Peter Matthiessen Excerpt, "November 15, 16, 17," from *The Snow Leopard* by Peter Matthiessen. Copyright© 1978 by Peter Matthiessen. Used by permission of Viking Penguin, a division of Penguin Books USA Inc.

Joseph Meeker "Nuclear Time," reproduced by permission of Joseph W. Meeker from his book, *Minding the Earth* (Alameda, CA: Latham Foundation, 1988).

Susan Mitchell "Dreaming in Public: A Provincetown Memoir" by Susan Mitchell. First published in *Provincetown Arts.* Copyright© 1987 by Susan Mitchell. Reprinted from *Best American Essays 1988,* ed. Annie Dillard (New York: Ticknor & Fields, 1988), pp. 191–200, by permission of the author and publisher.

N. Scott Momaday "An American Land Ethic," from *Ecotactics: The Sierra Club Handbook for Environmental Activists,* edited by John G. Mitchell and Constance L. Stallings (Trident Press, 1970). Reprinted by permission of the author.

John Muir "Prayers in Higher Mountain Temples, OR A Geologist's Winter Walk," from *Steep Trails* by John Muir. Copyright 1918 by Houghton Mifflin Company. Copyright renewed 1946 by Helen Muir Funk. Reprinted by permission of Houghton Mifflin Company. All rights reserved. Excerpt, journal entry (April 3, 1871), from *John of the Mountains: The Unpublished Journals of John Muir,* edited by Linnie Marsh Wolfe. Copyright 1938 by Wanda Muir Hanna. Copyright© renewed 1966 by John Muir Hanna and Ralph Eugene Wolfe. Reprinted by permission of Houghton Mifflin Co. All rights reserved. Letter to Mrs. Ezra S. Carr from *The Life and Letters of John Muir,* edited by William Frederic Badè. Copyright 1924 by Houghton Mifflin Co. Copyright© renewed 1952 by John Muir Hanna. Reprinted by permission of Houghton Mifflin Co. All rights reserved.

Richard Nelson "Oil and Ethics: Adrift on Troubled Waters," in the *Los Angeles Times,* April 9, 1989. Copyright© 1989 by Richard Nelson. Reprinted by permission of Susan Bergholz, Literary Agency.

John Nichols "Keep It Simple" published in *Buzzworm,* September/October 1990. Copyright© 1990 by John Nichols. Reprinted by permission of the publisher. *Buzzworm: The Environmental Journal* is an independent magazine providing balanced and comprehensive coverage of national and international environmental issues. *Buzzworm* is produced in Boulder, Colorado.

Georgia O'Keeffe Letter to Anita Politzer (September 11, 1916), from *Georgia O'Keeffe: Art and Letters,* edited by Jack Cowart, Juan Hamilton, and Sarah Greenough. Published by Little, Brown, 1987. Reprinted by permission of The Georgia O'Keeffe Foundation, P.O. Box 40, Abiquiu, NM 87510.

Michael Pollan "Why Mow? The Case Against Lawns," from the book, *Second Nature* by Michael Pollan. Copyright© 1991 by Michael Pollan. Used here with the permission of Atlantic Monthly Press.

Stephen J. Pyne "Monsoon Lightning," originally published in *Antaeus* 61, Autumn 1988, pp. 374–382. Reprinted by permission of the author.

David Quammen "The Face of a Spider," from *Flight of the Iguana* by David Quammen. Copyright© 1988 by David Quammen. Used by permission of Dell Books, a division of Bantam Doubleday Dell Publishing Group, Inc. "The White Tigers of Cincinnati: A Strabismic View of Zookeeping," in *Outside,* September 1991. Copyright© 1991 by David Quammen. Reprinted by permission of the author's agent, Rene Golden. "Dirty Word, Clean Place," in *Outside,* August 1991. Copyright© 1991 by David Quammen. Reprinted by permission of the author's agent, Rene Golden.

Chet Raymo "The Blandishments of Color," from the book, *The Soul of the Night,* by Chet Raymo. Copyright© 1985 by Chet Raymo. Used by permission of the publisher, Prentice Hall, a division of Simon & Schuster, Englewood Cliffs, New Jersey.

David Roberts "Five Days on Mount Huntington," copyright© David Roberts. "Five Days on Mount Huntington" reprinted with permission of the publisher from *Moments of Doubt*, by David Roberts (Seattle: The Mountaineers, 1986).

Scott Russell Sanders "Listening to Owls," copyright© 1982 by Scott Russell Sanders; first appeared in *The North American Review*; reprinted by permission of the author and Virginia Kidd, Literary Agent. "Cloud Crossing," copyright© 1981 by Scott Russell Sanders; first appeared in *The North American Review*; reprinted by permission of the author and Virginia Kidd, Literary Agent. "The Singular First Person," first published in *The Sewanee Review*, vol. 96, no. 4, Fall 1988. Reprinted with permission of the editor.

May Sarton "Mud Season" is reprinted from *Plant Dreaming Deep* by May Sarton, by permission of W. W. Norton & Company, Inc. Copyright© 1968 by May Sarton.

Leslie Marmon Silko Excerpts, "Through Stories We Hear Who We Are" and "The Migration Story," from *Antaeus* 57, 1986. Reprinted by permission of the author. All rights reserved.

Gary Soto "Blue" is used by permission of the author. Copyright© 1986 by Gary Soto.

John Tallmadge "In the Mazes of Quetico," first appeared in *Orion Magazine*, Summer 1984, pp. 24–35. Copyright© 1984 by The Myrin Institute. Reprinted with permission of the author and *Orion Magazine*.

Edwin Way Teale Excerpt from "October," in *Circle of the Seasons* (Dodd, Mead and Company, 1953). All rights reserved.

Lewis Thomas "Death in the Open," copyright© 1973 by The Massachusetts Medical Society, from *The Lives of a Cell* by Lewis Thomas. Used by permission of Viking Penguin, a division of Penguin Books USA Inc.

Alice Walker "Am I Blue?" from *Living by the Word*, copyright© 1986 by Alice Walker, reprinted by permission of Harcourt Brace Jovanovich, Inc.

Jonathan Weiner "The New Question" from *The Next One Hundred Years* by Jonathan Weiner. Copyright© 1990 by Jonathan Weiner. Used by permission of Bantam Books, a division of Bantam Doubleday Dell Publishing Group, Inc.

Eudora Welty "Some Notes on River Country" from *The Eye of the Story: Selected Essays & Reviews* by Eudora Welty. Copyright© 1978 by Eudora Welty. Reprinted by permission of Random House, Inc.

Joy Williams "Save the Whales, Screw the Shrimp," reprinted by permission of Joy Williams. Copyright© 1988 by Joy Williams. This article first appeared in *Esquire*.

Terry Tempest Williams "Yucca," reprinted with the permission of Charles Scribner's Sons, an imprint of Macmillan Publishing Company, from *Pieces of White Shell: A Journey to Navajoland* by Terry Tempest Williams. Copyright© 1983, 1984 Terry Tempest Williams.

Ann Zwinger "Fort Bottom to Turks Head" from *Run, River, Run*. Published in 1984 by Harper & Row. Reprinted by permission of Frances Collin, Literary Agent. Copyright© 1975 by Ann H. Zwinger.

Index